CONTENTS

PREFACE

Since its introduction in the mid-1960s, BASIC has become the most widely used programming language, especially among nonprofessional users. However, it has also evolved into one of the most nonstandard languages. Versions of BASIC are now in use on computers from the largest mainframes to the smallest microcomputers. This diversity naturally leads to vastly different implementations of BASIC. Unfortunately, even similar computers may offer very different forms of the language. To date, only minimal standards have been established for BASIC, and virtually every version of the language offers its own enhancements. This diversity of dialects can make it very difficult to find a text that is consistent with a specific BASIC. It is to this need for a general, generic treatment of the language that this book is aimed.

The text is intended for a one- or two-term course in introductory programming with BASIC. It is written with the general liberal arts student in mind who has had no prior experience with computers. The required mathematical background is minimal; except for some of the advanced mathematical functions described in Section 11-2 (which can be easily omitted), a one-year course in high school algebra is sufficient. While the book is geared toward the average college-level student, the approach is such that it could very well be used for programming courses in high schools or technical/vocational schools as well. It might also be used as a supplement in general survey or computer literacy courses that include programming with BASIC. (It was while teaching such a general survey course that the idea for this book was born.)

The approach to programming taken here is a mixture between traditional and structured. There are several reasons for not following the crowd and writing another book on structured programming. First, BASIC is frequently very unfriendly to the strictly structured approach in that many versions do not provide the special statements that are needed. Second, it has been my experience that students, especially the less able ones, progress faster, learning language syntax and programming strategies more quickly, when a more traditional approach is followed in the early phases of programming. Later, when the structured techniques are introduced, the students appreciate the obvious advantages of the new methods and take to them very quickly. (The structured procedures are taught as an *alternative* method, not as "the correct way and what you have been doing is all wrong.") Finally, while flowcharts are considered old-fashioned by some, they are still—in my opinion—the most effective means for illustrating program design to the beginning student. However, for those instructors who prefer a more structured approach, pseudocode is described in Section 2-5, and the blocked structures (blocked IF–THEN, IF–THEN–ELSE, REPEAT–UNTIL, and WHILE–DO) are discussed in detail in Chapter 7.

Developing the skill of writing programs is the most important part of any programming course. Chapters 1 and 2 work on dispelling fear and apprehension and letting the students know that "programming" is nothing new to them, that they are only applying some old skills to a new device. The presentation in the remainder of the text is highly example oriented. Discussions of new BASIC statements and program designs are usually based on short, easy-to-understand examples. Beginning with Chapter 3, each chapter contains at least one fully developed example. These always occupy a full section and contain the following:

1. The statement of a problem
2. An outlined verbal solution
3. A flowchart (or other schematic) diagram
4. A line-by-line analysis of the program

5. A complete program listing
6. A program run

There are 23 major examples in all, all of which relate to practical situations as do the programming problems at the end of each chapter.

The book is divided into four parts. Part I, consisting of Chapters 1 and 2, provides an introduction to computers and the programming process for those students who have had no previous experience. These two chapters might be omitted or covered very quickly for classes with more experienced students. Part II will form the heart of most short courses. It consists of Chapters 3 through 7 and gives the students a firm foundation in BASIC for handling the three fundamental operations: input/output, arithmetic, and logical. Chapters 8 through 10 constitute Part III, which covers additional program control structures, arrays, and subroutines and will be covered in most courses. Part IV consists of Chapters 11 through 15 and includes special functions, multidimensional arrays, file processing, and several other advanced topics. It is anticipated that topics from this part will be selectively covered according to the available time and individual preferences. However, depending on the depth of coverage desired, there is more than enough material in this part alone for a one-term course.

While the very nature of the subject demands a certain sequence of topics, there is a great deal of flexibility of coverage built into the book. It is impossible to delineate all the possibilities, but some of the most likely choices are as follows:

1. Depending on the general backgrounds and capabilities of the students, work can begin with Chapter 1, 2, or 3.
2. For instructors desiring a faster start, Chapters 3 and 4 can be covered as a single unit.
3. While Chapters 3 through 9 will normally be covered essentially in that order, several sections within these chapters can be either postponed or omitted without causing problems with continuity throughout Part III. These include Sections 5-8, 6-5 through 6-7, 7-6 through 7-8, 8-7 and 8-8, and 9-7 and 9-8. Some of the material in these sections may, however, be needed for certain advanced topics in Part IV or end-of-chapter programming problems.
4. Many instructors prefer to cover subroutines earlier in the course. Sections 10-1, 10-2, and 10-4 can easily be covered between Chapters 5 and 6, with Section 10-3 following Section 6-4. Section 8-5 must precede 10-5. The remaining two sections should follow Chapter 9 (but could be omitted, if desired).
5. After Chapter 9, the sequence of coverage is very flexible. Chapters 10 through 14 are relatively independent and can be covered or omitted as desired. Of course, Section 13-5 must follow Chapter 12. Chapter 11 can be covered at any time following Section 8-2, while Chapter 12 assumes Chapter 9.

This is more specifically detailed in Table P-1 on the following page.

This book is distinguished by a number of features that make it appropriate for a wide variety of courses and student abilities. These include the following:

Computer Independence. The development of BASIC is as computer independent as practical. Rules are given in general terms that apply to *most* versions of BASIC with common variations mentioned. This should make the text useful for users of most computer systems from mainframes to micros.

Full Treatment. The treatment of BASIC is as complete as practicality permits in a volume of this size. Only a few topics, namely those that are highly machine dependent, are abbreviated or omitted.

Unique Coverage. Several special topics, both on BASIC and on programming techniques, are included that are not frequently found in an introductory-level book on BASIC. Some examples of this are Sections 6-6, 8-7, 10-6, 13-1, 13-4, 13-5, 13-7, 14-5, 14-6, and 14-8, Chapter 15 and Appendix D.

TABLE P-1

Recommended Prerequisites by Chapter and Section

Chapter/Section	Prerequisite	Chapter/Section	Prerequisite
Chapter 1	None	Chapter 13	
Chapter 2	Chapter 1*	Sections 13-1 to 13-4	Chapter 9§
Chapter 3	Chapter 2*	Sections 13-5, 13-6	Section 12-5
Chapter 4	Chapter 3	Sections 13-7, 13-8	Section 8-7
Chapter 5	Chapter 4	Chapter 14	
Chapter 6	Section 5-7	Sections 14-1 to 14-5	Section 8-2
Chapter 7	Section 6-4	Sections 14-6, 14-7	Section 9-6
Chapter 8	Section 7-5	Section 14-8	Section 14-1
Chapter 9	Section 8-3	Chapter 15	
Chapter 10		Case Study 1	Section 8-5
Sections 10-1 to 10-4	Section 5-5†	Case Study 2	Chapter 9
Section 10-5	Section 8-5	Case Study 3	Chapters 10, 11
Sections 10-6, 10-7	Section 9-6	Case Study 4	Section 12-5
Chapter 11	Section 8-2‡	Case Study 5	Section 13-6
Chapter 12	Chapter 9	Case Study 6	Chapter 13

*Optional.
†Except for the example in Section 10-3 which is based on the one given in Section 6-4.
‡Except for the discussion of the CHANGE statement in Section 11-5.
§Except for the discussion of the pointer method in Section 12-4.

Flexibility. As discussed above, there is a great deal of flexibility available to the course instructor or independent user in approaching the material covered.

Abundant Examples. The development is highly example dependent. There are 23 fully developed examples. These are entire sections with a specific problem stated, the solution outlined in words and in flowchart (or other structural) form, and the program explained with emphasis on the new principles of the chapter. In addition, there is a much larger number of short programs or program segments used to explain individual concepts as they are introduced.

Realistic Applications. The examples in the text as well as the problems at the ends of the chapters are aimed at realistic, real-life situations.

Stepwise Approach. Each topic is introduced, often with an example, in a slow, careful manner so as not to overwhelm the student. New material is presented in small steps that are easy to analyze and correlate with previously learned features.

Depth of Coverage. Topics are discussed fully and in depth. As many of the various features of BASIC that are commonly available and relate to a given topic are mentioned as practicality permits.

Readability. The book is written in a relaxed and informal style that is easy for the student to follow. Topics are presented in a conversational rather than lecture manner.

Tables and Figures. The text is highlighted with numerous tables and figures to aid the student in understanding specific concepts. Tables are used throughout to summarize points covered in the text, present examples, and give data for programs. Figures, including many flowcharts, are included to reemphasize new programming structures and the strategy for the solution to the programs in the examples.

End-of-Chapter Aids. There is extensive end-of-chapter material for student aid and study. This includes the following:

1. The TROUBLESHOOTING section provides the student with examples of short programs that contain common errors.
2. The IMPORTANT TERMS lists all significant terms, features of BASIC, and concepts introduced in the chapter.

3. The EXERCISES provide the student with nonprogramming practice problems.
4. The PROGRAMMING PROBLEMS sections provide a large number of practical programming problems of varied difficulty.

End-of-Text Aids. Following the same computer-independent approach as the main text, the appendixes present a summary of several features of the BASIC language and environment. These include a summary of BASIC statements and functions and a general outline of the most commonly used interactive screen commands. There is also a summary of the most common BASIC error messages. A Glossary provides brief definitions for most of the terms listed in the IMPORTANT TERMS sections at the ends of the chapters. (BASIC statements listed in the IMPORTANT TERMS are covered in the appendixes.)

Wide Appeal. While the primary target group for this book is the student in the introductory college course (one or two terms) in BASIC—it assumes no prior study in computers or programming—the approach and flexible format should make the text valuable as well for high school courses, technical/vocational schools, and self-study.

An instructor's manual is available to accompany the text. It provides overviews and outlines for each chapter along with teaching suggestions and a suggested lecture outline for each chapter. Sample test questions are provided as well as answers to the TROUBLESHOOTING and EXERCISES sections in each chapter. A set of transparency masters is also included.

ACKNOWLEDGMENTS

It is impossible to remember and list all the many thoughtful friends and colleagues who have at various times expressed words of encouragement, given little suggestions, or simply provided a smile or pat on the back, often when it was most needed. You know who you are, and the fact that I cannot list each name individually in no way diminishes your valued contributions.

This entire project would, in all likelihood, still be in that overpopulated, underdeveloped land of planned-but-never-started/completed books were it not for the encouragement and continued support of my family, who deserve a very special word of thanks. Several close friends have also been very supportive of this work and deserve special mention; they are Mary Lane, Phillip Iloff, Debby James, and Raymond Kaiser.

Over the years, many students have contributed much to improving the overall presentation of the subject. While most of these must be placed in the first group above, three exceptional students have worked with dedication in helping to proofread and otherwise improve the final manuscript and merit special mention; they are Deborah Carpenter, Richard Drown, and Terisa Rodriguez. Terisa also provided invaluable assistance in the preparation of the index.

The final form of the manuscript reflects many very helpful suggestions from reviewers. The following persons have reviewed all or part of the manuscript as it was being written and prepared for publication: Sudesh K. Bhatia, Middlesex County College; Barbara Buhr, Fresno City College; Robert H. Dependahl, Jr., Santa Barbara City College; Richard Fleming, North Lake College; James Kasum, University of Wisconsin: Cynthia B. Kirby, Onondaga Community College; Anthony Malone, Raymond Walters College; David Newhall, North Shore Community College; Lawrence Seiford, The University of Texas at Austin; Rod Southworth, Laramie City Community College; and Paul Wolotkin, State University of New York at Farmingdale.

Finally, and certainly not least, a very special word of appreciation is due to McGraw-Hill for their expression of confidence in this book. The McGraw-Hill staff, most notably Eric Munson (for his initial faith in the project), Christina Mediate (for guiding the work to its successful conclusion), and Jo Satloff (for supervising the metamorphosis of a rough manuscript into a real book), have been especially helpful and a pleasure to work with during both the writing and production phases of this project.

Olen R. Pearson

PROGRAMMING WITH BASIC
A PRACTICAL APPROACH

PART ONE

PRELIMINARIES

CHAPTER 1

WHY BASIC?

Before we begin our study of BASIC and programming, we must take a look at computers and programming languages in general. In order to understand why BASIC is so frequently selected for study as a first language, you must know something about other languages and how they compare to BASIC. We will begin this chapter with a very brief look at computers and the processing of data. This will be followed by a discussion of the development of programming languages, concluding with a more detailed examination of the use of BASIC.

1-1 COMMUNICATING WITH A COMPUTER

A student was recently asked, "Have you ever used a computer?" He quickly replied, "I've never come in contact with one of those terrible things! They're only for geniuses anyway!" This response is all too typical of the false impression shared by many that computers are mysterious monsters, things to be feared and avoided, comprehensible only to the superintelligent. Nothing could be further from the truth! **Computerphobia**, or the fear of computers, is not uncommon among those who are unfamiliar with computers. There is, however, nothing to fear. Computers are no better or worse than those who use them. As we will see below, the real heart of a computer is not the electronic part, but the instructions that tell it what to do.

While you may never have actually touched a computer console or attempted to write a computer program, in a modern technological society we all interact with a computer in some way virtually every day of our lives. If you use the telephone, you must go through the phone company's computer system. Traffic lights in most large cities are computer controlled to optimize traffic flow. If you have a programmable stereo, microwave oven, watch, calculator, or other such gadget, whenever you use it, you interact with a tiny computer called a **microprocessor**. Most modern cars contain at least one microprocessor. If you have used an electronic banking machine, you were interacting directly with the bank's computer. Of course, the most obvious example is that of electronic games. The list goes on and on.

In all of the examples above (except possibly a programmable calculator), you are supplying **data**, or information, to be processed by the computer. The **program**, or set of instructions that directs the processing of the data, is already in the computer, and you have no control over this. It is the construction of these computer programs which will concern us in this book.

It is the programs (collectively known as **software**) that are most important in determining how well a computer performs a certain job. Without a program, a computer is no more than a collection of useless circuits. With a bad program, the computer may do a job, but incorrectly. Consider this analogy. Suppose that you have a very expensive component stereo system (the computer), but you have no records or tapes to play and no radio stations in your area to tune in (no program). Your stereo might look nice in the corner, but it is rather useless to you for producing music (processing data). Now suppose someone gives you some tapes and records (at last, some programs!), but they are very poor ones. You can now use your stereo to make music, but not very good music. Finally, a great FM station which you can receive with crystal clarity (a great program!!) is opened in a nearby town. You can now use your stereo to produce good quality music. The sources of music are the same to the stereo as the program is to the computer. Likewise, the quality of the music produced depends on the source, just as the information produced by a computer is only as good as the program that processes it.

Do not be afraid to interact with your computer and write programs. You will not hurt the computer, and it will not harm you! You will make mistakes, but even the most experienced programmers make errors in writing programs. It is important that you do not become discouraged when your programs do not work on the first, second, or even the third try. Programming is like anything else; it requires not only a basic knowledge of the subject but also *practice*. Write programs, and the more you do, the better you will get as a programmer.

1-2 THE COMPONENTS OF A COMPUTER

All computers, no matter how large or small, are composed of several basic sections as shown in Figure 1-1. Larger computers may offer more choices for a particular device, such as for input or output or auxiliary storage, have more memory, and be more complex in general design, but the component sections will not change. Let us look at each part individually.

Input Device. This is any unit that can be used to read information *into* the computer. In working with BASIC, you will probably use a **visual display terminal**, or **VDT**, which is a keyboard with a TV screen on which you can see what you type and the results of your work. Other common types of input devices include punch cards, paper tape, magnetic tape, magnetic disk, optical character readers, bar codes, and magnetic ink character readers.

Output Device. This is any unit that can be used to copy information *from* the computer. Again, with BASIC, you will probably use the VDT for most of your work, but use the printer when you need a copy on paper, a **hard copy**. Other common types of output devices include paper tape, magnetic tape, magnetic disk, and plotters.

Central Processor Unit. The **CPU** is the heart of the computer where all processing of data takes place. It is divided into three main sections: main memory, the control unit, and the arithmetic/logic unit (or ALU).

Main Memory. This includes storage locations *within* the computer for storing and processing data. Two types of information will normally be in main memory at any given time: the programs that control the processing and the data that the programs will process.

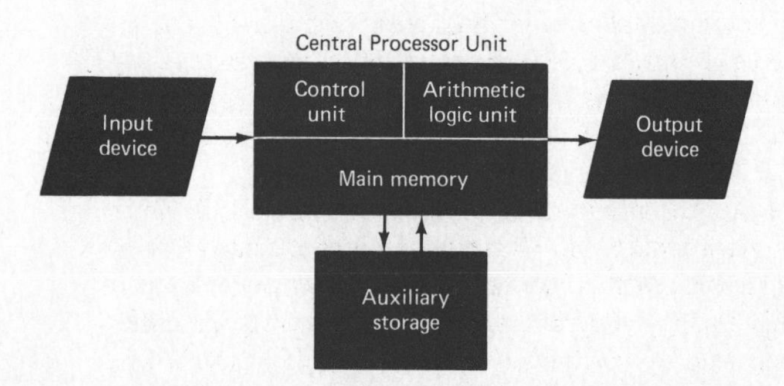

FIGURE 1-1
The primary components of a computer

Memory is normally measured in terms of **K**, which is 1024 storage locations. Thus, a 64K computer can store 64 × 1024, or 65,536, characters of information.

Control Unit. This section of the CPU directs the activities of the entire computer system under the control of one or more programs that have been placed in memory.

Arithmetic/Logic Unit. The **ALU** contains all the circuitry to perform two sets of operations. First, all arithmetic operations, such as addition, subtraction, multiplication, and division, are performed by this unit. Second, comparisons involving *less than, equal to,* or *greater than* conditions are handled by the ALU.

Auxiliary Storage. Data (or programs) that is to be available for processing but that cannot be placed into main memory for some reason—for example, a lack of space—can be placed on an auxiliary storage device from which they are retrieved as needed. For example, a typical small computer might have room in main memory for only a few million characters of data, whereas many *billions* can be stored on auxiliary devices, ready to be located, read into memory, and processed. The most commonly used auxiliary storage devices are magnetic tape and disk.

1-3 PROCESSING DATA

The primary function of any computer is to process data. This involves three ''simple'' steps:

$$\text{Input} \longrightarrow \text{process} \longrightarrow \text{output}$$

The first and last are usually fairly routine, except when the input is unreliable. In such cases, no matter what the processing, the output is likely to be poor as well; this is known as **GIGO**, garbage-in-garbage-out.

The first operation that usually occurs in processing data is that a program, possibly along with the data to be processed, is input to the main memory from an input device. This is under the direction of another program, such as the computer's operating system, that has already been loaded into the memory. The program is then read line by line, and the action called for at each line is directed to be carried out by the control unit. Suppose that we are processing a simple program that does only three things:

1. Reads two numbers
2. Adds the two numbers
3. Prints the sum of the two numbers

The control unit will (1) look to find the two numbers from the proper place and put them into memory, (2) direct the ALU to add the two numbers, and (3) output the sum as directed.

No matter how complex the processing is that occurs between input and output, it will consist of a combination of three basic types of operations:

1. Input/output (I/O)
2. Arithmetic
3. Logic

Let us look briefly at a few of the most common types of processing that you may encounter.

Input/Output. This is probably the simplest type of processing. It involves only the direct input and output of information, such as reading in a mailing list from a tape and printing it out on labels.

Calculations. Most processing will require some type of arithmetic operations to be performed between input and output.

Summary Reports. These are reports that accumulate totals or other summary information. Such a report, for example, might give the *number* of students in a class rather than a complete class roster.

Classifying. This process places data into certain categories according to specified conditions. An example would be classifying students as freshmen, sophomores, etc., by the number of hours earned, GPA, or other criteria.

Exception Reports. Such a report will print only those results that satisfy a certain condition, such as printing the names of those from the entire student body who are on the dean's list.

Updating. This is the process of using new data to bring old values up to date.

Sorting. This process puts a set of values into a specific sequence, such as alphabetical order or increasing or decreasing numerical order.

Control Break. The change in the value of a certain key variable is used to signal that processing should be temporarily interrupted (a control break) for a second type of processing, such as the printing of totals, to be performed before the first is resumed.

Searches. This involves the checking of a predetermined set of values to find a specific value from the group.

Merging. This is the process of combining two or more sets of data to form a single set.

Many programs will involve more than one of the above types of processing. While all are unique processes, some are dependent upon or usually associated with others. For example, before two sets of data are merged, they are usually sorted into the same type of sequence. Updating is frequently accompanied by sorting and merging of data.

1-4 THE DEVELOPMENT OF PROGRAMMING LANGUAGES

Today, there is a programming language available to suit almost anyone's special needs or desires, but it has not always been that way. In the very early days of experimental computers, programming was an awkward task that was slow to develop because it did not receive the attention that the electronics or **hardware** did. In the earliest computers, programs could not be stored in memory. Thus, if a job needed to be run 20 times, the program had to be entered into the computer 20 times! At least one popular computer of the late 1940s had to be partially rewired to be reprogrammed.

Things were not much better in the early 1950s when computers were first made commercially available. Thanks to the **stored program concept**, programs could be stored in memory along with the data; however, the actual task of writing programs was still very tedious. They had to be done in **machine language**, which involved expressing all operations in codes that the computer could interpret directly. All operations were written in **binary code**, a sequence of 0's and 1's. The programmer had to keep track of what was in memory, where it was, and exactly how much space it occupied. A typical machine language statement that might perform one simple operation could look something like this:

```
1Ø1ØØØ11Ø1Ø1Ø1ØØØØØØØØØØØØØØØ11ØØØ1ØØØØØØØØØ
```

Such programs were very **machine-specific** in that a program written on one machine would not run on another, usually not even on one of the same model.

In the early 1950s, a new type of programming language was developed called **assembly language**. Assembly languages use mnemonic codes to represent operations and symbolic addresses for memory locations. This means that the programmers can now use a code like ADD for addition or LD to load a value from one location into another. A simple assembly language program (for the popular Z80 microprocessor) that adds two numbers is shown below.

```
LD     A, (NUM1)
LD     HL, NUM2
ADD    A, (HL)
LD     (SUM), A
```

Assembly language programs are much easier to write, maintain, modify, and understand than machine language programs. Also, they will contain considerably fewer errors than equivalent-size machine programs. Imagine the possibility for error when a program is written in nothing but 0's and 1's! The primary disadvantage to an assembly program is that it must be translated into machine code before it can be run. This is done by a translator program called an **assembler**, which takes the assembly language version, or **source program**, and translates it into machine code, creating an **object program**, which the computer uses to execute the program. Each computer will have its own assembler, meaning that assembly language programs are (or should be) portable among computers of the same type. Assembly programs are not as fast as machine programs.

A **high-level language** is one that combines several operations into one (called a **macro**), allowing the programmer to express procedures in more human-friendly terms. Typical statements for adding two numbers in high-level language code are

```
160  LET S = N1 + N2              (BASIC)

SUM  = NUM1 + NUM2                (FORTRAN)

ADD  NUM1, NUM2 GIVING SUM.       (COBOL)
```

The high-level source program must also be translated into machine code for processing. This is done by either a **compiler** or an **interpreter**. A compiler is basically the same as an assembler; it translates the entire source program into machine code, forming an object program for use in processing. If the source program is changed in any way, it must be recompiled in order for the object program to also be changed. Compiled high-level programs are not as fast as assembly language programs. Interpreters translate and execute the source program line by line and do not create an object code program. While compiled programs are faster in execution time than interpreted programs, interpreters are normally faster for program development. Programs written in a high-level language were intended to be portable, or **machine-independent**, so that they would transfer from one machine to another, provided both had the proper compiler. Unfortunately, due to a number of problems, such as language enhancements by individual manufacturers, this feature has never been fully realized.

The concept of a high-level language was first realized in 1957 with the introduction by IBM of a special language called **FORTRAN** (FORmula TRANslation). Under development since 1954, FORTRAN was designed primarily for scientific and engineering applications. In 1958, **ALGOL** (ALGOrithmic Language) was introduced, followed by **COBOL** (COmmon Business-Oriented Language) in 1961. ALGOL is another scientific-oriented language, but COBOL took another approach. It was designed, as the name implies, for business applications. Its mathematical power is very limited, but operations in COBOL are expressed in English statements that make it easy to understand, even by those unfamiliar with the details of the language. **BASIC** appeared in 1964; we will discuss it in more detail in the next section.

By the mid-1960s a relatively large number of languages began to appear, and by the 1970s there was a virtual explosion. However, like anything else, only those that met the needs of the users survived. One real survivor is a derivative of ALGOL called **Pascal** (named for the French mathematician Blaise Pascal). It was developed in the late 1960s in Switzerland by Niklaus Wirth and is the first programming language developed specifically for structured programming. Pascal has become one of the most popular languages for educational uses. (Another ALGOL offshoot, **Ada**, has recently been developed by the Department of Defense. Its acceptance is yet to be determined.)

There are literally hundreds of other languages available for either general or specific applications. We have mentioned only those that hold an important place in the historical development of high-level languages or that have achieved outstanding acceptance. This does not mean that others, like PL/1, APL, LISP, PILOT, and C, are not equally worthy, but space does not permit a full discussion of all. Each language has been developed for a specific purpose and should be applied to that purpose. We will be concerned with BASIC, which was developed for the specific purpose of being an easy-to-learn first language.

1-5 THE BASIC ENVIRONMENT

BASIC (Beginners' All-purpose Symbolic Instruction Code) was developed in 1963–1964 by two professors at Dartmouth College, John Kemeny and Thomas Kurtz. While most languages up to that time had been compiled and designed to run on a **batch system**, BASIC was designed to be interpreted and run on a **time-sharing system** so that it would be **interactive** with the user. That is, rather than writing a program, punching it onto cards, and submitting it to the system for processing (compilation and execution), only to find that it contains errors and has to be corrected and resubmitted, BASIC programs could be checked and run as they were written. The original concept for BASIC was that it would be easy for the beginner to learn and would actually encourage the use of the computer. It was and is an unqualified success!

BASIC had come into widespread use by the mid-1970s. The introduction of microcomputers, virtually all of which used BASIC as the primary "house" language, brought computing (and BASIC) to literally everyone. Today, almost all computer makers offer a version of BASIC for their systems. The main problem with BASIC is that there is no real standard for the various versions. In 1978, **ANSI** (American National Standards Institute) did publish a minimal set of standards, but they are just that—*minimal*. And all computer makers offer extensions, frequently wide-ranging, among which there is little or no agreement. In this book an attempt is made to stay with the "most standard" BASIC, common variations being noted whenever appropriate.

Although BASIC was originally designed to work with an interpreter, there are currently many versions that function as compiled languages. The few real differences between the forms are not in the writing of programs, but in how programs are executed and errors detected. Whether a BASIC is interpreted or compiled, the system commands for interacting with the computer vary drastically from one computer to the next. No attempt will be made at this point to cover these. (A summary of the most commonly used interactive system commands is provided in Appendix C.) Most of the programs in this book are written for an interpreted BASIC, but they should run on a compiled version with few if any changes.

While it began as an educational tool for teaching programming, BASIC is now a true general-purpose language finding applications from business to science to education. One of the primary reasons for the expansion in BASIC applications was the microcomputer and its nearly exclusive use of BASIC in the late 1970s. For the first time, even a small business could afford a computer, one that talked BASIC. Hospitals, colleges, and commercial labs put BASIC-speaking microcomputers to work controlling scientific instruments and performing routine tests. Home computers allow people to balance their checkbooks and keep household records in BASIC. While the increased power of the micro has made other languages available—and languages such as Pascal have gained popularity recently as teaching languages—the proven ease of learning BASIC as a first language will preserve its place as one of the top languages for many years to come.

IMPORTANT TERMS

After studying this chapter, you should be familiar with the meaning and use of the following terms:

Computerphobia
Microprocessor
Data
Program
Software
Input device
VDT
Output device
Hard copy
Central processor unit
Main memory
K
Control unit
Arithmetic/logic unit
Auxiliary storage
GIGO
I/O operations
Arithmetic operations
Logic operations
Summary reports
Classifying
Exception reports
Updating
Sorting
Control breaks
Merging
Hardware
Stored program concept
Machine language
Binary code
Machine-specific
Assembly language
Assembler
Source program
Object program
High-level language
Macro
Compiler
Interpreter
Machine-independent
FORTRAN
ALGOL
COBOL
BASIC
Pascal
Ada
Batch system
Time-sharing system
Interactive system
ANSI

CHAPTER 2

YOU *ARE* A PROGRAMMER!

Before we begin our study of the BASIC programming language in Chapter 3, let us look at what is involved in planning a program. Before actually writing statements in any programming language, a programmer must first outline the logic of the solution to the problem. This will help to get the statements in the proper order. In this chapter, we will take a brief look at how to plan for a program and outline its solution. We will also examine the use of flowcharts as a planning tool, with a quick introduction to some alternative methods.

2-1 WHAT IS A PROGRAM?

A **program** can be defined as a sequence of instructions to accomplish a specific job. Note that the word *computer* does not appear in the definition. This is because a program need not have anything at all to do with a computer. A **computer program** is simply a program that is designed to be executed by a computer. Whether you are aware of it or not, even though you may never have touched a computer, you *are* already a programmer, and an experienced one at that. Let us look at some examples of *non*computer programming.

You have probably at some time been asked by someone for directions on getting to a specific place. When you replied, your directions were in the form of a sequence of steps to follow. They should have been clear, specific, and in the proper order. We have all had the misfortune of receiving ambiguous directions like "take a right by the wooden house" or "continue on this street until you come to a pine tree." If you have ever given anyone a recipe for preparing a certain dish, you were writing out a program that, if followed properly, would permit that person to recreate your masterpiece. Again, the steps must be clear, specific, and in the proper order. "How many cups of salt did you say to add?" "Are you sure that you stir the cake *after* it comes out of the oven?" You have also used many programs that were prepared by other people. Other than the examples relating to computers that were mentioned in Section 1-1, consider the following: The instructions on how to operate or assemble something are a type of program to guide you through a procedure. Have you ever used a programmed textbook? This is a text that has the subject broken into self-paced teaching segments that, if properly followed, will allow (program) you to learn the material on your own.

Computer programs are no more than programs to accomplish a task—as are the above examples—except now the task will be performed by a computer under your direction. You will decide on the procedure to solve the problem and then, using the programming language BASIC, instruct the computer on how to perform the solution. Just as there might be more than one way to reach a certain destination, and therefore more than one possible set of directions, there is usually more than one way to approach computerized problem solving. Of course, some solutions will be better than others, just as some directions give shorter or easier routes than others.

For the remainder of this chapter, we will examine the logic of constructing programs and look at some of the tools available to assist you in this.

2-2 THE PROGRAMMING PROCESS

All programs are different, and each will involve its own special conditions and problems to solve. We can, however, outline a series of steps that are normally followed in constructing programs. These are:

1. Clearly define the problem.
2. Outline the steps of the solution.
3. Translate the steps into program statements.
4. Test the program and make any necessary changes.
5. Put the program into use.

Let us examine each of these steps individually.

As a student, you will not be concerned with the actual formulation of the problem as might a professional programmer in an on-the-job assignment. You will be given specific problems and asked to write programs for their solution. From the start you must be absolutely certain that you understand the problem. Ask yourself such questions as: "What data is to be processed?" "What result is to be produced?" "What type of processing or calculations must be performed in order to obtain that result from the known data?" "What special conditions must be checked?" It is not necessary at this point to know exactly *how* to solve the problem, but you should know precisely *what* is to be done.

Once you have a firm understanding of what the problem requires, you are ready to begin constructing a solution. First, you should outline the logic or the general design of the program you will use to solve the problem. This will provide a pattern to follow when you write the actual program. It is this part of the program solution that will concern us for the remainder of this chapter.

Having outlined the solution, you are ready to translate it into a program. For our work in this book, this will mean a computer program written in BASIC. We will begin the translation phase in Chapter 3 and continue with program development for the remainder of the book.

The fourth step given above is actually a part of program development. It is a sad fact, but there will probably be errors in your programs. It will, of course, be necessary to eliminate these errors before your program will function properly. This is the purpose of the testing phase. As you write and test your program and find errors, you will need to **troubleshoot** or **debug** the program to eliminate them. The errors you find will fall into one of three general classes. These are syntax, runtime, and logic errors.

Syntax errors are those resulting from a mistake in the rules of the language. A simple example would be misspelling a command. **Runtime errors** occur when a program is executed but the computer runs into a command that it cannot execute. An example of a runtime error would be trying to read data when none has been entered. While syntax and runtime errors usually cause an error message to be printed to the screen, the third type of error, the **logic error**, normally does not. A logic error arises when you attempt to execute program steps in the wrong sequence. For example, suppose that you wish to add two numbers and print the sum, but you list the statement to print *before* the one that adds. Clearly, the sum cannot be printed before it is calculated. With this type of error, you usually just get the wrong results. Unfortunately, of the types of errors, logic errors are often the most difficult to track down.

The last step above simply means that once the program is running properly, you put it into use for the intended purpose. In your case as a student, that will usually mean submitting it to the instructor for an A!

2-3 THINKING IT OUT: THE ALGORITHM

Before you can successfully write programs in BASIC or any other language, you must learn to logically organize the steps of the program. This requires no more ability than you would need to organize the steps in writing out a set of directions or a recipe as described above. The problems you will be solving may be a little different to you, so you may have to think a bit more about organizing them than you would something with which you are already familiar, but you can do this with a little effort. The key to organizing any programming problem is to think it out in small steps: "How would I do this manually?" Trace through the solution as if you were the computer, performing each operation in turn, and see if it comes out properly.

The carefully defined, step-by-step outline solution for a problem is known as an **algorithm**. An algorithm can be more formally defined as a finite series of well-defined instructions for accomplishing a specific task. This should be clear except possibly for the term *finite,* which simply means that the algorithm must provide a method for completing the designated job in a countable number of steps. In other words, the algorithm must have an end. Let us look at some examples of writing algorithms.

We will begin by writing an algorithm for a very simple task: moving a pile of bricks, one brick at a time, from one place to another. First, think it through. How would you do this step by step? You would probably proceed something like this: Pick up a brick, carry it to the new pile, and put it down. Go back, get another brick, and continue the process until all the bricks have been moved. This can be expressed a little more formally as follows:

1. Get a brick from the old pile.
2. Carry it to the new pile.
3. Place it on the new pile.
4. Are there any more bricks to be moved? If so, go to step 1. If not, stop.

This sequence of steps states *exactly* the same thing stated in the text above, but more concisely and in a form that is easier to understand. This may not be apparent yet, but it will be as we look at some more complex examples.

As a second example, consider the problem of adding the integers 1 through 10. This sounds easy enough, but think it out. What steps are involved in finding the sum of $1 + 2 + 3 + 4 + 5 + 6 + 7 + 8 + 9 + 10$? You add 1 and 2 to get 3. Then add 3 to this, giving 6. To this sum, add 4, then 5, and so forth up to 10. Let us write an algorithm for finding this sum.

1. Set sum equal to 0.
2. Set number equal to 1.
3. Add number to sum.
4. Add 1 to number.
5. Is number greater than 10? If yes, go to the next step; otherwise, go to step 3.
6. State sum.
7. Stop.

Step 1 starts the sum at 0, and step 2 begins the series of numbers that we are to add at 1. Step 3 adds the number to the sum, while step 4 generates the next number. That is, for the first number, 1, 1 is added to 0 at step 3 to give 1; then at step 4, 1 is added to 1, giving 2, the next number to be added. Step 5 checks to see that we have not gone too far. As long as the numbers are not greater than 10, we continue to add to the sum at step 3. Hence, we go back to step 3 where 2 will be added to the sum, giving 3. At step 4, 1 is added to 2 to give the next number, 3, which is not greater than 10, so it is added to the sum at step 3, giving 6, and so on until the number reaches 11. The sum is stated, and the process stops. Try tracing it through; you should get a sum of 55.

As a final example, we will construct an algorithm for making change for any purchase up to \$1.00. You know how to do this. You give as many quarters as you can, then as many dimes, then nickels, and finally finish out with pennies. For example, if the purchase is for \$0.27, then change is \$1.00 − \$0.27 = \$0.73. Thus the change will be 2 × \$0.25 + 2 × \$0.10 + 3 × \$0.01 = two quarters plus two dimes plus three pennies. Now for an algorithm to accomplish this task:

1. Set the number of quarters, dimes, nickels, and pennies equal to 0.
2. Record purchase price.
3. Subtract purchase price from \$1.00. Call this change.
4. Is change less than \$0.25? If yes, go to step 8. If not, go to the next step.
5. Add 1 to the number of quarters in the change.
6. Subtract \$0.25 from the change.
7. Go to step 4.
8. Is change less than \$0.10? If yes, go to step 12. If not, go to the next step.
9. Add 1 to the number of dimes in the change.
10. Subtract \$0.10 from the change.
11. Go to step 8.
12. Is change less than \$0.05? If yes, go to step 16. If not, go to the next step.
13. Add 1 to the number of nickels in the change.
14. Subtract \$0.05 from the change.
15. Go to step 12.
16. Is change less than \$0.01? If yes, go to step 20. If not, go to the next step.
17. Add 1 to the number of pennies in the change.
18. Subtract \$0.01 from the change.
19. Go to step 16.
20. Give change using the number of quarters, dimes, nickels, and pennies counted.
21. Stop.

This may seem a bit long, but if you carefully trace it through, you will be able to see how the exact procedure for making change is detailed.

The verbal algorithm is but one method for outlining the solution to a problem. In the next section, we will look at flowcharts, which accomplish essentially the same result but in pictorial form.

2-4 FLOWCHARTING

In the last section, we saw how to outline the solution to a problem as a sequence of verbal instructions. There are, however, a number of other methods for expressing an algorithm. One very popular technique is the use of **flowcharts**. Flowcharts provide a pictorial illustration of the solution to a problem, which allows you to trace the steps to the solution in graphic form. This can, in many cases, provide a better overall view of the general procedure than the verbal algorithm. Figure 2-1 gives the six most commonly used flow-

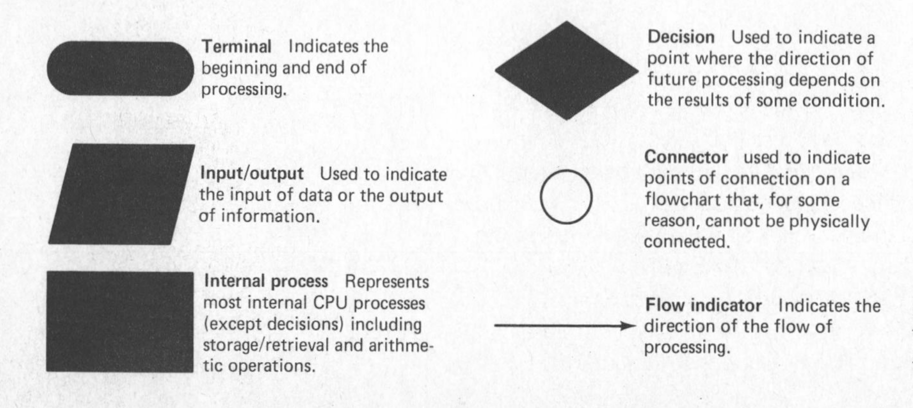

FIGURE 2-1
The six most commonly used flowcharting symbols

charting symbols along with an explanation of their use. Although we will occasionally find a need for certain other special symbols, these six will allow us to construct nearly all of the flowcharts we will need.

Let us look at the three examples from the previous section and construct flowcharts for these processes. The first problem, moving the pile of bricks, can be represented by the diagram shown in Figure 2-2. The first symbol is the start symbol. The second symbol is input or "get a brick from the old pile." The next is a process: "carry it to the new pile." The fourth symbol is output or "place it on the new pile." The diamond represents the decision, "Are there any more bricks to be moved?" If the answer is yes, then we go back to the input symbol and get another brick. If there are no more bricks, then move to the next symbol, which in this case is the stop symbol.

The second problem, that of adding the integers from 1 through 10 is diagrammed in Figure 2-3. Compare this to the algorithm given above. You should be able to follow the flowchart directly from the verbal statements.

Now we come to the final example, making change. This process consists of a brief initialization procedure for setting the number of each type of coin to zero and calculating the amount of change that is to be given (steps 1 to 3 in the verbal algorithm). This first part is shown as a section of a flowchart in Figure 2-4*a*. Next, there are four identical sections which determine the number of quarters (steps 4 to 7), dimes (steps 8 to 11), nickels (steps 12 to 15), and pennies (steps 16 to 19) that will make up the change. These four sets of instructions are exactly the same except for the type of coin processed. A flowchart section for quarters is illustrated in Figure 2-4*b*, but the others will have precisely the same structure. The final part of the process (steps 20 to 21) is to give the correct change as determined by the algorithm and to end. The completed flowchart illustrating the entire process is shown in Figure 2-5.

In the major examples in the chapters that follow, algorithms in both verbal and flowchart form will be presented along with a complete explanation of the program solution. In addition, flowcharts will be used extensively throughout the text to illustrate the various programming procedures and logic structures that we will study.

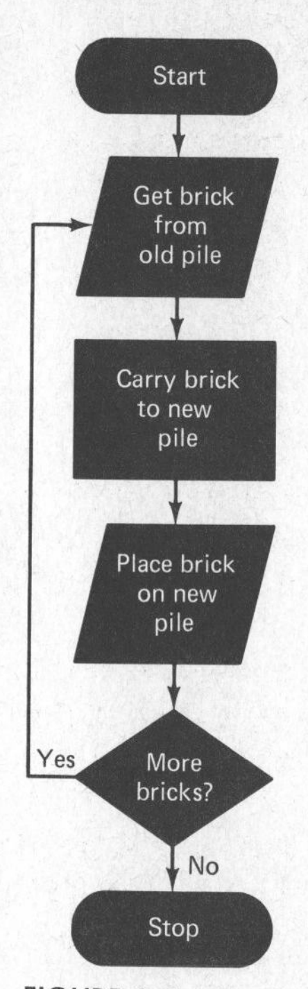

FIGURE 2-2
Flowchart for moving a pile of bricks

2-5 OTHER PROGRAM DESIGN TOOLS

While we will rely almost entirely on the two program design techniques discussed thus far, there are several others that are used, two of which deserve brief mention in this section. These are pseudocode and decision tables.

Pseudocode is another form of expressing a verbal algorithm; however, the statements used are a little more structured and more closely related to the actual *program* design. The algorithm for moving the pile of bricks might be expressed in pseudocode as follows:

```
WHILE there are bricks
        Get a brick from the old pile
        Carry it to the new pile
        Place it on the new pile
ENDWHILE
Stop
```

The procedure for adding the integers from 1 to 10 could be written as:

```
Set sum equal to 0
Set number equal to 1
IF number is not greater than 10
        THEN Add number to sum
                Add 1 to number
        ELSE State sum
ENDIF
Stop
```

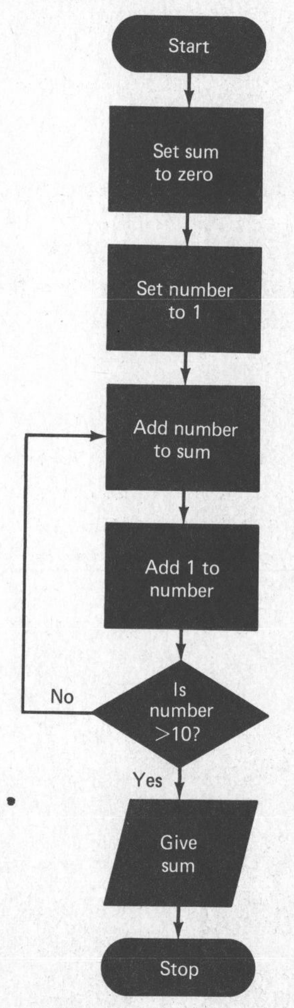

FIGURE 2-3
Flowchart for adding integers from 1 to 10

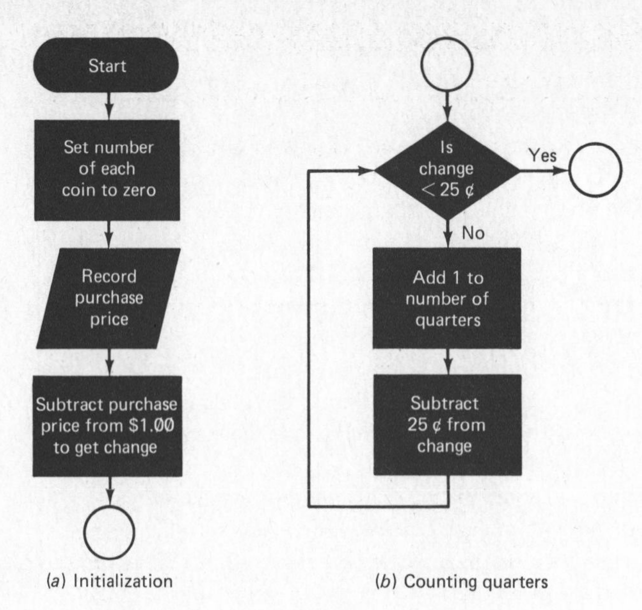

FIGURE 2-4
Sections from the flowchart for making change

Of course, as with the other types of algorithms, these, or most any processes, could be stated in a variety of ways.

The **decision table** differs slightly from what we have encountered so far. It consists of two basic parts: The first section lists the conditions that are to be tested as part of the algorithm, and the second part identifies (as with an X) the specific actions to be taken, given the results of the test of the condition. As an example, the algorithm for making change is illustrated in a decision table in Table 2-1. Note that the four conditions controlling the counts for the four types of coins are listed at the top of the table. The results for

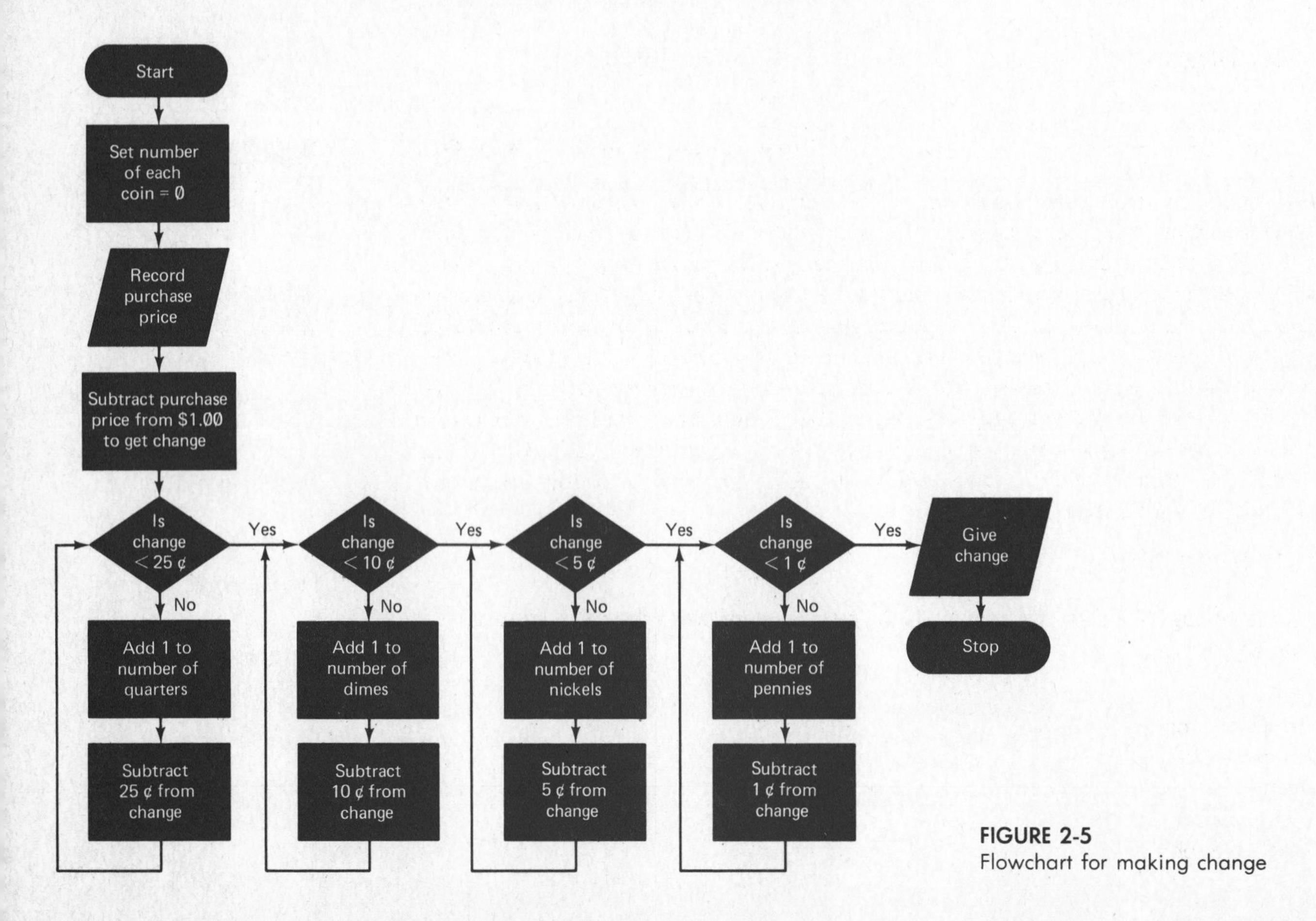

FIGURE 2-5
Flowchart for making change

TABLE 2-1

Brief Decision Table for Making Change Algorithm

Conditions						
Is change at least $0.25?		Y	N	N	N	N
Is change at least $0.10?			Y	N	N	N
Is change at least $0.05?				Y	N	N
Is change at least $0.01?					Y	N
Actions Taken						
Set number of quarters, dimes, nickels, and pennies equal to 0	X					
Record purchase price	X					
Subtract purchase price from $1.00. Call this change.	X					
Add 1 to number of quarters in change.		X				
Subtract $0.25 from change.		X				
Add 1 to number of dimes in change.			X			
Subtract $0.10 from change.			X			
Add 1 to number of nickels in change.				X		
Subtract $0.05 from change.				X		
Add 1 to number of pennies in change.					X	
Subtract $0.01 from change.					X	
Give change using number of quarters, dimes, nickels, and pennies counted.						X
Stop.						X

each condition are indicated by a Y or N (''yes'' or ''no'') in columns to the right. The possible actions are given in the second section of the table, with an action resulting from a specific condition indicated by an X. For example, as long as the change is *not* less than $0.25, the actions noted under that column (add 1 to the number of quarters in the change and subtract $0.25 from change) will be executed. The same procedure is followed for the other three conditions. In this particular example, only one condition at a time could be tested, and these only in a given sequence. This will not always be the case. In some problems, several conditions may have to be satisfied in order for a certain action to be true. It is for this type of problem that decision tables can be most useful. As with the other design techniques that we have discussed, different forms of decision tables are possible for a given problem.

IMPORTANT TERMS

After studying this chapter, you should be familiar with the meaning and use of the following terms:

Program
Computer program
Troubleshoot
Debug
Syntax error
Runtime error
Logic error
Algorithm
Flowchart
Pseudocode
Decision table

EXERCISES

For Exercises 1 to 8, write verbal algorithms and draw flowcharts to describe a solution to each problem.

1. Count the marbles in a bowl.
2. Count the *green* marbles in a bowl.
3. Find the sum of the even integers from 10 through 20.
4. Find the average of four test grades.
5. Read a set of three numbers and select the largest of the three.
6. Read a set of three numbers and arrange them in order of increasing size.
7. Examine a series of test grades and determine whether each is an A, B, C, D, or F.
8. Repeat the procedure in Exercise 7 but keep track of the number of tests of each grade and find the class average.

It is important that you learn how to operate your computer/terminal before you begin to write your own programs in the next chapter. For Exercises 9 to 12, type the given program into your computer exactly as it is written and run it. The programs are correct as given below. If you get an error message, such as Syntax Error in Line #, you probably have miscopied something. Retype the indicated line. If this does not eliminate the error message, consult your instructor for assistance.

9.
```
10 REM  PROGRAM TO FIND THE SUM OF TWO NUMBERS
20 REM
30 LET X = 12
40 LET Y = 17
50 LET Z = X + Y
60 PRINT X, Y, Z
70 END
```

10.
```
10 REM  PROGRAM TO ADD AND SUBTRACT ANY TWO NUMBERS
20 REM
30 INPUT "ENTER ANY NUMBER"; A
40 INPUT "ENTER ANOTHER NUMBER"; B
50 LET S = A + B
60 LET D = A - B
70 PRINT
80 PRINT "THE SUM OF YOUR NUMBERS IS"; S
90 PRINT "THE DIFFERENCE OF YOUR NUMBERS IS"; D
100 END
```

11.
```
10 REM  PROGRAM TO FIND THE SUM OF
20 REM  THE INTEGERS FROM 1 - 10
30 REM
40 LET S = 0
50 LET N = 1
60 LET S = S + N
70 LET N = N + 1
80 IF N < 11 GOTO 60
90 PRINT "THE SUM OF THE INTEGERS 1-10 ="; S
100 END
```

12.
```
10 REM  PROGRAM TO MAKE CHANGE
20 REM
30 LET NQ = 0
40 LET ND = 0
50 LET NN = 0
60 LET NP = 0
70 INPUT "ENTER AMOUNT IN CENTS (1-100)"; P
80 IF P < 1 OR P > 100 GOTO 310
90 LET C = 100 - P
100 IF C < 25 THEN 140
```

```
110   LET NQ = NQ + 1
120   LET C = C - 25
130 GOTO 100
140 IF C < 10 THEN 180
150   LET ND = ND + 1
160   LET C = C - 10
170 GOTO 140
180 IF C < 5 THEN 220
190   LET NN = NN + 1
200   LET C = C - 5
210 GOTO 180
220 IF C < 1 THEN 260
230   LET NP = NP + 1
240   LET C = C - 1
250 GOTO 220
260 PRINT
270 PRINT "AMOUNT OF",, " CHANGE AS NUMBER OF"
280 PRINT "PURCHASE", "QUARTERS","DIMES","NICKELS","PENNIES"
290 PRINT
300 PRINT P, NQ, ND, NN, NP
310 END
```

PART TWO

FUNDAMENTAL PROCEDURES

CHAPTER 3

GETTING STARTED

This chapter provides an introduction to the fundamentals of BASIC. You will learn how BASIC programs are constructed, the types of data handled by BASIC, how to select and name variables, some simple program statements and their functions, and, hopefully in this and every chapter, some good programming techniques.

Studying computer programming and a programming language is often compared to such other subject areas as mathematics or foreign languages. As with most analogies, this one has some degree of truth but is not perfect. There is one point, however, regarding the study of programming that holds true for studying most any subject: *Build and maintain a sound foundation*. Learn and understand (do not just memorize) the fundamental principles as they are introduced. Then, as new concepts are encountered, add these to your repertoire of skills so that you are continually building on your own ''mental program library.''

3-1 STATEMENTS IN BASIC

As with virtually all programming languages, programs in BASIC are constructed by writing a sequence of instructions that direct the action of the computer. Each **instruction** consists of a statement which must always be preceded by a line number; line numbers will be discussed in detail in Section 3-2. All statements in BASIC may be classified within two distinct (and disjoint) categories: executable statements and nonexecutable statements. An **executable** statement is a command that causes an action to occur; this can be the input or output of data, an arithmetic operation, a transfer of control to another part of the program, or *any* command that causes some type of process to take place. Such statements usually begin with an action **verb**, such as READ, PRINT, or GOTO, that provides a clue to their effect. Nearly all statements in BASIC are of the executable category.

The second classification of statements, the **nonexecutable** ones, are included in BASIC programs for special reasons, which will become clear as these statements are discussed. Because the nonexecutable statements by definition cause *no* action to occur and have no effect on the actual logic of the program execution, they may be placed at any convenient point in the program with *no* effect on the processing of the problem. The actual presence or absence of nonexecutable statements may affect the program; it is their physical placement that is flexible. There are very few such statements. We shall discuss one here and see one other at the beginning of Chapter 4.

One nonexecutable statement that is very important to all BASIC programmers is the **REM** (for REMark) statement. It has the general form:

ln **REM** *comment*

where *ln* represents the BASIC line number. With the REM statement, anything that is typed after the three letters REM will be printed on the program listing but will be ignored by the computer in processing the program. This statement is used to insert comments into the program at any point where they may be useful. Typical examples of the use of the REM statement would be to give the name of the programmer, identify the problem being coded, specify the variables used, or identify the functions of various parts of the program. The following are examples:

```
10 REM   INVENTORY UPDATE PROGRAM
20 REM   ACME HARDWARE
30 REM   WRITTEN BY JOHN SMITH
                  :
          (rest of program)
                  :
```

3-2 USE OF LINE NUMBERS

As mentioned at the beginning of the last section, *all* statements in BASIC *must* have a **line number**. The exact range of the numbers will vary with the computer being used, but the usual range is 1 to 99999. Some computers may accept 0 for a line number, while others may not allow numbers above a certain upper limit that is less than 99999, say 63999; however, negative numbers are never allowed, nor are numbers above 99999 or fractions. Table 3-1 illustrates some invalid line numbers. The function of the line number in BASIC is very simple: It is used to sequence the statements. In other words, the statements are placed in order according to the numerically *increasing* values of the line numbers. This is a very convenient feature once you get used to it. If you find that a statement is in the wrong place, it can be moved by simply changing (or rewriting) it so that it has a line number that will put it in the correct order in the program. Statements may be added by simply typing them into the computer with the proper line numbers. In all cases, the statements need not be typed originally or changes made in any certain order as long as the line numbers are assigned to the statements in the numerical order in which the statements are to be processed. The computer will automatically resequence the statements into order by line number.

The following is an example of the use of line numbers to move or rearrange statements in a BASIC program. Assume that a section of a program consists of five statements written like this:

```
120  statement 1
130  statement 2
140  statement 3
150  statement 4
160  statement 5
```

Now, suppose we discover that in order to make the program work properly we must (1) move statement 4 so that it is between statements 1 and 2 and (2) add a new statement 6 between statements 2 and 3. To do this, type:

```
125  statement 4
150    (blank)
135  statement 6
```

TABLE 3-1

Examples of Invalid BASIC Line Numbers

Invalid Line Number	Reason Why It Is Invalid
−120	No negative line numbers are permitted.
+ 120	No sign can be designated.
45.6	No fractional line numbers are allowed.
20A	Only the ten digits (0 to 9) may be used to write a line number.
2,000	No commas are allowed.
1245000	Number is too large.

The first line places statement 4 between statements 1 and 2. (Any line number from 121 through 129 could have been used.) The second line clears the old statement 4. (As an alternative to this, the DELETE command is available on some computers. If your system uses DELETE, refer to Appendix C for more information on this command.) Finally, the last line inserts the new statement. When this portion of the program is listed back, it will be in the required order:

```
120  statement 1
125  statement 4
130  statement 2
135  statement 6
140  statement 3
160  statement 5
```

When assigning line numbers to BASIC statements, *never* select consecutive numbers such as 1, 2, 3, 4, . . . , or 100, 101, 102, 103, ... Consecutive numbers allow no room between lines for inserting new statements should the need arise. The most common practice for line numbering is to number by tens: 10, 20, 30, 40, . . . , although any scheme may be used: 20, 40, 60, 80, . . . ; 100, 200, 300, 400, . . . ; 25, 50, 75, 100, . . . ; 20, 35, 80, 135, . . . ; or whatever seems good to you.

3-3 DATA REPRESENTATION

Data in BASIC is classified as either numeric or string (nonnumeric), A **numeric value** is one that is assigned to a number field, generally, but not necessarily, one that is to be used in mathematical operations. For example, values that might be handled as numeric are 123, 573.56, −92.665, and 0.045. Numeric data can contain only the ten digits (0 to 9), a plus or minus sign, and a decimal point as needed. Absolutely *no* letters or other special characters are permitted. A **string value** is used to handle anything that is not numeric. This would include data that contains other than the above-listed characters or that for some reason cannot be treated as numeric. Examples of string values are names; addresses; dates and social security numbers, if any dashes or other separators are used; CHAP3.BK1; and $$$$$. (The maximum size of numeric and string values varies with the computer being used; you will need to check to see what limits apply to your system.)

Data values are the information—names, numbers, dates, etc.—to be processed by the computer. **Data names** (commonly referred to as variables) are the symbols selected by you, the programmer, to *represent* the data values. A data value is usually, but not always, assigned to a specified data name. If the value assigned to a data name remains the same throughout the program run, it is referred to as a **constant**. If the value assigned is numeric, then it is a *numeric constant;* if it is string, then it is a *string constant*. Either a numeric or a string constant may be specified within the program without being assigned

TABLE 3-2

Examples of Valid and Invalid BASIC Data Names

Numeric	
X	Valid
A3	Valid
VT	Valid
7	Invalid—Contains only digit
8Y	Invalid—Begins with digit
G +	Invalid—Contains special symbol
TO	Invalid—Reserved word
RATE1	Invalid—Too long*
String	
Q$	Valid
FL$	Valid
K6$	Valid
PI	Invalid—No $
$DX	Invalid—$ not at end
4$	Invalid—Contains no letter
$	Invalid—Contains no letter
NAME$	Invalid—Too long*

*Some versions of BASIC will allow longer data names.

to a data name. These types of constants are referred to as numeric or string **literals;** we will discuss the use of literals in more detail in a later chapter.

If the value assigned to a data name changes during the course of a program run, the data name is referred to as a **variable**, either numeric or string, depending on the type of data assigned. Constant and variable data names and values are handled exactly the same by the computer and are indistinguishable as far as processing is concerned. In either case, the computer assigns a storage location to the data name (which you select) and places data in storage as you direct. Once you have specified the data name, you may change the value assigned as often as needed without being concerned with *where* the computer has placed it; in BASIC, the computer takes care of all storage bookkeeping chores automatically. In the case of a constant, the first value that is placed in storage remains there without ever being altered. If the data name represents a variable, the value in the storage area is changed as the processing dictates.

The rules for naming variables or constants in BASIC are simple. Any numeric value can be designated by (1) any single letter from A to Z, (2) any two-letter combination, or (3) any letter followed by one digit (0 to 9). Numeric data names must begin with a letter, may consist of one or two characters only, and cannot contain any special symbols. A few combinations of letters (referred to as **reserved words**) have a special interpretation by the computer and should be avoided; these include IF, TO, GO, ON, and FN. String values are designated by any valid numeric data name with a dollar sign ($) on the end. Table 3-2 gives several examples of both valid and invalid data names. (Some versions of BASIC allow data names of more than two characters.)

3-4 THE ASSIGNMENT (LET) STATEMENT

A specific value can be assigned to a data name by the use of the **LET** statement. The general form of this statement is:

ln **LET** *data name = expression*

Again, *ln* represents the line number. The expression may be a data value, another data name, or any valid BASIC mathematical expression. The latter two cases will be discussed in detail in Chapter 5; for now, the expression part of the LET statement will be confined to a single data value. Examples of typical LET statements are:

```
130  LET A = 12.5
145  LET DS = -5993.56
190  LET FL$ = "FIRST CARD"
```

These statements have the effect of assigning the values of 12.5 to the variable A, −5993.56 to DS, and FIRST CARD to FL$. In the above examples, note that either numeric or string values can be assigned by means of the LET statement. Also, observe that string values are placed in quotation marks while numeric data is not. Many computers consider the verb LET to be optional so that it can be omitted from the above statements without harm. These statements would then be written:

```
130  A = 12.5
145  DS = -5993.56
190  FL$ = "FIRST CARD"
```

The action of the LET statement within the computer's memory is shown in Figure 3-1.

With the LET statement, as with all other statements in most versions of BASIC, spaces are ignored and are added by the programmer for readability. The following statements would all be interpreted the same by BASIC:

```
50  LET CB = -42.7
50  LETCB=-42.7
50  CB = -42.7
50  CB=-42.7
50  CB      =       -42.7
```

The first and third are the easiest to read; the second and fourth are the most difficult; the fifth is simply awkward. There is no rule regarding spaces, but the general guideline is that spaces should be added as necessary to make statements easy to read and to avoid any possibility of confusion (on the part of the human user—not the computer!). The one notable exception to this involves spaces within quotation marks, meaning string constants or literals. A space within the quotes will be considered as part of the string constant and assigned as such. There will be more discussion of this in Chapter 6.

Before moving on to the PRINT statement, a word about error messages in is order. BASIC is designed to detect many of your programming errors as the program is executed, and as it does, an appropriate error message will be issued. We will discuss some of the types of errors and corresponding messages that you may encounter.

The **Syntax** error is probably the most common type of error message encountered. It normally occurs when a "grammatical" mistake, such as typing LTE for LET, has been made, an invalid data name has been used, or some other general rule of BASIC programming has been violated. It may, however, be issued for any type of problem which the computer cannot specifically classify; that is, it tends to be a catchall category. Another error that you may encounter in your early work in BASIC is the **Type Mismatch**. This error usually results from a mismatch between numeric and string data names and values. For example, it would occur if you were to type:

```
220  LET X1 = "DOG"
```

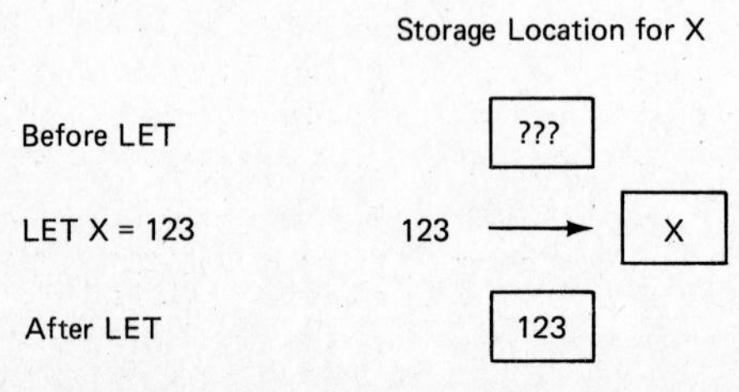

		Storage Location for X
Before LET		???
LET X = 123	123 ⟶	X
After LET		123

FIGURE 3-1
Internal effect of LET statement

The Type Mismatch is sometimes identified as a Syntax error. To complicate matters, all versions of BASIC do not treat and report the same errors in the same way. A Type Mismatch on one computer may well be reported as a Syntax problem on another. A general summary of BASIC error messages is provided in Appendix D.

3-5 PRODUCING OUTPUT: THE PRINT STATEMENT

Data output from a program is controlled by the **PRINT** Statement. The PRINT statement has many uses and forms in BASIC; however, for simple printing of data values, it has the general form:

ln **PRINT** *list*

where list represents a list of data names separated by commas. Typical PRINT statements are:

```
120  PRINT A, B, C
295  PRINT NA$, S$, R, H, P
```

PRINT statements can be used to print numeric data, string data, or both. Variables or constants can be printed, but the printing of literals will not be discussed until Chapter 6. Whenever a value is printed, only a copy of the data that is in storage is output, with the original value remaining in memory for future use if needed. This is illustrated in Figure 3-2.

While BASIC does provide some degree of control over the format (design) of the output data, in its simplest form the PRINT statement provides automatic spacing of the data on the output screen. When the PRINT statement is used with only a list of data names separated by commas, the data values to be printed are output to the screen in five **zones** (also referred to as *divisions* or *sections*). The number of screen columns included in each zone will depend on the computer and the version of BASIC being used. Most will range from 13 to 16 columns per zone. (We will be using 13 columns per zone in the examples that follow.) This means that the first value to be printed will appear in the first zone, the second in the second, etc., up to five values across the screen. If more than five values are listed in the print list, the sixth will appear back in the first zone under the first, the seventh will be in the next zone under the second, and so on. Within each zone, data values are always **left-justified**, meaning that they will always be printed beginning on the left side of the zone. String values will be printed beginning in the *first* column of each zone and continue for the length of the data value; there will be more about this later in this section. Numeric values usually begin in the *second* column of a zone, with the initial space being reserved for the printing of a plus or minus sign (if required). They are normally followed by at least one blank space and will print up to six to nine digits plus a decimal depending on the version of BASIC in use. These guidelines are not universal and may vary with your computer. Table 3-3 summarizes the screen zones and print positions for several of the most common formats.

TABLE 3-3

Summary of Screen Zones and Default Print Positions Employed by the PRINT Statement

Screen Zone	Column and Print Positions for Screen Zones of* 13 cols		14 cols		15 cols		16 cols	
1	1–13	1/ 2	1–14	1/ 2	1–15	1/ 2	1–16	1/ 2
2	14–26	14/15	15–28	15/16	16–30	16/17	17–32	17/18
3	27–39	27/28	29–42	29/30	31–45	31/32	33–48	33/34
4	40–52	40/41	43–56	43/44	46–60	46/47	49–64	49/50
5	53–65	53/54	57–70	57/58	61–75	61/62	65–80	65/66

*Shown as screen columns included for each zone, followed by columns in which string or numeric data will begin to print.

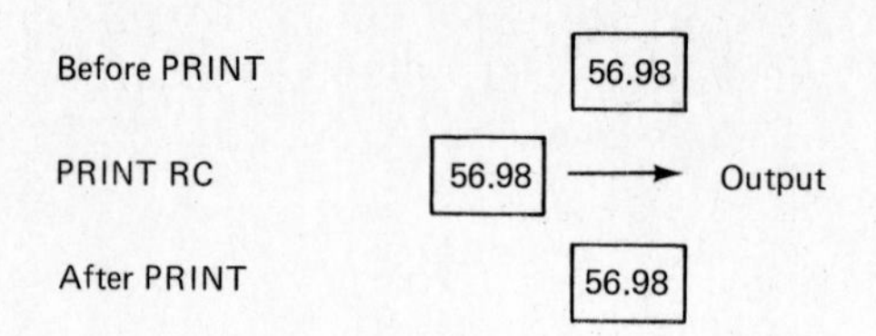

FIGURE 3-2
Internal action caused by PRINT

Let us look at a few examples of the PRINT statement. First, use the LET statement to assign values to several variables as follows:

```
10  LET N = 46508
20  LET NA$ = "MARY AMES"
30  LET H = 42.5
40  LET R = 7.45
50  LET SF$ = "YES"
60  LET K = 3
```

To print N, NA$, H, R, and SF$ in that order across the screen, write:

ln PRINT N, NA$, H, R, SF$

where *ln* is the proper line number. The output will look like this:

```
46508          MARY AMES       42.5              7.45              YES
```

To print the same values but in a different order, simply change the PRINT statement with the variables written in the order desired.

Sometimes it is necessary to print data on more than one line. There are six values above and only five zones on the screen; thus, to print all six of these values will (for now) require two PRINT statements. Maybe we would like to print N and NA$ on one line and the other four on a second line. The following PRINT statements will accomplish this:

ln1 PRINT N, NA$
ln2 PRINT H, R, SF$, K

producing a result on the screen as follows:

```
46508          MARY AMES
42.5            7.45            YES               3
```

The PRINT statement normally begins a new line of output on the screen. An exception to this occurs whenever the *immediately preceding* PRINT *ends* in a comma with no trailing data name. In this case, the variables listed in the new PRINT will be printed as though they were a continuation of the list in the previous PRINT. All of the following will yield the same output:

```
150  PRINT NA$, N, H, R, K

150  PRINT NA$, N,
155  PRINT H, R, K

150  PRINT NA$,
153  PRINT N, H, R,
157  PRINT K
```

There are several other possible variations which will produce the same result, that is:

```
MARY AMES      46508          42.5           7.45           3
```

A PRINT statement with *no* list of data names

ln PRINT

will cause a blank line to be printed unless it follows a PRINT that *ends* in a comma, in which case it has the effect of terminating the preceding print list and causing the next PRINT to begin on a new line.

It is also possible to skip over a zone on the screen without printing anything in it. Suppose you wanted NA$, N, and SF$ to appear in the first, second, and *fourth* zones, leaving the third empty. To do this, write:

ln PRINT NA$, N,, SF$

which will print on the screen

```
MARY AMES      46508                        YES
```

Note the extra comma after the N causes SF$ to be spaced *two* zones to the right instead of one. To print the same three variables in the second, third, and fifth zones write:

ln PRINT , NA$, N,, SF$

which prints

```
               MARY AMES      46508                        YES
```

One final note on the PRINT statement. If the value assigned to a data name is too long to fit into one screen zone, BASIC will take *two* (or more) zones to print the value, causing all subsequent items in that print line to be one additional zone to the right. If NA$ = WILLIAM CUNNINGHAM instead of MARY AMES, then the last two PRINT statements would produce the following results, respectively:

```
WILLIAM CUNNINGHAM            46508                        YES
```

and for the second statement:

```
               WILLIAM CUNNINGHAM            46508
YES
```

The YES in the last case is "reflected" back to the first screen zone because the long data value for the name has caused the YES to be pushed from the fifth position, where it was intended to be, into the sixth, which is printed under the first.

3-6 THE STOP AND END STATEMENTS

The last statement in any program should always be the **END** statement. It has the very simple form:

ln **END**

The END statement signals two things to the computer: (1) that program execution is complete and (2) that the physical end of the program has been encountered. In other words, when any program runs, the very last thing it should do is come to an END statement. The END statement should have the highest line number and be the last line of the program. All compiled and some interpreted versions of BASIC require that the END statement be physically present at the end of the program. Other BASIC interpreters do not and will stop execution with an **assumed END** when there are no more statements to be processed. Even on these systems, it is *always* advisable to end your programs with an END statement. This will help to assure that your program stops at the desired point.

Some interpreted BASICs will allow an END statement to be placed at the end of execution, even if this is not the very end of the program. This is *not* advised. The **STOP** statement is provided for the purpose of stopping a program in the middle of processing or at any point other than the very end. The STOP statement also has a very simple general form:

ln **STOP**

Because of their similarity in function and appearance, these two statements are frequently confused. There are, however, three basic differences between them: (1) Most forms of BASIC allow the program processing to continue (by typing **CONT**) at the point where it was interrupted with a STOP statement; this is not possible following an END statement. (2) A program may contain more than one STOP but can have only one END. (3) An interrupt caused by a STOP statement will usually cause a message, such as BREAK AT 250, to be printed on the screen, whereas END statements do not generate such messages.

3-7 AN EXAMPLE: CONSTRUCTING A PROGRAM

Now we are ready to put together what we have learned thus far, to construct a full program.

Problem: The values for a student's name, social security number, year in school, major, minor, and current GPA are to be assigned to appropriate variables. The data is then to be printed, with the social security number and name, in that order, on one line in the first and third positions and the remaining four values on a second line with the year, major, and minor in the first three positions, respectively, and the GPA in the fifth. The values to be assigned are:

Student Name: Brian Jones
Social Security Number: 449-01-8746
Year in School: Junior
Major: Chemistry
Minor: Biology
Current GPA: 2.78

A program to accomplish the above task consists of four distinct parts:

1. REM statements for documentation (not required for processing)
2. LET statements to assign the values to variables
3. PRINT statements for producing output
4. An END statement

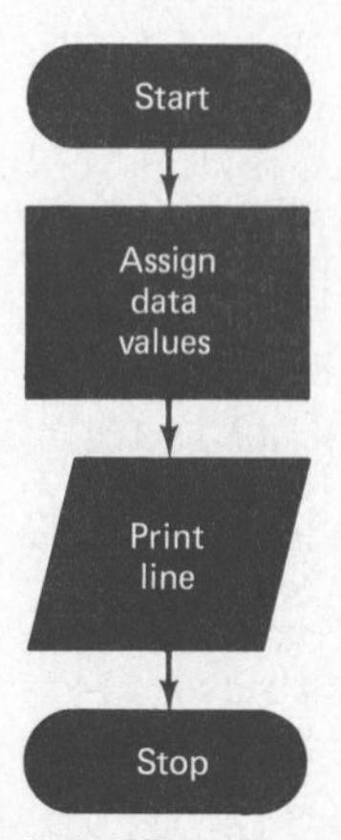

FIGURE 3-3
Flowchart for example

This example is a simple, straightforward sequence of statements and is illustrated in Figure 3-3.

To begin, the initial REM statements to identify the program and define the variables used might look something like this:

```
 10 REM  A FIRST PROGRAMMING EXAMPLE
 20 REM
 30 REM  VARIABLES ARE DEFINED AS --
 40 REM
 50 REM          SN$ = STUDENT NAME
 60 REM          SS$ = SOCIAL SECURITY NUMBER
 70 REM           Y$ = YEAR IN SCHOOL
 80 REM          MA$ = MAJOR
 90 REM          MI$ = MINOR
100 REM            G = GPA
110 REM
```

Note that all the variables *must* be string except G for the GPA. Other REM statements may be placed in the program as desired.

The six data values can be assigned to the designated variables by six LET statements:

```
140 LET SN$ = "BRIAN JONES"
150 LET SS$ = "449-01-8746"
160 LET Y$ = "JUNIOR"
170 LET MA$ = "CHEMISTRY"
180 LET MI$ = "BIOLOGY"
190 LET G = 2.78
```

Remember that string data values are always in quotes.

To print the results will require two PRINT statements. The social security number and name will be printed on the first line in the first and third positions by:

```
230  PRINT SS$,, SN$
```

The remaining four values are printed on a separate line with a blank fourth zone by:

```
240  PRINT Y$, MA$, MI$,, G
```

The final detail is the END statement:

```
250  END
```

Putting this all together along with a few additional REM statements for emphasis, the completed program listing is as follows:

```
 10 REM  A FIRST PROGRAMMING EXAMPLE
 20 REM
 30 REM  VARIABLES ARE DEFINED AS --
 40 REM
 50 REM          SN$ = STUDENT NAME
 60 REM          SS$ = SOCIAL SECURITY NUMBER
 70 REM           Y$ = YEAR IN SCHOOL
 80 REM          MA$ = MAJOR
 90 REM          MI$ = MINOR
100 REM            G = GPA
110 REM
120 REM  ASSIGN VALUES TO VARIABLES
130 REM
140 LET SN$ = "BRIAN JONES"
150 LET SS$ = "449-01-8746"
160 LET Y$ = "JUNIOR"
170 LET MA$ = "CHEMISTRY"
```

```
180 LET MI$ = "BIOLOGY"
190 LET G = 2.78
200 REM
210 REM  PRINT RESULTS AND END
220 REM
230 PRINT SS$,, SN$
240 PRINT Y$, MA$, MI$,, G
250 END
```

When this program is run, the output on the screen will be:

```
449-01-8746                      BRIAN JONES
JUNIOR         CHEMISTRY         BIOLOGY                      2.78
```

This example program consists of a total of 25 statements, only nine of which are executable. The 16 REM statements may seem like quite a number for such a short program, and there is some truth to that, but careful documentation becomes increasingly important as the programs become more and more complex. For that reason, it is best to develop at an early stage the habit of carefully documenting all programs so that it becomes part of your regular programming style.

TROUBLESHOOTING

Each of the following programs contains an error that prevents it from executing properly. Explain *specifically* what the problem is and what must be done to correct it. To assist you, a sample of what would happen should you attempt to run the program is provided after each listing. Refer to Appendix D for an explanation of BASIC error messages.

1.

```
 10 REM  TROUBLESHOOTING PROGRAM 3-1
 20 REM
 30 REM         NA = CUSTOMER NAME
 40 REM         AD = ACCOUNT ADJUSTMENT
 50 REM         BL = NEW BALANCE
 60 REM
 70 LET NA = "PETER SMITH"
 80 LET AD = 45.98
 90 LET BL = 372.79
100 PRINT NA, AD, BL
110 END

Type Mismatch in Line 70
```

2.

```
 10 REM  TROUBLESHOOTING PROBLEM 3-2
 20 REM
 30 REM         SN = STUDENT NUMBER
 40 REM         CN = CLASS NUMBER
 50 REM         IN = INSTRUCTOR NUMBER
 60 REM          G = GRADE
 70 REM
 80 LET SN = 190045
 90 LET CN = 4615
100 LET IN = 527
110 LET G = B
120 PRINT SN, CN, IN, G
130 END

190045         4615           527            0
```

3.

```
 10 REM  TROUBLESHOOTING PROBLEM 3-3
 20 REM
 30 REM         N$ = EMPLOYEE NAME
```

```
 40 REM        S$ = SOCIAL SECURITY NUMBER
 50 REM         A = AGE
 60 REM
 70 LET N$ = "ALICE KING"
 80 LET S$ = "388-91-0403"
 90 LET A = 67
100 PRINT N,, S,, A
110 END
```

```
0                            0                            67
```

4.

```
 10 REM  TROUBLESHOOTING PROBLEM 3-4
 20 REM
 30 REM        IV = INVENTORY NUMBER
 40 REM        N$ = ITEM NAME
 50 REM         Q = QUANTITY IN STOCK
 60 REM
 70 LET IV = 92330
 80 LET N$ = "CLAW HAMMER"
 90 LET Q = 218
100 PRNIT IV, N$, Q
110 END
```

```
Syntax Error in Line 100
```

5.

```
 10 REM  TROUBLESHOOTING PROBLEM 3-5
 20 REM
 30 REM        S$ = STUDENT'S NAME
 40 REM        A$ = ADVISOR'S NAME
 50 REM        M$ = MAJOR
 60 REM        L$ = MINOR
 70 REM
 80 LET S$ = "JACK OWENS"
 90 LET A$ = "DR. ANDERSON"
100 LET M$ = "ENGLISH"
110 LET M$ = "HISTORY"
120 PRINT S$
130 PRINT A$
140 PRINT M$, L$
150 END
```

```
JACK OWENS
DR. ANDERSON
HISTORY
```

6.

```
 10 REM  TROUBLESHOOTING PROBLEM 3-6
 20 REM
 30 REM        IV = INVENTORY NUMBER
 40 REM        N$ = ITEM NAME
 50 REM         Q = QUANTITY IN STOCK
 60 REM
 70 LET IV = 92330
 80 LET N$ = "CLAW HAMMER"
 90 LET Q = 218
100 REM PRINT IV, N$, Q
110 END
```

(No output)

IMPORTANT TERMS

After studying this chapter, you should be familiar with the meaning and use of the following terms and BASIC statements:

Instruction	BASIC verbs
Executable statements	Nonexecutable statements

REM statement
Line numbers
Numeric value
String value
Data value
Data name
Constant
Literal
Variable
Reserved word
LET statement
Syntax error
Type Mismatch error
PRINT statement
Print zones
Left-justified
END statement
Assumed END
STOP statement
CONT command

EXERCISES

1. Identify each of the following data values as numeric or string and assign to each an appropriate BASIC variable. Make all choices based on the appearance of the value, with no assumptions as to use.
   (a) Ralph (b) 288
   (c) 5th Ave. (d) 27559-0338
   (e) XIV (f) +17.226
   (g) 12/25/83 (h) Ed Jones
   (i) $377.00 (j) −0.2556
2. Consider the two consecutive statements:

   70 statement 1
   85 statement 2

   How many statements could be inserted between these two, and what line numbers or range of numbers are available for use?
3. Enter the sequence of statements that you would type to change the program segment in column A to that in column B.

Column A	Column B
200 statement 1	200 statement 1
210 statement 2	205 statement 6
220 statement 3	207 statement 4
230 statement 4	210 statement 2
240 statement 5	240 statement 5
250 statement 6	250 statement 3

For Exercises 4 to 7, use the following information:

Item to Print	Data Value	Data Name
College name	King College	C$
City	Yorkton	P$
State	Maine	S$
Enrollment	2378	E
Number of faculty	56	F
Code	U	K$

4. Describe the output produced by the following PRINT statements:
   (a)
   ```
   150 PRINT C$, P$, S$, E
   ```
   (b)
   ```
   235 PRINT C$
   240 PRINT P$, S$, E, F, K$
   ```

(c)
```
190  PRINT C$, P$, S$,, K$
200  PRINT E, F
```
(d)
```
312  PRINT C$,,,K$
314  PRINT E, F
316  PRINT C$, S$
```
(e)
```
220  PRINT C$, P$, S$,, K$, E, F
```
(f)
```
320  PRINT C$,
330  PRINT P$, S$,,K$
```
(g)
```
260  PRINT C$, P$, S$
265  PRINT
270  PRINT E, F
```
(h)
```
475  PRINT C$, P$, S$,, K$
480  PRINT
485  PRINT E,
490  PRINT F
```

5. Repeat Exercise 4 using a college name of Mountainview College.
6. Write PRINT statements that will produce the following results:
   (a) One line with college name, city, and enrollment.
   (b) A two-line report consisting of the college name, enrollment, and code in the first, third, and fifth screen zones, respectively, and a second with the city and state.
   (c) A three-line printout formatted to give college name, city, state, and code on the first line, with the code in the last zone, and the enrollment and number of faculty printed on separate lines.
   (d) A three-line report with the college name and code in the first and last zones of the first line, the city and state on the second line, and the enrollment and number of faculty in the last two zones of the third line.
   (e) Repeat parts (b) through (d), but insert a blank line between each line of output as described.
7. Repeat Exercise 6 using North Hillcrest College as the college name.

For Exercises 8 to 10, give the output that will be produced by the given programs. Then, type the programs into the computer, run them, and check the actual outputs against your predictions.

8.
```
10 LET A$ = "TIM REESE"
20 LET PC = 230.19
30 LET TB = 377.09
40 PRINT A$
50 PRINT PC,, TB
60 END
```
9.
```
10 LET S$ = "TOYS"
20 LET E$ = "E. R. EPPS"
30 LET A = 3298.36
40 PRINT S$, E$, A,, S$
50 END
```
10.
```
10 LET X = 100
20 LET Y = 200
30 LET Z = 400
40 LET T = -300
50 PRINT X, Z, Y, T, X
60 END
```

PROGRAMMING PROBLEMS

Write programs in BASIC to accomplish the tasks described by each of the following problems. Be sure to carefully document each program.

1. Assign the following data to appropriate BASIC variables and then print the results in the same order as assigned.

   Class Number: 3992
   Class Name: ENG 101
   Enrollment: 28
   Instructor's Name: T. R. Evans

2. Redo Problem 1 to print all data values on separate lines.
3. Print a dual report with *two* copies of the patient's name and room number, one under the other.

   Patient's Name: Robert Fox
   Room Number: 1320W

4. If you used two separate PRINT statements to complete Problem 3, try doing it with only one. (If you did use only one when you completed Problem 3, redo it now with two.)
5. Redo Problem 3 to print two duplicate reports *side by side*.

Use the following data for Problems 6 to 10:

Customer's Name: Kevin Ellis
Account Number: 21094
Street Address: 74 Main St.
City: Upton
State: CA
Zip Code: 91022
Telephone: 213-555-8309
Current Balance: 3288.09

6. Prepare a two-line report with the account number, name, and telephone number in the first, second, and fourth zones of the first line, and with the current balance being printed in the *last* zone of the second line.
7. A three-line report is to be produced showing the customer's name and account number on the first line; street address, city, state, and zip code on the second; and the current balance as a single entry on the third.
8. Prepare a six-line printout as follows: The first four lines present the account number, name, current balance, and street address as separate items; the fifth line shows the city, state, and zip code; and the final line gives the telephone number.
9. Repeat Problem 8, but print the account number as the first entry on *every* line. It need appear only once on the first line. The remaining five lines will have the information as described, but with the account number in the first section and everything else moved to the right.
10. The format of the report is often as important as what it contains. Print the above eight values with the account number and customer's name in the first and third zones on the first line. On the second line, print the current balance and address also in the first and third zones. On the third line, print the city, state, and zip code, *beginning* at the third zone. Finally, print the telephone number on the fourth line, third zone.
11. A report is to be produced that lists the data for three different input records. This is to be done by using only *three* variables and the alternate use of LET and PRINT statements. The data to be used is given below.

Record Number	Student Name	Year in School	Current GPA
1	Randy Jordan	Senior	2.18
2	Lucy Edwards	Freshman	2.53
3	Mike Fuller	Junior	2.91

Each record should be printed on a single line and separated by one blank line.

12. A program is needed that prints a salesperson's performance report for a 4-month period. The following data is to be used:
Program Constants:

Salesperson's Name: Jim Baxter
Department Name: Hardware
Store Branch: Northwood

Variables:

Month	Sales
September	6874.88
October	5981.20
November	8224.82
December	9127.06

No more than *five* data names should be used. The program constants can be assigned and not changed. The variables can be initially assigned the first set of values for the month and sales, the first month's report can be printed, then the variables can be reassigned for the second month, that month's report printed, and so on. The report for each month should show the month on the first line, the salesperson's name on the second, and the department, branch, and sales on the third line, with sales moved over to the fourth zone. There should be one blank line between each month's report.

13. Redo Problem 12 to print the program constants only once. To do this, print the salesperson's name, department, and branch *one* time at the beginning of the report. Then alternately assign and print the month and sales. The program constants should be separated from the rest of the report by two blank lines.

CHAPTER 4

PROCESSING MULTIPLE RECORDS

In Chapter 3, you learned how to construct simple programs in BASIC, but the techniques shown can be used to write programs that will process only a small number of data values. Most applications that require the processing power of a computer involve either the handling of a large amount of information or many repetitive calculations. In this chapter, we will explore some of the procedures that can be used to process multiple data records, a necessity in most programs.

4-1 DATA INPUT WITH THE READ AND DATA STATEMENTS

Probably the most common method of inputting data into the computer in BASIC is by means of the **READ** and **DATA** statements. The READ statement is used to list and specify the variables being used. It has the general form:

ln **READ** *variable list*

where **variable list** is a list of variables, separated by commas, to be read into the computer. A typical READ statement is:

```
80 READ N$, H, R, X$
```

This statement will read values for the four variables N$, H, R, and X$, which might represent such quantities as employee's name, hours worked, pay rate, and shift.

The READ obtains the values to assign to the variables in the list from the DATA statement, which has the form:

ln **DATA** *data list*

The **data list** is a list of data values, separated by commas, to be assigned to the variables in the READ statement. *The data values in the DATA statement* **must** *be in exactly the same order as the variables in the READ to which they are to be assigned.* For example, suppose the above READ were matched with the DATA statement

```
310 DATA "PETER DAVIS", 38.5, 8.15, "DAY"
```

Then the four variables would be assigned values in the same way as in the following four LET statements:

```
10  LET N$ = "PETER DAVIS"
15  LET H = 38.5
20  LET R = 8.15
25  LET X$ = "DAY"
```

Note that string variables are in quotes in the DATA statement just as with the LET. Like nearly all statements in BASIC, the READ is executable and must be placed in the program at the proper place. The DATA statement, however, is nonexecutable and therefore can be placed anywhere. General practice is to group all the DATA statements together, usually at the end of the program.

The advantage of the READ and DATA statement combination may not yet be apparent, but it will be shortly. First, consider what must be done if you need to assign several sets of data to the above four variables for processing. Using LET statements, you would have to write one set of LET statements as above, process the data, write a second set of LET statements, process again, and so on, until you had repeated the cycle for all the data. (See Programming Problems 11 to 13 at the end of Chapter 3.) This would create quite a long and boring program. With the READ and DATA statements, this problem is eliminated. Consider the following:

```
          :
          :
 80 READ N$, H, R, X$
          :
          :
310 DATA "PETER DAVIS", 38.5, 8.15, "DAY"
320 DATA "JOY EVANS", 42.6, 6.45, "EVENING"
330 DATA "BILL JACOBS", 40.0, 7.70, "DAY"
340 DATA "DEBBI SIMS", 43.0, 7.95, "NIGHT"
350 DATA "LUCY PYKE", 39.3, 6.05, "EVENING"
```

To process the five *sets* of values, the four variables in the READ statement are first assigned to the values in the first DATA statement as above. These values are processed and the program is directed back to the READ. (We will see how to do this in Section 4.2.) When the READ is processed a second time, the second set of values (in line 320) is paired with the four variables, replacing the first group. (This is known as a **destructive read**.) When the READ is processed a third time, the third set of four values is read, and so it goes until all the data has been processed.

As mentioned above, it is very important that the order of the variables in the READ and the data values in the DATA statements be exactly the same. Care must also be taken to ensure the correct matching of variables and data by *type*. That is, numeric variables must be matched to numeric data and string variables paired to string data. Mismatched data will not process correctly if at all.

It is not necessary to always group the variables and data as shown in the above example. All of the following are equivalent:

```
80  READ N$, H, R, X$

80  READ N$
85  READ H, R, X$

80  READ N$, H
85  READ R, X$

80  READ N$
82  READ H, R
84  READ X$
```

Each would function equally well with the above DATA statements.

Likewise, there are many ways of writing the data. The sequence shown above may be the most logical, but it is not always the most convenient. Consider the following two equivalent arrangements of the above DATA statements:

```
310 DATA "PETER DAVIS"
320 DATA 38.5, 8.18, "DAY"
330 DATA "JOY EVANS"
340 DATA 42.6, 6.45, "EVENING"
350 DATA "BILL JACOBS"
360 DATA 40.0, 7.70, "DAY"
370 DATA "DEBBI SIMS"
380 DATA 43.0, 7.95, "NIGHT"
390 DATA "LUCY PYKE"
400 DATA 39.3, 6.05, "EVENING"
```

```
310 DATA "PETER DAVIS", 38.5, 8.15, "DAY","JOY EVANS", 42.6, 6.45
320 DATA "EVENING","BILL JACOBS", 40.0, 7.70, "DAY","DEBBI SIMS"
330 DATA 43.0, 7.95, "NIGHT","LUCY PYKE", 39.3, 6.05, "EVENING"
```

While the READ and DATA statements work as a team, no single READ or DATA statement is paired specifically with another. The first READ to be processed reads the data corresponding to the variables in its list from the *first* values in the DATA statements; this may involve one or more DATA statements. The next READ to be processed takes its values from the data list *starting at the point where the last READ left off*. This procedure continues until the READs are no longer processed and the data list is exhausted. Consider the above example of reading the four variables N$, H, R, and X$. Suppose that prior to processing the values for these four quantities, we wish to read a single value for the date (as D$) and the department number (as DP) to be printed at the beginning of the report. A sequence of READ and DATA statements for this would be as follows:

```
      :
      :
 40 READ D$, DP
      :
      :
 80 READ N$, H, R, X$
      :
      :
300 DATA "JULY 31, 1983", 4261
310 DATA "PETER DAVIS", 38.5, 8.15, "DAY"
320 DATA "JOY EVANS", 42.6, 6.45, "EVENING"
330 DATA "BILL JACOBS", 40.0, 7.70, "DAY"
340 DATA "DEBBI SIMS", 43.0, 7.95, "NIGHT"
350 DATA "LUCY PYKE", 39.3, 6.05, "EVENING"
```

It is sometimes helpful to think of a **data pointer** that moves through the data list and *points* to the data value that is to be read next. For the first READ statement, the data pointer is always at the first item in the data list. For the READ at line 40 above, it will be at ''JULY 31, 1983'' in the DATA statement at 300. When the next READ is executed at line 80, the data pointer will be at ''PETER DAVIS'' in line 310. The data pointer continues *forward* through the data list, never moving backward unless a **RESTORE** statement is encountered. This statement causes the pointer to return to the beginning of the list so that the list will be reread. The action of the data pointer is illustrated in Figure 4-1.

4-2 THE GOTO STATEMENT

The repeat processing described in the preceding section is accomplished by means of the **GOTO** statement. The GOTO has the effect of directing the action of the processing to

```
 40  READ D$, DP
       :
       :
 80  READ N$, H, R, X$
       :
       :
300  DATA "JULY 31, 1983", 4261
310  DATA "PETER DAVIS", 38.5, 8.15, "DAY"
320  DATA "JOY EVANS", 42.6, 6.45, "EVENING"
330  DATA "BILL JACOBS", 40.0, 7.70, "DAY"
340  DATA "DEBBI SIMS", 43.0, 7.95, "NIGHT"
350  DATA "LUCY PYKE", 39.3, 6.05, "EVENING"
```

Position of data pointer before first READ at 40	300 DATA "JULY 31, 1983", 4261
Position of data pointer after READ at 40 and before first READ at 80	310 DATA "PETER DAVIS", 38.5, 8.15, "DAY"
Position of data pointer after first READ at 80	320 DATA "JOY EVANS", 42.6, 6.45, "EVENING"
Position of data pointer after second READ at 80	330 DATA "BILL JACOBS", 40.0, 7.70, "DAY"
Position of data pointer after third READ at 80	340 DATA "DEBBI SIMS", 43.0, 7.95, "NIGHT"

FIGURE 4-1
Action of data pointer in data list

another part of the program. This is done by simply specifying the line number of the statement to which you want program control to branch next. The general form of the GOTO statement is:

ln1 **GOTO** *ln2*

where *ln1* is the line number of the GOTO statement and *ln2* is the number of the statement to which you are directing the program. (If *ln2* is not a line number of a statement in the program, you will get an **Undefined Line** error message.)

As an example of the use of the GOTO, let us return to the example, given in the last section, of several input records using only one READ statement. We can see now that the GOTO is one method for sending the program back to the READ to process more records. The above example might be modified as follows to include a GOTO statement:

```
        :
        :
 80 READ N$, H, R, X$
        :
        :
170 GOTO 80
        :
        :
310 DATA "PETER DAVIS", 38.5, 8.15, "DAY"
320 DATA "JOY EVANS", 42.6, 6.45, "EVENING"
330 DATA "BILL JACOBS", 40.0, 7.70, "DAY"
340 DATA "DEBBI SIMS", 43.0, 7.95, "NIGHT"
350 DATA "LUCY PYKE", 39.3, 6.05, "EVENING"
```

The GOTO at 170 will direct the program flow back to the READ at 80 for the processing of more data. This creates a **loop**, and the process is referred to as *looping*.

4-3 AN EXAMPLE: AIRLINE FLIGHT SCHEDULE

A sample problem that combines the techniques described thus far in this chapter is presented below.

TABLE 4-1
Data for Airline Flight Schedule Example

Date: September 10, 1983 | Airline: Northern Air

Flight Number	Type Plane	Departure City	Departure Time	Arrival City	Arrival Time
1284	727	New York	8:15 AM	Atlanta	10:30 AM
738	737	St. Louis	9:50 AM	Los Angeles	12:35 PM
2105	DC9	Atlanta	11:45 AM	Boston	2:25 PM
301	727	Detroit	3:55 PM	Dallas	4:30 PM
911	DC10	Denver	5:10 PM	Chicago	9:45 PM
1744	L10	Dallas	8:20 PM	New York	1:05 AM

Problem: An airline flight schedule is to be printed. The report is to give the current date and name of the airline at the top of the printout, followed by a listing of all flights by number, plane type, departing city and time, and arrival city and time. The output should give the flight number and plane type on one line with the cities and times on a second line. Each flight record should be separated by one blank line. The date and airline should be separated from the flight listings by two blank lines. The data to be processed is given in Table 4-1.

The solution to this problem involves the following sequence of steps:

1. Read the date and airline name.
2. Print the date and airline name.
3. Read the individual flight data (flight number and departure and arrival cities and times).
4. Print the flight data.
5. Repeat steps 3 and 4 until all flights have been processed.

This process is illustrated pictorially by the flowchart in Figure 4-2.

The first part of the program is a series of REM statements to document the program and define the variables being used:

```
 10 REM  AIRLINE FLIGHT SCHEDULE
 20 REM
 30 REM  VARIABLES ARE DEFINED AS --
 40 REM
 50 REM        D$ = DATE
 60 REM        A$ = AIRLINE NAME
 70 REM         F = FLIGHT NUMBER
 80 REM        P$ = TYPE PLANE
 90 REM       DC$ = DEPARTURE CITY
100 REM       DT$ = DEPARTURE TIME
110 REM       AC$ = ARRIVAL CITY
120 REM       AT$ = ARRIVAL TIME
130 REM
```

Steps 1 and 2 above are accomplished by the following three statements:

```
160  READ D$, A$
170  PRINT D$
180  PRINT A$
```

Steps 3 through 5 translate into the following lines:

```
230  READ F, P$, DC$, DT$, AC$, AT$
               :
250  PRINT F, P$
260  PRINT DC$, DT$, AC$, AT$
270  GOTO 230
```

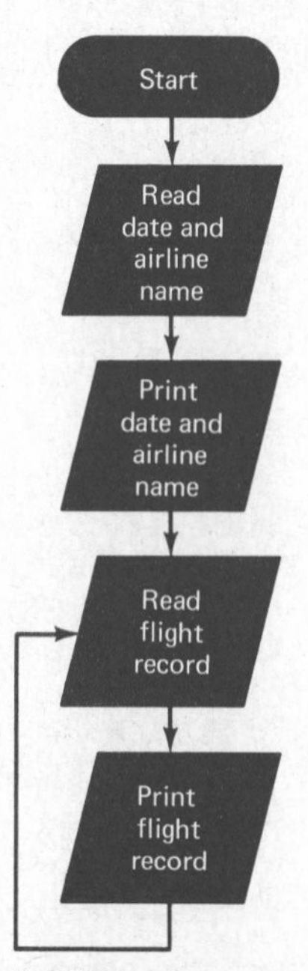

FIGURE 4-2
Flowchart for airline flight schedule problem

The flight data is read at line 230 and printed on two lines as required by lines 250 and 260. Line 270 is the GOTO statement that causes the processing to continue for additional records.

The completed program is shown below. REM statements have been inserted to identify the function of each section, and the END statement has been placed at line 999.

```
 10 REM  AIRLINE FLIGHT SCHEDULE
 20 REM
 30 REM  VARIABLES ARE DEFINED AS --
 40 REM
 50 REM          D$ = DATE
 60 REM          A$ = AIRLINE NAME
 70 REM           F = FLIGHT NUMBER
 80 REM          P$ = TYPE PLANE
 90 REM         DC$ = DEPARTURE CITY
100 REM         DT$ = DEPARTURE TIME
110 REM         AC$ = ARRIVAL CITY
120 REM         AT$ = ARRIVAL TIME
130 REM
140 REM  READ AND PRINT DATE AND AIRLINE NAME
150 REM
160 READ D$, A$
170 PRINT D$
180 PRINT A$
190 PRINT
200 REM
210 REM  READ AND PRINT FLIGHT DATA
220 REM
230 READ F, P$, DC$, DT$, AC$, AT$
240 PRINT
250 PRINT F, P$
260 PRINT DC$, DT$, AC$, AT$
270 GOTO 230
280 REM
290 REM  LIST DATA
300 REM
310 DATA "SEPTEMBER 10, 1983", "NORTHERN AIR"
320 DATA 1284,"727","NEW YORK","8:15 AM","ATLANTA","10:30 AM"
330 DATA 738,"737","ST. LOUIS","9:50 AM","LOS ANGELES","12:35 PM"
340 DATA 2105,"DC9","ATLANTA","11:45 AM","BOSTON","2:25 PM"
350 DATA 301,"727","DETROIT","3:55 PM","DALLAS","4:30 PM"
360 DATA 911, "DC10","DENVER","5:10 PM","CHICAGO","9:45 PM"
370 DATA 1744,"L10","DALLAS","8:20 PM","NEW YORK","1:05 AM"
999 END
```

The required blank lines are produced on the output by the PRINT statements at lines 190 and 240. The printout will appear as follows:

```
SEPTEMBER 10, 1983
NORTHERN AIR


 1284           727
NEW YORK        8:15 AM        ATLANTA        10:30 AM

 738            737
ST. LOUIS       9:50 AM        LOS ANGELES    12:35 PM

 2105           DC9
ATLANTA         11:45 AM       BOSTON         2:25 PM

 301            727
DETROIT         3:55 PM        DALLAS         4:30 PM
```

```
 911          DC10
DENVER        5:10 PM        CHICAGO        9:45 PM

 1744         L10
DALLAS        8:20 PM        NEW YORK       1:05 AM
```

4-4 THE PROBLEM OF INFINITE LOOPS

The example in Section 4-3 has one major flaw: It does not have a **logical end**. That is, the processing stops only when the computer runs out of data to process. In certain rare circumstances, this may be a satisfactory approach, but with BASIC it usually leads to an error message (**Out of Data in Line #**) and is considered *very* poor programming style. In Section 4-5, we will discuss a new BASIC statement that will allow us to signal the computer to stop processing data; in Section 4-6 we will learn how to use this statement to provide a logical end to a program to avoid this situation. For now, let us look at some of the problems that can arise from uncontrolled looping.

The situation encountered in the example in the preceding section is a very common one. If we examine a portion of the program, we can easily see what is happening.

```
                    :
                    :
230  READ F, P$, DC$, DT$, AC$, AT$
                    :
                    :
270  GOTO 230
                    :
                    :
```

The READ statement at 230, when first encountered, will read the first set of flight data values from the DATA statements. These are processed, then the GOTO at 270 sends the program back to the READ at 230 for more data to be processed. This procedure continues with no problems for six loops because there are six flight records to be processed. However, when the GOTO directs the program back to the READ for the *seventh* record, a problem arises because there is no seventh flight record. At this point, the computer is attempting to process a data record that does not exist; therefore, it issues an error message to inform you of the problem.

The Out of Data error message can be caused by several other conditions. One of these is the omission of one or more items from the data list. In the airline flight schedule example, there are 38 items in the data list: the date, the airline name, plus six flight records with six entries each. Suppose that one item has been accidentally left out, leaving only 37 in the list. When the computer tries to read the last (sixth) record, there will be only *five* values left in the list. This means that it will be out of data before it can complete reading the last record. A second situation can arise if a comma is omitted from the data list. This could cause two values to be incorrectly read as one and the remainder of the data list to be thrown out of sequence with the data names in the READ statements, thus leaving the data list one value short at the end. (An extra comma, especially at the end of a DATA statement, can cause problems of another sort.) Either of the above situations could lead to other error conditions as well, such as Syntax or Type Mismatch. Which error message is issued will depend on where the problem occurs and the type of data being processed.

Careless looping can bring about other, much more alarming conditions. One of the most traumatic situations for the beginner is to run a program with an infinite loop that the computer *will not stop* even with an error message. This can occur in the simplest of programs. Here is one example.

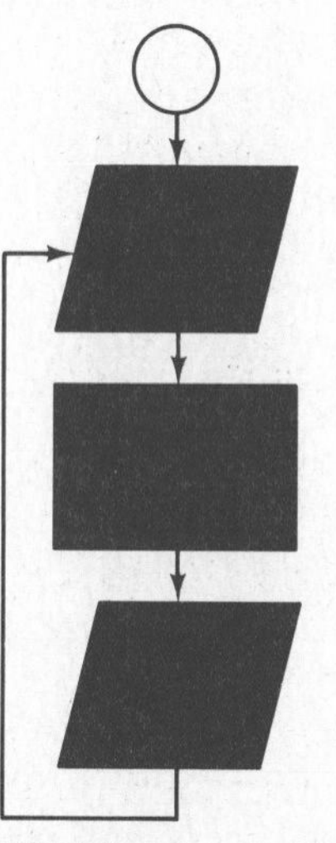

FIGURE 4-3
An uncontrolled loop

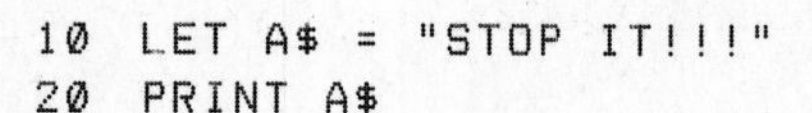

```
10  LET A$ = "STOP IT!!!"
20  PRINT A$
```

```
30 GOTO 10
40 END
```

When run, this little program will print

```
STOP IT!!!
STOP IT!!!
STOP IT!!!
STOP IT!!!
STOP IT!!!
STOP IT!!!
    :
    :
    :
```

until the computer breaks down or until you (or someone) does "STOP IT!!!" Nearly all computers have special keys or commands for stopping such infinite loops without the loss of your program or data.

This example seems so simple that you may be thinking "Nobody would ever do that!" Perhaps no one would in a situation as simple as the one shown, but sometimes uncontrolled loops can develop because of typos or from other unanticipated sources. Suppose that in the example in the last section, line 270 had been mistyped as GOTO 250 instead of GOTO 230. This would cause the program to read the first flight record, then continually print it over and over as follows:

```
SEPTEMBER 10, 1983
NORTHERN AIR

 1284         727
NEW YORK      8:15 AM      ATLANTA      10:30 AM
 1284         727
NEW YORK      8:15 AM      ATLANTA      10:30 AM
 1284         727
NEW YORK      8:15 AM      ATLANTA      10:30 AM
 1284         727
NEW YORK      8:15 AM      ATLANTA      10:30 AM
                           :
                           :
                           :
```

It is not always possible to prevent uncontrolled or infinite loops from getting into your programs; even experienced programmers have occasional unexpected problems with loops. It is wise, however, to take precautions when you write the program so as to prevent as many such problems as possible. In Section 4-6, we will discuss one technique for avoiding uncontrolled looping, with more to follow in later chapters. The best prevention, though, is careful and thoughtful programming.

4-5 THE IF–THEN STATEMENT

The GOTO statement discussed in Section 4-2 provides what is known as an **unconditional branch**. This means that when a program comes to a GOTO statement, control is transferred by the GOTO to the statement with the line number indicated, regardless of other conditions; thus, the transfer of control (or branch) is said to be unconditional. Many times, however, you may want to transfer the processing to another part of the program, but *only if a certain condition is met*. This is known as a **conditional branch**. Many methods exist for producing conditional branches in BASIC programs, and we will discuss them in detail in later chapters. For now, let us look at the simplest form, the **IF–THEN** statement.

TABLE 4-2

Summary of Relational Operators

Symbol	Meaning
=	Equal to
< >	Not equal to
<	Less than
< =	Less than or equal to
>	Greater than
> =	Greater than or equal to

The general form of the IF–THEN statement is

ln1 **IF** *condition* **THEN** *ln2*

where *ln1* is the line number of the IF–THEN statement, the **condition** specifies when a branch will take place, and *ln2* is the line number of the statement to which a branch will proceed if the condition is met (true). In other words, the condition is first tested; if it is met, program control branches to the statement indicated after the THEN; otherwise, processing continues with the next statement.

The condition part of an IF statement will be discussed in Chapter 7. For the present, we can limit our use to a form that involves a single data name and a single data value, related by one of the **relational operators** listed in Table 4-2. Examples of simple IF–THEN statements are:

```
210  IF X = 100 THEN 130
460  IF SF < 0 THEN 590
385  IF B$ = "STOP" THEN 480
```

Both numeric and string quantities may be used in constructing conditions with the following cautions: (1) The usual rules regarding type matching must be observed, (2) all string data values must be in quotes (as with the LET and DATA statements), and (3) while all relational operators in Table 4-2 may be used with numeric values, most computers allow only equal (=) and unequal (<>) to be used with string values. Table

TABLE 4-3

Conditional Branching with the IF–THEN Statement

Program Segment with IF–THEN Statement	Value of Variable	Action Caused by IF–THEN
210 IF A = 25 THEN 100 220 PRINT A	A = 25	Branches to 100
535 IF DN < 0 THEN 690 540 READ X, Y, Z	DN = −1	Branches to 690
380 IF H > 40 THEN 450 390 LET R = 7.25	H = 40	Continues to 390
265 IF FX$ = "FIRST" THEN 150 280 PRINT FX$, D, S$	FX$ = "FIRST"	Branches to 150
320 IF T => 100 THEN 195 330 READ U, X$	T = 100	Branches to 195
440 IF A$ <> "END IT" THEN 90 445 PRINT B, HG, F$,, P	A$ = "END IT"	Continues to 445

4-3 presents several IF–THEN statements with specified conditions, the values of the variables at the time of execution, and the action taken by the computer.

4-6 PROGRAM CONTROL WITH THE IF–THEN

We are now ready to see how to use the IF–THEN statement to insert a logical end into a program so that it will stop when we want it to without an error message instead of stopping only when there is no more data to process. The usual technique for this is to employ what is commonly known as a **sentinel,** or **trailer,** record. This is a special data record placed in the data list, usually at the end, to signal the computer that all the data has been processed. The sentinel record contains a special entry for one of the data values; an IF statement somewhere in the program checks for this entry as the data is read. When the special value is found, the THEN part of the IF–THEN executes, causing a branch that stops any more data from being read and ends the program. (Actually, the sentinel record does not always have to come at the end of the data list and cause the program to end. We will see why in later chapters.)

As an example of the use of the sentinel record, consider the following short program. It does nothing but read and print a series of three positive numbers:

```
10  READ A, B, C
20  PRINT A, B, C
30  GOTO 10
40  DATA 543, 757, 337, 889, 33, 5678, 5543, 455, 909
50  DATA 2500, 258, 2001, 68, 458, 79, 3256, 5578, 1248
60  END
```

If this program is run as it is, we will get:

```
543          757          337
889          33           5678
5543         455          908
2500         258          2001
68           458          79
3256         5578         1248

Out of Data in Line 10
```

The Out of Data error message could be avoided by inserting an IF–THEN to signal that all data has been processed. To do this, we must: (1) decide where to place the IF–THEN statement in the program, (2) select the variable to be used in the condition of the IF, (3) determine what value of the selected variable to use to signal the program end, (4) decide to what line the THEN part of the IF–THEN should send the program, and (5) be certain that the sentinel record has been added to the data list. Let us go through each of these steps to add a logical end to the above short program.

1. The first thing to do is to decide where to place the IF statement. Usually, but not always, it will be placed immediately after the READ containing the variable that the IF will use in its condition. In the above program, that would be between lines 10 and 20, say at line 15.

2. Normally, any of the variables in the READ list can be used in the **IF** condition. Sometimes, because of the way some of the variables are defined, it is more convenient to work with one variable than another; this will become clear with experience. In the above program, any of the three variables could be used with equal ease. We will use A.

3. Once the variable to be used has been selected, an appropriate value must be chosen to signal the end of the data. *Care must be taken to ensure that the value used in the IF condition is* **not** *part of the actual data*. Should this happen, the program will end prematurely. For the variable A, we are not certain what values will be processed, only

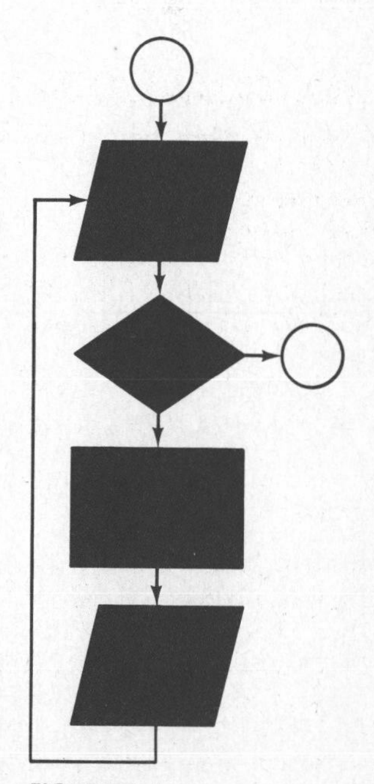

FIGURE 4-4
A controlled loop

that all values will be positive (greater than zero). In this case, it would be dangerous to just pick a number and hope that it is not one of the data values; since A is positive, however, we can use either zero or any negative value. Let us use A = 0 as our condition.

4. For this problem, at the end of the data, we will immediately stop processing; therefore, the THEN part of the IF–THEN will direct the processing to the END statement. Here it will send the program to line number 60. This completes the IF–THEN statement; it is 15 IF A = 0 THEN 60.

5. Finally, we must add the sentinel record to the end of the data list. This *must* contain the proper value for the selected variable, but the remainder of the values are unimportant as long as there are no type mismatches. We can add three zeros at the end of the data list by the DATA statement at 55.

With these modifications the above program now becomes

```
10  READ A, B, C
15  IF A = 0 THEN 60
20  PRINT A, B, C
30  GOTO 10
40  DATA 543, 757, 337, 889, 33, 5678, 5543, 455, 908
50  DATA 2500, 258, 2001, 68, 458, 79, 3256, 5578, 1248
55  DATA 0, 0, 0
60  END
```

If this modified program is run, we will get

```
543           757           337
889           33            5678
5543          455           908
2500          258           2001
68            458           79
3256          5578          1248
```

It now processes without errors—as it should.

As another example, let us alter the airline flight schedule program in Section 4-3 to process without an Out of Data message. The IF statement will go at line 235. We can use any of the six variables read at line 230; let us use P$ (type of plane) and stop the program for a value equal to NO PLANE sending the processing to the END statement at line 999. Another DATA statement will have to be added for the sentinel record. A partial listing of the program, showing only the pertinent sections with the additions, is provided below.

```
                :
                :
230 READ F, P$, DC$, DT$, AC$, AT$
235 IF P$ = "NO PLANE" THEN 999
240 PRINT
250 PRINT F, P$
260 PRINT DC$, DT$, AC$, AT$
270 GOTO 230
                :
                :
310 DATA "SEPTEMBER 10, 1983", "NORTHERN AIR"
320 DATA 1284,"727","NEW YORK","8:15 AM","ATLANTA","10:30 AM"
330 DATA 738,"737","ST. LOUIS","9:50 AM","LOS ANGELES","12:35 PM"
340 DATA 2105,"DC9","ATLANTA","11:45 AM","BOSTON","2:25 PM"
350 DATA 301,"727","DETROIT","3:55 PM","DALLAS","4:30 PM"
360 DATA 911, "DC10","DENVER","5:10 PM","CHICAGO","9:45 PM"
370 DATA 1744,"L10","DALLAS","8:20 PM","NEW YORK","1:05 AM"
380 DATA 0, "NO PLANE", "0", "0", "0", "0"
999 END
```

Note that in line 380, NO PLANE is in the second position as it must be to correspond to P$ in the READ at 230. The other five values are unimportant as far as specific content, provided they are of the proper type. In other words, the decision to enter 0 in those fields was totally arbitrary; we could have entered any value as long as the first value was numeric and the last four were string.

One final point on the logical end and the sentinel record: It is sometimes practical to read only *part* of the data record, test for the end-of-data condition, then read the remainder of the data record. For example, suppose that instead of reading all six values in the flight record at line 230, we read only as far as P$, the variable that serves as the test for the program end. After testing P$ at line 235, we can then read the remaining four values. This means that the sentinel record needs to have only *two* entries, those for F and P$. Written in this fashion, the above would be modified to read:

```
          :
          :
230  READ F, P$
235  IF P$ = "NO PLANE" THEN 999
237  READ DC$, DT$, AC$, AT$
          :
          :
380  DATA 0, "NO PLANE"
999  END
```

Clearly, this technique is of most value for READs with a long variable list and when used with a variable near the beginning of that list.

4-7 AN EXAMPLE: CLASS ROSTER

As a second example, we shall do a problem with both processing of multiple records *and* logical end.

Problem: A class roster is to be printed that presents the following information: At the top of the report is to be a three-line header that gives the current quarter on the first line, the course number and name on the second line, and the instructor's name on the third. After skipping one blank line, a class roster is to be printed that lists each student's ID number, name, class code, and enrollment status in that order, but with the third print zone empty. After all data has been processed, the program should end for a sentinel record containing a negative ID number. Data is given in Table 4-4.

TABLE 4-4

Data for Class Roster Example

Current Quarter: Fall, 1983 — Course Number: 3507
Instructor: Dr. T. A. Pool — Course Name: HIS 201

Student			
ID Number	**Name**	**Class Code**	**Enrollment Status**
22006	Y. C. Kelley	2	G
68429	L. M. Benson	3	G
31088	P. S. Harris	2	G
31940	A. N. Gibson	4	A
54338	F. G. Pyle	2	G
30116	W. R. Orr	2	P
59831	C. A. Smith	3	P
13943	T. J. Carver	2	G

The solution to this problem will follow these steps:

1. Read the course data (quarter, course number and name, and instructor's name).
2. Print the course data.
3. Read a student record.
4. Check to see if the last (sentinel) record has been reached. If it has, go to step 7; if it has not, proceed with the next step.
5. Print a student record.
6. Go to step 3 for more data.
7. Stop.

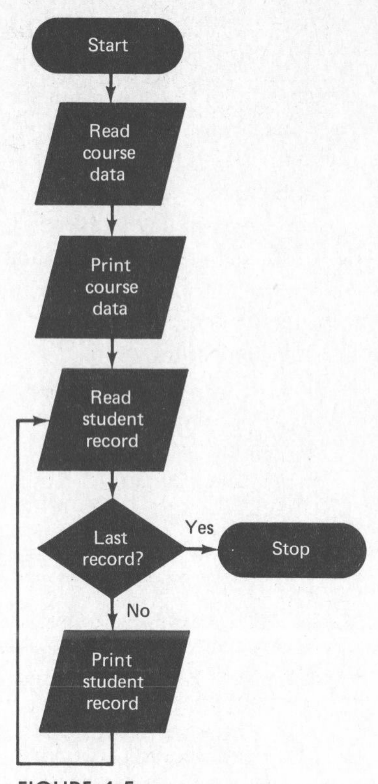

FIGURE 4-5
Flowchart for class roster problem

These seven steps are shown pictorially by the flowchart in Figure 4-5.

The program and variables are defined by the following series of REM statements:

```
10 REM   CLASS ROSTER
20 REM
30 REM   VARIABLES ARE DEFINED AS --
40 REM
50 REM          Q$ = CURRENT QUARTER
60 REM          CN = COURSE NUMBER
70 REM          C$ = COURSE NAME
80 REM          I$ = INSTRUCTOR'S NAME
90 REM          ID = STUDENT'S ID NUMBER
100 REM         S$ = STUDENT'S NAME
110 REM         CC = CLASS CODE
120 REM         E$ = ENROLLMENT STATUS
130 REM
```

Steps 1 and 2 are very similar to the example in Section 4-3 except for the print formatting. The statements which read and print the initial course data are:

```
160  READ Q$, CN, C$, I$
170  PRINT Q$
180  PRINT CN, C$
190  PRINT I$
```

The processing of the class roster, the heart of the program, is described by steps 3 through 7 above. These translate directly into the relatively short sequence of BASIC statements shown below:

```
240  READ ID, S$, CC, E$
250  IF ID < 0 THEN 410
260  PRINT ID, S$,, CC, E$
270  GOTO 240
          :
          :
410  END
```

The statements at lines 240 and 260 read and print, respectively, one student record for the roster. Line 250 provides a logical end to the program when the sentinel record with a negative value for the ID (ID $<$ 0) is found; note that a value of -1 has been placed in the last record of the data list for this purpose. When the sentinel record is found, the conditional statement at 250 ends the program by directing it to the END statement at line 410. Line 270 keeps the processing going until the logical end is executed.

A complete program listing follows.

```
 10 REM  CLASS ROSTER
 20 REM
 30 REM  VARIABLES ARE DEFINED AS --
 40 REM
 50 REM          Q$ = CURRENT QUARTER
 60 REM          CN = COURSE NUMBER
 70 REM          C$ = COURSE NAME
 80 REM          I$ = INSTRUCTOR'S NAME
 90 REM          ID = STUDENT'S ID NUMBER
100 REM          S$ = STUDENT'S NAME
110 REM          CC = CLASS CODE
120 REM          E$ = ENROLLMENT STATUS
130 REM
140 REM  READ AND PRINT COURSE DATA
150 REM
160 READ Q$, CN, C$, I$
170 PRINT Q$
180 PRINT CN, C$
190 PRINT I$
200 PRINT
210 REM
220 REM  PROCESS STUDENT ROSTER
230 REM
240 READ ID, S$, CC, E$
250 IF ID < 0 THEN 410
260 PRINT ID, S$,, CC, E$
270 GOTO 240
280 REM
290 REM  DATA LIST
300 REM
310 DATA "FALL. 1983", 3507, "HIS 201", "DR. T. A. POOL"
320 DATA 22006, "Y. C. KELLEY", 2, "G"
330 DATA 68429  "L. M. BENSON", 3, "G"
340 DATA 31088, "P. S. HARRIS", 2, "G"
350 DATA 31940, "A. N. GIBSON", 4, "A"
360 DATA 54338, "F. G. PYLE", 2, "G"
370 DATA 30116, "W. R. ORR", 2, "P"
380 DATA 59831, "C. A. SMITH", 2, "P"
390 DATA 13943, "T. J. CARVER", 2, "G"
400 DATA -1, "X", 0, "X"
410 END
```

When run, this program produces an output as follows:

```
FALL, 1983
 3507          HIS 201
DR. T. A. POOL

 22006         Y. C. KELLEY                  2            G
 68429         L. M. BENSON                  3            G
 31088         P. S. HARRIS                  2            G
 31940         A. N. GIBSON                  4            A
 54338         F. G. PYLE                    2            G
 30116         W. R. ORR                     2            P
 59831         C. A. SMITH                   3            P
 13943         T. J. CARVER                  2            G
```

4-8 THE INTERACTIVE INPUT STATEMENT

So far, we have seen two means of entering data into the computer for processing with a BASIC program. One is the LET statement, which was introduced in Chapter 3 and will be studied in more detail in Chapter 5; it is primarily used for single or one-time data value assignments. The other is the READ/DATA statement pair, presented in this chapter, which is valuable for processing multiple data records. A *third* method of data entry available in BASIC is to use the **INPUT** statement.

The simplest form of the INPUT statement is:

ln **INPUT** *variable list*

where variable list has the same meaning as with the READ statement; that is, a list of variables to be assigned values and separated by commas. Unlike the LET or READ/DATA statements, the INPUT allows data to be entered directly from the terminal keyboard during program execution. No entries are placed in the data list of the DATA statements for those values that are to be entered by means of INPUT statements.

Here is how the INPUT statement works. When an INPUT statement is placed in a program, program execution continues until the INPUT in encountered. At this point, the program will pause and send a question mark (?) to the screen as a **prompt** to signal you to enter data. You should then enter on the screen following the ? the data values for the variables listed in the INPUT statement *exactly as you would type them into a DATA statement, in the proper order and separated by commas*. After you have typed in the data, the program will resume its processing until another INPUT is encountered, at which time it will again pause and print ? to the screen to request data. There will be a ? prompt for each INPUT statement that is encountered.

Let us look at an example. Consider the following short program that simply reads and prints values for three variables. First, look at the program as it is written using the already familiar READ/DATA statements.

```
 10 REM   PROGRAM WITH READ/DATA STATEMENTS
 20 REM
 30 READ N$, A, S$
 40 IF N$ = "STOP" THEN 120
 50 PRINT S$,, N$,, A
 60 GOTO 30
 70 DATA "R SIMMONS", 67,  "463-77-6944"
 80 DATA "T HARRIS", 54,  "254-29-3922"
 90 DATA "L WILSON", 61,  "324-98-3196"
100 DATA "T JENKINS", 66,  "499-37-0902"
110 DATA "STOP", 0,  "0"
120 END
```

The program run will look like this:

```
463-77-6944                 R SIMMONS                  67
254-29-3922                 T HARRIS                   54
324-98-3196                 L WILSON                   61
499-37-0902                 T JENKINS                  66
```

If we rewrite this program to provide for data input with the INPUT statement, it might look something like this:

```
10 REM  PROGRAM WITH INPUT STATEMENT
20 REM
30 INPUT N$, A, S$
40 IF N$ = "STOP" THEN 70
50 PRINT S$,, N$,, A
60 GOTO 30
70 END
```

The only two changes that have been made are (1) the READ statement at line 30 has been replaced with an INPUT statement and (2) the DATA statements have been deleted. The program may look deceptively short with no DATA statements, but remember that the data is to be entered from the terminal during the run.

Let us now trace this last program through a run. When program execution begins, the first executable statement encountered is the INPUT at 30, and thus a ? will be the first thing to appear on the screen, followed by a pause for data. We must type in the first data record (corresponding to the values in the DATA statement at line 80 above), which will then be printed according to the PRINT at 50. The GOTO at 60 sends the program back to the INPUT which causes another ? to be sent to the screen for more data. This cycle repeats until all records have been processed and we type in a sentinel record to end the program. The program run will proceed as follows:

```
? "R SIMMONS", 67, "463-77-6944"
463-77-6944                R SIMMONS                          67
? "T HARRIS", 54, "254-29-3922"
254-29-3922                T HARRIS                           54
? "L WILSON", 61, "324-98-3196"
324-98-3196                L WILSON                           61
? "T JENKINS", 66, "499-37-0902"
499-37-0902                T JENKINS                          66
? "STOP", 0, "0"
```

There are several additional points to be made on the use of the INPUT statement. First, instead of a single INPUT statement, several can be used. In other words, the INPUT at line 30 above might be replaced by the following:

```
25  INPUT N$
30  INPUT A
35  INPUT S$
```

The only difference is that we would now see *three* ?'s (one for each INPUT) instead of one. Second, both INPUT and READ statements may be used in the same program, with data being entered directly from the terminal for those variables listed in the INPUT statements and DATA statements used for those listed with READs. Third, while programs that make use of the INPUT may appear to be shorter, it must be remembered that the data still has to be entered at the time of the run. In some cases, this may be helpful when processing unfamiliar data; however, if the program must be run several times, the data must be reentered each time, a time-consuming and tiresome task. Also, typographical errors in entering the data interactively from the terminal can invalidate a run. Finally, from the above comparison, you can see that the output is interrupted and broken up by the data input when using the INPUT statement. In many cases, this would be impractical.

For most of our work in the next few chapters, we will rely primarily on the READ/DATA combination for data entry; however, we will see many applications involving the use of the INPUT statement in these same chapters.

TROUBLESHOOTING

Each of the following programs contains an error that prevents it from executing properly. Explain *specifically* what the problem is and what must be done to correct it. To assist you, a sample of what would happen should you attempt to run the program is provided after each listing. Refer to Appendix D for an explanation of BASIC error messages.

1.

```
10 REM   TROUBLESHOOTING PROBLEM 4-1
20 REM
30 REM         N$ = PATIENT'S NAME
40 REM         I$ = INSURANCE NUMBER
50 REM          R = ROOM NUMBER
60 REM         D$ = DOCTOR'S NAME
70 REM
80 READ N$, I$, R, D$
```

```
 90 IF N$ = "STOP" THEN 160
100 PRINT I$, N$, D$, R
110 GOTO 80
120 DATA "TOM SMITH","288-4566",357,"DR. INMAN"
130 DATA "SARAH POE","392-9002",734,"DR. MITCHELL"
140 DATA "LARRY JONES","499-1022",529,"DR. EDMUND"
150 DATA "STOP"
160 END

TOM SMITH     288-4566      357          DR. INMAN
SARAH POE     392-9002      734          DR. MITCHELL
LARRY JONES   499-1022      529          DR. EDMUND

Out of Data in Line 80
```

2.

```
 10 REM  TROUBLESHOOTING PROBLEM 4-2
 20 REM
 30 REM        N$ = NAME
 40 REM        T$ = TELEPHONE NUMBER
 50 REM
 60 READ N$, T$
 70 IF N$ = "STOP-IT" THEN 900
 80 PRINT N$, T$,, N$, T$
 90 GOTO 60
100 DATA "JOE FRANKS", "212-555-4932"
110 DATA "LEE HENRY", "404-555-3817"
120 DATA "BOB WYNN", "906-555-4208"
130 DATA "STOP IT", "0"
900 END

JOE FRANKS    212-555-4932                 JOE FRANKS    212-555-4932
LEE HENRY     404-555-3817                 LEE HENRY     404-555-3817
BOB WYNN      906-555-4208                 BOB WYNN      906-555-4208
STOP IT       0                            STOP IT       0

Out of Data in Line 60
```

3.

```
 10 REM  TROUBLESHOOTING PROBLEM 4-3
 20 REM
 30 REM          A = ACCOUNT NUMBER
 40 REM          T = AMOUNT OF TRANSACTION
 50 REM         D$ = DATE OF TRANSACTION
 60 REM
 70 READ A, T, D$
 80 IF A < 0 THEN 160
 90 PRINT A, T, D$
100 GOTO 80
120 DATA 389220, 473.50, "8-10-83"
130 DATA 410034, 73.00,, "8-13-83"
140 DATA 462848, -127.75, "8-14-83
150 DATA -1, 0, "X"
160 END

389220        473.50       8-10-83
389220        473.50       8-10-83
389220        473.50       8-10-83
389220        473.50       8-10-83
                 :
                 :
                 :
```

4.

```
 10 REM  TROUBLESHOOTING PROBLEM 4-4
 20 REM
 30 REM        S$ = STUDENT'S NAME
 40 REM        ID = STUDENT'S ID NUMBER
 50 REM         G = CURRENT GPA
 60 REM
 70 READ ID, S$, G
 80 IF G > 4.0 THEN 999
 90 PRINT S$, ID, G
100 GOTO 70
110 DATA "PAUL YOUNG", 38198, 2.53
120 DATA "CAROL HALL", 46729, 3.41
130 DATA "LINDA DODD", 72044, 2.04
140 DATA "0", 0, 5
999 END

Syntax Error in Line 110
```

5.

```
 10 REM  TROUBLESHOOTING PROBLEM 4-5
 20 REM
 30 REM        L$ = LICENSE NUMBER
 40 REM        C$ = TYPE OF AUTO
 50 REM        V$ = VIOLATION
 60 REM
 70 READ L$, C$, V$
 80 IF L$ = "XXX" THEN 100
 90 PRINT L$, C$, V$
100 GOTO 70
110 DATA "AHF 372","79 FORD", "SPEEDING"
120 DATA "RSK 703", "82 BUICK", "PARKING"
130 DATA "JFL 774", "80 DODGE", "RED LIGHT"
140 DATA "XXX", "X", "X"
200 END

AHF 372       79 FORD       SPEEDING
RSK 703       82 BUICK      PARKING
JFL 774       80 DODGE      RED LIGHT

Out of Data in Line 70
```

6.

```
 10 REM  TROUBLESHOOTING PROBLEM 4-6
 20 REM
 30 REM        A$ = APPLICANT'S NAME
 40 REM         Y = YEARS EXPERIENCE
 50 REM         S = SALARY REQUIREMENTS
 60 REM         R = OVERALL RATING
 70 REM
 80 REM A$, Y, S, R
 90 IF Y < 0 THEN 160
100 PRINT A$, Y, S, R
110 GOTO 80
120 DATA "JERRY ELLIS", 7, 15000, 8
130 DATA "PAUL THOMAS", 11, 22000, 9
140 DATA "LYNN BERGER", 8, 16500, 7
150 DATA "X", -1, 0, 0
160 END

        0           0           0
        0           0           0
        0           0           0
        0           0           0
               :
               :
               :
```

7.

```
 10 REM  TROUBLESHOOTING PROBLEM 4-7
 20 REM
 30 REM          S$ = STUDENT'S NAME
 40 REM  T1 - T4 = FOUR TEST GRADES
 50 REM
 60 READ S$
 70 IF S$ = "END" THEN 200
 80 READ T1, T2, T3, T4
 90 PRINT S$, T1, T2, T3, T4
100 GOTO 60
110 DATA "JAN REESE", 88, 93, 78, 84,
120 DATA "ED HARRIS", 69, 82, 75, 79
130 DATA "TERRY OWENS", 74, 93, 83, 71, "END"
200 END

JAN REESE      88            93            78            84

Syntax Error in Line 120
```

8.

```
 10 REM  TROUBLESHOOTING PROBLEM 4-8
 20 REM
 30 REM          S$ = STUDENT'S NAME
 40 REM  T1 - T4 = FOUR TEST GRADES
 50 REM
 60 READ S$
 70 IF S$ = "END" THEN 200
 80 READ T1, T2, T3, T4
 90 PRINT S$, T1, T2, T3, T4
100 GOTO 80
110 DATA "JAN REESE", 88, 93, 78, 84
120 DATA "ED HARRIS", 69, 82, 75, 79
130 DATA "TERRY OWENS", 74, 93, 83, 71
140 DATA "END"
200 END

JAN REESE      88            93            78            84

Syntax Error in Line 120
```

IMPORTANT TERMS

After studying this chapter, you should be familiar with the meaning and use of the following terms and BASIC statements:

READ statement
DATA statement
Variable list
Data list
Destructive read
Data pointer
RESTORE statement
GOTO statement
Undefined Line error
Loop
Infinite loop
Logical end
Out of Data error
Unconditional branch
Conditional branch
IF–THEN statement
Condition (IF)
Relational operator
Sentinel (trailer) record
INPUT statement
Screen prompt

EXERCISES

1. Some computers do not require that string values in DATA statements be placed in quotes. This is, however, a dangerous practice and can lead to unexpected results.

Reexamine the example in Section 4-7 and determine whether any problems would occur if the quotes were omitted from around the string values. Explain your conclusions. (Even more serious problems could occur if the quotes were omitted from around the string values in the DATA statements in the example in Section 4-3 because of the presence of the colons, which have a special meaning in some versions of BASIC.)

2. What is wrong with the following program segments? Explain what will happen in each case and suggest a possible solution.

(a)
```
130  READ A, B, C
140  IF A = 0 THEN 170
150  PRINT A, B, C
160  GOTO 140
170  END
```
(b)
```
130  READ A, B, C
140  IF A = 0 THEN 140
150  PRINT A, B, C
160  GOTO 130
170  END
```
(c)
```
130  READ A, B, C
140  IF A = 0 THEN 160
150  PRINT A, B, C
160  GOTO 130
170  END
```
(d)
```
130  READ A, B, C
140  IF A = 0 THEN 150
150  PRINT A, B, C
160  GOTO 130
170  END
```
(e)
```
130  READ A, B, C
140  IF A = 0 THEN 160
150  PRINT A, B, C
160  GOTO 140
170  END
```
(f)
```
130  READ A, B, C
140  IF A = 0 THEN 170
150  GOTO 130
160  PRINT A, B, C
170  END
```

3. Write an IF–THEN statement that satisfies the following conditions:

(a) Branches to statement 255 if XF has a value of zero
(b) Branches to statement 310 when L$ is equal to STOP!
(c) Continues to the next statement whenever N is positive; otherwise, control is directed to line 170
(d) Branches to line 1260 when a value of 9999 is found
(e) Continues to the next statement unless ALL DONE is read from the data list

4. What statement will be processed after each of the following IF–THENs? The value of the variable in the IF condition is given in parentheses to the right.

(a) (W = 12)
```
180  IF W > 0 THEN 300
190  PRINT S$, G
```
(b) (H$ = "THE END")
```
320  IF H$ = "THE END" THEN 200
330  READ D, T, P$
```
(c) (P = 110)
```
525  IF P = 100 THEN 280
540  PRINT P, Q, R
```
(d) (D = 0)
```
220  IF D <= 0 THEN 390
230  PRINT F, GY, T$
```
(e) (F$ = "GO")
```
175  IF F$ <> "GO" THEN 100
180  LET A = 23.98
```
(f) (T = 0)
```
280  IF T > 0 THEN 655
285  PRINT T
```
(g) (E$ = "END-IT")
```
150  IF E$ = "END IT" THEN 360
155  LET X$ = "TRICKY!!"
```

For Exercises 5 to 7, give the output that will be produced by the given programs. Then, type the programs into the computer, run them, and check the actual outputs against your predictions.

5.
```
10 READ N$, A, C$
20 IF N$ = "STOP" THEN 100
30 PRINT C$, N$, A
40 GOTO 10
```

```
 50 DATA "JACKSON", 24, "DENVER"
 60 DATA "TIPPS", 41, "HOUSTON"
 70 DATA "WILSON", 33, "CHICAGO"
 80 DATA "DILLARD", 29, "BOSTON"
 90 DATA "STOP", 0, "0"
100 END
```

6.
```
 10 READ D$, S$
 20 PRINT D$
 30 PRINT S$
 40 PRINT
 50 READ A, PB, CB
 60 IF A = 0 THEN 150
 70 PRINT A,, PB, CB
 80 GOTO 50
 90 DATA "JUNE 3, 1984", "JIM DUNE"
100 DATA 28774, 267.34, 356.25
110 DATA 13055, 135.55, 468.96
120 DATA 31159, 846.25, 458.61
130 DATA 27797, 113.00, 219.54
140 DATA 0, 0, 0
150 END
```

7.
```
 10 READ C$, A, D$, IV
 20 PRINT C$, A
 30 PRINT D$,,, IV
 40 PRINT
 50 READ W$, N, L, W
 60 IF W$ = "Z" THEN 140
 70 PRINT W$
 80 PRINT N, L, W
 90 GOTO 50
100 DATA "AIMES CONSTRUCTION", 72283, "4-23-84", 46533
110 DATA "PINE", 20, 8, 2, "OAK", 35, 6, 2
120 DATA "CHERRY", 12, 4, 2, "REDWOOD", 25, 6, 1
130 DATA "Z", 0, 0, 0
140 END
```

8. (a) Rewrite the programs given in Exercises 5 to 7 above to provide for input using the INPUT statement instead of the READ/DATA statements.
   (b) Write out the runs for the three programs that you wrote in part (a), giving all information that will appear on the screen. Be careful to distinguish between the information which you type and that which is printed by the computer.

PROGRAMMING PROBLEMS

Write programs in BASIC to accomplish the tasks described by each of the following problems. Be sure to carefully document each program and provide a logical end for all processing.

Use the following data for problems 1 to 4.

Name of Course	Language Taught	Quarter Offered	Maximum Enrollment	Course Instructor
CS 201	BASIC	All	60	Dr. Wilson
CS 301	FORTRAN	Fall	30	Dr. Stevens
CS 311	Pascal	Winter	30	Dr. Stevens
CS 321	COBOL	Winter	20	Dr. Lewis
CS 322	COBOL	Spring	20	Dr. Lewis
CS 341	RPG II	Fall	20	Dr. Lewis
CS 351	Assembly	Spring	30	Dr. Stevens

1. Write a program to read and print the above data, producing a Programming Course Report with one line of output for each input record. You may select any convenient value to end your program.
2. Write a program to process the above data, preparing a two-line report with the course and language on the first line and the remaining three fields in the second. Each print record should be separated by one blank line. Use a negative value for the enrollment to end the program.
3. Prepare a report to present the above data, but with the name of the college, Parks College, and the academic year, 1983–1984, at the top, separated from the rest of the report by two blank lines. The format of the print lines and the logical end are left to you.
4. Revise your program for Problem 3 to read only the name of the course before checking for the end of the data.

The following data is to be used for problems 5 to 8.

Department Name	Number of Salespersons	Weekly Sales	Weekly Quota	Sales Rating
Hardware	5	$12,455	$16,500	Poor
Appliance	8	$67,598	$55,000	Excellent
Clothing	15	$43,677	$45,000	Good
Toys	4	$ 9,822	$10,000	Good
Electronics	8	$56,823	$50,000	Good
Garden	6	$ 3,670	$12,000	Poor
Automotive	12	$33,865	$22,500	Superior
Furniture	10	$29,040	$29,500	Good

5. Prepare a Weekly Sales Report from the above data. One print line should be allotted to each department, and your report should end for a sales rating of HELP.
6. Another sales report is to be prepared from the above data, but this one is to give the store name, Smythe's, and the date (you supply that) at the top of the report. This information is to be separated from the body of the report by *at least* one blank line; however, the exact details are left to you. The report should end for a number of salespersons equal to 0.
7. The above data is to be used to prepare a Weekly Sales Report according to the following requirements:
   (a) The data given below is to be printed at the top of the report, all on separate lines and spaced from the report by two blank lines.

   Store name: Smythe's
   Branch: Easthaven
   Manager: Michael Woods
   Date: (you supply)

   (b) Each department should show a report on two lines with the department name and the number of salespersons on the first line and the remaining three values on the second with the rating printed in the fifth zone. Each department record should be separated by one blank line.
   (c) Only the department name should be read before a check is made for the end of the data condition, which should be signaled by a department name of END.
8. Revise Problem 7 to provide for this additional condition:
   (d) After all data has been processed, the following two names should be printed on separate lines at the *bottom* of the report, spaced down three lines from the last department record.

Top salesperson: Peggy Aaron
Low salesperson: Jerry North

9. Write a program to produce a Passenger Usage Report from the data given below. The details of the design of the printout are left to you.

Company: Krawl Bus Lines
City: Philadelphia, PA

Owner: Stephen V. Lobolov
Week of: October 18, 1983

Route Number	Bus Number	Driver's Name	Miles per Week	Number of Passengers	Weekly Income
26	249	F. Neills	1855	132	2643.76
31	100	L. Boyd	2030	161	2788.02
36	542	L. Smith	1757	110	1682.26
49	298	H. Jones	2450	153	2338.53
58	206	J. Walker	1330	82	928.61
59	843	D. Nolan	1785	139	1304.25

10. Write a program to produce a personal telephone directory. This should begin with your name at the top, followed by two blank lines. The directory is to list the name and telephone number (with area code) in the first and fifth zones of one line, with the full address—street, city, state, and zip code—on a second line. Each entry should be separated by one blank line. You supply the data for at least six of your friends.
11. Prepare a program to print a Student Interest Summary Report, giving the results of a survey of at least eight of the students in your class. Your report should present the name of the school, the course name, and the current quarter at the top, followed by the name, year in school, major, minor, home state, and ''Yes'' or ''No'' in answer to the question: ''Do you own your own microcomputer?'' If the student has not yet declared a major or minor, enter ''Undecided'' in the appropriate place on the report. The report should have your name printed at the bottom. (Be sure to insert blank lines as needed.)
12. Prepare a program to print a Christmas card mailing list. Each entry on the list should provide for a name line, two lines for the street address, and a fourth line for the city, state, and zip code; that means *six* data values per entry. All data records will require six items in the data list corresponding to the six variables in the read list: one for the name, two for the street address, and one each for the city, state, and zip code. If an entry uses only one line for the street address, the extra one must be made to print as a blank; this can be accomplished by entering a '' '' in the data list at the proper place. Two blank lines should separate each entry. Use the names and addresses of at least six of your friends for data.

CHAPTER 5

ARITHMETIC OPERATIONS

One of the remarkable things about computers is their ability to work with an enormous quantity of numbers at high speeds. This includes making many thousands of mathematical calculations per second. Certainly, many of the most outstanding human achievements within the last two decades, such as the Apollo manned moon landings, would not have been possible without the processing power of the computer.

You will begin to learn in this chapter how to write programs that involve simple mathematical operations. As you complete the examples and problems that follow, you should begin to appreciate the real power of the computer to handle numbers. We will cover the mathematical features of BASIC that are needed to solve about 95 percent of all programming problems. Some advanced features, including special functions for working with problems that involve trigonometry and other higher mathematical tools, will be introduced in Chapter 11. You will also be introduced, in the chapters that follow, to many special programming techniques that use the mathematical operations covered in this chapter.

5-1 THE FUNDAMENTAL ARITHMETIC OPERATORS

Mathematical expressions in BASIC are constructed using variables and constants connected with the five fundamental **arithmetic operators** listed in Table 5-1. For example, to add *A* to the product of 25 and *W*, we would write

```
A + 25 * W
```

To divide *F* by 5 and subtract the product of *P* and *X* from the quotient would be written

```
F / 5 - P * X
```

TABLE 5-1

Summary of Fundamental Arithmetic Operators

Operator	Meaning	Examples of Use		
+	Addition	A + G	and	Y + 24 + T
−	Subtraction	V − S	and	L − R − 2.7
*	Multiplication	Y * P	and	1.23 * A4 * YX
/	Division	G / B	and	S / K / 100
^	Exponentiation†	R ^ I	and	NA ^ X ^ 3

†A few computers use ** instead of ^ for exponentiation

As with most statements in BASIC, spaces are inserted at the programmer's discretion to improve readability. The last expression could be written as F/5 − P*X or F/5−P*X.

Clearly, as in algebra, each operator must always join *two* numbers represented by either variables or constants. One *apparent* exception to this occurs when the minus sign is used for **negation** instead of subtraction, as in the case:

```
JX + (-M) * H4
```

In this expression, there is no number separating the two operators + and −; however, in any such case, there must always be a parenthesis between the negation and another operator. (Negation is the same as multiplying by the constant −1; in the last expression, −M = −1 * M.) Also, any two variables and/or constants must be separated by an operator. In algebra, you may indicate the product of two numbers, say 2 and x, by $2x$. To write this product in a BASIC expression, you *must* include the multiplication symbol; it would be written as 2 * X. (Be careful not to confuse two-character variables, such as JX or H4, with implied multiplication.)

Table 5-2 gives some examples of mathematical expressions before and after being "translated" into BASIC. (There will be more in Section 5-3 on writing expressions.) Also, remember that only the five operators listed in Table 5-1 may be used to construct mathematical expressions; any unauthorized characters, such as × (for multiplication) or ÷ (for division), will result in a Syntax error. (Some versions of BASIC permit a few additional special arithmetic operators.)

There are several general guidelines that you may find helpful when writing mathematical expressions in BASIC.

1. Always observe the order of operations, using parentheses to change the order whenever necessary. (This is discussed in the next two sections.)
2. Write expressions on single lines as you would type them.
3. *All* arithmetic operations must be explicitly indicated; unlike algebra, no assumed operations are permitted.
4. Two *adjacent* operators are never permitted; all operators must be separated by either a variable, constant, or parenthesis.
5. The number of left and right parentheses must be equal.
6. Mathematical expressions may not contain string variables or constants.

Table 5-3 gives some typical invalid expressions and the reason why each is incorrect.

TABLE 5-2

Writing Mathematical Expressions in BASIC

Algebraic Form	BASIC Form
$5t - 3$	`5 * T - 3`
$2x + 3y$	`2 * X + 3 * Y`
$a + \frac{b}{5}$	`A * B / 5`
$12(3r - p)$	`12 * (3 * R - P)`
$2x^2 - 7x + 4$	`2 * X * X - 7 * X + 4`
$\frac{a + 3b}{d - 11}$	`(A + 3 * B) / (D - 11)`
$t^5 - 7(t^3 - 22t)$	`T ^ 5 - 7 * (T ^ 3 - 22 * T)`
$\frac{79}{4a - 7} + 3b(a - 5)$	`79 / (4 * A - 7) + 3 * B * (A - 5)`

TABLE 5-3

Examples of Invalid BASIC Mathematical Expressions

Invalid Expression	Reason for Invalid Condition	Corrected Expression
2A + V - 7	Missing operator	2 * A + V - 7
5 * R + - 7 * S3	Two adjacent operators	5 * R + (- 7) * S3
(F - BT / U	Missing parenthesis	(F - BT) / U
56 - F2 / - 8	Two adjacent operators	56 - F2 / (- 8)
P + 6(Y1 - 66)	Missing operator	P + 6 * (Y1 - 66)
G - H$ * K / 12	String value present	G - H * K / 12
A X B + C / D	Undefined operator	A * B + C / D
(J - 15) / (-1) * N)	Missing parenthesis	(J - 15) / ((-1) * N)

Most errors that occur in mathematical expressions will be reported by the computer as Syntax errors, but there are a few special cases where the problem will be defined more specifically. One of these is the **Division by Zero** error. This occurs whenever a division is attempted with a denominator that has a value of zero. Sometimes the situation is obvious, as when a data value of zero has been read and assigned to a variable in a denominator. In other cases, the problem is caused by values that are calculated during program processing and is often considerably more difficult to find. Another error message that you may encounter is **Overflow**. This is produced when a data value is developed (usually in calculations) that is too large for the computer to handle. Limits on the size of the numbers that can be processed will vary with the computer, but they will always be large enough for most problems. You will need to check this for the system you are using.

5-2 THE ORDER OF OPERATIONS

Many times you will not have an expression to translate but will have to write your own. To do this properly, you must know something about the way the computer will evaluate the expression that you write. BASIC follows a very definite **order of operations** in performing arithmetic operations and in evaluating mathematical expressions. This order of operations is summarized as follows:

Step 1. All grouped terms are evaluated from inner to outer groupings.

Step 2. All exponentiations are performed from left to right.

Step 3. Negations are performed.

Step 4. All multiplications and divisions are performed from left to right.

Step 5. All additions and subtractions are performed from left to right.

Let us examine each of these steps.

We will leave a detailed discussion of Step 1 for Section 5-3. Step 2 means that in any expression, if exponents are to be evaluated, they will be calculated *first,* before any of the other four operations are performed. In each of the following expressions, X ^ 4 will be evaluated first.

```
3 * X ^ 4 + X * X - 11

X ^ 4 - 234 / X

75 * X * Y + R / X ^ 4
```

The phrase "performed from left to right" that appears in steps 2, 4, and 5 means that if more than one of the listed operations is present in the expression, the *leftmost* occurrence will be evaluated first, with successive evaluations moving to the right until all are done. In the case of exponentiation, consider the following expressions, which contain more than one exponent. First there is the case of unconnected (separated by another operator) exponentiations such as

```
N ^ 5 + 2 * N ^ 3 - 7 * N
```

N ^ 5 will be evaluated first, then N ^ 3, because N ^ 5 is to the left of N ^ 3. In this case, it really makes little difference which is done first.

As a somewhat more technical example, consider this:

```
Y ^ K ^ L
```

What is done first? According to the order of operations, Y ^ K is to the left and should be calculated first, with the result raised to the L power. If you want the exponents to be calculated in the reverse order, you must *group* part of the expression to indicate this preference. To cause K ^ L to be done first, write the above as

```
Y ^ (K ^ L)
```

Now the **grouped** part of the expression (in parentheses) will take precedence (step 1) and will be evaluated first despite the left to right rule.

Step 3 of the order of operations relates to taking the negative (changing the sign) of part or all of an expression. This was discussed in Section 5-1.

Step 4 follows essentially the same ideas as step 2 except that there are now *two* operations involved. As for the left to right evaluation of operations, there is no distinction between multiplication and division. For example, in evaluating the expression

```
R * S / T * Z
```

the computer will (1) multiply R by S, (2) divide that product by T, and (3) multiply the result of the division by Z. Suppose that we want to divide S by *both* T and Z. To do this, simply group T and Z in parentheses:

```
R * S / (T * Z)
```

Now the order will be (1) multiply T by Z, (2) multiply R by S, and (3) divide the result of (2) by (1).

As you probably noted, the difficulty in the order of the above expression arose because of the division. Had the expression been

```
R * S * T * Z
```

it still would be evaluated from left to right, but the final result would be the same regardless of the sequence in which the multiplications were performed. This is known as the **associative property of multiplication**. Stated a little more formally, it is:

```
A * (B * C) = (A * B) * C
```

which says that *when only multiplication is involved,* the result is the same whether you multiply from left to right or right to left. As an example of this, suppose that we wish to multiply three numbers: 4, 3, and 5. In left to right order (the right-hand side of the above property), we first multiply 4 by 3, giving 12. This result is multiplied by 5 to give a final product of 60. For right to left order (the left-hand side above), first 3 is multiplied by 5, giving 15. This result is then multiplied by the first number, 4, to yield the product of 60.

A written-out example of the associative property would be as follows:

```
4 * (3 * 5) = (4 * 3) * 5
    4 * 15 = 12 * 5
        60 = 60
```

Addition is also associative. The **associative property of addition** is stated:

```
A + (B + C) = (A + B) + C
```

which means that for addition alone the left to right sequence is unimportant.

Neither exponentiation, division, nor subtraction obeys an associative property. That is, with any of these three operators, left to right evaluation will not be the same as right to left. This can be stated as follows:

```
A ^ (B ^ C) ≠ (A ^ B) ^ C
A / (B / C) ≠ (A / B) / C
A - (B - C) ≠ (A - B) - C
```

To illustrate this, consider the division of three numbers: 24, 6, and 2. In left to right sequence, we first divide 24 by 6 to get 4; the 4 is then divided by 2, giving a final answer of 2. In reverse order, we would divide 6 by 2 to get 3; then 24 divided by the 3 would give 8, which is not the same as we got the other way. This can be expressed a little more mathematically as

```
24 / (6 / 2) ≠ (24 / 6) / 2
      24 / 3 ≠ 4 / 2
           8 ≠ 2
```

Step 5 in the order of operations involves the evaluation of additions and subtractions. We have already discussed these operators in general; the basic guidelines relating to their use are essentially the same as those for multiplications and divisions. Terms are evaluated from left to right with parentheses being used to change the order, if needed.

5-3 CHANGING THE ORDER OF OPERATIONS

We now turn to a discussion of expressions the evaluation of which will involve more than one step in the order of operations. This will also bring us back to step 1 in the above order, the one we temporarily postponed. Actually, we had some brief contact with the meaning of step 1 when we used parentheses to change the standard left to right order of evaluation; this same technique can be used to accomplish much more powerful results.

Let us consider a few examples of algebraic expressions and how they would be correctly written in BASIC. First, take the very simple expression

$$2x + 7$$

To write this in BASIC is easy; it is

```
2 * X + 7
```

which even has the proper order of operations: multiply, then add. And if the above expression had been written as

$$2(x + 7)$$

you should have no trouble transforming it to

```
2 * (X + 7)
```

or understanding that the parentheses cause the addition to be done before the multiplication, exactly as in the algebraic form. Unfortunately, things are not always so simple.

How would you translate this expression into BASIC to ensure the proper order of operations?

$$\frac{x + 5}{y - 2}$$

Your first try might be something like this:

```
X + 5 / Y - 2
```

But, recalling the order in which the operations will be done, you see that this will not work. In the algebraic form, first $x + 5$ and $y - 2$ are calculated, then the division takes place. In the BASIC expression, the division is first; Y is divided by 5, then the other operations are performed, giving a totally erroneous result. The addition and subtraction must be performed before the division, which changes the normal working sequence. To indicate this, both the X + 5 and the Y − 2 are placed in parentheses (grouped). The expression is correctly written:

```
(X + 5) / (Y - 2)
```

Another example, somewhat similar to the last one, is illustrated by the following:

$$a + b^{n+2}$$

This expression is evaluated by first raising only b to the $n + 2$ power, then adding a to that result. The order that must be followed is (1) calculate $n + 2$, (2) raise b to the $n + 2$ power, and (3) add a to the result of (2). This is expressed in BASIC as

```
A + B ^ (N + 2)
```

In this case, it would be incorrect to place parentheses around the A + B. Why?

As yet another example of using parentheses to group terms to change the order of operations, consider the following algebraic expression, which is a combination of the last two:

$$\frac{7p - r^{3x}}{11q + 29}$$

First, we must analyze the order of the operations needed to evaluate this expression. Exponents are done first; therefore, we must group the $3x$ so that it will be calculated *before* the exponentiation and treated as a single value. Then the numerator and denominator must be grouped in order to force the addition and subtraction involved to precede the final division. In summary, the steps are (1) group the $3x$—(3 * X); (2) raise r to the $3x$ power, R ^ (3 * X); (3) group the entire numerator, 7 * P − R ^ (3 * X), and the entire denominator, 11 * Q + 29 (after steps 1 and 2 the order will proceed normally within these two groups); and (4) divide. Combining all this into a single BASIC expression gives

```
(7 * P - R ^ (3 * X)) / (11 * Q + 29)
```

One final point relating to grouping terms is to remember that, according to step 1 of the order of operations, grouped terms are performed from inner to outer groupings. In other words, if there are parentheses *within* parentheses, evaluation of terms will begin with the innermost and work outward to the outermost. There is a very simple illustration of this in the last example. The exponent 3 * X is in parentheses, which in turn fall within the parentheses grouping the numerator. This means that the inner group, the 3 * X, will be evaluated before the rest of the numerator—but you already knew this! Consider one final example:

```
X * (R / (A + 5) - (B * (J - 11) + 7))
```

There are three levels of parentheses in this expression, the innermost one being (J - 11). This subtraction is done first. Next, the result is multiplied by B and added to 7, and (A + 5) is divided into R, removing the two middle layers of parentheses. Finally, these two results are subtracted to clear the outermost parentheses (the ''longest'' ones). This difference multiplied by X produces the final result.

5-4 MORE ON THE LET STATEMENT

In Section 3-4, you were introduced to the LET statement for the purpose of assigning specific values to data names; however, the LET is a much more versatile tool. As mentioned at that time, the general form of the LET is

ln **LET** *data name = expression*

A data name (variable) must *always* be to the left of the equals sign. The expression may be a constant (as was the case in Chapter 3), another variable, or a mathematical expression. In the case of constants and variables, both numeric and string are allowed, provided the usual cautions regarding type matching are observed.

With these comments in mind, consider the following examples of LET statements:

```
120  LET P = X
155  LET D$ = A3$
170  LET N = S * T - (R - 4) / 3
```

Table 5-4 gives some examples of invalid LET statements. Of course, the simple form of the assignment statement that we studied in Section 3-4 can still be used, if needed.

Before moving on to an example, let us look briefly at how the computer functions when you use a LET statement. In the simplest terms, the computer will take whatever is on the right-hand side of the equal sign, perform the necessary calculations, and assign

TABLE 5-4

Examples of Invalid LET Statements

Invalid Statement	Reason Why It Is Invalid	Possible Correction
150 LET S = F$	Type mismatch	150 LET S$ = F$ or 150 LET S = F
275 LET P$ = A + A - C	Type mismatch	275 LET P = A + A - C
190 LET F - 3 * H = X	Variable not on left	190 LET X = F - 3 * H
365 LET A * D / C	No = or assignment variable	365 LET R = A * D / C
220 LET Z = V + T = Q	Only one = allowed†	220 LET Z = V + T 225 LET Q = V + T

†Multiple = are allowed by some versions of BASIC under certain conditions

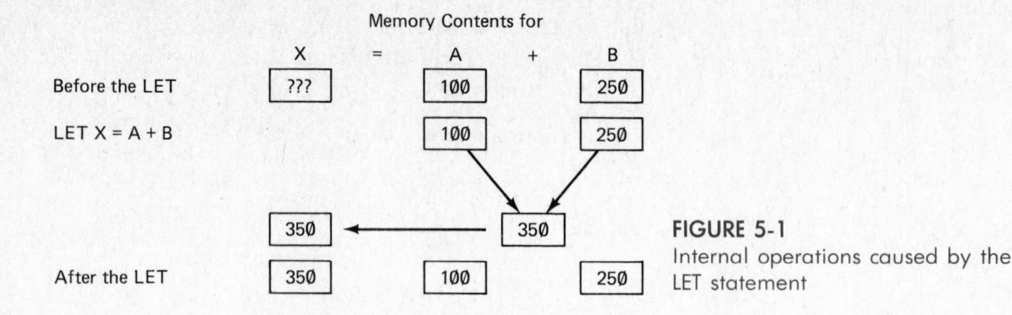

FIGURE 5-1
Internal operations caused by the LET statement

(hence the name **assignment statement**!) the resulting value to the variable on the left of the equals. Look at the following short program.

```
100 REM   EXAMPLE WITH MATH EXPRESSIONS
110 REM
120 READ A, B, C
130 IF A < 0 THEN 999
140 LET S = A + B + C
150 LET P = A * B * C
160 PRINT A, B, C, S, P
170 GOTO 120
180 DATA 3,7,2,8,12,5,9,10,4,-1,0,0
999 END
```

This will produce an output of

```
3          7          2          12         42
8          12         5          25         480
9          10         4          23         360
```

The values read for A, B, and C are added and assigned to S by the LET statement at line 140 and multiplied and assigned to P by the one at 150. Each time a new set of input values is processed, the resulting sum and product are assigned, respectively, to S and P replacing the old ones. Always keep in mind that the computer does *not* treat an = the same as in algebra; the computer uses it to assign the value on the right to the variable on the left. The normal rules of algebraic relations *do not apply*. The action is illustrated in Figure 5-1.

The same variable can appear on both sides of the equal sign in a LET statement. This usually means that the new value to be assigned depends on the old one in some way It is a common occurrence in calculating totals as we will see in Section 5-6.

5-5 AN EXAMPLE: CALCULATING COMPOUND INTEREST

For this example, let us first briefly discuss what is meant by compound interest. If you are already familiar with the concept, you may skip down to the beginning of the problem.

There are basically two types of interest: simple and compound. With simple interest you invest your money for a certain length of time at a given rate, and at the end of the time your money is returned along with the interest earned. With this type of investment, the interest is referred to as simple because it never draws interest on itself. With compound interest, once your money begins to draw interest, you will usually begin to draw interest on the interest that has already been earned. The formula for calculating compound interest is

$$p = a(1 + r/n)^{ny}$$

where a = the amount initially invested
r = the *annual* interest rate (as a decimal)
n = the number of times the interest is calculated (compounded) each year: $n = 1$ for annually, $n = 2$ for semiannually, $n = 4$ for quarterly, $n = 12$ for monthly, etc.
y = the total number of years for which the investment is made
p = the value of the investment after y years

This means that if you invest $1000.00 at 8 percent interest, compounded monthly for 3 years, at the end of that time you will have

$$\begin{aligned} p &= 1000(1 + 0.08/12)^{12\times 3} \\ &= 1000(1 + 0.00667)^{36} \\ &= 1000(1.00667)^{36} \\ &= 1000(1.27039) \\ &= 1270.39 \end{aligned}$$

(This figure is slightly off due to our *manual* calculations; the actual value is $1270.24.) The interest earned is found by subtracting the original investment from this figure ($i = p - a$), giving $270.39 for the above data. This compares favorably with the $240.00 that would have been earned for the same rate and time at simple interest.

Now let us tackle a programming problem dealing with compound interest.

Problem: A certain bank has investment certificates for sale that are available at several different interest rates and for varying lengths of time; however, all are compounded monthly. A report is to be prepared that summarizes the sales of these certificates for 1 day. The projected value at maturity and the total interest earned are to be calculated for each certificate. The report should show the name of the bank and the date at the top, followed after one blank line by a detailed printout for each certificate, giving the certificate number, face value (original investment), interest rate (as percent), and time of investment on one line, with the value at maturity and interest earned on a second line but beginning in the second print zone. Data may be found in Table 5-5.

The solution to this problem involves the following sequence of steps:

1. Read the bank name and date.
2. Print the bank name and date.
3. Assign the value for the compounding period to be monthly ($n = 12$).
4. Read one certificate record.
5. If the sentinel record has been reached, go to step 9; otherwise, continue to the next step.

TABLE 5-5

Data for Compound Interest Example

Bank Name: First National Date: July 25, 1983

Certificate Number	Amount of Investment	Interest Rate (%)	Investment in Years
377933	1000	8.50	1.0
267951	5000	10.50	3.0
160248	2500	9.25	2.5
684552	5000	9.25	0.5
610205	10000	12.50	4.0
493022	3000	9.00	2.0

6. Calculate the maturity value and the interest earned.
7. Print the report on one certificate.
8. Go to step 4.
9. Stop.

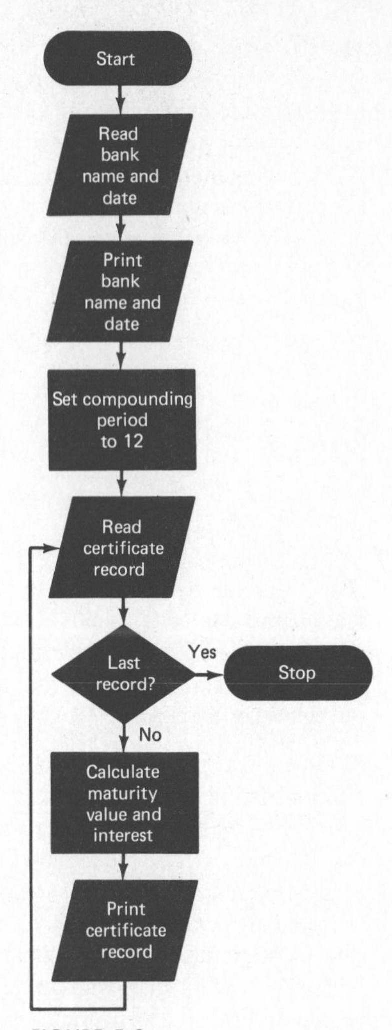

FIGURE 5-2
Flowchart for compound interest problem

This procedure is pictorially illustrated by the flowchart in Figure 5-2.

The variables to be used are defined in the complete program listing. By now you should be familiar with REM statements and their use, so we will not discuss these any further.

Steps 1 and 2 in the program solution outlined above are essentially the same as those we encountered in the two problems in Chapter 4; the statements corresponding to these are:

```
180  READ B$, D$
190  PRINT B$
200  PRINT D$
```

Step 3 involves a new idea—that of **initially assigning** a program constant for use in all the calculations that follow. There are many variations of this; we will see one in Section 5-6. In this case, we need to assign the number of times per year that the interest is to be compounded. Of course, this could have been included in the data record for each certificate, but that would have been a waste of effort since the value is the same for all certificates. The easiest way is to simply set the value at the beginning of the program by some convenient means; in this case, we are using a LET statement:

```
250  LET N = 12
```

You will see in Section 5-6 that we could have accomplished the same result by using a READ and placing the required value in the data list, much as we did with the bank name and date above.

We now come to steps 4 through 9, which comprise the heart of the program. In this part we read, process, and print the certificate information. The portion of the program that accomplishes this is:

```
290 READ C, A, RP, Y
300 IF C = 0 THEN 480
310 LET RD = RP / 100
320 LET P = A * (1 + RD / N) ^ (N * Y)
330 LET I = P - A
340 PRINT C, A, RP, Y
350 PRINT , P, I
360 GOTO 290
         :
         :
480 END
```

Line 290 reads a record of certificate data. Line 300 provides a logical end to the processing by directing the program to the END statement at line 480 when the sentinel record with a certificate number of 0 is found. Lines 340 and 350 provide for the printed output, and 360 continues the processing for multiple records. All of this is old business; now for the new. The interest rate is input and output as a *percentage* value, but it must be expressed as a *decimal* in order to be used in calculations. The LET statement at 310 converts the percent form to the decimal. (This could have been incorporated into line 320, but that would have made the expression more complicated and would have increased the chance of error.) Line 320 calculates the maturity value of the certificate, and line 330 gives the interest earned.

The complete program listing is shown opposite.

```
 10 REM  PROGRAM TO CALCULATE COMPOUND INTEREST
 20 REM
 30 REM  VARIABLES ARE DEFINED AS --
 40 REM
 50 REM         B$ = BANK NAME
 60 REM         D$ = DATE OF REPORT
 70 REM          C = CERTIFICATE NUMBER
 80 REM          A = ORIGINAL INVESTMENT
 90 REM         RP = INTEREST RATE IN PERCENT FORM
100 REM         RD = INTEREST RATE IN DECIMAL FORM
110 REM          Y = TIME OF INVESTMENT IN YEARS
120 REM          N = NUMBER OF COMPOUNDINGS PER YEAR
130 REM          P = VALUE AT MATURITY
140 REM          I = INTEREST EARNED
150 REM
160 REM  READ AND PRINT BANK NAME AND DATE
170 REM
180 READ B$, D$
190 PRINT B$
200 PRINT D$
210 PRINT
220 REM
230 REM  ASSIGN NUMBER OF COMPOUNDINGS PER YEAR
240 REM
250 LET N = 12
260 REM
270 REM  PROCESS CERTIFICATE AND CALCULATE VALUES
280 REM
290 READ C, A, RP, Y
300 IF C = 0 THEN 480
310 LET RD = RP / 100
320 LET P = A * (1 + RD / N) ^ (N * Y)
330 LET I = P - A
340 PRINT C, A, RP, Y
350 PRINT , P, I
360 GOTO 290
370 REM
380 REM  DATA LIST
390 REM
400 DATA "FIRST NATIONAL", "JULY 25, 1983"
410 DATA 377933,1000,8.50,1.0
420 DATA 267951,5000,10.50,3.0
430 DATA 160248,2500,9.25,2.5
440 DATA 684552,5000,9.25,0.5
450 DATA 610205,10000,12.50,4.0
460 DATA 493022,3000,9.00,2.0
470 DATA 0,0,0,0
480 END
```

The output is as follows:

```
FIRST NATIONAL
JULY 25, 1983

 377933         1000           8.5            1
                1088.39        88.3891
 267951         5000           10.5           3
                6841.89        1841.89
 160248         2500           9.25           2.5
                3147.63        647.635
 684552         5000           9.25           .5
                5235.75        235.75
 610205         10000          12.5           4
                16444.6        6444.56
 493022         3000           9              2
                3589.24        589.242
```

5-6 ACCUMULATING TOTALS

One of the most valuable programming techniques that you will learn is that of **accumulating totals**. In many programming applications, as data is processed, it is necessary to keep track of the sum of the values or number of values that have been processed (a "running total"). Since most programs use destructive reads (*see* Chapter 4) for processing data, it is not possible to calculate these totals at the end of the program; they must be continually updated as the other processing is done.

Most totals are calculated by using a LET statement of the following general form:

ln **LET** *total* = *total* + *value*

where *total* is the variable that is being used to accumulate the sum of *value*. For example, if we wish to find the total of all the commissions paid to a certain group of salespersons, we might write:

```
260  LET TC = TC + C
```

where C represents the commission and TC the sum of all the values assigned to C.

This last statement may look a little strange to you at first. Your algebra teacher will tell you that the relation

```
TC = TC + C
```

has no solution for TC (if $C \neq 0$), which is true *for an algebraic relationship*. But remember that the computer does not treat this the same as you would in algebra. The computer takes the result of the evaluation of the expression on the right and assigns it to the variable on the left. In this case, that means that the old total stored in TC will have C added to it (it will be *updated*); then the new value for TC replaces the old in storage. Assuming that TC started with a value of zero, this process will calculate the sum of all C's. This process is shown schematically in Figure 5-3.

Consider the following simple example of calculating totals. Suppose that we wish to read a series of two numbers and calculate the product of each pair of numbers. In

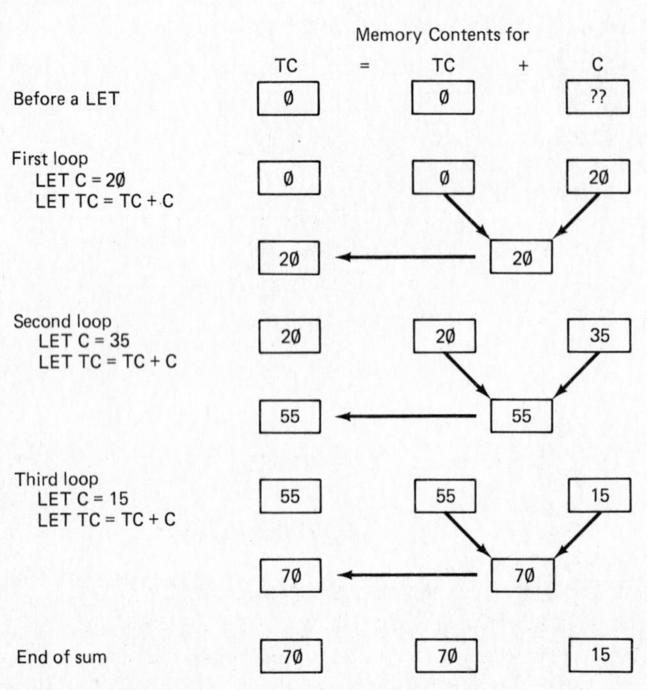

FIGURE 5-3
Internal transfer of data in accumulating a sum

addition, we need to find the *sum* of all the products that we have calculated and the total number of pairs of numbers processed. The following short program will do the job:

```
 10 REM   ILLUSTRATION OF ACCUMULATION TOTALS
 20 REM
 30 LET T = 0
 40 LET TP = 0
 50 READ X, Y
 60 IF X = 99999 THEN 120
 70 LET P = X * Y
 80 LET T = T + 1
 90 LET TP = TP + P
100 PRINT X, Y, P
110 GOTO 50
120 PRINT
130 PRINT T,, TP
140 DATA 4,8,5,9,12,6,10,5,15,4,99999,0
150 END
```

The first two lines set the variables T and TP, which represent the two totals, to 0 at the beginning of the program. (This is unnecessary with most forms of BASIC but is extremely good programming technique, since it is necessary with most other languages!)

Lines 50 through 110 form the processing loop. Line 50 reads the two numbers X and Y, line 60 checks for the logical end, while line 100 prints the results and line 110 sends the program back for more data. The product of the two numbers is calculated at line 70, and the sum of the products is accumulated at 90. Line 80 keeps track of the number of products that are calculated by adding 1 to the total each time a pair of numbers is processed. Since the total T started at 0, this will give the number of times the loop is executed. This type of total is referred to as a **counter**. We will learn more uses for counters in Chapter 7.

Notice that the IF at 60 does not send the program to the END statement at the end of processing. This is because when all the data has been processed, we still must print the totals that we have calculated. This is done by first going to line 120 to print the totals, then ending. When this program is run, we get:

```
4             8             32
5             9             45
12            6             72
10            5             50
15            4             60

5                           259
```

Totals or any other variables that must be initialized at the beginning of a program may be assigned their proper values by means of the READ statement instead of the LET, or a combination of the two may be used. If we use a READ in place of the two LET statements at lines 30 and 40 in the above program, we will have:

```
 30  READ T, TP
                        :
                        :
150  DATA 0,0,4,8,5,9,12,6,10,5,15,4,99999,0
```

We also have to add the initial values for the totals to the beginning of the data list. The action of the data pointer is shown in Figure 5-4.

There is no rule on which statement is best to use, but the general guideline on whether to use the LET or READ to initialize variables is as follows: If there are only a few values to be assigned, usually the LET is as easy as the READ, and it provides better

150 DATA 0, 0, 4, 8, 5, 9, 12, 6, 10, 5, 15, 4, 99999, 0

Position of data pointer <u>before</u> first READ

150 DATA 0, 0, 4, 8, 5, 9, 12, 6, 10, 5, 15, 4, 99999, 0

Position of data pointer <u>after</u> READ at line 30

FIGURE 5-4
Effect of initializing with READ statement

documentation. When there are many values involved, the READ has the advantage of convenience. However, when a variable must be reassigned *during the processing of the data,* the LET is usually the safest.

Let us look at the example in Section 5-5 and see how we would have to modify that program to calculate totals for the number of certificates sold, the total investments, and the total interest due. The new program listing with the required changes is below.

```
 10 REM  PROGRAM TO CALCULATE COMPOUND INTEREST
 15 REM     -- MODIFIED TO CALCULATE TOTALS --
 20 REM
 30 REM  VARIABLES ARE DEFINED AS --
 40 REM
 50 REM             B$ = BANK NAME
 60 REM             D$ = DATE OF REPORT
 70 REM              C = CERTIFICATE NUMBER
 80 REM              A = ORIGINAL INVESTMENT
 90 REM             RP = INTEREST RATE IN PERCENT FORM
100 REM             RD = INTEREST RATE IN DECIMAL FORM
110 REM              Y = TIME OF INVESTMENT IN YEARS
120 REM              N = NUMBER OF COMPOUNDINGS PER YEAR
130 REM              P = VALUE AT MATURITY
140 REM              I = INTEREST EARNED
142 REM             TC = TOTAL NUMBER OF CERTIFICATES
144 REM             TA = TOTAL AMOUNT INVESTED
146 REM             TI = TOTAL INTEREST DUE
150 REM
160 REM  READ AND PRINT BANK NAME AND DATE
170 REM
180 READ B$, D$
190 PRINT B$
200 PRINT D$
210 PRINT
220 REM
225 REM  INITIALIZE ALL FINAL TOTALS TO ZERO AND
230 REM  ASSIGN NUMBER OF COMPOUNDINGS PER YEAR
240 REM
242 LET TC = 0
244 LET TA = 0
246 LET TI = 0
250 LET N = 12
260 REM
270 REM  PROCESS CERTIFICATE AND CALCULATE VALUES
280 REM
290 READ C, A, RP, Y
300 IF C = 0 THEN 366
310 LET RD = RP / 100
320 LET P = A * (1 + RD / N) ^ (N * Y)
330 LET I = P - A
332 LET TC = TC + 1
334 LET TA = TA + A
336 LET TI = TI + I
340 PRINT C, A, RP, Y
```

```
350 PRINT , P, I
360 GOTO 290
362 REM
363 REM  PRINT TOTALS AND END
364 REM
366 PRINT
368 PRINT TC, TA, TI
370 REM
380 REM  DATA LIST
390 REM
400 DATA "FIRST NATIONAL", "JULY 25, 1983"
410 DATA 377933,1000,8.50,1.0
420 DATA 267951,5000,10.50,3.0
430 DATA 160248,2500,9.25,2.5
440 DATA 684552,5000,9.25,0.5
450 DATA 610205,10000,12.50,4.0
460 DATA 493022,3000,9.00,2.0
470 DATA 0,0,0,0
480 END
```

Aside from a few REM statements that have been changed or added, the modifications that were required were to (1) add three LET statements at lines 242, 244, and 246 to set the totals to zero initially; (2) add three LET statements at lines 332, 334, and 336 that will accumulate the totals; (3) insert PRINT statements before the END to print the totals; and (4) modify the IF at line 300 to direct the program at the end to the new PRINT statements instead of the just coming to a quick stop. The output will now have the totals added at the bottom:

```
FIRST NATIONAL
JULY 25, 1983

 377933         1000           8.5            1
                1088.39        88.3891
 267951         5000           10.5           3
                6841.89        1841.89
 160248         2500           9.25           2.5
                3147.63        647.635
 684552         5000           9.25           .5
                5235.75        235.75
 610205         10000          12.5           4
                16444.6        6444.56
 493022         3000           9              2
                3589.24        589.242

 6              26500          9847.47
```

It might have been more advantageous to have done the above modifications with a READ statement, especially since there is already one at line 180 that reads two initial values. There are two good approaches to this; these are both shown below along with program segments.

The first approach is to use a READ in place of the *four* LET statements at lines 242 through 250 to assign the three totals as well as N. To do this, the above program would be modified as follows:

```
                             :
                             :
     180 READ B$, D$
                             :
                             :
     250 READ TC, TA, TI, N
                             :
                             :
     400 DATA "FIRST NATIONAL", "JULY 25, 1983"
```

```
405 DATA 0,0,0,12
410 DATA 377933,1000,8.50,1.0
420 DATA 267951,5000,10.50,3.0
430 DATA 160248,2500,9.25,2.5
440 DATA 684552,5000,9.25,0.5
450 DATA 610205,10000,12.50,4.0
460 DATA 493022,3000,9.00,2.0
470 DATA 0,0,0,0
```

Besides replacing the four LETs with the READ, we have inserted the initial values of the four variables in the data list after the bank name and date.

The second approach takes advantage of the fact that there is already a READ at 180 that assigns the values to the bank name and the date. The two READs at 180 and 250 can be combined into one something like this:

```
180 READ B$, D$, TC, TA, TI, N
```

There would be no change in any other part of the program (except some REMs), including the PRINTs following 180 and the data list.

5-7 AN EXAMPLE: CLASS AVERAGE

In this example, we will look at a problem that involves performing calculations as well as accumulating totals.

Problem: A class average is to be calculated. The input consists of (1) class identification data—the names of the class and instructor and the quarter—and (2) student test data—each student's name and test scores from which all averages will be calculated. For each student, there are three tests and a final exam; the final is weighted twice as much as any one of the other tests. The average of the grades for each student is to be calculated along with the class average. The report will consist of three parts: (1) the class name, instructor's name, and quarter, all printed on separate lines at the top of the report; (2) a report line for each student, showing name and average in the first and third print zones, respectively; and (3) the total number of students in the class and the class average printed on separate lines at the bottom of the report. Each of the parts of the report should be separated by one blank line. Data is provided in Table 5-6.

The solution to this problem will involve the following sequence of steps:

1. Read the class identification data (class and instructor name and quarter).
2. Set all totals to 0.
3. Print the class identification data.

TABLE 5-6
Data for Class Average Example

Course Name: English Composition I
Instructor's Name: Dr. L. W. Williamson
Quarter: Winter, 1984

Student Name	Test 1	Test 2	Test 3	Final
S. Roull	65	73	52	68
W. Hannah	100	93	98	95
H. Langley	72	55	64	60
P. Smith	81	72	77	69
C. Berger	93	87	100	85
D. Jenkins	61	43	57	55
F. Larkins	88	74	84	80
P. Thompson	95	88	90	82

4. Read a student record (name and test data).
5. Check for the end-of-data condition. If it has been reached, go to step 10; otherwise, continue to the next step.
6. Calculate the average of the test scores for one student.
7. Update the totals for the number of students and the sum of the student averages.
8. Print a student report line.
9. Go to step 4.
10. Calculate the class average.
11. Print the total number of students and class average.
12. Stop.

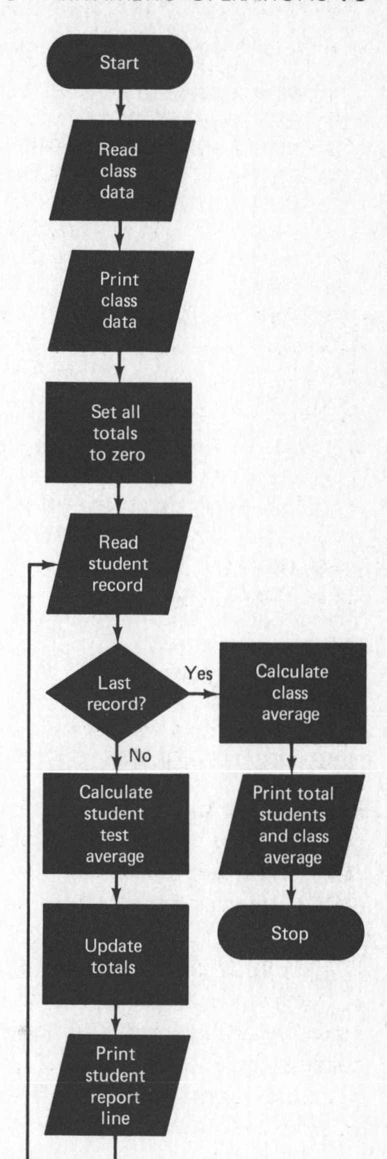

FIGURE 5-5
Flowchart for class average problem

This procedure is illustrated pictorially by the flowchart in Figure 5-5.

The report is to consist of three parts as described above; we will construct the program according to that. The first part will present the class identification data. This section of the program will involve steps 1 through 3 of the solution outline. We will use one READ statement to assign the three values to be initially printed and to set the two totals to zero. The program segment for this part is:

```
190  READ C$, I$, Q$, TS, TA
200  PRINT C$
210  PRINT I$
220  PRINT Q$
```

where the appropriate values to be assigned to the five variables in the READ statement at 190 have been placed at the head of the data list in the DATA statements beginning at line 440. This READ does double duty; it reads both the values to be printed in the first part of the report (C$, I$, and Q$) as well as setting the totals (TS and TA) to zero.

The middle portion of the report, steps 4 through 9 above, processes the student grades and updates all totals. This may be expressed by the following program sequence:

```
270 READ S$, T1, T2, T3, FL
280 IF S$ = "LAST" THEN 370
290 LET SA = (T1 + T2 + T3 + 2 * FL) / 5
300 LET TS = TS + 1
310 LET TA = TA + SA
320 PRINT S$,, SA
330 GOTO 270
```

The first statement reads the student name and test scores, while the individual student grade report is printed at line 320. Line 330 continues the processing until the end of data is signaled by the IF at 280; the program is then directed to line 370 where the class average is calculated and printed before the program ends. The average of the test scores for each student is calculated at line 290; note that the final exam (FL) is weighted twice. Line 300 represents a counter that keeps track of the number of students, and 310 sums all the students' averages.

The final section of the report prints the total number of students and the class average. The BASIC statements to accomplish this are:

```
370  LET CA = TA / TS
380  PRINT
390  PRINT TS
400  PRINT CA
```

The class average is calculated at line 370 by dividing the sum of all the students' averages by the total number of students. This is something we could not do until this point in the program because it requires the two totals, and they are not known until all the data has been processed. The remainder of the statements print the results.

Below is a complete program listing followed by a run.

```
10 REM  CALCULATING CLASS AVERAGE
20 REM
30 REM  VARIABLES ARE DEFINED AS --
40 REM
50 REM        C$ = COURSE NAME
60 REM        I$ = INSTRUCTOR'S NAME
70 REM        Q$ = QUARTER
80 REM        S$ = STUDENT'S NAME
90 REM   T1 - T3 = THREE TEST SCORES
100 REM       FL = FINAL EXAM SCORE
110 REM       SA = STUDENT AVERAGE
120 REM       TS = TOTAL STUDENTS
130 REM       TA = SUM OF STUDENT AVERAGES
140 REM       CA = CLASS AVERAGE
150 REM
160 REM  READ AND PRINT CLASS IDENTIFICATION DATA
170 REM  AND SET TOTAL ACCUMULATORS TO ZERO
180 REM
190 READ C$, I$, Q$, TS, TA
200 PRINT C$
210 PRINT I$
220 PRINT Q$
230 PRINT
240 REM
250 REM  PROCESS STUDENT TEST SCORES
260 REM
270 READ S$, T1, T2, T3, FL
280 IF S$ = "LAST" THEN 370
290 LET SA = (T1 + T2 + T3 + 2 * FL) / 5
300 LET TS = TS + 1
310 LET TA = TA + SA
320 PRINT S$,, SA
330 GOTO 270
340 REM
350 REM  CALCULATE AND PRINT CLASS AVERAGE
360 REM
370 LET CA = TA / TS
380 PRINT
390 PRINT TS
400 PRINT CA
410 REM
420 REM  DATA LIST
430 REM
440 DATA "ENGLISH COMPOSITION I","DR. L. W. WILLIAMS"
450 DATA "WINTER, 1984",0,0,"S. ROULL",65,73,52,68
460 DATA "W. HANNAH",100,93,98,95,"H. LANGLEY",72,55,64
470 DATA 60,"P. SMITH",81,72,77,69,"C. BERGER",93,87,100
480 DATA 85,"D. JENKINS",61,43,57,55,"F. LARKINS",88,74
490 DATA 84,80,"P. THOMPSON",95,88,90,82,"LAST",0,0,0,0
500 END
```

```
ENGLISH COMPOSITION I
DR. L. W. WILLIAMS
WINTER, 1984

S. ROULL                      65.2
W. HANNAH                     96.2
H. LANGLEY                    62.2
P. SMITH                      73.6
C. BERGER                     90
```

```
D. JENKINS                    54.2
F. LARKINS                    81.2
P. THOMPSON                   87.4

 8
 76.25
```

5-8 INTRODUCTION TO MATHEMATICAL FUNCTIONS

In Chapter 11, we will study the many special **functions** available which make BASIC such a powerful and versatile programming language. A few of these functions are very widely used and therefore will be introduced early so that you may make use of them as the need arises. We will look at four of the most commonly used functions in this section; another, the TAB function, will be discussed in the next chapter.

The four functions that we will discuss are summarized in Table 5-7. The first, the **SQR** function, is used to find the square root of a number. It has the general form:

SQR*(argument)*

where the **argument** may be any *numeric* constant or variable or any valid BASIC mathematical expression, provided that the value of the argument is *not less than zero*. The parentheses around the argument are required. The effect of SQR is to take the value of the argument, find its square root, then return the square root of the argument for further calculations. The SQR may appear alone on the right side of the equals sign in an assignment statement or be incorporated as part of a mathematical expression much like any variable. Here are several examples:

```
130 LET S = SQR(20)
210 LET X = SQR(P)
285 LET F4 = SQR(2 * A + TS / 10)
190 LET J = Z + 56 * B * SQR(W + Y / U)
455 LET A = SQR(N + M * (2 * X - 7))
```

The SQR is a *function*, not a *statement*. The difference is apparent if you look closely at the above examples. A function performs a certain job (in this case, it takes the square root) but is expressed as part of a BASIC statement (here, the LET). A function may *never* appear on a line by itself; it must always be incorporated as part of an appropriate executable statement.

As an example of the use of the SQR function, consider the following short program which reads two numbers, finds the square roots of the two numbers, as well as the square root of the *sum* of the two numbers.

TABLE 5-7

Commonly Used Mathematical Functions

Function	Description	Example
SQR(X)	Returns the square root of X	SQR(25) = 5 SQR(2) = 1.41421
INT(X)	Returns the largest integer less than or equal to X	INT(3.2) = 3 INT(1.98) = 1
ABS(X)	Returns the absolute value of X	ABS(12) = 12 ABS(−11.4) = 11.4
RND	Returns a random number between 0 and 1	PRINT RND .330827

```
 10 REM   EXAMPLE OF USE OF SQR FUNCTION
 20 REM
 30 READ A, B
 40 IF A < 0 THEN 999
 50 LET X = SQR(A)
 60 LET Y = SQR(B)
 70 LET Z = SQR(A + B)
 80 PRINT A, B, X, Y, Z
 90 GOTO 30
100 DATA 9,16,36,4,10,26,6.5,8,12,7.2
110 DATA 1.5,0.81,1255,380,0.006,0.02,-1,0
999 END
```

At lines 50 and 60, the SQR function is used to find the square roots of A and B, and these results are assigned to X and Y, respectively. At line 70, the square root of the *sum* of A and B is found and assigned to Z. A program run produces:

```
9              16             3              4              5
36             4              6              2              6.32456
10             26             3.16228        5.09902        6
6.5            8              2.54951        2.82843        3.80789
12             7.2            3.4641         2.68328        4.38178
1.5            .81            1.22474        .9             1.51987
1255           380            35.426         19.4936        40.4351
.006           .02            .0774597       .141421        .161245
```

The above results have been illustrated using what is known as **six-digit** format (or **single-precision**), which means that numeric values are displayed with six **significant** (accurate) digits being shown. A seventh digit is maintained in storage to provide the full six digits as significant. We will use the six-digit form in our work, but the number of digits displayed will vary from six to nine with the version of BASIC being used; you will need to check to see how many digits your computer displays. In Section 11-1 we will talk more about the handling of very large or very small numbers for which six digits are not enough.

Above, we stated that the argument of the SQR function cannot be less than zero. This is, of course, because the square root of a negative number is undefined. If you attempt to take the square root of a negative value, you will get an error message. On many systems, this will produce a **Function Call** error. This may arise because one of your original data values was negative, but more likely it will be due to a negative value that is the result of a calculation during processing.

The second function is the **INT** (for INTeger) function. It has the general form:

INT(*argument*)

where the argument may be any numeric constant, variable, or mathematical expression. The function returns the largest integer that is less than or equal to the argument. This is referred to as the **truncated** value as opposed to the more familiar **rounding** to the nearest whole number. Truncation means that the fractional part of the number is dropped to leave only the integer part (or next lowest integer); with rounding, the number is converted to the nearest integer. Table 5-8 gives several numbers and their corresponding rounded and truncated values.

The third function is the **ABS** (for ABSolute value) function and has a form similar to the first two:

ABS(*argument*)

As with the INT function, the argument may be any numeric constant, variable, or mathematical expression. The value returned is numerically the same as the argument but *always with a positive sign*. This is also illustrated in Table 5-8.

TABLE 5-8

Comparison of Truncation and Rounding

Original Number	Rounded Value	Truncated Value	Absolute Value
2.2	2	2	2.2
2.7	3	2	2.7
0.9	1	0	0.9
0.4	0	0	0.4
−6.3	−6	−7	−6.3
−6.8	−7	−7	−6.8

The last function that we will examine in this section is **RND**, or the random number generator. While the above three functions are standard with all BASICs, RND is not. We will use the most commonly available form of the random number generator for the examples that follow and discuss the most frequent variations at the end of the section.

Most versions of BASIC provide the argument-free form of RND. This will automatically produce a random number *between* 0 and 1 whenever it is used. For example, the following short program will print three random numbers:

```
10  REM   PRINT RANDOM NUMBERS
20  REM
30  PRINT RND
40  PRINT RND
50  PRINT RND
60  END
```

The actual numbers that will be printed will vary with the BASIC that is being used, but it will look something like this:

```
.194873
.873394
.388335
```

Unfortunately, if we run the same program again, we will get the same sequence of numbers. This may be good or bad depending on what you are doing. To get a different set of numbers for each run, we can use the **RANDOMIZE** *statement* before the random numbers are printed. This would modify the above program to be

```
10  REM   PRINT RANDOM NUMBERS
20  REM
25  RANDOMIZE
30  PRINT RND
40  PRINT RND
50  PRINT RND
60  END
```

Now each run will be different. The first run will produce the same three numbers as above, but all subsequent runs will generate a different set of three numbers.

It is frequently convenient to produce random numbers that are within intervals other than 0 to 1. Suppose that we multiply RND by A:

```
200  LET N = A * RND
```

This will produce random numbers between 0 and A. The expression

```
250  LET M = A * RND + B
```

will yield random numbers between B and A + B. If only integer results are desired,

```
350  LET I = INT((A + 1) * RND + B)
```

will give only *integers* from B to A + B including A and B. The following program will print four columns of random numbers; the first will be between 0 and 1, the second between 0 and 3, the third between 5 and 8, and the fourth will print random integers from 5 through 8.

```
 10 REM  PRINTING RANDOM NUMBERS
 20 REM
 30 LET C = 1
 40 LET R1 = RND
 50 LET R2 = 3 * RND
 60 LET R3 = 3 * RND + 5
 70 LET R4 = INT(4 * RND + 5)
 80 PRINT R1, R2, R3, R4
 90 LET C = C + 1
100 IF C < 6 GOTO 40
110 END

.390223         1.22903       6.33987      5
.190265         1.00987       5.92563      7
.987356         .644377       6.98247      7
.0984673        2.89467       6.2871       8
.298357         1.89233       7.92244      6
```

Some systems require an argument for RND giving different random numbers for different arguments. Others may require a **seed** to generate different sequences of random numbers as with the RANDOMIZE statement. A seed is just a number (supposedly random) that is used as input to the random number generator to provide a starting point for generating a sequence of numbers.

TROUBLESHOOTING

Each of the following programs contains an error that prevents it from executing properly. Explain *specifically* what the problem is and what must be done to correct it. To assist you, a sample of what would happen should you attempt to run the program is provided after each listing. Refer to Appendix D for an explanation of BASIC error messages.

1.

```
 10 REM  TROUBLESHOOTING PROBLEM 5-1
 20 REM
 30 REM            E$ = EMPLOYEE'S NAME
 40 REM             H = HOURS WORKED
 50 REM             R = PAY RATE
 60 REM             D = DEDUCTIONS
 70 REM             P = NET PAY
 80 REM
 90 READ E$, H, R, D
100 IF E$ = "END" THEN 190
120 LET P = H X R - D
130 PRINT E$, H, R, D, P
140 GOTO 90
150 DATA "JOE EGAN", 45, 6.50, 87.75
160 DATA "JILL KELLY", 40, 6, 60
170 DATA "SARAH JONES", 42, 7.5, 110.25
180 DATA "END", 0, 0, 0
190 END

Syntax Error in Line 120
```

2.

```
 10 REM  TROUBLESHOOTING PROBLEM 5-2
 20 REM
 30 REM        S$ = SALESPERSON'S NAME
 40 REM  S1 - S4 = FOUR WEEKLY SALES TOTALS
 50 REM        SA = AVERAGE WEEKLY SALES
 60 REM
 70 READ S$, S1, S2, S3, S4
 80 IF S1 < 0 THEN 160
 90 LET SA = S1 + S2 + S3 + S4 / 4
100 PRINT S$,, SA
110 GOTO 70
120 DATA "GEORGE REED",2576.77,1288.25,3844.54,978.21
130 DATA "KAREN HIX",2155.00,2148.23,1552.25,3255.15
140 DATA "PHILIP SIMMS",948.44,2561.84,2149.76,875.46
150 DATA "X",-1,0,0,0
160 END

GEORGE REED                    7954.11
KAREN HIX                      6669.27
PHILIP SIMS                    5878.91
```

3.

```
 10 REM  TROUBLESHOOTING PROBLEM 5-3
 20 REM
 30 REM          U = COMPUTER USER'S ID CODE
 40 REM          H = NUMBER OF HOURS OF USE
 50 REM          R = COST PER HOUR OF USE
 60 REM          C = CHARGE TO USER
 70 REM          T = TOTAL NUMBER OF USERS
 80 REM         TC = TOTAL COST TO ALL USERS
 90 REM
100 LET T = 0
110 LET TC = 0
120 READ U, H, R
130 IF U = 0 THEN 190
140 LET C = H * R
150 LET T = T + U
160 LET TC = TC + C
170 PRINT U, H, R, C
180 GOTO 120
190 PRINT
200 PRINT T,,, TC
210 DATA 25613,23,45,32556,28,35,35415,19,40,0,0,0
220 END

25613         23          45          1035
32556         28          35          980
35415         19          40          760

93584                                 2775
```

4.

```
 10 REM  TROUBLESHOOTING PROBLEM 5-4
 20 REM
 30 REM          A = STUDENT'S AVERAGE
 40 REM         TS = TOTAL NUMBER OF STUDENTS
 50 REM         TA = TOTAL OF STUDENT AVERAGES
 60 REM         CA = CLASS AVERAGE
 70 REM
 80 READ TS, TA
 90 READ A
100 IF A < 0 THEN 130
110 LET TA = TA + A
120 GOTO 90
130 LET CA = TA / TS
```

```
140 PRINT CA
150 DATA 0,0,75,80,65,92,88,52,100,71,96,83,68,46,-1
160 END
```

```
Division by Zero in Line 130
```

5.

```
 10 REM  TROUBLESHOOTING PROBLEM 5-5
 20 REM
 30 REM        N$ = SALESPERSON'S NAME
 40 REM         B = BASE PAY
 50 REM        TS = TOTAL SALES
 60 REM        CR = COMMISSION RATE (AS %)
 70 REM         C = COMMISSION EARNED
 80 REM         T = TOTAL SALESPERSONS
 90 REM        TC = TOTAL COMMISSIONS PAID
100 REM
110 READ CR, T, TC
120 READ N$, B, TS
130 IF N$ = "STOP" THEN 240
140 LET C = B + TS * CR / 100
150 LET T = T + 1
160 LET TC = TC + C
170 PRINT N$, TS, B, C
180 GOTO 120
190 PRINT
200 PRINT T,,, TC
210 DATA 2.5,0,0,"TOM JAFFE",300,17500
220 DATA "DAVID LEE",450,22550
230 DATA "KATHY BYRD",375,20250,"STOP",0,0
240 END
```

```
TOM JAFFE      17500        300          737.5
DAVID LEE      22550        450          1013.75
KATHY BYRD     20250        375          881.25
```

(No totals)

6.

```
 10 REM  TROUBLESHOOTING PROBLEM 5-6
 20 REM
 30 REM         U = COMPUTER USER'S ID CODE
 40 REM         H = NUMBER OF HOURS OF USE
 50 REM         R = COST PER HOUR OF USE
 60 REM         C = CHARGE TO USER
 70 REM         T = TOTAL NUMBER OF USERS
 80 REM        TC = TOTAL COST TO ALL USERS
 90 REM
100 READ T, TC
110 READ U, H, R
120 IF U = 0 THEN 180
130 LET C = H * R
140 LET T = T + 1
150 LET TC = TC + C
160 PRINT U, H, R, C
170 GOTO 100
180 PRINT
190 PRINT T,,, TC
200 DATA 0,0,25613,23,45,32556,28,35,35415,19,40,0,0,0
210 END
```

```
25613         23            45            1035
35            65415         19            672885
```

```
Out of Data in Line 110
```

IMPORTANT TERMS

After studying this chapter, you should be familiar with the meaning and use of the following terms and BASIC statements:

Mathematical expression
Arithmetic operators
Exponentiation
Negation
Division by Zero error
Overflow error
Order of operations
Left to right order
Grouped terms
Associative property of multiplication
Associative property of addition
Assignment statement
Initializing values
Accumulating totals
Updating
Counter
BASIC functions
SQR function
Argument
Six-digit format
Single-precision
Significant digit
Function Call error
INT function
Truncation
Rounding
ABS function
RND function
RANDOMIZE statement
Seed

EXERCISES

1. Write the following as BASIC expressions:

(a) $3y - 8$

(b) $7b + 13f$

(c) $5(2x + y)$

(d) $a(3r - 7t) + \frac{w}{n}$

(e) $\frac{2t - 13}{9}$

(f) $45 - \frac{11}{12c - 5d}$

(g) $\frac{m + 5(m - 2)}{3(m - 2)}$

(h) $\frac{6r - 13}{11(r + 3) - 8} - 7(r - 4)$

(i) $x^2 - 2x + 3$

(j) $(h - 7)^3 - (h - 7)$

(k) $vt - .5gt^2$

(l) $(d - 3n^3)^2$

(m) $\frac{4(2s + 5)}{x^2 - 16}$

(n) $\sqrt{\frac{y^{n+3} - 1}{n + 3}}$

(o) $\frac{\sqrt{w + 8}}{5v + 2u - 12}$

(p) $\frac{z^3 - z + 11}{z^2 + 25} - 10z + 7$

(q) $(a^2 + b^2)^{1/2}$

(r) $\frac{-1}{(r + s)^{r+s}}$

(s) $\frac{2(x - 4) - 6(3t - 8)}{x^2 - t^2 - 3(5t - 2x)}$

(t) $\frac{a}{b + c} - \frac{b}{a + c} - \frac{c}{a + b}$

(u) $\sqrt{|x + 6|}$

(v) $\sqrt{a} + \sqrt{b} + \sqrt{c}$

(w) $|x - 3|\sqrt{y + 11}$

(x) $\sqrt{\sqrt{J} + 2(k + 4n)}$

(y) $\frac{\sqrt{v + z}}{\sqrt{v} + \sqrt{z}}$

(z) $\sqrt{\frac{|p - 2|}{p^2 + 3p - 2}}$

2. For each of the expressions in Exercise 1, list the sequence in which the arithmetic operations will be performed.
3. Verify the associative property of multiplication for the following sets of numbers:
   (a) 3, 6, and 2 (b) 5, 4, and 7
   (c) −5, 8, and 3 (d) 10, 4, and −6
4. Verify the associative property of addition for the following sets of numbers:
   (a) 30, 16, and 12 (b) 15, 45, and 70
   (c) −52, 28, and 36 (d) 110, −134, and −169
5. Using the following sets of numbers, show that division does not obey an associative property:
   (a) 12, 6, and 2 (b) 100, 20, and 5
   (c) 144, 12, and 4 (d) 512, 128, and 16
6. Using the following sets of numbers, show that subtraction does not obey an associative property:
   (a) 22, 36, and 12 (b) 60, 25, and 55
   (c) 144, 82, and 114 (d) 112, 158, and 216
7. Using the following sets of numbers, show that exponentiation does not obey an associative property:
   (a) 2, 3, and 2 (b) 3, 2, and 3

For Exercises 8 to 12, give the output that will be produced by the given programs. Then, type the programs into the computer, run them, and check the actual outputs against your predictions.

8.
```
10 READ A, B, C
20 IF A = 0 THEN 80
30 LET X = A + B - C
40 LET Y = A * C - B
50 PRINT A, B, C, X, Y
60 GOTO 10
70 DATA 6,3,1,2,3,9,12,7,1,2,15,6,0,0,0
80 END
```

9.
```
10 READ W, H
20 IF W = 0 THEN 70
30 LET A = H * W ^ 2
40 PRINT W, H, A
50 GOTO 10
60 DATA 2, 3, 3, 4, 5, 3, 2, 6, 3, 2, 0, 0
70 END
```

10.
```
 10 LET S = 0
 20 READ ID, P, R
 30 IF ID < 0 THEN 80
 40 LET T = P + R
 50 LET S = S + T
 60 PRINT ID, P, R, T
 70 GOTO 20
 80 PRINT
 90 PRINT S
100 DATA 65812, 125, 12, 65944, 138, 15
110 DATA 56981, 85, 16, 86552, 105, 15, -1, 0, 0
120 END
```

11.
```
10 READ T, TN, TS
20 READ N
30 IF N = 0 THEN 100
40 LET S = N * N
50 PRINT , N, S
```

```
 60 LET T = T + 1
 70 LET TN = TN + N
 80 LET TS = TS + S
 90 GOTO 20
100 PRINT
110 PRINT T, TN, TS
120 DATA 0, 0, 0, 4, 7, 11, 5, 8, 0
130 END
```

12.
```
 10 READ TS, N
 20 READ N$, T1, T2, T3
 30 IF T1 = 999 THEN 90
 40 LET AV = (T1 + T2 + T3) / 3
 50 LET TS = TS + AV
 60 LET N = N + 1
 70 PRINT N$, AV
 80 GOTO 20
 90 LET CA = TS / N
100 PRINT
110 PRINT N, CA
120 DATA 0, 0, "S. STEVENS", 75, 82, 71
130 DATA "L. CAMPBELL", 76, 64, 80
140 DATA "G. CHURCH", 94, 88, 96
150 DATA "X", 999, 0, 0
160 END
```

13. Write an expression that will generate random numbers in the following ranges:
(a) 0 to 10 (b) 7 to 21 (c) 1 to 8
(d) 3 to 103 (e) −1 to 1 (f) −5 to 25

14. Repeat Exercise 13 but write an expression that will generate *integers* over the given ranges.

PROGRAMMING PROBLEMS

Write programs in BASIC to accomplish the tasks described by each of the following problems. Be sure to carefully document each program.

1. The Johnson Co. is having a sale with selected merchandise at 25 percent off the regular price. A program is needed that will calculate the sale price of each item. The output should give the store name followed by the stock number, item name, the original price, and the sale price for each sale item. Data is provided below.

Stock Number	Item Name	Regular Price
10658	Alarm Clock	19.95
19568	35mm Camera	149.00
29564	Toaster	17.95
35608	LCD Watch	49.50
35591	Table Lamp	34.50
49622	Umbrella	5.50
50015	Computer	99.00
51223	Stereo	349.00

2. A Payroll Report for The Parkham Co. is to be prepared from the data below. Each employee's gross pay is to be calculated as the product of the hours worked and the pay rate. The input data plus the gross pay should be printed for each employee. Final

totals for the number of employees, hours worked, and gross pay should be accumulated and printed at the end of the report. The company name should be printed at the top of the report.

Employee Name	Hours Worked	Pay Rate
Sam Olson	38.6	7.50
Julie Fried	42.7	6.65
Ben Ickard	40.0	6.50
Jeff Berk	39.1	6.70
Beth Ingles	44.6	7.35
Diane Royce	40.0	6.90

Use the following data for Problems 3 to 6. Each of these programs should have the company name and the date printed at the top of the report.

Company: Southside Loan   Date: August 10, 1983

Investment Number	Amount of Investment	Interest Rate (%)	Years of Investment
130256	5000.00	9.50	2.5
215454	10000.00	12.00	4.0
312246	3500.00	8.75	3.0
381996	7500.00	11.00	3.5
465809	12500.00	13.50	4.5
640016	2500.00	8.50	2.0

3. Simple interest is calculated by the formula

$$i = prt$$

where p is the amount invested, r is the yearly rate of interest (as a decimal), and t is the number of years of the investment. Write a program to calculate the interest earned on the investments described in the table above. The printout should show the investment number, the original amount invested, the rate (as a percentage), the number of years, and the interest earned.
4. Repeat Problem 3 but calculate the compound interest earned on each investment. You may assume that the interest is compounded monthly.
5. Write a program that will calculate both simple and compound interest for the investments given and then find the difference in the two. In other words, this program will provide information on how much *more* will be earned with compound interest than with simple. The output should give all the original investment data on one line with the calculated values for the interest on a second.
6. So far we have only worked with compound interest that is compounded monthly, but a number of other periods are used. Write a program to calculate simple interest and *three* compound interest values, using periods of quarterly, monthly, and daily ($n = 365$). The output should give all the original investment data on one line with the calculated values for the interest on a second.
7. An updated Billing Report is to be prepared for the current month for Bill's Hardware from the data below. The new balance on each customer's account is to be calculated by taking the previous balance and adding the new charges, then subtracting any payments. The report should print the store name and month at the top along with all input data and the new balance for each customer.

Account Number	Previous Balance	Payments Made	New Charges
12583	538.56	50.00	89.41
19765	0.00	167.26	167.26
25681	106.84	25.00	189.56
26543	311.09	100.00	0.00
32149	33.10	33.10	67.24
41219	219.64	50.00	11.19
51369	0.00	0.00	106.59
65074	79.16	10.00	38.47

8. Modify your program from Problem 7 to provide for a finance charge of 1.5 percent on the previous unpaid balance.

9. Modify your program from either Problem 7 or 8 to give the final totals for the number of customers, the previous balance, payments made, new charges, and the new balance. The total customers should be printed under the account number, with the other totals under their respective columns. One blank line should separate the total line from the rest of the report.

10. A Mileage Report for the Haul-a-way Trucking Co. is needed that computes the number of miles per gallon that is being obtained for each truck that the company operates. This is found by taking the number of miles driven and dividing by the gallons of gas used. The report should show for each truck the number of miles traveled, the number of gallons of fuel used, and the mileage. Totals for the number of trucks, miles driven, and fuel used should be found, with an average mileage figure for the entire company calculated from the total miles driven and gallons used by all trucks. The name of the company should appear at the head of the report. Data is provided below.

Truck Number	Miles Driven	Gallons Used	Truck Number	Miles Driven	Gallons Used
1	2510.3	210.8	5	6529.1	436.0
2	9860.9	620.0	6	1203.8	72.0
3	4623.4	296.6	7	3946.3	279.6
4	3125.7	196.5	8	5469.7	366.6

11. A Daily Temperature Report is to be produced which gives the time of day and the temperature at each time in *both* Fahrenheit and Celsius form. The input data (given below) provides only Fahrenheit values; therefore, the program will have to calculate the Celsius values. The formula to convert from Fahrenheit to Celsius is

$$C = \frac{5}{9}(F - 32)$$

At the end of the report, the average daily temperature should be given in both forms. Also, remember to print the city and date at the top of the report.

City: Atlanta, GA — Date: April 21, 1983

Time of Day	Temperature	Time of Day	Temperature
2:00 AM	56	2:00 PM	81
4:00 AM	54	4:00 PM	79
6:00 AM	53	6:00 PM	73
8:00 AM	62	8:00 PM	65
10:00 AM	69	10:00 PM	61
12:00 PM	76	12:00 AM	58

12. Write a program to read a series of numbers and calculate the square, square root, and reciprocal of each number. Print all the numbers along with the calculated values. Use the following set of numbers for input data: 4, 10, 25, 200, 0.04, 5000, 0.007, 19.6.

13. Bob's Carpet Store is having a carpet sale and needs a program to process the sales data. All carpets are priced by the square foot, and the discount on each sale differs depending on the type of carpet. To find the sale price, multiply the length of the carpet by the width to determine the number of square feet, then multiply this figure by the price per square foot to find the nondiscounted price. To find the sale price, subtract the appropriate discount according to the percentage given for that particular carpet. Finally, all carpets carry an additional $50.00 installation fee. The program should print the store name at the top of the report and for each sale, the customer's name, the number of square feet of carpet purchased, the cost per square foot, the discount rate, and the sale price. Totals should be accumulated and printed for the number of customers, the number of square feet of carpet sold, and the total sales. Data is provided below.

Customer's Name	Carpet Size (ft) Length	Width	Cost Per Sq Ft	Discount Rate (%)
Nancy Scott	18	15	1.25	25
Gayle Burke	14	10	0.95	10
Paul Mann	15	12	1.50	30
Gary Wilcox	25	18	1.25	25
Mary Lane	21	16	1.15	15
Debby Hamby	12	9	1.20	20
Linda Keller	24	20	1.25	25
Henry Long	18	14	1.50	30

14. The interest rate (in % form) that is being charged on a loan can be found from the formula

$$r = 200\frac{ni}{a(t + 1)}$$

where n = the number of payments per year, i = the total interest paid, a = the original amount of the loan, and t = the total number of payments made. Write a program to calculate the interest rate for loans as described by the data given below. (Assume all loans are for monthly payments or 12 payments per year.) Your output should show the input data plus the calculated values for r.

Company: Ace Loan　　　Branch: N. Lincoln
Manager: Pete Fox　　　Date: 10-19-83

Loan Number	Amount of Loan	Total Interest	Number of Payments
12469	5000	1256	36
21599	10000	2287	36
36842	5000	1684	48
39451	7500	1733	36
45806	1500	298	24
54397	25000	8728	60
56499	3500	616	24
60076	10000	3512	60

15. The time that it takes a pendulum to make one swing (called the period) is given by the formula:

$$T = 6.28\sqrt{\frac{l}{980}}$$

where T is the period in seconds and l is the length of the pendulum in centimeters (cm). Write a program that reads pendulum lengths, calculates the respective periods, then *numbers* the pendulums in increasing sequence (1, 2, 3, etc.), while printing both length and period for each. Use the following values for pendulum lengths (in cm): 10, 17.5, 25, 44.3, 100, 200, 500, and 1000.

16. The *hypotenuse* of a right triangle is the side opposite the right angle and is given in terms of the other two sides, the *legs,* by the famous Pythagorean relation:

$$h = \sqrt{x^2 + y^2}$$

where h is the hypotenuse and x and y are the two legs. Write a program to read the legs of each of a series of right triangles and calculate each hypotenuse. The output should number the triangles and print the three sides. Input data is given below.

Leg 1	Leg 2	Leg 1	Leg 2
3	4	4	6
12	9	10	10
0.6	0.4	5	12
15	8	24	19
6.9	8.4	119	211
30	35	31.6	47.5

17. Write a program that will simulate the toss of two dice. The output should show two random integers from 1 through 6 and should be different with each "toss" (run).

18. Check to see just how "random" your BASIC's random number generator really is. Set up a program to generate a series of random numbers and accumulate a total of all numbers produced. At the end, divide the total by the number of random numbers generated and print this "average random number." The nearer the middle of the interval over which the numbers are generated, the better. That is, if your numbers are random between 0 and 1, the average should be close to 0.50. Try this for totals of 10, 100, and 1000 random numbers.

CHAPTER 6

PRODUCING A REPORT

In the last three chapters, you have learned how to write programs that process simple reports. The printouts produced made sense to you because you knew at the time what was represented by each value that was printed. On the other hand, if the output from one of the examples in those chapters or from one of your own programs were to be handed to someone not already familiar with it, that person would have a hard time figuring out what all the printed values represented.

In Chapter 3, we stressed the importance of carefully documenting your programs with REM statements. In this chapter, we will see how to do the same for program outputs. We will explore many additional features and uses of the PRINT statement which will allow us to label printouts in such a way that most any reader of a report, even one who is inexperienced in programming, can read the printed result with full comprehension.

6-1 PRINTING LITERALS

Remember the general form of the PRINT statement:

ln **PRINT** *list*

Until now, we have restricted the list to data names. It may, however, contain other types of entries which we will discuss in this chapter. One such entry is the **literal**.

A literal is any numeric or string value used in a program but not specifically assigned to a data name. We saw several examples of numeric literals in the last chapter. Whenever a number is given explicitly in a mathematical expression, it is a numeric literal. For example, in the statement:

```
190 LET F = 2 * X - 3.14
```

there are two numeric literals, 2 and 3.14. (We will discuss string literals below.) To print a numeric literal is simple. If we wish to print the number 15.66, we would write:

```
265 PRINT 15.66
```

which, when executed, would print:

```
 15.66
```

Numeric literals may be inserted at any place in the print list, and they obey the same general rules as data names.

Most of our work in this chapter will be concerned with printing string literals. These will be used as report headings, column headings, total (and other) identifiers, special messages, and any other place that some sort of specific identification is needed. Normally, they will be used on the printout, but they can also be employed in a number of other areas, such as producing special messages to the screen, instructions to the operator, or error messages. String literals are printed in the same way as numeric ones. To print the phrase IT WORKS!, we would write:

```
230  PRINT "IT WORKS!"
```

which will print:

```
IT WORKS!
```

when the above PRINT statement is executed. Note that string literals in the print list are enclosed in quotation marks as they are elsewhere in the program.

Let us look at a short program that uses string literals. The following program will print the numbers from 1 to 10, each after the phrase THE NUMBER IS NOW =. At the end of the program, we will print an appropriate message.

```
10 REM  USING STRING LITERALS
20 REM
30 LET N = 0
40 LET N = N + 1
50 PRINT "THE NUMBER IS NOW =", N
60 IF N < 10 THEN 40
70 PRINT
80 PRINT "PROCESSING COMPLETED"
90 END
```

When this little program is run, we will get:

```
THE NUMBER IS NOW =          1
THE NUMBER IS NOW =          2
THE NUMBER IS NOW =          3
THE NUMBER IS NOW =          4
THE NUMBER IS NOW =          5
THE NUMBER IS NOW =          6
THE NUMBER IS NOW =          7
THE NUMBER IS NOW =          8
THE NUMBER IS NOW =          9
THE NUMBER IS NOW =          10

PROCESSING COMPLETED
```

The spacing between the = and the numbers exists because the literal is too long to fit into one screen zone; therefore, it is automatically printed in the first two, but it is not long enough to fill both. The numbers are then pushed over into the third zone. We could rewrite the literal to make it fit exactly into one zone so the numbers would fall next to it, but BASIC provides a better way: **the semicolon** (;).

If a semicolon is used in place of a comma in a print list, the two items on either side of the semicolon will be printed immediately next to each other on the output without regard for the normal zones. If we rewrite the PRINT at line 50 using a semicolon as:

```
50  PRINT "THE NUMBER IS NOW ="; N
```

the printout will be:

```
THE NUMBER IS NOW = 1
THE NUMBER IS NOW = 2
THE NUMBER IS NOW = 3
THE NUMBER IS NOW = 4
THE NUMBER IS NOW = 5
THE NUMBER IS NOW = 6
THE NUMBER IS NOW = 7
THE NUMBER IS NOW = 8
THE NUMBER IS NOW = 9
THE NUMBER IS NOW = 10

PROCESSING COMPLETED
```

Note that there is not a space after the = in the literal in the PRINT in line 50, but there is one in the output. This is because numeric values are printed with a preceding (and following) blank space in case a sign is needed. If you want more than one space or expect to have a sign printed, you must add spaces accordingly. This space *will not be present* with string values so you will have to insert one. For example, consider this:

```
10  LET A$ = "CLARK KENT"
20  PRINT "SUPERMAN'S SECRET IDENTITY IS"; A$; "!!"
```

As written, this will print:

```
SUPERMAN'S SECRET IDENTITY ISCLARK KENT!!
```

with no space separating IS and CLARK. It should be written with a space after the IS in the literal in the print list:

```
20  PRINT "SUPERMAN'S SECRET IDENTITY IS "; A$; "!!"
```

This will produce a more desirable result:

```
SUPERMAN'S SECRET IDENTITY IS CLARK KENT!!
```

A space is not inserted before the ! !, so it *will* print immediately after the T of CLARK KENT.

While the remainder of this chapter will be devoted to the **formatting of output**, there is one important use of string literals that applies to input; this is in providing special screen prompts when the interactive INPUT is used. Consider the following short program and run that appeared in Section 4-8:

```
10 REM  PROGRAM WITH INPUT STATEMENT
20 REM
30 INPUT N$, A, S$
40 IF N$ = "STOP" THEN 70
50 PRINT S$,, N$,, A
60 GOTO 30
70 END
```

```
? "R SIMMONS", 67, "463-77-6944"
463-77-6944                R SIMMONS                67
? "T HARRIS", 54, "254-29-3922"
254-29-3922                T HARRIS                 54
? "L WILSON", 61, "324-98-3196"
324-98-3196                L WILSON                 61
? "T JENKINS", 66, "499-37-0902"
499-37-0902                T JENKINS                66
? "STOP", 0, "0"
```

If the ? prompt that is automatically supplied by the INPUT statement is not explicit enough for a given situation, you can print your own special prompt to the screen in either of two ways. First, immediately before the INPUT(s), a PRINT statement can be inserted into the program that prints a message asking for data entry. In the above program, this can be done by placing a PRINT at line 25 as follows:

```
10 REM  PROGRAM WITH INPUT STATEMENT
20 REM
25 PRINT "ENTER NAME, AGE, & SS NUMBER"
30 INPUT N$, A, S$
40 IF N$ = "STOP" THEN 70
50 PRINT S$,, N$,, A
60 GOTO 25
70 END
```

The run would then proceed like this:

```
ENTER NAME, AGE, & SS NUMBER
? "R SIMMONS", 67, "463-77-6944"
463-77-6944                     R SIMMONS                      67
ENTER NAME, AGE, & SS NUMBER
? "T HARRIS", 54, "254-29-3922"
254-29-3922                     T HARRIS                       54
                                    :
                                    :
                                    :
```

The second method involves the INPUT statement itself. The INPUT statement has the following, more general, form:

ln **INPUT** *"prompt"* ; *variable list*

where **prompt** is the message to appear on the screen which must be enclosed in quotes and separated from the variable list by a semicolon. This form allows the prompt to be placed directly in the INPUT statement at the beginning of the variable list. This can be done in the above program if, instead of the PRINT statement at line 25, the INPUT at 30 is modified as follows:

```
30 INPUT "ENTER NAME, AGE, & SS NUMBER"; N$, A, S$
```

This will produce a run that is similar to the one above except that now the special prompt message is on the *same* line as the ? prompt and input data.

```
ENTER NAME, AGE, & SS NUMBER? "R SIMMONS", 67, "463-77-6944"
463-77-6944                R SIMMONS                 67
ENTER NAME, AGE, & SS NUMBER? "T HARRIS", 54, "254-29-3922"
254-29-3922                T HARRIS                  54
                              :
                              :
                              :
```

Of course, multiple INPUTs and prompt messages may be used to provide more explicit screen directions as needed.

6-2 PRODUCING REPORT AND COLUMN HEADINGS

Probably the best way to learn how to print headings and other literals on a printout is by an example. Let us take a short program that has no special literals for documentation and add them one by one. First, consider the following program, which reads a series of salespersons' names, total sales, and commission rates; calculates the commissions earned; and prints detailed lines with the input data plus the calculated value for each salesperson. Totals are accumulated and printed for the number of salespersons, sales, and commissions paid. The program listing for this is:

```
 10 REM  ADDING LITERALS TO REPORTS FOR DOCUMENTATION
 20 REM
100 READ T, TS, TC
110 READ S$, S, CR
120 IF S < 0 THEN 190
130 LET C = S * CR / 100
140 LET T = T + 1
150 LET TS = TS + S
160 LET TC = TC + C
170 PRINT S$, S, CR, C
180 GOTO 110
190 PRINT
200 PRINT T
210 PRINT TS
220 PRINT TC
230 DATA 0, 0, 0
240 DATA "PETER FONG", 26500, 3
250 DATA "LUCY LAW", 32950, 3.5
260 DATA "JOHN WAYNE", 29440, 3
270 DATA "MARK OHM", 22890, 2.5
280 DATA "BO HOWARD", 29750, 3.5
290 DATA "0", -1, 0
300 END
```

As it is now written, the output will be:

```
PETER FONG     26500          3              795
LUCY LAW       32950          3.5            1153.25
JOHN WAYNE     29440          3              883.2
MARK OHM       22890          2.5            572.25
BO HOWARD      29750          3.5            1041.25

5
141530
4444.95
```

Nothing to this point should be new to you.

The first thing we will add to the above program will be headings. Basically, there are two types of headings that will appear on most printouts: (1) **report headings**, which are like titles at the top of the page, identifying the general subject of the report, and (2) **column headings**, which appear at the top of each column of data to be printed and define what is printed in each column. PRINT statements to produce headings are nearly always placed near the beginning of a program before the section (or loop) that processes the main data. In the current example, this would be before the READ at line 110.

Let us do the column headings first. The following set of PRINT statements will get us started:

```
70 PRINT "EMPLOYEE","TOTAL","COMMISSION","COMMISSION"
80 PRINT "NAME","SALES","RATE","EARNED"
90 PRINT
```

This will produce a two-line set of column headings with the PRINT at 90 providing a blank line to separate the headings from the lines on which the data is printed. Our printout will now appear as follows:

```
EMPLOYEE       TOTAL          COMMISSION     COMMISSION
NAME           SALES          RATE           EARNED

PETER FONG      26500          3              795
LUCY LAW        32950          3.5            1153.25
JOHN WAYNE      29440          3              883.2
MARK OHM        22890          2.5            572.25
BO HOWARD       29750          3.5            1041.25

5
141530
4444.95
```

What is wrong with this? If you look closely, you will see that some of the headings are not centered over the columns. In the second line of the headings, NAME, RATE, and EARNED need to be moved to the right so that they will be centered under EMPLOYEE, COMMISSION, and COMMISSION, respectively, in the first line. Also, the first three full headings (both lines) are not centered over their associated columns and need to be adjusted. With the exception of centering the heading over the third column, we can make all the required adjustments by inserting spaces into the literals in the above PRINT statements.

```
70  PRINT " EMPLOYEE"," TOTAL","COMMISSION","COMMISSION"
80  PRINT "   NAME"," SALES","    RATE","  EARNED"
```

The third heading needs to be moved to the *left* to be centered, but this would mean the *removal* of spaces, something we cannot do. An alternative approach is to move the *data* to the *right*. This can be done by rewriting the PRINT at 170 as:

```
170  PRINT S$, S, "   "; CR, C
```

With the spaces inserted as shown, the printout will now be:

```
 EMPLOYEE      TOTAL         COMMISSION     COMMISSION
   NAME        SALES            RATE          EARNED

PETER FONG     26500            3             795
LUCY LAW       32950            3.5           1153.25
JOHN WAYNE     29440            3             883.2
MARK OHM       22890            2.5           572.25
BO HOWARD      29750            3.5           1041.25

5
141530
4444.95
```

which looks much better.

The report heading can be added by the following set of statements:

```
30  PRINT , "   COMMISSION REPORT"
40  PRINT , "  TED'S FURNITURE CO."
50  PRINT
60  PRINT
```

which place the title at the top of the report:

```
                       COMMISSION REPORT
                      TED'S FURNITURE CO.


 EMPLOYEE       TOTAL        COMMISSION     COMMISSION
   NAME         SALES           RATE          EARNED

PETER FONG      26500           3            795
LUCY LAW        32950           3.5          1153.25
JOHN WAYNE      29440           3            883.2
MARK OHM        22890           2.5          572.25
BO HOWARD       29750           3.5          1041.25

5
141530
4444.95
```

Finding the spacing required to center the report heading is a matter of determining the width of the printout (in spaces) and of the *widest* line in the heading, subtracting, and then dividing this difference by 2 to distribute the spaces equally on the right and left. Our output is 49 spaces wide. The second line of the title, TED'S FURNITURE CO., is the longest at 19 spaces. Half the difference of these values is 15, so the second line of the heading should begin in the 16th column. The comma at the beginning of the print list provides for 13 spaces (one zone), and 2 spaces are added to the literals to bring the total to 15. Other lines in the heading are centered from this one.

There are two more improvements that we can make to the program. The first one you may have foreseen. We need to add appropriate literals to specify what the three totals represent. This can be accomplished by rewriting the three PRINTs at lines 200 through 220 as:

```
200 PRINT "TOTAL NUMBER OF EMPLOYEES ="; T
210 PRINT "TOTAL SALES BY ALL EMPLOYEES = $"; TS
220 PRINT "TOTAL COMMISSIONS PAID = $"; TC
```

The totals at the end of the report will now be printed as:

```
TOTAL NUMBER OF EMPLOYEES = 5
TOTAL SALES BY ALL EMPLOYEES = $ 141530
TOTAL COMMISSIONS PAID = $ 4444.95
```

The second improvement that we can make is to add dollar and percent signs to the numbers in the second, third, and fourth columns. To do this, we must revise the PRINT at 170 to insert the proper symbols:

```
170 PRINT S$, "$"; S, "   "; CR; "%", "$"; C
```

Each detailed line will now have dollar and percent signs like this:

```
LUCY LAW      $ 32950       3.5 %        $ 1153.25
```

Any such changes will normally cause the headings to have to be realigned; however, in this case, we are lucky in that no other adjustments are required. A complete program listing and printout, including the last two modifications, are given below.

```
10 REM  ADDING LITERALS TO REPORTS FOR DOCUMENTATION
20 REM
30 PRINT , "   COMMISSION REPORT"
40 PRINT , "  TED'S FURNITURE CO."
```

```
 50 PRINT
 60 PRINT
 70 PRINT " EMPLOYEE"," TOTAL","COMMISSION","COMMISSION"
 80 PRINT "   NAME"," SALES","    RATE","   EARNED"
 90 PRINT
100 READ T, TS, TC
110 READ S$, S, CR
120 IF S < 0 THEN 190
130 LET C = S * CR / 100
140 LET T = T + 1
150 LET TS = TS + S
160 LET TC = TC + C
170 PRINT S$, "$"; S, "    "; CR; "%", "$"; C
180 GOTO 110
190 PRINT
200 PRINT "TOTAL NUMBER OF EMPLOYEES ="; T
210 PRINT "TOTAL SALES BY ALL EMPLOYEES = $"; TS
220 PRINT "TOTAL COMMISSIONS PAID = $"; TC
230 DATA 0, 0, 0
240 DATA "PETER FONG", 26500, 3
250 DATA "LUCY LAW", 32950, 3.5
260 DATA "JOHN WAYNE", 29440, 3
270 DATA "MARK OHM", 22890, 2.5
280 DATA "BO HOWARD", 29750, 3.5
290 DATA "0", -1, 0
300 END
```

```
                     COMMISSION REPORT
                    TED'S FURNITURE CO.


 EMPLOYEE       TOTAL        COMMISSION    COMMISSION
   NAME         SALES           RATE          EARNED

PETER FONG     $ 26500          3 %         $ 795
LUCY LAW       $ 32950          3.5 %       $ 1153.25
JOHN WAYNE     $ 29440          3 %         $ 883.2
MARK OHM       $ 22890          2.5 %       $ 572.25
BO HOWARD      $ 29750          3.5 %       $ 1041.25

TOTAL NUMBER OF EMPLOYEES = 5
TOTAL SALES BY ALL EMPLOYEES = $ 141530
TOTAL COMMISSIONS PAID = $ 4444.95
```

6-3 THE TAB FUNCTION

What we have learned so far about the PRINT statement is sufficient to allow us to design the printouts of most problems. We can even fit more than five columns of data on the screen by using combinations of variables and spaces in quotes separated by semicolons, but this can be very awkward. BASIC provides an alternative, often much more convenient, way of positioning print values in complex reports. This is by means of the **TAB** function.

The TAB function has the general form:

TAB(*argument)*

where the **argument** can be a numeric constant or variable or a mathematical expression, the value of which cannot be less than zero. The parentheses around the argument are required. The TAB may appear *only* in the list of a PRINT statement and is normally followed by a semicolon and an entry in the list. The action of the TAB function is similar to that of the TAB key on a typewriter; that is, it gives the column (by the argument) at which the entry in the print list that immediately follows will begin to be printed. To print A$, B, and C in columns 5, 30, and 45, respectively, we would write:

```
300  PRINT TAB(5); A$; TAB(30); B; TAB(45); C
```

Note the use of semicolons throughout this statement. If commas were used, they would cause the next values in the print list to be printed in the *next* print zone; if the arguments of any subsequent TABs specified closer columns, they would be overridden by the commas. In any PRINT statement, the numerical values of the arguments of *all* TAB functions in the print list must increase to the right. If they do not, the items in the list that are out of order will not appear in the proper columns, possibly affecting other entries as well, and perhaps the entire line. Had the above statement been mistyped as:

```
300  PRINT TAB(5); A$; TAB(30); B; TAB(25); C
```

A$ and B would still be in columns 5 and 30 as they should, but the PRINT cannot back up to column 25 for C, so it would be printed immediately following B. An even more severe case would arise had the first TAB been accidentally entered as TAB(55) instead of TAB(5); in this case, none of the three values would appear in the proper column! [A few computers print values beginning in the column immediately *after* the one specified by the TAB so that the above would print A$, B, and C starting in columns 6, 31, and 46, respectively. This is easily corrected for by tabbing back one column from where you want the value to print. Most versions of BASIC number the print columns beginning with 1, but some number from 0 so that TAB(N) = column N + 1.]

We shall use the TAB extensively in the example in Section 6-4. Keep in mind, however, that it is just another tool intended to supplement, not to replace, the printing techniques already learned. You should always format a print line by the simplest method available. If the standard print zones, with a little modification, will do, by all means use them; if not, then the TAB is there to help you find a screen design to satisfy your needs. In Section 6-7, we will study yet another form of the PRINT statement, the PRINT USING, which gives us even more control over the output—in this case, over the format of specific values as they are printed.

6-4 AN EXAMPLE: AIR POLLUTION REPORT

This example will combine all that we have studied so far in this chapter about producing a well-documented report. You will also be introduced to a new technique for placing variables in headings.

Problem: The air pollution count for several major cities has been collected for one 5-day period, and this data is to be used to produce an air pollution report. The daily average for each city is to be calculated as well as the average for all cities. The report should show all the input data, the calculated averages, and the number of cities reporting. The printout should have all appropriate headings and other literals; however, the beginning and ending dates of the report should be included in the main heading. Data is given in Table 6-1.

The outline solution to this problem is as follows:

1. Read the dates of the report.
2. Set all total accumulators to zero.
3. Print the main and column headings with the dates of the report included in the title.
4. Read a pollution record for a city.
5. Check for the end of processing. At the end, go to step 10; otherwise, continue to the next step.
6. Calculate the average of the daily pollution values for a city.

TABLE 6-1

Data for Air Pollution Report Example

Beginning Date: 6-13-83 Ending Date: 6-17-83

Reporting City	Pollution Count for Monday	Tuesday	Wednesday	Thursday	Friday
New York	67	89	55	145	112
Chicago	90	125	177	132	231
Miami	35	51	37	44	21
Pittsburgh	47	73	88	108	94
Denver	12	24	19	7	16
San Francisco	57	88	84	118	103
Boston	46	77	112	64	89
Detroit	98	145	132	87	134

7. Update the totals for the number of cities processed and the total of all the daily averages for each city.
8. Print a detailed line for a city record.
9. Go to step 4.
10. Calculate the average of the daily averages for all cities reporting.
11. Print the total number of cities reporting and the average of all the daily averages.
12. Stop.

Refer to the flowchart in Figure 6-1 for a pictorial illustration of the above procedure.

The first two steps involve nothing new and can be accomplished by a single program statement:

```
160 READ D1$, D2$, N, TA
```

We must read the dates *before* we print the headings because they are to be printed in the main headings. The totals could have been initialized after the headings were done, but it is easier to go ahead and do it now.

Step 3, printing the headings, translates into a set of statements that look much more complicated than they actually are. Let us examine these in two parts. First, we will look at the lines that print the main heading at the top of the report:

```
200 PRINT TAB(23); "AIR POLLUTION REPORT"
210 PRINT TAB(22); D1$; TAB(31); "THRU "; D2$
220 PRINT
230 PRINT
```

This will produce a two-line heading. AIR POLLUTION REPORT is printed on the first line by the statement at line 200. The PRINT at 210 places the dates of the report in the second line of the title. These headings will appear like this:

```
AIR POLLUTION REPORT
6-13-83  THRU 6-17-83
```

The positions on the screen given by the TABs must be calculated from the *longest* line to be printed. In order to determine the proper spacing, you may need to make a sketch of how the printout will appear on the screen. Such a sketch need not be an actual program listing or output, but it should be detailed enough for you to figure the column numbers for all variables and literals to be printed. There are special printout design forms available to help you with this.

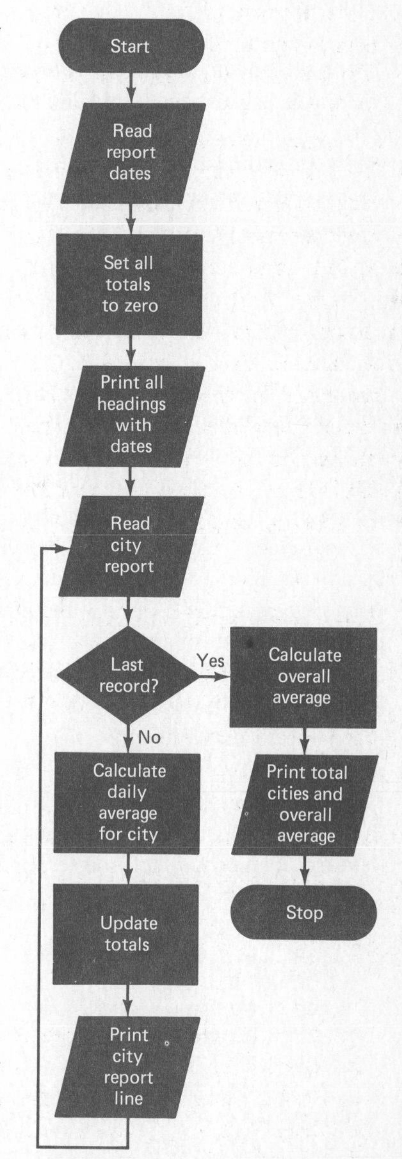

FIGURE 6-1
Flowchart for air pollution report problem

For this problem, the longest line is the second line of the column heads; it is 64 characters wide (see below). The first line of the above heading is 20 characters in length. This means that it should have (64 − 20) / 2 = 22 spaces before it if it is to be centered, or it should *begin* at column 23—hence the TAB(23). The second line is a little more complex. The dates are only seven characters in length, but we must allow for eight in the case of a two-digit month. This means that the length of the second line will be a maximum of 2 × 8 + 6 = 22 characters. The first date will begin at column 22. Allowing for the full eight characters in this date plus a blank space, the remainder of the line will print from column 31.

The column headings are printed by the following lines:

```
240 PRINT "   REPORTING"; TAB(27); "POLLUTION COUNT FOR";
250 PRINT TAB(59); "DAILY"
260 PRINT "     CITY"; TAB(21); "MON"; TAB(28); "TUE";
270 PRINT TAB(35); "WED"; TAB(42); "THU"; TAB(49); "FRI";
280 PRINT TAB(58); "AVERAGE"
290 PRINT
```

These statements produce a two-line column heading. Lines 240 and 250 print the first line of the column heads and 260 through 280 print the second. If you look closely at lines 240, 260, and 270, you will see that all three *end* with a semicolon. This has a similar effect to ending a PRINT with a comma; that is, the next PRINT statement acts as a continuation of the preceding one and continues to print on the same line. The column headings will print as:

```
REPORTING                   POLLUTION COUNT FOR                DAILY
  CITY                MON      TUE     WED     THU     FRI      AVERAGE
```

The choice as to where to place the column headings must be made in combination with the placement of the data to be printed. There are no rules about this, but there are some general guidelines that you can follow. First, you must decide what is to be printed and how many columns of data you will need. Next, you must determine the spacing of the data on the screen. If the normal zones will do, fine; if not, then you must divide the screen to allow enough room for each column as well as spacing in between. This should be done in such a way that the data is not too crowded and is easy to read. You must use your own judgment here. Although there are occasional exceptions, the spacing will normally be determined by the size of the largest (longest) value to be printed in a given set of data. You should take care to allow for the maximum size value that *might* reasonably be expected to occur in general processing, not just the one that is present in the data that you are currently processing. We will discuss this in more detail below. Finally, remember to provide for totals, main headings, and any other special features, being sure that they are properly placed with vertical blanks included as needed.

This brings us to steps 4 through 9, which describe the processing of the pollution data for each city. These correspond to the BASIC statements:

```
330 READ C$
340 IF C$ = "END" THEN 450
350 READ P1, P2, P3, P4, P5
360 LET A = (P1 + P2 + P3 + P4 + P5) / 5
370 LET N = N + 1
380 LET TA = TA + A
390 PRINT C$; TAB(20); P1; TAB(27); P2; TAB(34); P3;
400 PRINT TAB(41); P4; TAB(48); P5; TAB(58); A
410 GOTO 330
```

The processing described by these lines is routine; nothing is new except for the two PRINT statements. Lines 390 and 400 print a single report line because of the semicolon at the end of line 390. The TABs establish the positions of the data on the screen, which are aligned with those set for the column heads above.

The setting of the print columns is, to a great extent, arbitrary, a matter of opinion. Here is the reasoning followed in establishing the seven columns as shown in this example. The city name is printed first and is assumed to be no more than about 13 spaces. The five daily pollution values are assumed to be no larger than a three-digit integer, while the daily average can be assumed to be a maximum of five spaces: three before the decimal, the decimal, and one after. (This is because we are dividing by 5; any integer divided by 5 must be either another integer or have a decimal part of .2, .4, .6, or .8.) We have used a total of 33 spaces so far.

The number of spaces that you can insert between columns will frequently depend on your screen size or how wide you want to make the output. At other times, you will have the luxury of selecting the number of spaces and letting the width follow. Here, we were able to separate the columns by a convenient amount with the overall width coming out to 64 spaces. The five pollution counts are each separated by four spaces; for emphasis, we have placed a few (about three) extra spaces in the gaps before and after this group of columns. This means that the city name, plus about seven spaces for separation, places the first pollution count at say column 21. Then, with three spaces for the number and four for separation, the next four values will come at seven-column intervals: 28, 35, 42, and 49. Finally, the daily average has been spaced over to column 59. If we want the numbers to actually appear in these columns, we must set the tabs *one position to the left*—remember that numeric values are usually preceded (and followed) by one blank space. This means that the arguments of the TABs should be 20, 27, 34, 41, 48, and 58, respectively.

A quick count reveals that this extends only to column 63, not 64. In all of this, we need to remember that the column headings must also be considered. If they are the same size or smaller than the data fields, there is rarely a problem; however, when a heading is longer, there may be difficulties. You may, in fact, have to position the heading rather than the data. None of our headings is longer than the corresponding data except the last one; this causes it to ''hang over'' one column on either side of the daily average values, thus extending to column 64!

Finally, steps 10 through 12 process the totals and end the program. For our program, this is accomplished by the following group of statements:

```
450  LET AA = TA / N
460  PRINT
470  PRINT "NUMBER OF CITIES SURVEYED ="; N
480  PRINT "AVERAGE COUNT FOR ALL CITIES ="; AA
```

Line 450 calculates the average of all the daily averages for all cities surveyed. The PRINTs at 470 and 480 print the number of cities reporting in the survey and the overall average, but with appropriate identifying literals.

A complete program listing followed by a printout is given below.

```
 10 REM  AIR POLLUTION REPORT
 20 REM
 30 REM  VARIABLES ARE DEFINED AS --
 40 REM
 50 REM         D1$ = DATE AT BEGINNING OF REPORT
 60 REM         D2$ = DATE AT END OF REPORT
 70 REM          C$ = NAME OF CITY
 80 REM    P1 - P5 = DAILY POLLUTION COUNTS
 90 REM           A = AVERAGE OF DAILY POLLUTION COUNTS
100 REM           N = TOTAL NUMBER OF CITIES SURVEYED
110 REM          TA = TOTAL OF DAILY AVERAGES
120 REM          AA = AVERAGE COUNT FOR ALL CITIES
130 REM
140 REM  READ DATES AND INITIALIZE TOTALS
```

```
150 REM
160 READ D1$, D2$, N, TA
170 REM
180 REM  PRINT HEADINGS
190 REM
200 PRINT TAB(23); "AIR POLLUTION REPORT"
210 PRINT TAB(22); D1$; TAB(31); "THRU "; D2$
220 PRINT
230 PRINT
240 PRINT "  REPORTING"; TAB(27); "POLLUTION COUNT FOR";
250 PRINT TAB(59); "DAILY"
260 PRINT "    CITY"; TAB(21); "MON"; TAB(28); "TUE";
270 PRINT TAB(35); "WED"; TAB(42); "THU"; TAB(49); "FRI";
280 PRINT TAB(58); "AVERAGE"
290 PRINT
300 REM
310 REM  PROCESS POLLUTION COUNT DATA
320 REM
330 READ C$
340 IF C$ = "END" THEN 450
350 READ P1, P2, P3, P4, P5
360 LET A = (P1 + P2 + P3 + P4 + P5) / 5
370 LET N = N + 1
380 LET TA = TA + A
390 PRINT C$; TAB(20); P1; TAB(27); P2; TAB(34); P3;
400 PRINT TAB(41); P4; TAB(48); P5; TAB(58); A
410 GOTO 330
420 REM
430 REM  CALCULATE FINAL AVERAGE AND PRINT TOTALS
440 REM
450 LET AA = TA / N
460 PRINT
470 PRINT "NUMBER OF CITIES SURVEYED ="; N
480 PRINT "AVERAGE COUNT FOR ALL CITIES ="; AA
490 REM
500 REM  DATA LIST
510 REM
520 DATA "6-13-83", "6-17-83", 0, 0
530 DATA "NEW YORK", 67, 89, 55, 145, 112
540 DATA "CHICAGO", 90, 125, 177, 132, 231
550 DATA "MIAMI", 35, 51, 37, 44, 21
560 DATA "PITTSBURGH", 47, 73, 88, 108, 94
570 DATA "DENVER", 12, 24, 19, 7, 16
580 DATA "SAN FRANCISCO", 57, 88, 84, 118, 103
590 DATA "BOSTON", 46, 77, 112, 64, 89
600 DATA "DETROIT", 98, 145, 132, 87, 134
610 DATA "END", 0, 0, 0, 0, 0
620 END
```

```
                      AIR POLLUTION REPORT
                     6-13-83  THRU 6-17-83


  REPORTING                 POLLUTION COUNT FOR              DAILY
    CITY             MON    TUE    WED    THU    FRI        AVERAGE

NEW YORK             67     89     55     145    112         93.6
CHICAGO              90     125    177    132    231         151
MIAMI                35     51     37     44     21          37.6
PITTSBURGH           47     73     88     108    94          82
DENVER               12     24     19     7      16          15.6
SAN FRANCISCO        57     88     84     118    103         90
```

```
BOSTON                  46      77      112     64      89          77.6
DETROIT                 98      145     132     87      134         119.2

NUMBER OF CITIES SURVEYED = 8
AVERAGE COUNT FOR ALL CITIES = 83.325
```

6-5 MATH EXPRESSIONS AND THE PRINT STATEMENT

Thus far, we have seen that the list of the PRINT statement may contain data names or literals, either of which may be numeric or string, as well as the TAB function. In addition, the print list may have mathematical expressions as one or more of its entries. As an example of this, consider the following program which appeared in the last chapter as an example of writing mathematical expressions in BASIC programs:

```
100 REM  EXAMPLE WITH MATH EXPRESSIONS
110 REM
120 READ A, B, C
130 IF A < 0 THEN 999
140 LET S = A + B + C
150 LET P = A * B * C
160 PRINT A, B, C, S, P
170 GOTO 120
180 DATA 3,7,2,8,12,5,9,10,4,-1,0,0
999 END
```

The values calculated in the two LET statements at lines 140 and 150 could be incorporated directly into the list of the PRINT at 160 eliminating the need for the two LETs. The program would then read:

```
100 REM  MATH EXPRESSIONS IN A PRINT LIST
110 REM
120 READ A, B, C
130 IF A < 0 THEN 999
160 PRINT A, B, C, A + B + C, A * B * C
170 GOTO 120
180 DATA 3,7,2,8,12,5,9,10,4,-1,0,0
999 END
```

which would work equally well. But before you become too enthusiastic about this technique, read on.

There are two very important cautions about placing mathematical expressions directly into the print list. First, it should be done only when the expression is relatively simple, never with complex expressions or when the print list itself is involved, as with the use of many TABs. Second, and most important, *any value calculated and printed only within a print list cannot be used in any other way within the program, such as in accumulating totals, without first being recalculated* (see Figure 6-2). Following is an-

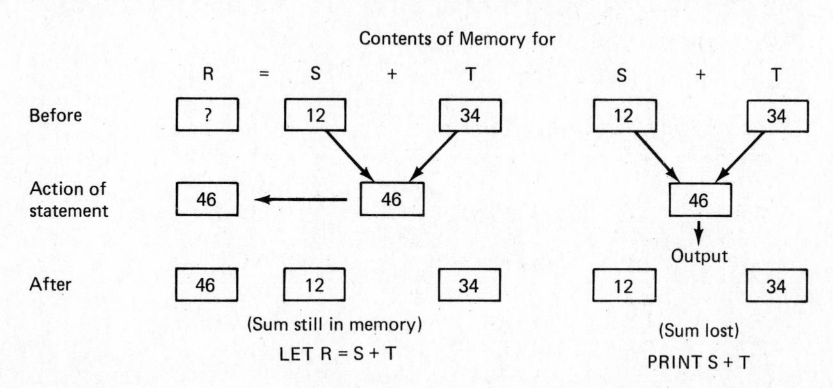

FIGURE 6-2
Comparison of addition with LET and in PRINT list

other program that appeared in the last chapter, one that was used to illustrate the accumulation of totals:

```
 10 REM   ILLUSTRATION OF ACCUMULATION TOTALS
 20 REM
 30 LET T = 0
 40 LET TP = 0
 50 READ X, Y
 60 IF X = 99999 THEN 120
 70 LET P = X * Y
 80 LET T = T + 1
 90 LET TP = TP + P
100 PRINT X, Y, P
110 GOTO 50
120 PRINT
130 PRINT T,, TP
140 DATA 4,8,5,9,12,6,10,5,15,4,99999,0
150 END
```

Here, if we replace P in the print list in line 100 with the explicit product X * Y, *we* ***cannot*** *delete the LET at* 70 *unless we also replace P with X * Y at line* 90 *and anywhere else in the program it might occur*. This might be rewritten as:

```
              :
              :
 50  READ X, Y
 60  IF X = 99999 THEN 120
 80  LET T = T + 1
 90  LET TP = TP + X * Y
100  PRINT X, Y, X * Y
110  GOTO 50
              :
              :
```

This was not too difficult in such a simple example, but you are able to see from this just how complicated things can get in a more involved problem. As one final illustration, consider this program segment from the example on calculating compound interest as it was modified in Section 5-6 to accommodate several totals:

```
                    :
                    :
290 READ C, A, RP, Y
300 IF C = 0 THEN 362
310 LET RD = RP / 100
320 LET P = A * (1 + RD / N) ^ (N * Y)
330 LET I = P - A
332 LET TC = TC + 1
334 LET TA = TA + A
336 LET TI = TI + I
340 PRINT C, A, RP, Y
350 PRINT , P, I
360 GOTO 290
                    :
                    :
```

This could have been written as:

```
                    :
                    :
290 READ C, A, RP, Y
300 IF C = 0 THEN 362
310 LET RD = RP / 100
```

```
332 LET TC = TC + 1
334 LET TA = TA + A
336 LET TI = TI + A * (1 + RD / N) ^ (N * Y)
340 PRINT C, A, RP, Y
350 PRINT , A * (1 + RD / N) ^ (N * Y),
355 PRINT A * (1 + RD / N) ^ (N * Y) - A
360 GOTO 290
                        :
                        :
```

The second version is more difficult to understand than the first and would be subject to more errors. Also, although the new version *appears* to be shorter than the original, it will actually require *more* computer memory space. Of course, had we not removed the LET at 320 that defines I, we would not necessarily have had to replace all of the occurrences of I in the remainder of the program.

Placing mathematical expressions in print lists is often tricky and can get you into trouble if you are not very careful. You are cautioned to do so only when you are certain that the circumstances are appropriate; if in doubt, avoid the practice. In summary, you should consider placing a mathematical expression in the print list only in situations where (1) there is no possibility of confusion, (2) it does not make the program more complicated, (3) the resulting value is only printed and not required for other calculations, and (4) the expression is not too complex.

6-6 MORE ON SPACING WITH THE TAB FUNCTION

In our earlier discussion of the TAB function, we said that the argument could be a numeric variable or mathematical expression as well as a numeric constant, which was the only case we examined in Section 6-3. Using variables or expressions in the TAB can provide some very convenient methods for column spacing.

Let us look once more at the air pollution report example from Section 6-4. If for some reason, such as a very long city name, we had to move all of the columns, beginning with the second one, three spaces to the right, this would mean retyping *all* of the values in the TABs for the column heads, the detail line, and probably the title lines as well. There are some special techniques for indicating columns with the TAB that will help eliminate some of these problems.

The general idea is to specify a **reference** column and write all other column numbers in relation to it. In our example, we might take column 20 (the second column of data) as our reference and call it R. Then the third column of data, which begins at column 27, would be indicated by R + 7, the fourth at column 34 by R + 14, the fifth at column 41 by R + 21, the sixth at column 48 by R + 28, and the last at column 58 by R + 38. Using this method, all the columns (except the first) can be moved to the right or left by simply changing the value of R to the proper value; to move the columns three spaces to the right, set R equal to 23. (The first column could be written as R − 19, in which case it would shift as well, but care must be taken to ensure that subtraction does not produce a negative value.) Of course, all of the TABs for the headings can also be written with values relative to R so that they will automatically shift too. Here is a portion of the program from Section 4 with the TABs rewritten using a reference value of 20 (to produce the same output as before, not to move the columns to the right).

```
                        :
                        :
163 REM  SET REFERENCE VALUE FOR TABS
165 LET R = 20
                        :
                        :
200 PRINT TAB(R + 3); "AIR POLLUTION REPORT"
210 PRINT TAB(R + 2); D1$; TAB(R + 11); "THRU "; D2$
```

```
220 PRINT
230 PRINT
240 PRINT "  REPORTING"; TAB(R + 7); "POLLUTION COUNT FOR";
250 PRINT TAB(R + 39); "DAILY"
260 PRINT "     CITY"; TAB(R + 1); "MON"; TAB(R + 8); "TUE";
270 PRINT TAB(R + 15); "WED"; TAB(R + 22); "THU";
280 PRINT TAB(R + 29); "FRI"; TAB(R + 38); "AVERAGE"
290 PRINT
                              :
                              :
390 PRINT C$; TAB(R); P1; TAB(R + 7); P2; TAB(R + 14); P3;
400 PRINT TAB(R + 21); P4; TAB(R + 28); P5; TAB(R + 39); A
                              :
                              :
```

Note that the list of the PRINT statements at lines 270 and 280 have been slightly adjusted due to the length of 270. Individual columns can still be adjusted, if necessary, by simply changing the **shift factor** or the amount that is added or subtracted from the reference value.

The use of a reference column can be of value on many printouts that require the use of the TAB. There is one other technique that is of particular value for outputs which have equally spaced columns; this is the use of a **column width** indicator. In the air pollution example, the five daily values form five identical columns, each of which is seven spaces wide. If we wanted to increase this to eight spaces, we would have to rewrite all of the involved TABs, even with the reference column in use. However, if we indicate the columns as a multiple of a column width, we need only change the width value. Suppose we let W be the column width, which is seven for our problem. Then, the first daily value (second column of data) will still be indicated by R. The second daily value will now be R + W, the third by R + 2 * W, the fourth by R + 3 * W, and the fifth by R + 4 * W. (The last column is unchanged.) Any equally spaced column headings may be specified likewise, except that when they do not begin in the same columns as the data, a shift factor will have to be added or subtracted to adjust for proper alignment. Either the headings or the data columns may be shifted, depending on which is used as a source of the reference column number. Rewriting the above program segment using this technique yields:

```
                              :
                              :
163 REM  SET REFERENCE VALUE AND COLUMN WIDTH FOR TABS
165 LET R = 20
167 LET W = 7
                              :
                              :
200 PRINT TAB(R + 3); "AIR POLLUTION REPORT"
210 PRINT TAB(R + 2); D1$; TAB(R + 11); "THRU "; D2$
220 PRINT
230 PRINT
240 PRINT "  REPORTING"; TAB(R + 7); "POLLUTION COUNT FOR";
250 PRINT TAB(R + 39); "DAILY"
260 PRINT "     CITY"; TAB(R + 1); "MON"; TAB(R + 1 + W); "TUE";
270 PRINT TAB(R + 1 + 2 * W); "WED"; TAB(R + 1 + 3 * W); "THU";
280 PRINT TAB(R + 1 + 4 * W); "FRI"; TAB(R + 38); "AVERAGE"
290 PRINT
                              :
                              :
390 PRINT C$; TAB(R); P1; TAB(R + W); P2; TAB(R + 2 * W); P3;
400 PRINT TAB(R + 3 * W); P4; TAB(R + 4 * W); P5; TAB(R + 38); A
                              :
                              :
```

Since the five column headings for the daily values all begin one space to the right of the data, we had to compensate by adding one to R to properly position these headings. An alternative method would be to define a *second* reference value, say R1, which has a value of 21: R1 = R + 1 = 21. This would change the above to be:

```
                                   :
                                   :
166  LET R1 = R + 1
                                   :
                                   :
260  PRINT "     CITY"; TAB(R1); "MON"; TAB(R1 + W); "TUE";
270  PRINT TAB(R1 + 2 * W); "WED"; TAB(R1 + 3 * W); "THU";
280  PRINT TAB(R1 + 4 * W); "FRI"; TAB(R + 38); "AVERAGE"
                                   :
                                   :
```

The TABs in the other headings have been left written in terms of R because there was no advantage to changing them to R1. You should be aware that, while using more than one reference does simplify the TABs somewhat, any adjustments to the output may require changing *all* references. Here, we have avoided this by writing R1 in terms of R at line 166.

While either of these methods of spacing can be of significant value to you in both designing and adjusting your printouts, you should be careful not to overuse either one. It is very easy to spend too much time trying to develop a perfect system of tabbing (none exists!), resulting in TABs that are more complex than the original program! In fact, one could argue with some justification that the TABs used in the second example above are overdone for a relatively simple program. In Chapter 11, we will see how the TAB can be used in combination with other BASIC functions to achieve special control over otherwise difficult data fields, such as in the centering of variable length values.

6-7 FORMATTING WITH THE PRINT USING STATEMENT

There is yet another method for designing output that is provided by some versions of BASIC. This is by means of the **PRINT USING** statement. Unfortunately, this statement is not a standard part of the BASIC language and therefore is not available on many computer systems, especially smaller microcomputers. To make the problem even worse, since there is no language standard for the statement, PRINT USING, when available, will vary widely in general format and usage from computer to computer. In this section, the most common forms and variations of the PRINT USING statement will be given; however, you should consult your instructor for specific differences that apply to your computer's BASIC.

While the TAB function, when used with the PRINT statement, provides a great deal of control over the *position* of a field on the print line, it gives little or no control over the field itself. It is this additional control over the formatting of the *individual output fields* that is provided by the PRINT USING statement, *without the loss of positional control* provided by the TAB.

As mentioned above, the PRINT USING statement does not have a standard format; however, we will look at two of the most commonly encountered forms. The first has the general form:

ln **PRINT USING** *format* , *print list*

where *format* is a string variable or literal that describes the print format of the items in the print list. Some of the most common **formatting symbols** are given in Table 6-2 along with an explanation and examples of the use of each. (Some of the symbols in Table 6-2 may not be available on your computer, while additional or alternative ones may be. Ask your instructor for a specific list for your system.)

TABLE 6-2

Summary of Most Commonly Available Format Field Indicators Used with the PRINT USING Statement

Format Symbol	Summary of Meaning and Uses of Formatting Symbols	Sample Format	Input Field	Printed Field
#	Indicates the presence of a character in a field. String fields are left-justified and numeric ones are right-justified. Extra spaces are filled with blanks except to the right in numeric fields which are completed with zeros.	########### ########	JOHN SMITH 12345	JOHN SMITH 12345
<	Left-justifies a string field.	<##########	ABCDE	ABCDE
>	Right-justifies a string field.	>##########	ABCDE	ABCDE
.	Indicates the position of a decimal in a numeric field. If the number of formatted places to the right of the decimal is less than that in the input number, the number is rounded to the indicated position.	###.## ###.## ##.####	45.86 60.5288 19.433	45.86 60.53 19.4330
,	Used to place commas in numbers over 999.	##,###.##	5962.45	5,962.45
$	Places a dollar sign before a numeric field. Two or more adjacent dollar signs at the beginning of the format cause the $ to "float" to the right against the first nonzero digit or last $ in the field.	$###,## $$$#.## $$$$,$$#.##	34.95 65.98 5788.05	$ 34.95 $65.98 $5,788.05
+	Places a plus sign before/after a positive number and a negative sign before/after a negative number. Two or more adjacent plus signs at the beginning of the format will cause the sign to "float" to the right in the same manner as the $.	+##.### +##,### ###,###+ +++++++#.#### +$$,$$$,$$#.##	2.733 −1734 45600 504.3 50012	+ 2.733 - 1,743 45,600+ +504.3000 + $50,012.00
−	Places a minus sign before/after a negative number. Two or more adjacent minus signs at the beginning of the format will cause the sign to "float" to the right in the same manner as the $.	−#.#### −#.#### ###.##− −−−−−−−−#.# −$$$,$$#	3.1416 −5.332 −90.168 −311.4 −4502	3.1416 -5.3320 90.17- -311.4 - $4,502
^	Placing four ^ at the end of a format outputs a number in exponential (scientific) notation (which we will discuss in Chapter 11).	#.##^^^^ +#.####^^^^	200 125127	2.00E+02 +1.2513E+05
*	The asterisk is not used to format data, but its appearance in an output field indicates that the data is too large or otherwise inconsistent with the format.	##.## ++##	354.98 12345	**.** ****

The use of the PRINT USING statement is best illustrated by an example. Consider the following short program and output:

```
10 LET Y = 100
20 LET M = Y / 6
30 PRINT "$"; Y, "$"; M
40 END
```

```
$ 100          $ 16.6667
```

This is okay except that if we are printing dollars and cents, it would be better to have the last field print as 16.67, rounded to the nearest cent. This is where PRINT USING is of value. If the program is revised as follows to include a PRINT USING statement at line 30, the result will be as shown:

```
10  LET Y = 100
20  LET M = Y / 6
30  PRINT USING "$####          $###.##", Y, M
40  END
```

```
$ 100        $ 16.67
```

Note that the format description for the two values to be printed is given at the beginning of the PRINT USING statement. This particular format is written to make this output identical to that above except for the round-off in the second field. It could have been easily modified to make the two values print closer together or farther apart, to have a floating dollar sign or comma, to add a sign, etc.

When there are several variables to be printed, the format may become too long to be placed in the PRINT USING statement itself. In such cases, the format description can be assigned to a string variable, which is in turn placed in the proper position in the PRINT USING statement. The last program could have been written:

```
10  LET Y = 100
20  LET M = Y / 6
25  LET S$ = "$####          $###.##"
30  PRINT USING S$, Y, M
40  END
```

There are far too many possible format descriptions to cover them all here, but let us look at a few. Consider the above program but with different numbers and formats:

```
10  LET Y = 50000
20  LET M = Y / 125
25  LET S$ = "$###,###          $##,###.##"
30  PRINT USING S$, Y, M
40  END
```

This will print:

```
$ 50,000     $    400.00
```

If line 25 is modified to have the following format:

```
25  LET S$ = "$$$$,$$#          $$$,$$#.##"
```

the dollar sign will **float** to the right to the first nonzero digit or the position of the last $. With this format, the last program will print:

```
 $50,000     $    400.00
```

The plus and minus signs can be made to float in much the same way as the dollar sign, but while most symbols can be combined in a given **field format**, *there cannot be two* ***floating*** *symbols in the same field.*

The second version of the PRINT USING statement that is frequently encountered uses a nonexecutable **format** or **image line** for the format description of the output fields. The general form of this statement is:

ln1 **PRINT USING** *ln2* , *print list*

where *ln2* is the line number of the corresponding format line which has the form:

ln2: *format description*

The **format line** is signaled by a **colon** immediately following the line number. Since this is a nonexecutable statement, it can be placed at any point in the program and need not necessarily follow a PRINT USING statement. If the last program (with the floating $) were rewritten to employ this version of PRINT USING, it would appear as follows:

```
10  LET Y = 50000
20  LET M = Y / 125
25: $$$$,$$#              $$$,$$#.##
30  PRINT USING 25, Y, M
40  END
```

which will print the same result as above:

```
$50,000      $    400.00
```

As a final example of the use of the PRINT USING statement, we will rewrite the air pollution report example given earlier in this chapter so that the output is formatted with PRINT USING. The new program listing with the corresponding run is as follows:

```
 10 REM   AIR POLLUTION REPORT WITH PRINT USING
 20 REM
 30 REM   VARIABLES ARE DEFINED AS --
 40 REM
 50 REM            D1$ = DATE AT BEGINNING OF REPORT
 60 REM            D2$ = DATE AT END OF REPORT
 70 REM             C$ = NAME OF CITY
 80 REM       P1 - P5 = DAILY POLLUTION COUNTS
 90 REM              A = AVERAGE OF DAILY POLLUTION COUNTS
100 REM              N = TOTAL NUMBER OF CITIES SURVEYED
110 REM             TA = TOTAL OF DAILY AVERAGES
120 REM             AA = AVERAGE COUNT FOR ALL CITIES
130 REM
140 REM   READ DATES AND INITIALIZE TOTALS
150 REM
160 READ D1$, D2$, N, TA
170 REM
180 REM   PRINT HEADINGS
190 REM
200 PRINT USING 480
210 PRINT USING 490, D1$, D2$
220 PRINT
230 PRINT
240 PRINT USING 500
250 PRINT USING 510
260 PRINT
270 REM
270 REM   PROCESS POLLUTION COUNT DATA
290 REM
300 READ C$
310 IF C$ = "END" THEN 420
320 READ P1, P2, P3, P4, P5
330 LET A = (P1 + P2 + P3 + P4 + P5) / 5
340 LET N = N + 1
350 LET TA = TA + A
360 PRINT USING 520, C$, P1, P2, P3, P4, P5, A
370 GOTO 300
```

```
380 REM
390 REM  CALCULATE FINAL AVERAGE AND PRINT TOTALS
400 REM
410 LET AA = TA / N
420 PRINT
430 PRINT USING 530, N
440 PRINT USING 540, AA
450 REM
460 REM  FORMATS FOR PRINT USING STATEMENTS
470 REM
480:                          AIR POLLUTION REPORT
490:                        >######## THRU ########
500:  REPORTING                  POLLUTION COUNT FOR                   DAILY
510:     CITY              MON      TUE      WED      THU      FRI       AVERAGE
520:###############        ###      ###      ###      ###      ###        ###.#
530:NUMBER OF CITIES SURVEYED = ##
540:AVERAGE COUNT FOR ALL CITIES = ###.##
550 REM
560 REM  DATA LIST
570 REM
580 DATA "6-13-83", "6-17-83", 0, 0
590 DATA "NE ERR YORK", 67, 89, 55, 145, 112
600 DATA "CHICAGO", 90, 125, 177, 132, 231
610 DATA "MIAMI", 35, 51, 37, 44, 21
620 DATA "PITTSBURGH", 47, 73, 88, 108, 94
630 DATA "DENVER", 12, 24, 19, 7, 16
640 DATA "SAN FRANCISCO", 57, 88, 84, 118, 103
650 DATA "BOSTON", 46, 77, 112, 64, 89
660 DATA "DETROIT", 98, 145, 132, 87, 134
670 DATA "END", 0, 0, 0, 0, 0
680 END
```

```
                        AIR POLLUTION REPORT
                        6-13-83 THRU 6-17-83


  REPORTING                  POLLUTION COUNT FOR                  DAILY
     CITY             MON     TUE      WED      THU      FRI      AVERAGE

NEW YORK               67      89       55      145      112        93.6
CHICAGO                90     125      177      132      231       151.0
MIAMI                  35      51       37       44       21        37.6
PITTSBURGH             47      73       88      108       94        82.0
DENVER                 12      24       19        7       16        15.6
SAN FRANCISCO          57      88       84      118      103        90.0
BOSTON                 46      77      112       64       89        77.6
DETROIT                98     145      132       87      134       119.2

NUMBER OF CITIES SURVEYED =  8
AVERAGE COUNT FOR ALL CITIES =  83.33
```

All PRINT statements have been replaced with PRINT USING statements, with the corresponding format lines grouped at program lines 480 to 540. The first two format lines relate to the PRINT USING statements at lines 200 and 210 and provide for the main heading with the two dates printed by the second line. Note the right-justification of the first date in the format at line 490. The column heads are printed by lines 240 and 250 with the formats described at lines 500 and 510. The detailed line is printed by line 360 with its image at 520. The totals, corresponding to the last two format lines are printed at lines 430 and 440. Compare the printout to the one in Section 6-4. The values are all the same, as they must be; we have not changed the actual program. However, the output is neater in appearance. The more complex the report, the more valuable is PRINT USING for formatting the output. (While we have used the second version of the PRINT USING statement described above, it would have been equally easy to rewrite the program with the first form.)

By now you should have some idea of the power of the PRINT USING statement. Because of the problems with the nonuniformity of the statement, to minimize confusion, we will continue in later chapters to use the standard PRINT, with TABs as needed, to produce printouts and to avoid the PRINT USING as much as possible. This should not, however, deter you from using the PRINT USING that is available on your computer. It is a powerful statement that borrows much from other languages and should (and probably soon will) be a standard part of all versions of BASIC.

TROUBLESHOOTING

Each of the following programs contains an error that prevents it from executing properly. Explain *specifically* what the problem is and what must be done to correct it. To assist you, a sample of what would happen should you attempt to run the program is provided after each listing. Refer to Appendix D for an explanation of BASIC error messages.

1.

```
 10 REM   TROUBLESHOOTING PROBLEM 6-1
 20 REM
 30 REM            N$ = APPLICANT'S NAME
 40 REM            H$ = HIGHEST DEGREE
 50 REM             Y = YEARS EXPERIENCE
 60 REM            D$ = DATE AVAILABLE
 70 REM
 80 PRINT "    NAME","DEGREE","EXP","AVAILABLE"
 90 PRINT
100 READ N$, H$, Y, D$
110 IF N$ = "ALL" THEN 180
120 PRINT N$,, H$, Y, D$
130 GOTO 80
140 DATA "ALAN CRUZ", "M. S.", 7, "SEPTEMBER"
150 DATA "JANET ELROD", "PH. D.", 11, "AUGUST"
160 DATA "PEDRO LOPEZ", "ED. S.", 9, "OCTOBER"
170 DATA "ALL", "X", 0, "X"
180 END
```

```
    NAME                        DEGREE         EXP          AVAILABLE

ALAN CRUZ                       M. S.           7           SEPTEMBER
    NAME                        DEGREE         EXP          AVAILABLE

JANET ELROD                     PH. D.          11          AUGUST
    NAME                        DEGREE         EXP          AVAILABLE

PEDRO LOPEZ                     ED. S.          9           OCTOBER
    NAME                        DEGREE         EXP          AVAILABLE
```

2.

```
 10 REM TROUBLESHOOTING PROBLEM 6-2
 20 REM
 30 REM          E$ = EMPLOYEE'S NAME
 40 REM           W = WEEKLY SALES
 50 REM           C = COMMISSION EARNED
 60 REM          TE = TOTAL NUMBER OF EMPLOYEES
 70 REM          TS = TOTAL WEEKLY SALES
 80 REM          TC = TOTAL COMMISSIONS PAID
 90 REM
100 PRINT "EMPLOYEE", " SALES", "COMMISSION"
110 PRINT
```

```
120 READ E$, W, C
130 IF W < 0 THEN 190
140 PRINT E$, "$"; W, " $"; C
150 LET T = T + 1
160 LET TS = TS + W
170 LET TC = TC + C
180 GOTO 120
190 PRINT
200 PRINT "TOTAL EMPLOYEES = $; T"
210 PRINT "TOTAL WEEKLY SALES = $; TS"
220 PRINT "TOTAL COMMISSIONS PAID = $; TC"
230 DATA "F. PRICE", 21356, 587.29
240 DATA "L. ROPPER", 19033, 523.41
250 DATA "C. TYRE", 28654, 787.99
260 DATA "0", -1, 0
270 END
```

```
EMPLOYEE       SALES          COMMISSION

F. PRICE       $ 21356          $ 587.29
L. ROPPER      $ 19033          $ 523.41
C. TYRE        $ 28654          $ 787.99

TOTAL EMPLOYEES = $; T
TOTAL WEEKLY SALES = $; TS
TOTAL COMMISSIONS PAID = $; TC
```

3.

```
 10 REM  TROUBLESHOOTING PROBLEM 6-3
 20 REM
 30 REM          N$ = APPLICANT'S NAME
 40 REM          H$ = HIGHEST DEGREE
 50 REM           Y = YEARS EXPERIENCE
 60 REM          D$ = DATE AVAILABLE
 70 REM
 80 READ N$, H$, Y, D$
 90 IF N$ = "ALL" THEN 180
100 PRINT "    NAME","DEGREE","EXP","AVAILABLE"
110 PRINT
120 PRINT N$,, H$, Y, D$
130 GOTO 80
140 DATA "ALAN CRUZ", "M. S.", 7, "SEPTEMBER"
150 DATA "JANET ELROD", "PH. D.", 11, "AUGUST"
160 DATA "PEDRO LOPEZ", "ED. S.", 9, "OCTOBER"
170 DATA "ALL", "X", 0, "X"
180 END
```

```
   NAME                      DEGREE       EXP          AVAILABLE

ALAN CRUZ                    M. S.         7           SEPTEMBER
   NAME                      DEGREE       EXP          AVAILABLE

JANET ELROD                  PH. D.        11          AUGUST
   NAME                      DEGREE       EXP          AVAILABLE

PEDRO LOPEZ                  ED. S.        9           OCTOBER
```

4.

```
 10 REM  TROUBLESHOOTING PROBLEM 6-4
 20 REM
 30 REM          C$ = NAME OF CITY
 40 REM           N = NUMBER OF OFFICES
 50 REM           E = NUMBER OF EMPLOYEES
 60 REM           S = TOTAL SALES
 70 REM
```

```
 80 PRINT TAB(8); "CITY", TAB(22); "OFFICES",
 90 PRINT TAB(33); "EMPLOYEES", TAB(50); "TOTAL SALES"
100 PRINT
110 READ C$, N, E, S
120 IF C$ = "END" THEN 200
130 PRINT TAB(4); C$, TAB(24); N, TAB(36); E,
140 PRINT TAB(50); "$"; S
150 GOTO 110
160 DATA "DALLAS", 5, 41, 956288
170 DATA "PHILADELPHIA", 3, 33, 655430
180 DATA "LONDON", 4, 35, 703994
190 DATA "END", 0, 0, 0
200 END
```

```
     CITY              OFFICES                EMPLOYEES    TOTAL SALES

   DALLAS                 5             41               $ 956288.29
   PHILADELPHIA               3               33               $ 655430.83
   LONDON                 4             35               $ 703994.70
```

5.

```
 10 REM  TROUBLESHOOTING PROBLEM 6-5
 20 REM
 30 REM          C$ = CITY
 40 REM          S$ = STATE
 50 REM          N$ = FM STATION NAME
 60 REM           F = BROADCAST FREQUENCY
 70 REM           R = REFERENCE COLUMN FOR TAB
 80 REM
 90 LET R = 15
100 PRINT " STATION"; TAB(R + 2); "FREQUENCY";
110 PRINT TAB(R - 14); "CITY"; TAB(R - 24); "STATE"
120 PRINT
130 READ N$, F, C$, S$
140 IF F = 0 THEN 220
150 PRINT TAB(R + 11); N$; TAB(R); F; TAB(R - 11); C$
160 PRINT TAB(R - 26); S$
170 GOTO 130
180 DATA "KHTC", 89.5, "HELENA", "MT"
190 DATA "WLVH", 93.7, "HARTFORD", "CT"
200 DATA "WPFR", 102.7, "TERRE HAUTE", "IN"
210 DATA "0", 0, "0", "0"
220 END
```

```
 STATION        FREQUENCYCITYSTATE

                           KHTC 89.5 HELENAMT
                           WLVH 93.7 HARTFORDCT
                           WPFR 102.7 TERRE HAUTEIN
```

IMPORTANT TERMS

After studying this chapter, you should be familiar with the meaning and use of the following terms and BASIC statements:

Literal
Semicolon (in PRINT)
Format of output
Message prompt
Report headings
Column headings
TAB function
Argument (of TAB)
Reference column
Shift factor
Column width
PRINT USING statement
Formatting symbol
Floating character
Field format
Format (or image) line
Colon (in format line)

EXERCISES

For the following exercises, use the print zone that is standard on your system.

1. Write PRINT statements to center each of the following headings over a report of the indicated width.

Heading	Report Width
(a) PAYROLL REPORT	56 columns
(b) GRADUATING SENIORS	44 columns
(c) PROSPECTIVE RETIREMENT ROSTER	65 columns
(d) MONTHLY SALES REPORT	72 columns
(e) DEAN'S SCHOLARS FALL, 1983	36 columns
(f) ECONOMIC FORECASTS FOR 1984–1985 VAN ISHING INVESTMENTS, INC.	132 columns
(g) STATISTICAL SUMMARY USFL TEAMS FOR 1983 SEASON	80 columns
(h) UNEMPLOYMENT APPLICATIONS REPORT LOS ANGELES, CALIFORNIA SEPTEMBER, 1983	75 columns

2. Write statements that will place the following variables or literals at the indicated columns.

(a) N$ at column 1
N at column 31
P at column 41
X1 at column 55

(b) A at column 3
K at column 11
H at column 25
Q$ at column 35
A$ at column 50

(c) NAME at column 6
NUMBER at column 21
AGE at column 28
DOCTOR at column 36
DIAGNOSIS at column 50
CHARGES at column 66

(d) X$ at column 4
Y$ at column 24
TA at column 50
TB at column 55
TC at column 60

(e) F$ in column 1
X1 through X5 in five equal columns of 9 spaces width with the first beginning at column 26

(f) BRANCH at column 4
The twelve, three-letter abbreviations for the months of the year in equal columns 6 spaces wide with the first to begin at column 23
TOTAL UNITS at column 102

3. Give the column at which each entry in the print list of the following PRINT statements will appear.

```
(a) 190  PRINT , "    INVENTORY REPORT"
(b) 320  PRINT "   NAME","RATING",,"GRADE"
(c) 285  PRINT A3$; TAB(25); C$; TAB(40); SX
(d) 410  PRINT TAB(4); S; TAB(9); F; TAB(24); Z$; TAB(55); U
(e) 195  PRINT "    "; CX,, R$; TAB(75); K
(f) 220  LET J = 18
    230  PRINT P$; TAB(J); T; TAB(J + 11); Q; TAB(J + 23); Y
(g) 110  LET R = 35
    420  PRINT TAB(R - 29); E$; TAB(R); F$; TAB(R + 15); L
(h) 310  LET X = 25
    405  PRINT TAB(X - 21); A$; TAB(X - 10); V; TAB(X); W;
    410  PRINT TAB(X + 9); R1$; TAB(X + 32); GA$
(i) 180  LET A = 26
    190  LET B = 12
    320  PRINT X$; TAB(A); W1; TAB(A + B); W2;
    330  PRINT TAB(A + 2 * B); W3; TAB(A + 40); TW
```

(j)
```
210  LET Z = 30
220  LET N = 9
370  PRINT TAB(Z - 18); LA$; TAB(Z - N); K1; TAB(Z);
380  PRINT K2; TAB(Z + N); K3; TAB(Z + 2 * N); K4;
390  PRINT TAB(Z + 3 * N + 5); TK
```

4. Give the output that will be produced by the following PRINT USING statements:

(a)
```
170  LET X = 319.5
180  LET Y = 6 * X
190  PRINT USING "$###.##          $##,###.##", X, Y
```

(b)
```
440  LET P$ = "RONALD THOMAS"
450  LET C = 367.98
450  LET R = 0.1
460  LET D = C * R
470  LET S$ = "####################          $$$$#.##"
480  PRINT USING S$, P$, D
```

(c)
```
390  LET A = 467
400  LET B = 756
410  LET S = A + B
420  LET D = A - B
430  S$ = "+####       +####      +#####      +#####"
440  PRINT USING S$, A, B, S, D
```

(d)
```
220  LET N = 200
230  LET K = N * N
240  PRINT USING  "-$$,$$#          $$,$$$,$##", N, K
```

(e)
```
100  LET M$ = "123-546"
110  LET T = 3.7697
120  LET R = T / 5
130  LET E = T * 500
140  PRINT USING 150, T, R, E
150: ##.##        #.###        #.##^^^^        >###########
```

PROGRAMMING PROBLEMS

Write programs in BASIC to accomplish the tasks described by each of the following problems. Be sure to carefully document each program.

1. Rewrite the program for Programming Problem 1 at the end of Chapter 4 to have appropriate title and column headings.
2. Write a program to prepare an inventory report for Sam's Market from the data below.

Item Name	Unit Size	Unit Price	Quantity	Order
Bologna	12 oz	1.59	13	7
Cheese	16 oz	2.79	26	14
Ham	3 lb	11.99	14	6
Bread	6 oz	1.25	32	18
Milk	1 qt	1.09	26	19
Ice Cream	2 qt	3.09	21	9

3. Revise the program for Programming Problem 6 of Chapter 4 to provide headings. Note that the name of the store should appear at the top of the report in the main heading.
4. Redo the program for Programming Problem 7 of Chapter 5 so that it will produce all appropriate headings on the output. Also, place dollar signs in front of all appropriate columns.
5. Modify the program for Programming Problem 2 of Chapter 5 to include all necessary headings and other literals. The store name should appear in the title.

6. Revise the program for Programming Problem 11 of Chapter 5 to include all necessary headings and other literals. Both the city and date should appear in the main heading.
7. A computer usage report is to be prepared for the Databyte Co. from the following data.

User's Name	Classification	Sign-ons	CPU Time
Youngblood's	Commercial	13	12:27.63
Gigi's	Commercial	2	0:25.71
Jock University	Educational	524	201:11.54
Payroll	Administrative	2	3:16.76
Tenth National Bank	Commercial	72	324:46.49
Bolt High School	Educational	216	63:48.34
First Church	Special	1	2:05.27
Hook's Pharmacy	Commercial	7	3:28.19

Write a program to print the report with all headings. The date of the report (you supply that) should be assigned to a variable and then printed as part of the main heading.
8. Modify the program for Programming Problem 9 of Chapter 4 to print the six columns of data all on one print line. Also, remember to provide for all appropriate headings.
9. Write a program to read two numbers and calculate the sum, difference, product, and quotient of the two numbers plus the reciprocal of each. Print the original two numbers and the six calculated values on one line with column headings.
10. Rewrite the program for Programming Problem 5 of Chapter 5 to print on a single print line all seven values to be printed. Remember to print all headings and other appropriate literals.
11. Revise the program for Programming Problem 13 of Chapter 5 to print all five of the input data fields plus the two calculated values all on one line. Also, be sure to provide for all headings and other necessary literals.
12. A Cassette Tape Sales Report is to be prepared from the following data.

Brand of Tape	Number of Tapes Sold of Length (Minutes)			
	46	60	90	120
Maxell	134	534	894	378
TDK	678	1655	2304	1732
Hissalot	309	987	578	112
Sony	465	890	1425	576
Memorex	538	1008	1521	798
BASF	843	1782	2833	1689

The total sales for each brand of tape is to be calculated as well as final totals for each tape length and total sales. The input data plus the total sales for each brand should be printed on one line, with the five totals on a single line at the bottom of the report. All headings and other literals should be included as needed.
13. Another inventory report for Sam's Market (see Problem 2) is needed. The new report should calculate the total cost of each of the items *to be ordered* as well as accumulating totals for the number of items in stock, the number of items to be ordered, and the total cost of all the items to be ordered. There should be only one print line for each inventory item. Headings and other literals must be included on the report.

14. Prepare an Absentee Summary Report for Knoall College. The data, as given below, provides daily absentee figures by department for one week. The report will need to include the following calculated values: the sum *and* average of the absentee data by department, the sum *and* average by day, and an overall sum and average figure. The departmental data, including the two calculated values, should be printed all on a single line; the daily sums and averages should be printed on two total lines at the end of the report. The dates of the report should be read and printed in the main heading.

Report Dates: 2-20-84 through 2-24-84

Department Name	Number of Reported Absentees for				
	Monday	**Tuesday**	**Wednesday**	**Thursday**	**Friday**
History	79	71	62	55	72
Business	51	43	46	52	66
English	87	86	76	81	94
Mathematics	37	36	29	37	42
Chemistry	31	26	29	30	35
Psychology	33	24	27	33	30
Biology	43	38	34	36	49
Education	36	31	38	47	55

CHAPTER 7

PROGRAM CONTROL. PART I

All computer processing procedures, no matter how complex, are composed of a combination of three basic operations: input/output, arithmetic, and logic. In Chapters 3, 4, and 6, we studied various methods that are available in BASIC for the input and output of data. Chapter 5 was an introduction to arithmetic operations. In this chapter and in Chapter 8, we will look at the third type of fundamental operation. These two chapters will be devoted to a survey of the several statements in BASIC and programming techniques that allow us to check a condition, such as the value of a certain variable, and vary the sequence of the program on the basis of the results of the check. We have already seen one simple example of this in the use of the IF–THEN statement to provide a logical end to our programs. We will begin with a more complete discussion of the uses of the IF–THEN statement.

7-1 CONDITIONAL BRANCHING WITH THE IF–THEN STATEMENT

The IF–THEN statement has two basic forms. The first is:

ln1 **IF** *condition* **THEN** *ln2*

which we have been using since Chapter 4 to provide a logical end to our programs. The second form of the IF–THEN statement has the general form:

ln1 **IF** *condition* **THEN** *statement*

where *condition* has the same meaning as in the first form, and *statement* can be any *executable* BASIC statement (except END in compiled BASICs). Unlike the first form of the IF–THEN, which always redirects the program on the basis of the results of the condition, this form will usually proceed to the next step following the IF–THEN regardless of the results of the condition. The difference here is that the statement at the end of the IF–THEN will be executed *only if the condition is true*. As an example of this, consider the following set of statements:

```
340  IF T < 10 THEN LET S = S + T
350  LET F = F + T
```

No matter what the value of T, the statement at line 350 will be executed, and T will be added to F. However, T will be added to S only when it has a value less than 10. Both IF–THEN structures are illustrated in Figure 7-1.

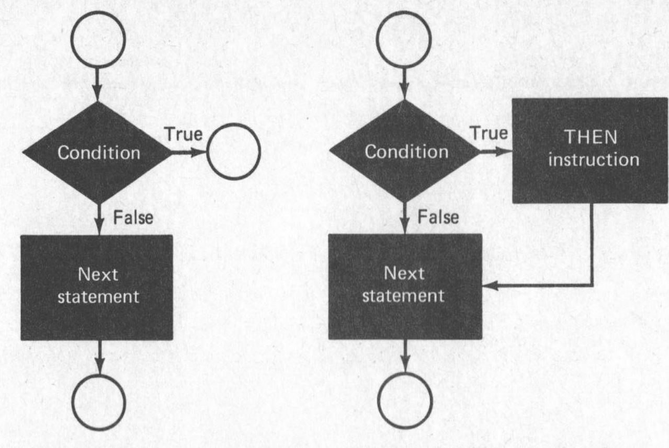

(a) The IF-THEN line number form (b) The IF-THEN statement form

FIGURE 7-1
The IF-THEN structures

Let us examine two short programs using the IF–THEN statement. First, consider the following program that simply finds the sum of the integers from 1 through 100.

```
 10 REM  THIS PROGRAM FINDS THE SUM OF
 20 REM  THE FIRST 100 POSITIVE INTEGERS
 30 REM
 40 LET S = 0
 50 LET N = 0
 60 LET N = N + 1
 70 LET S = S + N
 80 IF N < 100 THEN 60
 90 PRINT "THE SUM OF THE FIRST 100"
100 PRINT "POSITIVE INTEGERS IS"; S
110 END
```

```
THE SUM OF THE FIRST 100
POSITIVE INTEGERS IS 5050
```

Here, N is used as a **counter** to count off the numbers, and S keeps a continuous sum of the numbers. The statement at line 80 is used to stop the program when the counter reaches the maximum desired value. In other words, as long as N is less than 100, the program is directed back to line 60 where N is **incremented** (increased) by 1 until it reaches 100, at which time the sum is printed and the program ends. This process is shown in the flowchart in Figure 7-2. (See Section 6-1 for a similar example.)

As a second example, the following program reads a list of integers and finds the total number of positive numbers, negative numbers, and zeros.

```
 10 REM  THIS PROGRAM WILL READ A LIST OF NUMBERS
 20 REM  AND FIND THE TOTAL NUMBER OF NEGATIVE NUMBERS,
 30 REM  POSITIVE NUMBERS, AND ZEROS IN THE LIST
 40 REM
 50 READ TN, TZ, TP
 60 READ N
 70 IF N = 99999 THEN 190
 80 IF N < 0 THEN TN = TN + 1
 90 IF N = 0 THEN TZ = TZ + 1
100 IF N > 0 THEN TP = TP + 1
110 GOTO 60
120 PRINT "THE LIST CONTAINS"; TN; "NEGATIVE NUMBERS"
130 PRINT "THE LIST CONTAINS"; TZ; "ZEROS"
140 PRINT "THE LIST CONTAINS"; TP; "POSITIVE NUMBERS"
150 DATA 0,0,0,45,387,-76,4,-8,0,-42,9,-21,0,-7,-39
160 DATA 55,4,8,-3,0,7,-11,-8,0,0,-44,78,-3,0,12,-1
```

```
170 DATA -833,71,0,-19,-9165,-7,23,-81,1,54,1,125
180 DATA 34,-104,0,89,34,112,58,-214,-9,66,99999
190 END

THE LIST CONTAINS 20 NEGATIVE NUMBERS
THE LIST CONTAINS 8 ZEROS
THE LIST CONTAINS 22 POSITIVE NUMBERS
```

The three IF statements at lines 80, 90, and 100 are the key to this program. At line 80, 1 is added to TN, the total of the negative numbers, *only if N is less than zero*. Likewise, the total number of zeros, TZ, is increased by 1 at line 90 whenever N is zero; and TP, the total number of positive numbers, is incremented by 1 at line 100 if N is greater than zero. This procedure is illustrated in Figure 7-3.

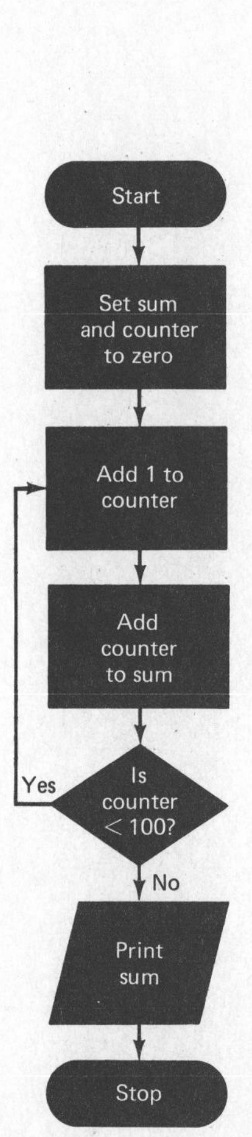

FIGURE 7-2
Flowchart for adding first 100 positive integers

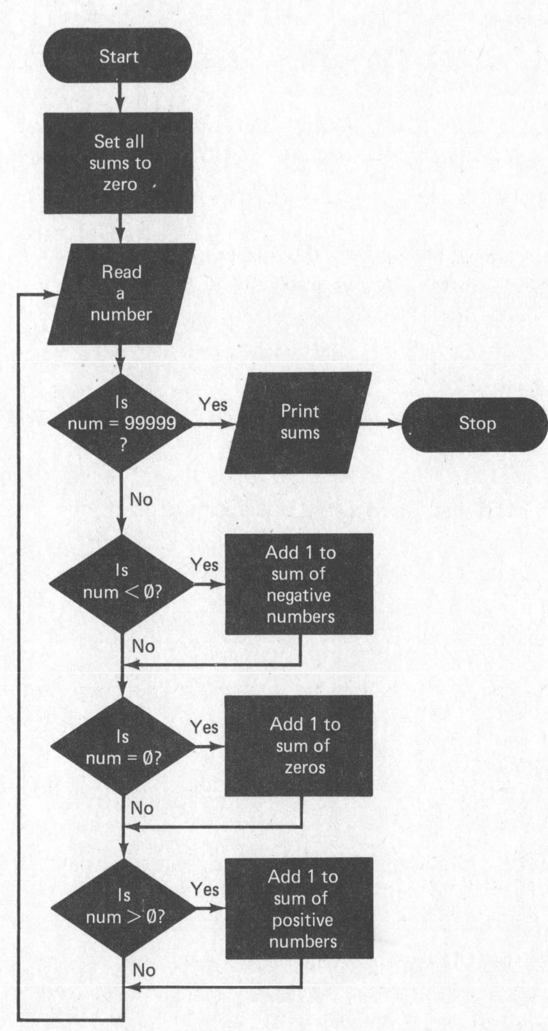

FIGURE 7-3
Flowchart for finding sum of positives, negatives, and zeros

7-2 AN EXAMPLE: PAYROLL REPORT

This section presents an example that illustrates a simple use of the IF-THEN statement other than to provide a logical end to a program.

Problem: A payroll report is to be prepared that calculates each employee's weekly pay, taking into account overtime earnings. Input will be the employee's name, hours worked, and hourly pay rate. Output will be the input data plus the weekly pay. The pay is calculated according to the following:

TABLE 7-1

Data for Weekly Payroll Report Problem

Employee Name	Hours Worked	Hourly Pay Rate
Ed Jones	35.2	5.25
Mary Epps	40	6.5
Paul Wyre	32	7.25
Gail Pope	40.4	5.25
Lucy Ing	43.6	5.5
Al Napper	36	4.75
Fred King	44	6.25

1. If the number of hours worked does not exceed 40, the pay is the hours worked times the hourly rate.
2. If the number of hours worked is more than 40, the employee receives the regular rate for the first 40 hours, with time-and-a-half (1.5 times the hourly rate) for all hours over 40.

Totals are to be accumulated for the number of employees, the number of employees with overtime, and the total payroll. Data for this problem is provided in Table 7-1.

The solution to this problem is outlined by the following sequence of steps:

1. Print report and column headings.
2. Set total accumulators for number of employees, employees with overtime, and total payroll equal to zero.
3. Read an employee pay record.
4. Check to see if this is the last record. If it is, go to step 13; if not, proceed to the next step.
5. Check to see if the hours worked is over 40. If so, go to step 8; otherwise, go on to the next step.
6. Calculate the weekly pay as hours times rate without overtime.
7. Go to step 10.
8. Calculate the weekly pay to include overtime.
9. Add 1 to the total number of employees receiving overtime.
10. Print a detailed line giving employee pay data.
11. Add 1 to the total number of employees, and add the pay to the total payroll.
12. Go to step 3.
13. Print totals for number of employees, employees with overtime, and total payroll.
14. Stop.

This procedure is pictorially illustrated by the flowchart in Figure 7-4.

There is nothing new in this program through the READ at 270, that is, the part corresponding to steps 1 through 3 above. The IF at 280,

```
280 IF H < 0 THEN 550
```

provides for a logical end to the program in the same manner as in the previous examples.

The part of this program that merits our attention involves lines 320 through 510, which are shown below with the REM statements deleted.

```
320 IF H > 40 THEN 420
                     :
360 LET P = H * R
370 GOTO 480
                     :
420 LET P = 40 * R + 1.5 * R * (H - 40)
```

```
430 LET TV = TV + 1
                        :
480 PRINT E$, H, " $"; R, "$"; P
490 LET TE = TE + 1
500 LET TP = TP + P
510 GOTO 270
```

These lines relate to steps 5 through 12. At line 320, a check is made to see if the employee has worked more than 40 hours. If the answer is yes (H > 40), then the program branches to line 420 where pay is calculated *to include overtime*. Line 430 updates the total number of employees earning overtime. Processing then proceeds to lines 480 through 510 where the detailed line is printed at 480, the total number of employees and total payroll are updated at 490 and 500, and processing is sent back to the READ by 510 for the next record. On the other hand, if the number of hours worked is *not* greater than 40, then the program is *not* sent to 420 but continues to 360 where pay *without* overtime is calculated. Note that the GOTO at 370 directs the program to line 480, causing it to skip over the section that processes for overtime, but, like the overtime branch, it will proceed through lines 480 to 510. In other words, all employees are processed by the statements

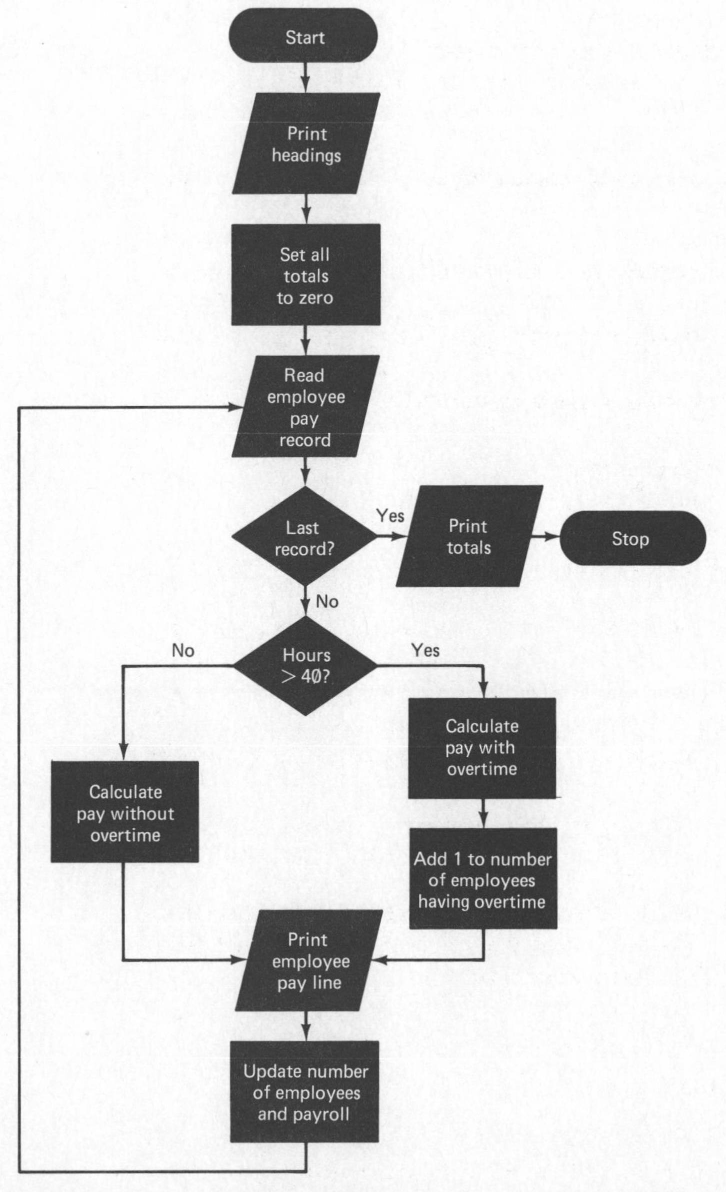

FIGURE 7-4
Flowchart for weekly payroll report problem

through 320 and from 480 on, but *only* overtime earners are processed by the statements at lines 420 and 430, and only nonovertime earners are processed by the statements at lines 360 and 370.

The remainder of the program beyond line 510 involves the printing of the final totals and the data list; this is nothing new. A complete program listing and run follow.

```
 10 REM   PAYROLL REPORT
 20 REM
 30 REM   VARIABLES ARE DEFINED AS --
 40 REM
 50 REM             E$ = EMPLOYEE NAME
 60 REM              H = HOURS WORKED
 70 REM              R = HOURLY PAY RATE
 80 REM              P = WEEKLY PAY
 90 REM             TE = TOTAL EMPLOYEES
100 REM             TV = TOTAL EMPLOYEES WITH OVERTIME
110 REM             TP = TOTAL PAYROLL
120 REM
130 REM   PRINT HEADINGS AND SET TOTALS TO ZERO
140 REM
150 PRINT , "WEEKLY PAYROLL REPORT"
160 PRINT
170 PRINT
180 PRINT " EMPLOYEE", "HOURS", " HOURLY", " WEEKLY"
190 PRINT "   NAME", "WORKED", "PAY RATE", "  PAY"
200 PRINT
210 LET TE = 0
220 LET TV = 0
230 LET TP = 0
240 REM
250 REM   READ AND PROCESS PAYROLL DATA
260 REM
270 READ E$, H, R
280 IF H < 0 THEN 550
290 REM
300 REM   CHECK FOR OVERTIME
310 REM
320 IF H > 40 THEN 420
330 REM
340 REM   CALCULATE PAY WHEN NO OVERTIME IS DUE
350 REM
360 LET P = H * R
370 GOTO 480
380 REM
390 REM   CALCULATE PAY AND UPDATE NUMBER
400 REM   OF EMPLOYEES WHO EARNED OVERTIME
410 REM
420 LET P = 40 * R + 1.5 * R * (H - 40)
430 LET TV = TV + 1
440 REM
450 REM   PRINT RESULTS AND UPDATE TOTAL EMPLOYEES
460 REM   AND TOTAL PAY FOR ALL EMPLOYEES PROCESSED
470 REM
480 PRINT E$, H, " $"; R, "$"; P
490 LET TE = TE + 1
500 LET TP = TP + P
510 GOTO 270
520 REM
530 REM   PRINT FINAL TOTALS
540 REM
550 PRINT
560 PRINT "TOTAL EMPLOYEES ="; TE
```

```
570 PRINT "TOTAL WITH OVERTIME ="; TV
580 PRINT "TOTAL PAYROLL = $"; TP
590 REM
600 REM  DATA LIST
610 REM
620 DATA "ED JONES", 35.2, 5.25, "MARY EPPS", 40, 6.5
630 DATA "PAUL WYRE", 32, 7.25, "GAIL POPE", 40.4, 5.25
640 DATA "LUCY ING", 43.6, 5.5, "AL NAPPER", 36, 4.75
650 DATA "FRED KING", 44, 6.25, "Z", -1, 0
660 END
```

```
          WEEKLY PAYROLL REPORT


 EMPLOYEE     HOURS        HOURLY       WEEKLY
   NAME       WORKED      PAY RATE       PAY

ED JONES       35.2        $ 5.25      $ 184.8
MARY EPPS      40          $ 6.5       $ 260
PAUL WYRE      32          $ 7.25      $ 232
GAIL POPE      40.4        $ 5.25      $ 213.15
LUCY ING       43.6        $ 5.5       $ 249.7
AL NAPPER      36          $ 4.75      $ 171
FRED KING      44          $ 6.25      $ 287.5

TOTAL EMPLOYEES = 7
TOTAL WITH OVERTIME = 3
TOTAL PAYROLL = $ 1598.15
```

7-3 LOGICAL (CONDITIONAL) EXPRESSIONS

The condition that determines what action will be taken by an IF–THEN statement is actually a much more complex expression than we have seen thus far. In this and later sections of this chapter, we will explore some of the more complex features of this part of the IF statement.

What we have thus far been calling a condition is actually more formally known as a **logical** or **conditional expression** and has the general form:

expression relational operator expression

Here either expression is any legal BASIC variable, literal, or mathematical expression where both must be of the same type: string or numeric. The **relational operator** is any of the six operators that were given in Table 4-2. Let us look at some examples of more general logical expressions.

In all of our work to this point, we have written only logical expressions of the form:

variable relational operator literal

which means expressions like:

```
A < 100
P$ = "FINI"
```

While the variable does not actually have to be listed first with the literal second, this is the most common way of writing logical expressions connecting a variable and literal.

A relational operator may connect two variables like this:

```
X => Y
N$ <> J$
```

Or, in the case of numeric values, a variable and mathematical expression or two mathematical expressions may be compared as shown below:

```
R <> (A + B) / 2
X + Y > X * Y
```

Again, when a variable is compared to a mathematical expression, the variable does not have to be written first; however, that is the usual way of writing this type of logical expression. In logical expressions that involve mathematical expressions, the mathematical operations are performed *before* the comparison is made. We will discuss the order of operations in logical expressions in more detail in Section 7-4.

When evaluated, a logical expression can have only one of two values; it must be either *true* or *false*. This is referred to as the **truth value** of the expression. If the expression has a truth value of true, the THEN part of the IF–THEN statement is executed; if the truth value is false, the THEN part is skipped. The following short program will illustrate this:

```
10 REM   PROGRAM TO ILLUSTRATE TRUTH VALUE
20 REM
30 INPUT "ENTER TWO NUMBERS"; A, B
40 IF A = 0 THEN 90
50 LET TV$ = "FALSE"
60 IF A + B < A * B THEN LET TV$ = "TRUE"
70 PRINT "THE LOGICAL EXPRESSION IS ";TV$
80 GOTO 30
90 END
```

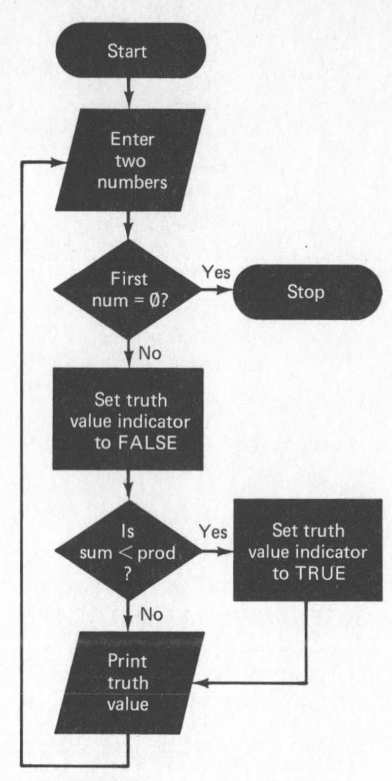

FIGURE 7-5
Flowchart for truth value example

This program asks for two numbers to be entered by means of the interactive INPUT statement. A message, TV$, is set to FALSE at line 50 and is changed to TRUE at 60 *only if the logical expression is evaluated to have a truth value of true*. Therefore, at line 70, TRUE will be printed if the logical expression in 60 is true; otherwise, FALSE will be printed. Let us look at a run for several pairs of numbers.

```
ENTER TWO NUMBERS? 1,2
THE LOGICAL EXPRESSION IS FALSE
ENTER TWO NUMBERS? 2,3
THE LOGICAL EXPRESSION IS TRUE
ENTER TWO NUMBERS? 4,2
THE LOGICAL EXPRESSION IS TRUE
ENTER TWO NUMBERS? 3,1
THE LOGICAL EXPRESSION IS FALSE
ENTER TWO NUMBERS? 2,2
THE LOGICAL EXPRESSION IS FALSE
ENTER TWO NUMBERS? 0,0
```

Note that the logical expression $A + B < A * B$ in the IF at line 60 asks the simple question, Is the sum of the two numbers less than the product? For the first pair of numbers, 1 and 2, the sum is 3 while the product is only 2; hence the logical expression (sum < product) is false. In the second case, the sum is 5 while the product is 6; this makes the condition true. Check the other three pairs of numbers to see that the proper truth values have been printed.

7-4 LOGICAL OPERATORS

Many problems require that more than one condition be tested in order for the proper programming sequence to be followed. For example, suppose that a list of numbers is to be read and only those between 0 and 100 are to be printed. This would require that a test be made to see if the number is greater than zero plus a second check to verify that the same number is less than 100. This might mean two IF statements, something like those in the following program:

```
 10 REM   PROGRAM WITH MULTIPLE CONDITIONS
 20 REM
 30 READ N
 40 IF N = -9999 THEN 100
 50 IF N <= 0 THEN 30
 60 IF N => 100 THEN 30
 70 PRINT N,
 80 GOTO 30
 90 DATA 45,1,165,0,99,-65,14,100,83,587,-9999
100 END
```

which will print:

```
45              1               99              14              83
```

The IF at line 50 throws out any number that is less than or equal to (not greater than) 0, while that at 60 disregards all values that are equal to or greater than (not less than) 100. If *either* condition is found to be false, the number is omitted from the list. This might have been written with the two IFs at lines 50 and 60 combined into a *single* statement as follows:

```
 10 REM   PROGRAM WITH COMPOUND CONDITION
 20 REM
 30 READ N
 40 IF N = -9999 THEN 100
 50 IF N <= 0 OR N => 100 THEN 30
 70 PRINT N
 80 GOTO 30
 90 DATA 45,1,165,0,99,-65,14,100,83,587,-9999
100 END
```

The new IF statement at 50 states the condition more as you would say it in words: IF either N <= 0 OR N => 100, THEN go to line 30 and read the next value for N.

The condition in the IF at line 50 in the last example is an illustration of how two (or more) simple conditions can be combined by using a **logical operator** to form what is called a **compound condition** or **compound logical expression**. (These conditions are also referred to as **Boolean expressions**.) Table 7-2 gives a summary of the most commonly used logical operators and their meanings. Table 7-3 summarizes the truth values that the compound conditions will have if the truth values of the individual expressions are known. Let us look at some examples that should help to clarify the use of compound conditions.

Consider the following compound logical expression:

```
A < 10 AND K > 25
```

When will this be true? Let us consider the following cases:

1. A = 3 and K = 31
2. A = 18 and K = 45
3. A = 37 and K = 19

From Tables 7-2 and 7-3, we can see that since the two individual conditions are linked with **AND**, the combined condition will be true only when *both* are true; that is, only when A has a value that is less than 10 *AND* K has a value that is greater than 25. For the

TABLE 7-2

Summary of Logical Operators

Operator	Meaning	Operator	Meaning
NOT	Reverses the truth value of a logical expression. A false expression becomes true and vice versa.	XOR*	Connects two logical expressions so that the compound expression is true whenever *only one*—*not both*—of the individual expressions is true and is false otherwise.
AND	Connects two logical expressions so that the compound expression is true *only* when *both* of the individual expressions are true and is false otherwise.	IMP*	Connects two logical expressions so that the compound expression is always true except when the first condition is true *and* the second is false.
OR	Connects two logical expressions so that the compound expression is true whenever *either* or *both* of the individual expressions are true and is false otherwise.	EQV*	Connects two logical expressions so that the compound expression is true whenever both individual conditions have the *same* truth value.

*This operator is not available on all forms of BASIC.

first set of values, both conditions are satisfied, hence the combined expression will be true. In the second and third cases, one and both, respectively, of the two individual conditions are false, which yields a false truth value for a logical expression linked with AND.

Now, consider the same compound expression as above but with OR as the logical operator:

```
A < 10 OR K > 25
```

Again, from Tables 7-2 and 7-3, we see that a compound expression with **OR** is true in all cases except when *both* individual conditions are false. Using the above three sets of values for A and K, we can see that this expression will be true for the first and second pairs of numbers and false for the third because only with the third pair will *both* conditions be false.

The three remaining operators, **XOR**, **IMP**, and **EQV**, are less frequently used and are not available on many systems. They are included here primarily for reference. If we write the above compound expression using the logical operator XOR, we have:

```
A < 10 XOR K > 25
```

TABLE 7-3

Truth Values for Compound Logical Expressions

Exp1	Exp2	Exp1 AND Exp2	Exp1 OR Exp2	Exp1 XOR Exp2	Exp1 IMP Exp2	Exp1 EQV Exp2
True	True	True	True	False	True	True
True	False	False	True	True	False	False
False	True	False	True	True	True	False
False	False	False	False	False	True	True

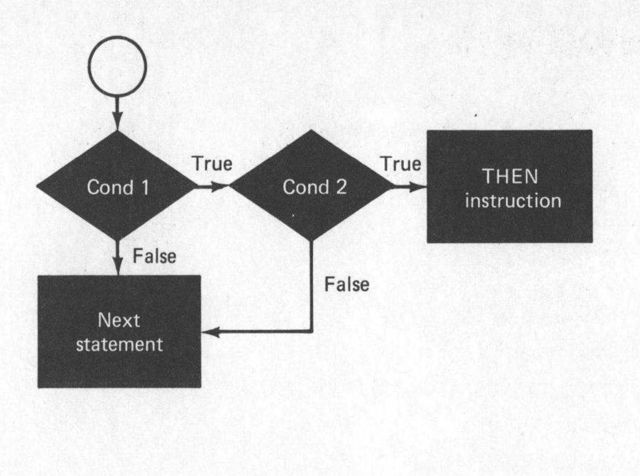

(*a*) Condition with AND

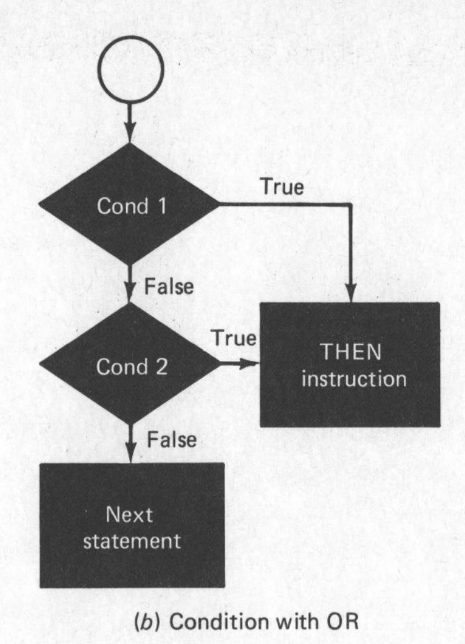

(*b*) Condition with OR

FIGURE 7-6
Comparison of logic for AND and OR

XOR is known as the **exclusive OR**, meaning that the case where both conditions are true is false instead of true as it is with the more common OR, or the **inclusive OR**. This means that, for the above pairs of numbers, only the middle set will yield a truth value of true for this expression with XOR. Using IMP, the expression becomes:

```
A < 1Ø IMP K > 25
```

which is known as an **implication**; that is, the first condition *implies* the second. Such an expression is always true except when the first condition is true and the second is false; a true assumption cannot lead to a false conclusion. Thus, this implication is true for all three of the above sets of values. With the final operator, EQV, the above expression becomes:

```
A < 1Ø EQV K > 25
```

which is known as an **equivalence**, which means that either condition implies the other. An EQV is true only when both conditions have the same truth value. This expression is true for the first and third pairs of values and false for the second one. Some additional examples of compound logical expressions and their truth values are given in Table 7-4.

As one final point on compound logical expressions before we return to the use of IF statements in programs, you should be aware that more than one logical operator can

TABLE 7-4

Examples of Compound Logical Expressions

Compound Expression	Values of Variables	Truth Value
F = Ø AND Y < 1ØØ	F = 0 and Y = 0	True
V <> Ø OR Z$ = "XXX"	V = 0 and Z$ = "XXX"	True
Q <= 75 XOR R = 1ØØ	Q = 53 and R = 100	False
S$ = "FLAG" AND P = Ø	S$ = "FLAG" and P = 1	False
T => 9 OR N > 19	T = 9 and N = 80	True
H = Ø XOR L <> Ø	H = 0 and L = 0	True
H < 1Ø OR PT > Ø	H = 20 and PT = 0	False
R > S IMP R > Ø	R = 10 and S = 5	True
A < B EQV B > 4	A = 6 and B = 2	True
N = -M IMP N > Ø	N = −14 and M = 14	False

appear in a single expression. That is, such compound conditions as the following are permitted by most versions of BASIC:

```
X = Ø AND Y < 1ØØ AND T = P
F = G OR R <> Ø OR X$ = "PRINT-IT"
E < Ø AND T = X OR AX <> U
J = K + N OR S <> Ø AND Z > (3 * Q - W) / B
```

When multiple logical operators appear in the same expression, there is the question of which is done first? If only one type of operator is present, as in the first two examples above, there is no problem; AND, OR, and XOR all obey associative properties (see Section 5-1) so that the order in which the operations are performed does not matter. It is a different matter, however, when two *different* operators are involved, as in the last two examples. Here, order is important, and we must establish another order of operations for logical operations.

In evaluating complex logical expressions, the following order of operations should be observed:

1. Evaluate all mathematical expressions according to the order of operations given in Section 5-2.
2. NOT operators are evaluated from left to right.
3. AND operators are evaluated from left to right.
4. OR operators are evaluated from left to right.
5. XOR operators are evaluated from left to right.
6. IMP operators are evaluated from left to right.
7. EQV operators are evaluated from left to right.

As with mathematical expressions, the order of steps 2 through 7 can be changed with the use of parentheses to group operations.

While it is possible to construct very complex logical expressions by using a combination of several operators in a single expression, this is not a wise practice for the beginning programmer. Until you have more programming experience, you would be well advised to avoid using more than one or two operators in a single expression or mixing operator types.

7-5 AN EXAMPLE: RETIREMENT ELIGIBILITY LIST

The example that follows illustrates a problem whose programming solution requires the use of multiple IF statements.

Problem: A retirement eligibility list is to be prepared from an employee data list. Input will consist of the employee's name, age, years with the company, and accumulated merit points. Output will be a list of employee names with YES printed beside the names of those who qualify to retire and NO by all others. In order to be eligible to retire, an employee must satisfy the following conditions:

1. Be at least 55 years of age

and

2. Have at least 20 years experience with the company *or* have accumulated at least 500 merit points

The percentage of all employees eligible to retire is to be printed at the bottom of the report. Data is given in Table 7-5.

TABLE 7-5

Data for Retirement Eligibility Problem

Employee Name	Employee Age	Years with Company	Merit Points
R. Henson	57	18	487
Y. Franklin	54	26	645
A. Thomas	61	29	377
T. Underwood	59	19	426
C. Williams	51	22	475
P. Lockhart	64	31	734
N. Roberts	49	22	583

The solution to this problem is outlined as follows:

1. Print report and column headings.
2. Set totals for number of all employees and number eligible to retire equal to zero.
3. Read an employee data record.
4. Check for the last record. If found, go to step 14; otherwise, continue to the next step.
5. If employee's age is less than 55, go to step 10.
6. If the employee has less than 20 years experience with the company *and* fewer than 500 merit points, go to step 10.
7. Add 1 to the number of employees eligible to retire.
8. Set retirement eligibility message equal to YES.
9. Go to step 11.
10. Set retirement eligibility message equal to NO.
11. Print a detailed line showing an employee's name and retirement eligibility status.
12. Add 1 to the total number of employees.
13. Go to step 3.
14. Calculate percentage of employees eligible to retire.
15. Print percentage eligible to retire.
16. Stop.

This procedure is illustrated pictorially by the flowchart shown in Figure 7-7.

Before analyzing this program, let us be sure that you understand what is required for an employee to be eligible to retire. First, he or she must be at least 55 years of age; if not, then there is no retirement no matter how many years experience or merit points. If the age requirement is met, then the employee must have *either* 20 years or more with the company *or* at least 500 merit points; both are not necessary. In other words, the first condition (age) *plus* either one of the second two (experience or merit points) must be satisfied.

Steps 1 through 4 of the above outlined solution, corresponding to the program steps below through 280, involve no new processing techniques and should give you no trouble. The IF statements that form the heart of this program and direct the processing to select the employees who qualify for retirement are at lines 320 and 330. The section of the program with which we are most concerned is listed here (with REMs omitted).

```
320 IF A < 55 THEN 440
330 IF Y < 20 AND M < 500 THEN 440
                    :
380 LET TR = TR + 1
390 LET M$ = "YES"
400 GOTO 490
                    :
440 LET M$ = "NO"
                    :
490 PRINT N$,, "    "; M$
500 LET TE = TE + 1
510 GOTO 270
```

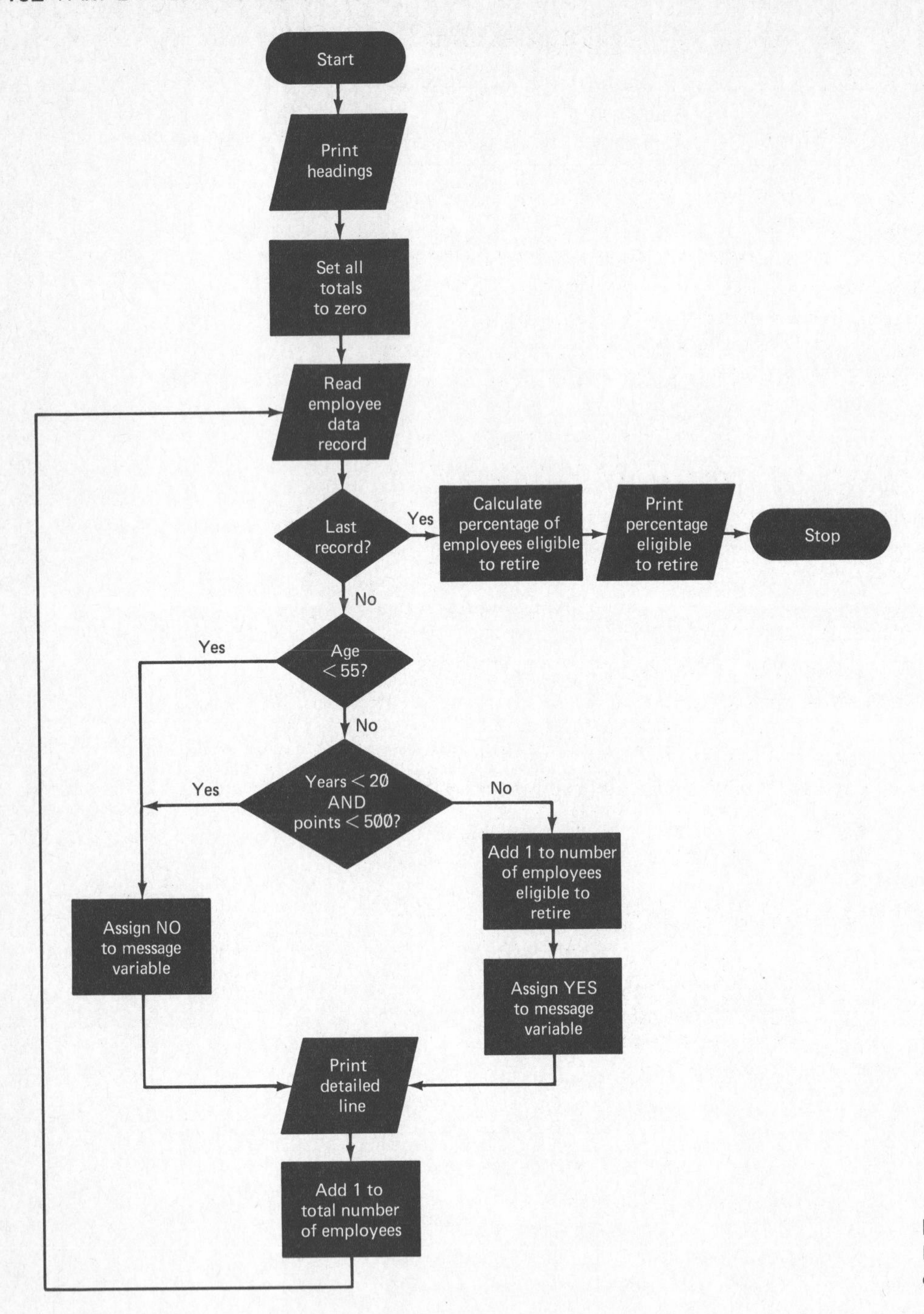

FIGURE 7-7
Flowchart for retirement eligibility problem

Since the age requirement must be met by all employees, the IF at 320 checks for this first. If the age is less than 55, then the employee does not qualify for retirement, hence the program is sent directly to line 440 where NO is assigned to a message variable that will indicate the retirement eligibility status. Since no other checks are required for this employee, processing drops straight through to lines 490 to 510 where the detailed line is printed, the total number of employees updated, and the program redirected back to the READ for the next employee's record. On the other hand, if the employee is 55 or older, then a second test must be made for the other conditions. This is done by the IF at line 330. Let us look at this statement a little more closely.

To understand what is happening at line 330, remember that a compound logical expression that involves AND is true only when all involved conditions are true. Look again at the expression in the IF in 330:

```
Y < 20 AND M < 500
```

This is true only when *both* of the second conditions are *not* met. That is, when this condition is true, the employee is not eligible for retirement, and a branch to 440 occurs with the same results as when the age was less than 55. Whenever either (or both) the number of years experience is 20 or more or the merit points amount to at least 500, one (or both) of the conditions will be false, and the branch to 440 will not occur. Processing will then continue with the number of employees eligible to retire updated at line 380 and YES assigned to the message variable at 390. Line 400 directs the program to the common statements at 490 through 510.

The remainder of the program simply processes the percentage of the employees eligible for retirement and contains no new programming concepts. The following is a complete program listing followed by a run:

```
 10 REM  COMPANY RETIREMENT ELIGIBILITY LIST
 20 REM
 30 REM  VARIABLES ARE DEFINED AS --
 40 REM
 50 REM         N$ = EMPLOYEE NAME
 60 REM          A = EMPLOYEE AGE
 70 REM          Y = YEARS WITH COMPANY
 80 REM          M = ACCUMULATED MERIT POINTS
 90 REM         TE = TOTAL EMPLOYEES
100 REM         TR = TOTAL ELIGIBLE FOR RETIREMENT
110 REM         PR = PERCENTAGE ELIGIBLE FOR RETIREMENT
120 REM         M$ = RETIREMENT MESSAGE INDICATOR
130 REM
140 REM  PRINT HEADINGS AND SET TOTALS TO ZERO
150 REM
160 PRINT "      RETIREMENT ELIGIBILITY LIST"
170 PRINT
180 PRINT
190 PRINT " EMPLOYEE",, " ELIGIBLE"
200 PRINT "   NAME",, "TO RETIRE?"
210 PRINT
220 LET TE = 0
230 LET TR = 0
240 REM
250 REM  READ AND PROCESS RETIREMENT DATA
260 REM
270 READ N$, A, Y, M
280 IF A < 0 THEN 550
290 REM
300 REM  CHECK FOR RETIREMENT ELIGIBILITY
310 REM
320 IF A < 55 THEN 440
330 IF Y < 20 AND M < 500 THEN 440
340 REM
350 REM  ADD 1 TO NUMBER OF ELIGIBLE RETIREES
360 REM  AND ASSIGN PROPER PRINT MESSAGE
370 REM
380 LET TR = TR + 1
390 LET M$ = "YES"
400 GOTO 490
410 REM
420 REM  ASSIGN PRINT MESSAGE FOR NON-RETIREE
430 REM
```

```
440 LET M$ = "NO"
450 REM
460 REM  PRINT NAME AND RETIREMENT ELIGIBILITY STATUS
470 REM  AND UPDATE TOTAL NUMBER OF ALL EMPLOYEES
480 REM
490 PRINT N$,, "   "; M$
500 LET TE = TE + 1
510 GOTO 270
520 REM
530 REM  PRINT PERCENTAGE ELIGIBLE FOR RETIREMENT
540 REM
550 LET PR = TR / TE * 100
560 PRINT
570 PRINT "PERCENTAGE EMPLOYEES ELIGIBLE"
580 PRINT "FOR RETIREMENT IS ";PR;"%"
590 REM
600 REM  DATA LIST
610 REM
620 DATA "R HENSON",57,18,487,"Y FRANKLIN",54,26,645
630 DATA "A THOMAS",61,29,377,"T UNDERWOOD",59,19,426
640 DATA "C WILLIAMS",51,22,475,"P LOCKHART",64,31,734
650 DATA "N ROBERTS",49,22,583,"X",-1,0,0
660 END
```

```
    RETIREMENT ELIGIBILITY LIST


 EMPLOYEE                     ELIGIBLE
   NAME                      TO RETIRE?

R HENSON                        NO
Y FRANKLIN                      NO
A THOMAS                        YES
T UNDERWOOD                     NO
C WILLIAMS                      NO
P LOCKHART                      YES
N ROBERTS                       NO

PERCENTAGE EMPLOYEES ELIGIBLE
FOR RETIREMENT IS 28.5714 %
```

There is one additional point that should be mentioned before leaving this example; this is in regard to the use of the **message variable**. In this program we could just as easily have used two separate PRINT statements. This might have modified the program something like this:

```
320 IF A < 55 THEN 490
330 IF Y < 20 AND M < 500 THEN 490
                      :
380 LET TR = TR + 1
390 PRINT N$,, "   YES"
400 GOTO 500
                      :
490 PRINT N$,, "   NO"
500 LET TE = TE + 1
510 GOTO 270
```

While it is true that we do not really benefit in this program from the use of the message variable, it is a very valuable tool, most useful when several different messages are involved and the PRINT statements are complex. We will see this technique again in the next chapter. (Where else in *this* chapter did we use a message variable?)

7-6 MORE ON WRITING IF–THEN STATEMENTS

As you have probably already guessed, there is almost always more than one way to write a logical expression. In this section, we will review the two IFs at lines 320 and 330 of the program in Section 7-5 and examine several alternative ways of expressing the conditions.

Once again, look at the two statements as they were expressed in the preceding example:

```
320  IF A < 55 THEN 440
330  IF Y < 20 AND M < 500 THEN 440
```

The compound condition at line 330 could have been avoided by the use of three IF statements, possibly something like this:

```
320  IF A < 55 THEN 440
330  IF Y => 20 THEN 380
335  IF M < 500 THEN 440
```

Line 320 is unchanged. Line 330 determines whether the employee has enough years experience to be eligible to retire. If so, processing is directed to 380 where the retirees are processed, skipping the last condition at 335. If not, then merit points are checked at 335 with the appropriate action being taken.

Of course, all three conditions could be included in one compound expression written as follows:

```
320  IF (A < 55) OR (Y < 20 AND M < 500) THEN 440
```

This simply combines the two separate statements into a single one. It states exactly the same conditions; this is, if either A < 55 or Y < 20 AND M < 500, then no retirement. Since AND operations are performed before ORs, the parentheses are unnecessary, but they are included here to make the expression more readable. This is probably a little more complex than you will want to tackle for now, but such statements are possible and not uncommon. With a bit more experience, you will find them less impressive.

One point about writing conditions that we have not yet discussed involves **logical negations** and the use of **NOT**. Above, we first wrote the conditions as:

```
320  IF A < 55 THEN 440
330  IF Y < 20 AND M < 500 THEN 440
```

We expressed all conditions in *negative* terms. That is, we wrote each expression in terms of the conditions that were necessary *not* to retire. What is the age requirement *to* retire? Age must be at least 55, or A => 55. The negation of this is what was written above, A < 55, or:

```
NOT(A => 55) = A < 55
```

In the same manner, the second condition *to* retire could be written as Y => 20 OR M => 500. The negative of this is then:

```
NOT(Y => 20 OR M => 500) = Y < 20 AND M < 500
```

or our two IFs might have been written as:

```
320  IF NOT (A => 55) THEN 440
330  IF NOT (Y => 20 OR M => 500) THEN 440
```

Table 7-6 summarizes some of the relations between an expression and its corresponding negation.

TABLE 7-6

Summary of Effects of Negations (NOT)

Original Expression	Negation NOT (Exp)
Single Expressions	
X = Y	X <> Y
X <>Y	X = Y
X < Y	X => Y
X > Y	X <= Y
X <= Y	X > Y
X => Y	X < Y
Compound Expressions	
Exp1 AND Exp2	NOT(Exp1) OR NOT(Exp2)
Exp1 OR Exp2	NOT(Exp1) AND NOT(Exp2)

7-7 THE IF–THEN–ELSE STRUCTURE

The IF–THEN statement introduced at the beginning of this chapter can be expressed in a **blocked structured** form something like the following:

```
IF   condition
        THEN   statement group 1
ENDIF
statement group 2
```

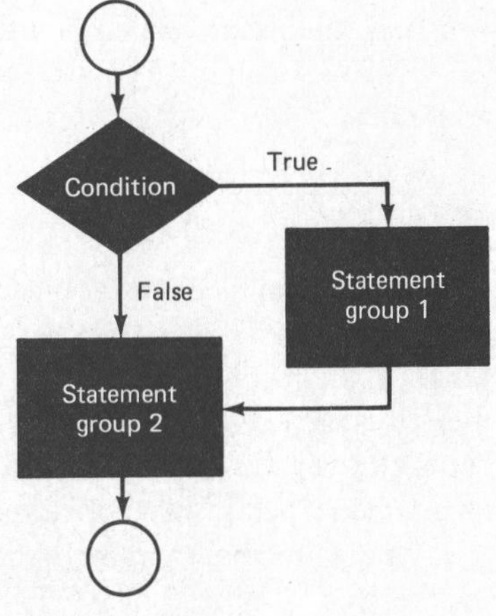

FIGURE 7-8
Blocked IF-THEN structure

where statement group 1 is executed whenever the condition in the IF is true, and statement group 2 logically follows the IF–THEN and is always executed. Figure 7-8 shows this in a flowchart.

It is usually very easy to translate the blocked structure into program statements if statement group 1 consists of a single statement. This, unfortunately, is usually not the case. When group 1 consists of several statements, it is frequently easier to state the condition as the *negation* of the original condition so that this group will be executed whenever the condition is *false* rather than true. The following short program is an example of this structure.

```
 10 REM  BLOCKED IF-THEN STRUCTURE
 20 REM
 30 READ N$, C
 40 IF N$ = "END" THEN 120
 50 IF C < 1000 THEN 80
 60    LET D = .1 * C
 70    LET C = C + D
 80 PRINT N$, "$"; C
 90 GOTO 30
100 DATA "TOM YAP", 700, "SARA NUNN", 1100
110 DATA "ED TUBB", 950, "ZACK COX", 1200, "END", 0
120 END

TOM YAP         $ 700
SARA NUNN       $ 1210
ED TUBB         $ 950
ZACK COX        $ 1320
```

In this program, lines 60 and 70 form statement group 1 (shown indented for clarity) in that their execution depends on the results of the condition in the IF at line 50. No matter what the value of C, processing always goes through to lines 80 and 90, either directly or

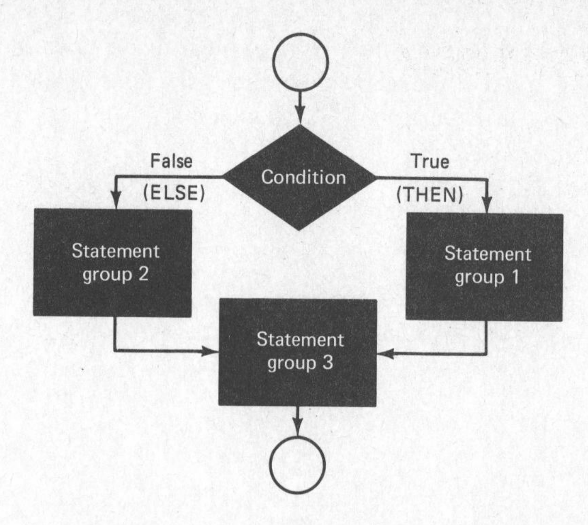

FIGURE 7-9
IF-THEN-ELSE structure

through lines 60 and 70. Lines 60 and 70 (statement group 1) are executed when the condition C < 1000 is false (or when *its* negation, C => 1000, is true). Lines 80 and 90 make up statement group 2.

The **IF–THEN–ELSE** structure, illustrated in Figure 7-9, is similar to the blocked IF–THEN except that it has *two* separate branches of statements that are executed depending on the results of the condition, each branch coming together at a later point in the processing. This structure can be outlined as:

```
IF  condition
        THEN  statement group 1
        ELSE  statement group 2
ENDIF
statement group 3
```

Here statement group 1 is executed if the condition is true, statement group 2 is executed when the condition is false, and statement group 3 follows the IF and whichever of the other two sets of statements that was performed. Here is an example.

```
 10 REM   IF-THEN-ELSE STRUCTURE
 20 REM
 30 READ N$, C
 40 IF N$ = "END" THEN 160
 50 IF C < 1000 THEN 90
 60   LET D = .2 * C
 70   LET Q$ = " "
 80 GOTO 110
 90   LET D = .1 * C
100   LET Q$ = "UNDER QUOTA"
110 LET C = C + D
120 PRINT N$, "$"; C, Q$
130 GOTO 30
140 DATA "TOM YAP", 700, "SARA NUNN", 1100
150 DATA "ED TUBB", 950, "ZACK COX", 1200, "END", 0
160 END
```

```
TOM YAP         $ 770          UNDER QUOTA
SARA NUNN       $ 1320
ED TUBB         $ 1045         UNDER QUOTA
ZACK COX        $ 1440
```

If the condition in the IF at line 50 is true, then the statements (group 1) at lines 90 and 100 are executed; if the condition is false, then the statements at lines 60 to 80 (group 2) are performed. In either case, processing goes to lines 110 to 130 (group 3).

Before leaving the IF–THEN–ELSE, let us look back through this chapter at the examples to see this structure in use. Both of the major examples in Sections 7-2 and 7-5 employ this structure. Look first at a segment from the first example.

```
320 IF H > 40 THEN 420
                    :
360 LET P = H * R
370 GOTO 480
                    :
420 LET P = 40 * R + 1.5 * R * (H - 40)
430 LET TV = TV + 1
                    :
480 PRINT E$, H, " $"; R, "$"; P
490 LET TE = TE + 1
500 LET TP = TP + P
510 GOTO 270
```

Can you pick out the three statement groups before reading any further? Group 1 consists of the statements at lines 420 and 430, group 2 consists of lines 360 and 370, and group 3 includes the four statements at lines 480 to 510. Now, here is a similar segment from the second example. See if you can locate the three statement groups for each IF.

```
320 IF A < 55 THEN 440
330 IF Y < 20 AND M < 500 THEN 440
                    :
380 LET TR = TR + 1
390 LET M$ = "YES"
400 GOTO 490
                    :
440 LET M$ = "NO"
                    :
490 PRINT N$,, "    "; M$
500 LET TE = TE + 1
510 GOTO 270
```

For both IFs, line 440 is statement group 1 while lines 490 to 510 form group 3. For the first IF, lines 330 to 400 are group 2, but since 330 is the second IF, its group 2 consists only of lines 380 to 400.

An actual IF–THEN–ELSE *statement* is available only with some versions of BASIC. Ask your instructor if your system has this statement and, if it does, to show you its exact format.

7-8 THE REPEAT–UNTIL AND WHILE–DO STRUCTURES

We have previously discussed and used loops in designing programming solutions. In this section, design of loop structures will be outlined a little more formally.

We will look at two basic loop structures: **REPEAT–UNTIL** and **WHILE–DO**. These are similar in general design, but the REPEAT–UNTIL has the IF for loop control at the bottom of the loop, whereas a WHILE–DO loop has it at the beginning. Let us look at the REPEAT–UNTIL first.

The general structure of a REPEAT–UNTIL loop is:

```
REPEAT
        statements
UNTIL   condition
next statement
```

This is just as simple as it looks. A block of statements is repeated until a condition is satisfied; once the condition becomes true, processing moves out of the loop to the next statement. As with the blocked IF, it is frequently more convenient to write the condition as a negation so that the loop is executed while the condition is *true* and exited when it becomes *false*. We saw one very good example of this—the program for adding the first 100 positive integers—in the first section of this chapter. Here it is again:

```
 10 REM  PROGRAM WITH REPEAT-UNTIL STRUCTURE
 20 REM
 30 LET S = 0
 40 LET N = 0
 50    LET N = N + 1
 60    LET S = S + N
 70    IF N < 100 THEN 50
 80 PRINT "THE SUM OF THE FIRST 100"
 90 PRINT "POSITIVE INTEGERS IS"; S
100 END
```

FIGURE 7-10
The REPEAT-UNTIL structure

The REPEAT–UNTIL loop involves statements 50 to 70 (again indented for emphasis). The statements on lines 50 and 60 will be repeated until (hence the name) the condition given in the last statement of the loop is no longer true. Then, lines 80 to 100 will be processed. In other words, we really want to exit the loop when it is true that we have reached 100, or when N => 100 is true. But it is easier to use the negation, N < 100, and then exit with a false condition. This program can be outlined with a REPEAT–UNTIL structure as follows:

```
Initialize values
REPEAT
        Increase the number counter by 1
        Add the number to the sum
UNTIL the number is not less than 100
Print final sum
```

The REPEAT–UNTIL loop is illustrated in Figure 7-10.

The second loop structure, illustrated in Figure 7-11, is the WHILE–DO and has a general design as follows:

```
WHILE  condition  DO
        statements
ENDWHILE
next statement
```

This is very similar to the above except that the condition is at the top of the loop. Once the condition is no longer met and becomes false, processing branches to the next statement below the loop; otherwise, as long as the condition is true, the block of statements

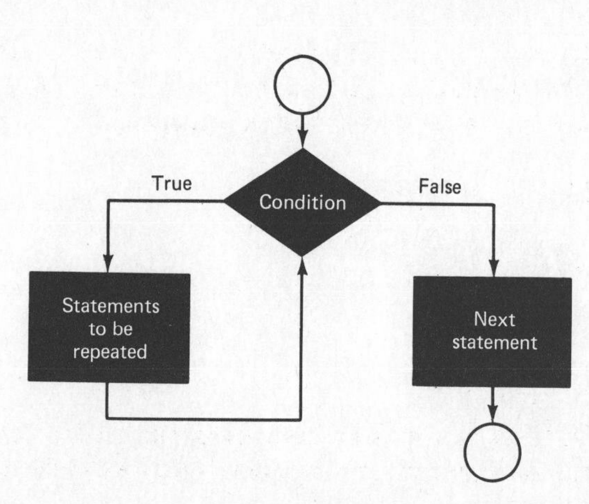

FIGURE 7-11
The WHILE-DO structure

within the loop is repeated. As with the blocked IF–THEN and the REPEAT–UNTIL structures, it is often more convenient to express the condition as a negation. The above program can easily be rewritten to show the WHILE–DO structure:

```
 10 REM   PROGRAM WITH WHILE-DO STRUCTURE
 20 REM
 30 LET S = 0
 40 LET N = 0
 45   IF N => 100 THEN 80
 50   LET N = N + 1
 60   LET S = S + N
 70   GOTO 45
 80 PRINT "THE SUM OF THE FIRST 100"
 90 PRINT "POSITIVE INTEGERS IS"; S
100 END
```

This program is one line longer, with the loop being the four statements on lines 45 to 70. The loop is repeated until N = 100, at which time a branch to line 80, the next statement after the loop, occurs and the cycle ends. This program can be outlined with a WHILE-DO structure as follows:

```
Initialize values
WHILE  the number is less than 100  DO
       Increase the number counter by 1
       Add the number to the sum
ENDWHILE
Print final sum
```

Like the IF–THEN–ELSE structure, many versions of BASIC provide no specific statements designed to directly implement either of the above loop structures; however, some systems will offer special statements for this purpose, such as the WHILE–WEND or others. Check with your instructor to see if any special statements for the REPEAT–UNTIL or WHILE–DO loops are available on your computer.

TROUBLESHOOTING

Each of the following programs contains an error that prevents it from executing properly. Explain *specifically* what the problem is and what must be done to correct it. To assist you, a sample of what would happen should you attempt to run the program is provided after each listing. Refer to Appendix D for an explanation of BASIC error messages.

1.

```
 10 REM   TROUBLESHOOTING PROBLEM 7-1
 20 REM
 30 REM         N = ANY INTEGER
 40 REM
 50 READ N
 60 IF N = 0 THEN 130
 70 IF N < 0 THEN 80
 80 PRINT N; "IS A POSITIVE INTEGER"
 90 GOTO 50
100 PRINT N; "IS A NEGATIVE INTEGER"
110 GOTO 50
120 DATA 12,45,-17,-23,0
130 END
```

```
 12 IS A POSITIVE INTEGER
 45 IS A POSITIVE INTEGER
-17 IS A POSITIVE INTEGER
-23 IS A POSITIVE INTEGER
```

2.

```
 10 REM  TROUBLESHOOTING PROBLEM 7-2
 20 REM
 30 REM          N = ANY INTEGER
 40 REM          S = NUMBER OF INTEGERS IN LIST FROM 1-100
 50 REM
 60 READ N
 70 IF N = 9999 THEN 110
 80 IF N < 1 AND N > 100 THEN 60
 90 LET S = S + 1
100 GOTO 60
110 PRINT "THE LIST CONTAINS"; S; "INTEGERS"
120 PRINT "IN THE RANGE BETWEEN 1 AND 100"
130 DATA 25,198,-11,73,533,-267,2455,-45,49,9999
140 END
```

```
THE LIST CONTAINS 9 INTEGERS
IN THE RANGE BETWEEN 1 AND 100
```

3.

```
 10 REM  TROUBLESHOOTING PROBLEM 7-3
 20 REM
 30 REM         E$ = EMPLOYEE'S NAME
 40 REM          S = TOTAL SALES
 50 REM          Q = QUOTA
 60 REM         TE = TOTAL EMPLOYEES
 70 REM         TS = TOTAL SALES
 80 REM         TQ = TOTAL EMPLOYEES REACHING QUOTA
 90 REM
100 READ TE, TS, TQ
110 READ E$, S, Q
120 IF E$ = "STOP" THEN 170
130 LET TE = TE + 1
140 LET TS = TS + S
150 IF S => Q LET TQ = TQ + 1
160 GOTO 110
170 PRINT "TOTAL EMPLOYEES ="; TE
180 PRINT "TOTAL REACHING QUOTA ="; TQ
190 PRINT "TOTAL SALES = $"; TS
200 DATA 0,0,0,"Q REESE",4665,5000,"C DAVIS",3655,3500
210 DATA "T GEORGE",4329,4000,"STOP",0,0
220 END
```

```
Syntax Error in Line 150
```

4.

```
 10 REM  TROUBLESHOOTING PROBLEM 7-4
 20 REM
 30 REM  A AND B = ANY TWO NUMBERS
 40 REM
 50 READ A, B
 60 IF A = 0 THEN 120
 70 IF A + B < A * B THEN LET TV$ = "TRUE"
 80 LET TV$ = "FALSE"
 90 PRINT "THE LOGICAL EXPRESSION IS ";TV$
100 GOTO 50
110 DATA 2,1,3,2,4,2,2,2,0,0
120 END
```

```
THE LOGICAL EXPRESSION IS FALSE
THE LOGICAL EXPRESSION IS FALSE
THE LOGICAL EXPRESSION IS FALSE
THE LOGICAL EXPRESSION IS FALSE
```

5.

```
 10 REM  TROUBLESHOOTING PROBLEM 7-5
 20 REM
 30 REM          N = POSITIVE INTEGERS THROUGH 100
 40 REM         SN = SUM OF INTEGERS THROUGH 100
 50 REM         SQ = SUM OF SQUARES
```

```
60 REM
70 LET SN = 0
80 LET SQ = 0
90 LET N = 0
100 LET N = N + 1
110 LET SN = SN + N
120 LET SQ = SQ + N * N
130 IF N => 100 THEN 100
140 PRINT "SUM OF INTEGERS 1-100 =";SN
150 PRINT "SUM OF SQUARES 1-100 ="; SQ
160 END
```

```
SUM OF INTEGERS 1-100 = 1
SUM OF SQUARES 1-100 = 1
```

6.

```
10 REM   TROUBLESHOOTING PROBLEM 7-6
20 REM
30 REM          N = POSITIVE INTEGERS THROUGH 100
40 REM         SN = SUM OF INTEGERS THROUGH 100
50 REM         SQ = SUM OF SQUARES
60 REM
70 LET SN = 0
80 LET SQ = 0
90 LET N = 0
100 IF N=> 100 THEN 150
110 LET N = N + 1
120 LET SN = SN + N
130 LET SQ = SQ + N * N
140 GOTO 110
150 PRINT "SUM OF INTEGERS 1-100 =";SN
160 PRINT "SUM OF SQUARES 1-100 ="; SQ
170 END
```

(No output—goes into an infinite loop)

IMPORTANT TERMS

After studying this chapter, you should be familiar with the meaning and use of the following terms and BASIC statements:

IF–THEN ln
IF–THEN statement
Counter
Increment
Logical (or conditional) expressions
Relational operator
Truth value
Logical operator
Compound condition
Boolean expression
AND
OR
XOR
IMP
EQV
Exclusive OR
Inclusive OR
Implication
Equivalence
Message variable
Logical negation
NOT
Blocked IF–THEN structure
IF–THEN–ELSE structure
REPEAT–UNTIL structure
WHILE–DO structure

EXERCISES

1. Give the value of X that will be produced after each of the following sets of statements:

(a)
```
100  LET X = 1
110  IF X < 0 THEN LET X = X + 1
120  LET X = X + 1
```

(b)
```
200 LET X = 1
210 IF X > 0 THEN LET X = X + 1
220 LET X = X + 1
```
(c)
```
340 LET S = 0
350 LET X = 10
360 LET S <> 0 THEN LET X = X + S
370 LET X = 2 * X
```
(d)
```
140 LET S = 5
150 LET X = 10
160 IF S <> 0 THEN LET X = X + S
170 LET X = 2 * X
```
(e)
```
190 LET X = 2
200 LET Y = X + 3
210 IF X > 0 THEN LET Y = X * Y
220 LET X = X + Y
```
(f)
```
400 LET F = 0
410 LET A = 3
420 LET X = 2 * A - 1
430 IF A <> X THEN LET F = X - A
440 LET X = F
```

2. Determine whether the following compound expressions will be true or false given the indicated values of the variables.

Expression	Values
(a) `V <> 12 AND Y < 99`	V = 10 and Y = 0
(b) `C = 0 OR D => 0`	C = D = 0
(c) `FL < 0 AND P$ = "END"`	FL = 0 and P$ = "END"
(d) `Z = 0 XOR B <> 0`	Z = 0 and B = 900
(e) `N <> 0 AND J <> N`	N = 45 and J = 13
(f) `LN => 40 OR F$ = "PAGE"`	LN = 9 and F$ = "NO PAGE"
(g) `F5 = 5 XOR T < 100`	F5 = 7 and T = 67
(h) `N > 0 OR R <> 0`	N = R = 0
(i) `A < 25 AND B => 10 AND C > 0`	A = 15, B = 10, and C = 100
(j) `J <> 100 OR K > 0 OR L <= 50`	J = 45, K = 63, and L = 0
(k) `R > 45 AND N = 0 OR W < 20`	R = 65, N = 0, and W = 12
(l) `FL$ = "FIRST" OR SV < 0 AND T => 100`	FL$ = "LAST", SV = 13, and T = 99

3. Verify the associative property for AND for the following expression and sets of values:

```
A < 100 AND Y <> 0 AND P => 20
```

(a) A = 50, Y = −11, and P = 20
(b) A = 15, Y = 0, and P = 100
(c) A = 212, Y = 25, and P = 79

4. Repeat Exercise 3 for OR instead of AND.
5. Repeat Exercise 3 for XOR instead of AND.
6. Verify from Table 7-6 that

NOT(*exp1* AND *exp2*) = NOT(*exp1*) OR NOT(*exp2*)

for the following expressions and values:
(a) exp1 = Q <= 0 and exp2 = R > 0 for R = Q = 0
(b) exp1 = A < 10 and exp2 = K <> R for A = 5 and K = 4

7. Repeat Exercise 6 for

NOT(*exp1* OR *exp2*) = NOT(*exp1*) AND NOT(*exp2*)

For Exercises 8 to 13, give the output that will be produced by the given programs. Then type the programs into the computer, run them, and check the actual outputs against your predictions.

8.

```
 10 READ N$, S, Q
 20 IF N$ = "STOP" THEN 100
 30 LET M$ = " "
 40 IF S < Q THEN LET M$ = "BELOW QUOTA"
 50 PRINT N$, S, Q, M$
 60 GOTO 10
 70 DATA "F JONES", 3454, 2500, "P SMITH", 2744, 3000
 80 DATA "Q WILLS", 3288, 3500, "Y UPPS", 3676, 3000
 90 DATA "R BEVINS", 3988, 3500, "STOP", 0, 0
100 END
```

9.

```
 10 READ S$, GPA
 20 IF S$ = "END" THEN 70
 30 LET TS = TS + 1
 40 IF GPA < 1.5 THEN LET TP = TP + 1
 50 IF GPA > 3.5 THEN LET TD = TD + 1
 60 GOTO 10
 70 PRINT "TOTAL STUDENTS ON PROBATION ="; TP
 80 PRINT "TOTAL STUDENTS ON DEAN'S LIST ="; TD
 90 PRINT "TOTAL STUDENTS REPORTED ="; TS
100 DATA "D GARY", 2.56, "P EVANS", 3.78
110 DATA "L POOL", 3.44, "F HARRIS", 1.32
120 DATA "T REED", 2.84, "K THOMAS", 3.68
130 DATA "R SIMMS", 2.77, "END", 0
140 END
```

10.

```
 10 READ X
 20 IF X = 0 THEN 120
 30 IF X < 0 THEN 70
 40 LET Y = 2 * X + 1
 50 LET Z = X
 60 GOTO 90
 70 LET Y = 3 - 2 * X
 80 LET Z = -X
 90 PRINT X, Y, Z
100 GOTO 10
110 DATA 2, 5, -3, 1, -2, -3, 4, 0
120 END
```

11.

```
 10 READ N
 20 IF N = -9999 THEN 80
 30 IF N < 0 OR N > 100 THEN 10
 40 LET Z = N / 5
 50 PRINT N, Z
 60 GOTO 10
 70 DATA 35,0,125,-22,67,40,-177,95,544,-9999
 80 END
```

12.

```
 10 LET S = 0
 20 LET N = 1
 30 LET N = N + 2
 40 LET S = S + N
 50 IF N < 20 THEN 30
 60 PRINT "THE SUM IS"; S
 70 END
```

13.

```
 10 LET F = 1
 20 LET N = 0
 30 IF N > 10 THEN 80
 40 LET F = F + N
 50 LET N = N + 1
 60 PRINT N, F
 70 GOTO 30
 80 END
```

PROGRAMMING PROBLEMS

Write programs in BASIC to accomplish the tasks described by each of the following problems. Be sure to carefully document each program and include all appropriate report headings and other literals.

1. Write a program that calculates the *product* of the first 10 positive integers.
2. I agree to work for you for 25 days for 1 cent on the first day, 2 cents on the second, 4 cents on the third, and so forth, with my daily pay doubling each day. Write a program to calculate what you will owe me at the end of the 25 days. (Did you make a good deal?)
3. Print a Height Conversion Chart that can be used to convert a person's height from inches to centimeters. Your chart should range from 48 through 84 inches. (1 inch = 2.54 centimeters)
4. Write a program to read a series of test grades and find the average for each student. The output should give the student's name, test average, and for those students with an average below 60, the message FAILING—ON PROBATION. The total number of students processed as well as the number on probation should appear at the bottom of the report. Data is provided below.

Name	Test 1	Test 2	Test 3	Test 4
G. Lawson	88	75	81	80
P. Crawford	90	82	88	76
L. Hubbard	62	48	56	58
R. Stimpson	58	71	67	62
T. Bennefield	72	72	68	84
D. Duckworth	33	53	49	61
R. Young	89	95	98	78
S. Spencer	73	62	0	32

5. The Winston Company needs an inventory control program that will keep track of how many of a particular item need to be ordered. Input to the program will be the item number, quantity on hand, and the stock level, which is the minimum number that should be in stock at any given time. If the quantity on hand is less than the stock level, the difference in the two values plus 20 percent of the stock level is the number to be ordered. If the quantity on hand is *not* less than the stock level, nothing is to be ordered. The output should give the input data plus the number to be ordered for each item. Data is provided below.

Item Number	Quantity on Hand	Stock Level	Item Number	Quantity on Hand	Stock Level
210365	205	250	651178	56	50
256443	315	300	786653	265	300
300215	489	500	798650	72	75
456325	131	125	800400	176	200

6. The First Bank is offering a special new savings account to its customers. The basic interest rate for this account is 5.5 percent unless you have at least $500 in your account, in which case you will receive 6.0 percent. Input data is given below. The output should provide the input plus the interest rate paid on each account and the interest earned. Assume that all interest is compounded monthly and calculated for one year. (See Section 5-5 for a review of compound interest.)

Account Number	Current Balance	Account Number	Current Balance
22202	462.96	56632	4610.51
28665	512.00	65532	23.00
32559	1036.51	68555	684.10
40059	500.00	69204	327.82

7. The Upushit Rent-a-Wreck Company rents used cars by the day. The basic charge is $8 per day for the first week and $6 each day for all days beyond the seventh. From the data in the table below, write a program to calculate the charges for each customer. The output should show all input data plus the calculated charges.

Customer Name	Days Used	Customer Name	Days Used
L. Sloan	3	P. Lowe	8
Q. Adams	9	T. Perkins	7
G. Lewis	14	T. Kwik	1
H. Popp	2	F. Smith	8

8. The Hendenburg Wholesale Company is having a going out of business sale. As part of the sale, it is offering quantity discounts to any of its retail customers who buy items in quantity. A 10 percent discount is given on the total cost of any item when 10 or more are purchased, and a 25 percent discount is given whenever the customer purchases at least 25 of any given item. That is, if 10 or more alarm clocks are bought, the customer will get a 10 percent discount on *all* clocks, but if he or she buys 25 or more, the discount on all the clocks will be 25 percent. Prepare an invoice for the customer whose total purchase is shown below. The printout should provide all customer data at the top, detailed lines with item number and description, unit price, quantity, discount (if any), and net price, which is calculated as the quantity times the unit price minus any discount. Totals should be taken for number of items, total quantity, and total price.

Company Name: Lloyds Discount, Inc.
Account Number: 4566-778 Date: June 28, 1984

Item Number	Item Description	Unit Price	Quantity Purchased
110330	Typewriter	120.00	10
112568	Alarm clock	14.50	40
125463	SLR camera	110.00	5
225315	Calculator	7.50	150
321065	Table lamp	28.00	25
406653	LCD watch	43.50	30
532007	Color TV	200.00	7
655532	Smoke alarm	11.00	200

9. A Sales Commission Report is to be prepared from the data provided below. A salesperson's net sales is found by subtracting the returns from the sales. The commission is then calculated as follows:

(a) If the net sales is less than or equal to zero, then no commission is earned, and the message EXCESSIVE RETURNS—NO COMMISSION EARNED should appear on the print line following the salesperson's name.

(b) If the net sales is positive but less than the quota, then the commission is 5 percent of the net sales.

(c) If the net sales is equal to or greater than the quota, then the commission is 5 percent of the quota plus the bonus plus 7 percent of all sales over the quota.

Except when the net sales is not positive [case (a)], the printout should show the salesperson's name, the net sales, and the commission earned. Totals should be accumulated for number of salespersons, net sales, and commissions paid.

Name	Sales	Returns	Bonus	Quota
F. Harris	10550	1200	350	10000
E. Lobo	17992	3292	500	12500
J. Suggs	8944	654	200	7500
Y. Amos	6299	299	150	6000
L. Franks	10345	734	500	10000
P. McKay	3290	5166	200	5000
L. Ogleby	12560	60	500	12500
H. Busch	8900	321	350	7500

10. A Graduation List is to be prepared for Rockhead College from a list of potential graduates. In order to graduate, a student must have satisfied all of the following requirements: (1) have an overall GPA of at least 2.00, (2) have accumulated at least 180 quarter hours credit, and (3) have a GPA of at least 2.5 in subjects in the major. The printout is a simple list of the graduates with a percentage of those graduating printed at the bottom of the list. Data is provided below.

Student Name	Overall GPA	Total Hours	GPA in Major
K. A. Johnson	2.56	185	3.13
J. T. Williams	1.97	190	2.05
H. R. Goldstein	3.45	210	3.89
R. D. Thompson	3.75	170	3.90
D. T. Anderson	3.11	180	2.97
E. A. Graham	2.39	195	2.50
T. L. Greene	2.38	220	2.43
R. R. Polczynski	3.37	205	3.66

11. Rockhead College also needs a Tuition Charges Report for its students. Students at Rockhead are charged according to (1) whether they are full-time or part-time and (2) by their residence status as in-state or out-of-state. Full-time students are those who are taking 12 quarter hours or more and are charged a flat rate of $600. A part-time student is one taking less than 12 hours and charged $50 per quarter hour. Out-of-state students are charged at double the rate of those from in-state. Calculate the appropriate tuition for each student from the data below. The printout should give the input data, a column stating whether the student is full-time or part-time, plus the tuition charged. Totals are to be accumulated for total students and tuition in each of the four possible classifications as well as a grand total for all students and tuition (that makes *10* totals!!).

Student Name	Hours Taken	Residence Status
K. A. Johnson	15	In-state
J. T. Williams	10	Out-of-state
H. R. Goldstein	15	Out-of-state
R. D. Thompson	20	In-state
D. T. Anderson	5	In-state
E. A. Graham	12	In-state
T. L. Greene	15	In-state
R. R. Polczynski	12	Out-of-state

12. Write a program to read a series of grades and add the total number of grades as well as the total at each letter grade; that is, the number with a grade of A, with a B, etc. Use the following list of grades for data: 85, 90, 75, 56, 88, 70, 63, 76, 81, 45, 94, 100, 86, 77, 73, 84, 60, 76, 73, 84, 59, 78, 70, 81, 67, 78, 62, 96.

13. A loan for $500 is made under the conditions that interest of 1 percent *per month* on the unpaid balance will be charged and monthly payments of $35 will be made. Write a program that prints a summary of the repayment schedule for the first year. The output should show the number of the month (1 to 12), the balance at the beginning of the month, and the balance at the end of the month. The balance at the end of the month is the balance at the beginning plus the interest minus the payment. For example, for the first month, the initial value is $500. To this, add 1 percent, or $5, for the interest and subtract the $35 payment giving a balance of $470, which becomes the initial value for the second month. This is repeated for the remaining 11 months. The detail lines should be preceded by specifics on the loan, such as the amount, interest rate, and monthly payment. At the end of the report, print the total amount paid, total interest paid, and amount remaining on the loan.

14. Write a program that will process the following list of names and print only those that are either male and aged 21 to 30 or female and 18 to 25 years of age. Each print line should give the name, age, and the sex as MALE or FEMALE, not M or F, as the data is entered.

Name	Age	Sex	Name	Age	Sex
G. Potter	19	M	T. Quinton	25	F
R. Townsend	23	M	L. Kellogg	21	F
R. Sanders	22	F	A. Nelson	17	F
Y. Bergen	28	F	H. Walker	26	M
D. Evans	31	M	J. Matthews	20	F
I. Fong	27	M	K. Lester	27	F

15. Write a program to evaluate the following equation and find y beginning with $x = 0$ and continuing with $x = 1, 2, 3, \ldots$ until $y \geq 100$.

$$y = x^2 - 8x + 12$$

For each evaluation, print x and the corresponding value for y.

16. Write a program to evaluate both of the following expressions, beginning with $x = -5$ and continuing until either $y_1 = y_2$ or $x > 10$.

$$y_1 = 5x - 3$$
$$y_2 = 1 + 4x$$

Print either the value of x at which $y_1 = y_2$ or an appropriate message that no such value was found.

PART THREE

INTERMEDIATE TECHNIQUES

CHAPTER 8

PROGRAM CONTROL. PART II

In the last chapter, we studied several methods for program control using the IF-THEN statement. These might be called manual methods in that the programmer must specify with one or more logical conditions all controls necessary to make the program execute properly. In this chapter we will look at two BASIC statements, the FOR-NEXT and ON-GOTO. These can, under certain conditions, take the place of IF statements to make the processing more automatic and, hopefully, easier. We will then take a brief look at the concept of input data editing and, finally, conclude the chapter with a special type of program called a control break.

8-1 THE FOR-NEXT LOOP

One of the most useful statements in BASIC is the FOR-NEXT statement pair. It is generally used to cause the execution of a certain group of statements to be repeated a specified number of times. The general form of the FOR-NEXT statement pair is:

ln1 FOR *var* = *num1* TO *num2* STEP *num3*

:

Statements to be repeated

:

ln2 NEXT *var*

where the two statements must always appear together and *ln2* is greater than *ln1*, that is, the NEXT must be below the FOR in the program. The *var* is any numeric variable and must be the same in both the NEXT and FOR. The three values, *num1*, *num2*, and *num3* may be any numeric constant or variable or a mathematical expression. The variable, *var*, is the **loop counter** or **index**. The three numbers represented by *num1*, *num2*, and *num3* are the **initial value,** the **test value,** and the **step** or increment, respectively. The statements provide a simple loop structure in which the counter ranges from the specified initial value to the end or test value by the indicated increment. Let us look at some examples.

Consider the following short program:

```
10 FOR X = 1 TO 10
20    PRINT "X ="; X
30 NEXT X
40 END
```

This will begin with X having a value of 1, it will execute the PRINT statement, then repeat for X = 2, X = 3, and so on, until X reaches 10. The output will be:

```
X = 1
X = 2
X = 3
X = 4
X = 5
X = 6
X = 7
X = 8
X = 9
X = 10
```

Suppose the above program was modified to include a STEP 3 in the FOR statement at line 10. This would read:

```
10  FOR X = 1 TO 10 STEP 3
20     PRINT "X ="; X
30  NEXT X
40  END
```

This will now process for values of X = 1, 4, 7, and 10. The STEP 3 causes only every *third* value for X to be used. The output is now:

```
X = 1
X = 4
X = 7
X = 10
```

If the step is such that it does not end on the test value exactly, then the next lower value will be the last to be used. The upper limit is *never* exceeded. For example, if the step were 4 in the above program, the output would be:

```
X = 1
X = 5
X = 9
```

It will not go on to X = 13 since 13 is beyond the loop test value of 10.

In the last chapter, we looked at a program that found the sum of the first 100 positive integers. First, here is the program as we wrote it using an IF statement:

```
 10 REM  THIS PROGRAM FINDS THE SUM OF
 20 REM  THE FIRST 100 POSITIVE INTEGERS
 30 REM
 40 LET S = 0
 50 LET N = 0
 60 LET N = N + 1
 70 LET S = S + N
 80 IF N < 100 THEN 60
 90 PRINT "THE SUM OF THE FIRST 100"
100 PRINT "POSITIVE INTEGERS IS"; S
110 END
```

Now, let us rewrite it using FOR-NEXT statements:

```
 10 REM  THIS PROGRAM FINDS THE SUM OF
 20 REM  THE FIRST 100 POSITIVE INTEGERS
 30 REM
```

```
 40 LET S = 0
 50 FOR N = 1 TO 100
 70   LET S = S + N
 80 NEXT N
 90 PRINT "THE SUM OF THE FIRST 100"
100 PRINT "POSITIVE INTEGERS IS"; S
110 END
```

The IF at line 80 is gone as are the LETs at 50 and 60, which initialize N to 0 then increment it by 1. The functions of both of these statements are performed by the FOR-NEXT statements. N ranges from 1 to 100, each value being added to S at line 70.

Before proceeding to a detailed discussion of the FOR-NEXT statements, a word about the flowcharting symbol that is used to represent this structure is needed. Unfortunately, there is no one symbol that is universally used for this. Figure 8-1 shows four of the most commonly used ones. Each symbol is the same except for its shape and the way the dividing lines are drawn. All four are divided into three parts to give the initial value of the loop, the increment, and a test condition. In our work, we will use the form illustrated in Figure 8-1*a*; however, this is only a matter of choice, and your instructor may prefer another. A flowchart for the above example is given in Figure 8-2.

To avoid improper combinations, careful attention should be given to the three numbers in the FOR statement. A few general guidelines for establishing proper numbering in FOR-NEXT statements can be outlined as follows:

1. If the step option is not used, then *num1* should be less than *num2*. If it is not, the loop will be executed only once for *num1*.
2. If the step option is used, then the following will apply:
   (a) If *num1* $<$ *num2*, the step *num3* must be positive (forward step) and vice versa.

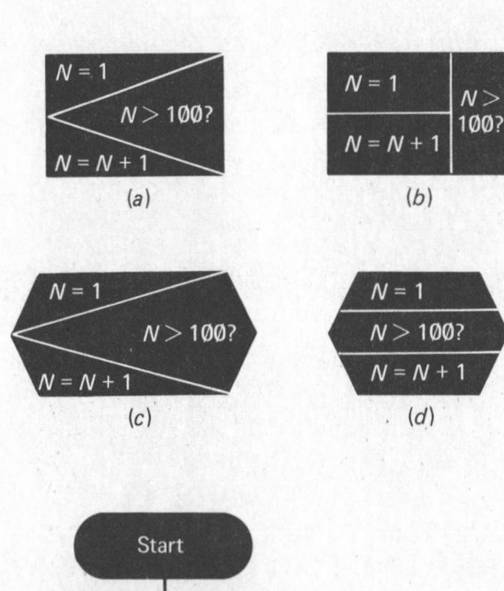

FIGURE 8-1
Common flowchart symbols for FOR-NEXT structure

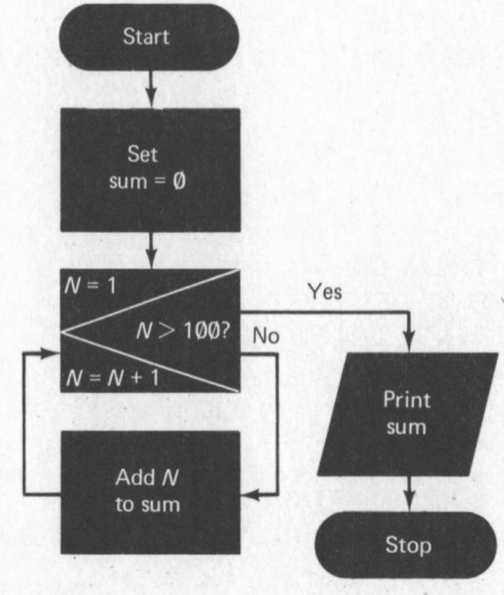

FIGURE 8-2
Flowchart with FOR-NEXT loop

(b) If *num1* > *num2*, the step *num3* must be negative (backward step) and vice versa.
(c) The step *num3* should not be larger than the difference of *num1* and *num2*. If it is, the loop will be executed only once for *num1*.
(d) A zero step causes an infinite loop at *num1*.

3. If *num1* = *num2*, the loop will be executed only once at *num1*.

Some deviations from the above guidelines may exist with your particular version of BASIC. Several examples of invalid FOR-NEXT statements are given in Table 8-1.

Care must be taken not to alter the value of the counter within a FOR-NEXT loop. The counter may be used as part of a mathematical calculation, but it may not appear on the left-hand side of the equals sign in a LET statement. For example, the following is permitted:

```
10  FOR N = 1 TO 5
20    LET S = N * N
30    PRINT N, S
40  NEXT N
50  END
```

because the counter N is only used in a calculation and is not altered within the loop. On the other hand, this is not valid:

```
10  FOR N = 1 TO 10
20    LET N = N / 3
30    PRINT N
40  NEXT N
50  END
```

The results of such calculations can be very unpredictable, varying with the version of BASIC that is in use.

One additional caution involving FOR-NEXT loops relates to branching into or out of the loop. *Never branch from elsewhere in the program into the* ***middle*** *of a* FOR-NEXT *loop*. This can create any number of problems. The computer will think there is no FOR

TABLE 8-1

Examples of Invalid FOR-NEXT Statements

Invalid Statement	Reason Why Invalid	Possible Correction
200 FOR X = 1 TO 10 : 250 NEXT Y	Variables in FOR and NEXT statements do not match.	200 FOR X = 1 TO 10 : 250 NEXT X
160 FOR A = 10 TO 1 : 220 NEXT A	Second value must be greater than the first unless a negative step is used.	160 FOR A = 10 TO 1 STEP -1 : 220 NEXT A
300 FOR S$ = 5 TO 17 : 370 NEXT S$	String variables (or constants) are not allowed.	300 FOR S = 5 TO 17 : 370 NEXT S
185 FOR R = 2 TO 20 STEP 20 : 230 NEXT R	Step is too large. Loop will be executed only for R = 2.	185 FOR R = 2 TO 20 STEP 2 : 230 NEXT R
430 FOR K = -50 TO 50 STEP -5 : 510 NEXT K	Cannot have a negative step when the second value is greater than the first.	430 FOR K = -50 TO 50 STEP 5 : 510 NEXT K
290 FOR B = 1 TO 5 STEP 0 : 355 NEXT B	A zero step generates an infinite loop at B = 1.	290 FOR B = 1 TO 5 STEP 0.1 : 355 NEXT B

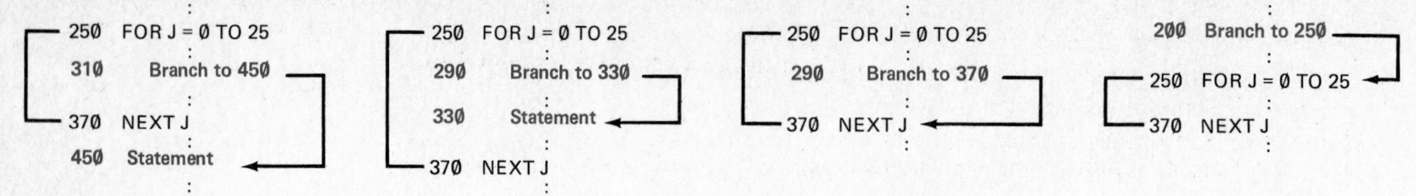

FIGURE 8-3 Examples of valid branches with FOR-NEXT loops

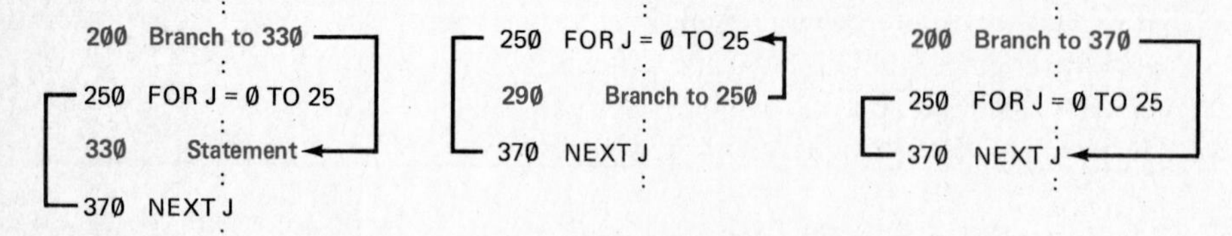

FIGURE 8-4 Examples of invalid branches with FOR-NEXT loops

statement for the NEXT and will issue a NEXT without FOR error message (see below). Branching *within* a loop or *out of* a loop is permitted, but once out of the loop, *you may not reenter except at the* FOR *statement*. Some examples of valid and invalid branches with FOR-NEXT loops are given in Figures 8-3 and 8-4.

Of course, not all IF statements are replaceable by FOR-NEXT loops. Generally, those that function to control counters can be most readily substituted with FOR-NEXT statements. Both types of statements have a place in BASIC programs and each should be used as appropriate.

Before moving on to the next section and an example, a word is in order on special error messages that are associated with the FOR-NEXT statements. You are likely to encounter either of two types of error messages that are issued especially for FOR-NEXT error conditions. Both are similar and occur whenever an attempt is made to use one of the two statements without the other. If a FOR is in a program without an accompanying NEXT, a **FOR without NEXT** error message will occur. On the other hand, if the FOR is omitted, the error message will read **NEXT without FOR**. As described above, the same errors can occur when improper branches involving FOR-NEXT loops are attempted.

8-2 AN EXAMPLE: ITEM DEPRECIATION

The example that is presented in this section illustrates a simple use of the FOR-NEXT loop.

Problem: The yearly depreciation of an item is to be calculated for the anticipated lifetime of the item. Two different methods are to be used to calculate the depreciation. The first is the straight-line method, which involves dividing the initial value of the item by the lifetime and subtracting this constant amount each year. This means that a \$100 item that is expected to last 5 years would be depreciated by \$100/5 = \$20 each year. The second method is the double-declining balance method. With this method, a constant percentage of the *remaining* value of the item is subtracted. This is calculated as 2 divided by the lifetime of the item times the value at the *beginning* of the year. For the above \$100 item, the first year's depreciation would be \$100 × 2/5 = \$40, or the item would be worth only \$60 at the beginning of the second year. For that year, the depreciation is \$60 × 2/5 = \$24 leaving a value of \$36, and so on. The program will be run for a \$5000 computer that is to last 10 years. The printout should give the input at the head of the report, detailed lines giving the year number and initial value at the beginning of the year and the yearly depreciation for both methods, and the depreciated value after the anticipated lifetime.

The solution to this problem is outlined as follows:

1. Input the item name, initial value, and anticipated lifetime.
2. Print report and column headings to include printing the input data from step 1.

3. Assign initial value of item for each depreciation method.
4. For years ranging from 1 through the anticipated lifetime, perform steps 5 to 8. When this is completed, go to step 9.
5. Calculate the yearly depreciation by each method.
6. Print a detailed line showing the year number and yearly value and depreciation for both methods.
7. Subtract the depreciations from the respective yearly values to obtain the next yearly value.
8. Return to step 4.
9. Print the depreciated value remaining after the lifetime by each method.
10. Stop.

The solution is illustrated pictorially by the flowchart shown in Figure 8-5.

Since this program requires the entry of only three data values, INPUT statements have been used for data entry instead of the usual READs. These are at lines 140 to 160.

```
140  INPUT "ENTER NAME OF ITEM"; I$
150  INPUT "ENTER INITIAL VALUE"; V
160  INPUT "ENTER ANTICIPATED LIFETIME IN YEARS"; L
```

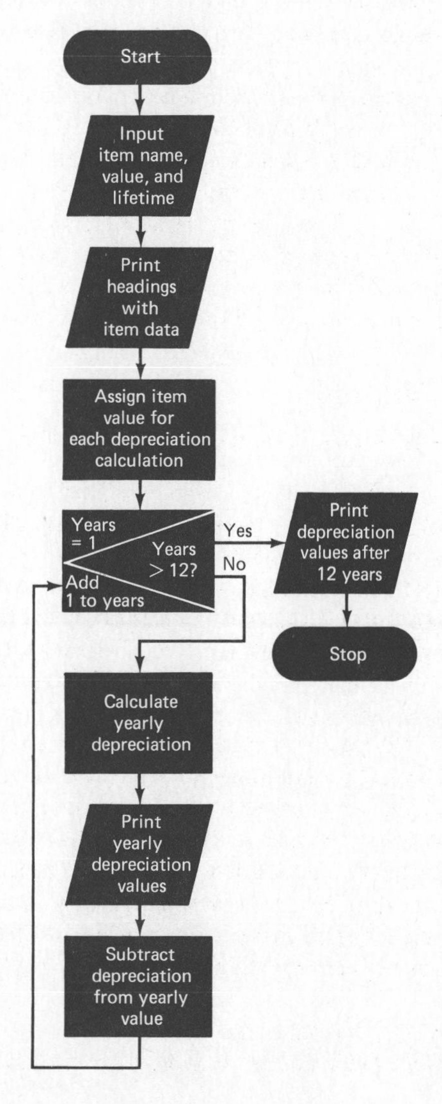

FIGURE 8-5
Flowchart for item depreciation problem

Lines 210 to 380 are for printing the headings and the input values at the top of the report.

```
210 PRINT
220 PRINT
230 PRINT
240 PRINT , "    ITEM DEPRECIATION"
250 PRINT , "  TWO METHODS COMPARED"
260 PRINT
270 PRINT
280 PRINT "ITEM TO BE DEPRECIATED:   "; I$
290 PRINT "INITIAL VALUE OF ITEM:   $"; V
300 PRINT "ANTICIPATED LIFETIME IN YEARS: "; L
310 PRINT
320 PRINT TAB(18); "STRAIGHT-LINE"; TAB(42);
330 PRINT "DOUBLE-DECLINING"
340 PRINT TAB(21); "METHOD"; TAB(43); "BALANCE METHOD"
350 PRINT
360 PRINT " YEAR", "YEARLY", "DEPRECI-", "YEARLY", "DEPRECI-"
370 PRINT "NUMBER", "VALUE", " ATION", "VALUE", " ATION"
380 PRINT
```

This is essentially the same as we have done in previous chapters except that the headings for this program are much more complex. Lines 240 and 250 print the main report heading. Lines 280 to 300 print the input data following the heading. The remainder print column headings. Lines 320 to 340 identify which columns are for each depreciation method, and lines 360 and 370 print the primary column headings. The lines with *blank* PRINT statements as at 210 to 230 provide for blank lines as usual.

The main processing occurs in lines 420 to 500, corresponding to steps 3 through 8.

```
420 LET V1 = V
430 LET V2 = V
440 FOR N = 1 TO L
450    LET D1 = V / L
460    LET D2 = V2 * 2 / L
470    PRINT " "; N, "$"; V1, "$"; D1, "$"; V2, "$"; D2
480    LET V1 = V1 - D1
490    LET V2 = V2 - D2
500 NEXT N
```

The two LET statements at lines 420 and 430 are to assign the initial value of the item to two initial yearly values to be used in the two depreciation calculations. The FOR-NEXT loop from 440 to 500 counts the years from 1 through the lifetime represented by the variable L. The depreciations are calculated at lines 450 and 460. The detailed line is printed at 470. At lines 480 and 490, the calculated depreciations are subtracted from the respective yearly values to give the updated new yearly depreciated value. The FOR-NEXT statements provide for these calculations to be automatically repeated from the first year (*num1* = 1) until the lifetime (*num2* = L) has been reached. Here the step is unspecified so it is assumed to be 1.

The last section of the program is straightforward.

```
540 PRINT
550 PRINT "VALUE OF "; I$; " AFTER"; L; "YEARS IS --"
560 PRINT
570 PRINT "     $"; V1; "BY THE STRAIGHT-LINE METHOD"
580 PRINT "     $"; V2; "BY THE DOUBLE-DECLINING BALANCE METHOD"
590 END
```

This simply prints the value of the item that remains after the lifetime according to the two depreciation methods.

Here is a complete program listing:

```
 10 REM  ITEM DEPRECIATION -- TWO METHODS COMPARED
 20 REM
 30 REM  VARIABLES ARE DEFINED AS --
 40 REM
 50 REM          I$ = ITEM NAME
 60 REM           V = INITIAL VALUE
 70 REM V1 AND V2 = YEARLY DEPRECIATED VALUES
 80 REM D1 AND D2 = YEARLY DEPRECIATIONS
 90 REM           Y = ANTICIPATED LIFETIME
100 REM           N = YEAR NUMBER
110 REM
120 REM  ENTER DATA ON ITEM TO BE DEPRECIATED
130 REM
140 INPUT "ENTER NAME OF ITEM"; I$
150 INPUT "ENTER INITIAL VALUE"; V
160 INPUT "ENTER ANTICIPATED LIFETIME IN YEARS"; L
170 REM
180 REM  PRINT REPORT AND COLUMN HEADINGS ALONG WITH
190 REM  THE BASIC ITEM DATA THAT WAS INPUT ABOVE
200 REM
210 PRINT
220 PRINT
230 PRINT
240 PRINT , "   ITEM DEPRECIATION"
250 PRINT , "  TWO METHODS COMPARED"
260 PRINT
270 PRINT
280 PRINT "ITEM TO BE DEPRECIATED:  "; I$
290 PRINT "INITIAL VALUE OF ITEM:  $"; V
300 PRINT "ANTICIPATED LIFETIME IN YEARS: "; L
310 PRINT
320 PRINT TAB(18); "STRAIGHT-LINE"; TAB(42);
330 PRINT "DOUBLE-DECLINING"
340 PRINT TAB(21); "METHOD"; TAB(43); "BALANCE METHOD"
350 PRINT
360 PRINT " YEAR", "YEARLY", "DEPRECI-", "YEARLY", "DEPRECI-"
370 PRINT "NUMBER", "VALUE", " ATION", "VALUE", " ATI
380 PRINT
390 REM
400 REM  CALCULATE AND PRINT DEPRECIATION DATA
410 REM
420 LET V1 = V
430 LET V2 = V
440 FOR N = 1 TO L
450   LET D1 = V / L
460   LET D2 = V2 * 2 / L
470   PRINT " "; N, "$"; V1, "$"; D1, "$"; V2, "$"; D2
480   LET V1 = V1 - D1
490   LET V2 = V2 - D2
500 NEXT N
510 REM
520 REM  PRINT FINAL RESULTS
530 REM
540 PRINT
550 PRINT "VALUE OF "; I$; " AFTER"; L; "YEARS IS --"
560 PRINT
570 PRINT "    $"; V1; "BY THE STRAIGHT-LINE METHOD"
580 PRINT "    $"; V2; "BY THE DOUBLE-DECLINING BALANCE METHOD"
590 END
```

The run will consist of a short session to enter the data followed by the output:

```
ENTER NAME OF ITEM? "COMPUTER"
ENTER INITIAL VALUE? 5000
ENTER ANTICIPATED LIFETIME IN YEARS? 10
```

```
                ITEM DEPRECIATION
               TWO METHODS COMPARED


ITEM TO BE DEPRECIATED:  COMPUTER
INITIAL VALUE OF ITEM:  $ 5000
ANTICIPATED LIFETIME IN YEARS:  10
```

	STRAIGHT-LINE METHOD		DOUBLE-DECLINING BALANCE METHOD	
YEAR NUMBER	YEARLY VALUE	DEPRECI- ATION	YEARLY VALUE	DEPRECI- ATION
1	$ 5000	$ 500	$ 5000	$ 1000
2	$ 4500	$ 500	$ 4000	$ 800
3	$ 4000	$ 500	$ 3200	$ 640
4	$ 3500	$ 500	$ 2560	$ 512
5	$ 3000	$ 500	$ 2048	$ 409.6
6	$ 2500	$ 500	$ 1638.4	$ 327.68
7	$ 2000	$ 500	$ 1310.72	$ 362.144
8	$ 1500	$ 500	$ 1048.58	$ 209.715
9	$ 1000	$ 500	$ 838.861	$ 167.772
10	$ 500	$ 500	$ 671.089	$ 134.218

```
VALUE OF COMPUTER AFTER 10 YEARS IS --

    $ 0 BY THE STRAIGHT-LINE METHOD
    $ 536.871 BY THE DOUBLE-DECLINING BALANCE METHOD
```

8-3 NESTED FOR-NEXT STRUCTURES

It is frequently necessary to have two or more simultaneous counters in a program. Such problems can frequently be solved by the use of **nested FOR-NEXT** loops; that is, one FOR-NEXT loop inside another. Let us look at some examples.

First, consider the simple problem of printing a list of products something like A TIMES B EQUALS C where all the possible combinations of A and B are multiplied and the results printed. Therefore, if A = 1 to 3 and B = 1 to 4, there will be 12 products to be printed. This can be accomplished by the following short program:

```
10 REM  EXAMPLE WITH NESTED FOR-NEXT LOOPS
20 REM
30 FOR A = 1 TO 3
40    FOR B = 1 TO 4
50       LET C = A * B
60       PRINT A; "TIMES"; B; "EQUALS"; C
70    NEXT B
80 NEXT A
90 END
```

The printout will look like this:

```
1 TIMES 1 EQUALS 1
1 TIMES 2 EQUALS 2
1 TIMES 3 EQUALS 3
1 TIMES 4 EQUALS 4
2 TIMES 1 EQUALS 2
```

```
2 TIMES 2 EQUALS 4
2 TIMES 3 EQUALS 6
2 TIMES 4 EQUALS 8
3 TIMES 1 EQUALS 3
3 TIMES 2 EQUALS 6
3 TIMES 3 EQUALS 9
3 TIMES 4 EQUALS 12
```

The outer FOR-NEXT loop is first entered at line 30 and A is set equal to 1. The first statement within this loop is another FOR-NEXT at 40. Here B begins at 1. The product (1 × 1) is calculated at 50 and printed at 60. At line 70, the NEXT B causes the program to loop back to 40 (the corresponding FOR) where B is incremented to 2, and the product, 1 × 2, is processed. This continues until B reaches its test value of 4. When this occurs, the NEXT at 70 no longer directs the processing back to the FOR at 40, but the program continues to the next statement, which in this case is another NEXT. This is the NEXT A, which is paired with the FOR at 30, hence A is now incremented to 2. The FOR-NEXT at 40 for B is now begun anew with B at 1 again, and the cycle repeats. The sequence of the numbers for A and B can be easily seen from the output. The process is illustrated in Figure 8-6.

Progression of the counters in nested FOR-NEXT loops is outlined below:

Outer Loop	Inner Loop
Counter first set to initial value	Counter goes from initial to test value by steps and exits loop
Counter moves up by one step	Counter goes from initial to test value by steps and exits loop
Counter moves up by one step	Counter goes from initial to test value by steps and exits loop
This process continues until . . .	
Counter reaches test value	Counter goes from initial to test value by steps and exits loop
Exits loop	

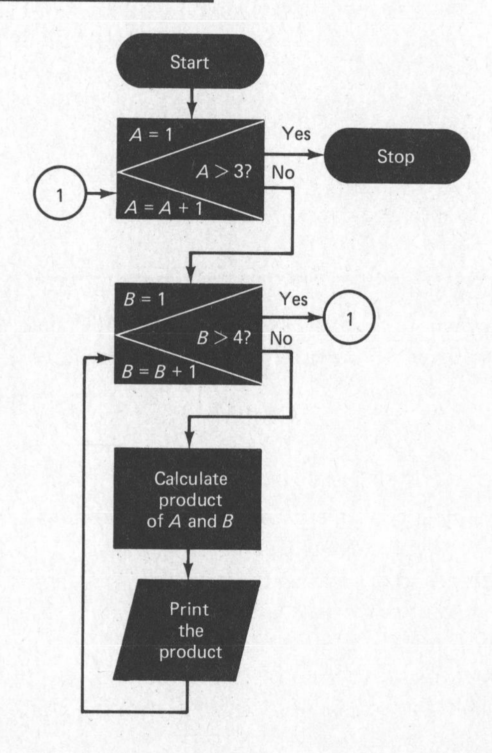

FIGURE 8-6
Flowchart for nested FOR-NEXT structures

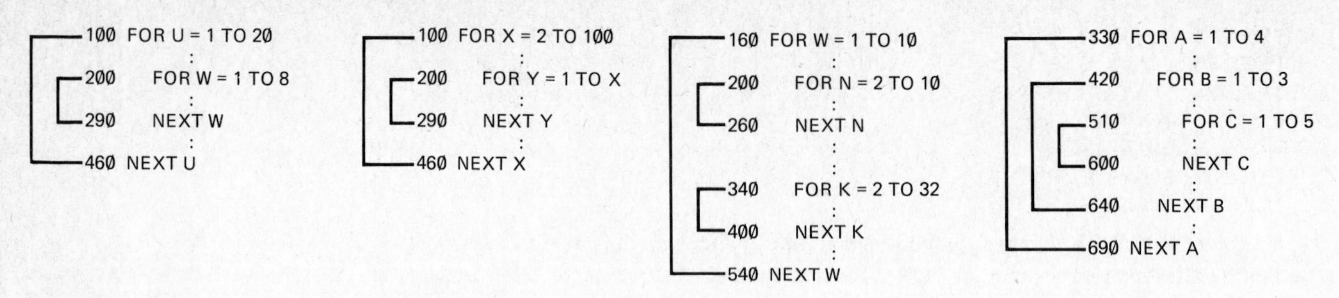

FIGURE 8-7 Examples of valid nested FOR-NEXT structures

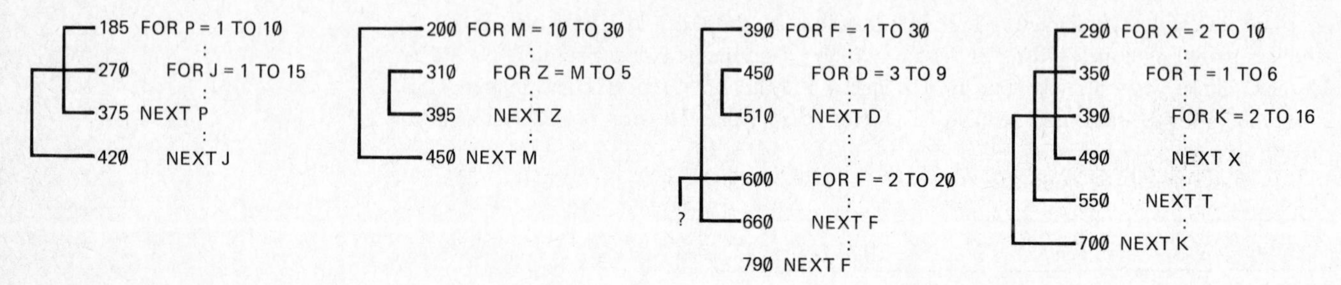

FIGURE 8-8 Examples of invalid nested FOR-NEXT structures

When using nested FOR-NEXT loops, care must be taken to ensure that the structures are properly constructed. You should be aware of two very common types of improperly nested FOR-NEXT constructions. The first involves overlapping loops. Loops must *never* overlap. The first loop opened must be the last closed. The second problem relates to counters. Disjoint (nonnested) loops may use the same variable for a counter provided the variable, or a specific value of the first counter, is not used elsewhere in the program within or below the second loop. However, nested loops may *never* use the same variable for a counter. Think about that. We said in Section 8-1 that the value of the counter cannot be altered within the loop. This is exactly what happens when nested loops have a common counter. Figures 8-7 and 8-8 give some examples of valid and invalid nested and multiple FOR-NEXT loops.

8-4 THE ON-GOTO STATEMENT

It is frequently necessary to perform different processes depending on the value of a certain variable or mathematical expression. In some cases, the **ON-GOTO** statement can be of great value in constructing the required program branches. The statement has the general form:

ln ON *expression* GOTO *ln1, ln2, ln3, . . .*

where *expression* is any numeric variable or mathematical expression and *ln1, ln2, ln3,* etc., are the lines to which a branch will proceed depending on the value of the expression. That is, if *expression* = 1, a branch to *ln1* occurs; if *expression* = 2, then control is directed to *ln2;* when *expression* = 3, processing is sent to *ln3,* and so forth. The number of line numbers that may appear in a single ON-GOTO statement is limited only by the physical length of the statement line. For now, we will restrict our discussion to cases where the expression is only a variable and consider the situation of using mathematical expressions later in this section. (The exact form of the ON-GOTO statement varies with the version of BASIC that is in use. You will need to consult your instructor as to the precise syntax of the statement that is available on your system. No matter what the form of your ON-GOTO statement, all of the general features of that statement and its uses described in the remainder of this section should apply.)

A typical ON-GOTO statement is as follows:

```
250  ON N GOTO 300, 410, 750, 500, 100, 999
```

This is equivalent to the following *six* IF statements:

```
250  IF N = 1 THEN 300
251  IF N = 2 THEN 410
252  IF N = 3 THEN 750
253  IF N = 4 THEN 500
254  IF N = 5 THEN 100
255  IF N = 6 THEN 999
```

From this, it should be clear that the ON-GOTO is little more than a special extended case of the IF-THEN allowing multiple comparisons and branches but using an equal condition only. A flowchart illustrating an ON-GOTO structure with four branches is shown in Figure 8-9.

Care must be taken to ensure that the value of the variable does not fall outside of the range for which there are line numbers. That is, in the above example, N can have only values of 1, 2, 3, 4, 5, and 6. If any other values are used, problems will result, but the exact nature of the difficulty will depend on the version of BASIC in use. If a value of N is used that is less than 1 or greater than 6, some systems will issue an appropriate error message, something like **Function Call** or **Value out of Range** error. Other systems will simply pass processing on to the next statement following the ON-GOTO. Some BASICs will do unusual things like treating a value of 7 as if it were 1, 8 like 2, and so forth. Fractional values are either truncated or rounded, depending on the version of BASIC, and are then handled as integers. Truncation can be forced by means of the INT function; see Section 5-8.

As a final point in this section, we return to the use of mathematical expressions in the ON-GOTO statement. There should be relatively little trouble with such expressions as long as they are kept simple and the above-mentioned cautions regarding the range of values and fractions are observed. With a little practice, often an expression can be constructed that will allow one range of values to be converted to another. For example, suppose that the input to a program for a certain variable, J, ranges from 0 through 3. We could then use J in an ON-GOTO as follows:

```
320  ON J + 1 GOTO 450, 560, 200, 600
```

where J + 1 ranges from 1 to 4.

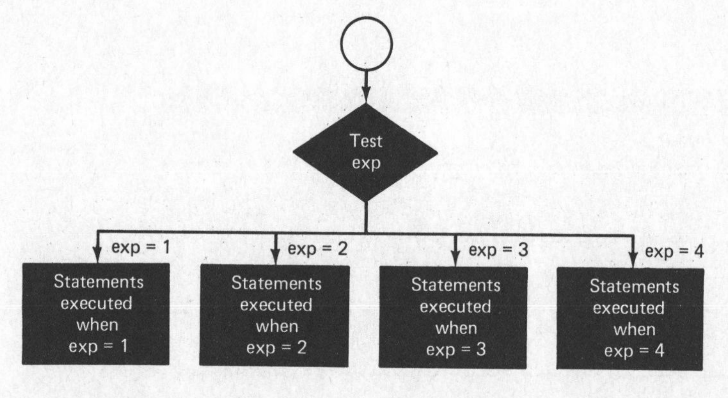

FIGURE 8-9
Flowchart for ON-GOTO structure

As another example, consider the following situation in which test grades are converted to a format suitable for use in the ON-GOTO. A variable, T, is used to input test grades that may range from 0 to 100. The following pair of statements will form a set of directions for controlling the processing of the grades:

```
         :
210  IF T < 60 THEN 300
220  ON (T - 60) / 10 + 1 GOTO 400, 500, 600, 700, 700
         :
300  (processes failing grades)
         :
400  (processes grades of D)
         :
500  (processes grades of C)
         :
600  (processes grades of B)
         :
700  (processes grades of A)
         :
```

Here, we have assumed that fractions are truncated. The IF at line 210 catches all failing grades (T 60) and sends the program to line 300 where these are processed. The expression (T − 60) / 10 + 1 in the ON-GOTO statement converts all the remaining grades to range 1 to 5. Remember that only grades 60 to 100 remain after line 210. Subtracting 60 from these places them in the range 0 to 40. Dividing by 10 converts this to 0 to 4. The +1 is to convert this to 1 to 5, which is a valid range for the ON-GOTO. This means that all grades in the range 60 to 69 will translate into a 1 (assuming truncation); all grades of 70 to 79 into a 2; all of 80 to 89 into a 3; all between 90 to 99 into a 4; and any grades of 100 into a 5. Since both values of 4 and 5 will correspond to a grade of A, both direct processing to line 700.

8-5 AN EXAMPLE: FACULTY SALARY UPDATE

This example will illustrate a typical problem that makes use of the ON-GOTO statement.

Problem: A Faculty Salary Update report is to be prepared that processes salary raises for the faculty of Luckyduck College. There are four faculty ranks at the college that are represented by faculty rank codes 1 to 4 which correspond to academic ranks as given in Table 8-2. Each faculty member will receive a raise to the new salary scale based on the following formula:

$$p = s \times b + m \times y$$

where p = new salary
s = salary scale factor
b = old base salary
m = experience multiplier
y = years experience

TABLE 8-2

Faculty Salary Update Program Parameters

Rank Code	Academic Rank	Salary Scale Factor	Experience Multiplier
1	Instructor	1.05	25
2	Asst Prof	1.10	50
3	Assoc Prof	1.15	75
4	Professor	1.20	100

TABLE 8-3

Data for Faculty Salary Update Example

Faculty Name	Years Experience	Academic Rank Code	Original Base Pay
W. Tower	8	2	15,500
Y. Lee	8	3	18,800
M. Jones	3	1	12,500
H. Bowen	22	4	23,500
P. Swank	6	3	17,900
W. Aaron	14	4	21,500
D. Smith	5	2	14,500
R. Thomas	4	2	14,500
P. Lewis	12	3	19,900
C. Wamble	6	2	15,500

The salary scale factor and experience multiplier have different values depending on the rank and are given in Table 8-2. Input to the program will consist of the faculty member's name, old base salary, years experience, and rank code (Table 8-3). The program should process each faculty member's record and calculate the new salary. The detailed line should print the faculty member's name, years experience, academic rank, and new salary. Totals are to be accumulated for all faculty at each rank (four totals), all faculty, and the total payroll.

The solution to the above problem is outlined below.

1. Print report and column headings.
2. Set all total accumulators equal to zero.
3. Read a faculty pay record.
4. If this is the last record, go to step 25; otherwise, go to the next step.
5. For faculty rank codes of 1, 2, 3, and 4, go to steps 6, 10, 14, and 18, respectively.
6. Assign the proper values from Table 8-2 for the salary scale factor and the experience multiplier for an instructor.
7. Set the academic rank message variable equal to INSTRUCTOR.
8. Add 1 to the number of instructors.
9. Go to step 21.
10. Assign the proper values from Table 8-2 for the salary scale factor and the experience multiplier for an assistant professor.
11. Set the academic rank message variable equal to ASST PROF.
12. Add 1 to the number of assistant professors.
13. Go to step 21.
14. Assign the proper values from Table 8-2 for the salary scale factor and the experience multiplier for an associate professor.
15. Set the academic rank message variable equal to ASSOC PROF.
16. Add 1 to the number of associate professors.
17. Go to step 21.
18. Assign the proper values from Table 8-2 for the salary scale factor and the experience multiplier for a professor.
19. Set the academic rank message variable equal to PROFESSOR.
20. Add 1 to the number of professors.
21. Calculate the new salary.
22. Add 1 to the total faculty and the new salary to the total payroll.
23. Print a detailed line giving faculty and new salary information.
24. Go to step 3.
25. Print totals for faculty at each rank, all faculty, and payroll.
26. Stop.

This procedure is illustrated pictorially in Figure 8-10.

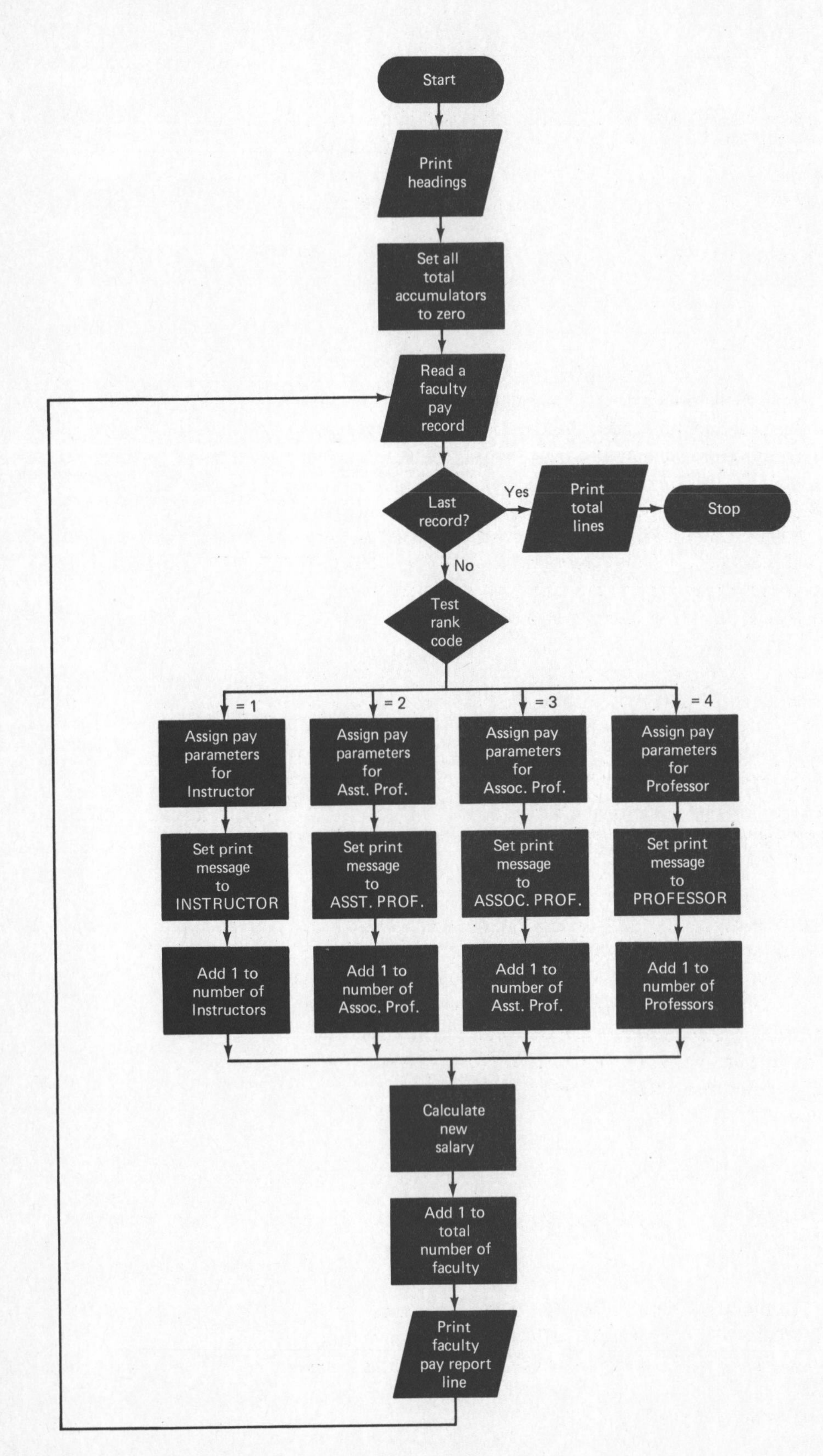

FIGURE 8-10
Flowchart for faculty salary update problem

The program is routine through the statement at line 310. This part of the program corresponds to steps 1 to 4 above. The part of the program that merits our attention begins with the ON-GOTO statement at line 390.

```
390  ON K GOTO 430, 510, 590, 670
```

This provides that, for faculty rank codes of 1 to 4, program control will be directed to lines 430 (K = 1), 510 (K = 2), 590 (K = 3), and 670 (K = 4). In this program, these four branches are all the same except that the first at 430 processes for instructors, the second at 510 for assistant professors, 590 processes associate professors, and the last at 670 takes care of full professors. Let us look at these branches.

The first branch for instructors (steps 6 to 9) beginning at line 430 involves the following set of statements:

```
430  LET S = 1.05
440  LET M = 25
450  LET M$ = "INSTRUCTOR"
460  LET T1 = T1 + 1
470  GOTO 770
```

The two LET statements at lines 430 and 440 assign the values for the salary scale factor and the experience multiplier, respectively. The LET at 450 sets the academic rank message variable equal to INSTRUCTOR. The last LET updates the total number of instructors. The GOTO at line 470 directs processing to a common part of the program where the new salary will be calculated for all faculty, total faculty and payroll will be updated, and a detailed line will be printed.

The second branch for assistant professors (steps 10 to 13) begins at line 510 and consists of the following segment:

```
510  LET S = 1.1
520  LET M = 50
530  LET M$ = "ASST PROF"
540  LET T2 = T2 + 1
550  GOTO 770
```

A quick comparison of this group of statements with those above will show that they are exactly the same except for the various values assigned to the variables. This is also true for the segment for associate professors at lines 590 to 630 and professors at lines 670 to 700. The single exception is that the last group of statements for professors does not end in a GOTO 770 because the next executable statement in the program *is* line 770.

All four branches come back together at line 770 at which point the following set of statements (steps 21 to 24 above) is processed for *all* faculty:

```
770  LET P = S * B + M * Y
780  LET TP = TP + P
790  LET TF = TF + 1
800  PRINT N$, Y, M$, "$"; P
810  GOTO 300
```

The LET at line 770 calculates the new salary, the next two LETs update the totals for all faculty and payroll, and the PRINT at 800 produces a detailed line with faculty data and the new salary. The remainder of the program prints the totals and involves no new processing.

Here is a complete program listing followed by a run:

```
 10 REM  FACULTY SALARY UPDATE
 20 REM
 30 REM  VARIABLES ARE DEFINED AS --
 40 REM
 50 REM          N$ = FACULTY NAME
 60 REM           Y = YEARS EXPERIENCE
 70 REM           K = ACADEMIC RANK CODE
 80 REM          M$ = MESSAGE VARIABLE TO PRINT RANK
 90 REM           S = SALARY SCALE FACTOR
100 REM           M = EXPERIENCE MULTIPLIER
110 REM           B = ORIGINAL BASE PAY
120 REM           P = NEW BASE PAY
130 REM     T1 - T4 = TOTAL FACULTY AT EACH RANK
140 REM          TF = TOTAL FACULTY
150 REM          TP = TOTAL PAYROLL
160 REM
170 REM  PRINT REPORT AND COLUMN HEADINGS
180 REM  AND SET ALL TOTALS EQUAL TO ZERO
190 REM
200 PRINT , " FACULTY SALARY UPDATE"
210 PRINT
220 PRINT
230 PRINT "FACULTY","YEARS"," ACADEMIC","  NEW"
240 PRINT " NAME", " EXP","   RANK", " SALARY"
250 PRINT
260 READ T1, T2, T3, T4, TF, TP
270 REM
280 REM  READ AND PROCESS FACULTY DATA
290 REM
300 READ N$, Y, K, B
310 IF Y < 0 THEN 850
320 REM
330 REM  THE ON-GOTO DIRECTS THE PROGRAM TO THE PROPER
340 REM  SECTION FOR PROCESSING EACH FACULTY RANK.  IN
350 REM  EACH SECTION, VALUES FOR CALCULATING PAY ARE
360 REM  ASSIGNED, THE RANK IS ASSIGNED TO THE PRINT
370 REM  MESSAGE VARIABLE, AND THE PROPER TOTAL UPDATED.
380 REM
390 ON K GOTO 430, 510, 590, 670
400 REM
410 REM  PROCESS THIS SECTION IF INSTRUCTOR
420 REM
430 LET S = 1.05
440 LET M = 25
450 LET M$ = "INSTRUCTOR"
460 LET T1 = T1 + 1
470 GOTO 770
480 REM
490 REM  PROCESS THIS SECTION IF ASSISTANT PROFESSOR
500 REM
510 LET S = 1.1
520 LET M = 50
530 LET M$ = "ASST PROF"
540 LET T2 = T2 + 1
550 GOTO 770
560 REM
570 REM  PROCESS THIS SECTION IF ASSOCIATE PROFESSOR
580 REM
590 LET S = 1.15
600 LET M = 75
610 LET M$ = "ASSOC PROF"
620 LET T3 = T3 + 1
630 GOTO 770
```

```
 640 REM
 650 REM  PROCESS THIS SECTION IF FULL PROFESSOR
 660 REM
 670 LET S = 1.2
 680 LET M = 100
 690 LET M$ = "PROFESSOR"
 700 LET T4 = T4 + 1
 710 REM
 720 REM  THIS SECTION IS PROCESSED FOR ALL FACULTY:
 730 REM  PAY IS CALCULATED, TOTALS FOR ALL FACULTY
 740 REM  AND TOTAL PAYROLL ARE UPDATED AND A
 750 REM  DETAILED LINE IS PRINTED.
 760 REM
 770 LET P = S * B + M * Y
 780 LET TP = TP + P
 790 LET TF = TF + 1
 800 PRINT N$, Y, M$, "$"; P
 810 GOTO 300
 820 REM
 830 REM  PRINT TOTALS
 840 REM
 850 PRINT
 860 PRINT "TOTAL INSTRUCTORS ="; T1
 870 PRINT "TOTAL ASST PROF ="; T2
 880 PRINT "TOTAL ASSOC PROF ="; T3
 890 PRINT "TOTAL PROFESSORS ="; T4
 900 PRINT "TOTAL ALL FACULTY ="; TF
 910 PRINT "TOTAL PAYROLL = $"; TP
 920 REM
 930 REM DATA LIST
 940 REM
 950 DATA 0,0,0,0,0,0,"W TOWER",8,2,15500
 960 DATA "Y LEE",8,3,18800,"M JONES",3,1,12500
 970 DATA "H BOWEN",22,4,23500,"P SWANK",6,3,17900
 980 DATA "W AARON",14,4,21500,"D SMITH",5,2,14500
 990 DATA "R THOMAS",4,2,14500,"P LEWIS",12,3,19900
1000 DATA "C WAMBLE",6,2,15500,"X",-1,0,0
1010 END
```

```
                FACULTY SALARY UPDATE


FACULTY        YEARS           ACADEMIC       NEW
 NAME           EXP              RANK        SALARY

W TOWER         8             ASST PROF     $ 17450
Y LEE           8             ASSOC PROF    $ 22220
M JONES         3             INSTRUCTOR    $ 13200
H BOWEN         22            PROFESSOR     $ 30400
P SWANK         6             ASSOC PROF    $ 21035
W AARON         14            PROFESSOR     $ 27200
D SMITH         5             ASST PROF     $ 16200
R THOMAS        4             ASST PROF     $ 16150
P LEWIS         12            ASSOC PROF    $ 23785
C WAMBLE        6             ASST PROF     $ 17350

TOTAL INSTRUCTORS = 1
TOTAL ASST PROF = 4
TOTAL ASSOC PROF = 3
TOTAL PROFESSORS = 2
TOTAL ALL FACULTY = 10
TOTAL PAYROLL = $ 204990
```

Before leaving this example, it should be mentioned that the several branches produced by an ON-GOTO statement need not necessarily come back together at a common point. They did in the above example because the processing for all the values of the variable K was almost identical. If this were not the case, the branches might not reconverge.

As an example of this from the above program, let us look again at the two IF statements at lines 310 and 390.

```
310  IF Y < THEN O 850
              :
              :
390  ON K GOTO 430, 510, 590, 670
```

If we used K in the sentinel record as the test variable used to stop the program instead of Y, this check could be incorporated into the ON-GOTO as follows:

```
390  ON K GOTO 430, 510, 590, 670, 850
```

In this case, the program will branch to line 850 to print the totals and end when K = 5 just as it would with the original IF at 310 when Y < 0.

8-6 A WORD ABOUT INPUT DATA EDITING

It is very important that the data entered into any program be accurate. We have all heard the stories of the telephone bill for $50,000 or the million dollar paycheck, all because of a misplaced decimal. (In the early days of the space program, a satellite was lost because of a missing decimal point!) Checking the accuracy of the data that is entered into the computer for processing is known as **input data editing**. It is simply not possible to catch all errors, but many of the obvious ones can be trapped rather easily. We will look at an example of input data editing in this section and summarize some of the more common editing checks. Additional examples will appear in the chapters that follow, with more discussion on editing in general in Section 11-6.

In the last two sections, we saw the importance of keeping the variable used in the ON-GOTO within the specified range. This can be achieved with a simple editing check before the ON-GOTO is encountered in the program. Consider the following segment from the program in the last section:

```
300  READ N$, Y, K, B
310  IF Y < 0 THEN 850
                :
                :
390  ON K GOTO 430, 510, 590, 670
```

If it is modified as follows:

```
300 READ N$, Y, K, B
310 IF Y < 0 THEN 850
312 IF K => 1 AND K <= 4 THEN 390
314 PRINT N$, "INVALID RANK CODE -- NOT PROCESSED"
316 GOTO 300
              :
              :
390 ON K GOTO 430, 510, 590, 670
```

the IF checks to insure that K is within the proper range. If it is, processing is sent to the ON-GOTO as before. If, on the other hand, a value of K is found that is not from 1 through 4 (false condition), the next sentence is executed, printing the faculty member's name and a message indicating the error condition. The next line directs the program back to the READ for the next record. Suppose that line 980 in the program in the last section had read as follows:

```
980 DATA "W AARON",14,4,21500,"D SMITH",2,5,14500
```

where the years experience and rank code for D Smith have been accidentally switched. Now the printout will look like this:

```
              FACULTY SALARY UPDATE


FACULTY        YEARS            ACADEMIC         NEW
 NAME          EXP                RANK          SALARY

W TOWER        8              ASST PROF       $ 17450
Y LEE          8              ASSOC PROF      $ 22220
M JONES        3              INSTRUCTOR      $ 13200
H BOWEN        22             PROFESSOR       $ 30400
P SWANK        6              ASSOC PROF      $ 21035
W AARON        14             PROFESSOR       $ 27200
D SMITH        INVALID RANK CODE -- NOT PROCESSED
R THOMAS       4              ASST PROF       $ 16150
P LEWIS        12             ASSOC PROF      $ 23785
C WAMBLE       6              ASST PROF       $ 17350

TOTAL INSTRUCTORS = 1
TOTAL ASST PROF = 3
TOTAL ASSOC PROF = 3
TOTAL PROFESSORS = 2
TOTAL ALL FACULTY = 9
TOTAL PAYROLL = $ 188790
```

The error message appears on the line with Smith's name, and the totals do not include data for Smith.

Edit checks are not necessarily limited to the input data; they can be applied to intermediate calculation or final values as well. The number of checks that are included in any given program is limited only by the specific requirements of the program and the ingenuity of the programmer. Here are three of the most common and easiest to apply edit checks that you might now begin to include in some of your programs.

Range Check: Tests to verify that the given value falls within a specified (known) range of values. The above edit check was a range check.

Value Check: Checks to verify that the given value of a variable is one of a specified set of allowed values. In the above example, we could have performed a value check by testing *each* the four possible values of K individually.

Limit Check: A check to see if a certain value falls within *reasonable* limits. In the above example, we might have checked the calculated salaries to see that none was more than some upper limit, say $50,000. (This could be used to prevent those million dollar phone bills!)

8-7 CONTROL BREAK PROCESSING

Control break processing is a very common and important type of procedure, especially in business-oriented applications. Basically, a **control break** program is one in which one type of processing is temporarily interrupted for a second. For example, a program might be calculating the average daily sales for each salesperson in a department of a store.

Then, when the department changes, before continuing on to the next one, some types of totals or other summary information for the first department could be printed. Here, the report of the sales for each salesperson is temporarily stopped to print the data for the department before continuing with salespersons in the next department; that reflects a control break. Of course, control breaks need not always occur for printing totals, but this seems to be the most common usage.

A control break takes place whenever there is a change in the value of some **key variable** (or **control field**). To check for this change, the previous value must be saved to a **compare variable** to which the current value of the key variable can be compared. When there is a change, the control break takes place and **minor totals** are printed. That is, if the department number changes, then minor totals for the department just processed will be printed; then the new department is processed. There is the problem: To what do you compare the *first* department number? Since there is no value to compare it to, we must provide a method to prevent minor totals from being printed for some nonexistent department. This can be accomplished by the use of a **flag** (or **switch**). This is a variable to which we assign a known value and then, at the proper point in the program, test for that value and branch accordingly. In this case, we will assign some value to our **first record flag** to allow the key variable to be saved to the compare variable but prevent any minor totals from being printed. Since the first record occurs only once, we will change the value of the flag after it is processed so it will not affect any future control breaks. At the end of the report, after all records have been processed, **final** or **grand totals** may be printed.

Clearly, the data values for the key variable must be in a specific sequence before control break processing can be performed. For now, we will assume that the data is prearranged into the proper sequence; however, in Section 12-2 we will learn how to sort or arrange the sequence of a series of data values.

Control breaks can occur in other situations, such as when the key variable assumes a specific value rather than changes, but the general idea of control break processing remains the same. For an example of a different type of control break, see Programming Problem 22 at the end of this chapter. The best way to learn about control breaks is by an example. The next section presents a control break program in detail.

8-8 AN EXAMPLE: INSTRUCTOR'S GRADE REPORT

The example that follows will illustrate the main features of control break processing.

Problem: An Instructor's Grade Report is to be prepared from the data in Table 8-4. Input consists of the class name, student name, three test grades, and a final exam grade. Each student's average is to be calculated by finding the average of the four grades with the final counted twice. A detailed line should print the class name, student name, and test average. A control break is to be taken whenever there is a change in the class name, at which time a minor total line is to be printed with the class average. Final totals at the end of the report should give the total number of classes and students taught. The instructor's name and the current quarter are to appear at the head of the report.

The outline solution to this problem is as follows:

1. Set all minor and final total accumulators equal to zero.
2. Read instructor's name and current quarter.
3. Set the first record control flag equal to a known value, in this case, FIRST.
4. Set the compare variable for the class name (key variable) equal to an initial value, in this case, SAVE-IT.
5. Print main and column headings along with the instructor's name and the current quarter.
6. Read a student record.

TABLE 8-4

Data for Instructor's Grade Report Example

Instructor: E. F. FRANKLIN Quarter: FALL, 1984

Class Name	Student Name	Test 1	Test 2	Test 3	Final Exam
ENG 211	S. Smith	87	69	74	67
ENG 211	R. Brown	93	88	92	85
ENG 211	G. Aimes	77	63	47	64
ENG 365	T. Crump	85	66	74	57
ENG 365	W. Foxx	85	91	78	85
ENG 365	S. Mock	46	52	64	35
ENG 365	H. Peters	79	94	100	88
LIT 401	K. Lang	88	79	93	77
LIT 401	F. Brentt	68	73	76	68
LIT 401	R. Timms	93	100	86	92

7. Compare the current class name to the previous name stored in the compare variable. If it is different, go to step 12. If it is the same, go to the next step.
8. Calculate the student's test average.
9. Print a detailed line with the class name, student name, and test average.
10. Update the minor totals by adding 1 to the number of students in the class and the test average to the total of the averages.
11. Go to step 6.
12. Check to see if this is the first record (test the first record control flag). If it is, go on to the next step; otherwise, go to step 15.
13. Change the value of the test flag.
14. Go to step 20.
15. Calculate class average.
16. Print class average (minor total line).
17. Update final totals by adding 1 to total number of classes and number of students in last class to total in all classes.
18. In this the last record? If so, go to step 22; otherwise, continue to the next step.
19. Reset minor total accumulators for number of students and sum of test grades equal to zero.
20. Set compare variable equal to new class name.
21. Go to step 8.
22. Print final totals for number of classes and students taught.
23. Stop.

This process is illustrated by the flowchart in Figure 8-11.

The first three steps in the above outlined procedure correspond to the following three program statements, respectively:

```
240 READ TS, TA, TC, TT, N$, Q$
250 LET FL$ = "FIRST"
260 LET CP$ = "SAVE-IT"
```

Line 240 initializes all totals to zero and reads the instructor's name and the current quarter. Line 250 sets the first record control flag equal to FIRST. Both the variable FL$ and the value FIRST are arbitrary choices. We could have selected any variable, even a numeric one, and assigned any initial value. The use for this flag will become apparent shortly. The LET at 260 initialized the compare variable; we could have set it equal to anything *except the **first** data value for the key variable.*

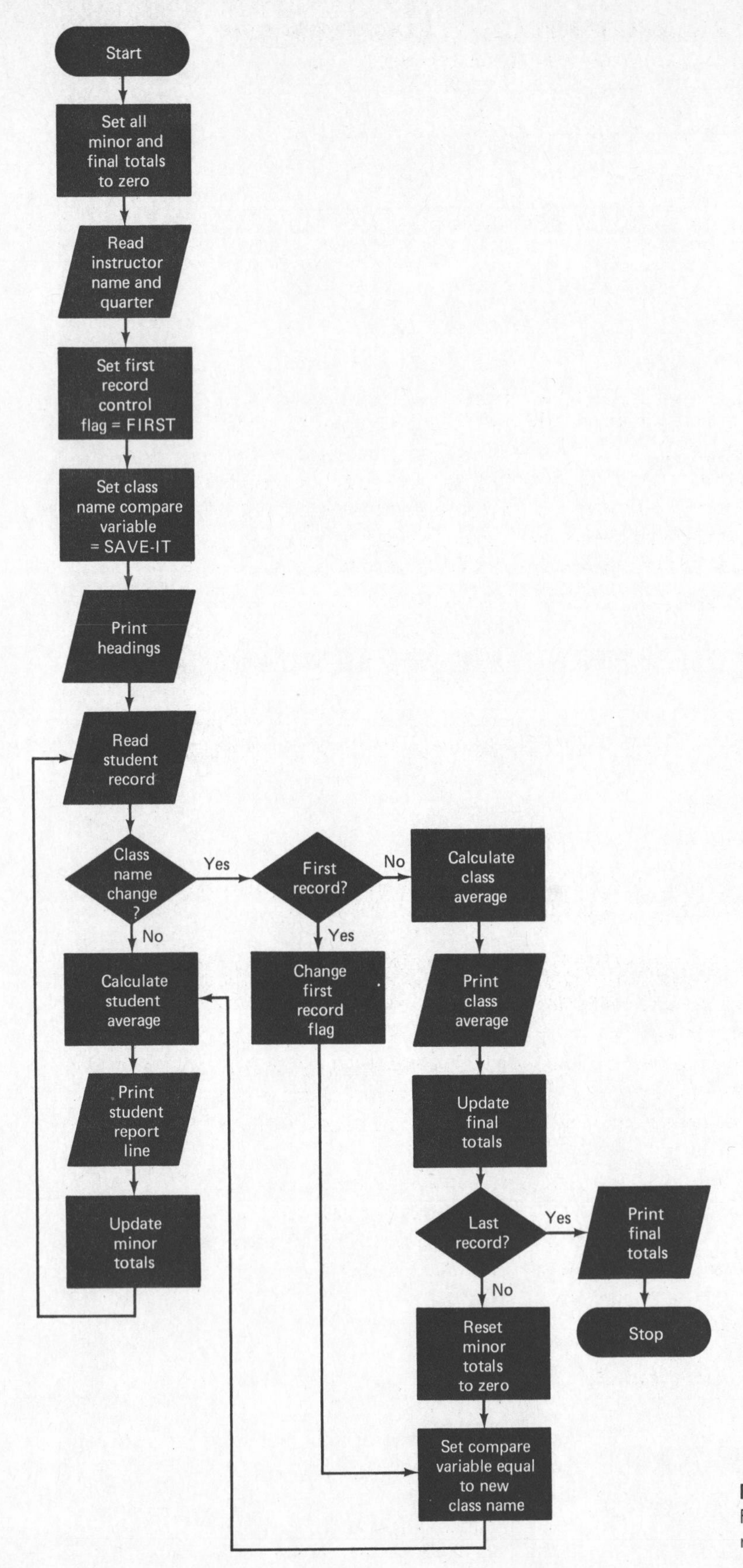

FIGURE 8-11
Flowchart for instructor's grade report problem

The next part of the program is routine through line 430. The IF that tests for a change in the key variable and forces a control break to occur is at line 470.

```
430 READ C$, S$, T1, T2, T3, F
                 :
470 IF C$ <> CP$ THEN 610
                 :
510 LET AV = (T1 + T2 + T3 + 2 * F) / 5
520 PRINT C$, S$, AV
530 LET TS = TS + 1
540 LET TA = TA + AV
550 GOTO 430
```

Immediately after a new record is read, the new value for the class name is compared to the previous one that is stored in the compare variable. If they are *not* equal, control branches to line 610 where the minor totals are processed; we will get to that later. If there is no change in the class name, processing continues to lines 510 to 550 where the individual record is processed. Line 510 calculates the test average, 520 prints a detailed line, and 530 and 540 update the total accumulators for number of students and averages in a class. The GOTO at line 550 directs the program back to the READ at 430 for the next record. This completes the loop that is executed when there is no change in the class name.

Whenever there *is* a change in the class name, the IF at line 470 directs the program to 610 for the control break.

```
610  IF FL$ <> "FIRST" THEN 670
620  LET FL$ = "NOT FIRST"
630  GOTO 790
                :
                :
790  LET CP$ = C$
800  GOTO 510
```

The first thing we do is check for the first record by testing the value of the flag at line 610. If it is not equal to the value that we initially set, it is *not* the first record, and we branch to line 670 to process the minor total line. If it is the first record, then we change the value from FIRST to anything else and will *never* change it back because only *one* first record is ever processed. At line 790, the first value for the class name is assigned to the compare variable for use with the next record. Line 800 directs the program back to 510 to complete the processing of the first record.

Once we have passed the problem of the first record, future minor totals are processed by lines 670 to 800. Of course, processing is first directed to line 610 for a check for the first record; since it is no longer the first record, processing is directed to 670 where the class average is calculated. The minor total line is then printed at 690.

```
670 LET CA = TA / TS
680 PRINT
690 PRINT "CLASS AVERAGE FOR "; CP$; " IS"; CA
700 PRINT
710 LET TC = TC + 1
720 LET TT = TT + TS
                :
760 IF C$ = "LAST" THEN 840
770 LET TS = 0
780 LET TA = 0
790 LET CP$ = C$
800 GOTO 510
```

The two LETs at line 710 and 720 update the final totals for the number of classes and students. The minor total accumulators for number of students and test average sum are reset to zero at lines 770 and 780 so that they will give the correct sums for the next class. The new class name is assigned to the compare variable at 790, and the program is directed back to 510 to complete the processing of the first record for the new class.

The IF at line 760 checks for the sentinel record and provides for a logical end to the program. This is a new position for this statement. It could have been placed immediately following the READ at 430; however, before the final totals can be printed, the minor totals for the *last* class must be processed. This would mean that we would have to rewrite some of the statements that process the minor totals immediately before the final totals. Placing the check for the sentinel record in the section of the program that does the minor totals allows the sentinel record to be initially treated like any other class name change, then it is intercepted during the process of the minor totals and branches to print the final totals. The final totals are printed by lines 840 and 850.

A complete program listing and a run follow:

```
10 REM   INSTRUCTOR'S GRADE REPORT
20 REM
30 REM   VARIABLES ARE DEFINED AS --
40 REM
50 REM            N$ = INSTRUCTOR'S NAME
60 REM            Q$ = QUARTER OF REPORT
70 REM            C$ = CLASS NAME
80 REM            S$ = STUDENT NAME
90 REM       T1 - T3 = TEST GRADES
100 REM            F = FINAL EXAM GRADE
110 REM           AV = STUDENT TEST AVERAGE
120 REM           TS = TOTAL STUDENTS IN CLASS
130 REM           TA = SUM OF STUDENT AVERAGES
140 REM           CA = CLASS AVERAGE
150 REM           TC = TOTAL CLASSES
160 REM           TT = TOTAL STUDENTS IN ALL CLASSES
170 REM          FL$ = FIRST RECORD FLAG
180 REM          CP$ = CLASS NAME SAVE VARIABLE
190 REM
200 REM  SET ALL TOTALS EQUAL TO ZERO, INITIALIZE THE
210 REM  FIRST RECORD FLAG AND CLASS NAME SAVE VARIABLE,
220 REM  AND READ INSTRUCTOR'S NAME AND QUARTER
230 REM
240 READ TS, TA, TC, TT, N$, Q$
250 LET FL$ = "FIRST"
260 LET CP$ = "SAVE-IT"
270 REM
280 REM  PRINT MAIN AND COLUMN HEADINGS
290 REM  AND INSTRUCTOR NAME AND QUARTER
300 REM
310 PRINT "      INSTRUCTOR'S GRADE REPORT"
320 PRINT
330 PRINT
340 PRINT "INSTRUCTOR:    "; N$
350 PRINT "QUARTER:       "; Q$
360 PRINT
370 PRINT " CLASS", "STUDENT", " TEST"
380 PRINT " NAME", " NAME", "AVERAGE"
390 PRINT
400 REM
410 REM  READ STUDENT RECORD
420 REM
430 READ C$, S$, T1, T2, T3, F
440 REM
450 REM CHECK FOR CHANGE IN CLASS NAME
```

```
460 REM
470 IF C$ <> CP$ THEN 610
480 REM
490 REM  PROCESS RECORD WITH NO CLASS CHANGE
500 REM
510 LET AV = (T1 + T2 + T3 + 2 * F) / 5
520 PRINT C$, S$, AV
530 LET TS = TS + 1
540 LET TA = TA + AV
550 GOTO 430
560 REM
570 REM  PROCESS CONTROL BREAK WHEN CLASS NAME CHANGES
580 REM
590 REM  FIRST CHECK FOR FIRST RECORD
600 REM
610 IF FL$ <> "FIRST" THEN 670
620 LET FL$ = "NOT FIRST"
630 GOTO 790
640 REM
650 REM  PROCESS MINOR TOTALS
660 REM
670 LET CA = TA / TS
680 PRINT
690 PRINT "CLASS AVERAGE FOR "; CP$; " IS"; CA
700 PRINT
710 LET TC = TC + 1
720 LET TT = TT + TS
730 REM
740 REM  CHECK FOR LAST RECORD
750 REM
760 IF C$ = "LAST" THEN 840
770 LET TS = 0
780 LET TA = 0
790 LET CP$ = C$
800 GOTO 510
810 REM
820 REM  PROCESS FINAL TOTALS
830 REM
840 PRINT "TOTAL CLASSES TAUGHT ="; TC
850 PRINT "TOTAL STUDENTS TAUGHT ="; TT
860 REM
870 REM  DATA LIST
880 REM
890 DATA 0, 0, 0, 0, "E F FRANKLIN", "FALL, 1984"
900 DATA "ENG 211", "S SMITH", 87, 69, 74, 67
910 DATA "ENG 211", "R BROWN", 93, 88, 92, 85
920 DATA "ENG 211", "G AIMES", 77, 63, 47, 64
930 DATA "ENG 365", "T CRUMP", 85, 66, 74, 57
940 DATA "ENG 365", "W FOXX", 85, 91, 78, 85
950 DATA "ENG 365", "S MOCK", 46, 52, 64, 35
960 DATA "ENG 365", "H PETERS", 79, 94, 100, 88
970 DATA "LIT 401", "K LANG", 88, 79, 93, 77
980 DATA "LIT 401", "F BRENTT", 68, 73, 76, 68
990 DATA "LIT 401", "R TIMMS", 93, 100, 86, 92
1000 DATA "LAST", "Z", 0, 0, 0, 0
1010 END
```

```
      INSTRUCTOR'S GRADE REPORT


INSTRUCTOR:   E F FRANKLIN
QUARTER:      FALL, 1984
```

```
CLASS          STUDENT          TEST
NAME            NAME          AVERAGE

ENG 211       S SMITH          72.8
ENG 211       R BROWN          88.6
ENG 211       G AIMES          63

CLASS AVERAGE FOR ENG 211 IS 74.8

ENG 365       T CRUMP          67.8
ENG 365       W FOXX           84.8
ENG 365       S MOCK           46.4
ENG 365       H PETERS         89.8

CLASS AVERAGE FOR ENG 365 IS 72.2

LIT 401       K LANG           82.8
LIT 401       F BRENTT         70.6
LIT 401       R TIMMS          92.6

CLASS AVERAGE FOR LIT 401 IS 82

TOTAL CLASSES TAUGHT = 3
TOTAL STUDENTS TAUGHT = 10
```

TROUBLESHOOTING

Each of the following programs contains an error that prevents it from executing properly. Explain *specifically* what the problem is and what must be done to correct it. To assist you, a sample of what would happen should you attempt to run the program is provided after each listing. Refer to Appendix D for an explanation of BASIC error messages.

1.

```
 10 REM  TROUBLESHOOTING PROBLEM 8-1
 20 REM
 30 REM           N = INTEGERS FROM 1-10
 40 REM           S = SUM OF VALUES OF N
 50 REM
 60 LET S = 0
 70 FOR N = 1 TO 10
 80    LET N = N + 1
 90    LET S = S + N
100 NEXT N
110 PRINT "THE SUM OF THE INTEGERS"
120 PRINT "FROM 1-10 IS"; S
130 END

THE SUM OF THE INTEGERS
FROM 1-10 IS 30
```

2.

```
 10 REM  TROUBLESHOOTING PROBLEM 8-2
 20 REM
 30 REM           N = ACCOUNT NUMBER
 40 REM           R = QUARTERLY INTEREST RATE
 50 REM           A = AMOUNT IN ACCOUNT
 60 REM           Q = QUARTERLY COUNTER
 70 REM          M$ = INVALID RATE INDICATOR
 80 REM
 90 READ N, R, A
100 PRINT N, "$"; A, R; "%"
110 IF N < 0 THEN 240
120 IF R => 1 AND R <= 3 THEN 150
130 LET M$ = "RATE OUT OF RANGE"
```

```
140 GOTO 180
150 LET M$ = " "
160 FOR Q = 1 TO 4
170   LET A = A + R * A / 100
180   PRINT Q, "$"; A, M$
190 NEXT Q
200 PRINT
210 GOTO 90
220 DATA 23554, 1.5, 1500, 25443, .5, 1750
230 DATA 43985, 2, 1600, -1, 0, 0
240 END
```

```
23554        $ 1500        1.5 %
1            $ 1522..5
2            $ 1545.34
3            $ 1568.52
4            $ 1598.05

25443        $ 1750         .5 %
5            $ 1750       RATE OUT OF RANGE
```

NEXT without **FOR** in Line 190

3.

```
10 REM  TROUBLESHOOTING PROBLEM 8-3
20 REM
30 REM        A = FIRST NUMBER
40 REM        B = SECOND NUMBER'
50 REM        C = PRODUCT OF A AND B
60 REM
70 FOR A = 1 TO 6
80   FOR B = 1 TO 6
90     LET C = A * B
100    PRINT C; "="; A; "X"; B
110  NEXT A
120 NEXT B
130 END
```

```
1 = 1 X 1
2 = 2 X 1
3 = 3 X 1
4 = 4 X 1
5 = 5 X 1
6 = 6 X 1
```

NEXT without **FOR** in Line 120

4.

```
10 REM  TROUBLESHOOTING PROBLEM 8-4
20 REM
30 REM        J = FIRST NUMBER
40 REM          K = SECOND NUMBER
50 REM          P = PRODUCT OF J AND K
60 REM
70 FOR J = 1 TO 5
80   FOR K = 5 TO J
90     LET P = J * K
100    PRINT "THE PRODUCT OF"; J; "AND"; K; "IS"; P
110  NEXT K
120 NEXT J
130 END
```

```
THE PRODUCT OF 1 AND 5 IS 5
THE PRODUCT OF 2 AND 5 IS 10
THE PRODUCT OF 3 AND 5 IS 15
THE PRODUCT OF 4 AND 5 IS 20
THE PRODUCT OF 5 AND 5 IS 25
```

5.

```
 10 REM  TROUBLESHOOTING PROBLEM 8-5
 20 REM
 30 REM        N$ = STUDENT NAME
 40 REM         G = GPA
 50 REM        M$ = PRINT MESSAGE
 60 REM        T1 = TOTAL EXCLUDED
 70 REM        T2 = TOTAL ON PROBATION
 80 REM        T3 = TOTAL ON DEAN'S LIST
 90 REM        T4 = TOTAL SPECIAL SCHOLARS
100 REM
110 READ T1, T2, T3, T4
120 READ N$, G
130 IF G < 0 THEN 300
140 ON G GOTO 150, 180, 210, 230, 260
150 LET M$ = "EXCLUSION"
160 LET T1 = T1 + 1
170 GOTO 280
180 LET M$ = "PROBATION"
190 LET T2 = T2 + 1
200 GOTO 280
210 LET M$ = " "
220 GOTO 280
230 LET M$ = "DEAN'S LIST"
240 LET T3 = T3 + 1
250 GOTO 280
260 LET M$ = "SPECIAL SCHOLAR"
270 LET T4 = T4 + 1
280 PRINT N$, G, M$
290 GOTO 120
300 PRINT
310 PRINT "TOTAL EXCLUDED ="; T1
320 PRINT "TOTAL ON PROBATION ="; T2
330 PRINT "TOTAL ON DEAN'S LIST ="; T3
340 PRINT "TOTAL SPECIAL SCHOLARS ="; T4
350 DATA 0, 0, 0, 0, "E BOND", 3.99, "R HOBBS", 2.89
360 DATA "R CRAIG", 0.89, "W UPTON", 3.63
370 DATA "J REESE", 2.24, "W ADAMS", 1.57, "X", -1
380 END
```

```
E BOND        3.99
R HOBBS       2.89          PROBATION
R CRAIG       .89           EXCLUSION
W UPTON       3.63
J REESE       2.24          PROBATION
W ADAMS       1.57          EXCLUSION

TOTAL EXCLUDED = 2
TOTAL ON PROBATION = 2
TOTAL ON DEAN'S LIST = 0
TOTAL SPECIAL SCHOLARS = 0
```

6.

```
 10 REM  TROUBLESHOOTING PROBLEM 8-6
 20 REM
 30 REM  P AND R = TWO INTEGERS
 40 REM        A = AVERAGE OF P AND R
 50 REM
 60 FOR P = -4 TO 12 STEP 4
 70   FOR R = 2 TO P STEP P / 2
 80     LET A = (P + R) / 2
 90     PRINT "THE AVERAGE"; P;"AND"; R; "IS"; A
100   NEXT R
110 NEXT P
120 END
```

```
THE AVERAGE OF-4 AND 2 IS-1
THE AVERAGE OF-4 AND 0 IS-2
THE AVERAGE OF-4 AND-2 IS-3
THE AVERAGE OF-4 AND-4 IS-4
THE AVERAGE OF 0 AND 2 IS 1
THE AVERAGE OF 0 AND 2 IS 1
THE AVERAGE OF 0 AND 2 IS 1
THE AVERAGE OF 0 AND 2 IS 1
THE AVERAGE OF 0 AND 2 IS 1
                :
                :
                :
                :
```

IMPORTANT TERMS

After studying this chapter, you should be familiar with the meaning and use of the following terms and BASIC statements:

FOR-NEXT loop
Loop counter
Index
Initial value
Test value
Step
FOR without NEXT error
NEXT without FOR error
Nested FOR-NEXT structures
ON-GOTO statement
Value out of Range error
Input data editing
Range check
Value check
Limit check
Control break
Key variable
Control field
Compare value for key variable
Minor totals
Flag
Switch
First record control
Grand (or final) totals

EXERCISES

1. Write FOR-NEXT statements that will count:
   (a) From 2 to 24
   (b) From 1 to 15 by 2s
   (c) From 0 to 100 by 5s
   (d) 10, 9, 8, 7, 6, 5, 4, 3, 2, 1
   (e) Backwards from 100 to −100 by 10s
   (f) From 4 to 5 by 0.1
   (g) Backwards from 6 to 2 by 0.4
   (h) 15, 21, 27, 33, 39, 45
   (i) 95, 60, 25, −10, −25, −80, −115
   (j) 10.0, 9.8, 9.6, 9.4, 9.2, 9.0, 8.8, 8.6, 8.4

2. Give the sequence of numbers that the counter will assume for each of the following FOR-NEXT statements:

(a)
```
FOR X = 1 TO 12
      :
NEXT X
```
(b)
```
FOR P = 3 TO 18 STEP 3
          :
NEXT P
```
(c)
```
FOR S = -12 TO 12 STEP 4
          :
NEXT S
```

(d)
```
FOR A = 75 TO -30 STEP -15
         :
NEXT A
```
(e)
```
FOR I = 10 TO 12 STEP .2
         :
NEXT I
```
(f)
```
FOR Z = 1 TO -1 STEP .1
         :
NEXT Z
```
(g)
```
FOR N = 1 TO 5
   FOR M = 1 to 3
         :
   NEXT M
NEXT N
```
(h)
```
FOR J = 1 to 4
   FOR K = 1 to J
         :
   NEXT K
NEXT J
```
(i)
```
FOR X = 2 TO 4
   FOR Y = X TO 5
         :
   NEXT Y
NEXT X
```
(j)
```
FOR D = 1 TO 3
   FOR E = D TO 4
      FOR F = 1 TO 2
         :
      NEXT F
   NEXT E
NEXT D
```

3. Write mathematical expressions to convert the range of the given variables to a range that is suitable for use with the ON-GOTO statement. (Assume truncation of fractions.)

(a) $0 \leqslant B \leqslant 5$ (b) $-2 \leqslant V \leqslant 2$
(c) $0 \leqslant N \leqslant 50$ (d) $-40 \leqslant F \leqslant 40$
(e) $100 \leqslant X \leqslant 200$ (f) $-50 \leqslant J \leqslant 250$
(g) $50 < R < 300$ (h) $-500 < W < 200$

For Exercises 4 to 7, give the output that will be produced by the given programs. Then, type the programs into the computer, run them, and check the actual outputs against your predictions.

4.
```
10 FOR X = -3 TO 5
20    LET Y = 2 * X - 1
30    PRINT X, Y
40 NEXT X
50 END
```
5.
```
10 FOR X = -4 TO 4
20    IF X <> 0 THEN 50
30    PRINT "X = 0 -- Y IS UNDEFINED!!"
40    GOTO 70
50    LET Y = 1 / X
60    PRINT X, Y
70 NEXT X
80 END
```
6.
```
10 FOR N = 2 TO 5
20    FOR M = 1 TO 4
```

```
30        LET R = 2 * N - 3 * M
40        PRINT N, M, R
50     NEXT M
60 NEXT N
```

7.
```
10 FOR A = 2 TO 8 STEP 2
20    FOR B = 2 TO A STEP 2
30       LET C = (A + B) / 2
40       PRINT "THE AVERAGE"; A; "AND"; B; "IS"; C
50    NEXT B
60 NEXT A
70 END
```

PROGRAMMING PROBLEMS

Write programs in BASIC to accomplish the tasks described by each of the following problems. Be sure to carefully document each program and include all appropriate report headings and other literals.

1. Rewrite the program for Programming Problem 2 of Chapter 7 using a FOR-NEXT loop to keep count of the days rather than an IF statement.
2. Rewrite the program for Programming Problem 3 of Chapter 7 using a FOR-NEXT loop to control the limits of the table instead of an IF statement.
3. Write a program to find the sum of the first 250 *even* positive integers.
4. Write a program to input an item and its current cost and then print a series of values projecting what the cost of the item will be for each of the next 20 years at constant inflation rates of 3, 6, 9, and 12 percent. To calculate the inflated value of a $100.00 item at 3 percent, in the first year the cost will increase by $100.00 + 0.03 × $100.00 = $103.00. In the second year the increase is $103.00 + 0.03 × $103.00 = $106.09 and so forth. The printout should have columns for the years (printed as *years,* not just numbers) and one for each of the four inflation rates. The name, initial value, and current year should appear at the top of the report. You supply the data for this one.
5. Revise your program for Programming Problem 13 of Chapter 7 to use a FOR-NEXT loop to count the months.
6. Rewrite your program for Programming Problem 16 of Chapter 7 using a FOR-NEXT loop to control the limits of x rather than an IF statement.
7. A certain author is to be paid royalties on book sales at the following rates:

   10 percent on the first 10,000 copies
   15 percent on all sales from 10,000 to 15,000 copies
   20 percent on all sales beyond 15,000 copies

   Thus, if a book sells 18,000 copies, the author will receive 10 percent for 10,000 copies, 15 percent for the next 5000, and 20 percent for the last 3000. Write a program to input the author's name, title of the book, and price. The printout should provide a list of the number of copies by increments of 1000 from 1000 through 25,000, with the net sales and the royalties due the author for each increment. (The net sales is simply the number of copies times the base price.) For input, use *Answers to Everything* by I. Knoh Itall at $25.00 per copy.
8. Write a program to calculate and print the sum, difference, product, and quotient of all possible combinations of two integers in the range 10 to 15. Print the two integers followed by the four calculated values.
9. Ignatz has just opened a retirement account which pays 1 percent per month to which he plans to deposit $100 each month with an extra $500 at the end of each year. Write a program to calculate and print how much Ignatz will have in his account at the end of each of the next 20 years.

10. A combination lock to a safe has only eight digits on the dial, 0 to 7. It is also known that the combination to the safe consists of only three digits. Write a program to print all possible three-digit combinations of the eight digits and give the total number. The printout should be folded with five combinations per print line.
11. A certain company has employees that work in three shifts who have base pay rates of \$6.00, \$6.75, and \$7.50 per hour and are identified by shift codes of 1, 2, and 3, respectively. Write a program to produce a Payroll Report from the data below. Each detailed line should give the employee's name, shift code, and pay (with overtime, if earned). Totals are to be printed for the number of employees on each shift, all employees, and total payroll.

Employee Name	Shift Code	Hours Worked
R. Harris	1	37
T. Yetter	2	40
A. Towns	1	43
S. Craig	3	36
T. Lewis	2	28
B. Morton	3	38
J. Lang	1	40
S. Agnew	2	42

12. Revise your program for Problem 12 from Chapter 7 to use an ON-GOTO statement. Refer to the method outlined at the end of Section 8-4 for assistance.
13. The following students attend Greenwood College:

Student Name	Total Hours	Student Name	Total Hours
H. Gibson	55	R. Roam	45
Y. Friend	180	S. Roam	165
R. Davis	15	P. Lewis	95
E. Smith	110	Y. Young	40
T. Horne	125	T. Wilson	190
R. King	155	T. Clarke	90
F. Jones	135	A. Moore	65
S. Anders	70	L. Timms	105

Write a program to read the student names and total quarter hours credit and print a list of the students, identifying each by class as follows:

0–45 hours	Freshman
46–90 hours	Sophomore
91–135 hours	Junior
136–180 hours	Senior

No student should have more than 180 hours. An edit check should be performed for this with the message EXCESS HOURS printed for any student failing this check. The total number of students in each class as well as the total of all students is to be printed at the end of the list. Data is provided above.
14. The Wooton Company has four classifications of employees identified by class codes of 1 to 4 corresponding to the following payment methods:

Class Code	Employee Classification	Method Used to Determine Employee's Salary
1	Management	\$1250 + 1.5% of sales
2	Salaried	\$750 + 1.0% of sales
3	Commissioned	6.0% of sales
4	Trainee	4.0% of sales

Write a program to process the data below and produce a Monthly Payroll Report. Input will be the employee's name, class code, and total sales. Output should be the employee's name, classification, and salary. Totals are to be accumulated for the number of employees and salary paid for each classification as well as totals for all employees and salary. An edit check should be performed to verify that only proper codes are input, with the message INVALID CODE—RECORD NOT PROCESSED printed for bad codes.

Employee Name	Class Code	Total Sales	Employee Name	Class Code	Total Sales
P. Smith	1	15,500	R. Wilkes	2	17,500
T. Robson	2	12,500	W. Cruz	5	13,500
R. Eason	3	15,000	F. Carson	1	16,500
K. Quinn	1	17,500	T. Langley	3	22,500
T. Wong	2	10,000	L. Wiley	4	8,000
F. Watson	4	7,500	R. Monroe	3	15,500

15. A Checking Account Statement is to be prepared for the customers of the Last National Bank. The customer's name, account number, and beginning balance are to be printed at the top of the report. Transaction records giving the date, code, and amount of each transaction are then to be processed. Detailed lines are to show the date, amount of the transaction in the proper column, and the updated balance. There are three types of transactions that are to be considered. They are identified by codes of 1 to 3 as follows:

Code	Type of Transaction	Action Taken
1	Deposit	Credited to account
2	Withdrawal	Subtracted from account
3	Other charges	Same as withdrawal

There will be five possible fields on each detailed line, but only *three* will be used on any one line because each can only represent one type of transaction. At the end of the report, print the total number and amount of the transactions of each type and the final balance.

Customer's Name: E Kendra Harrison
Account Number: 22-78-003 Beginning Balance: 336.59

Date	Code	Amount	Date	Code	Amount
2/02/84	2	21.78	2/22/84	2	63.84
2/03/84	2	126.43	2/24/84	2	118.55
2/03/84	2	55.06	2/27/84	1	150.00
2/13/84	2	9.14	2/28/84	2	11.65
2/16/84	3	10.00	2/29/84	2	79.05
2/16/84	1	300.00	2/29/84	3	5.00
2/17/84	2	250.00	2/29/84	1	540.00

16. From the data at the top of the next page, which provides the department name, salesperson's name, and total weekly sales, prepare a program to produce a Department Sales Report. This will be a control break program that reprints the individual sales data but also gives departmental totals for number of salespersons and total sales whenever there is a change in department number. Final totals should be printed at the end of the report for total number of departments, salespersons, and sales.

Department Name	Salesperson Name	Total Sales
Furniture	T. J. Evans	3677.34
Furniture	R. K. Love	6455.02
Furniture	A. L. Nunn	5766.30
Appliances	W. W. Davis	7944.36
Appliances	P. H. Butts	2465.00
Toys & Games	T. N. Jolly	6488.38
Clothing	Y. F. Howe	7533.03
Clothing	D. H. Lewis	980.77
Clothing	P. T. Vann	3788.90
Clothing	R. K. Scott	4377.56

17. An Expense Account Report is to be prepared for the sales representatives of the Databit Computer Company. Input consists of the salesperson's name, type of expense, and amount. A salesperson may have more than one expense to declare; therefore, a total of all expenses for each salesperson must be taken. A detailed line is to be printed that lists each expense claim. A control break is to be taken whenever there is a change of salesperson, with the total number and amount of expenses being printed before resuming the processing of the next salesperson. If any salesperson has total expenses in excess of $1000, the warning message OVERDRAWN should appear on the minor total line. Final totals should be printed for the number of salespersons and total amount of all expenses claimed. Data is provided below.

Salesperson Name	Type of Expense	Amount of Expense
T. K. Lee	Car Rental	135.65
T. K. Lee	Food	27.88
T. K. Lee	Hotel	136.28
F. A. Collins	Food	37.19
H. L. Newton	Hotel	368.98
H. L. Newton	Food	105.39
H. L. Newton	Car Rental	203.74
H. L. Newton	Airline	528.00
R. R. Towns	Car Rental	57.36
R. R. Towns	Food	25.85

18. Revise your program for Problem 17 to produce what is called a **group printed** report. For this report, *no* detailed lines are printed, only summary information as minor total lines which in this case should include the salesperson's name, total number of claims, total amount of claims, and overdrawn message as appropriate.
19. An Invoice Summary Report is to be prepared from a list of sales receipts for a given date. The input is to consist of the customer's account number, the item number, the unit price, and the quantity. The total purchase price for each item is to be calculated as the unit price times the quantity sold. A control break will occur whenever there is a change in the customer account number. The input data plus the total price are to be printed on each detailed line. Minor totals are to be accumulated for the number of items sold, the total quantity, and total price. Final totals are to be found for the total number of customers and total sales. Data is given at the top of page 185.
20. Revise your program for Problem 19 to produce what is called a **group indicated** report. In this form of report, the key variable (in this case the account number) should appear only on the first of the detailed lines and is suppressed (left blank) on all subsequent lines. When there is a control break, the new value is printed once for the new group of detailed lines.

Account Number	Item Number	Unit Price	Quantity Sold
38894	783990	18.90	5
38894	892002	120.00	2
38894	911226	67.50	1
40022	166591	22.50	8
40022	233356	2.98	200
40022	325568	35.00	15
40022	865549	49.00	1
53312	166591	22.50	20
74001	325568	35.00	10
74001	568411	52.50	4
74001	783990	18.90	15
74001	884568	195.00	1

21. A program is needed to produce a Depreciated Value Inventory Report for Jonesboro, Inc. Input will be the department number, item number, original value, anticipated lifetime, and age in years. The present value for each item is to be calculated by the double-declining balance method (see Section 8-2) and printed on the detailed line following the department and item numbers and age of the item. If an item's age has exceeded its projected lifetime, a message BEYOND LIFETIME should appear on that line of the printout. A control break is to occur whenever there is a change in the department number, with minor totals printed for number of items in the department and total depreciated value. Final totals are to be accumulated for the number of departments, total items in all departments, and total depreciated value for all items. Data is given below.

Department Number	Item Number	Original Value	Anticipated Lifetime	Current Age
263	147879	100.00	10	4
263	195673	250.00	25	12
263	213564	175.00	5	8
263	296653	75.00	10	14
471	284653	99.00	5	1
471	394562	1,500.00	25	16
471	500689	435.00	15	15
471	621358	200.00	10	12
471	246531	450.00	15	6
501	164475	900.00	15	17
501	111256	3,750.00	30	9
501	204300	65.00	10	10

22. Assume that the data for Problem 14 is arranged so that each manager is listed first, followed by all employees in his or her group. Revise your program to take a control break whenever a management-level employee is encountered, printing the number of employees of each class and the total sales for each group as a minor total. At the end of the report, print the total number of employees of each type, total employees, total sales, and total commissions paid.

CHAPTER 9

ARRAYS

If you were to ask professional programmers to name the one most useful feature available in any high-level language such as BASIC, the most frequent response would be its ability to represent data as subscripted variables. This capability of arranging sets of data values into arrays provides some of the most powerful processing techniques offered by computers. In this chapter, we will look at some of the fundamental techniques involved in handling simple arrays; in Chapters 12 and 13, we will study more advanced arrays.

9-1 SUBSCRIPTED VARIABLES: THE DIM STATEMENT

It is possible to assign *more than one* data value to the same data name. This is done with the use of **subscripted variables**. A subscripted variable has the general form:

variable(subscript)

where the *variable* is designated, with most BASICs, in the same way as any other variable and can be either string or numeric. The **subscript** is any positive numeric constant, variable, or mathematical expression and is used to specify which value of the variable is to be used. Examples of subscripted variables are:

A(7)	(the seventh value of A)
TJ(43)	(the forty-third value of TJ)
F$(17)	(the seventeenth value of F$)

The above three values are read "A sub 7," "TJ sub 43," and "F$ sub 17," respectively.

Before a variable is used in the program, the computer must be notified that the specific variable is to be subscripted and to what **dimension** (the number of values). This is done by means of the **DIM** (for DIMension) statement. The DIM statement is nonexecutable and has the general form:

DIM *var(sub) list*

where *var(sub) list* is a list of subscripted variables separated by commas. Most versions of BASIC require that subscripts used in the DIM statement be numeric *constants*. Subscripts here *must* provide for the maximum number of values that are to be assigned to the corresponding variable. Suppose that we are to have three subscripted variables, A, R$, and NH, in a program, and A is to have 20 values, R$ 35, and NH 15. The DIM statement for this might be:

```
DIM A(20), R$(35), NH(15)
```

Of course, the variables could all be in separate DIM statements:

```
DIM A(20)
DIM R$(35)
DIM NH(15)
```

or any combination between. All DIM statements need not be placed at the same point in a program; however, a subscripted variable must be dimensioned before it is used, and then it *cannot be redimensioned*. (Many versions of BASIC will automatically dimension a variable up to 10. If this is available on your system, it is a convenience for small arrays, but we will not assume it here.)

An **array** is the collected set of values assigned to any one subscripted variable. A **table** consists of one or more related arrays. Frequently these terms are used interchangeably. For example, the subscripted variable X may be referred to as the array X. Figure 9-1 illustrates an array for the 12 values of the subscripted variable M that has been dimensioned as follows:

```
DIM M(12)
```

This array has 12 possible values, all of which do not have to be used, as we will see later in this chapter. The *position* of a value in the array is indicated by the subscript. For the array shown in Figure 9-1, the *fifth* value in the array is 18.4 and is denoted by the variable M(5). Note that the subscript is 5 for the fifth value. Be careful to distinguish between the subscript and the data value stored in a given location. The subscript only indicates *where* in the array a particular value is to be found and has no numerical relation to the value it locates. In fact, an array may store string values in which case the subscript may designate the location of a name, address, or other string value.

Care must always be taken to ensure that the value of a subscript never exceeds the value for which the array was dimensioned. For the array shown in Figure 9-1, the subscript may have values from 1 through 12. Subscripts may *never* be negative or beyond the value specified in the DIM statement for the given subscripted variable. Most versions of BASIC include a **zeroth position** for all arrays. Thus, if a variable is dimensioned for 20, on these systems you actually have *21* locations in the array numbered from 0 through 20. For the array M in Figure 9-1, this would add an extra position, M(0), at the top of the array. The use of the zeroth location can be confusing and can increase the number of

Subscripted Variable	Value Stored	Relation of Array to Values
M (1)	34.2	M (1) = 34.2
M (2)	19.54	M (2) = 19.54
M (3)	-2.33	M (3) = -2.33
M (4)	733	M (4) = 733
M (5)	18.4	M (5) = 18.4
M (6)	0.89	M (6) = 0.89
M (7)	0	M (7) = 0
M (8)	177.3	M (8) = 177.3
M (9)	-9368	M (9) = -9368
M (10)	22	M (10) = 22
M (11)	83.57	M (11) = 83.57
M (12)	3.447	M (12) = 3.447

FIGURE 9-1
The relation of an array to the stored data

subscript errors because a subscript of 5, for example, will denote the *sixth* location in the array rather than the fifth. Even if available, this extra position may be ignored and used only when there is a specific use for it. (If you have the **OPTION BASE** statement on your system, you may select whether arrays are numbered from 0 or 1.) Since it is not standard with all BASICs, we will not assume the zeroth position here; however, for the benefit of those who have this feature on their system, some uses for the zeroth location will be illustrated in several of the examples throughout the remainder of this chapter.

As stated earlier in this section, the subscript may also be a numeric variable or mathematical expression. The following are examples of subscripted variables with subscripts expressed as nonconstants:

```
G5(N)
V$(K + 2)
YF(2 * X - 1)
```

In such cases, even more care must be taken to ensure that the value of the subscript remains within the proper range. Should the value be negative or too large, an error message such as **Invalid Subscript** or **Subscript Out of Range** will result. The presence of fractional values as subscripts presents yet another danger. As with the ON–GOTO statement (see Section 8-4), some versions of BASIC will round the fraction, and others will truncate it. You will have to check to see what your system does. We will assume truncation.

9-2 INPUT AND OUTPUT WITH ARRAYS

The first thing to remember when working with subscripted variables and arrays is that every individual value of the variable for each subscript (each **element** of the array) is a variable in its own right and is to be treated as such. This means that each can be read, printed, used in mathematical calculations, compared as part of a logical expression, or used in any other way that you would use a nonsubscripted variable. Let us look at some examples.

Normally, the first thing that one needs to do with an array is to assign values to the designated locations. This can be done much as it would be with regular variables except that now we have many more values to assign. For example, the 12 values for M in Figure 9-1 could be assigned by 12 LET statements:

```
200 LET M(1) = 34.2
210 LET M(2) = 19.54
220 LET M(3) = -2.33
230 LET M(4) = 733
240 LET M(5) = 18.4
250 LET M(6) = 0.89
260 LET M(7) = 0
270 LET M(8) = 177.3
280 LET M(9) = -9368
290 LET M(10) = 22
300 LET M(11) = 83.57
310 LET M(12) = 3.447
```

We could also use READ/DATA statements as follows:

```
200 READ M(1), M(2), M(3), M(4), M(5), M(6)
210 READ M(7), M(8), M(9), M(10), M(11), M(12)
                    :
                    :
900 DATA 34.2,19.54,-2.33,733,18.4,0.89
910 DATA 0,177.3,-9368,22,83.57,3.447
```

or even INPUT statements:

```
200 INPUT M(1), M(2), M(3)
205 INPUT M(4), M(5), M(6)
210 INPUT M(7), M(8), M(9)
215 INPUT M(10), M(11), M(12)
```

These techniques are awkward for subscripted variables. They are not too bad for small arrays, but can you imagine trying to use any one of these methods for an array of 100 or 1000 elements? There are better ways for working with large arrays.

The array in Figure 9-1 could easily be ''loaded'' by the following short program segment:

```
200 FOR J = 1 TO 12
210    READ M(J)
220 NEXT J
                  :
                  :
900 DATA 34.2,19.54,-2.33,733,18.4,0.89
910 DATA 0,177.3,-9368,22,83.57,3.447
```

The FOR–NEXT loop steps the array through each element, reading them one by one. At first, J = 1 so M(1) is read as 34.2. The next J is 2 so M(2) is read and so forth through J = 12 or M(12). This accomplishes the same task as the two READ statements above; however, had the array M consisted of 1200 elements instead of just 12, we would need only to change the 12 in the FOR–NEXT loop to 1200. With individual READs, we would have pages of nothing but READ statements!

Printing an array is just as easy as reading it. To print M, we would write:

```
500  FOR J = 1 TO 12
510     PRINT M(J)
520  NEXT J
```

which would print:

```
 34.2
 19.54
-2.33
 733
 18.4
 .89
 0
 177.3
-9368
 22
 83.57
 3.447
```

We are not restricted to the input or output of a single subscripted variable at a time. For example, the following FOR–NEXT loop is equivalent to the above four INPUT statements:

```
200  FOR I = 1 TO 12 STEP 3
210     INPUT M(I), M(I + 1), M(I + 2)
220  NEXT I
```

When I = 1, the INPUT statement will accept values for M(1), M(2), and M(3). Because the step is 3, the next I is 4, hence the next INPUT will take values of M(4), M(5), and M(6). Each cycle through the FOR–NEXT loop will cause the INPUT statement to accept the next *three* values for M. In like manner, we can print more than one value of a subscripted variable on a single print line. The following loop will cause the array M to be printed with four values to a line:

```
500  FOR P = 1 TO 12 STEP 4
510     PRINT M(P), M(P + 1), M(P + 2), M(P + 3)
520  NEXT P
```

This will print M as follows:

```
 34.2          19.54         -2.33          733
 18.4          .89           0              177.3
-9368          22            83.57          3.447
```

Sometimes, we might not know the exact number of values that we wish to place into an array, or the value may change from run to run. Suppose, for example, that we want to load array M without the knowledge that it will contain exactly 12 values. We can first dimension M for a value that we are certain will be large enough for any possible situation that might arise; for M that might be:

```
150  DIM M(50)
```

We can terminate the reading of values into the array by the conventional method of using a sentinel value, thus using only as much of the array as needed. This is done as follows:

```
200  FOR J = 1 TO 50
210     READ M(J)
220     IF M(J) = 99999 THEN 240
230  NEXT J
240  LET M(0) = J - 1
                   :
                   :
900  DATA 34.2,19.54,-2.33,733,18.4,0.89
910  DATA 0,177.3,-9368,22,83.57,3.447,99999
```

The FOR–NEXT loop is set to read up to the maximum of 50 values for which M was dimensioned; however, the input is ended when the *13th*, or sentinel, value is encountered. The program is then directed out of the loop to line 240. This line gives (J − 1) the actual number of data values that we have stored in the array and stores this in the zeroth location of M for later reference. (Of course, another variable can be used for this if you do not have the zeroth position with your BASIC or just do not wish to use it.) Line 240 is not required because the sentinel value is stored in the array and can be used again to find the end of the array, but if we know how many values we are working with in an array, we can use that knowledge to control FOR–NEXT loops, which is easier than having to include IF statements to check for the sentinel value.

9-3 ARITHMETIC WITH ARRAYS

All or part of an array may be set equal to a certain value. The following three statements will set all of the elements of the array T equal to zero:

```
350  FOR K = 1 TO 20
355     LET T(K) = 0
360  NEXT K
```

This is useful for initializing an array, the elements of which are to be used as total accumulators. One array may be set equal to another as follows:

```
250  FOR K = 1 TO 20
255     LET R2(K) = R1(K)
260  NEXT K
```

which sets the elements of array R2 equal to the corresponding ones of R1.

The sum of the elements of array M from Figure 9-1 can be found by the following set of statements:

```
400  LET S = 0
410  FOR X = 1 TO 12
420     LET S = S + M(X)
430  NEXT X
```

which adds M(1), M(2), M(3), and so forth up to M(12) to S. If the zeroth location for an array is available with your BASIC, you could use M(0) to store the sum instead of S. This would change the above set of statements to read as follows:

```
400  LET M(0) = 0
410  FOR X = 1 TO 12
420     LET M(0) = M(0) + M(X)
430  NEXT X
```

One array may be added to another. The following short segment adds the elements of array M from Figure 9-1 to a second array Y.

```
330  FOR J = 1 TO 12
340     LET Y(J) = Y(J) + M(J)
350  NEXT J
```

Each element of M is added to the corresponding element of Y, and the result is stored in Y. This is illustrated in Figure 9-2*a*. A third array can be used to hold the sums of the addition. This could be accomplished by the following loop:

```
330  FOR J = 1 TO 12
340     LET Q(J) = Y(J) + M(J)
350  NEXT J
```

as is illustrated in Figure 9-2*b*.

Arrays need not always be processed in the same order in which the data is stored. For example, the following short program will read the data for array M and print it in the *reverse* order:

```
 10 DIM M(12)
 20 FOR J = 1 TO 12
 30    READ M(J)
 40 NEXT J
 50 FOR K = 12 TO 1 STEP -1
 60    PRINT M(K)
 70 NEXT K
 80 DATA 34.2,19.54,-2.33,733,18.4,0.89
 90 DATA 0,177.3,-9368,22,83.57,3.447
100 END
```

Let us add arrays M and Y once again, but this time we will reverse the order and add the first element of M to the last of Y, the second of M to the next-to-last of Y, and so forth

Location	Array *M*	Array *Y* before Adding *M*	Array *Y* after Adding *M*
1	34.2	40.6	74.8
2	19.54	6.75	26.29
3	-2.33	11.6	9.27
4	733	-125	608
5	18.4	-88.22	-69.82
6	0.89	31.5	32.39
7	0	837.5	837.5
8	177.3	51.8	229.1
9	-9368	164	-9204
10	22	9.5	31.5
11	83.57	-28	55.57
12	3.447	42.75	46.197

(*a*) Storing the sum in array *Y*

Location	Array *M*	Array *Y*	Array *Q*
1	34.2	40.6	74.8
2	19.54	6.75	26.29
3	-2.33	11.6	9.27
4	733	-125	608
5	18.4	-88.22	-69.82
6	0.89	31.5	32.39
7	0	837.5	837.5
8	177.3	51.8	229.1
9	-9368	164	-9204
10	22	9.5	31.5
11	83.57	-28	55.57
12	3.447	42.75	46.197

(*b*) Storing the sum in a third array *Q*

FIGURE 9-2
Adding array *M* to array *Y*

until we get to the last element of M and the first of Y. This can be accomplished by the following loop:

```
300  FOR X = 1 TO 12
310     LET Q(X) = M(X) + Y(13 - X)
320  NEXT X
```

When X = 1, the first element of M, M(1), is added to the last element of Y, Y(12) (12 = 13 − 1), with the sum stored in the first location of Q. For the next value of X, the second element of M, M(2), is added to Y(11). With the next loop, M(3) is added to Y(10), and so forth moving "down" in M and "up" in Y. Finally, when X = 12, the last element of M, M(12), is added to the first of Y, Y(1), to complete the addition. This process is illustrated in Figure 9-3*a*.

Location	Array *M*	Array *Y*	Array *Q*
1	34.2	40.6	76.95
2	19.54	6.75	-8.46
3	-2.33	11.6	7.17
4	733	-125	897
5	18.4	-88.22	70.2
6	0.89	31.5	838.39
7	0	837.5	31.5
8	177.3	51.8	89.08
9	-9368	164	-9493
10	22	9.5	33.6
11	83.57	-28	90.32
12	3.447	42.75	44.047

(*a*) Adding the elements in reverse order

Location	Array *M*	Array *Y*	Array *Q*
1	34.2	40.6	74.8
2	19.54	6.75	12.79
3	-2.33	11.6	-27.03
4	733	-125	5.864
5	18.4	-88.22	-69.82
6	0.89	31.5	-30.61
7	0	837.5	0
8	177.3	51.8	3.42278
9	-9368	164	-9204
10	22	9.5	12.5
11	83.57	-28	-2339.96
12	3.447	42.75	0.0806316

(*b*) Alternately adding, subtracting, multiplying, and dividing the elements

FIGURE 9-3
Other operations on arrays *M* and *Y*

As a final example in this section of operations with arrays, consider the following loop:

```
450  FOR L = 1 TO 12 STEP 4
460     LET Q(L) = Y(L) + M(L)
470     LET Q(L + 1) = Y(L + 1) - M(L + 1)
480     LET Q(L + 2) = Y(L + 2) * M(L + 2)
490     LET Q(L + 3) = Y(L + 3) / M(L + 3)
500  NEXT L
```

On the first pass through the loop, L = 1. At line 460 the first elements of M and Y are added; at 470 the *second* (L + 1) elements are subtracted; the *third* (L + 2) are multiplied at 480; and at 490 the *fourth* (L + 3) are divided. This completes the first loop. Since the step is 4, the second loop will begin with L = 5 and process the next four elements at array positions 5 through 8, adding at 5, subtracting at 6, multiplying at 7, and dividing at 8. The final loop will repeat the process for the last four elements of the two arrays. This process is illustrated in Figure 9-3*b*.

Before leaving this section and looking at a major example, it should be pointed out that IF statements and manual counters can be used to control arrays as well as FOR–NEXT loops. (In fact, some programmers actually *prefer* the use of IFs to the FOR–NEXT loop.) As examples of using IF statements for this purpose, the last two loops above could be written with IFs as follows:

```
300  LET X = 1
310     LET Q(X) = M(X) + Y(13 - X)
320  LET X = X + 1
330  IF X <= 12 THEN 310
```

and

```
450  LET L = 1
460     LET Q(L) = Y(L) + M(L)
470     LET Q(L + 1) = Y(L + 1) - M(L + 1)
480     LET Q(L + 2) = Y(L + 2) * M(L + 2)
490     LET Q(L + 3) = Y(L + 3) / M(L + 3)
500  LET L = L + 4
510  IF L <= 12 THEN 460
```

While we will continue to use primarily the FOR–NEXT loop in the examples that follow, you should be aware that either technique is available and equally applicable.

9-4 AN EXAMPLE: GASOLINE SALES REPORT

The following example illustrates both the use and convenience of arrays in processing data.

Problem: A Gasoline Sales Report is needed for the Phossil Oil Company to produce a summary of the sales of all branch locations in a given city. Input will consist of the branch name plus sales in gallons for a 7-day period. The program is to calculate the weekly total sales for each branch as well as total sales for each day and for all branches for the full week. The detailed line should show the branch name with the seven daily sales and weekly total for each branch. At the end of the report, the daily and weekly totals for all branches are to be printed under the corresponding columns. Data is provided in Table 9-1.

TABLE 9-1

Data for Gasoline Sales Report Problem

Branch Name	Daily Sales in Gallons for Mon	Tue	Wed	Thu	Fri	Sat	Sun
FIRST ST.	1554	896	2088	1554	2887	3244	2766
N. EXPWY	2566	4655	3776	6554	3445	6215	5784
EASTLAKE	1355	1677	2004	1657	3566	4200	3846
NORTHSIDE	943	855	1254	765	2445	1866	2456
MILL RD.	3546	4511	5488	4351	5033	6524	2453
OLD PINES	1033	1542	845	1665	2150	1866	2488
FIFTH AVE	2010	1568	1755	2305	1433	3154	2766
I-905	4588	3458	2975	4886	7844	9786	8754

The solution to this problem is outlined as follows:

1. Print report and column headings.
2. Set branch weekly total and total weekly sales accumulators to zero.
3. Dimension daily total accumulator array.
4. Set daily total accumulator array to zero.
5. Dimension daily sales array.
6. Read branch name.
7. If this is the last record, go to step 15; otherwise, continue to the next step.
8. Read the seven daily sales values into the daily sales array. As each value is read, perform steps 9 and 10; after the last value is processed, go to step 11.
9. Add the daily sales to the branch total.
10. Add the daily sales to the corresponding total in the daily total array.
11. Add the branch weekly sales to the total weekly sales.
12. Print detailed line with branch name with daily sales data and the weekly total.
13. Reset the branch weekly total to zero.
14. Go to step 6.
15. Print daily and weekly totals.
16. Stop.

This procedure is illustrated pictorially by the flowchart shown in Figure 9-4.

While you may wish to review the use of the TAB function (Section 6-3), there is nothing new in this program until line 290 (step 3).

```
270 LET BT = 0
280 LET TW = 0
290 DIM TD(7)
300 FOR X = 1 TO 7
310    LET TD(X) = 0
320 NEXT X
```

Lines 270 and 280 set the nonsubscripted total accumulators to zero as we have done previously. Lines 300 to 320 do exactly the same for the seven daily total accumulators represented by the array TD. The DIM at 290 dimensions TD. It could have been placed earlier in the program, but it *must* precede the use of TD.

The heart of the program, in which the gasoline sales data is processed, corresponds to steps 5 to 14 above and translates into the following program segment:

```
360 DIM DS(7)
370 READ B$
380 IF B$ = "END" THEN 530
390 FOR X = 1 TO 7
```

```
400     READ DS(X)
410     LET BT = BT + DS(X)
420     LET TD(X) = TD(X) + DS(X)
430 NEXT X
440 LET TW = TW + BT
450 PRINT B$; TAB(15); DS(1); TAB(23); DS(2); TAB(31); DS(3);
460 PRINT TAB(39); DS(4); TAB(47); DS(5); TAB(55); DS(6);
470 PRINT TAB(63); DS(7); TAB(73); BT
480 LET BT = 0
490 GOTO 370
```

Line 360 serves to dimension the daily sales array. Lines 370 and 380 read the branch name and check for the end of processing, respectively. The FOR–NEXT loop from 390 to 430 performs three functions. First, data is read into the daily sales array. As each *day* is processed, that day's sales is added to the branch weekly total at line 410 and to the daily total of 420. Thus, when Monday's sales (X = 1) for a particular branch is read, it is also added to the branch weekly total and the daily total. Then Tuesday's value is processed, then Wednesday's, and so forth through Sunday's sales. At line 440, the

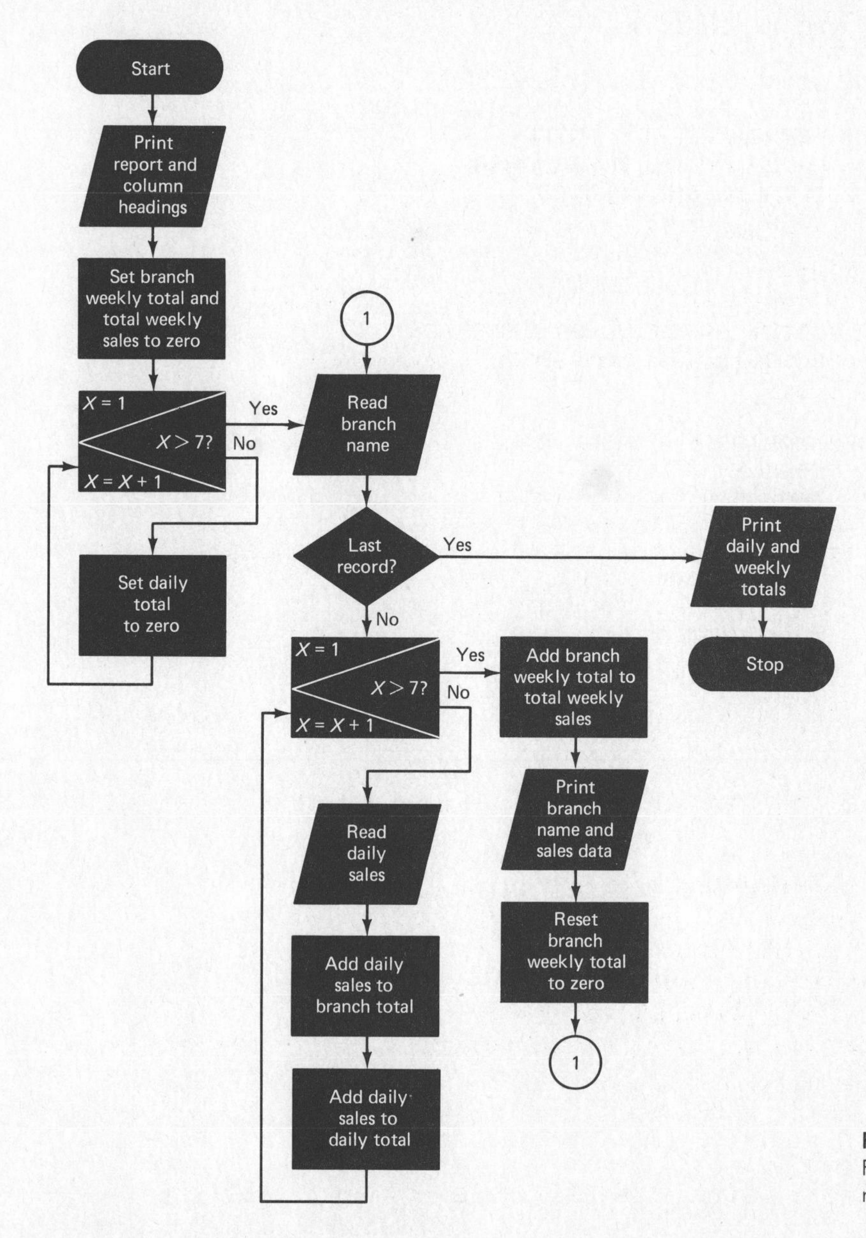

FIGURE 9-4
Flowchart for gasoline sales report problem

branch total is added to the weekly total for all branches. The next three lines, 450 to 470, simply print the detailed line. Monday's value is printed as DS(1), Tuesday's as DS(2), etc. Line 480 resets the branch total back to zero. This is necessary since the next line directs the program back to read data for another branch.

The final section prints the daily and weekly totals for all branches. This is accomplished by the following lines:

```
530  PRINT
540  PRINT "TOTALS:   "; TAB(15); TD(1); TAB(23); TD(2);
550  PRINT TAB(31); TD(3); TAB(39); TD(4); TAB(47); TD(5);
560  PRINT TAB(55); TD(6); TAB(63); TD(7); TAB(73); TW
```

This is essentially the same as the detailed line with Monday's total printed by TD(1), Tuesday's by TD(2), etc.

A complete program listing followed by a run is as follows:

```
 10 REM  GASOLINE SALES REPORT
 20 REM
 30 REM  VARIABLES ARE DEFINED AS --
 40 REM
 50 REM          B$ = BRANCH LOCATION NAME
 60 REM          DS = DAILY SALES (IN GALLONS) ARRAY
 70 REM          BT = BRANCH WEEKLY TOTAL
 80 REM          TD = DAILY TOTAL SALES ARRAY
 90 REM          TW = TOTAL WEEKLY SALES
100 REM           X = LOOP INDEX
110 REM
120 REM  PRINT HEADINGS
130 REM
140 PRINT TAB(27); "DAILY GASOLINE SALES REPORT"
150 PRINT TAB(31); "PHOSSIL OIL COMPANY"
160 PRINT
170 PRINT
180 PRINT " BRANCH"; TAB(29); "DAILY SALES IN GALLONS FOR";
190 PRINT TAB(74); "WEEKLY"
200 PRINT "   NAME"; TAB(16); "MON"; TAB(24); "TUE";
210 PRINT TAB(32); "WED"; TAB(40); "THU"; TAB(48); "FRI";
220 PRINT TAB(56); "SAT"; TAB(64); "SUN"; TAB(74); "SALES"
230 PRINT
240 REM
250 REM  INITIALIZE TOTALS TO ZERO
260 REM
270 LET BT = 0
280 LET TW = 0
290 DIM TD(7)
300 FOR X = 1 TO 7
310    LET TD(X) = 0
320 NEXT X
330 REM
340 REM  READ AND PROCESS DAILY SALES DATA
350 REM
360 DIM DS(7)
370 READ B$
380 IF B$ = "END" THEN 530
390 FOR X = 1 TO 7
400    READ DS(X)
410    LET BT = BT + DS(X)
420    LET TD(X) = TD(X) + DS(X)
430 NEXT X
440 LET TW = TW + BT
450 PRINT B$; TAB(15); DS(1); TAB(23); DS(2); TAB(31); DS(3);
```

```
460 PRINT TAB(39); DS(4); TAB(47); DS(5); TAB(55); DS(6);
470 PRINT TAB(63); DS(7); TAB(73); BT
480 LET BT = 0
490 GOTO 370
500 REM
510 REM  PRINT TOTAL SALES LINE
520 REM
530 PRINT
540 PRINT "TOTALS:  "; TAB(15); TD(1); TAB(23); TD(2);
550 PRINT TAB(31); TD(3); TAB(39); TD(4); TAB(47); TD(5);
560 PRINT TAB(55); TD(6); TAB(63); TD(7); TAB(73); TW
570 REM
580 REM  DATA LIST
590 REM
600 DATA "FIRST ST.",1554,896,2088,1554,2887,3244,2766
610 DATA "N. EXPWY",2566,4655,3776,6554,3445,6215,5784
620 DATA "EASTLAKE",1355,1677,2004,1657,3566,4200,3846
630 DATA "NORTHSIDE",943,855,1254,765,2445,1866,2456
640 DATA "MILL RD.",3546,4511,5488,4351,5033,6524,2453
650 DATA "OLD PINES",1033,1542,845,1665,2150,1866,2488
660 DATA "FIFTH AVE",2010,1568,1755,2305,1433,3154,2766
670 DATA "I-905",4588,3458,2975,4886,7844,9786,8754,"END"
680 END
```

```
                    DAILY GASOLINE SALES REPORT
                       PHOSSIL OIL COMPANY


 BRANCH                     DAILY SALES IN GALLONS FOR                 WEEKLY
  NAME         MON     TUE     WED     THU     FRI     SAT     SUN       TOTALS

FIRST ST.      1554    896     2088    1554    2887    3244    2766      14989
N. EXPWY       2566    4655    3776    6554    3445    6215    5784      32995
EASTLAKE       1355    1677    2004    1657    3566    4200    3846      18305
NORTHSIDE      943     855     1254    765     2445    1866    2456      10584
MILL RD.       3546    4511    5488    4351    5033    6524    2453      31906
OLD PINES      1033    1542    845     1665    2150    1866    2488      11589
FIFTH AVE      2010    1568    1755    2305    1433    3154    2766      14991
I-905          4588    3458    2975    4886    7844    9786    8754      42291

TOTALS:        17595   19162   20185   23737   28803   36855   31313     177650
```

9-5 TABLE SEARCHES

It is frequently necessary to determine whether a certain value is present as one of the elements of an array and, if so, at what location. First, let us look at some of the techniques for searching through the elements of an array; then, we will see how we might apply this procedure.

Suppose that we wish to determine where in array A the value V is located. The following loop searches the elements of A one by one (called a **sequential** search) until a match with V is found.

```
300 FOR N = 1 TO 20
310    IF V = A(N) THEN 330
320 NEXT N
330 (Next statement)
```

Although this works in theory, it is not very useful in practice because at line 330 we cannot be sure whether or not a match was found until the result is processed, by which time it may be too late. The following is basically the same as the above sequential search, but it is more helpful:

```
300  FOR N = 1 TO 20
310     IF V = A(N) THEN 400
320  NEXT N
330  PRINT "VALUE NOT FOUND"
                :
400  (Process match from array)
```

If a match is found, the program is directed to line 400 where this information is used to continue processing. The *position* in the array A of the matching element is indicated by N. Corresponding values in other arrays can now be located by using N. In other words, suppose that A represents account numbers and a match is found at N = 14. The customer's name, address, or any other information can now be found from the proper arrays at location number 14. If the entire array is searched without locating a value equal to V, a statement to that effect is printed and the program is sent to the proper place, possibly back to the READ for more data.

Frequently, we need to know not only if a certain value is contained within an array but how many times. This can be accomplished by a program segment similar to the following:

```
200  LET C = 0
210  FOR N = 1 TO 20
220     IF V = A(N) THEN LET C = C + 1
230  NEXT N
240  IF C = 0 THEN PRINT "VALUE NOT FOUND"
250  IF C > 0 THEN PRINT "VALUE FOUND"; C; "TIMES"
```

At line 220, the counter C is incremented by 1 every time a match is found. Line 240 is executed if the value is not present. If it is found, line 250 gives the number of times. Of course, with only a slight modification, this same procedure can be used to determine the number of values in an array that are less than or greater than a certain value. To find the number of elements of A that are *less than* V, we would write:

```
200  LET C = 0
210  FOR N = 1 TO 20
220     IF V > A(N) THEN LET C = C + 1
230  NEXT N
240  IF C = 0 THEN PRINT "A IS NEVER LESS THAN V"
250  IF C > 0 THEN PRINT C; "ELEMENTS OF A ARE LESS THAN V"
```

[This might be another use for that zeroth position; A(0) could be used in place of C as the counter.]

Let us now look at some of the uses for array searches. Table 9-2 lists a series of pay rate codes and the corresponding hourly pay rates. This constitutes a pay rate *table*. Such tables are very convenient in processing large numbers of records. Suppose that a company has 1000 employees that work on 12 different pay rates. When the time comes to give all the employees a pay raise, if the individual pay rates are recorded on each record, all 1000 employee pay records will have to be updated. However, if the rates are kept in a pay rate table with the rate *codes* recorded in the employee pay records, only the 12 values in the table need be changed to process the raise.

Such a table is easily incorporated into a program for processing the pay data. Let us see how to calculate an employee's pay with the employee's name, hours, and *pay code* as

TABLE 9-2

Employee Pay Rate Table

Rate Code	Hourly Rate	Rate Code	Hourly Rate
1004	4.65	4330	7.55
1145	5.65	4723	8.05
3228	6.15	6213	8.55
3466	6.75	6493	9.00
3663	7.00	7443	9.25
4229	7.30	7853	9.85

input, using the above table to find the proper pay rate. This can be done (without headings, etc.) by the following program:

```
 10 REM  PROCESSING PAY WITH PAY RATE TABLE
 20 REM
 30 DIM PC(12), PR(12)
 40 FOR J = 1 TO 12
 50    READ PC(J), PR(J)
 60 NEXT J
 70 READ E$, H, C
 80 IF H < 0 THEN 250
 90 FOR K = 1 TO 12
100    IF C = PC(K) THEN 140
110 NEXT K
120 PRINT E$, "INVALID PAY CODE -- RECORD NOT PROCESSED"
130 GOTO 70
140 LET P = H * PR(K)
150 IF H > 40 THEN P = (40 + 1.5 * (H - 40)) * PR(K)
160 PRINT E$, H, PR(K), P
170 GOTO 70
180 DATA 1004,4.65,4330,7.55,1145,5.65,4723,8.05
190 DATA 3228,6.15,6213,8.55,3466,6.75,6493,9.00
200 DATA 3663,7.00,7443,9.25,4229,7.30,7853,9.85
210 DATA "J SMITH",35,3466,"R REESE",40,4330
220 DATA "G DAVIS",38,1004,"T YOUNG",44,6493
230 DATA "W JONES",40,7442,"P OWENS",37,1145
240 DATA "R LEWIS",42,4330,"XXX",-1,0
250 END
```

The first thing that must be done is to dimension the two arrays that make up the pay rate table and read the data into the arrays. This is done at lines 30 to 60 with the data for the table in the DATA statements at lines 180 to 200. The employee pay record with the pay code C is read at line 70. Lines 90 to 110 check the pay code from the input record against each pay code in the table until a match is found. If no match is found after the entire pay code array has been checked, the message at line 120 is printed, and the next record is processed.

When the code in the table is found that matches the input code, the program branches to line 140 to calculate the pay. At line 140, the pay is computed assuming no overtime (hours over 40). If overtime is due, the pay is recalculated at 150 to include the overtime. The two pay calculations use the pay rate from the table that corresponds to the input pay code. When a match for the code is found at line 100 and the program branches to 140, the value of the subscript K *for which the match was found* is used to designate the pay rate. That is, the pay rate that is used corresponds to the pay code because the same subscript will yield corresponding values. The first code to be input for J SMITH is 3466.

This is the *seventh* code in the data list; therefore, it will be stored in the array to have a subscript of 7 (K = 7). The *seventh* pay rate is 6.75, which will also have a subscript of 7. The output from the above program is

```
J SMITH        35              6.75             236.25
R REESE        40              7.55             302
G DAVIS        38              4.65             176.7
T YOUNG        44              9                414
W JONES       INVALID PAY CODE -- RECORD NOT PROCESSED
P OWENS        37              5.65             209.05
R LEWIS        42              7.55             324.65
```

The example in the next section will give a much more detailed illustration of table searches and their applications.

9-6 AN EXAMPLE: INVOICE PREPARATION

The example that follows illustrates a practical application of table searches.

Problem: Cindy's Cameras needs a program to produce an invoice for each mail order received. The input for each invoice will consist of the customer's name, address, account number, and date of purchase, along with the stock number and quantity of each item ordered. An inventory table must then be searched for each stock number to find the corresponding item name and unit cost. The quantity purchased and unit price are multiplied to give the total cost. These are, in turn, added to produce the total amount due. The customer's name, address, account number, and date of purchase should appear at the top of the invoice. For each item purchased, the stock number, item name, quantity purchased, unit cost, and total cost should be printed. The total amount due is to be printed at the bottom of the invoice. Use the interactive INPUT statement for data entry. Data for the inventory table is provided in Table 9-3. Customer data to be processed is given in Table 9-4.

The solution to the problem is outlined as follows:

1. Input customer's name, address, account number, and date of purchase.
2. Dimension input stock number and quantity arrays.
3. Input the stock number and quantity of the item purchased.
4. Repeat step 3 until either 20 items have been processed or a stock number of zero has been encountered.

TABLE 9-3

Data for Inventory Table for Cindy's Cameras

Stock Number	Item Name	Unit Cost	Stock Number	Item Name	Unit Cost
11543	Enlarger	350.00	23223	Developer	22.50
23980	35MM Camera	275.00	24511	W/A Lens	215.00
25002	Tele Lens	165.00	25134	Zoom Lens	320.00
30020	B/W Film	2.50	30030	Color Film	4.50
30040	Slide Film	5.75	42090	Disk Camera	45.00
43376	Flash	135.00	44354	Camera Case	45.25
44632	Slide Proj	270.00	45201	Proj Screen	55.75
45355	Movie Proj	550.00	45744	Movie Film	6.25
46001	Mini Camera	100.00	53223	Tripod	57.50
54202	UV Filter	5.50	54322	Polarizer	17.50
60330	Cable Rel	2.75	62332	Cam Strap	4.25
63556	Cam Battery	2.75	65447	Lens Clnr	4.50

TABLE 9-4

Data for Invoice Preparation Problem

Customer's Name: George R. Bradford
Street Address: 7813 Poppyseed Lane
City: Chicago State: IL Zip Code: 60613
Account Number: 28822 Date of Purchases: August 19, 1984

Stock Number	Quantity Purchased	Stock Number	Quantity Purchased
23980	1	52332	1
25134	1	30030	5
43376	1	30040	5
44354	1	63556	3

5. Set size of the two input arrays equal to the number of items purchased.
6. Print main and column headings with the customer's name, address, account number, and date of purchase between.
7. Dimension the stock number, item name, and unit cost arrays for the inventory table.
8. Read a stock number, item name, and unit cost into the inventory table.
9. Repeat step 8 until either 100 items have been processed or a negative stock number is found.
10. Set the size of the three inventory arrays to the number of items read.
11. For each item purchased, perform steps 12 to 19.
12. Compare the stock number of the item purchased with those in the stock number array of the inventory table.
13. If a match is found, go to step 16.
14. If the stock number is not in the inventory table, print an appropriate message.
15. Return to step 12 and process the next item.
16. Calculate the cost of the item as the quantity purchased times the unit price from the inventory table.
17. Print a detailed line giving the stock number, item name, quantity purchased, unit cost, and total cost.
18. Update the total cost of the order.
19. Return to step 12 and process the next item.
20. Print the total amount due for the invoice.
21. Stop.

This procedure is illustrated pictorially by the flowchart shown in Figure 9-5.

We are to use the INPUT statement to enter the data on the customer and the items purchased. This must be done *before* the headings are printed so that the printout will not be interrupted. Lines 280 to 340 of the program provide for the input of the customer's name, address, account number, and date of purchase. The stock number and quantity for each item purchased are entered into the proper arrays by the following sequence of statements:

```
370 DIM N(20), Q(20)
380 PRINT "ENTER PURCHASE DATA -- MAXIMUM OF 20 ITEMS:"
390 PRINT "(TERMINATE ENTRY WITH A STOCK NUMBER OF ZERO)"
400 PRINT
410 FOR X = 1 TO 20
420   INPUT "      STOCK NUMBER"; N(X)
430   IF N(X) = 0 THEN 460
440   INPUT "      QUANTITY"; Q(X)
450 NEXT X
460 LET XM = X - 1
```

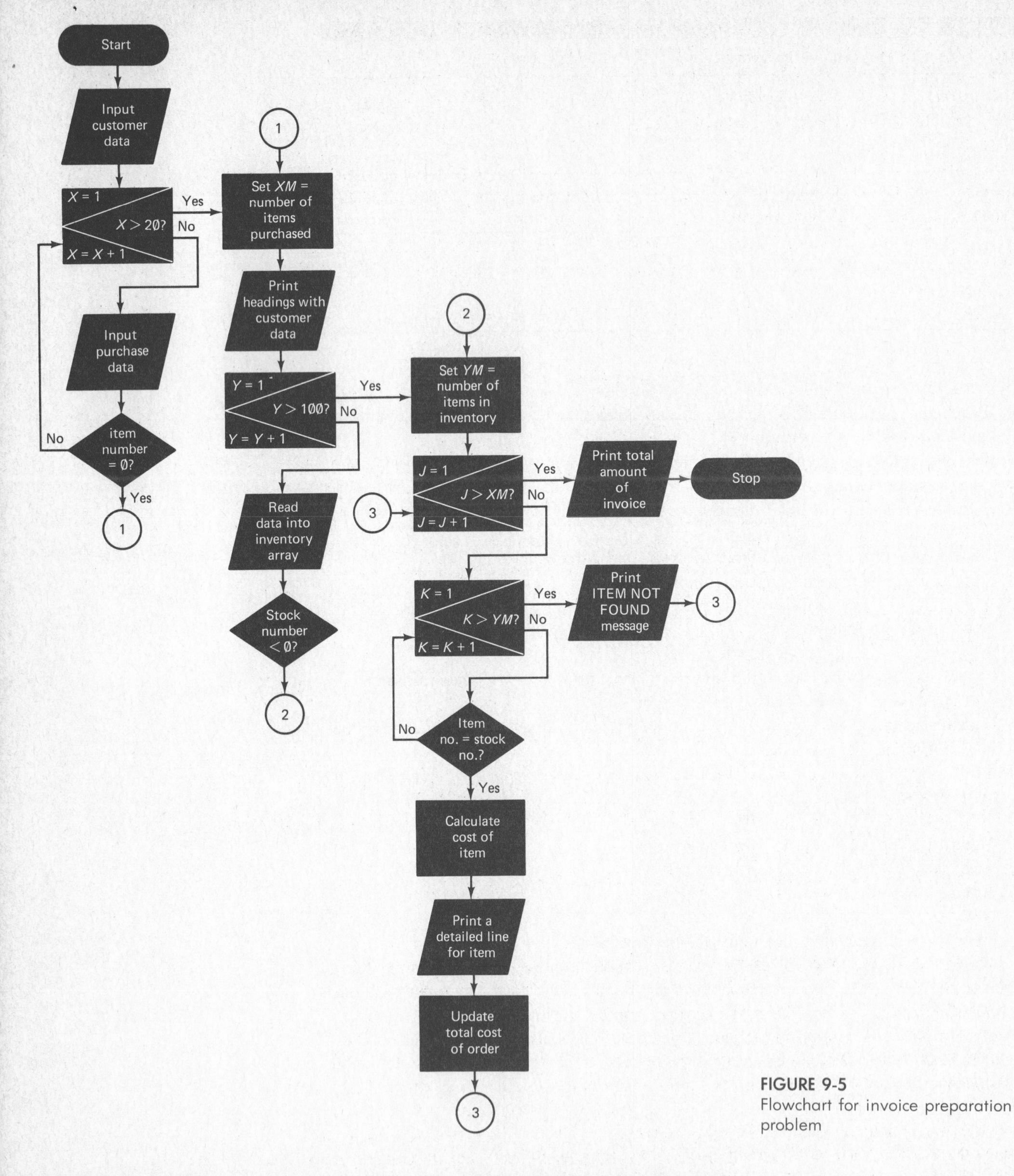

FIGURE 9-5
Flowchart for invoice preparation problem

Line 370 serves to dimension the arrays for the stock number and quantity, respectively. Although we do not know how many items a customer will purchase, we will set a limit of 20 per invoice and dimension the two arrays accordingly. The FOR–NEXT loop at lines 410 to 450 is used to input the stock numbers at line 420 and the corresponding quantities at line 440 into the proper arrays. Since most customers will not purchase 20 items, line 430 terminates the input when a stock number of 0 is encountered. Line 460 sets XM equal to the number of items purchased. When a stock number equal to zero is found, we have gone one loop too far. This means that the number of items purchased is one less than the value of X, hence XM = X − 1. In the event that the maximum of 20 items is purchased, line 460 should still give XM = 20 with most versions of BASIC. Most BASICs exit a completed FOR–NEXT loop with the counter at one increment (or step) beyond the last one processed. Thus, if 20 items are processed, X should be *21* at line 460.

Lines 510 to 660 print the headings and the customer's name, address, account number, and date of purchase between the main and column headings. This is similar to the printout for the item depreciation example in Section 8-2.

The inventory table consists of three arrays; these are for the stock number, the item name, and the unit price. The following program segment loads the inventory table:

```
700  DIM SN(100), I$(100), U(100)
710  FOR Y = 1 TO 100
720     READ SN(Y), I$(Y), U(Y)
730     IF SN(Y) < 0 THEN 750
740  NEXT Y
750  LET YM = Y - 1
```

Again, we do not know the exact number of items that are in inventory at any one time; therefore, we must dimension the arrays for a sufficiently large value. The DIM statement at line 700 does this. The FOR–NEXT loop reads data into the three inventory arrays until a negative (sentinel) value is found, at which point processing is directed to line 750 which sets YM equal to the number of items in inventory. This line functions the same as line 460 for the number of items purchased. (Note that the only DATA statements in this program provide data for the inventory table.)

The main processing (steps 12 to 19) is accomplished by the following set of statements:

```
790 LET TC = 0
800 FOR J = 1 TO XM
810    FOR K = 1 TO YM
820       IF N(J) = SN(K) THEN 860
830    NEXT K
840    PRINT N(J); "   UNIDENTIFIED STOCK NUMBER -- PLEASE RE-ORDER!"
850    GOTO 890
860    LET C = Q(J) * U(K)
870    PRINT N(J), I$(K), "    "; Q(J), U(K), "$"; C
880    LET TC = TC + C
890 NEXT J
```

Line 790 sets the accumulator for the total cost of the order to zero. The outside FOR–NEXT loop (lines 800 to 890) controls the processing of each item purchased. That is, the counter J will go from 1 to XM, which is the number of items purchased. Any subscript J within this loop will indicate a particular stock number or quantity from the two arrays holding the purchase data. For each item purchased, we must search the inventory table for a match. The little inner loop at lines 810 to 830 does this. The stock number of each item purchased, N(J), is compared at line 820 to that of every item in the inventory table, SN(K), until a match is found. For the first item purchased, N(1) = 23980. This is compared to each stock number in the array SN until a match is located. In this case, it is found when K = 3 or at SN(3). The second item has N(2) = 25134 and is located at SN(6). Thus, while J keeps track of the input items, K will indicate the location of the item stock number and corresponding values in the inventory table (arrays). If no match is found, the appropriate message is printed at 840 and the program directed to process the next item.

When the proper stock number is found in the inventory stock number array, SN, line 820 directs processing to line 860 to process the item. At 860, the total cost for that item is found by multiplying the quantity purchased, Q(J) (from the input quantity array) by the unit price, U(K), from the unit price array of the inventory table. That is:

```
860  LET C = Q(J) * U(K)
```

We get the proper quantity because J keeps track of the items as they are processed; therefore, it indicates the current item being processed and will select the correct quantity from that array. In like manner, K gives the position of the stock number in the inventory table; hence it also indicates the proper unit price. The detailed line is printed as:

```
870  PRINT N(J), I$(K), "     "; Q(J), U(K), "$"; C
```

where, as above, the subscripts J and K extract the proper values from the indicated arrays. Finally, line 880 updates the total cost for the order by adding the cost for the current item to that for all the others, while 890 continues processing for the next item.

Note that the values XM and YM that indicate the number of values to be processed and the number of items in the inventory table, respectively, have been used to control the FOR–NEXT loops. Of course, the sentinel values used to stop the loops earlier in the program could have been used again here; however, the use of maximum values such as XM and YM is easier. (You might use one of the zeroth array locations for these values.) It should be very strongly emphasized that this type of processing will work *only if the arrays are loaded properly. Corresponding values must be loaded together; that is, they must be placed in corresponding positions in their respective arrays*. If values are not loaded properly, then a particular subscript from one array cannot produce a related value from another array.

The remainder of the program involves only the printing of the total amount due for the invoice. A complete program listing follows.

```
 10 REM   INVOICE PREPARATION
 20 REM
 30 REM   VARIABLES ARE DEFINED AS --
 40 REM
 50 REM          N$ = CUSTOMER NAME
 60 REM          S$ = STREET ADDRESS
 70 REM          C$ = CITY
 80 REM         ST$ = STATE
 90 REM          Z$ = ZIP CODE
100 REM           A = ACCOUNT NUMBER
110 REM          D$ = DATE PURCHASES MADE
120 REM           N = STOCK NUMBER OF ITEMS PURCHASED ARRAY
130 REM           Q = QUANTITY PURCHASED ARRAY
140 REM          SN = STOCK NUMBER ARRAY
150 REM          I$ = ITEM DESCRIPTION ARRAY
160 REM           U = UNIT PRICE ARRAY
170 REM           C = COST FOR EACH ITEM PURCHASED
180 REM          TC = TOTAL COST OF ALL ITEMS PURCHASED
190 REM           X = COUNTER TO INPUT PURCHASES
200 REM          XM = NUMBER OF ITEMS PURCHASED
210 REM           Y = COUNTER TO LOAD INVENTORY ARRAYS
220 REM          YM = NUMBER OF ITEMS IN INVENTORY
230 REM           J = COUNTER TO PROCESS PURCHASES
240 REM           K = COUNTER TO LOCATE ITEM IN INVENTORY LIST
250 REM
260 REM   INPUT CUSTOMER DATA
270 REM
```

```
280 PRINT "ENTER THE FOLLOWING CUSTOMER DATA:"
290 PRINT
300 INPUT "      NAME"; N$
310 INPUT "      STREET ADDRESS"; S$
320 INPUT "      CITY, STATE, AND ZIP CODE"; C$, ST$, Z$
330 INPUT "      ACCOUNT NUMBER"; A
340 INPUT "      DATE OF PURCHASE"; D$
350 PRINT
360 PRINT
370 DIM N(20), Q(20)
380 PRINT "ENTER PURCHASE DATA -- MAXIMUM OF 20 ITEMS:"
390 PRINT "(TERMINATE ENTRY WITH A STOCK NUMBER OF ZERO)"
400 PRINT
410 FOR X = 1 TO 20
420   INPUT "      STOCK NUMBER"; N(X)
430   IF N(X) = 0 THEN 460
440   INPUT "      QUANTITY"; Q(X)
450 NEXT X
460 LET XM = X - 1
470 PRINT
480 PRINT
490 PRINT
500 REM
510 REM  PRINT HEADINGS AND CUSTOMER DATA
520 REM
530 PRINT TAB(23);  "I N V O I C E"
540 PRINT TAB(22); "CINDY'S CAMERAS"
550 PRINT
560 PRINT
570 PRINT "ACCOUNT NUMBER: "; A
580 PRINT "DATE OF PURCHASE:  "; D$
590 PRINT
600 PRINT "SOLD TO:", N$
610 PRINT , S$
620 PRINT , C$; ", "; ST$, Z$
630 PRINT
640 PRINT "STOCK", "DESCRIPTION", "QUANTITY", " UNIT", " TOTAL"
650 PRINT "NUMBER", "  OF ITEM", "PURCHASED", " COST", "  COST"
660 PRINT
670 REM
680 REM  LOAD INVENTORY ARRAYS
690 REM
700 DIM SN(100), I$(100), U(100)
710 FOR Y = 1 TO 100
720   READ SN(Y), I$(Y), U(Y)
730   IF SN(Y) < 0 THEN 750
740 NEXT Y
750 LET YM = Y - 1
760 REM
770 REM  PROCESS PURCHASES
780 REM
790 LET TC = 0
800 FOR J = 1 TO XM
810   FOR K = 1 TO YM
820     IF N(J) = SN(K) THEN 860
830   NEXT K
840   PRINT N(J); "  UNIDENTIFIED STOCK NUMBER -- PLEASE RE-ORDER!"
850   GOTO 890
860   LET C = Q(J) * U(K)
870   PRINT N(J), I$(K), "  "; Q(J), U(K), "$"; C
880   LET TC = TC + C
890 NEXT J
```

```
 900 REM
 910 REM  PRINT FINAL AMOUNT DUE
 920 REM
 930 PRINT
 940 PRINT "TOTAL AMOUNT DUE THIS INVOICE:  $"; TC
 950 REM
 960 REM  DATA FOR INVENTORY ARRAYS
 970 REM
 980 DATA 11543,"ENLARGER",350,23223,"DEVELOPER",22.5
 990 DATA 23980,"35MM CAMERA",275,24511,"W/A LENS",215
1000 DATA 25002,"TELE LENS",165,25134,"ZOOM LENS",220
1010 DATA 30020,"B/W FILM",2.5,30030,"COLOR FILM",4.5
1020 DATA 30040,"SLIDE FILM",5.75,42090,"DISK CAMERA",45
1030 DATA 43376,"FLASH",135,44354,"CAMERA CASE",45.25
1040 DATA 44632,"SLIDE PROJ",270,45201,"PROJ SCREEN",55.75
1050 DATA 45355,"MOVIE PROJ",550,45744,"MOVIE FILM",6.25
1060 DATA 46001,"MINI CAMERA",100,53223,"TRIPOD",57.5
1070 DATA 54202,"UV FILTER",5.5,54322,"POLARIZER",17.5
1080 DATA 60330,"CABLE REL",2.75,62332,"CAM STRAP",4.25
1090 DATA 63556,"CAM BATTERY",2.75,65447,"LENS CLNR",4.5
1100 DATA -1,"X",0
1110 END
```

The interactive session to input the customer data for producing the invoice is as follows:

```
ENTER THE FOLLOWING CUSTOMER DATA:

      NAME? "GEORGE R. BRADFORD"
      STREET ADDRESS? "7813 POPPYSEED LANE"
      CITY, STATE, AND ZIP CODE? "CHICAGO","IL","60613"
      ACCOUNT NUMBER? 28822
      DATE OF PURCHASE? "AUGUST 19, 1984"


ENTER PURCHASE DATA -- MAXIMUM OF 20 ITEMS:
(TERMINATE ENTRY WITH A STOCK NUMBER OF ZERO)

      STOCK NUMBER? 23890
      QUANTITY? 1
      STOCK NUMBER? 25134
      QUANTITY? 1
      STOCK NUMBER? 43376
      QUANTITY? 1
      STOCK NUMBER? 44354
      QUANTITY? 1
      STOCK NUMBER? 52332
      QUANTITY? 1
      STOCK NUMBER? 30030
      QUANTITY? 5
      STOCK NUMBER? 30040
      QUANTITY? 5
      STOCK NUMBER? 63556
      QUANTITY? 3
      STOCK NUMBER? 0
```

The invoice produced from the above data will be:

```
                    I N V O I C E
                   CINDY'S CAMERAS

ACCOUNT NUMBER:  28822
DATE OF PURCHASE:  AUGUST 19, 1984

SOLD TO:      GEORGE R. BRADFORD
              7813 POPPYSEED LANE
              CHICAGO, IL  60613

STOCK         DESCRIPTION  QUANTITY    UNIT       TOTAL
NUMBER          OF ITEM    PURCHASED   COST       COST

 23980        35MM CAMERA      1       275        $ 275
 25134        ZOOM LENS        1       220        $ 220
 43376        FLASH            1       135        $ 135
 44354        CAMERA CASE      1       45.25      $ 45.25
 52332    UNIDENTIFIED STOCK NUMBER -- PLEASE RE-ORDER!
 30030        COLOR FILM       5       4.5        $ 22.5
 30040        SLIDE FILM       5       5.75       $ 28.75
 63556        CAM BATTERY      3       2.75       $ 8.25

TOTAL AMOUNT DUE THIS INVOICE:   $ 714.75
```

9-7 FINDING MAXIMUM AND MINIMUM VALUES

One problem that frequently faces programmers is that of finding the largest or smallest value from those contained in an array. The following routine searches an array A to find the largest value:

```
300  LET EX = A(1)
310  FOR N = 2 TO 35
320     IF A(N) > EX THEN LET EX = A(N)
330  NEXT N
```

The variable EX is used to find large values in the array until the largest is located. We begin by assuming that the first element of the array, A(1), is the largest value, and we set EX = A(1). Next, we compare the elements of the array, beginning with A(2), until a value larger than EX is found. Since EX is to be the *largest* value, we must set it equal to the larger value that has just been found. This is all accomplished at line 320. Thus, by the time we reach the last element in the array, EX will be equal to the largest element in A.

The above search finds the largest value in an array, but it tells us nothing about *where* in the array that value is located. This procedure can be modified as follows to find not only the maximum value but the subscript that gives its location as well.

```
300 LET EX = A(1)
305 LET NX = 1
310 FOR N = 2 TO 35
315    IF A(N) <= EX THEN 330
320    LET EX = A(N)
325    LET NX = N
330 NEXT N
```

This will locate the largest value in the same manner as above. As long as A(N) is not greater than EX, no change is made; when a larger value is found, it is stored in EX. In addition, we initially set NX, the subscript of the largest value, equal to 1. Whenever a larger value is found, it is set equal to the subscript of that value. Thus, at the end of the search, while EX will be the largest value, NX will be its location in A; in other words,

EX = A(NX). If there are two or more elements in the array that are equal to the largest value, the above procedure will yield the location of the *first* such element. To find the *last* largest element, simply rewrite line 315 as:

```
315  IF A(N) < EX THEN 330
```

All of the above procedures can be rewritten to find *smallest* elements by simply reversing the *greater than* signs to *less than* and vice versa. It is possible to construct a combined routine that will simultaneously find both maximum and minimum values in an array. Such a procedure is used in the example in the next section and will be illustrated at that time.

9-8 AN EXAMPLE: PLACEMENT TEST REPORT

This example provides another illustration of table searches; however, in this case, rather than looking for a specific value, we will be searching for the maximum and minimum values. The problem also illustrates some additional techniques for using subscripts for locating array elements and another method for the use of arrays for accumulating totals.

Problem: A certain university gives a placement test to all incoming students, and a program is needed to process the results of the test. The test consists of eight sections: English, Math, Music, Reading, History, Art, Science, and Skills. Input to the program will consist of each student's name and score on each section of the test as shown in Table 9-5. For each student's test results, the highest and lowest scores and the corresponding areas of the test should be found along with the total score on all sections. This information, with the student's name, should be printed on each detailed line. At the end of the listing of the individual student's test results, a second summary is to be printed that lists each area of the test and the total number of students who scored highest in that area and the total number scoring lowest.

The solution to this problem is outlined as follows:

1. Print main and column headings.
2. Set student test total to zero.
3. Dimension test area name array and two arrays for holding totals for number of students scoring highest and lowest on each area of the test.
4. Load the test area array with the names of the sections of the test.
5. Set to zero the two arrays for accumulating totals of number of students scoring highest and lowest in each area.

TABLE 9-5

Data for Placement Test Report Problem

Student	Score Made on							
Name	English	Math	Music	Reading	History	Art	Science	Skills
R. Harris	34	43	26	20	49	54	44	65
T. Newton	75	54	23	23	55	43	12	54
S. Clarke	45	35	53	33	28	26	73	43
W. Andrews	26	17	36	12	31	30	28	33
L. Cummings	39	65	45	33	45	14	32	33
E. Fuller	46	27	22	52	71	43	27	29
R. Quincy	27	52	23	42	39	37	30	14
S. Hawkins	32	18	24	34	17	21	42	26
L. Smith	29	43	37	77	53	22	48	31
N. Vincent	26	31	32	44	36	54	43	55
P. Miller	23	44	61	33	41	17	53	55
J. Holmes	38	41	32	43	22	28	36	21

6. Dimension the array for reading each student's eight test scores.
7. Read the student's name.
8. If this is the last record, go to step 29; otherwise, go to the next step.
9. Read a test score into the test score array.
10. Add the test score to the test score total.
11. Repeat steps 9 and 10 until all scores for the student have been processed.
12. Set the subscript to locate the highest score equal to 1.
13. Set the highest score equal to the first score.
14. Set the subscript to locate the lowest score equal to 1.
15. Set the lowest score equal to the first score.
16. Beginning with the second test score and continuing through the last one, perform steps 17 to 23.
17. If the present test score is not greater than the current highest score, go to step 20.
18. Set the subscript to find the position of the highest score to that of the present score.
19. Set the highest score equal to the present score.
20. If the present test score is not less than the current lowest score, go to step 23.
21. Set the subscript to find the position of the lowest score to that of the present score.
22. Set the lowest score equal to the present score.
23. Go to step 16 to process any remaining values.
24. Update the total for the number of students scoring highest for the appropriate area of the test.
25. Update the total for the number of students scoring lowest for the appropriate area of the test.
26. Print a detailed line showing the student's name, highest and lowest test scores and corresponding areas, and sum of test scores.
27. Reset total of eight test scores to zero.
28. Go to step 7.
29. Print summary of test results giving each area of the test along with the total number of students who scored highest in that area and the total number scoring lowest.
30. Stop.

This procedure is illustrated pictorially by the flowchart shown in Figure 9-6.

The first part of the program involves only the printing of headings and is routine. The first section that relates to the techniques of this chapter is:

```
300 LET TS = 0
310 DIM A$(8), TH(8), TL(8)
320 FOR N = 1 TO 8
330    READ A$(N)
340    LET TH(N) = 0
350    LET TL(N) = 0
360 NEXT N
```

Line 300 sets the total accumulator for the sum of the eight test scores for each student to zero; this is not new. The three arrays for the names of the test areas, the totals of the students scoring highest on each area, and the totals of those scoring lowest are dimensioned at 310. The FOR–NEXT loop at lines 320 to 360 reads the names of the test areas into this array at 330 and sets all of the elements of the other two arrays (remember these are totals!) to zero. The data for A$ is found at lines 910 and 920.

```
910  DATA "ENGLISH","MATH","MUSIC","READING"
920  DATA "HISTORY","ART","SCIENCE","SKILLS"
```

The test section names must be listed in the same order as the test scores.

A student record of test data is read at lines 400 to 460.

```
400 DIM T(8)
410 READ S$
420 IF S$ = "LAST" THEN 780
430 FOR N = 1 TO 8
440    READ T(N)
450    TS = TS + T(N)
460 NEXT N
```

The array that holds each student's eight test scores is dimensioned at line 400. The next two lines read the student's name and check for the sentinel record. The eight test scores are read into the test score array by the FOR–NEXT loop. Also, as each score is read, the score is added to the total of the eight scores at line 450.

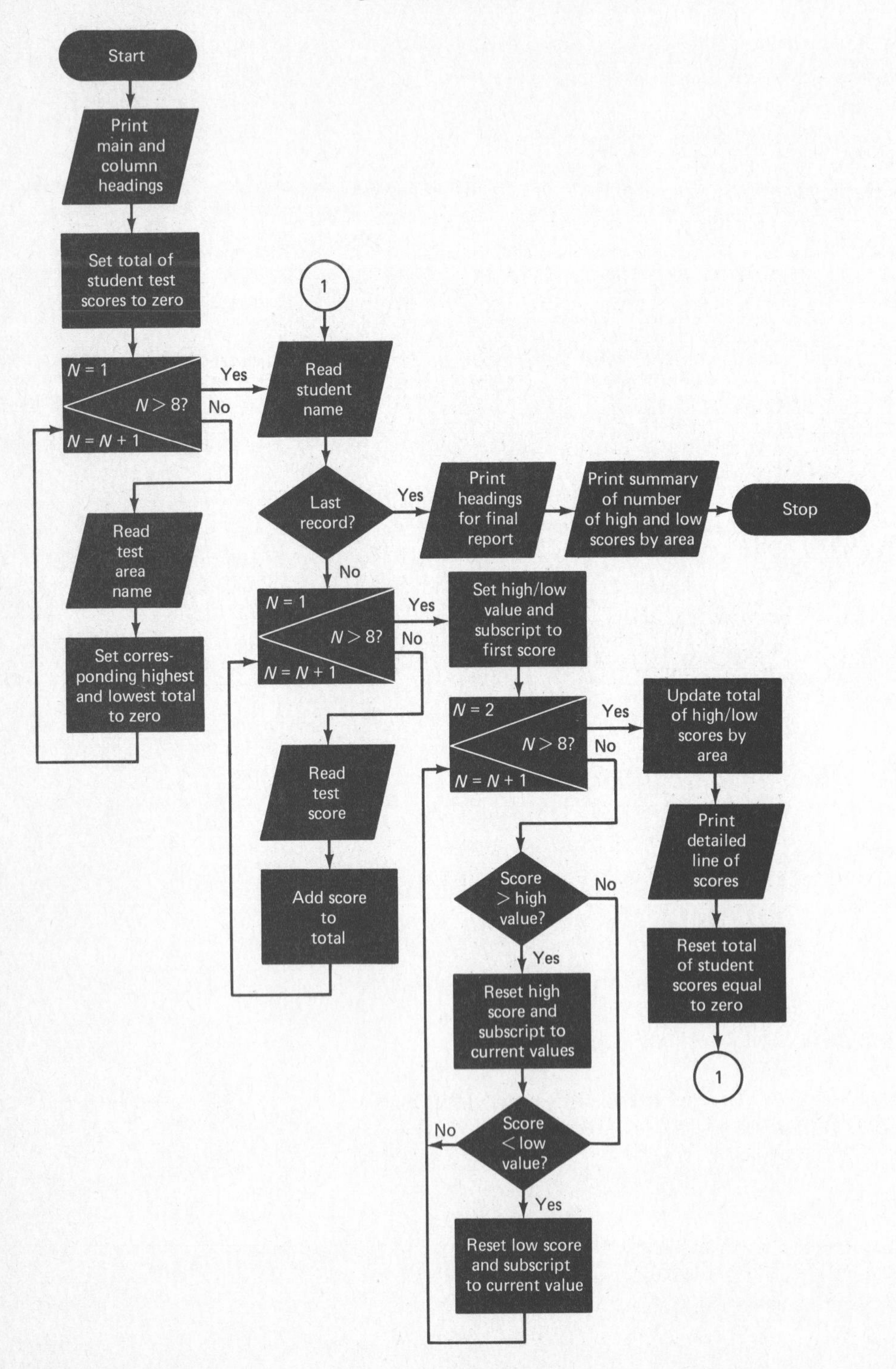

FIGURE 9-6
Flowchart for placement test report problem

Now that the tests have been read into the test array and summed, we must find the highest and lowest scores. The processing that accomplishes this is described by the following:

```
510 LET NH = 1
520 LET HS = T(1)
530 LET NL = 1
540 LET LS = T(1)
550 FOR N = 2 TO 8
560    IF T(N) <= HS THEN 590
570    LET NH = N
580    LET HS = T(N)
590    IF T(N) => LS THEN 620
600    LET NL = N
610    LET LS = T(N)
620 NEXT N
```

Line 510 sets the subscript that will locate the position of the highest score equal to 1, and line 520 sets the highest score equal to the first test score. The next two lines do the exact same thing for the low score. The FOR–NEXT loop at lines 550 to 620 searches through the test array to find the two extreme values. Line 560 checks to verify that the test score is not higher than the current highest one, in which case line 590 checks to verify that it is not lower. If the score is neither higher nor lower than the current high and low scores, then no changes are made and the next score is checked. If a score is found that *is* higher (false condition at 560), the values for the subscript and high score are updated at 570 and 580, respectively. In like manner, when a lower score is found, the corresponding subscript and low value are updated at 600 and 610. [Note that only *one* of the conditions in the above loop can be false for any one score. Since HS is never less than LS, if T(N) is greater than HS, it *cannot* be less than LS!]

The two subscripts, NH and NL, give the position of the highest and lowest scores, respectively, in the test array or any other related array, such as the test area name array or the highest and lowest totals arrays. For example, the first student had a high score of 65 on the last section of the test, Skills, and a low score of 20 on the fourth part, Reading. This means that NH = 8 and NL = 4, and these can be used to select the corresponding positions in other arrays. In updating the total number of students scoring highest or lowest on each section, we can write:

```
660  LET TH(NH) = TH(NH) + 1
670  LET TL(NL) = TL(NL) + 1
```

This means that for the first student, 1 will be added to TH(8) or the number scoring highest on the eighth area, and 1 will be added to TL(4) or the number scoring lowest on the fourth section. Verify that, for the second student, NH = 1 and NL = 7.

The detailed line is printed as follows:

```
710  PRINT S$; TAB(20); HS; "ON "; A$(NH);
720  PRINT TAB(38); LS; "ON "; A$(NL); TAB(60); TS
```

This is relatively straightforward. As with the totals above, the proper areas of the test for the highest and lowest scores are located by means of NH and NL. It might be mentioned that, since HS = T(NH) and LS = T(NL), the above PRINT statements could have been written as:

```
710  PRINT S$; TAB(20); T(NH); "ON "; A$(NH);
720  PRINT TAB(38); T(NL); "ON "; A$(NL); TAB(60); TS
```

The processing is routine until the final section, which prints the summary of the number of students scoring highest and lowest on each section of the test. Except for a new set of headings (lines 780 to 840), this is done as follows:

```
850 FOR N = 1 TO 8
860    PRINT A$(N), "   "; TH(N), "   "; TL(N)
870 NEXT N
```

This simply prints the three arrays giving each test section name with the corresponding number of students who have scored highest and lowest on that section.

A complete program listing followed by a run is given below.

```
 10 REM  UNIVERSITY PLACEMENT TEST REPORT
 20 REM
 30 REM  VARIABLES ARE DEFINED AS --
 40 REM
 50 REM           S$ = STUDENT NAME
 60 REM            T = TEST SCORES ARRAY
 70 REM           TS = SUM OF SCORES
 80 REM           A$ = TEST AREA NAMES ARRAY
 90 REM           TH = HIGH SCORE ACCUMULATORS ARRAY
100 REM           TL = LOW SCORE ACCUMULATORS ARRAY
110 REM           HS = HIGH SCORE MARKER
120 REM           LS = LOW SCORE MARKER
130 REM            N = LOOP COUNTER
140 REM           NH = POSITION OF COUNTER AT HIGHEST SCORE
150 REM           NL = POSOTION OF COUNTER AT LOWEST SCORE
160 REM
170 REM  PRINT HEADINGS
180 REM
190 PRINT TAB(19); "PLACEMENT TEST SCORE SUMMARY"
200 PRINT
210 PRINT
220 PRINT " STUDENT"; TAB(24); "HIGHEST";
230 PRINT TAB(43); "LOWEST"; TAB(60); "TOTAL"
240 PRINT "  NAME"; TAB(21); "SCORE AND AREA";
250 PRINT TAB(39); "SCORE AND AREA"; TAB(60); "SCORE"
260 PRINT
270 REM
280 REM  INTITALIZE TOTALS
290 REM
300 LET TS = 0
310 DIM A$(8), TH(8), TL(8)
320 FOR N = 1 TO 8
330   READ A$(N)
340   LET TH(N) = 0
350   LET TL(N) = 0
360 NEXT N
370 REM
380 REM  READ PLACEMENT TEST DATA
390 REM
400 DIM T(8)
410 READ S$
420 IF S$ = "LAST" THEN 780
430 FOR N = 1 TO 8
440   READ T(N)
450   TS = TS + T(N)
460 NEXT N
470 REM
480 REM  FIND HIGHEST AND LOWEST SCORES AND
490 REM  LOCATE CORRESPONDING TEST AREAS
500 REM
```

```
 510 LET NH = 1
 520 LET HS = T(1)
 530 LET NL = 1
 540 LET LS = T(1)
 550 FOR N = 2 TO 8
 560   IF T(N) <= HS THEN 590
 570   LET NH = N
 580   LET HS = T(N)
 590   IF T(N) => LS THEN 620
 600   LET NL = N
 610   LET LS = T(N)
 620 NEXT N
 630 REM
 640 REM  UPDATE TOTALS FOR HIGH AND LOW SCORES
 650 REM
 660 LET TH(NH) = TH(NH) + 1
 670 LET TL(NL) = TL(NL) + 1
 680 REM
 690 REM  PRINT INDIVIDUAL TEST RESULTS
 700 REM
 710 PRINT S$; TAB(20); HS; "ON "; A$(NH);
 720 PRINT TAB(38); LS; "ON "; A$(NL); TAB(60); TS
 730 LET TS = 0
 740 GOTO 410
 750 REM
 760 REM  PROCESS TOTAL SUMMARY
 770 REM
 780 PRINT
 790 PRINT
 800 PRINT "SUMMARY OF TOTAL NUMBER SCORING HIGHEST"
 810 PRINT "AND LOWEST ON EACH AREA OF TEST --"
 820 PRINT
 830 PRINT "  AREA", "HIGHEST", "LOWEST"
 840 PRINT
 850 FOR N = 1 TO 8
 860   PRINT A$(N), "  "; TH(N), "  "; TL(N)
 870 NEXT N
 880 REM
 890 REM  DATA FOR SUBJECT AREA ARRAY
 900 REM
 910 DATA "ENGLISH","MATH","MUSIC","READING"
 920 DATA "HISTORY","ART","SCIENCE","SKILLS"
 930 REM
 940 REM  DATA TO BE PROCESSED
 950 REM
 960 DATA "R HARRIS",34,43,26,20,49,54,44,65
 970 DATA "T NEWTON",75,54,23,23,55,43,12,54
 980 DATA "S CLARKE",45,35,53,33,28,26,73,43
 990 DATA "W ANDREWS",26,17,36,11,31,30,28,33
1000 DATA "L CUMMINGS",39,65,45,33,45,14,32,33
1010 DATA "E FULLER",46,27,22,52,71,43,27,29
1020 DATA "R QUINCY",27,52,23,42,39,37,30,14
1030 DATA "S HAWKINS",32,18,24,34,17,21,42,26
1040 DATA "L SMITH",29,43,37,77,53,22,48,31
1050 DATA "N VINCENT",26,31,32,44,36,54,43,55
1060 DATA "P MILLER",23,44,61,33,41,17,53,55
1070 DATA "J HOLMES",38,41,32,43,22,28,36,21,"LAST"
1080 END
```

```
                    PLACEMENT TEST SCORE SUMMARY


 STUDENT                 HIGHEST              LOWEST              TOTAL
  NAME               SCORE AND AREA      SCORE AND AREA           SCORE

R HARRIS             65 ON SKILLS        20 ON READING             335
T NEWTON             75 ON ENGLISH       12 ON SCIENCE             339
S CLARKE             73 ON SCIENCE       26 ON ART                 336
W ANDREWS            36 ON MUSIC         11 ON READING             212
L CUMMINGS           65 ON MATH          14 ON ART                 306
E FULLER             71 ON HISTORY       22 ON MUSIC               317
R QUINCY             52 ON MATH          14 ON SKILLS              264
S HAWKINS            42 ON SCIENCE       17 ON HISTORY             214
L SMITH              77 ON READING       22 ON ART                 340
N VINCENT            55 ON SKILLS        26 ON ENGLISH             321
P MILLER             61 ON MUSIC         17 ON ART                 327
J HOLMES             43 ON READING       21 ON SKILLS              261


SUMMARY OF TOTAL NUMBER SCORING HIGHEST
AND LOWEST ON EACH AREA OF TEST --

  AREA          HIGHEST           LOWEST

ENGLISH            1                 1
MATH               2                 0
MUSIC              2                 1
READING            2                 2
HISTORY            1                 1
ART                0                 4
SCIENCE            2                 1
SKILLS             2                 2
```

TROUBLESHOOTING

Each of the following programs contains an error that prevents it from executing properly. Explain *specifically* what the problem is and what must be done to correct it. To assist you, a sample of what would happen should you attempt to run the program is provided after each listing. Refer to Appendix D for an explanation of BASIC error messages.

1.

```
 10 REM  TROUBLESHOOTING PROBLEM 9-1
 20 REM
 30 REM        C$ = COLLEGE NAME ARRAY
 40 REM         E = ENROLLMENT ARRAY
 50 REM         S = SUM OF ENROLLMENTS
 60 REM         A = AVERAGE OF ENROLLMENTS
 70 REM         D = DEVIATION FROM AVERAGE
 80 REM
 90 DIM C$(12), E(12)
100 FOR N = 1 TO 20
110   READ C$(N), E(N)
120   IF E(N) < 0 THEN 150
130   LET S = S + E(N)
140 NEXT N
150 LET NX = N - 1
160 LET A = S / NX
170 FOR K = 1 TO NX
180   LET D = A - E(K)
190   PRINT C$(K),, E(K), D
200 NEXT K
```

```
210 DATA "STONEWOOD", 2455, "HIGH FALLS", 982
220 DATA "TREEMONT", 1766, "ELSON", 439
230 DATA "PINE ST.", 6443, "DONNAH", 1722
240 DATA "PHILLS", 399, "LYNNWOOD", 822
250 DATA "PEAH U.", 3902, "ELM HILLS", 2911
260 DATA "WINDOHM", 2910, "RUSH U.", 7994
270 DATA "WILLOW ST.", 9220, "MUNSEY ST.", 8993
280 DATA "JYNX U.", 3992, "XXX", -1
290 END
```

```
Subscript Out of Range in Line 110
```

2.

```
 10 REM  TROUBLESHOOTING PROBLEM 9-2
 20 REM
 30 REM        C$ = CLASS NAME
 40 REM        S$ = STUDENT NAME ARRAY
 50 REM
 60 DIM S$(30)
 70 READ C$
 80 FOR J = 1 TO 30
 90   READ S$(J)
100   IF S$ = "LAST" THEN 120
110 NEXT J
120 LET JM = J - 1
130 PRINT C$
140 PRINT
150 FOR J = 1 TO JM STEP 4
160   PRINT S$(J), S$(J +1), S$(J + 2), S$(J + 3)
170 NEXT J
180 DATA "CHEMISTRY 121","M UPSON","S FULTON","W RING"
190 DATA "L LEE","R GRIGGS","W CULP","R TIMMS",D WILSON"
200 DATA "A HAMPTON","R AMOS","H PETERS","E DREWE","LAST"
210 END
```

```
Out of Data in Line 90
```

3.

```
 10 REM  TROUBLESHOOTING PROBLEM 9-3
 20 REM
 30 REM        C$ = CLASS NAME
 40 REM         G = GRADE ARRAY
 50 REM
 60 DIM G(30)
 70 READ C$
 80 FOR N = 1 TO 30
 90   READ G(N)
100   IF G(N) < 0 THEN 120
110 NEXT N
120 PRINT C$
130 PRINT
140 FOR N = 1 TO 30
150   PRINT G(N),
160 NEXT N
170 DATA "HISTORY 312",78,90,82,56,95,78,100
180 DATA 94,88,49,76,78,91,85,73,65,81,62,-1
190 END
```

```
HISTORY 312

 78          90          82          56          95
 78          100         94          88          49
 76          78          91          85          73
 65          81          62         -1           0
 0           0           0           0           0
 0           0           0           0           0
```

4.

```
 10 REM  TROUBLESHOOTING PROBLEM 9-4
 20 REM
 30 REM        C$ = CLASS NAME
 40 REM         G = GRADE ARRAY
 50 REM         H = HIGHEST GRADE
 60 REM         L = LOWEST GRADE
 70 REM
 80 DIM G(100)
 90 READ C$
100 FOR J = 1 TO 100
110   READ G(J)
120   IF G(J) < 0 THEN 140
130 NEXT J
140 LET JM = J - 1
150 LET H = G(1)
160 LET L = G(1)
170 FOR J = 2 TO JM
180   IF H < G(J) THEN LET G(J) = H
190   IF L > G(J) THEN LET G(J) = L
200 NEXT J
210 PRINT "THE HIGHEST GRADE IN "; C$; " IS"; H
220 PRINT "THE LOWEST GRADE IN "; C$; " IS"; L
230 DATA "PSYCHOLOGY 101",78,72,91,48,84,75,96,63,59,73
240 DATA 78,84,86,79,92,83,56,81,67,83,50,94,63,79,80,-1
250 END

THE HIGHEST GRADE IN PSYCHOLOGY 101 IS 78
THE LOWEST GRADE IN PSYCHOLOGY 101 IS 78
```

5.

```
 10 REM  TROUBLESHOOTING PROBLEM 9-5
 20 REM
 30 REM        C$ = CLASS NAME
 40 REM         G = GRADE ARRAY
 50 REM         F = NUMBER OF FAILING GRADES
 70 REM
 80 DIM G(100)
 90 READ C$
100 FOR J = 1 TO 100
110   READ G(J)
120   IF G(J) < 0 THEN 140
130 NEXT J
140 LET JM = J - 1
150 LET F = 0
170 FOR J = 1 TO JM
180   IF G(JM) < 60 THEN F = F + 1
200 NEXT J
220 PRINT "THERE ARE";F;"FAILING GRADES"
230 DATA "PSYCHOLOGY 101",78,72,91,48,84,75,96,63,59,73
240 DATA 78,84,86,79,92,83,56,81,67,83,94,63,79,80,50,-1
250 END

THERE ARE 25 FAILING GRADES
```

IMPORTANT TERMS

After studying this chapter, you should be familiar with the meaning and use of the following terms and BASIC statements:

Subscripted variable	Array
Subscript	Table
Dimension	Zeroth position
DIM statement	OPTION BASE statement

Invalid Subscript error
Subscript Out of Range error
Array element
Table search
Sequential search
Maximum element
Minimum element

EXERCISES

1. Explain the meaning of the following DIM statements:
   (a) `120 DIM A(20), H(35)`
   (b) `200 DIM V$(25)`
   (c) `165 DIM N(12), N$(12), XN(36)`
   (d) `130 DIM CN$(100), PT(100)`
   `140 DIM K(25), J(25), L$(50)`
   (e) `100 DIM Z(18), A$(24)`

```
        :
310 DIM TV(75), Y(20), R$(250)
```

2. Write DIM statements to set up the following array(s);
   (a) A with 20 elements and B with 30 elements
   (b) PD with 55 elements and D$ with 15 elements
   (c) C$ with 16 elements, X$ with 16 elements, and FY with 40 elements
   (d) WA with 150 elements, FT with 100 elements, L$ with 250 elements, and W$ with 200 elements
   (e) H$ with 75 elements, R$ with 65 elements, and R and Q, both with 1200 elements
3. Write BASIC statements to accomplish the following tasks:
   (a) Read data into a 20 element array beginning at the last element and ending at the first.
   (b) Add the nonzero elements of a 200 element array.
   (c) Add every other element of a 99 element array beginning with the first element.
   (d) Print the 40 elements of an array four to a print line.
   (e) Combine the elements of a 50 element array into a 10 element array by adding 5 elements at a time from the first array and placing the sums into a single element of the second array.
   (f) Print only the elements of a 100 element array that are greater than −15 and less than 35.
   (g) Count the elements of an array with P elements that are either greater than 100 or less than 0.
   (h) Multiply every fourth element of a 200 element array, beginning with the third element.
   (i) Add and subtract the elements of a 100 element array in pairs, placing the sums and differences in the corresponding positions in a second 100 element array. In other words, add and subtract the first two elements, placing these results in positions 1 and 2 of the second array. Next, add and subtract elements 3 and 4 of the second array, placing these results in locations 3 and 4 of the second array. Continue working with pairs of elements until the entire array has been processed.
   (j) Create a symmetrical array by reading the first data value into the first and last positions, the second value into the second and next-to-last positions, etc., working toward the center of the array. This may result in either of two situations: the last value read may appear once or twice in the array. Write program segments to create symmetrical arrays for 20 data values, with the last value appearing (1) twice in the array and (2) only once in the array.
4. It is possible to process variable length records with arrays. For example, suppose that we need to process class rosters for a college. The first class might be a freshman course with 200 students while the second is a senior course with only 20 in the class.

(a) Explain how arrays are especially useful for processing this type of data.
(b) Write a short section of program code to accept data for processing a class roster. The input record will consist of the class name, instructor, and the list of the names, ID numbers, and classifications of the students in the class, allowing for a varied number students in each class.

For Exercises 5 to 9, give the output that will be produced by the given programs. Then type the programs into the computer, run them, and check the actual outputs against your predictions.

5.
```
10 DIM N(12)
20 FOR J = 1 TO 12
30    READ N(J)
40 NEXT J
50 FOR K = 1 TO 12
60    PRINT N(13 - K)
70 NEXT K
80 DATA 37,44,28,90,76,54,37,43,28,72,13,28
90 END
```

6.
```
10 DIM N(20), S(20)
20 FOR A = 1 TO 20
30    LET N(A) = A
40    LET S(A) = A * A
50 NEXT A
60 FOR P = 1 TO 20 STEP 2
70    PRINT N(P), S(P),, N(P + 1), S(P + 1)
80 NEXT P
90 END
```

7.
```
10 DIM X(100)
20 FOR I = 1 TO 100
30    READ X(I)
40    IF X(I) = 9999 THEN 70
50    IF X(I) < 0 OR X(I) > 100 THEN I = I - 1
60 NEXT I
70 LET IM = I - 1
80 FOR I = 1 TO IM STEP 2
90    PRINT I, X(I),, I + 1, X(I + 1)
100 NEXT I
110 DATA 21,453,68,0,4,-55,34,211,13,877,23,-3
120 DATA 355,100,829,74,38,-54,119,54,29,9999
130 END
```

8.
```
10 DIM ZT(50)
20 FOR N = 1 TO 50
30    READ ZT(N)
40    IF ZT(N) = 9999 THEN 60
50 NEXT N
60 LET NM = N - 1
70 LET A = ZT(1)
80 LET Z = ZT(1)
90 FOR N = 2 TO NM
100    IF ZT(N) > A THEN A = ZT(N)
110    IF ZT(N) < Z THEN Z = ZT(N)
120 NEXT N
130 PRINT A, Z
140 DATA 21,453,68,0,4,-55,34,211,13,877,23,-3
150 DATA 355,100,829,74,38,-54,119,54,29,9999
160 END
```

PROGRAMMING PROBLEMS

Write programs in BASIC to accomplish the tasks described by each of the following problems. Be sure to carefully document each program and include all appropriate report headings and other literals.

1. Store the number 10 in the first position of an array that has been dimensioned for 20 elements. Now, multiply 10 by the subscript of each position in the array and store the product in the corresponding location. Print the resulting array.
2. The Barney Cahl Yacht Company needs a report to compare the month in which an order for a custom yacht is received and the month in which the work is actually started. Input will be a project number, the number (1 to 12) of the month in which the order was placed, and the number of the month in which the work on the yacht actually started. Output should give the project number, the *names* of the two months in question, and the number of months between. Data is given below. (The month names should be stored in the proper sequence in an array from which they may be retrieved *without* a table search.)

Project Number	Order Placed	Work Begun	Project Number	Order Placed	Work Begun
16548	5	8	30212	11	1
18220	4	8	32391	9	12
20199	2	5	42002	12	4
23902	10	12	49215	3	6
27299	7	10	62990	7	10

3. A Grade Analysis Report is needed for the grades in a remedial math class in which quizzes are given each week of the quarter. Input will be each student's name plus nine quiz grades. The program should find the average grade for each student as well as the class average for *each* of the nine quizzes and the final averages. Output should provide detail lines showing the input data plus the students' averages. Class averages should be printed at the bottom of the report under the proper columns. Data is provided below.

Student	Week Number								
Name	1	2	3	4	5	6	7	8	9
J. Gibbons	78	85	65	94	73	79	82	81	55
F. Carson	85	86	71	61	94	76	85	100	94
H. Nelson	52	64	70	45	59	64	71	32	49
L. Braddock	68	74	100	89	81	71	76	73	94
Y. Smith	84	78	80	73	75	89	74	65	79
M. Ellis	65	65	61	89	75	71	60	84	72
L. Morgan	64	75	56	60	53	71	38	69	71
T. Dudley	100	95	98	84	92	86	91	76	92
R. Nunn	58	53	85	65	75	80	73	62	45
T. Kelley	84	70	71	85	100	84	91	76	82
N. Bruce	71	75	60	62	88	76	91	86	62
K. Andrews	84	86	92	75	81	62	68	76	82

4. The Gopher Green Golf Course has had several complaints from its members that some of its holes have par values that are improperly assigned. The current pars for the 18 holes are as follows:

Hole	Par	Hole	Par	Hole	Par
1	4	7	4	13	4
2	3	8	3	14	3
3	3	9	5	15	4
4	5	10	4	16	3
5	4	11	6	17	5
6	4	12	4	18	4

The course manager has agreed to hire 12 pros to play the course and to use the results of their scores on each hole to decide if adjustments to the individual pars are justified. A program is needed to analyze the pros' scores and single out those holes that may need attention. The *average* of the scores of all 12 pros on *each* hole is to be compared to the current pars. If the average on a particular hole is more than 0.50 over par, then the hole number, the present par, the pros' average, the amount that the pros differ from par, and the message TOO HARD should be printed. If the pros score more than 0.50 under par on a hole, the same information should be printed except with the message TOO EASY. The pros' scores are given below.

Pro	Score Made on Hole Number																	
Number	1	2	3	4	5	6	7	8	9	10	11	12	13	14	15	16	17	18
1	4	3	4	4	4	4	4	4	5	4	5	4	4	4	4	4	4	4
2	4	3	4	5	4	5	4	4	6	5	7	5	5	2	4	3	4	4
3	3	3	3	5	4	4	5	5	6	5	6	4	5	3	5	3	3	5
4	3	2	4	7	3	3	5	3	4	4	6	4	6	3	3	3	5	4
5	4	3	5	6	4	4	4	4	5	4	9	4	5	2	5	3	5	4
6	6	4	3	5	3	6	3	3	5	4	4	5	5	2	4	4	3	3
7	3	2	3	4	2	4	4	4	5	3	6	3	6	3	4	3	4	3
8	4	4	4	5	3	3	7	3	5	7	6	3	4	4	4	4	4	3
9	4	2	3	3	4	4	4	4	6	4	5	5	3	1	5	5	4	5
10	4	3	4	4	3	4	4	5	3	4	7	2	4	4	4	3	5	4
11	3	4	3	6	3	3	3	3	7	5	7	4	5	3	4	2	4	4
12	4	3	3	5	4	5	4	3	5	3	6	4	4	3	3	3	4	5

5. The following is a list of seniors at Primate College:

Name	GPA	Name	GPA	Name	GPA
L. Martin	2.67	R. Jones	1.85	D. Townes	1.92
O. Jordan	3.11	T. Benson	2.91	G. Hill	3.29
R. Yancy	2.15	W. Adams	3.82	R. Nolan	3.61
L. French	3.57	M. Greene	2.73	B. Mammey	2.29
J. Lewis	3.42	R. Ross	3.50	Y. Peoples	3.71
R. Evans	2.66	V. Land	1.79	C. Palmer	3.22
T. Poole	3.77	D. Fischer	2.92	M. Church	2.52

The dean needs a program that will search the list of seniors and provide the following three separate reports:

(a) The name of the senior with the highest GPA.

(b) A list of all seniors with a GPA of 3.50 or above—these are potential honor graduates.

(c) A list of all seniors with a GPA of less than 2.00—these are in danger of not graduating.

The following is a list of courses offered by the computer science department of Binary College. It is for use with Problems 6 to 8.

Course Code	Course Description	Instructor in Charge	Course Code	Course Description	Instructor in Charge
CS 101	Computer Literacy	Franklin	CS 311	Prog Lang Theory	Conrad
CS 201	Intro to Comp Sci	Edwards	CS 321	Operating Systems	Conrad
CS 211	Prog in BASIC	Lovejoy	CS 341	Database Systems	Freeman
CS 251	Prog in COBOL I	Henderson	CS 401	Systems Analysis I	Henderson
CS 252	Prog in COBOL II	Henderson	CS 402	Systems Analysis II	Henderson
CS 261	Prog in RPG	Henderson	CS 421	Data Structures	Freeman
CS 281	Prog in FORTRAN	Freeman	CS 431	Comp Architecture	Conrad
CS 291	Numerical Computing	Freeman	CS 481	Directed Project	Staff
CS 301	Assembly Language	Conrad	CS 491	Selected Topics	Staff

6. Both Professors Henderson and Freeman are leaving Binary College at the end of the current academic year. For the purpose of searching for replacement faculty, a program is needed that will search the departmental course listing and print all courses that are taught by either Henderson or Freeman.
7. It has been decided that the courses listed in the following table will be taught next quarter at the indicated times and places. Write a program to prepare a schedule that gives the following for each class to be offered: the time it is offered, the course code, the course description, the instructor, and the place taught. (Note that some courses are not offered, while others may be offered at more than one time and should be listed each time.)

Time Taught	Course Code	Where Taught	Time Taught	Course Code	Where Taught
8:00 AM	CS 101	A-125	10:00 AM	CS 401	A-101
8:00 AM	CS 261	A-101	11:00 AM	CS 251	A-212
8:00 AM	CS 481	TBA	11:00 AM	CS 291	A-123
9:00 AM	CS 211	A-125	11:00 AM	CS 431	A-322
9:00 AM	CS 301	A-318	12 NOON	CS 211	A-125
9:00 AM	CS 421	A-123	12 NOON	CS 311	A-101
10:00 AM	CS 101	A-201	1:00 PM	CS 201	A-125
10:00 AM	CS 201	A-125	1:00 PM	CS 281	A-123

8. The computer science department has several students who lack only one course to complete their major in computer science. A program is needed to check the proposed schedule given in Problem 7 to see if the needed courses will be offered next quarter. Input will be each student's name and needed course as given below. The schedule must then be searched for each course to determine whether it is to be offered. If the course is on the schedule, print the student's name, course, the message OFFERED AT, and the time that the course is to be given. If the course is not on the schedule, print the student's name and course with the message NOT OFFERED.

Student Name	Course Needed	Student Name	Course Needed
G. Pollock	CS 281	L. Craine	CS 431
T. Murphy	CS 481	H. Williams	CS 421
A. Dobbins	CS 311	N. Kulp	CS 291
Y. Smith	CS 402	W. Brown	CS 421
P. Thorpe	CS 421	L. Whindom	CS 341
T. Brewer	CS 481	N. Holmes	CS 291

9. **Merging** is the process of combining the contents of two or more arrays into a single array. Write a program that will read the names of 12 persons into one array, their respective telephone numbers into a second, then merge the two sets of values into a third array with each name followed by the corresponding phone number. The printout should first list the name and phone number arrays, each printed with four elements to a line. This should be followed by the merged array with two names and phone numbers per line. You supply the data for this one.

Use the following inventory table for Steve's Stereos in working with Problems 10 to 13. All four columns of data may not be needed for all problems.

Item Number	Item Name	Unit Price	Quantity in Stock	Item Number	Item Name	Unit Price	Quantity in Stock
110234	Tape Deck	245.00	7	164679	Analyzer	295.00	0
112892	Receiver	310.00	11	167011	Power Amp	210.00	3
114299	Amplifier	295.00	6	170114	Pre-amp	175.00	4
120002	Tuner	235.00	7	182001	FM Antenna	45.00	2
121178	Turntable	175.50	12	201190	Cartridge	85.00	17
127338	Timer	75.50	1	217782	Stylus	21.75	59
129002	Cabinet	220.00	2	219822	Cables	5.50	172
132822	8-Track	65.00	21	219928	Cassette	4.50	358
135288	Car Stereo	155.00	19	219930	Cas X 10	40.00	26
142882	Speaker	185.00	12	237783	Cas Clnr	12.75	38
156643	Mini-spkr	85.50	16	246689	Rec Clnr	17.50	47
156877	Equalizer	125.00	3	246690	Rec Brush	6.00	8

10. Steve's Stereos has just received a shipment of new equipment shown in the table below. Prepare a program to update the inventory table to reflect the additional quantities of equipment. Output will be the updated inventory table.

Item Name	Quantity	Item Name	Quantity
Timer	5	Amplifier	1
Equalizer	3	Analyzer	2
Cabinet	4	Rec Brush	30
Speaker	8	FM Antenna	4

11. Unlike Cindy's Cameras, where all orders are processed as they are received, Steve's Stereos waits and batch processes all orders at the end of the day. A program is needed that will give a summary of all sales and at the same time update the inventory. As each item is processed, the quantity sold must be subtracted from the quantity in stock and the new quantity stored in the inventory. The input will be the order number, the item number, and the quantity purchased. The printout will give the order number, the item number, item name, quantity ordered, unit price, and total price. The following special situations must be considered:
    (a) If there is an insufficient number of an item to fill an order, the number available should be shipped with the message INCOMPLETE, added to that line.
    (b) If the stock of a certain item has been completely depleted, then the order number, item number, and item name are printed with the message OUT OF STOCK.
    (c) If an item number is not in the inventory table, only the order and item numbers are to be printed with the message STOCK NUMBER NOT FOUND.

    At the end of the report, print the total amount of the sales for the day. Items that were out of stock or missing as part of an incomplete order are not to be included in the final total.

Order Number	Item Number	Number Ordered	Order Number	Item Number	Number Ordered
12128	112892	1	12136	156643	4
12129	156877	1	12137	114288	1
12130	127338	1	12138	201190	1
12131	182001	1	12139	112892	1
12132	246690	3	12140	142882	2
12133	219930	2	12141	182001	2
12134	135288	1	12142	219822	6
12135	164679	1	12143	127338	1

12. Prepare a Daily Sales Summary Report for each salesperson at Steve's Stereos. Input will consist of each salesperson's name, the number of each item sold, and the quantity. The output should give only one line per salesperson, showing the salesperson's name, the number of items sold, the total quantity, and the total sales. This means that a control break (see Chapter 8) will occur when there is a change in salesperson name. At the end of the report, the total sales for the day should be printed. Data is provided below.

Salesperson Name	Item Number	Quantity Sold	Salesperson Name	Item Number	Quantity Sold
H. Broche	219930	2	W. Dawson	110234	1
H. Broche	246690	1	W. Dawson	114299	1
H. Broche	182001	1	W. Dawson	120002	1
H. Broche	237783	1	W. Dawson	129002	1
L. Perry	135288	1	W. Dawson	219930	2
L. Perry	219928	5	F. Wilson	112892	1
L. Perry	246690	1	F. Wilson	142882	2

13. Prepare a Sales Commission Report for Steve's Stereo. Each salesperson works on a commission that is given in the following table:

Salesperson Name	Commission Rate (%)
H. Broche	7.25
W. Dawson	8.00
M. Kline	7.50
L. Perry	8.50
H. Truman	7.00
F. Wilson	7.75

Using the data from Problem 12, write a program to calculate the commission earned by each salesperson on the given day. The commission is found by multiplying the total sales by the commission rate. Print a single line for each salesperson showing the salesperson's name, total sales, commission rate, and commission earned. At the end of the report, print the total sales and commissions earned for the day.

14. The chairman of the education department wishes to know if students tend to do better work toward the beginning or the end of a quarter. She plans to give a test each week of a 9-week quarter and determine at what point during the term most students tend to have their highest or lowest grades. A program is needed that will find the highest and lowest grade for each student's tests, incrementing the appropriate weekly totals. In other words, a count is to be made of *how many* students score their highest or lowest grade each week. The input will be each student's name and nine test scores. Output will consist of the *week numbers* in which the most and least high scores were made and the *week numbers* in which the most and least low scores were made. The number of highest or lowest scores should also be printed with the respective week numbers. Use the data given for Problem 3.

15. Rewrite the program for the Gasoline Sales Report given in Section 9-4 to print the branch name, the day of highest sales, the day of lowest sales, and the total sales for the week on the detailed line. At the end of the report, print the names of the two branches that have the highest and lowest total sales for the week.

16. In many sporting events which are judged by a panel of judges, often the highest and lowest marks are dropped with the final score being the sum of the remaining judges' marks. The table below provides the results for a certain competition that was judged by a panel of eight judges. Write a program that will score each participant by the method just described and determine the winner. The printout should give each participant's name and total score with the winner (highest score) printed at the end of the report.

Name of Participant	Mark by Judge Number							
	1	2	3	4	5	6	7	8
H. G. Ruiz	8.5	8.8	7.9	8.4	8.5	9.1	7.6	8.4
B. N. Borsky	9.3	9.2	9.1	8.9	9.1	9.0	9.1	9.4
H. L. Hughes	8.6	8.1	8.3	8.0	7.6	8.9	7.1	8.2
J. T. Knight	7.2	7.1	6.4	7.6	7.5	7.1	6.9	7.0
L. W. Chen	9.5	9.2	9.4	8.8	9.0	9.1	9.4	9.3
P. T. Koa	6.1	5.8	6.5	6.4	5.9	6.7	6.6	6.2
T. N. Epstein	8.9	9.0	9.4	8.7	8.6	9.3	9.1	8.9
Y. F. Fritch	8.1	8.7	7.9	8.6	8.2	8.4	8.6	8.0

CHAPTER 10
SUBROUTINES

The use of subroutines has always been a valuable technique available to programmers, especially for the processing of program segments that have to be repeated several times during the course of a program. However, during the past few years, the growth of interest in structured programming and the construction of modular programs has generated a dramatic increase in the use of subroutines in programs. In this chapter, we will learn some of the many uses for subroutines.

10-1 THE GOSUB STATEMENT

A **subroutine** is a self-contained set of statements that performs one or more specific functions. In BASIC, subroutines are **called** by means of the **GOSUB** statement, which has the very simple general form:

ln1 **GOSUB** *ln2*

where *ln2* is the line number of the first statement of the subroutine. The subroutine has the form:

ln2 First statement
:
Statements in subroutine
:
ln3 RETURN

The first statement of the subroutine is at *ln2* to which the GOSUB has directed processing. All statements in the subroutine will be executed in the regular manner until the **RETURN** statement is encountered. The RETURN statement signals the end of the subroutine at which point processing *returns to the next statement immediately following the* GOSUB *that called the subroutine*. Let us look at a simple example.

Consider the following short program, which simply reads a series of two numbers and performs some calculations:

```
 10 REM  PROGRAM WITHOUT SUBROUTINE
 20 REM
 30 READ A, B
 40 IF A = B THEN 110
 50 LET C = 2 * A + 3 * B
 60 LET D = A - B
 70 LET E = C / D
 80 PRINT A, B, C, D, E
 90 GOTO 30
100 DATA 6,3,4,9,8,0,5,4,4,4
110 END
```

We can rewrite this to incorporate the three LET statements at lines 50 to 70 into a short subroutine as follows:

```
 10 REM   PROGRAM WITH SUBROUTINE
 20 REM
 30 READ A, B
 40 IF A = B THEN 130
 50 GOSUB 90
 60 PRINT A, B, C, D, E
 70 GOTO 30
 80 DATA 6,3,4,9,8,0,5,4,4,4
 90 LET C = 2 * A + 3 * B
100 LET D = A - B
110 LET E = C / D
120 RETURN
130 END
```

This performs the exact same task as the first version except that the mathematical operations have now been placed into the subroutine at lines 90 to 120. In their place at line 50 is a GOSUB statement that calls (directs processing to) the subroutine at line 90. The program continues from line 90 until the RETURN is encountered at 120, at which point control returns to the next statement following the calling GOSUB. In this case, this means that the PRINT at line 60 will be executed immediately after the subroutine. This is illustrated in Figure 10-1*a*.

You should not be bothered by the fact that the program with the subroutine is a little longer than the one without. Shorter programs are not always better programs, as we will see in Section 10-3. However, with some programs the use of subroutines will make the program shorter. This frequently occurs when a single subroutine is called from more than one point in the program. For example, suppose that the above program had repeated the calculations as follows:

```
 10 REM   PROGRAM WITHOUT SUBROUTINE
 20 REM
 30 READ A, B
 40 IF A = B THEN 180
 50 LET C = A + B
 60 LET D = A - B
 70 LET E = C / D
 80 PRINT A, B, C, D, E
 90 LET A = C
100 LET B = D
110 LET C = A + B
120 LET D = A - B
130 LET E = C / D
140 PRINT A, B, C, D, E
150 PRINT
160 GOTO 30
170 DATA 6,3,4,9,8,6,5,4,4,4
180 END
```

Lines 50 to 80 and 110 to 140 are exactly the same. Both sets of statements can be incorporated into the *same* subroutine as shown in the following modification of the above program:

```
10 REM   PROGRAM WITH SUBROUTINE
20 REM
30 READ A, B
40 IF A = B THEN 170
50 GOSUB 120
```

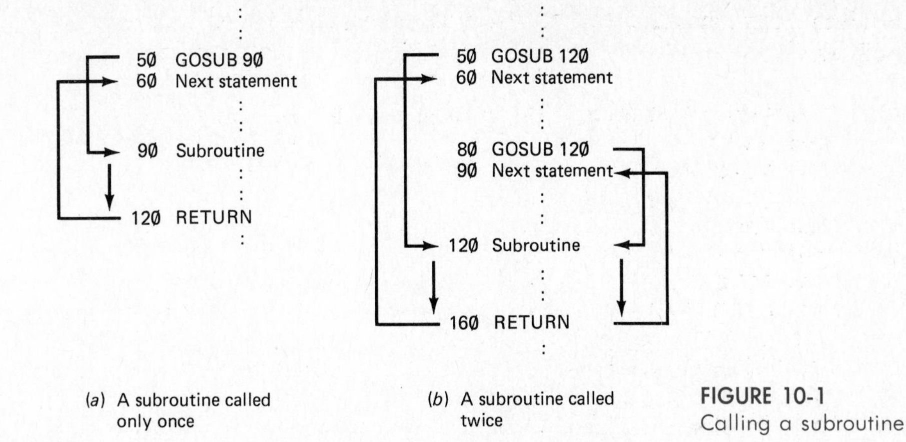

(a) A subroutine called only once

(b) A subroutine called twice

FIGURE 10-1
Calling a subroutine

```
 60 LET A = C
 70 LET B = D
 80 GOSUB 120
 90 PRINT
100 GOTO 30
110 DATA 6,3,4,9,8,6,5,4,4,4
120 LET C = A + B
130 LET D = A - B
140 LET E = C / D
150 PRINT A, B, C, D, E
160 RETURN
170 END
```

The four statements are written only once in the subroutine beginning at line 120. When the statements are needed at lines 50 and 80, a GOSUB calls the subroutine. Remember that the RETURN causes processing to return to the line following the *calling* GOSUB. This means that program control will automatically return to the line following the GOSUB that called the subroutine even if it was called several times from different locations in the program. This is illustrated in Figure 10-1*b*.

As seen in the last example, a single subroutine can be called more than once. In like manner, a single RETURN statement can serve as the end of more than one subroutine. For example, suppose that we need to call only part of a subroutine. The GOSUB can branch to any point before the RETURN and execute only part of the statements of the subroutine. Also, a GOTO can be used to jump directly to the RETURN, skipping over part of the subroutine. Care must always be taken, however, to ensure that a RETURN statement is never encountered without it being part of a *called* subroutine. If a subroutine is simply entered "from the top" without being called, when the RETURN is encountered, the program will not know where in the program it should return to and will issue a **RETURN without GOSUB** error message. Finally, a program may have as many subroutines as the programmer feels are needed.

10-2 GOSUB VERSUS GOTO

While the GOSUB statement does provide for a type of unconditional branch, it is *not* the same as the GOTO statement and should not be confused with it. The GOSUB with a RETURN provides for the automatic return to the next statement as described in Section 10-1; the GOTO cannot do this. GOSUBs are provided especially for processing with subroutines, which should never be constructed using GOTOs. Consider the following two examples.

In some simple cases, it may actually be possible to produce a very similar result by using only GOTO statements. For example, the subroutine described by Figure 10-1*a* can

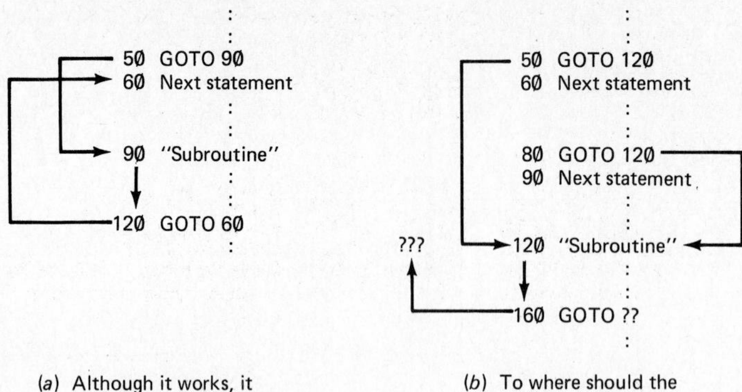

FIGURE 10-2
GOTOs do *not* produce subroutines

be written with GOTOs as shown in Figure 10-2*a*. This will work only for the very simplest cases. If we try to rewrite Figure 10-1*b* with *two* calls of the same subroutine, we are already in trouble. To which *Next statement* does the GOTO at the end of the subroutine return processing?

10-3 MODULAR PROGRAMMING

One of the recent trends in programming is that of writing **modular programs**. A modular program is constructed by writing the program as a series of self-contained segments or **modules**, each of which performs a specific task. If the definition of a module sounds very much like that of a subroutine, it is because subroutines are used extensively in constructing modular programs.

Consider the following very simple program outline:

Print headings
Read data
Perform calculations
Print detailed line
Print Totals

Let us see how such a simple set of tasks might be organized into a modular program outline. While there are no set rules as to what should be in a module (other than a self-contained task), most modular programs will have a **main** or **controlling module** from which all other modules are called as subroutines. The above might be set up as follows:

```
Main module
        Call subroutine to print headings
        Call subroutine to process data
        Call subroutine to print totals
End processing

Subroutine to print headings
        Statements to print headings
        RETURN

Subroutine to process data
        Read data
        Perform calculations
        Print detailed line
        RETURN

Subroutine to print totals
        Statements to print totals
        RETURN
```

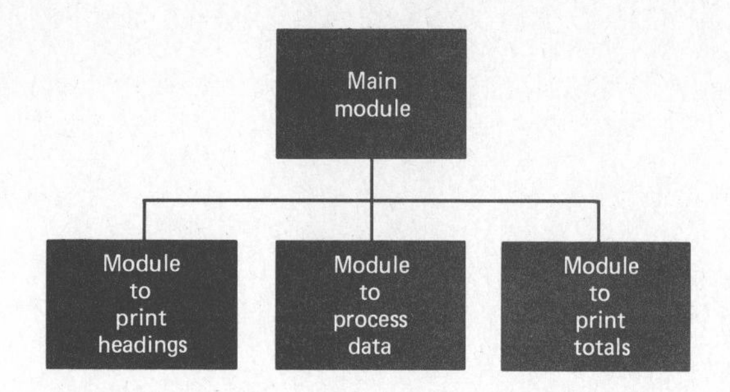

FIGURE 10-3
A simple modular structure

This will produce four modules as shown: the main module and the three subroutines. The organization of the four modules is shown schematically in Figure 10-3.

Let us look at an example of a program written in modular form. The Air Pollution Report example given in Section 6-4 has a very similar structure to that outlined above. You should review the program as it was written in Chapter 6 with the conventional method. It is rewritten below in modular form.

```
 10 REM  AIR POLLUTION REPORT
 20 REM
 30 REM  VARIABLES ARE DEFINED AS --
 40 REM
 50 REM        D1$ = DATE AT BEGINNING OF REPORT
 60 REM        D2$ = DATE AT END OF REPORT
 70 REM         C$ = NAME OF CITY
 80 REM    P1 - P5 = DAILY POLLUTION COUNTS
 90 REM          A = AVERAGE OF DAILY POLLUTION COUNTS
100 REM          N = TOTAL NUMBER OF CITIES SURVEYED
110 REM         TA = TOTAL OF DAILY AVERAGES
120 REM         AA = AVERAGE COUNT FOR ALL CITIES
130 REM
140 REM  MAIN PROGRAM MODULE
150 REM
160 READ D1$, D2$, N, TA
170 GOSUB 350
180 GOSUB 490
190 GOSUB 620
200 GOTO 700
210 REM
220 REM  DATA LIST
230 REM
240 DATA "6-13-83", "6-17-83", 0, 0
250 DATA "NEW YORK", 67, 89, 55, 145, 112
260 DATA "CHICAGO", 90, 125, 177, 132, 231
270 DATA "MIAMI", 35, 51, 37, 44, 21
280 DATA "PITTSBURG", 47, 73, 88, 108, 94
290 DATA "DENVER", 12, 24, 19, 7, 16
300 DATA "SAN FRANCISCO", 57, 88, 84, 118, 103
310 DATA "BOSTON", 46, 77, 112, 64, 89
320 DATA "DETROIT", 98, 145, 132, 87, 134
330 DATA "END", 0, 0, 0, 0, 0
340 REM
350 REM  MODULE TO PRINT HEADINGS
360 REM
370 PRINT TAB(23); "AIR POLLUTION REPORT"
380 PRINT TAB(22); D1$; TAB(31); "THRU "; D2$
390 PRINT
400 PRINT
410 PRINT "  REPORTING"; TAB(27); "POLLUTION COUNT FOR";
420 PRINT TAB(59); "DAILY"
```

```
430 PRINT "     CITY"; TAB(21); "MON"; TAB(28); "TUE";
440 PRINT TAB(35); "WED"; TAB(42); "THU"; TAB(49); "FRI";
450 PRINT TAB(58); "AVERAGE"
460 PRINT
470 RETURN
480 REM
490 REM  MODULE TO PROCESS POLLUTION COUNT DATA
500 REM
510 READ C$
520 IF C$ = "END" THEN 600
530 READ P1, P2, P3, P4, P5
540 LET A = (P1 + P2 + P3 + P4 + P5) / 5
550 LET N = N + 1
560 LET TA = TA + A
570 PRINT C$; TAB(20); P1; TAB(27); P2; TAB(34); P3;
580 PRINT TAB(41); P4; TAB(48); P5; TAB(58); A
590 GOTO 510
600 RETURN
610 REM
620 REM  MODULE TO CALCULATE FINAL
630 REM  AVERAGE AND PRINT TOTALS
640 REM
650 LET AA = TA / N
660 PRINT
670 PRINT "NUMBER OF CITIES SURVEYED ="; N
680 PRINT "AVERAGE COUNT FOR ALL CITIES ="; AA
690 RETURN
700 END
```

The main module is at lines 140 to 200. It consists of a READ to initialize certain values (see Section 6-4), three GOSUBs to call the three subroutines, and a GOTO to the END statement. (Some programmers prefer to use a STOP statement at line 200 instead of the GOTO.) The three subroutines to print headings, process data, and print totals are at lines 350 to 470, 490 to 600, and 620 to 690, respectively. This organization is identical to the one shown in Figure 10-3. The data has been placed following the main module. That is an arbitrary choice; it could have been placed at any point in the program.

The advantage of modular programming is difficult to appreciate with short programs. With longer programs, the modular approach improves a program in several ways. First, it makes a program easier to read and understand. Each task that the program performs is isolated into a separate module and, if properly documented, can be quickly located. Second, troubleshooting to find errors is easier due to the separation and isolation of functions into modules. Finally, modular programs are easier to maintain. If a program is in use for any length of time, it is very likely that a change will have to be made. The modular separation of processes makes it easier to find the places in the program where changes must be made. (The process of developing programs, beginning from a central controlling module and working downward through the program with modules to represent specific tasks, is sometimes referred to as **top-down design**.)

It may not yet be clear to you exactly *what* should be included within a module. Unfortunately, there are no set rules, and any two programmers will disagree, one including more or less than the other. There are, however, some general guidelines that you can follow. First, if it is a repeated process that you would place into a subroutine, it is a prime candidate for a module. Second, any self-contained process, such as printing headings, processing totals, etc., is easily modularized. Finally, the length of modules will vary with the process, but a module of one or two lines is probably too short, and it would be better to incorporate it into another module. Long modules of 20 or more lines likely perform multiple tasks and should be broken down into smaller units. With a little practice, you will develop a feel for forming modules.

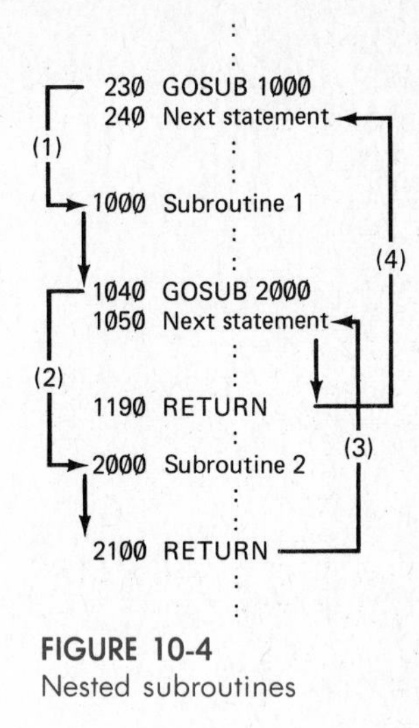

FIGURE 10-4
Nested subroutines

10-4 NESTED GOSUBS

It is possible to call a subroutine while within another subroutine. Consider the following:

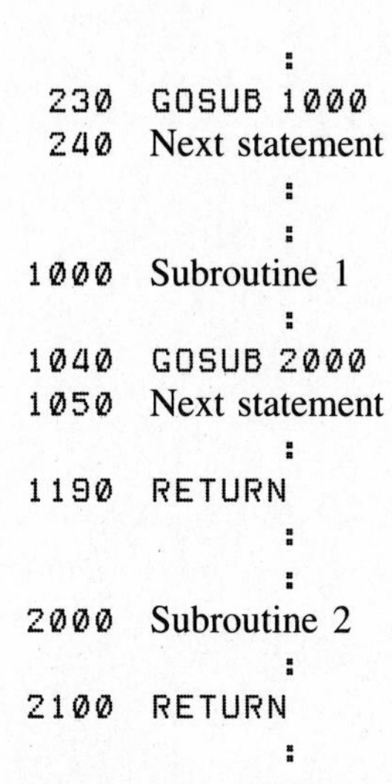

```
      :
 230  GOSUB 1000
 240  Next statement
      :
      :
1000  Subroutine 1
      :
1040  GOSUB 2000
1050  Next statement
      :
1190  RETURN
      :
      :
2000  Subroutine 2
      :
2100  RETURN
      :
```

The first subroutine at lines 1000 to 1190 is called at line 230. However, within this subroutine—at line 1040—a second subroutine is called. The sequence of processing is as you would expect. The first subroutine called (lines 1000 to 1190) is executed until the GOSUB at line 1040 calls a second subroutine. Processing is then transferred to the subroutine beginning at line 2000 and continues until the RETURN statement at 2100, at which point control returns to the next statement following the *calling* GOSUB, which is line 1050. We are still in the first subroutine where processing continues until the RETURN at line 1190 when control transfers back to line 240, the statement following the first GOSUB. Note that the terms *first* and *second* subroutines refer to the order in which they are called and not to their physical placement in the program. The procedure is illustrated in Figure 10-4.

In general, with nested subroutines (**nested GOSUBs**), the RETURNs will be executed in the opposite order to which the subroutines are called. However, you should take care not to nest routines too many times. Some versions of BASIC are especially sensitive to subroutines that are too deeply nested. Two or three levels are usually sufficient for most problems. If you find yourself with more than that, look again; there is probably a better way.

10-5 THE ON–GOSUB VARIATION OF THE ON–GOTO

Just as the GOSUB provides for an unconditional branch like the GOTO but with an automatic return to the next statement, there is a similar variation of the ON–GOTO known as the **ON–GOSUB** statement. It has the general form:

ln **ON** *expression* **GOSUB** *ln1*, *ln2*, *ln3*, . . .

which is identical to the ON–GOTO statement except that branches to *subroutines* at the indicated line numbers are executed on the basis of the value of the expression. Processing will then return to the next statement following the ON–GOSUB. Consider the following example:

```
 290  ON X GOSUB 1000, 2000, 3000
 300  Next statement
        :
        :
1000  Subroutine executed for X = 1
        :
1080  RETURN
        :
        :
2000  Subroutine executed for X = 2
        :
2130  RETURN
        :
        :
3000  Subroutine executed for X = 3
        :
3090  RETURN
        :
```

For values of X of 1, 2, and 3, respectively, the subroutines beginning at lines 1000, 2000, and 3000 will be executed. Unlike the simple ON–GOTO statement, control will return to the statement at line 300 following each subroutine.

In Section 8-5, we looked at an example that made use of the ON–GOTO statement. That program is rewritten below in modular form using the ON–GOSUB statement.

```
 10 REM   FACULTY SALARY UPDATE
 20 REM
 30 REM   VARIABLES ARE DEFINED AS --
 40 REM
 50 REM           N$ = FACULTY NAME
 60 REM            Y = YEARS EXPERIENCE
 70 REM            K = ACADEMIC RANK CODE
 80 REM           M$ = MESSAGE VARIABLE TO PRINT RANK
 90 REM            S = SALARY SCALE FACTOR
100 REM            M = EXPERIENCE MULTIPLIER
110 REM            B = ORIGINAL BASE PAY
120 REM            P = NEW BASE PAY
130 REM    T1 - T4 = TOTAL FACULTY AT EACH RANK
140 REM           TF = TOTAL FACULTY
150 REM           TP = TOTAL PAYROLL
160 REM
170 REM   MAIN PROGRAM MODULE
180 REM
190 GOSUB 240
200 GOSUB 360
210 GOSUB 800
220 GOTO 990
230 REM
240 REM   MODULE TO PRINT THE REPORT AND COLUMN
250 REM   HEADINGS AND SET ALL TOTALS EQUAL TO ZERO
260 REM
270 PRINT , " FACULTY SALARY UPDATE"
280 PRINT
290 PRINT
300 PRINT "FACULTY","YEARS"," ACADEMIC","  NEW"
310 PRINT " NAME", " EXP","   RANK", " SALARY"
320 PRINT
330 READ T1, T2, T3, T4, TF, TP
340 RETURN
350 REM
360 REM   MODULE TO READ AND PROCESS DATA
```

```
370 REM
380 READ N$, Y, K, B
390 IF Y < 0 THEN 460
400 ON K GOSUB 480, 560, 640, 720
410 LET P = S * B + M * Y
420 LET TP = TP + P
430 LET TF = TF + 1
440 PRINT N$, Y, M$, "$"; P
450 GOTO 380
460 RETURN
470 REM
480 REM  MODULE TO PROCESS INSTRUCTORS
490 REM
500 LET S = 1.05
510 LET M = 25
520 LET M$ = "INSTRUCTOR"
530 LET T1 = T1 + 1
540 RETURN
550 REM
560 REM  MODULE TO PROCESS ASSISTANT PROFESSORS
570 REM
580 LET S = 1.1
590 LET M = 50
600 LET M$ = "ASST PROF"
610 LET T2 = T2 + 1
620 RETURN
630 REM
640 REM  MODULE TO PROCESS ASSOCIATE PROFESSORS
650 REM
660 LET S = 1.15
670 LET M = 75
680 LET M$ = "ASSOC PROF"
690 LET T3 = T3 + 1
700 RETURN
710 REM
720 REM  MODULE TO PROCESS FULL PROFESSORS
730 REM
740 LET S = 1.2
750 LET M = 100
760 LET M$ = "PROFESSOR"
770 LET T4 = T4 + 1
780 RETURN
790 REM
800 REM  MODULE TO PRINT TOTALS
810 REM
820 PRINT
830 PRINT "TOTAL INSTRUCTORS ="; T1
840 PRINT "TOTAL ASST PROF ="; T2
850 PRINT "TOTAL ASSOC PROF ="; T3
860 PRINT "TOTAL PROFESSORS ="; T4
870 PRINT "TOTAL ALL FACULTY ="; TF
880 PRINT "TOTAL PAYROLL = $"; TP
890 RETURN
900 REM
910 REM DATA LIST
920 REM
930 DATA 0,0,0,0,0,0,"W TOWER",8,2,15500
940 DATA "Y LEE",8,3,18800,"M JONES",3,1,12500
950 DATA "H BOWEN",22,4,23500,"P SWANK",6,3,17900
960 DATA "W AARON",14,4,21500,"D SMITH",5,2,14500
970 DATA "R THOMAS",4,2,14500,"P LEWIS",12,3,19900
980 DATA "C WAMBLE",6,2,15500,"X",-1,0,0
990 END
```

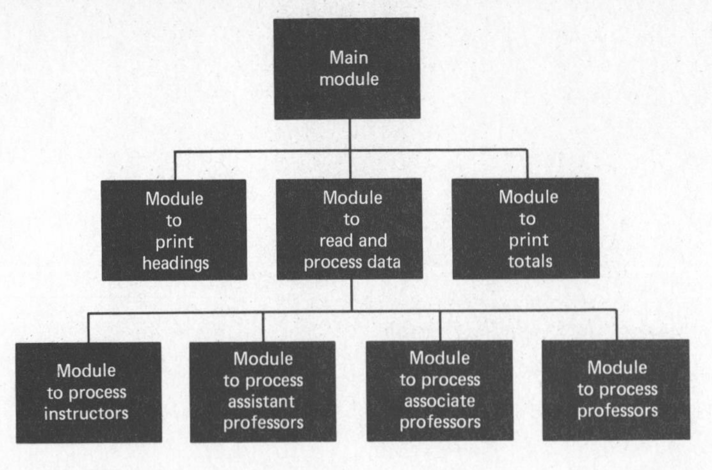

FIGURE 10-5
Modular organization of faculty salary update program

The main program module at lines 170 to 220 serves to call three subroutines to print the headings and initialize totals, read and process the data, and print the totals, respectively. The GOTO 990 at line 220 sends the program to the END statement. The first module called to print the headings and initialize the totals to zero is at lines 240 to 340. The second module that reads and processes the data is at lines 360 to 460. This is the heart of the program and contains the ON–GOSUB statement; we will look at it more closely below. The last module to print the final totals is at lines 800 to 890. Each of the three modules is processed in turn, after which the GOTO at line 200 ends the program.

The middle module to read and process data contains the ON–GOSUB statement at line 400:

```
400  ON K GOSUB 480, 560, 640, 720
```

This statement calls one of four possible subroutines beginning at the four indicated lines. These subroutines are located at lines 480 to 540, 560 to 620, 640 to 700, and 720 to 780, respectively. No matter which of the four modules is executed, processing will return to the statement immediately following the ON–GOSUB, which is line 410, and will continue from there. Lines 410 to 450 following the ON–GOSUB in the modular version above correspond to lines 770 to 810 in the program in Section 8-5. The organization of the modules is illustrated in Figure 10-5.

10-6 THE USE OF MENUS

Many interactive programs are **menu-driven**; that is, they provide the user with a **menu** of the possible program options that are available for selection. For example, a typical inventory control program might present a menu that looks something like the one below.

```
INVENTORY PROCESSING OPTIONS ARE --

     1 -- ADD AN ITEM TO THE STOCK
     2 -- DELETE AN ITEM FROM STOCK
     3 -- CHANGE THE UNIT PRICE OF AN ITEM
     4 -- REVIEW A SINGLE ITEM
     5 -- PRINT ENTIRE INVENTORY
     6 -- EXIT PROGRAM

ENTER NUMBER OF PROCESS DESIRED?
```

A menu such as the one above is usually self-explanatory and easy for the user to understand. This is why menus are very frequently incorporated into programs that will be used by a variety of individuals who may or may not be experienced in programming.

To produce a menu is reasonably simple; it is usually no more than a series of PRINT statements with an INPUT statement to allow the entry of the number of the desired process. The above menu would be produced by the following set of statements:

```
300 PRINT , "INVENTORY PROCESSING OPTIONS ARE --"
310 PRINT
320 PRINT , "      1 -- ADD AN ITEM TO THE STOCK"
330 PRINT , "      2 -- DELETE AN ITEM FROM STOCK"
340 PRINT , "      3 -- CHANGE THE UNIT PRICE OF AN ITEM"
350 PRINT , "      4 -- REVIEW A SINGLE ITEM"
360 PRINT , "      5 -- PRINT ENTIRE INVENTORY"
370 PRINT , "      6 -- EXIT PROGRAM"
380 PRINT
390 PRINT , "ENTER NUMBER OF PROCESS DESIRED";
400 INPUT N
```

Once the number of the process to be performed has been chosen, an ON–GOSUB statement can be used to direct the program to the proper module to perform the requested processing. For the above menu, we might have an ON–GOSUB like this:

```
450 ON N GOSUB 1000, 2000, 3000, 4000, 5000
```

Thus, for the five possible processes that can be performed, there are five corresponding subroutines that are called by the ON–GOSUB, depending on the selected value for N. (A separate subroutine is not needed for N = 6 since this simply directs processing to the end of the program.) To add an item to the inventory (N = 1), the subroutine at line 1000 is called; to delete an item (N = 2), the subroutine at 2000 is called, and so on for the five processes and subroutines. Each of the subroutines will incorporate one or more modules, depending on how complex the process is.

10-7 AN EXAMPLE: AIRLINE FLIGHT RESERVATIONS

The example that follows will illustrate the construction of a program that is both modular and menu-driven. While it is not necessarily the case that a menu-driven program must be modular, or vice versa, the modular structure of a program works exceptionally well whenever menus are used.

Problem: Albatross Airlines needs a menu-driven program that will allow reservations agents to perform the following tasks:

1. Make a reservation on a certain flight
2. Cancel a reservation
3. Review the status of an individual flight
4. Review the entire flight schedule for all flights

For the first two processes, the agent must be able to distinguish between first class and economy seats. The program must confirm that the reservation was made or cancelled or, if there are not enough seats for a reservation, print an appropriate message. Data for the flight table is provided in Table 10-1 and consists of the flight number, departure and arrival cities and times, and the number of available seats in both first and economy class. The input data will vary with the menu selection and is given in Table 10-2.

Since this program is to be menu-driven, a modular approach to the program design is best. For this reason, we will analyze the solution somewhat differently than usual. Other than the use of subroutines, there is no new BASIC required for the program solution; therefore, we will concentrate on the modular structure of the program and its general organization. Before we begin a discussion of the division of this program into modules, remember that there are no set rules as to exactly what should be in any specific

TABLE 10-1

Data for Flight Schedule Table for Albatross Airlines

Flight Number	Departure City	Arrival City	Departure Time	Arrival Time	1st Class Seats	Economy Seats
129	NYC	BOS	7:10A	7:35A	5	23
642	ATL	DET	8:05A	8:55A	11	37
805	ALB	CHI	9:20A	9:50A	8	12
375	DAL	BOS	10:00A	1:25P	3	0
492	DET	STL	11:30A	12:35P	7	31
102	BOS	ATL	12:05P	2:35P	4	2
388	LAX	DEN	1:45P	3:10P	14	42
487	MIA	NYC	2:25P	4:50P	0	0
500	CIN	DAL	3:55P	5:40P	9	23
311	DEN	CIN	5:35P	8:50P	5	18
149	NYC	LAX	8:10P	10:25P	14	87
902	CHI	MIA	9:50P	1:05A	12	42

module. This means that the structure of the modules described below (or for any program) is somewhat arbitrary and that there are others that would be equally suitable.

All processes are controlled through menu selections, hence the menu and its process selection will be the primary operation contained within the main program module. Although it may (and will) call other modules, this module must call the subroutines to load the flight table and perform the above four processes. From each of the first three tasks, a flight number must be entered to select a flight. This means that a subroutine that searches the flight table for the proper flight must be called from the corresponding module. You should begin to get the idea of the structure. Let us outline the major modules and their relationships to each other.

```
Main program module
    Call subroutine to load flight table
    Depending on menu selection
        Call subroutine to make reservation
        Call subroutine to cancel reservation
        Call subroutine to review single flight
        Call subroutine to print flight table

Module to make flight reservation
    Call subroutine to search flight table
RETURN

Module to cancel reservation
    Call subroutine to search flight table
RETURN

Module to review single flight
    Call subroutine to search flight table
RETURN

Module to print flight table
RETURN

Module to load flight table
RETURN

Module to search flight table
RETURN
```

Except for the main program module, which is not a subroutine, the actual order of the modules is unimportant since each as a subroutine will function as a self-contained

TABLE 10-2

Data to be Processed for Flight Reservation Example

Process Number	Flight Number	Seat Class	Number of Seats
1	311	2	6
2	492	1	2
1	102	2	4
3	102	N/A	N/A
1	500	2	3
2	129	2	5
4	N/A	N/A	N/A
5	N/A	N/A	N/A

unit. We now have seven modules; the final program will have thirteen. The remaining six modules will be inserted for such things as printing error messages, handling processes that are repeated at different points in the program, or just simplifying a program section. We will see how these modules are used as the program develops. An overall outline of all modules is given later.

The main program module consists of the following lines:

```
190 REM   MAIN PROGRAM MODULE
200 REM
210 DIM N(12), AC$(12), DC$(12), AT$(12), DT$(12), F(12), E(12)
220 GOSUB 1050
230 GOSUB 1120
240 INPUT "ENTER PROCESS DESIRED (1-5)"; P
250 IF P => 1 AND P <= 5 THEN 280
260 GOSUB 1610
270 GOTO 240
280 IF P = 5 THEN 1880
290 ON P GOSUB 320, 610, 860, 960
300 GOTO 230
```

This begins at line 220 with GOSUB 1050 to call the subroutine to load the flight data table. This subroutine is written as:

```
1050 REM   MODULE TO LOAD FLIGHT DATA TABLE
1060 REM
1070 FOR J = 1 TO 12
1080    READ N(J), DC$(J), AC$(J), DT$(J), AT$(J), F(J), E(J)
1090 NEXT J
1100 RETURN
```

The next line calls a subroutine beginning at line 1120. This subroutine is used to print the selection menu and appears as:

```
1120 REM   MODULE TO PRINT SELECTION MENU
1130 REM
1140 PRINT
1150 PRINT "SCHEDULING OPTIONS ARE AS FOLLOWS --"
1160 PRINT
1170 PRINT , "1 -- MAKE PASSENGER RESERVATION"
1180 PRINT , "2 -- CANCEL PASSENGER RESERVATION"
1190 PRINT , "3 -- REVIEW STATUS OF SPECIFIC FLIGHT"
1200 PRINT , "4 -- REVIEW ALL AVAILABLE FLIGHTS"
1210 PRINT , "5 -- EXIT PROGRAM"
1220 PRINT
1230 RETURN
```

Of course, both of these sets of statements could have been incorporated directly into the main program module; however, by placing them in separate modules, the main module is much simpler and easier to follow.

Line 240 follows the printing of the menu and is used to enter the selection to be processed. Line 250 provides an edit to ensure that only proper numbers were entered, and control continues to line 280 for valid entries only. Line 260 calls a subroutine at 1610 to print an error message for invalid entries. It is as follows:

```
1610  REM   MODULE TO SIGNAL INVALID ENTRIES
1620  REM
1630  PRINT
1640  PRINT "INVALID ENTRY -- RE-ENTER"
1650  PRINT
1660  RETURN
```

This is placed into a subroutine because the same message can be used elsewhere in the program. Line 270 allows for reentry after an invalid value. Line 280 sends the program to the END statement when option 5 is selected (see menu). Line 290 calls the four subroutines that process the first four processes listed on the menu, respectively. We will now look at these four modules individually.

The first process is to make a flight reservation. This is processed by the following module:

```
320 REM   MODULE TO MAKE A FLIGHT RESERVATION
330 REM
340 PRINT
350 INPUT "ENTER FLIGHT NUMBER"; NF
360 GOSUB 1370
370 PRINT
380 PRINT "DO YOU NEED FIRST CLASS (1)"
390 INPUT "OR ECONOMY (2) SEATS"; C
400 IF C = 1 OR C = 2 THEN 430
410 GOSUB 1610
420 GOTO 380
430 PRINT
440 INPUT "HOW MANY SEATS ARE NEEDED"; NS
450 IF C = 1 AND NS <= F(J) THEN 500
460 IF C = 2 AND NS <= E(J) THEN 530
470 PRINT
480 PRINT "REQUESTED SEATING UNAVAILABLE"
490 GOTO 580
500 LET F(J) = F(J) - NS
510 LET NS$ = "FIRST CLASS"
520 GOTO 550
530 LET E(J) = E(J) - NS
540 LET NS$ = "ECONOMY"
550 PRINT
560 PRINT "RESERVATION OF"; NS; NS$; " SEATS
570 PRINT "ON FLIGHT"; NF; "IS CONFIRMED"
580 GOSUB 1680
590 RETURN
```

This module is a little long and might be broken up; however, it does process a *single* function. The module begins at line 350 by requesting the number of the flight for which reservations are needed. The next line calls a subroutine at line 1370 that performs a search of the flight table for a flight with the requested number. That module is:

```
1370 REM   MODULE TO SEARCH FLIGHT TABLE FOR
1380 REM   MATCH TO ENTERED FLIGHT NUMBER
1390 REM
```

```
1400 FOR J = 1 TO 12
1410    IF NF = N(J) THEN 1450
1420 NEXT J
1430 GOSUB 1540
1440 GOTO 1400
1450 RETURN
```

This module is a simple table search; however, it calls a special subroutine at 1540 to print a message for invalid flight numbers and permits reentry as follows:

```
1540 REM  MODULE TO PROCESS INVALID FLIGHT NUMBER
1550 REM
1560 PRINT
1570 PRINT "FLIGHT NUMBER"; NF; "NOT FOUND"
1580 INPUT "RE-ENTER"; NF
1590 RETURN
```

Returning to the flight reservations module, the next step is to determine the class of the requested seating. Line 400 performs an edit check on this entry, with the error subroutine at 1610 being called at 410 for invalid entries. The remainder of the module requests the number of seats needed (line 440), checks this against the number available (450 and 460), and either prints a message that seating is unavailable (line 480) or subtracts the number of seats needed from the number available in the proper class (500 and 530). It then sets a print message variable equal to the proper class (510 and 540) and prints a confirmation message (550 to 570).

The GOSUB 1680 at the end of the module calls the following subroutine:

```
1680  REM  MODULE TO CONTINUE AND RETURN TO SELECTION MENU
1690  REM
1700  PRINT
1710  INPUT "HIT <RETURN> TO CONTINUE"; R$
1720  RETURN
```

This stops any action on the screen until the agent is ready to continue, at which point hitting the RETURN key will return the program to the main program module and the selection menu. Trace this through. Following line 1710 is a RETURN which returns processing to the next statement after the calling GOSUB, which is the RETURN at 590 at the end of the flight reservations module, so that processing returns to the main module. The next statement after the calling statement (which was the ON–GOSUB) in the main module is line 300, which is GOTO 230. Line 230, in turn, calls the subroutine to print the menu!

The second module is the one to cancel a reservation. It is given below:

```
610 REM  MODULE TO CANCEL A RESERVATION
620 REM
630 PRINT
640 INPUT "ENTER FLIGHT NUMBER"; NF
650 GOSUB 1370
660 PRINT
670 PRINT "ARE SEATS IN FIRST CLASS (1)"
680 INPUT "OR ECONOMY (2) SECTION"; C
690 IF C = 1 OR C = 2 THEN 720
700 GOSUB 1610
710 GOTO 670
720 PRINT
730 INPUT "HOW MANY SEATS ARE RESERVED"; NS
740 IF C = 2 THEN 780
750 LET F(J) = F(J) + NS
760 LET NS$ = "FIRST CLASS"
770 GOTO 800
```

```
780 LET E(J) = E(J) + NS
790 LET NS$ = "ECONOMY"
800 PRINT
810 PRINT "RESERVATION OF"; NS; NS$; " SEATS
820 PRINT "ON FLIGHT"; NF; "IS CANCELLED"
830 GOSUB 1680
840 RETURN
```

A comparison of this module to the one for making a reservation will reveal that they are very similar. Of course, there is no message for unavailable seating, and canceled seats are *added* to the number of available seats (lines 750 and 780) instead of subtracted. Note the GOSUB 1680 at line 830 at the end of the subroutine; it controls the printing of the menu as in the first module. It will also be at the end of the other two subroutines that are called from the menu.

The third module permits the reservations agent to select a specific flight and review its status, including available seating. This module is written as:

```
860 REM  MODULE TO REVIEW STATUS OF ONE FLIGHT
870 REM
880 PRINT
890 INPUT "ENTER FLIGHT NUMBER"; NF
900 GOSUB 1370
910 GOSUB 1250
920 GOSUB 1470
930 GOSUB 1680
940 RETURN
```

We have seen before the subroutine at 1370; it searches the flight table for the input flight number. The subroutine at 1250 prints headings for the flight data. It is as follows:

```
1250 REM  MODULE TO PRINT HEADINGS FOR FLIGHT TABLE
1260 REM
1270 PRINT
1280 PRINT "FLIGHT"; TAB(12); "DEP"; TAB(22); "ARV";
1290 PRINT TAB(31); "DEP"; TAB(41); "ARV"; TAB(52); "1 CLS";
1300 PRINT TAB(62); "ECON"
1310 PRINT "NUMBER"; TAB(12); "CITY"; TAB(22); "CITY";
1320 PRINT TAB(31); "TIME"; TAB(41); "TIME"; TAB(52);
1330 PRINT "SEATS"; TAB(62); "SEATS"
1340 PRINT
1350 RETURN
```

The subroutine at 1470 is:

```
1470 REM  MODULE TO PRINT FLIGHT DATA
1480 REM
1490 PRINT " "; N(J); TAB(12); DC$(J); TAB(22); AC$(J);
1500 PRINT TAB(30); DT$(J); TAB(40); AT$(J); TAB(53); F(J);
1510 PRINT TAB(63); E(J)
1520 RETURN
```

which actually prints the data. The reason for writing these as subroutines rather than placing the statements directly into the third module will be apparent shortly.

The fourth and last module to be processed directly from the menu is the following:

```
 960 REM  MODULE TO PRINT ENTIRE FLIGHT SCHEDULE
 970 REM
 980 GOSUB 1250
 990 FOR J = 1 TO 12
1000    GOSUB 1470
```

```
1010 NEXT J
1020 GOSUB 1680
1030 RETURN
```

which prints the entire flight table. Notice that the two subroutines at 1250 and 1470 that were used in the last process to print a single flight's status are also used here. The only real difference between this module and the last is the FOR–NEXT loop that causes the entire flight table to be printed rather than a single flight.

Before presenting the complete program listing and a sample run, let us take one last look at the organization of the modules. This is illustrated schematically in Figure 10-6. All thirteen modules of the program are shown below in the order that they are listed in the program (which, as we said earlier, is unimportant). Also shown is the module from which each is called.

Main program module
- Call subroutine to load flight table
- Call subroutine to print menu
- Call subroutine for invalid entry
- Depending on menu selection
  - Call subroutine to make reservation
  - Call subroutine to cancel reservation
  - Call subroutine to review single flight
  - Call subroutine to print flight table

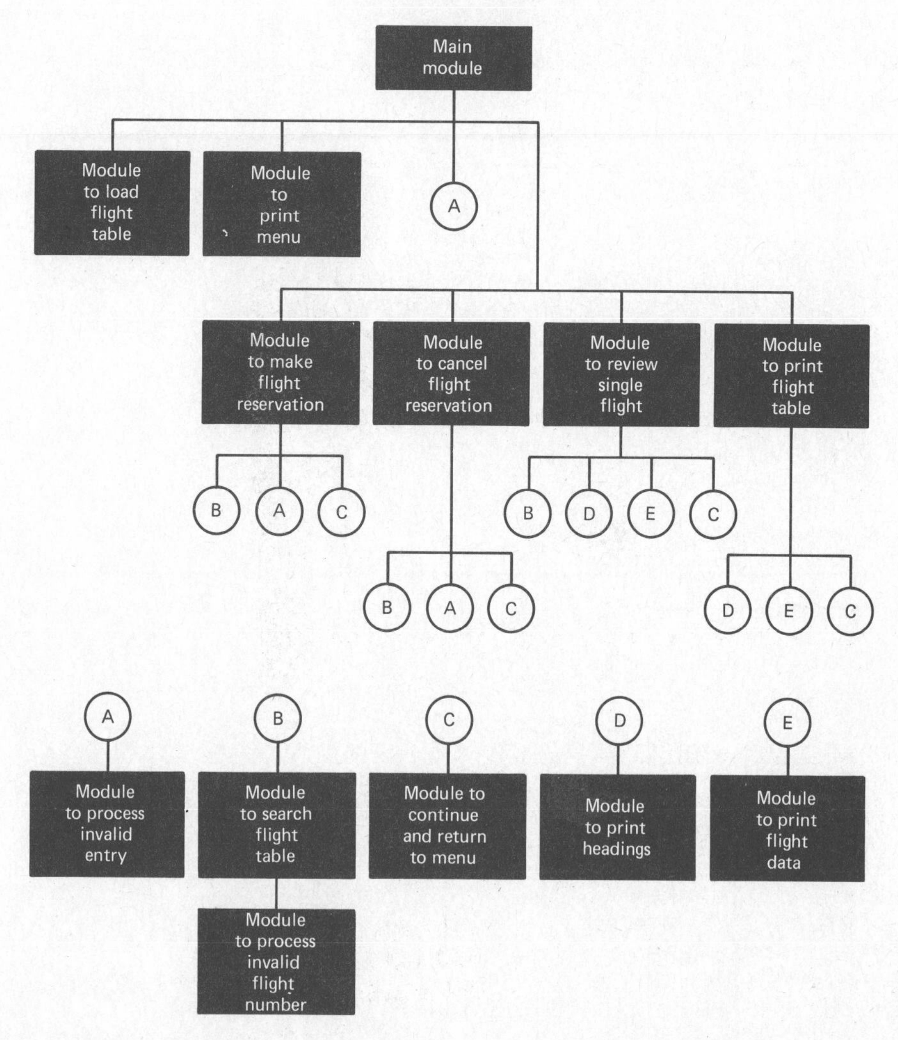

FIGURE 10-6
Modular structure for flight reservation program

Module to make flight reservation
    Call subroutine to search flight table
    Call subroutine for invalid entry
    Call subroutine to continue and return to menu
RETURN

Module to cancel reservation
    Call subroutine to search flight table
    Call subroutine for invalid entry
    Call subroutine to continue and return to menu
RETURN

Module to review single flight
    Call subroutine to search flight table
    Call subroutine to print headings
    Call subroutine to print flight data
    Call subroutine to continue and return to menu
RETURN

Module to print flight table
    Call subroutine to print headings
    Call subroutine to print flight data
    Call subroutine to continue and return to menu
RETURN

Module to load flight table
RETURN

Module to print selection menu
RETURN

Module to print headings for flight data
RETURN

Module to search flight table
    Call subroutine for invalid flight number
RETURN

Module to print flight data
RETURN

Module to process invalid flight number
RETURN

Module to signal invalid entry
RETURN

Module to continue and return to menu
RETURN

The complete program listing is provided below.

```
 10 REM  AIRLINE FLIGHT RESERVATIONS
 20 REM
 30 REM  VARIABLES ARE DEFINED AS --
 40 REM
 50 REM        N = FLIGHT NUMBER ARRAY
 60 REM      AC$ = ARRIVAL CITY ARRAY
 70 REM      DC$ = DEPARTURE CITY ARRAY
 80 REM      AT$ = ARRIVAL TIME ARRAY
 90 REM      DT$ = DEPARTURE TIME ARRAY
100 REM        F = NUMBER OF FIRST CLASS SEATS ARRAY
```

```
110 REM          E = NUMBER OF ECONOMY SEATS ARRAY
120 REM          P = PROCESS SELECTION VARIABLE
130 REM         NF = NUMBER OF SEATS TO BE PROCESSED
140 REM          C = CLASS INDICATOR
150 REM        NF$ = CLASS PRINT FIELD
160 REM         R$ = CONTINUE SIGNAL
170 REM          J = LOOP COUNTER/ARRAY INDEX
180 REM
190 REM  MAIN PROGRAM MODULE
200 REM
210 DIM N(12), AC$(12), DC$(12), AT$(12), DT$(12), F(12), E(12)
220 GOSUB 1050
230 GOSUB 1120
240 INPUT "ENTER PROCESS DESIRED (1-5)"; P
250 IF P => 1 AND P <= 5 THEN 280
260 GOSUB 1610
270 GOTO 240
280 IF P = 5 THEN 1880
290 ON P GOSUB 320, 610, 860, 960
300 GOTO 230
310 REM
320 REM  MODULE TO MAKE A FLIGHT RESERVATION
330 REM
340 PRINT
350 INPUT "ENTER FLIGHT NUMBER"; NF
360 GOSUB 1370
370 PRINT
380 PRINT "DO YOU NEED FIRST CLASS (1)"
390 INPUT "OR ECONOMY (2) SEATS"; C
400 IF C = 1 OR C = 2 THEN 430
410 GOSUB 1610
420 GOTO 380
430 PRINT
440 INPUT "HOW MANY SEATS ARE NEEDED"; NS
450 IF C = 1 AND NS <= F(J) THEN 500
460 IF C = 2 AND NS <= E(J) THEN 530
470 PRINT
480 PRINT "REQUESTED SEATING UNAVAILABLE"
490 GOTO 580
500 LET F(J) = F(J) - NS
510 LET NS$ = "FIRST CLASS"
520 GOTO 550
530 LET E(J) = E(J) - NS
540 LET NS$ = "ECONOMY"
550 PRINT
560 PRINT "RESERVATION OF"; NS; NS$; " SEATS
570 PRINT "ON FLIGHT"; NF; "IS CONFIRMED"
580 GOSUB 1680
590 RETURN
600 REM
610 REM  MODULE TO CANCEL A RESERVATION
620 REM
630 PRINT
640 INPUT "ENTER FLIGHT NUMBER"; NF
650 GOSUB 1370
660 PRINT
670 PRINT "ARE SEATS IN FIRST CLASS (1)"
680 INPUT "OR ECONOMY (2) SECTION"; C
690 IF C = 1 OR C = 2 THEN 720
700 GOSUB 1610
710 GOTO 670
720 PRINT
730 INPUT "HOW MANY SEATS ARE RESERVED"; NS
```

```
 740 IF C = 2 THEN 780
 750 LET F(J) = F(J) + NS
 760 LET NS$ = "FIRST CLASS"
 770 GOTO 800
 780 LET E(J) = E(J) + NS
 790 LET NS$ = "ECONOMY"
 800 PRINT
 810 PRINT "RESERVATION OF"; NS; NS$; " SEATS"
 820 PRINT "ON FLIGHT"; NF; "IS CANCELLED"
 830 GOSUB 1680
 840 RETURN
 850 REM
 860 REM  MODULE TO REVIEW STATUS OF ONE FLIGHT
 870 REM
 880 PRINT
 890 INPUT "ENTER FLIGHT NUMBER"; NF
 900 GOSUB 1370
 910 GOSUB 1250
 920 GOSUB 1470
 930 GOSUB 1680
 940 RETURN
 950 REM
 960 REM  MODULE TO PRINT ENTIRE FLIGHT SCHEDULE
 970 REM
 980 GOSUB 1250
 990 FOR J = 1 TO 12
1000   GOSUB 1470
1010 NEXT J
1020 GOSUB 1680
1030 RETURN
1040 REM
1050 REM  MODULE TO LOAD FLIGHT DATA TABLE
1060 REM
1070 FOR J = 1 TO 12
1080   READ N(J), DC$(J), AC$(J), DT$(J), AT$(J), F(J), E(J)
1090 NEXT J
1100 RETURN
1110 REM
1120 REM  MODULE TO PRINT SELECTION MENU
1130 REM
1140 PRINT
1150 PRINT "SCHEDULING OPTIONS ARE AS FOLLOWS --"
1160 PRINT
1170 PRINT , "1 -- MAKE PASSENGER RESERVATION"
1180 PRINT , "2 -- CANCEL PASSENGER RESERVATION"
1190 PRINT , "3 -- REVIEW STATUS OF SPECIFIC FLIGHT"
1200 PRINT , "4 -- REVIEW ALL AVAILABLE FLIGHTS"
1210 PRINT , "5 -- EXIT PROGRAM"
1220 PRINT
1230 RETURN
1240 REM
1250 REM  MODULE TO PRINT HEADINGS FOR FLIGHT DATA
1260 REM
1270 PRINT
1280 PRINT "FLIGHT"; TAB(12); "DEP"; TAB(22); "ARV";
1290 PRINT TAB(31); "DEP"; TAB(41); "ARV"; TAB(52); "1 CLS";
1300 PRINT TAB(62); "ECON"
1310 PRINT "NUMBER"; TAB(12); "CITY"; TAB(22); "CITY";
1320 PRINT TAB(31); "TIME"; TAB(41); "TIME"; TAB(52);
1330 PRINT "SEATS"; TAB(62); "SEATS"
1340 PRINT
1350 RETURN
1360 REM
1370 REM  MODULE TO SEARCH FLIGHT TABLE FOR
```

```
1380 REM  MATCH TO ENTERED FLIGHT NUMBER
1390 REM
1400 FOR J = 1 TO 12
1410   IF NF = N(J) THEN 1450
1420 NEXT J
1430 GOSUB 1540
1440 GOTO 1400
1450 RETURN
1460 REM
1470 REM  MODULE TO PRINT FLIGHT DATA
1480 REM
1490 PRINT " "; N(J); TAB(12); DC$(J); TAB(22); AC$(J);
1500 PRINT TAB(30); DT$(J); TAB(40); AT$(J); TAB(53); F(J);
1510 PRINT TAB(63); E(J)
1520 RETURN
1530 REM
1540 REM  MODULE TO PROCESS INVALID FLIGHT NUMBER
1550 REM
1560 PRINT
1570 PRINT "FLIGHT NUMBER"; NF; "NOT FOUND"
1580 INPUT "RE-ENTER"; NF
1590 RETURN
1600 REM
1610 REM  MODULE TO SIGNAL INVALID ENTRIES
1620 REM
1630 PRINT
1640 PRINT "INVALID ENTRY -- RE-ENTER"
1650 PRINT
1660 RETURN
1670 REM
1680 REM  MODULE TO CONTINUE AND RETURN TO SELECTION MENU
1690 REM
1700 PRINT
1710 INPUT "HIT <RETURN> TO CONTINUE"; R$
1720 RETURN
1730 REM
1740 REM  DATA TO LOAD FLIGHT TABLE
1750 REM
1760 DATA 129,"NYC","BOS","7:10A","7:35A",5,23
1770 DATA 642,"ATL","DET","8:05A","8:55A",11,37
1780 DATA 805,"ALB","CHI","9:20A","9:50A",8,12
1790 DATA 375,"DAL","BOS","10:00A","1:25P",3,0
1800 DATA 492,"DET","STL","11:30A","12:35P",7,31
1810 DATA 102,"BOS","ATL","12:05P","2:35P",4,2
1820 DATA 388,"LAX","DEN","1:45P","3:10P",14,42
1830 DATA 487,"MIA","NYC","2.25P","4:50P",0,0
1840 DATA 500,"CIN","DAL","3:55P","5:40P",9,23
1850 DATA 311,"DEN","CIN","5:35P","8:50P",5,18
1860 DATA 149,"NYC","LAX","8:10P","10:25P",14,87
1870 DATA 902,"CHI","MIA","9:50P","1:05A",12,42
1880 END
```

The run of the program is interactive, with the reservations agent continually making selections from the menu and responding to the screen prompts. A typical session corresponding to the data given in Table 10-2 follows.

```
SCHEDULING OPTIONS ARE AS FOLLOWS --

              1 -- MAKE PASSENGER RESERVATION
              2 -- CANCEL PASSENGER RESERVATION
              3 -- REVIEW STATUS OF SPECIFIC FLIGHT
              4 -- REVIEW ALL AVAILABLE FLIGHTS
              5 -- EXIT PROGRAM
```

```
ENTER PROCESS DESIRED (1-5)? 1

ENTER FLIGHT NUMBER? 311

DO YOU NEED FIRST CLASS (1)
OR ECONOMY (2) SEATS? 2

HOW MANY SEATS ARE NEEDED? 6

RESERVATION OF 6 ECONOMY SEATS
ON FLIGHT 311 IS CONFIRMED

HIT <RETURN> TO CONTINUE?

SCHEDULING OPTIONS ARE AS FOLLOWS --

             1 -- MAKE PASSENGER RESERVATION
             2 -- CANCEL PASSENGER RESERVATION
             3 -- REVIEW STATUS OF SPECIFIC FLIGHT
             4 -- REVIEW ALL AVAILABLE FLIGHTS
             5 -- EXIT PROGRAM

ENTER PROCESS DESIRED (1-5)? 2

ENTER FLIGHT NUMBER 492

ARE SEATS IN FIRST CLASS (1)
OR ECONOMY (2) SECTION? 1

HOW MANY SEATS ARE RESERVED? 2

RESERVATION OF 2 FIRST CLASS SEATS
ON FLIGHT 492 IS CANCELLED

HIT <RETURN> TO CONTINUE?

SCHEDULING OPTIONS ARE AS FOLLOWS --

             1 -- MAKE PASSENGER RESERVATION
             2 -- CANCEL PASSENGER RESERVATION
             3 -- REVIEW STATUS OF SPECIFIC FLIGHT
             4 -- REVIEW ALL AVAILABLE FLIGHTS
             5 -- EXIT PROGRAM

ENTER PROCESS DESIRED (1-5)? 1

ENTER FLIGHT NUMBER? 102

DO YOU NEED FIRST CLASS (1)
OR ECONOMY (2) SEATS? 2

HOW MANY SEATS ARE NEEDED? 4

REQUESTED SEATING UNAVAILABLE

HIT <RETURN> TO CONTINUE?

SCHEDULING OPTIONS ARE AS FOLLOWS --

             1 -- MAKE PASSENGER RESERVATION
             2 -- CANCEL PASSENGER RESERVATION
             3 -- REVIEW STATUS OF SPECIFIC FLIGHT
             4 -- REVIEW ALL AVAILABLE FLIGHTS
             5 -- EXIT PROGRAM
```

```
ENTER PROCESS DESIRED (1-5)? 6

INVALID ENTRY -- RE-ENTER

ENTER PROCESS DESIRED (1-5)? 3

ENTER FLIGHT NUMBER? 102

FLIGHT      DEP        ARV        DEP        ARV          1 CLS      ECON
NUMBER      CITY       CITY       TIME       TIME         SEATS      SEATS

  102       BOS        ATL       12:05P     2:35P           4          2

HIT <RETURN> TO CONTINUE?

SCHEDULING OPTIONS ARE AS FOLLOWS --

             1 -- MAKE PASSENGER RESERVATION
             2 -- CANCEL PASSENGER RESERVATION
             3 -- REVIEW STATUS OF SPECIFIC FLIGHT
             4 -- REVIEW ALL AVAILABLE FLIGHTS
             5 -- EXIT PROGRAM

ENTER PROCESS DESIRED (1-5)? 1

ENTER FLIGHT NUMBER? 500

DO YOU NEED FIRST CLASS (1)
OR ECONOMY (2) SEATS? 2

HOW MANY SEATS ARE NEEDED? 3

RESERVATION OF 3 ECONOMY SEATS
ON FLIGHT 500 IS CONFIRMED

HIT <RETURN> TO CONTINUE?

SCHEDULING OPTIONS ARE AS FOLLOWS --

             1 -- MAKE PASSENGER RESERVATION
             2 -- CANCEL PASSENGER RESERVATION
             3 -- REVIEW STATUS OF SPECIFIC FLIGHT
             4 -- REVIEW ALL AVAILABLE FLIGHTS
             5 -- EXIT PROGRAM

ENTER PROCESS DESIRED (1-5)? 2

ENTER FLIGHT NUMBER? 139

FLIGHT NUMBER 139 NOT FOUND
RE-ENTER? 129

ARE SEATS IN FIRST CLASS (1)
OR ECONOMY (2) SECTION? 2

HOW MANY SEATS ARE RESERVED? 5

RESERVATION OF 5 ECONOMY SEATS
ON FLIGHT 129 IS CANCELLED

HIT <RETURN> TO CONTINUE?
```

```
SCHEDULING OPTIONS ARE AS FOLLOWS --

              1 -- MAKE PASSENGER RESERVATION
              2 -- CANCEL PASSENGER RESERVATION
              3 -- REVIEW STATUS OF SPECIFIC FLIGHT
              4 -- REVIEW ALL AVAILABLE FLIGHTS
              5 -- EXIT PROGRAM

ENTER PROCESS DESIRED (1-5)? 4

FLIGHT     DEP       ARV       DEP       ARV        1 CLS     ECON
NUMBER     CITY      CITY      TIME      TIME       SEATS     SEATS

  129      NYC       BOS       7:10A     7:35A        5         23
  642      ATL       DET       8:05A     8:55A        11        37
  805      ALB       CHI       9:20A     9:50A        8         12
  375      DAL       BOS       10:00A    1:25P        3         0
  492      DET       STL       11:30A    12:35P       7         31
  102      BOS       ATL       12:05P    2:35P        4         2
  388      LAX       DEN       1:45P     3:10P        14        42
  487      MIA       NYC       2.25P     4:50P        0         0
  500      CIN       DAL       3:55P     5:40P        9         23
  311      DEN       CIN       5:35P     8:50P        5         12
  149      NYC       LAX       8:10P     10:25P       14        87
  902      CHI       MIA       9:50P     1:05A        12        42

HIT <RETURN> TO CONTINUE?

SCHEDULING OPTIONS ARE AS FOLLOWS --

              1 -- MAKE PASSENGER RESERVATION
              2 -- CANCEL PASSENGER RESERVATION
              3 -- REVIEW STATUS OF SPECIFIC FLIGHT
              4 -- REVIEW ALL AVAILABLE FLIGHTS
              5 -- EXIT PROGRAM

ENTER PROCESS DESIRED (1-5)? 5
```

As a final note, at the end of Section 10-4 we said that two or three levels of subroutines are usually enough for most problems. All of the examples in this chapter have been completed using only *two* levels with the single exception that in the table search module in the last example, the call of the invalid flight number subroutine sent processing to a third level. This could, however, have been easily avoided by simply incorporating the error routine into the table search module.

TROUBLESHOOTING

Each of the following programs contains an error that prevents it from executing properly. Explain *specifically* what the problem is and what must be done to correct it. To assist you, a sample of what would happen should you attempt to run the program is provided after each listing. Refer to Appendix D for an explanation of BASIC error messages.

1.

```
10 REM  TROUBLESHOOTING PROBLEM 10-1
20 REM
30 REM          C = CAR NUMBER
40 REM         D$ = DRIVER NAME
50 REM          M = MILES DRIVEN
60 REM          G = GALLONS OF GAS USED
70 REM         MG = MILES PER GALLON
80 REM
```

```
 90 READ C, D$, M, G
100 IF C < 0 THEN 190
110 LET MG = M / G
120 PRINT C, D$, M, G, MG
130 RETURN
140 GOSUB 90
150 DATA 2354, "DICK LOVE", 1278, 61
160 DATA 3422, "NANCY TODD", 1765, 74
170 DATA 4399, "BOB PERRY", 1483, 63
180 DATA -1, "X", 0, 0
190 END

 2354          DICK LOVE      1278          61            20.9508

RETURN without GOSUB in Line 130
```

2.

```
 10 REM  TROUBLESHOOTING PROBLEM 10-2
 20 REM
 30 REM         N$ = STUDENT NAME
 40 REM  T1 - T3 = TEST GRADES
 50 REM          A = AVERAGE OF TEST GRADES
 60 REM         M$ = MESSAGE VARIABLE
 70 REM          N = NUMBER OF STUDENTS BELOW PASSING
 80 REM
 90 LET N = 0
100 READ N$, T1, T2, T3
110 IF N$ = "LAST" THEN 150
120 GOSUB 180
130 PRINT N$, M$
140 GOTO 100
150 PRINT
160 PRINT "TOTAL BELOW PASSING ="; N
170 GOTO 250
180 LET M$ = " "
190 LET A = (T1 + T2 + T3) / 3
200 IF A < 60 THEN LET M$ = "BELOW PASSING"
210 IF A < 60 THEN LET N = N + 1
220 DATA "R E LEWIS",67,88,72,"T F GARY",87,73,65
230 DATA "L A BOGGS",54,76,42,"W N REESE",75,53,66
240 DATA "A M POPE",78,68,93,"LAST",0,0,0
250 END
```

(No output)

3.

```
 10 REM  TROUBLESHOOTING PROBLEM 10-3
 20 REM
 30 REM          N = INTEGER
 40 REM          S = SUM OF INTEGERS
 50 REM         SQ = SUM OF SQUARES OF INTEGERS
 60 REM         SR = SUM OF RECIPROCALS OF INTEGERS
 70 REM
 80 LET S = 0
 90 LET SQ = 0
100 LET SR = 0
110 FOR N = 1 TO 10
120   GOSUB 170
130 NEXT N
140 PRINT "SUM OF INTEGERS 1-10 ="; S
150 PRINT "SUM OF SQUARES 1-10 ="; SQ
160 PRINT "SUM OF RECIPROCALS ="; SR
170 LET S = S + N
180 LET SQ = SQ + N * N
190 LET SR = SR + 1 / N
200 RETURN
210 END
```

```
SUM OF INTEGERS 1-10 = 55
SUM OF SQUARES 1-10 = 385
SUM OF RECIPROCALS = 2.92897

RETURN without GOSUB in Line 200
```

4.

```
 10 REM  TROUBLESHOOTING PROBLEM 10-4
 20 REM
 30 REM        N = INTEGER
 40 REM        S = SUM OF INTEGERS
 50 REM       SQ = SUM OF SQUARES OF INTEGERS
 60 REM
 70 LET N = 0
 80 LET S = 0
 90 LET SQ = 0
100 IF N = 100 THEN 150
110 LET N = N + 1
120 LET S = S + N
130 LET SQ = SQ + N * N
140 GOSUB 100
150 PRINT "SUM OF INTEGERS 1-100 ="; S
160 PRINT "SUM OF SQUARES 1-100 ="; SQ
170 END

Out of Memory in Line 130
```

IMPORTANT TERMS

After studying this chapter, you should be familiar with the meaning and use of the following terms and BASIC statements:

Subroutine
Calling a subroutine
GOSUB statement
RETURN statement
RETURN without GOSUB error
Modular program
Module
Main (or controlling) module
Top-down design
Nested GOSUBs
ON–GOSUB statement
Menu-driven program
Menu

EXERCISES

Review the following examples from the last three chapters, decide how each can be divided into modules, and draw a diagram showing the organization of the modules.

1. Payroll Report from Section 7-2
2. Retirement Eligibility List from Section 7-5
3. Item Depreciation from Section 8-2
4. Instructor's Grade Report from Section 8-8
5. Gasoline Sales Report from Section 9-4
6. Invoice Preparation from Section 9-6
7. Placement Test Report from Section 9-8

PROGRAMMING PROBLEMS

Write programs in BASIC to accomplish the tasks described by each of the following problems. Be sure to carefully document each program and include all appropriate report headings and other literals.

For Problems 1 to 18, rewrite the indicated program using subroutines and the modular approach to program development.

1. Problem 4 from Chapter 7
2. Problem 8 from Chapter 7
3. Problem 9 from Chapter 7
4. Problem 11 from Chapter 7
5. Problem 13 from Chapter 7
6. Problem 11 from Chapter 8 (Use the ON–GOSUB.)
7. Problem 14 from Chapter 8 (Use the ON–GOSUB.)
8. Problem 15 from Chapter 8
9. Problem 17 from Chapter 8
10. Problem 22 from Chapter 8
11. Problem 3 from Chapter 9
12. Problem 4 from Chapter 9
13. Problem 5 from Chapter 9 (Make this one menu-driven.)
14. Problem 7 from Chapter 9
15. Problem 11 from Chapter 9
16. Problem 12 from Chapter 9
17. Problem 13 from Chapter 9
18. Problem 16 from Chapter 9
19. Steve's Stereos (see the problems at the end of Chapter 9) needs a menu-driven program that will perform the following functions:
    1. Change the unit cost of an item
    2. Update the quantity of an item that is in stock
    3. Review the current status of any one item
    4. Print the entire inventory
    5. Exit the program

    Data to be processed is given below.

Process Number	Stock Number	New Unit Cost	Quantity Adjustment
1	182001	49.50	N/A
3	182001	N/A	N/A
2	127338	N/A	+10
3	127338	N/A	N/A
1	246690	5.25	N/A
3	246690	N/A	N/A
1	156877	140.00	N/A
3	156877	N/A	N/A
4	N/A	N/A	N/A

20. The dean of Crookshank College needs a menu-driven program that will search the student information table and provide the following information options:
    1. List all students in any class
    2. List all students with a GPA below a given value
    3. List all students with a GPA above a given value
    4. List a specific student's record
    5. List entire student file
    6. Exit program

Data for the student information table is given below, followed by data for an interactive session with your program.

Data for Student Information Table

Student ID	Student Name	Class Code	Current GPA	Student ID	Student Name	Class Code	Current GPA
11209	W T Jackson	1	3.12	13001	D N Crewes	2	3.67
11729	F H Nelson	3	1.89	13171	N N Brewster	2	2.92
11820	Y A Peters	2	2.32	13228	L A Henson	1	3.20
11920	W W Simmons	3	3.11	13342	H M Young	3	2.56
12106	P J Lopez	1	2.67	13545	W A Chen	3	3.98
12119	C A Lewis	4	2.67	13625	E E Franklin	4	1.94
12143	F B Miller	2	2.47	14388	V H Satloff	2	2.78
12194	A S Philips	1	3.00	14850	E T Johnson	4	3.11
12287	P T Andrews	1	1.46	14920	R R Quinton	4	2.49
12291	F A Smith	4	3.78	15193	S M Graci	1	2.89
12456	S H Thomas	3	2.19	15266	J P Morris	2	3.97
12633	L M Reed	1	2.33	15633	D B Fuller	1	1.66

Data for Interactive Session

Option Number	Student ID	Class Code	Given GPA
1	N/A	4	N/A
2	N/A	N/A	2.00
4	12287	N/A	N/A
4	15633	N/A	N/A
3	N/A	N/A	3.50
4	13545	N/A	N/A
4	15266	N/A	N/A
4	12291	N/A	N/A
1	N/A	1	N/A
5	N/A	N/A	N/A

PART FOUR

ADVANCED FEATURES

CHAPTER 11

SPECIAL FUNCTIONS

As with most high-level programming languages, BASIC provides a number of **special** or **library functions** for various applications. However, primarily because of its general applicability to so many different types of problems, BASIC provides a much wider variety of such functions than most languages. In Section 5-8, we studied four of the most frequently used mathematical functions, and in Chapter 6, we examined the many uses of the TAB function for output formatting. In this chapter, we will look at most of the other functions that are commonly available with BASIC along with some typical applications.

Before beginning our survey of the many BASIC library functions, we will take a quick look, as promised in Chapter 5, at how BASIC handles very large and small numbers.

11-1 EXPONENTIAL NOTATION

It is often the case that we need to work with numbers that are either too large or too small to be conveniently represented by the normal output mode that we have been using. That is, a number such as 1234500000000 would have too many digits to be expressed in the usual way; whereas 0.00000000000234 has too many leading zeros. BASIC expresses such large and small numbers using **exponential** (or **scientific**) **notation**. Large numbers are converted to exponential notation by (1) moving the decimal to the *left* so that it is between the first two digits from the left, (2) counting the number of places that the decimal has been moved, and (3) writing the number as a product of the new number (which will always be equal to or greater than 1 but less than 10) and 10 raised to a power equal to the number of places that the decimal was moved. The above number could then be expressed in exponential form as 1.2345×10^{12}. Small numbers are converted by a similar procedure except that the decimal is moved to the *right* and 10 is raised to a power that is the negative of the number of times that the decimal was moved. In exponential format, the number given above would be 2.34×10^{-12}.

To express exponential notation in BASIC, we use what is known as the **E format**. To write a number in E format, the number is first written in exponential notation. The first part of the number is expressed exactly the same in both forms. The power of 10 is usually written in a form something like *Esnn*, where *s* is a + or − sign and *nn* is a two-digit number representing the exponent of the 10. The two numbers above would be expressed in E format as 1.2345E+12 and 2.34E−12, respectively. Table 11-1 gives some examples of large and small numbers, how each would be written in exponential notation, and the BASIC equivalent. Most BASICs do not require a + sign or both digits if they are not needed, while some may permit more than two digits.

The E format as shown in the third column of Table 11-1 will be used with BASIC for the output of any numbers that are too large or small for the normal print format. As

TABLE 11-1

Exponential Notation

Regular Notation	Exponential Form	Expression in E Format
34880000	3.488×10^{7}	3.488E+07
873398844	8.73398844×10^{8}	8.73399E+08
34557000000000000000	3.4557×10^{19}	3.4557E+19
0.00098655	9.8655×10^{-4}	9.8655E−04
0.0022872663	2.2872663×10^{-3}	2.28727E−03
0.000000000000000067443	6.7443×10^{-17}	6.7443E−17

an example of this, consider the following short program which simply raises the first ten positive integers to their own power and prints the original integer, the power, and the reciprocal of the power.

```
10 REM   EXPONENTIAL FORMAT
20 REM
30 FOR X = 1 TO 10
40    LET E = X ^ X
50    LET R = 1 / E
60    PRINT X, E, R
70 NEXT X
80 END
```

which will print:

```
1             1             1
2             4             .25
3             27            .037037
4             256           3.90625E-03
5             3125          .00032
6             46656         2.14335E-05
7             823544        1.21427E-06
8             1.67772E+07   5.96046E-08
9             3.87421E+08   2.58117E-09
10            1E+10         1E-10
```

Here, we are still assuming six-digit BASIC. The printout from your computer may treat the E format somewhat differently. For example, only the last number in the middle column would appear in exponential form with *nine*-digit BASIC. Also, all the following numbers are equivalent:

1.67772E+07
1.67772E+7
1.67772E07
1.67772E7

Whichever form your system uses to express output, it should recognize any of these for input.

As a final note on the E format, it can also be used for the input of numeric data values that are very large or small, either through direct interactive entry with the INPUT statement or as part of a regular data list. In such a case, the items to be entered are simply typed in their E-format equivalent. They will be read and processed as any other numeric value would be. The output will be in E format only if needed.

Before beginning our discussion of special functions, we need to look once again at the number of significant digits provided by BASIC. As mentioned in Section 5-8, we have been using a six-digit, single-precision output format which limits the numeric data to only six significant digits. If you need more digits than are provided by the normal single-precision format, some BASICs offer a **double-precision** option which may provide up to *sixteen* digits. This can be obtained by any of several possible methods, depending on the particular BASIC in use. Sometimes variables are declared as double-precision by a special statement. In other systems, a function is used to convert to and from single- and double-precision. Finally, some BASICs provide a **D format** that functions exactly like the E format described above except that it produces double-precision data. One or more of these methods may be available on your system. Check with your instructor for details.

11-2 MORE MATH FUNCTIONS

We will begin by taking a survey of some of the many additional mathematical functions that are normally available with BASIC. Many of these require a more advanced mathematical background than you have needed thus far or will need for any future work in this book. Unfortunately, we will be able to discuss only the functions as they apply to programming. Time and space do not permit a discussion of the mathematics behind the functions; this would require a book within itself! If you have not had enough prior math to understand the functions or will have no immediate need for the functions to be discussed in this section, you may skip ahead to Section 11-3 without any problem.

Appendix B lists more than two dozen mathematical functions that are available with various BASICs. You will not have all of the listed functions on your system, but you may have some that are not listed. In this section, we will look at the most commonly available functions and some typical applications. Table 11-2 lists the mathematical functions that are most frequently provided and used.

Most functions have the general form:

function(argument)

TABLE 11-2

Most Commonly Available Math Functions

Function	Description
ABS(X)	Takes the absolute value of X.
ATN(X)	Returns in radians the arctangent of X.
COS(X)	Returns the cosine for X in radians.
DEG(X)	Converts X from radians to degrees.
EXP(X)	Raises the natural base e to the X power.
INT(X)	Returns the truncated value of X.
LOG(X)	Gives the natural (base e) logarithm for $X > 0$.
PI	Gives the value of $\pi = 3.141592654\ldots$. The number of digits returned will depend on the system.
RAD(X)	Converts X from degrees to radians.
RND(X)	Generates a random number between 0 and 1. The exact response of RND to the values of X will depend on the version of BASIC that is in use. Many versions do not require an argument for RND.
SGN(X)	Returns the sign of X according to the following: Returns 1 when $X > 0$ Returns 0 when $X = 0$ Returns -1 when $X < 0$.
SIN(X)	Returns the sine for X in radians.
SQR(X)	Returns the square root for $X \geq 0$.
TAN(X)	Returns the tangent for X in radians.

where **function** is the function name and **argument** is a numeric constant, variable, or mathematical expression. Some functions apply natural restrictions to the argument, such as that the argument of SQR cannot be negative, as we saw in Section 5-8. Another example is the argument of LOG, the natural logarithm function, which must always be greater than zero. (Recall that the logarithm of any number less than or equal to zero is undefined, as is the square root of a negative number.) Also, there are a few functions that do not require an argument. The RND function described in Section 5-8 is one example. The **PI** function, which simply returns the value of π (3.141592654 . . .), is another. Finally, mathematical functions can be used in mathematical expressions in very much the same way as any regular BASIC variable, with the one exception that in most BASICs, they may not appear on the left side of the equal sign in an assignment statement. (Some of the newest forms of BASIC will allow this with certain functions.)

Let us look at two short programs that make use of several of the special mathematical functions. First, in Section 5-5 we examined a program for calculating compound interest. The formula that we used at that time:

$$P = a(1 + r/n)^{ny}$$

applies only to *discrete* or *countable* compounding periods which are indicated by n. Many banks advertise *continuous* compounding, which means that interest is *constantly* compounded. The above formula is useless for this. A new formula is needed; it is:

$$P = a\ e^{ry}$$

where p, a, r, and y have the same meaning as above. The value e is an irrational number equal to 2.718281828459045 . . . , which is the base of natural logarithms. The following program calculates compound interest for an investment of \$1000 at 10 percent for 1 to 10 years. Values are calculated for quarterly ($n = 4$), monthly ($n = 12$), daily ($n = 365$), and continuously at lines 120, 130, 140, and 150, respectively. The above formula for continuous compounding translates into the statement:

```
150  LET C = A * EXP(R * Y)
```

where the EXP function is used to perform operations requiring the very important number ***e***. The output is shown following the program listing.

```
 10 REM  EXAMPLE USING EXPONENTIAL (EXP) FUNCTION
 20 REM
 30 LET A = 1000
 40 LET R = 10
 50 PRINT "FOR $"; A; "INVESTED AT"; R; "% YEARLY,"
 60 PRINT "ACCUMULATED VALUES FOR EACH METHOD WILL BE:"
 70 PRINT
 80 PRINT "YEAR", "QUARTERLY", " MONTHLY", "  DAILY", "CONTINUOUSLY"
 90 PRINT
100 LET R = R / 100
110 FOR Y = 1 TO 10
120    LET Q = A * (1 + R / 4) ^ (4 * Y)
130    LET M = A * (1 + R / 12) ^ (12 * Y)
140    LET D = A * (1 + R / 365) ^ (365 * Y)
150    LET C = A * EXP(R * Y)
160    PRINT Y, "$"; Q, "$"; M, "$"; D, " $"; C
170 NEXT Y
180 END
```

```
FOR $ 1000 INVESTED AT 10 % YEARLY,
ACCUMULATED VALUES FOR EACH METHOD WILL BE:

YEAR          QUARTERLY     MONTHLY       DAILY         CONTINUOUSLY

 1            $ 1103.81     $ 1104.71     $ 1105.12     $ 1105.17
 2            $ 1218.4      $ 1220.39     $ 1221.28     $ 1221.4
 3            $ 1344.89     $ 1348.18     $ 1349.65     $ 1349.86
 4            $ 1484.5      $ 1489.36     $ 1491.52     $ 1491.82
 5            $ 1638.61     $ 1645.31     $ 1648.31     $ 1648.72
 6            $ 1808.72     $ 1817.6      $ 1821.57     $ 1822.12
 7            $ 1996.49     $ 2007.92     $ 2013.04     $ 2013.75
 8            $ 2203.75     $ 2218.18     $ 2224.64     $ 2225.54
 9            $ 2432.52     $ 2450.45     $ 2458.49     $ 2459.6
 10           $ 2685.05     $ 2707.05     $ 2716.91     $ 2718.28
```

As a second example, consider projectile motion. The range *R* or horizontal distance that an object (such as a cannon shell or football pass) will travel is given by the formula:

$$R = \frac{v^2 \sin(2a)}{g}$$

where v is the initial velocity of the projectile, a is the angle at which it is initially "thrown" with respect to the horizontal, and g is the acceleration due to the earth's gravity, which is 9.8 meters per second square. The program below prints the range for a projectile with an initial velocity of 500 meters per second for angles of 5° through 50° in 5° increments. The program and output are as follows:

```
 10 REM   EXAMPLE USING A TRIGONOMETRIC (SIN) FUNCTION
 20 REM
 30 LET V = 500
 40 PRINT "MUZZLE VELOCITY ="; V;"METERS/SEC"
 50 PRINT
 60 PRINT "ANGLE IN",  " RANGE IN"
 70 PRINT "DEGREES",  "KILOMETERS"
 80 PRINT
 90 FOR A = 5 TO 50 STEP 5
100    LET D = RAD(A)
110    LET R = V * V * SIN(2 * D) / 9.8
120    R = R / 1000
130    PRINT "   "; A, R
140 NEXT A
150 END
```

```
MUZZLE VELOCITY = 500 METERS/SEC

ANGLE IN       RANGE IN
DEGREES       KILOMETERS

   5           4.4298
   10          8.72501
   15          12.7551
   20          16.3976
   25          19.542
   30          22.0925
   35          23.9718
   40          25.1226
   45          25.5102
   50          25.1226
```

Since the trigonometric functions provided by BASIC normally require an argument expressed in radians, we must convert the degrees to radians. The RAD function may be used to make the conversion directly. This was done at line 100. Line 110 calculates the range using the above formula, and line 120 converts this result from meters to kilometers. Of course, all three of these lines could be combined into one expression like:

```
110 LET R = V * V * SIN(2 * RAD(A)) / 9.8 / 100
```

which is more difficult to understand but illustrates that one function can contain another within its argument.

If your BASIC does not provide the RAD function, you must make the conversion from degrees to radians manually. This is accomplished by the relationship:

$$\frac{d}{180} = \frac{r}{\pi}$$

If you have the PI function, you can write the equivalent of line 100 above as:

```
100 LET D = A * PI / 180
```

If you do not have the PI function either, then all you have to do is insert the numerical value for pi into the last statement:

```
100 LET D = A * 3.14159 / 180
```

The number of decimal places that you use may be limited by your system; however, the more accurate the value of pi that you use, the better will be the calculated results.

11-3 USER-DEFINED FUNCTIONS

Although BASIC provides a very wide variety of special functions for various applications, there is not always one for every occasion. Many times you will find that you have a particular expression that must be evaluated that cannot be expressed using one or more of the regular library functions. For such an application, BASIC provides the convenience of the **user-defined** functions, which allow the programmer to define the exact nature of a function. This is done by means of the **DEF** (for DEFinition) statement. It has the general form:

ln **DEF** FN*letter(dummy argument) = expression*

where *letter* is any letter A through Z (or combination of letters and digits allowed by some systems), *dummy argument* is any numeric BASIC variable name, and *expression* is any mathematical expression which may contain regular library or other user-defined functions. Examples of DEF statements to create user-defined functions are the following:

```
130 DEF FNA(X) = 2 * X - 5
210 DEF FNS(Z) = 4 * Z ^ 3 - Z * Z + 11 * Z - 7
195 DEF FNC(D1) = SQR(ABS(64 - D1 * D1))
100 DEF FNK(K) = INT((K - 60) / 10 + 1)
```

Once a function has been defined, it can be referenced at any time, anywhere in the program by simply using its three-letter function name. The DEF statement is nonexecutable but must appear in the program *before* the function that it defines is first used. User-defined functions can appear alone, in mathematical expressions, or in combination with other functions—either library or other user-defined—in any way that a regular BASIC library function may be used, even in the DEF statement that defines another user-defined function. When a function is actually used in a statement, it appears in the form:

FN*letter(argument)*

which is treated essentially the same as a regular library function. The functions defined above might appear in LET statements as follows:

```
200  LET F1 = FNA(N)
330  LET R = FNC(K + 1) - FNC(K)
510  LET MN = FNS(FNK(75))
405  LET W = 3 * FNA(ABS(D - C)) + FNC(D) / FNK(C + D)
390  LET A = 2 * J * J + 3 * SQR(ABS(FNA(3 * J - 4)))
```

When a function appears in an expression, it is said to *call* the DEF statement which defines that function. The value of the argument is sent to the dummy argument, the function is evaluated, and the result is returned to the point at which it appears in an expression. This is essentially the same procedure that is followed by the predefined library functions except that the definition of the function is supplied for you.

Above, when defining the DEF statement, we referred to the argument as a *dummy* argument. This means that whatever variable is used as the argument to define the function is used only for that purpose in the DEF statement and has no effect on any other variable elsewhere in the program. Therefore, if we use X as the dummy argument in the definition of a function, then X can be used as a variable in the regular way elsewhere in the program. Variables that appear as dummy arguments are referred to as **local variables**, as opposed to **global variables**, which are those that are defined in the usual way. Consider the following:

```
                    :
100  LET X = 3
                    :
130  DEF FNB(X) = X * X - 3 * X - 4
                    :
170  LET Y = FNB(X)
                    :
210  LET X = 5
220  LET Y = FNB(X)
                    :
290  LET R = -4
300  LET Y = FNB(R)
                    :
```

The variable X is set equal to 3 at line 100. *The DEF statement at line* 130, *which uses X as a dummy argument, has no effect on the value of X*. When statement 170 is executed, X will still have the value of 3 so that FNB(3) will be calculated as −4 and this value assigned to Y. X is reassigned as 5 at 210 and a new value of the function, FNB(5), is calculated and assigned to Y at 220. The last two statements illustrate that *any* variable can be used as the argument of a function. X at line 130 is local, but the X elsewhere is global as are Y and R.

The definition of a function may contain variables other than the dummy argument. All variables other than the dummy argument are considered to be global. Consider the following:

```
150 DEF FNL(X) = M * X + B
```

Here, X is local and M and B are global. This means that whatever value is assigned to the argument of FNL whenever it is called will be assigned to X. M and B need not have values specifically assigned as an argument but will assume the values in effect for those variables whenever the function is called. (All variables in a function, whether local or global, are sometimes collectively referred to as **parameters**.) Some versions of BASIC permit **argument-free** functions to be defined. In this case, FNL might be defined as:

```
150  DEF FNL = M * X + B
```

With such functions, all variables are global, and a function is called by simply placing the function name in the appropriate place as the following lines illustrate:

```
230  LET Y = FNL
310  LET FV = 3 - 5 * FNL
275  LET U = ABS(INT(FNL)))
```

Some versions of BASIC also permit functions to be defined that have more than one argument. For example, we might have:

```
110  DEF FNR(X,Y,Z) = A * X + B * Y + C * Z + D
```

Here, X, Y, and Z are all local, while A, B, C, and D are all global. Such a function is called in exactly the same value as described except that *three* arguments must be specified:

```
190  LET R = FNR(R,T,V)
280  LET E = FNR(J * K / L, J * L / K, K * L / J)
420  LET Z1 = (FNR(X,0,0) + FNR(0,Y,0) + FNR(0,0,Z)) / 3
220  LET Q = INT(FNR(P,-W,H)) - P + 2 * W + 3 * H - 7 * D
```

Functions with multiple arguments may be mixed as needed with those with no arguments or with only one.

11-4 STRING FUNCTIONS

BASIC provides an extensive set of functions for handling string data; these are collectively known as **string functions**. Table 11-3 summarizes some of the most commonly encountered string functions. A function of nearly every type is listed in Table 11-3; however, as with everything else in BASIC, there are many different functions and variations available. For example, the INDEX function is implemented on some systems under the names IDX or SER. If you do not find some functions that are on your system, refer to Appendix B for a more complete list of string functions.

In the same way that numeric functions help in handling numeric values, string functions increase our ability to manipulate string data. However, just as string values are very different from numeric values, string functions operate on their arguments in an entirely different manner from their numeric counterparts. Let us look at some of the simplest and most common string functions. Consider the functions **LEFT$** and **RIGHT$**, which have the general forms:

LEFT$(*str*, N)

RIGHT$(*str*, N)

These two functions will define a **substring** from the string *str* that consists of the first N characters from the left with LEFT$ and from the right with RIGHT$. The function **MID$** (for MIDdle) with the form:

MID$(*str*, N1, N2)

TABLE 11-3

Most Commonly Available String Functions

Function	Description	Example*
ASC(str)	Gives the ASCII code for the first character in *str*.†	ASC(B$) = 66
CHR$(N)	Returns a single ASCII character corresponding to the value of N.†	CHR$(66) = "B"
INDEX(str1, str2)	Determines whether or not *str1* contains *str2* and if so, at what position in *str1*.	INDEX(B$, L$) = 4 INDEX(P$, B$) = 16
INSTR(N, str1, str2)	Similar to INDEX except the search of *str1* begins at the position specified by N.	INSTR(1, P$, L$) = 2 INSTR(3, P$, L$) = 19
LEFT$(str, N)	Returns the first N characters of *str* beginning from the left.	LEFT$(B$, 1) = "B" LEFT$(X$, 4) = "JOHN"
LEN(str)	Returns the length (in characters) of *str*.	LEN(X$) = 10
MID$(str, N1, N2)	Returns N2 characters beginning at the N1 position from the left of *str*.	MID(X$, 5, 1) = "S" MID(P$, 6, 4) = "JOHN"
RIGHT$(str, N)	Returns the first N characters of *str* beginning from the right.	RIGHT$(B$, 1) = "C" RIGHT$(X$, 5) = "SMITH"
STR$(N)	Converts a numeric expression to a string expression.	STR$(1234) = "1234"
SPACE$(N)	Causes the insertion of N spaces.	SPACE$(5) = " "
STRING$(N, "str")	Prints the single character, *str*, N times. The string character can be represented by its ASCII code *not in quotes*.†	STRING$(4, "*") = "****" STRING$(4, 42) = "****"
VAL(str)	Converts a string expression to a numeric one provided *str* contains only numeric characters.	VAL("1234") = 1234

*For these examples, L$ = "I", B$ = "BASIC", X$ = "JOHN SMITH", and P$ = "WILL JOHN TAKE BASIC?"
†Refer to Appendix E for a list of the most commonly used ASCII codes.

defines a substring of *str* that starts at character N1 and is N2 characters long. (MID$ is sometimes implemented as CPY$ or a similar function, SEG$.) The following short program illustrates how these three functions work.

```
 10 REM  WORKING WITH STRING FUNCTIONS
 20 REM
 30 LET N$ = "DEBBIE L. THOMPSON"
 40 LET F$ = LEFT$(N$, 6)
 50 LET M$ = MID$(N$,8, 2)
 60 LET L$ = RIGHT$(N$, 8)
 70 PRINT "FIRST NAME IS    :  "; F$
 80 PRINT "MIDDLE INITIAL IS:  "; M$
 90 PRINT "LAST NAME IS     :  "; L$
100 END
```

```
FIRST NAME IS    :  DEBBIE
MIDDLE INITIAL IS:  L.
LAST NAME IS     :  THOMPSON
```

Of course, this is a very primitive use of the three string functions. To run the program with another name would mean changing the number of characters that each function uses to define its substring. In the next section, we will study better techniques for using string functions to break up and build strings.

The two functions **INDEX** (sometimes IDX) and **INSTR** can be used to locate the position of one string within another. They have the form:

INDEX(*str*1, *str*2)

INSTR(N, *str*1, *str*2)

Each function locates and gives the position of the string *str2* within the string *str1*. INSTR has the added convenience that the search can be started at any character in *str1* designated by N. For example, the following set of statements will locate the position of the first letter R in the string R$.

```
10  LET R$ = "THE THEORY OF RELATIVITY"
20  LET F = INDEX(R$, "R")
30  PRINT F
```

This will print 9 as the location in R$ of the first R. To find the second R is a little more difficult with INDEX, but just as easy as the first with INSTR. To find the first R with INSTR is exactly the same as with INDEX:

```
10  LET R$ = "THE THEORY OF RELATIVITY"
20  LET F = INSTR(1, R$, "R")
30  PRINT F
```

where the search begins at the first (N = 1) character. To find the second character, simply set N = 10 to "jump" past the first one. This would be:

```
10  LET R$ = "THE THEORY OF RELATIVITY"
20  LET F = INSTR(10, R$, "$")
30  PRINT F
```

which will now give 15 for the location of the second R. [INSTR is also found as a similar function, POS (for POSition).]

We can determine how long a string is (how many characters it contains) by using the **LEN** function. This is a very straightforward function that simply returns a numeric value that is the number of characters in the string in its argument. For example, LEN("DAVID") is 5 and LEN(R$) from the last example is 24. The LEN function cannot be applied to a numeric value. However, if we need to find the length of a numeric field, it can be converted to string by means of the **STR$** function. If we write:

```
210  LET J = 1234
220  LET J$ = STR$(J)
```

J$ will be "1234" (or maybe " 1234"—remember that extra space that comes with numeric values on many systems). We can then find LEN(J$) as 4. Provided they contain only numeric digits, string values can be converted to numeric by means of the **VAL** function. That is, if we have:

```
180  LET F$ = "45.63"
190  LET F = VAL(F$)
```

F will have the numeric value 45.63, which may be treated as any other numeric data.

BASIC provides two functions that allow a character to be expressed as its **ASCII** code (see Appendix E) or vice versa. The first, **ASC** (ORD on some systems), returns the ASCII code for the *first* character of its string argument. The second, **CHR$**, performs the reverse process, returning the character that corresponds to the ASCII code in its argument. The following short program prints the alphabet using ASCII codes.

```
10  REM  USING ASCII CHARACTERS
20  REM
30  FOR A = 65 TO 90
40     PRINT CHR$(A);
50  NEXT A
60  END
```

The output is simply:

```
ABCDEFGHIJKLMNOPQRSTUVWXYZ
```

The limits on the counter of the FOR–NEXT loop are the ASCII codes for a capital A and Z.

The last two functions that we will discuss in this section are **SPACE$** and **STRING$**. SPACE$ has a numeric argument and produces the number of spaces indicated by its argument. SPACE$(12) will provide 12 blank spaces. The second function, STRING$, is used to repeat a character a specified number of times and has two possible variations. It has the general form:

STRING$(N, "*str*")

where "*str*" is a *one-character* string that is to be repeated N times. The one-character string, "*str*", can be replaced by its ASCII code *not in quotes*. Both of the following statements will print a row of 65 equal signs:

```
300  PRINT STRING$(65, "=")
300  PRINT STRING$(65, 61)
```

As with mathematical functions, one string function can appear in the argument of another as long as the usage is consistent. In fact, certain mathematical functions, such as INT and ABS, can also be very useful in controlling values in the arguments of some string functions. All of the following are legal combinations of functions:

```
140  LET L = LEN(LEFT$(P$, X))
220  LET S$ = RIGHT$(H$, LEN(K))
310  LET V$ = MID$(LEFT$(E$, V), INT(V/3), 3)
275  LET N = INDEX(A$, ASC(76))
440  LET P2 = INSTR(P1, MID$(Y$, T, LEN(X$)), "**")
```

As we have seen in two examples above, string functions, like mathematical ones, can also be incorporated into the print list of PRINT statements.

Before going on to the next section and some applications involving the manipulation of string values, let us take a look at the **CHANGE** statement which is available on some BASICs. This statement has two forms; the first is:

ln **CHANGE** *string* **TO** *numeric array*

where *string* is any *string* variable and *numeric array* is a *numeric, subscripted* variable. The statement has the effect of assigning the ASCII codes of the individual characters of the string to the individual elements of the array variable. As an example, consider the following short program and run:

```
10 DIM N(6)
20 LET N$ = "CHANGE"
30 CHANGE N$ TO N
40 FOR X = 1 TO 6
50   LET C$ = MID$(N$, X, 1)
60   LET X$ = RIGHT$(STR$(X), 1)
70   PRINT C$; "  FROM N$ IS SENT TO N("; X$; ") AS "; N(X)
80 NEXT X
90 END

C  FROM N$ IS SENT TO N(1) AS  67
H  FROM N$ IS SENT TO N(2) AS  72
```

```
A   FROM N$ IS SENT TO N(3) AS  65
N   FROM N$ IS SENT TO N(4) AS  78
G   FROM N$ IS SENT TO N(5) AS  71
E   FROM N$ IS SENT TO N(6) AS  69
```

From the output, we can see that each character of the string "CHANGE" is stored in the corresponding element of the numeric array *as its ASCII counterpart*. The second form of the CHANGE statement is:

ln **CHANGE** *numeric array* **TO** *string*

which performs the exact reverse operation to the first form. That is, it "builds" a string from the ASCII codes stored in a numeric array. On systems that do not have the CHANGE statement, it can be simulated by the ASC or STR$ function with an appropriate loop.

11-5 MANIPULATING STRINGS

In this section, we will look at some of the techniques that can be used along with string function to manipulate string values. As a first example, in Section 6-4 we discussed how to *manually* center a value on a printout. We can now write a statement that will calculate this for us automatically. Remember from Section 6-4 that we must insert a number of spaces before a field to be centered equal to one-half the difference in the length of the field and the width of the longest print line. Suppose that we have a printout that is W characters wide and a heading of H$. The heading can be centered by the statements:

```
200  LET H = INT((W - LEN(H$)) / 2) + 1
210  PRINT TAB(H); H$
```

Of course, H$ may be expressed as a string literal rather than a variable with the same results.

As a second example, let us revise the first program in the last section to divide *any* name into the first name, middle initial, and last name. This can be done as follows:

```
 10 REM  WORKING WITH STRING FUNCTIONS -- AGAIN!
 20 REM
 30 READ N$
 40 IF N$ = "END" THEN 190
 50 PRINT "NAME ENTERED AS  "; N$
 60 PRINT
 70 LET P1 = INSTR(1, N$, " ")
 80 LET P2 = INSTR(P1 + 1, N$, " ")
 90 LET F$ = LEFT$(N$, P1 - 1)
100 LET M$ = MID$(N$, P1 + 1, P2 - P1)
110 LET L$ = RIGHT$(N$, LEN(N$) - P2)
120 PRINT , "FIRST NAME IS       "; F$
130 PRINT , "MIDDLE INITIAL IS   "; M$
140 PRINT , "LAST NAME IS        "; L$
150 PRINT
160 GOTO 30
170 DATA "ROBERT F. STEPHENSON", "ELIZABETH H. ORR"
180 DATA "WILLIAM T. HARRIS", "LINDA K. SIMMS", "END"
190 END
```

which will produce an output of:

```
NAME ENTERED AS  ROBERT F. STEPHENSON

          FIRST NAME IS         ROBERT
          MIDDLE INITIAL IS     F.
          LAST NAME IS          STEPHENSON

NAME ENTERED AS  ELIZABETH H. ORR

          FIRST NAME IS         ELIZABETH
          MIDDLE INITIAL IS     H.
          LAST NAME IS          ORR

NAME ENTERED AS  WILLIAM T. HARRIS

          FIRST NAME IS         WILLIAM
          MIDDLE INITIAL IS     T.
          LAST NAME IS          HARRIS

NAME ENTERED AS  LINDA K. SIMMS

          FIRST NAME IS         LINDA
          MIDDLE INITIAL IS     K.
          LAST NAME IS          SIMMS
```

A name is read and assigned to the string variable N$ at line 30. The location of the first space (that between the first name and middle initial) is found by the INSTR function at line 70 and assigned to P1. Counting from the next position beyond the first space, P1 + 1, the INSTR function at line 80 locates the second space (between the middle initial and last name) and assigns this to P2. The first name is then assigned to F$ at line 90 as the substring of N$ consisting of the first P1 − 1 characters from the left. We take the first P1 − 1 characters because P1 is the location of the *space* between the first name and the initial; the first name ends one character before this. Likewise, M$ at line 100 defines a substring that is the middle initial, and L$ at 110 is the last name. The three substrings that represent the parts of the original name are printed, respectively, at lines 120 to 140.

Once a substring has been defined as in the last example, it is a string in its own right and should be treated as such. The following short program is a modification of the one above, except that at line 100 a check is made to see if the last name starts with the letter S. Only names that begin with S are printed. These are given in reverse order with last name first, first name, middle initial.

```
 10 REM   WORKING WITH STRING FUNCTIONS -- AGAIN!
 20 REM
 30 READ N$
 40 IF N$ = "END" THEN 140
 50 LET P1 = INSTR(1, N$, " ")
 60 LET P2 = INSTR(P1 + 1, N$, " ")
 70 LET F$ = LEFT$(N$, P1 - 1)
 80 LET M$ = MID$(N$, P1 + 1, P2 - P1)
 90 LET L$ = RIGHT$(N$, LEN(N$) - P2)
100 IF LEFT$(L$, 1) = "S" THEN PRINT L$; ", "; F$; " "; M$
110 GOTO 30
120 DATA "ROBERT F. STEPHENSON", "ELIZABETH H. ORR"
130 DATA "WILLIAM T. HARRIS", "LINDA K. SIMMS", "END"
140 END
```

```
STEPHENSON, ROBERT F.
SIMMS, LINDA K.
```

In the last example, at line 100 the print list 'built'' the name in reverse order by listing each part in the proper order with spaces and a comma inserted as needed. Some versions of BASIC allow a string to be defined as the "sum" of several other strings. That is, the reversed name could have been printed as follows where the new line 95 has been inserted to define the variable NR$:

```
                      :
 95  LET NR$ = L$ + ", " + F$ + " " + M$
100  IF LEFT$(L$, 1) = "S" THEN PRINT NR$
                      :
```

The operation of building a string from smaller substrings as at line 95 is referred to as **concatenation**. The plus sign is called the **concatenation operator**. *It does not mean addition in the usual sense*. The following program illustrates traditional numeric addition:

```
10  REM  NUMERIC ADDITION
20  REM
30  LET A = 11
40  LET B = 22
50  LET C = 33
60  LET S = A + B + C
70  PRINT A, B, C, S
80  END

 11            22            33            66
```

Now, look at a similar program that concatenates the same values, but as strings.

```
10  REM  CONCATENATION
20  REM
30  LET A$ = "11"
40  LET B$ = "22"
50  LET C$ = "33"
60  LET S$ = A$ + B$ + C$
70  PRINT A$, B$, C$, S$
80  END

11             22            33            112233
```

A concatenated expression is to string data as a mathematical expression is to numeric calculations. Such an expression may only appear in appropriate BASIC statements and may never be placed on the left of an assignment statement. Any string constant, variable, substring, or string function (that returns a string) may appear in a concatenated expression.

As a final remark on string manipulations, some versions of BASIC permit the definition of user-defined *string* functions. Such functions are defined in much the same way as their numeric counterparts by using the DEF statement. These functions may have either string or numeric arguments but *must return a string value*. The same rules apply to local and global variables as with numeric user-defined functions. We can rewrite the program above to list only names that begin with S in reverse order using a user-defined string function.

```
10 REM  WORKING WITH STRING FUNCTIONS -- AGAIN!
20 REM
25 DEF FNR$(A$, B$, C$) = A$ + ", " + B$ + " " + C$
30 READ N$
40 IF N$ = "END" THEN 140
50 LET P1 = INSTR(1, N$, " ")
60 LET P2 = INSTR(P1 + 1, N$, " ")
```

```
 70 LET F$ = LEFT$(N$, P1 - 1)
 80 LET M$ = MID$(N$, P1 + 1, P2 - P1)
 90 LET L$ = RIGHT$(N$, LEN(N$) - P2)
100 IF LEFT$(L$, 1) = "S" THEN PRINT FNR$(L$, F$, M$)
110 GOTO 30
120 DATA "ROBERT F. STEPHENSON", "ELIZABETH H. ORR"
130 DATA "WILLIAM T. HARRIS", "LINDA K. SIMMS", "END"
140 END
```

```
STEPHENSON, ROBERT F.
SIMMS, LINDA K.
```

Note that user-defined string functions must be named with a $ appended to the end of the name as with regular variable names.

11-6 MORE ON DATA EDITING

In Section 8-6, we examined some of the most common techniques used for editing numeric data. In this section, we will look at additional methods that can be applied to string values.

One of the easiest checks that can be made on a field is a check to ensure that it fits certain length requirements as to the number of characters entered. This may be quite easy if it is known that a value will always be the same length. For example, social security numbers usually appear in the 11-character form, xxx-xx-xxxx. The LEN function can be used to check that the social security number is exactly 11 characters long. Often, the exact length of a field is not known, but a check can be made to ensure that it is not too long (or too short). For example, we may wish to enter names that we want to be no more than 25 but not less than 10 characters in length.

Another very important check is to verify that a field contains only the proper type characters. In the case of the social security number, we can check each character in the field to verify that it is either a digit (0 to 9) or a dash (−) and nothing else. The following loop performs this task for SS$:

```
200  FOR C = 1 TO LEN(SS$)
210    LET A = ASC(MID$(SS$, C, 1))
220    IF A => 48 AND A <= 57 OR A = 45 THEN 300
230    (Process bad fields here)
                    :
300  NEXT C
```

The loop is executed for the number of digits in the field, up to LEN(SS$). At line 210, the ASCII code of the character is found. At line 220, a check is made to see that the code is either between 48 and 57 (the ASCII codes for the ten digits) or equal to 45 (the code for a dash). If the character fails the test, an error message is printed or some other action taken beginning at line 230. Otherwise, the next character is checked.

Let us look at a short program that incorporates these techniques (plus a little more).

```
 10 REM  CHECKING A STRING FOR INVALID CHARACTERS
 20 REM
 30 INPUT "ENTER STRING"; A$
 40 IF LEN(A$) <= 20 THEN 80
 50 PRINT "        ----->  STRING '"; A$; "'"
 60 PRINT , "IS"; LEN(A$) - 20; "CHARACTERS TOO LONG"
 70 GOTO 170
 80 FOR C = 1 TO LEN(A$)
 90   LET C$ = MID$(A$, C, 1)
100   IF ASC(C$) => 65 AND ASC(C$) <= 90 THEN 150
```

```
110    IF ASC(C$) = 46 OR ASC(C$) = 32 THEN 150
120    PRINT "      ----->  '"; A$; "' CONTAINS AN INVALID"
130    PRINT , "CHARACTER OF '"; C$; "' AT POSITION"; C
140    GOTO 170
150 NEXT C
160 PRINT "      ----->  STRING '"; A$; "' IS OK"
170 INPUT "      ENTER ANOTHER STRING (Y/N)"; Q$
180 IF LEFT$(Q$, 1) = "Y" THEN 30
190 IF LEFT$(Q$, 1) = "N" THEN 220
200 PRINT "      **INVALID ENTRY -- RE-ENTER**"
210 GOTO 170
220 END
```

A string is entered at line 30 as A$, and a check is made at line 40 to ensure that it does not exceed 20 characters in length. Lines 50 and 60 print an error message for strings that are too long. The loop from 80 to 150 is used to verify that the string contains only certain characters, in this case, only letters A through Z, spaces, and periods. Line 90 selects one character from the string at a time. A check is first made at line 100 for the letters A through Z, and at 110 for spaces and periods. The remainder of the loop prints an error message for a string containing an invalid character. Line 160 prints a message for valid entries. A question is asked at line 170 to allow for the entry of another string or to terminate the program. Line 180 checks to see if the entry begins with a Y. Y, YES, YEP, and YHVFJ will all work and send the program back to line 30 for entry of another string. The same thing happens at line 190 for entries beginning with N, ending the program. Any entry that begins with anything other than a Y or N will cause the error message at line 200 to be printed and another to be requested. A sample run is given below.

```
ENTER STRING? "PETER RABBIT"
      ----->  STRING 'PETER RABBIT' IS OK
      ENTER ANOTHER STRING (Y/N)? Y
ENTER STRING? "JOHN Q. SMITH"
      ----->  STRING 'JOHN Q. SMITH' IS OK
      ENTER ANOTHER STRING (Y/N)? YES
ENTER STRING? "BARBARA ELAINE SIMPSON"
      ----->  STRING 'BARBARA ELAINE SIMPSON'
              IS 2 CHARACTERS TOO LONG
      ENTER ANOTHER STRING (Y/N)? Y
ENTER STRING? "NEW Y0RK CITY"
      ----->  'NEW Y0RK CITY' CONTAINS AN INVALID
              CHARACTER OF '0' AT POSITION 6
      ENTER ANOTHER STRING (Y/N)? T
      **INVALID ENTRY -- RE-ENTER**
      ENTER ANOTHER STRING (Y/N)? Y
ENTER STRING? "FIVE-HUNDRED"
      ----->  'FIVE-HUNDRED' CONTAINS AN INVALID
              CHARACTER OF '-' AT POSITION 5
      ENTER ANOTHER STRING (Y/N)? YEP
ENTER STRING? "THAT IS ENOUGH"
      ----->  STRING 'THAT IS ENOUGH' IS OK
      ENTER ANOTHER STRING (Y/N)? N
```

We have discussed only a few of the more commonly used edit checks. With a little thought, you can probably think of others. While editing is an important technique that should be incorporated into programs as needed, care should be taken not to get carried away and overedit everything. All input, calculated, or output fields should be edited *only when there is a need or reason to do so*. If you overedit, it is very possible to have more program statements devoted to editing than to the processing of the problem that you are trying to solve.

11-7 AN EXAMPLE: PLOTTING THE GRAPH OF A FUNCTION

Even without using special graphics features that are available with some BASICs, we can plot a rough graph of even complex mathematical expressions. The use of the library functions is not necessary for this, but as you will see, their use adds much to our ability to "draw" the graph.

Before we look at a specific example, let us examine some of the difficulties in plotting a graph on a printer. Figure 11-1 shows what we might expect if we were to plot points from 0 through 7 for the function:

$$y = x^3 - 10x^2 + 25x$$

as we would normally plot them on graph paper with a vertical y axis and a horizontal x axis. If we were to attempt to reproduce our manual procedure on a printer, the problem would clearly be: How do we get the printer to move *up and down* to print the points? If we go all the way down to print the first point at $x = 0$, we cannot get the printer to reverse and move back up to print the next point at $x = 1$. One possible answer is to print the graph from bottom to top instead of from top to bottom. That might work with some curves, but look again at Figure 11-1. Where would you start to print so that you did not have to reverse at some point? This problem is not new and was solved long ago. The answer is to print the graph on its side with the y axis horizontal at the top and the x axis vertical to the left. (In other words, simply turn or rotate the graph in Figure 11-1 by 90° or one-quarter turn clockwise.) Then, as we print down, we will print each successive function value for each x, and since each x is always greater than the last we will never have to backtrack. The function values are printed horizontally across the print line. The graph from Figure 11-1 is shown in Figure 11-2 as it would be "drawn" by a printer using this technique.

Problem: A program is needed that will plot a first quadrant (both x and y positive) graph of the function

$$y = a\left[\frac{(x + b)^3}{x^2 + c} + d\right]$$

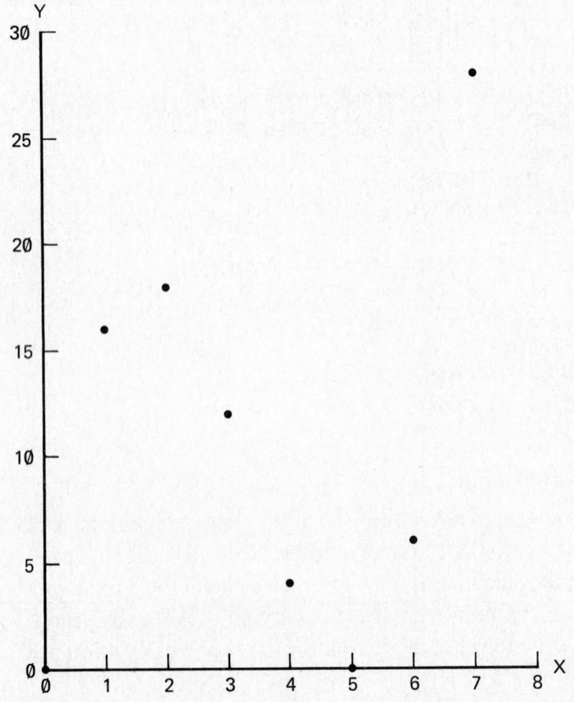

FIGURE 11-1
Common way of graphing a function

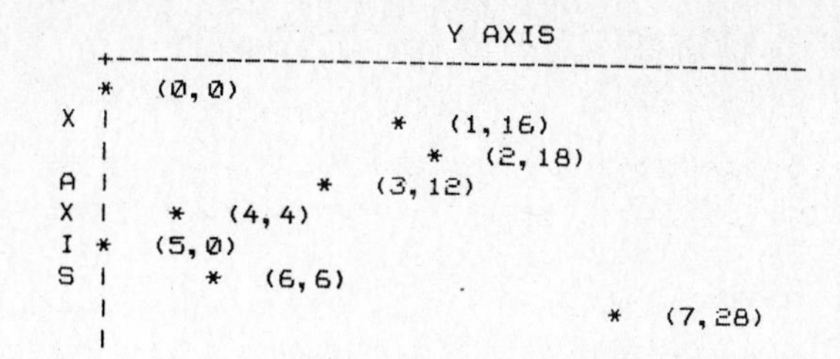

FIGURE 11-2
Graphing on a printer

for x equal to the integers from 1 through 10. Values for a, b, c, and d for up to four different graphs are given in Table 11-4; these should be entered interactively, using the INPUT statement. The graph should have an appropriate heading *that includes the function with the current values for all parameters* as well as the coordinate axes properly labeled. (All headings should automatically center.) Each point should have its corresponding coordinate values indicated. All necessary editing checks should be included. After each graph, a question should be asked as to whether another run is desired.

The solution to this problem is outlined as follows:

1. Define the required user-defined functions.
2. Define a user-defined string function to represent the required function as a string value.
3. Enter the screen width.
4. Enter values for the parameters in Table 11-4.
5. Define string values for the four parameters in step 4.
6. Print a general heading to include the function to be plotted.
7. Print the y axis properly labeled.
8. For values of x equal to 1 through 10, perform steps 9 through 11.
9. Calculate the function value y.
10. Check to verify that y is within the limits of the graph. If so, go to the next step; if not, go to step 13.
11. Print a line showing a section of the x axis (properly labeled), the graph point, and the coordinate values.
12. Go to step 15.
13. Print a message to indicate that the graph was aborted because the function value was out of the allowed range. Give the values of x and y at this point.
14. Go to step 16.
15. Print a message to indicate that the graph is complete.
16. Check for another run. If another is desired, go to step 4; otherwise, stop.

This procedure is pictorially illustrated by the flowchart shown in Figure 11-3.

The first thing to do is to define two user-defined functions as follows:

```
220  DEF FNA(X) = A * ((X + B) ^ 3 / (X * X + C) + D)
230  DEF FNA$ = A$ + " * ((X +" + B$ + ") ^ 3 / (X * X +" + C$ + ") + " + D$ + ")"
```

TABLE 11-4
Parameters for Function

Run No.	Values to be Processed for A	B	C	D
1	10	4	5	−20
2	10	4	3	−30
3	10	4	3	−25
4	20	4	4	−24

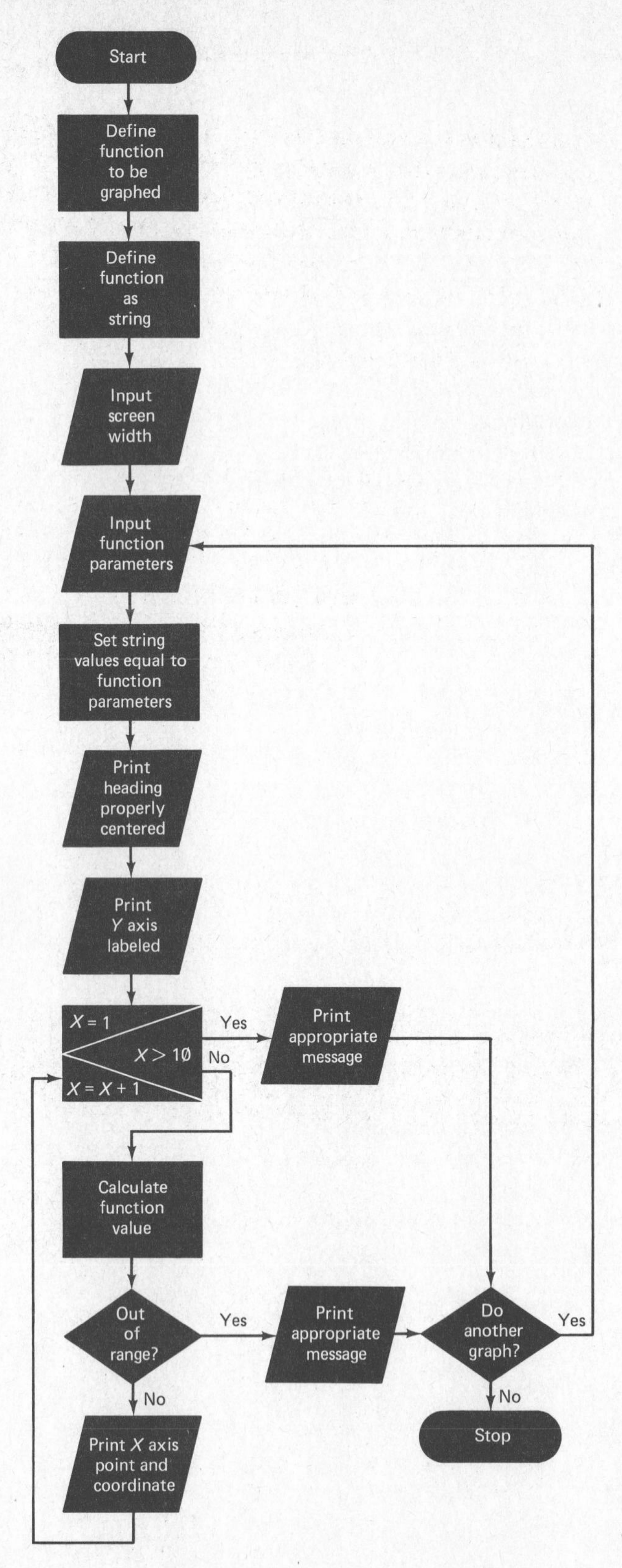

FIGURE 11-3
Flowchart for plotting a function example

The first defines the functions to be graphed as a mathematical function FNA(X), where X is a local variable and A, B, C, and D are all global. The second is a string function that will be used to print the function in the heading. Note that this function has no arguments so that all variables are global.

The next step is to enter the width of the screen (or printer) on which the graph is to be drawn.

```
240  INPUT "ENTER WIDTH OF SCREEN"; W
```

This allows the same program to be used on output devices that have different screen or paper widths. Next the values for the global parameters for FNA(X) (from Table 11-4) are entered and the corresponding string values defined. This is done at lines 260 and 290 to 320, respectively. The string values are needed, of course, for use by the function FNA$.

The headings for this one are a little more complex than usual and deserve some special attention. The first line of the heading is processed by lines 360 to 380.

```
360  LET H$ = "GRAPH OF FUNCTION"
370  LET H = INT((W - LEN(H$)) / 2) + 1
380  PRINT TAB(H); H$
```

Line 360 sets H$ equal to what is to be printed on the first line. The position at which H$ will be centered is calculated at 370, and it is printed at 380. At line 390, the string function defined at line 230 is concatenated with another literal to construct the string that will print the function in the second line of the heading.

```
390  LET H$ = "Y = " + FNA$
400  LET H = INT((W - LEN(H$)) / 2) + 1
410  PRINT TAB(H); H4
```

This is then centered and printed in the next two lines. Lines 420 to 440 process the third line of the heading and 470 and 480 the label Y AXIS in the same manner. Line 490, which is:

```
490  PRINT "   +"; STRING$(W - 3, "-")
```

actually prints the *y* axis. Note the use of the STRING$ function to print a series of W − 3 dashes. If the screen width is entered as 80, then 77 dashes will be printed.

The printing of the *x* axis is a little more difficult in that it must be printed in pieces as each function value is plotted. This will not, however, prove to be too difficult. The first step toward this occurs at line 500:

```
500  LET XA$ = "  X AXIS  "
```

The reason for the extra spaces will become apparent shortly. Each line is then processed by the following loop:

```
550 FOR X = 1 TO 10
560    LET Y = INT(FNA(X) + .5)
570    IF Y < 1 OR Y > W - 12 THEN 690
580    LET C$ = MID$(XA$, X, 1)
590    LET X$ = RIGHT$(STR$(X), LEN(STR$(X)) - 1)
600    LET Y$ = RIGHT$(STR$(Y), LEN(STR$(Y)) - 1)
610    LET P$ = "   (" + X$ + "," + Y$ + ")"
620    PRINT C$; " I"; TAB(Y + 3); "*"; P$
630 NEXT X
640 GOTO 740
```

The function values are calculated at line 560. The .5 added to FNA(X) within the INT function ensures that the values returned will be *rounded* rather then *truncated*. A check is made at line 570 to ensure that the calculated value is not outside the limits of the graph, for example, off the screen or paper. At line 580, C$ extracts a one-character substring from the string XA$ defined at line 500; this is done so that each time the loop is executed, C$ is the *next* character in the string. The next two lines may not be necessary with all versions of BASIC. They are included here to express the X and Y values as strings and remove that leading space that frequently accompanies numeric values when printed. These two string values are concatenated with the appropriate literals at line 610 to form one string that will print the coordinate value of the point. Line 620 prints a graph line. Four items are printed. The first two things to be printed are the appropriate character from XA$ followed by the literal " I" that creates the *x* axis. Next the graph point is "plotted" as an asterisk at the position given by the TAB. Finally, the coordinate values are printed as the literal that was "built" in the preceding line.

Lines 700 to 720 print the message for an aborted graph whenever a function value is out of range. Line 790 prints when a graph is successfully completed, and 810 to 860 provide for either ending the program or plotting another graph with different parameters.

A complete program listing, followed by a run for the data given in Table 11-4, is provided below.

```
 10 REM  PLOTTING THE GRAPH OF AN EQUATION
 20 REM
 30 REM  VARIABLES ARE DEFINED AS --
 40 REM
 50 REM          H$ = STRING FOR MAIN HEADING
 60 REM           H = TAB POSITION FOR HEADING
 70 REM           X = X COORDINATE (INDEPENDENT VARIABLE)
 80 REM               (ALSO DUMMY ARGUMENT OF FUNCTION)
 90 REM           Y = Y COORDINATE (DEPENDENT VARIABLE)
100 REM         XA$ = STRING TO PRINT "X AXIS"
110 REM    A THRU D = GLOBAL PARAMETERS OF FUNCTION
120 REM A$ THRU D$ = STRING VALUES FOR A THRU D
130 REM          C$ = SINGLE CHARACTER FROM XA$
140 REM          X$ = STRING VALUE OF X
150 REM          Y$ = STRING VALUE OF Y
160 REM          P$ = COORDINATE VALUE
170 REM           W = WIDTH OF SCREEN
180 REM
190 REM  DEFINE FUNCTION AND INPUT SCREEN
200 REM  WIDTH AND VALUES FOR A, B, C, AND D
210 REM
220 DEF FNA(X) = A * ((X + B) ^ 3 / (X * X + C) + D)
230 DEF FNA$ = A$ + " * ((X +" + B$ + ") ^ 3 / (X * X +" + C$ + ") + " + D$ + ")"
240 INPUT "ENTER WIDTH OF SCREEN"; W
250 PRINT
260 INPUT "ENTER VALUES FOR A, B, C, AND D"; A, B, C, D
270 PRINT
280 PRINT
290 LET A$ = STR$(A)
300 LET B$ = STR$(B)
310 LET C$ = STR$(C)
320 LET D$ = STR$(D)
330 REM
340 REM  PRINT HEADINGS AND Y AXIS
350 REM
360 LET H$ = "GRAPH OF EQUATION"
370 LET H = INT((W - LEN(H$)) / 2) + 1
380 PRINT TAB(H); H$
390 LET H$ = "Y = " + FNA$
400 LET H = INT((W - LEN(H$)) / 2) + 1
410 PRINT TAB(H); H$
```

```
420 LET H$ = "FOR X = 1 TO 10"
430 LET H = INT((W - LEN(H$)) / 2) + 1
440 PRINT TAB(H); H$
450 PRINT
460 PRINT
470 LET H = INT((W - LEN("X AXIS")) / 2) + 1
480 PRINT TAB(H + 1); "Y AXIS"
490 PRINT "  +"; STRING$(W - 3, "-")
500 LET XA$ = "  X AXIS  "
510 REM
520 REM  CALCULATE AND PRINT ("PLOT") FUNCTION VALUES
530 REM  ALONG WITH X AXIS AND COORDINATES OF POINTS
540 REM
550 FOR X = 1 TO 10
560   LET Y = INT(FNA(X) + .5)
570   IF Y < 1 OR Y > W - 12 THEN 690
580   LET C$ = MID$(XA$, X, 1)
590   LET X$ = RIGHT$(STR$(X), LEN(STR$(X)) - 1)
600   LET Y$ = RIGHT$(STR$(Y), LEN(STR$(Y)) - 1)
610   LET P$ = "   (" + X$ + "," + Y$ + ")"
620   PRINT C$; " |"; TAB(Y + 3); "*"; P$
630 NEXT X
640 GOTO 740
650 REM
660 REM  PRINT ERROR MESSAGE IF FUNCTION
670 REM  VALUE IS OUT OF RANGE OF GRAPH
680 REM
690 PRINT
700 PRINT "*** GRAPH ABORTED ***"
710 PRINT "FUNCTION OUT OF RANGE AT X = "; X
720 PRINT "AT THIS POINT, Y = "; Y
730 GOTO 800
740 PRINT
750 PRINT
760 REM
770 REM  PERMIT ANOTHER RUN
780 REM
790 PRINT "GRAPH COMPLETED --"
800 PRINT
810 PRINT "DO YOU WISH ANOTHER RUN WITH DIFFERENT"
820 INPUT "VALUES FOR A, B, C, OR D (Y/N)"; Q$
830 IF LEFT$(Q$, 1) = "Y" THEN 250
840 IF LEFT$(Q$, 1) = "N" THEN 870
850 PRINT"  *** INVALID ENTRY -- RE-ENTER ***"
860 GOTO 810
870 END
```

```
ENTER WIDTH OF SCREEN? 80

ENTER VALUES FOR A, B, C, AND D? 10, 4, 5, -20
```

```
                              GRAPH OF FUNCTION
                  Y =  10 * ((X + 4) ^ 3 / (X * X + 5) + -20)
                               FOR X = 1 TO 10
```

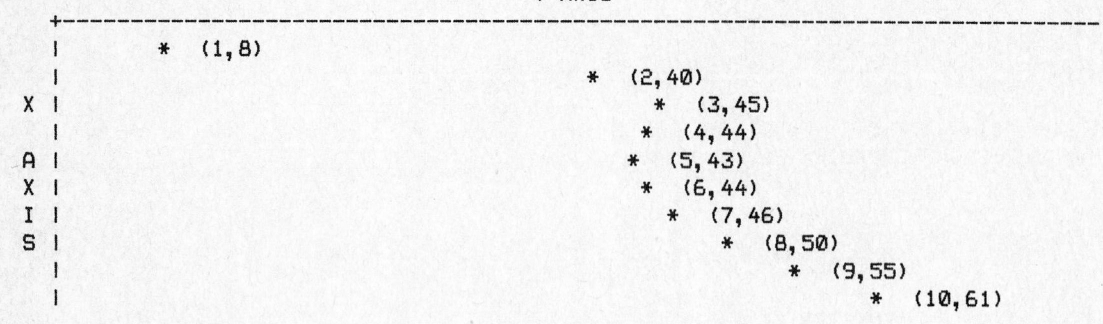


```
GRAPH COMPLETED --

DO YOU WISH ANOTHER RUN WITH DIFFERENT
VALUES FOR A, B, C, OR D (Y/N)? Y

ENTER VALUES FOR A, B, C, AND D? 10, 4, 3, -30


                              GRAPH OF FUNCTION
                  Y =  10 * ((X + 4) ^ 3 / (X * X + 3) + -30)
                               FOR X = 1 TO 10


                                    Y AXIS
  +-----------------------------------------------------------------------------
  I         *  (1,12)
  I       *  (2,9)

*** GRAPH ABORTED ***
FUNCTION OUT OF RANGE AT X =  3
AT THIS POINT, Y = -14

DO YOU WISH ANOTHER RUN WITH DIFFERENT
VALUES FOR A, B, C, OR D (Y/N)? Y

ENTER VALUES FOR A, B, C, AND D? 10, 4, 3, -25
```

```
                               GRAPH OF FUNCTION
                  Y =  10 * ((X + 4) ^ 3 / (X * X + 3) + -25)
                                FOR X = 1 TO 10


                                      Y AXIS
  +-----------------------------------------------------------------------------
  I                                                              *  (1,62)
  I                                                           *  (2,59)
X I                                   *  (3,36)
  I                   *  (4,19)
A I         *  (5,10)
X I     *  (6,6)
I I     *  (7,6)
S I       *  (8,8)
  I           *  (9,12)
  I               *  (10,16)


GRAPH COMPLETED --

DO YOU WISH ANOTHER RUN WITH DIFFERENT
VALUES FOR A, B, C, OR D (Y/N)? T
  *** INVALID ENTRY -- RE-ENTER ***
DO YOU WISH ANOTHER RUN WITH DIFFERENT
VALUES FOR A, B, C, OR D (Y/N)? YES

ENTER VALUES FOR A, B, C, AND D? 20, 4, 4, -24


                               GRAPH OF FUNCTION
                  Y =  20 * ((X + 4) ^ 3 / (X * X + 4) + -24)
                                FOR X = 1 TO 10
```

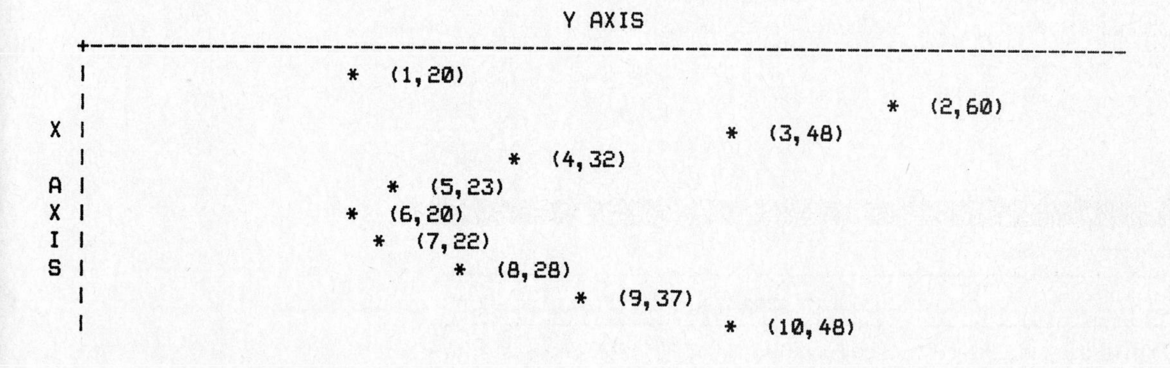

```
                                      Y AXIS
  +-----------------------------------------------------------------------------
  I                   *  (1,20)
  I                                                           *  (2,60)
X I                                               *  (3,48)
  I                               *  (4,32)
A I                      *  (5,23)
X I                   *  (6,20)
I I                     *  (7,22)
S I                           *  (8,28)
  I                                    *  (9,37)
  I                                               *  (10,48)
```

```
GRAPH COMPLETED --

DO YOU WISH ANOTHER RUN WITH DIFFERENT
VALUES FOR A, B, C, OR D (Y/N)? N
```

You may have realized by now that the above problem could have been done without having to employ user-defined functions or string concatenation. While that is true in this case, it might not be in another. The added abilities afforded to the programmer by these new features added much power to the programming process and is best appreciated by their actual use. In your solutions to the programming problems at the end of the chapter, you are encouraged to make use of user-defined functions and concatenation of string values whenever possible.

11-8 OTHER FUNCTIONS

There are a number of BASIC library functions that perform special tasks. Some of these are described in this section. Others that relate to matrix operations are discussed at the end of Chapter 12, while those dedicated to file processing are covered in Chapter 14.

Table 11-5 lists some of the miscellaneous functions available with many versions of BASIC. One function, **SPC**, is very similar to one that we have already examined, SPACE$, in that it creates the number of blank spaces indicated by its argument; however, SPC may only be used in a PRINT statement. All of the following PRINT statements are equivalent:

```
200  PRINT TAB(11); "10 SPACES"

200  PRINT SPACE$(10); "10 SPACES"

200  PRINT SPC(10); "10 SPACES"
```

All will print 10 SPACES beginning in the *eleventh* column.

The two functions **POKE** and **PEEK** are most frequently found on microcomputer BASICs. These two functions allow the user to interact with the computer at the machine language level by directly addressing memory locations. PEEK returns the ASCII code of the character stored in the memory location indicated by its argument. Suppose that the letter F is stored at address 1834; PEEK(1834) will return 70. POKE performs the opposite operation to PEEK and allows a specified character to be placed in a given memory location. In order to place F in location 1834, we would write POKE(1834,70). (Actually POKE is more properly classified as a BASIC *statement;* however, it is discussed here along with PEEK for convenience.)

Two other functions, **DATE$** and **TIME$**, which are found under several other names (see Appendix B), provide the programmer with the ability to insert into the program the current date or time as needed. DATE$ returns the data as a string of the form mm-dd-yyyy, which gives the current month, day, and year. TIME$ also returns the time as a string but of the form hh:mm:ss, providing the hour, minute, and second in a *24-hour* format. If the two functions were incorporated into a print list as follows:

```
120  PRINT DATE$, TIME$
```

TABLE 11-5
Additional BASIC Library Functions

Function	Description
DATE$	Gives the current data as a string value as month, day, and year in a format something like mm-dd-yyyy. Some systems use DATE.
INKEY$	Permits the entry of a character from the terminal *during program execution* without the need to press the RETURN key.
INPUT$(N)	Permits the entry of N characters from the terminal without pressing the RETURN key.
PEEK(N)	Gives the ASCII code of the character located at the memory address given by N. Most frequently found on microcomputer BASICs.
POKE(N1, N2)	Places the character with the ASCII code N2 into the memory address given by N1. Most frequently found on microcomputer BASICs.*
SPC(N)	Similar to SPACE$ except this function may only be used in a PRINT statement.
TIME$	Gives the current time of day as a string value in hours, minutes, and seconds in a 24-hour format something like hh:mm:ss.

*More properly classified as a statement.

We would get something like:

```
10-12-1985  16:35:21
```

which means 35 minutes and 21 seconds after 4 p.m. in the afternoon of October 12, 1985.

The final two functions that we will discuss in this chapter are **INKEY$** and **INPUT$**. These are very different from anything that we have seen so far. Both functions provide for interactive input from the terminal *without having to use the RETURN (or ENTER) key*. The first function, INKEY$, permits the input of a single character to the program to occur *without program execution having to stop to accept it*. It retains the *last* character entered from the keyboard but does not echo the image to the screen. As an example of the use of this function, consider the following short program:

```
10 LET C$ = ""
20 FOR N = 1 TO 100000
30   PRINT "THE NUMBER IS NOW"; N
40   IF INKEY$ <> C$ THEN 60
50 NEXT N
60 END
```

Line 10 set C$ equal to "" (no character). The loop is clear; it will print for a long time! However, at line 40 a check is made on each loop to see if a character has been typed. If it has not, the looping continues. If a character—any character—has been typed, a branch to the END statement will be executed. This can be easily modified to terminate the loop when only a specific character has been typed. The following would end only if the letter K is typed:

```
10 LET C$ = "K"
20 FOR N = 1 TO 100000
30   PRINT "THE NUMBER IS NOW"; N
40   IF INKEY$ = C$ THEN 60
50 NEXT N
60 END
```

Of course, more than one branch can be executed depending on the character typed. Without this type of nonstop input, fast-action video games would not be possible.

The function INPUT$ permits the entry of a specific string of characters (also not echoed), the length of which is given by its argument. Unlike INKEY$, processing must stop for INPUT$. One of the most common uses of INPUT$ is the familiar TYPE ANY KEY TO CONTINUE control built into many programs. This works as follows:

```
             :
300 PRINT "TYPE ANY KEY TO CONTINUE"
310 LET A$ = INPUT$(1)
             :
```

The program will pause at line 310 until a character is typed. When *one* character is typed, processing will continue to the next line. Unlike INKEY$, INPUT$ will accept strings longer than one character from which any processing possible with a string value can be performed.

Before ending our discussion of special functions, there is one additional BASIC *statement* that should be mentioned that is very handy for processing string data. This is the **LINE INPUT** statement (also called LINPUT or INPUT LINE on some systems), which permits the interactive entry of a single string that contains *any* characters. LINE INPUT is used like the regular INPUT to enter strings but with the following differences:

(1) Only one string can be entered with each statement. (2) No automatic prompt (?) or space is provided, but one may be manually inserted as with the regular INPUT. (3) The string may contain any characters, including quotation marks (“). As an example, consider the following very short program that simply reads and prints a single string:

```
10  LINE INPUT "WHAT DID YOU SAY? "; A$
20  PRINT A$
30  END

WHAT DID YOU SAY? I SAID:  "HE SAID, 'LET'S GO NOW'"
I SAID:  "HE SAID, 'LET'S GO NOW'"
```

Note that the string A$ = I SAID: “HE SAID, 'LET'S GO NOW' ” contains characters such as “ and , (and maybe :) that would normally be unacceptable in a string with the regular INPUT statement.

TROUBLESHOOTING

Each of the following programs contains an error that prevents it from executing properly. Explain *specifically* what the problem is and what must be done to correct it. To assist you, a sample of what would happen should you attempt to run the program is provided after each listing. Refer to Appendix D for an explanation of BASIC error messages.

1.

```
 10 REM  TROUBLESHOOTING PROBLEM 11-1
 20 REM
 30 REM     A & B = USER'DEFINED FUNCTIONS
 40 REM         X = X-COORDINATE
 50 REM              (ALSO DUMMY ARGUMENT)
 60 REM         Y = Y-COORDINATE
 70 REM
 80 DEF FNA(X) = 2 * X - 1
 90 DEF FNB(X) = 7 - 2 * X
100 FOR X = -10 TO 10
110   IF FNA(X) <> FNB(X) THEN 150
120   PRINT "POINT OF INTERSECTION"
130   PRINT "IS AT X ="; X;"AND Y ="; Y
140   GOTO 180
150 NEXT X
160 PRINT "LINES DO NOT INTERSECT"
170 PRINT "ON INTERVAL [-10,10]"
180 END

POINT OF INTERSECTION
IS AT X = 2 AND Y = 0
```

2.

```
 10 REM  TROUBLESHOOTING PROBLEM 11-2
 20 REM
 30 REM          C = CENTER OF PRINT PATTERN
 40 REM          S = NUMBER OF LEADING SPACES
 50 REM          N = NUMBER OF CHARACTERS TO PRINT
 60 REM          X = CHARACTER COUNTER
 70 REM         X$ = STRING VALUE OF X
 80 REM
 90 LET C = 10
100 FOR X = 0 TO 9
110   LET S = C - 2 * X
120   LET N = 4 * X + 1
130   LET X$ = RIGHT$(STR$(X), 1)
140   PRINT SPACE$(S); STRING$(N, X$)
150 NEXT X
160 END
```

```
          0
         11111
        222222222
       3333333333333
      44444444444444444
    555555555555555555555

Illegal Function Call in Line 140
```

3.

```
 10 REM  TROUBLESHOOTING PROBLEM 11-3
 20 REM
 30 REM        N$ = NAME
 40 REM        C$ = CHARACTER IN NAME
 50 REM         C = CHARACTER COUNTER
 60 REM
 70 READ N$
 80 LET S = 1
 90 IF N$ = "STOP" THEN 220
100 PRINT N$
110 FOR C = 1 TO LEN(N$)
120   LET C$ = MID$(N$, C, 1)
130   IF C$ <> " " THEN 160
140   PRINT MID$(N$, C, C - S)
150   LET S = C + 1
160 NEXT C
170 PRINT RIGHT$(N$, LEN(N$) - S + 1)
180 PRINT
190 GOTO 70
200 DATA "PETER L. JOHNSON", "SANDRA T. HARRIS"
210 DATA "JENNIFER L. KELLOGG", "STOP"
220 END

PETER L. JOHNSON
 L. J
 J
JOHNSON

SANDRA T. HARRIS
 T. HA
 H
HARRIS

JENNIFER L. KELLOGG
 L. KELL
 K
KELLOGG
```

4.

```
 10 REM  TROUBLESHOOTING PROBLEM 11-4
 20 REM
 30 REM        S$ = A STRING
 40 REM         W = NUMBER OF WORDS IN S$
 50 REM         P = POSITION OF SPACE IN S$
 60 REM
 70 READ S$
 80 IF S$ = " " THEN 240
 90 LET W = 0
100 P = 1
110 LET P = INSTR(P, S$, " ")
120 IF P = 0 THEN 150
130 LET W = W + 1
140 GOTO 110
150 LET W = W + 1
160 PRINT "THERE ARE"; W; "WORDS IN THE STRING"
170 PRINT  S$
```

```
180 PRINT
190 GOTO 70
200 DATA "MARY HAD A LITTLE LAMB"
210 DATA "THE MOON IS MADE OF GREEN CHEESE"
220 DATA "SHE SELLS SEA SHELLS BY THE SEA SHORE"
230 DATA " "
240 END
```

(No output)

5.

```
 10 REM   TROUBLESHOOTING PROBLEM 11-5
 20 REM
 30 REM        T$ = TELEPHONE NUMBER
 40 REM        C$ = CHARACTER IN T$
 50 REM         C = CHARACTER COUNTER
 60 REM         N = SUM OF DIGITS IN T$
 70 REM
 80 READ T$
 90 IF T$ = "###" THEN 200
100 LET N = 0
110 FOR C = 1 TO LEN(T$)
120   LET C$ = MID$(T$, C, 1)
130   IF ASC(C$) < 48 OR ASC(C$) > 57 THEN 150
140   LET N = N + ASC(C$)
150 NEXT C
160 PRINT T$; TAB(24); N
170 GOTO 80
180 DATA "404-555-3256", "(212)-555-8903"
190 DATA "555-9003", "806/555-2180", "###"
200 END
```

```
404-555-3256           519
(212)-555-8903         520
555-9003               363
806/555-2180           520
```

IMPORTANT TERMS

After studying this chapter, you should be familiar with the meaning and use of the following terms and BASIC statements:

Special function
Library function
Exponential notation
Scientific notation
E format
Double-precision
D format
Math function
Argument
pi
e
User-defined function
DEF statement
Dummy argument
Local variable
Global variable
Parameter
Argument-free function
String function
Substring
ASCII code
CHANGE statement
Concatenation
Concatenation operator
LINE INPUT statement

In addition to the terms listed above, you should be familiar with the BASIC functions that are available on your system. These are summarized in this chapter in Tables 11-2, 11-3, and 11-5. A more extensive list is provided in Appendix B.

EXERCISES

1. Write the following numbers in exponential notation. Assume whatever number of digits your system displays.
   (a) 6540000 (b) 909220000
   (c) 288933678 (d) 2000000000000000000000000
   (e) 62887968939000 (f) 4229840000000000000
   (g) 0.00000000456 (h) 0.000467788
   (i) 0.00000000000007665 (j) 0.0000067676767676767
   (k) 0.0000000075421388 (l) 0.000000000000009776844578
2. Write the numbers in Exercise 1 in E format.
3. Express the following in expanded form.
   (a) 9E+09 (b) 2.9998E+08
   (c) 3.45663E+13 (d) 6.023E+23
   (e) 6.93662E+19 (f) 1.992E+30
   (g) 2.8773E−05 (h) 6.67E−11
   (i) 3.02E−06 (j) 1.602E−19
   (k) 7.23882E−15 (l) 1.6625E−24

For Exercises 4 to 6, use the following strings as needed:

```
A$ = "T"
B$ = "THE"
C$ = "BOTTOM OF THE WELL"
D$ = "WHAT IS AT THE BOTTOM OF THE WELL?"
```

4. Give the strings or other values that will be returned by the functions given below.
   (a) `LEFT$(C$, 6)` (b) `LEFT$(D$, 9)`
   (c) `RIGHT$(B$, 2)` (d) `RIGHT$(D$, 5)`
   (e) `MID$(C$, 11, 3)` (f) `MID$(D$, 16, 6)`
   (g) `INDEX(C$, B$)` (h) `INDEX(D$, C$)`
   (i) `INSTR(8, D$, B$)` (j) `INSTR(1, D$, "AT")`
   (k) `LEN(C$)` (l) `ASC(A$)`
5. Give the strings or other values that will be returned by the functions given below.
   (a) `RIGHT$(D$, LEN(C$))`
   (b) `MID$(D$, INDEX(D$, B$), LEN(B$))`
   (c) `LEFT$(MID$(C$, 4, 8), 3)`
   (d) `LEFT$(RIGHT$(D$, LEN(C$) + 1), 6)`
   (e) `INDEX(MID$(D$, 6, 16), MID$(B$, 2, 1))`
   (f) `INSTR(INT(LEN(D$) / 2) + 1, D$, RIGHT$(B$, 1))`
6. Write string expressions or BASIC statements to produce the following results:
   (a) Find how much longer D$ is than C$.
   (b) Find the location of B$ within C$.
   (c) Find the *third* occurrence of A$ in D$.
   (d) Remove C$ from D$.
   (e) Count the number of T's in D$.
   (f) Break D$ into individual words.
7. What will be the result of each of the following?
   (a) `CHR$(80)` (b) `STRING$(24, "+")`
   (c) `PEEK(26338)` (d) `STR$(ASC("%"))`
   (e) `POKE(11802, 126)` (f) `STRING$(40, 88)`
   (g) `VAL(CHR$(54))` (h) `SPACE$(15)`
   (i) `VAL(LEFT$("123 EASY ST.", 3))`

For Exercises 8 to 13, give the output that will be produced by the given programs. Then, type the programs into the computer, run them, and check the actual outputs against your predictions.

8.
```
 10 REM  YOU WILL NEED A CALCULATOR FOR THIS ONE
 20 REM
 30 READ X, Y, Z
 40 LET P = X * Y * Z
 50 IF P = 0 THEN 120
 60 LET R = 1 / P
 70 PRINT X, Y, Z, P, R
 80 GOTO 30
 90 DATA 35766,3.44E+07,7779,20993,5.99332E+08,299817
100 DATA 3.589E+08,2.29E+16,9882,21198,22193,3.9928E+09
110 DATA 7992,5.84E+11,9.12E+06,98822,90005,12239,0,0,0
120 END
```

9.
```
 10 DEF FNL(X) = A * X * X + B * X + C
 20 LET A = 1
 30 LET B = -8
 40 LET C = 20
 50 FOR X = 1 TO 20
 60   IF FNL(X) <> FNL(0) THEN 90
 70   PRINT "SECOND VALUE FOUND AT X ="; X
 80   GOTO 110
 90 NEXT X
100 PRINT "SECOND VALUE NOT FOUND"
110 END
```

10.
```
10 LET N$ = "GEORGE WASHINGTON"
20 FOR P = 1 TO LEN(N$)
30   LET C$ = LEFT$(N$, P)
40   LET S = LEN(N$) - P
50   PRINT C$; STRING$(S, "*")
60 NEXT P
70 END
```

11.
```
10 INPUT "ENTER SCREEN WIDTH"; W
20 FOR P = 1 TO 2 * W - 1
30   LET S = W - ABS(W - P)
40   LET C$ = RIGHT$(STR$(S), 1)
50   PRINT SPACE$(S - 1); C$
60 NEXT P
70 END
```

12.
```
10 INPUT "ENTER SCREEN WIDTH"; W
20 LET C$ = ""
30 FOR P = 1 TO W
40   LET C$ = C$ + RIGHT$(STR$(P), 1)
50   PRINT C$
60 NEXT P
70 END
```

13.
```
 10 INPUT "ENTER TERMINAL WIDTH"; W
 20 FOR T = 1 TO INT(W / 10)
 30   LET T$ = MID$(STR$(T), 2, 1)
 40   PRINT SPACE$(9); T$;
 50 NEXT T
 60 PRINT
 70 FOR U = 1 TO W
 80   LET U$ = RIGHT$(STR$(U), 1)
 90   PRINT U$;
100 NEXT U
110 END
```

PROGRAMMING PROBLEMS

Write programs in BASIC to accomplish the tasks described by each of the following problems. Be sure to carefully document each program and include all appropriate report headings and other literals.

1. The square root of a number can be approximated by using the following procedure:
   (a) Divide the number by a guess at the square root.
   (b) Find the average of the guess and quotient from step 1. This becomes the new guess.
   (c) Repeat steps 1 and 2 until the difference in two consecutive guesses is less than the desired accuracy.

   Use this procedure to find the square root of a series of numbers. Repeat the procedure until the difference in two guesses is less than 0.001. Print the original number, your calculated square root, the number of guesses required, and the actual square root calculated by the SQR function. You supply the data.
2. The value of e, the base of the natural logarithm, can be calculated by the following series:

$$e = 2 + \frac{1}{2!} + \frac{1}{3!} + \frac{1}{4!} + \frac{1}{5!} + \frac{1}{6!} + \cdots$$

   where the ! means *factorial;* $6! = 6 \times 5 \times 4 \times 3 \times 2 \times 1 = 720$. Write a program to calculate e using the above series. Using EXP(1), compare the accumulated value and terminate your program whenever your sum is equal to or greater than EXP(1). Print both your accumulated value and EXP(1) as well as the number of terms that were required.
3. The second example in Section 11-2, which calculated the range of a projectile, used a formula for range, the derivation of which is based on the following trigonometric identity:

$$\sin 2x = 2 \sin x \cos x$$

   Write a program to verify this relationship for all angles from 0° to 360° in 10° increments.
4. Write a program to read the list of names below and print the names along with the corresponding three initials.

Name	Name
Nancy C. Jordan	Laurie T. Evans
Gary R. Larson	Teresa F. Freeman
Carol A. Morrison	Jon H. Carr
Jack L. Nix	V. Allan Hart
T. David Moore	Eleanor T. Hill

5. The Ionu Security Agency needs a program that will encode and decode the characters in a string. Write a program that will read a string, code the string as its corresponding ASCII codes, and then decode the string. The program should print the original string *before* it is encoded, the coded string of ASCII codes, and the *decoded* string. A check should be made to ensure that each string is properly decoded without errors. Process the strings below.

Mary Falkner
123 Easy St.
212-555-2711
Jack's Photo Lab
Box # 12673-B at Main Br.
Deposit of $15,500 on 4/12/85

6. Write a program to read a string and print both the original string as well as the string in reverse order. Use the strings given below to test your program.

BASIC
Abraham Lincoln
California
%#xhs(−+ **9a0j@!! $!^h)
Peter Piper Picked a Peck of What??
Beginner's All-purpose Symbolic Instruction Code

7. A *palindrome* is a string that reads the same from either direction. The string "abcba" is an example. Write a program to read a string and examine it to determine whether or not it is a palindrome. The output should print the string with an appropriate message as to whether or not it is a palindrome. Strings for testing are provided below.

Mom	Radar
Adadada	(** ?? **)
11-55-11	Ted Bob Ted
⟨⟨⟨ ERROR ⟩⟩⟩	Star Rats
1881	Pop saw was pop

8. A program is needed that will calculate and print the grades on a multiple choice test. The test has 20 questions, each of which has 5 possible choices labeled A through E. Input will consist of each student's name plus one 20-character string containing that student's answers to the test questions. The program must select and compare each answer (character in the string) to the correct answer and calculate a grade as a percent of the number correct. The output should give each student's name, the number correct, the number wrong, and the grade. Data is provided in the table below.

Correct Answers: ABDACEEDBCDAAEADCBBB

Student Name	Answers to Questions
James R. Cleveland	ABCACEDDCBCAAEADCBBA
Brenda N. Sykes	ADDADEEDBBDAAEACBBBB
Deborah A. Norris	ABCACEEDCCDAAEADBCBB
Robert W. Cummings	ABDACEEDBCDAAEADCBBB
Walter C. Riley	ABDBEBECBCDAAEDDCBBD
F. Janet Sanders	ABCACEEDBCDAAEADCBBA
Thomas D. Smith	ABDADEEDBCDAAEADCBBB
Linda T. Maxwell	BBDCCEEDBCDAADADCBBB

9. Social security numbers are normally written in the form xxx-xx-xxxx, with dashes inserted as indicated. The numbers below do not have dashes. Write a program to read the numbers and rewrite them with dashes in the proper places.

Number	Number	Number
211563522	213655325	332011025
765326598	233648950	320036527
215985566	541263325	326511065
356662157	651039953	216586322
332610025	321045809	224223682
210065943	651302456	659445321
322165036	322546621	321153356

10. Write a program to accomplish the same result with the dashes in the social security numbers as in Problem 9, except the input data for this one may have dashes or any other characters at any location in the number. There is also no information as to the exact length of the string of characters. Input data is provided below. (You may assume that each number contains exactly nine digits in addition to the other characters.)

Number	Number
125-652-668	44-665-66X-55
256,6601706	12335.3325C
2145-66-523V	561/22/65-52
5460,55,556	2233325-66-X
6884X665-55	65,2-566/33N6
465/56/6658B	321/56/966i5

11. The seven Roman numerals and their corresponding values in the Arabic system are M = 1000, D = 500, C = 100, L = 50, X = 10, V = 5, and I = 1. The Roman system is generally simply the sum of the values of the digits *as long as the digits decrease to the right*. That is, MCCLXXXVI would be 1286. Whenever a digit of smaller value appears to the left, it is subtracted from the digit to its immediate right. Only C, X, and I may subtract; C will subtract from M or D, X from C or L, and I from X or V. The number MCDXCII is 1492. Write a program to read and translate Roman numerals into Arabic numerals. The input is to consist of the Roman numerals in the table below. The output should give both the Roman and Arabic form.

Roman Numeral	Roman Numeral	Roman Numeral
DCCLXV	MCMLXI	MCDXIV
MMCCCXXXIII	DCXLII	CMXLVII
MDCCLXXVIII	CCLIV	MMMCDXCIX
MMMXXII	CCCXCIV	MMMCMLXXIV
MMDCCLXVIII	CDXLIII	MCDLXXXIX

12. Write a program to print asterisks in the following patterns: square, rectangle, diamond, and circle. Make your program menu-driven to allow the user to select the pattern that he or she would like to see.
13. Modify your program for Problem 12 to permit the user to select the dimension(s) of the figure (number of print lines or columns) to be printed.

For Problems 14 to 19, write a program to plot a graph of the indicated function. You may wish to experiment a little with the number of points to plot and the increment between points.

14. $y = |2x^2 - 15x + 8|$
15. $y = \sqrt{2x^3 + 25}$
16. $y = \dfrac{60}{x} - 5$
17. $y = (x - 4)^2 + 3$
18. $y = 12 \sin x + 25$
19. $y = 25e^{-(x-5)^2/4}$
20. Write a menu-driven program that will print *any one* of the functions listed in Problems 14 to 19 upon request by the user. The function that is being plotted should appear at the top of the graph in the heading.

CHAPTER 12

MORE ON ARRAYS

In Chapter 9, we saw how to handle data using subscripted variables and one-dimensional arrays. We have, thus far, only scratched the surface of the programming power afforded by arrays. In this chapter, we will study techniques for working with two-dimensional arrays, in which the data is arranged into rows and columns. In Chapter 13, you will encounter some additional, very powerful, advanced array processing techniques.

12-1 TWO-DIMENSIONAL ARRAYS

Data can be arranged and processed as a **two-dimensional array** by using a subscripted variable of the general form:

variable(sub1, sub2)

where *variable* is any legal *subscripted* variable name, and *sub1* and *sub2* are *two* subscripts. Two-dimensional arrays are named in the same way as one-dimensional arrays, but once a variable name has been used, it cannot be repeated even for an array of a different dimension. As with one-dimensional arrays, two-dimensional arrays may represent either numeric or string data and must be properly dimensioned in a DIM statement. Both one- and two-dimensional arrays may appear in the same DIM statement.

With a two-dimensional array, the data is arranged in a table with **rows** and **columns**. The first subscript *(sub1)* gives the *row* in which a particular value is to be found, while the second *(sub2)* gives the *column*. The above general expression for a two-dimensional dimensional array can be written as:

variable(row, column)

The numbering of the subscripts in a two-dimensional array with four rows and five columns is illustrated in Figure 12-1. This is called a 4 by 5 array (also written 4 × 5).

	Col. 1	Col. 2	Col. 3	Col. 4	Col. 5
Row 1	(1, 1)	(1, 2)	(1, 3)	(1, 4)	(1, 5)
Row 2	(2, 1)	(2, 2)	(2, 3)	(2, 4)	(2, 5)
Row 3	(3, 1)	(3, 2)	(3, 3)	(3, 4)	(3, 5)
Row 4	(4, 1)	(4, 2)	(4, 3)	(4, 4)	(4, 5)

FIGURE 12-1
Pattern of subscripts in a two-dimensional array

Just as an element in a one-dimensional array is located by designating the proper subscript, an element is located in a two-dimensional array by specifying *two* subscripts, the first for the row and the second for the column. For example, to indicate the element at the fourth row and second column of the array X, we would write X(4, 2). In like manner, if we have X(3, 5), we know that we are working with the element on row three at column five.

A one-dimensional array can be thought of as a two-dimensional pattern with only one row or column. An array that is dimensioned as:

```
200 DIM K(1, 12)
```

would have only *one* row with *twelve* columns. This arrangement is referred to as a **row vector**. On the other hand, had K been dimensioned as:

```
200 DIM K(12, 1)
```

it would have *twelve* rows with only *one* column, which forms what is known as a **column vector**. Either of these arrangements can be made, with care, to be equivalent to the one-dimensional array:

```
200 DIM K(12)
```

The row vector is, however, normally considered to be more closely equivalent to a one-dimensional array because it is the form that BASIC assumes when performing automatic operations with two-dimensional arrays—as with the MAT statements described in the last two sections of this chapter.

As with one-dimensional arrays, many BASICs provide a *zeroth* element for *each* subscript in a two-dimensional array. This means that an array R that is dimensioned as:

```
180 DIM R(15, 25)
```

will actually have *16* rows (0 to 15) and *26* columns (0 to 25). For the same reasons as with one-dimensional arrays, the zeroth positions are frequently not used or, if they are, only for special values. Also, many BASICs provide for the automatic dimensioning of two-dimensional arrays up to ten rows and ten columns (not counting the zeroth positions). Thus, the array Y(6, 3) would not have to be dimensioned with these BASICs. We will continue to dimension all arrays.

12-2 OPERATIONS WITH TWO-DIMENSIONAL ARRAYS

Data is read into a two-dimensional array in much the same way as it is read into a one-dimensional array; that is, by "stepping" through the values of a subscript; however, we now must "step through" two subscripts. This is done by using nested FOR–NEXT loops (or other control structures) to control the two subscripts. We must load the array in an orderly manner by either row or column order. The following reads values into an array, X, with three rows and four columns (3 by 4):

```
100 FOR R = 1 TO 3
110    FOR C = 1 TO 4
120       READ X(R, C)
130    NEXT C
140 NEXT R
          :
900 DATA 23,54,12,-7
910 DATA 14,8,-11,43
920 DATA 3,13,-27,15
```

Here, R counts the rows and C the columns. At line 100, R is first set equal to 1 or the first row. The inner loop then steps C from 1 through 4 for the four columns, which causes line 120 to read values into the four positions in the first row. Thus, the four data values in the DATA statement at line 900 will be assigned to X(1, 1), X(1, 2), X(1, 3), and X(1, 4), respectively. R is next set to 2 and the inner loop repeats for the four values of the *second* row. Finally, for R = 3 values are read into the third row. The arrangement of the values in array X is illustrated in Figure 12-2.

The data was read into the array by rows or in what is known as **row-priority order**. This means that the data was loaded into the array one row at a time. The data could be loaded into the array by columns or in **column-priority order**. This can be done by the following statements:

```
100 FOR C = 1 TO 4
110    FOR R = 1 TO 3
120       READ X(R, C)
130    NEXT R
140 NEXT C
          :
900 DATA 23,14,3
910 DATA 54,8,13
920 DATA 12,-11,-27
930 DATA -7,43,15
```

The column is first set to 1, and the three rows are read down by the inner loop, reading values into X(1, 1), X(2, 1), and X(3, 1), respectively. This continues for the four rows. Note that the data in the DATA statements had to be rearranged to place the values in the same locations as with the row-priority method. The two methods can be used for other procedures, such as printing, table searches, and accumulating totals. While either method is acceptable, unless the problem dictates the use of column priority, we will use row priority when there is a choice. This is primarily because this is the form used by automatic processes in BASIC, such as MAT statements, for working with arrays (see Sections 12-6 and 12-7). However you enter the data, *be sure you know how you are doing it, because if you enter it in the wrong way (by columns instead of rows), you will end up with the values assigned to the wrong array elements.*

Of course, any other statement that can be used for entering data, such as the LET or INPUT, can be used for input in place of the READ above. To print array X, we write:

```
200 FOR R = 1 TO 3
210    FOR C = 1 TO 4
220       PRINT X(R, C)
230    NEXT C
240 NEXT R
```

which will print:

```
 23
 54
 12
-7
 14
 8
-11
 43
 3
 13
-27
 15
```

	Col. 1	Col. 2	Col. 3	Col. 4
Row 1	23	54	12	-7
Row 2	14	8	-11	43
Row 3	3	13	-27	15

FIGURE 12-2
Data stored in array X

We can print the array in rows and columns much as it appears in Figure 12-2 as follows:

```
200  FOR R = 1 TO 3
210    FOR C = 1 TO 4
220      PRINT X(R, C),
230    NEXT C
235    PRINT
240  NEXT R
```

```
23              54              12              -7
14              8               -11             43
3               13              -27             15
```

The comma at the end of line 220 causes values to continue to be printed on the same line until a row has been completed. At that point, the PRINT at 235 "cancels" the comma and permits the next row to begin on a new line.

As with one-dimensional arrays, more than one array may appear in the variable list of a READ, INPUT, or PRINT statement. For example, the following statements will read data into two arrays, X and Y$:

```
100 FOR R = 1 TO 3
110    FOR C = 1 TO 4
120       READ X(R, C), Y$(R, C)
130    NEXT C
140 NEXT R
                    :
900 DATA 23,"A",54,"C",12,"F",-7,"A"
910 DATA 14,"C",8,"B",-11,"B",43,"F"
920 DATA 3,"B",13,"C",-27,"D",15,"D"
```

This will read one element into X, then one into Y$, alternately, until both arrays are filled. Similarly, arrays can be printed in alternate fashion. Obviously this method can be used only when the arrays are of the *same* size. If two arrays have been dimensioned to different sizes, then they must be processed by separate loops.

A two-dimensional array can be set equal to zero (or any other constant) by the following:

```
130  FOR R = 1 TO 3
140    FOR C = 1 TO 4
150      LET T(R, C) = 0
160    NEXT C
170  NEXT R
```

One array can be set equal to another, element by element, by:

```
130  FOR R = 1 TO 3
140    FOR C = 1 TO 4
150      LET T(R, C) = X(R, C)
160    NEXT C
170  NEXT R
```

which will make the new array, T, identical to X. The new array can be created with the elements in a different arrangement. For example, the following produces T with rows the same as the *columns* of X and columns equal to the *rows* of X:

```
130  FOR R = 1 TO 3
140    FOR C = 1 TO 4
150      LET T(C, R) = X(R, C)
160    NEXT C
170  NEXT R
```

	Col. 1	Col. 2	Col. 3
Row 1	23	14	3
Row 2	54	8	13
Row 3	12	-11	-27
Row 4	-7	43	15

FIGURE 12-3
Transposed form of X

The array T is called the **transpose** of X. It is shown in Figure 12-3.

It should be clear that operations with two-dimensional arrays are very similar to those with one-dimensional arrays except for the extra subscript. As with the one-dimensional type, always remember that all array elements are variables and should be treated as such. That is, they can be used in arithmetic operations and expressions, logical expressions and conditions, or in any other way that you would use a nonsubscripted variable. Before we look at searches and accumulating sums by rows and columns, let us pause for an example that employs two-dimensional arrays.

12-3 AN EXAMPLE: TELEPHONE USAGE REPORT

The example presented below illustrates the use of two-dimensional arrays for processing data in general and for the accumulating of totals.

Problem: The local telephone company needs a program that will calculate and print a summary of telephone usage for a 1-day period. As shown in Table 12-1, the phone company has 12 different basic rates that depend on the way the call was placed and the type of customer making the call. The basic rates given in the table are for daytime calls. Evening calls are 75 percent of this rate, while nighttime calls are 50 percent of the stated rate. The time period of the call is to be indicated by a code number as follows:

code of 1 = daytime call = full rate

code of 2 = evening call = 75 percent of rate

code of 3 = nighttime call = 50 percent of rate

Charges for a call are calculated as 1.5 times the appropriate rate for the first minute plus the applicable rate for all additional minutes. The report is to give for each of the 12 possible combinations of customer classifications and types of calls the following totals: (1) the total number of calls made, (2) the total time of all calls in hours and minutes, and (3) the total of all charges. Data on calls made is given in Table 12-2.

The solution to this problem is outlined as follows:

1. Dimension arrays for customer class, method of call, rate, total number of calls, total charges, and total time.
2. Read customer classes into customer class array.
3. Read calling methods into method of call array.

TABLE 12-1
Telephone Rate Table (Charges per Minute)

	Business	Residential	Nonprofit
Direct-dial	$0.96	$0.56	$0.42
Credit-card	$1.08	$0.64	$0.48
Person-to-person	$1.44	$0.84	$0.72
Collect	$1.24	$0.72	$0.64

TABLE 12-2

Data for Telephone Usage Report Example

Calling Codes for				Calling Codes for				Calling Codes for			
Class	Method	Time	Length of Call	Class	Method	Time	Length of Call	Class	Method	Time	Length of Call
1	1	2	14	1	2	1	15	3	3	3	5
2	1	1	18	1	2	3	27	1	3	1	28
1	1	1	32	3	2	2	8	1	2	2	48
2	1	2	6	1	1	1	27	1	3	1	39
1	2	3	24	1	1	2	18	1	2	3	22
2	1	1	19	2	1	3	51	1	3	2	3
1	3	2	19	4	1	2	15	1	1	1	16
1	1	1	47	3	1	1	17	3	1	2	21
2	2	2	1	2	2	1	19	1	1	2	38
2	1	3	25	2	2	1	9	2	1	1	7
4	1	3	25	2	1	1	53	1	2	3	28
2	1	1	5	1	1	2	37	3	3	1	22
2	1	2	10	1	1	2	16	1	1	2	53

4. Read rates into rate array.
5. Set all elements of arrays for totals of number of calls, charges, and time equal to zero.
6. Read a record for a call giving codes for method of call, customer class, and time period and the length of the call in minutes.
7. Check for the end of processing. If the end, go to step 14; otherwise, go to the next step.
8. If the time period code = 1, set the rate equal to that from the appropriate place in the rate table; if the code = 2, set the rate equal to 0.75 times the value from the table; and if the code = 3, set the rate equal to 0.50 times the table value.
9. Calculate the charges for a call.
10. Add 1 to the appropriate element in the array for the total number of calls.
11. Add the time of the call to the appropriate element in the array for the total time of calls.
12. Add the charges to the appropriate element in the array for the total charges of calls.
13. Go to step 6.
14. Print main and column headings giving the customer classes in the column headings.
15. Print detailed lines giving the method of call and the total number of calls, time, and charges for each customer class.
16. Stop.

This procedure is illustrated pictorially by the flowchart in Figure 12-4.

Steps 1 through 5 above are accomplished by the following set of statements:

```
250 DIM C$(3), M$(4), RT(4, 3), TN(4, 3), TT(4, 3), TC(4, 3)
260 FOR J = 1 TO 3
270    READ C$(J)
280 NEXT J
290 FOR J = 1 TO 4
300    READ M$(J)
310    FOR K = 1 TO 3
320       READ RT(J, K)
330       LET TN(J, K) = 0
340       LET TT(J, K) = 0
350       LET TC(J, K) = 0
360    NEXT K
370 NEXT J
```

All arrays are dimensioned at line 250. Notice that both one- and two-dimensional arrays are handled by the samė DIM statement. The class code array is loaded by the loop at 260 to 280. The nested loop from 290 to 370 accomplishes the rest. The rate array is loaded at line 320 (row-priority order) and the three total accumulator arrays are zeroed at the next

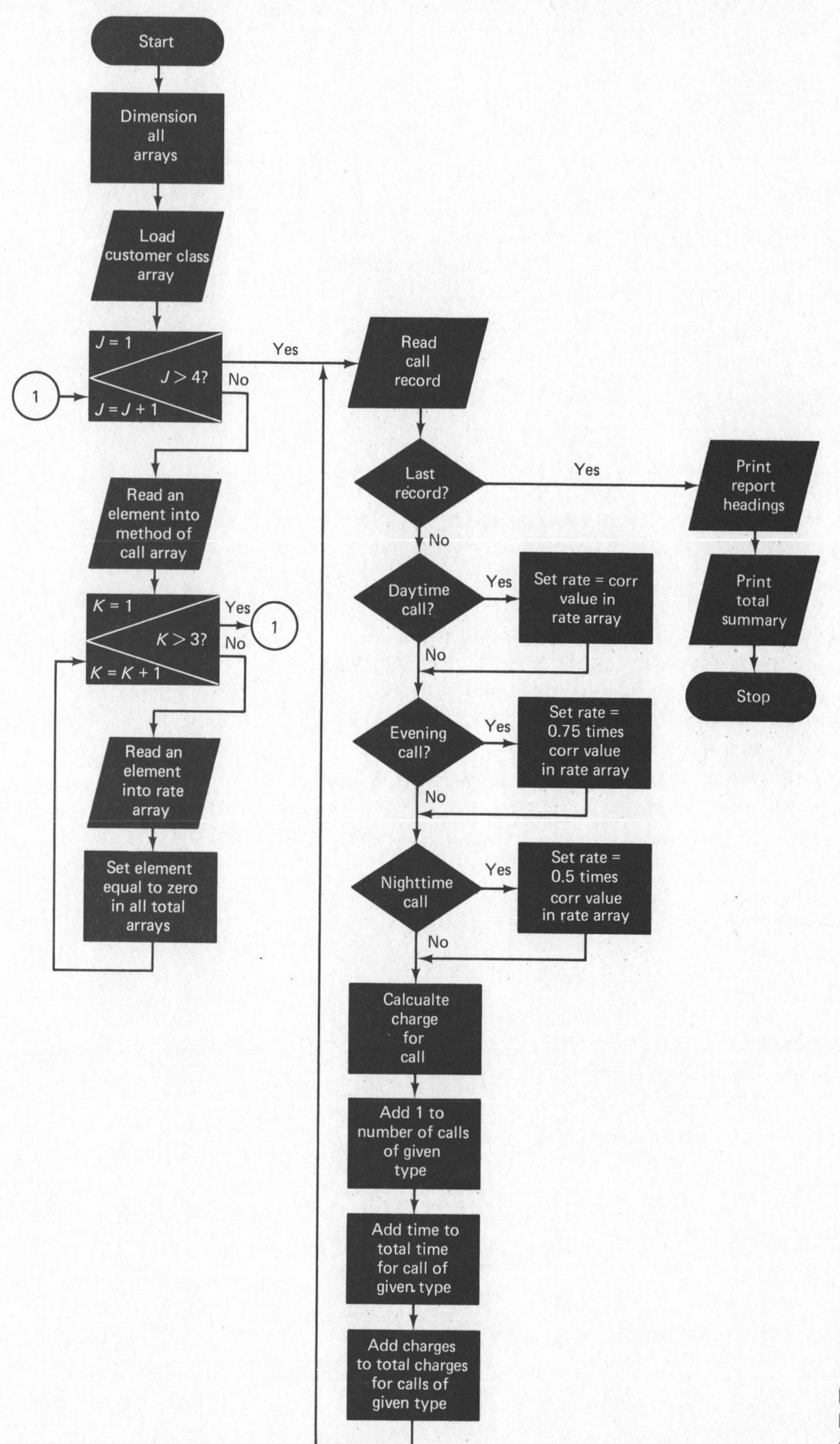

FIGURE 12-4
Flowchart for telephone usage report example

three lines. The method of call array is loaded at line 300. Note that it is included within the *outer* loop only.

The individual record of a call is processed by steps 6 to 9, which can be coded into BASIC as:

```
410 READ MC, CC, CT, T
420 IF CT = 0 THEN 570
430 IF CT = 1 THEN LET R = RT(MC, CC)
440 IF CT = 2 THEN LET R = .75 * RT(MC, CC)
450 IF CT = 3 THEN LET R = .5 * RT(MC, CC)
460 LET CH = 1.5 * R + R * (T - 1)
```

Lines 430 to 450 determine the proper rate from the code for the period of the call, CT, by extracting the basic rate from the rate table as R(MC, CC) and multiplying this by the appropriate factor. R(MC, CC) is found by using the codes for the method of call and customer class (MC and CC) as subscripts. The three arrays that accumulate the totals for number of calls, total time of calls, and total charges are updated at lines 500, 510, and 520, respectively.

```
500  LET TN(MC, CC) = TN(MC, CC) + 1
510  LET TT(MC, CC) = TT(MC, CC) + T
520  LET TC(MC, CC) = TC(MC, CC) + CH
```

Again, MC and CC are used as subscripts to locate the proper elements in the arrays.

The headings are printed at 570 to 660. This is a different position in the program for printing the headings; it is usually done near the beginning. They could be printed earlier; however, since this is a summary report in which nothing is printed until all data is processed, there is no need to print the headings until now. The headings are relatively routine, involving no two-dimensional arrays. Note the loop at lines 610 to 640 that prints the customer classes in the column heads. Line 620 calculates the appropriate positions for the TAB for this. (See Section 6-6 for a detailed discussion of the arithmetic calculation of tab positions in print lines.)

The printing of the detailed lines for this one is fairly complex. Here is how the first *set* of lines should appear (column headings are shown for clarity):

```
                BUSINESS     RESIDENTIAL  NON-PROFIT

DIRECT-DIAL     10 CALLS       6 CALLS       4 CALLS
               4 HR 58 MIN  2 HR 44 MIN  1 HR 29 MIN
                $ 247.92      $ 57.89       $ 35.805
```

For direct-dial calls from businesses, we must give the three totals. Likewise, for direct-dial calls from residential customers, there are three totals to be printed, and so on for all 12 combinations of methods of calling and customer classes. This is accomplished by lines 700 to 890:

```
700 FOR J = 1 TO 4
710    PRINT M$(J);
720    FOR K = 1 TO 3
730       LET P = 22 + 15 * (K - 1)
740       PRINT TAB(P); TN(J, K); "CALLS";
750    NEXT K
760    FOR K = 1 TO 3
770       LET H = INT((TT(J, K)) / 60)
780       LET M = TT(J, K) - 60 * H
790       LET P = 21 + 15 * (K - 1)
800       PRINT TAB(P); H; "HR"; M; "MIN";
810    NEXT K
```

```
820     PRINT
830     FOR K = 1 TO 3
840       LET P = 23 + 15 * (K - 1)
850       PRINT TAB(P); "$"; TC(J, K);
860     NEXT K
870     PRINT
880     PRINT
890 NEXT J
```

The outer loop controls the method of calling or the *rows* of the arrays; the inner loops print across the rows by column number. Line 710 prints the method of calling from that array. Lines 720 to 750 print the values from the total number of calls array. The loop at 760 to 810 prints the total time of calls. The total time in *minutes* is converted to *hours and minutes* by lines 770 and 780. The third total array for the total charges is printed by lines 830 to 860. Note the arithmetic calculation of the tab positions at lines 730, 790, and 840. Also, note the use of semicolons at the end of most PRINT statements to allow several values to print on the same line.

A complete program listing and run follow:

```
 10 REM  TELEPHONE USAGE REPORT
 20 REM
 30 REM  VARIABLES ARE DEFINED AS --
 40 REM
 50 REM          C$ = CUSTOMER CLASS ARRAY
 60 REM          M$ = METHOD OF CALL ARRAY
 70 REM          RT = RATE ARRAY
 80 REM          TT = TOTAL TIME OF CALLS ARRAY
 90 REM          TC = TOTAL CHARGES ARRAY
100 REM          TN = TOTAL NUMBER OF CALLS ARRAY
110 REM          MC = METHOD OF CALL CODE
120 REM          CC = CUSTOMER CLASS CODE
130 REM          CT = TIME OF CALL CODE
140 REM           T = TIME OF CALL
150 REM           R = RATE ADJUSTED FOR CT
160 REM          CH = CHARGE FOR EACH CALL
170 REM           P = PRINT POSITION
180 REM           H = TOTAL HOURS OF CALLS
190 REM           M = TOTAL MINUTES OF CALLS
200 REM     J AND K = LOOP COUNTERS
210 REM
220 REM  DIMENSION ARRAYS, LOAD ALL TABLES, AND
230 REM  SET ALL TOTAL ACCUMULATOR ARRAYS TO ZERO
240 REM
250 DIM C$(3), M$(4), RT(4, 3), TN(4, 3), TT(4, 3), TC(4, 3)
260 FOR J = 1 TO 3
270   READ C$(J)
280 NEXT J
290 FOR J = 1 TO 4
300   READ M$(J)
310   FOR K = 1 TO 3
320     READ RT(J, K)
330     LET TN(J, K) = 0
340     LET TT(J, K) = 0
350     LET TC(J, K) = 0
360   NEXT K
370 NEXT J
380 REM
390 REM  READ CALL RECORD AND CALCULATE CHARGE
400 REM
410 READ MC, CC, CT, T
420 IF CT = 0 THEN 570
```

```
430 IF CT = 1 THEN LET R = RT(MC, CC)
440 IF CT = 2 THEN LET R = .75 * RT(MC, CC)
450 IF CT = 3 THEN LET R = .5 * RT(MC, CC)
460 LET CH = 1.5 * R + R * (T - 1)
470 REM
480 REM  UPDATE TOTAL TIME AND CHARGES ARRAYS
490 REM
500 LET TN(MC, CC) = TN(MC, CC) + 1
510 LET TT(MC, CC) = TT(MC, CC) + T
520 LET TC(MC, CC) = TC(MC, CC) + CH
530 GOTO 410
540 REM
550 REM  PRINT REPORT HEADINGS
560 REM
570 PRINT TAB(21); "TELEPHONE USAGE REPORT"
580 PRINT TAB(21); "TOTAL TIME AND CHARGES"
590 PRINT
600 PRINT
610 FOR J = 1 TO 3
620   LET P = 22 + 15 * (J - 1)
630   PRINT TAB(P); C$(J);
640 NEXT J
650 PRINT
660 PRINT
670 REM
680 REM  PRINT TOTAL NUMBER, TIME, AND CHARGES ARRAYS
690 REM
700 FOR J = 1 TO 4
710   PRINT M$(J);
720   FOR K = 1 TO 3
730     LET P = 22 + 15 * (K - 1)
740     PRINT TAB(P); TN(J, K); "CALLS";
750   NEXT K
760   FOR K = 1 TO 3
770     LET H = INT((TT(J, K)) / 60)
780     LET M = TT(J, K) - 60 * H
790     LET P = 21 + 15 * (K - 1)
800     PRINT TAB(P); H; "HR"; M; "MIN";
810   NEXT K
820   PRINT
830   FOR K = 1 TO 3
840     LET P = 23 + 15 * (K - 1)
850     PRINT TAB(P); "$"; TC(J, K);
860   NEXT K
870   PRINT
880   PRINT
890 NEXT J
900 REM
910 REM  DATA LIST FOR ARRAYS
920 REM
930 DATA " BUSINESS", "RESIDENTIAL", "NON-PROFIT"
940 DATA "DIRECT-DIAL", .96, .56, .42
950 DATA "CREDIT-CARD", 1.08, .64, .48
960 DATA "PERSON-TO-PERSON", 1.44, .84, .72
970 DATA "COLLECT", 1.24, .72, .64
980 REM
990 REM  DATA TO BE PROCESSED
1000 REM
1010 DATA 1,1,2,14,2,1,1,18,1,1,1,32,2,1,2,6,1,2,3,24
1020 DATA 2,1,1,19,1,3,2,19,1,1,1,47,2,2,2,1,2,1,3,25
1030 DATA 4,1,3,25,2,1,1,5,2,1,2,10,1,2,1,15,1,2,3,27
1040 DATA 3,2,2,8,1,1,1,27,1,1,2,18,2,1,3,51,4,1,2,15
1050 DATA 3,1,1,17,2,2,1,19,2,2,1,9,2,1,1,53,1,1,2,37
1060 DATA 1,1,2,16,3,3,3,5,1,3,1,28,1,2,2,48,1,3,1,39
```

```
1070 DATA 1,2,3,22,1,3,2,3,1,1,1,16,3,1,2,21,1,1,2,38
1080 DATA 2,1,1,7,1,2,3,28,3,3,1,22,1,1,2,53,0,0,0,0
1090 END
```

```
                    TELEPHONE USAGE REPORT
                    TOTAL TIME AND CHARGES


                     BUSINESS        RESIDENTIAL      NON-PROFIT

DIRECT-DIAL          10 CALLS          6 CALLS          4 CALLS
                    4 HR 58 MIN      2 HR 44 MIN      1 HR 29 MIN
                     $ 247.92         $ 57.89          $ 35.805

CREDIT-CARD           9 CALLS          3 CALLS          0 CALLS
                    3 HR 14 MIN      0 HR 29 MIN      0 HR 0 MIN
                     $ 168.21         $ 19.28          $ 0

PERSON-TO-PERSON      2 CALLS          1 CALLS          2 CALLS
                    0 HR 38 MIN      0 HR 8 MIN       0 HR 27 MIN
                     $ 48.42          $ 5.355          $ 18.18

COLLECT               2 CALLS          0 CALLS          0 CALLS
                    0 HR 40 MIN      0 HR 0 MIN       0 HR 0 MIN
                     $ 30.225         $ 0              $ 0
```

12-4 MORE SUMMING AND SEARCHING

In Chapter 9, we studied various ways to search and sum the elements of a one-dimensional array. In this section, we will see how to extend these techniques to handle data that is organized into a two-dimensional array. In such cases, we can sum or search the entire array or just by rows or columns. Let us look at searching first.

Consider the 3 by 4 array X given in Figure 12-2. We can search a *single* row or column by using one FOR–NEXT loop with the required row or column fixed and by letting the loop counter range over the other subscript. The following will find the number of values in the second row that are greater than 10:

```
370 FOR C = 1 TO 4
380    IF X(2, C) > 10 THEN T = T + 1
390 NEXT C
```

We can search the entire array X to find the number of negative values by:

```
400 FOR R = 1 TO 3
410    FOR C = 1 TO 4
420       IF X(R, C) < 0 THEN N = N + 1
430    NEXT C
440 NEXT R
```

First, row 1 is searched, then row 2, and finally, row 3. This search was by row priority. It could have been as easily done by column priority.

The largest or smallest value in a two-dimensional array can be found in a very similar way as in a one-dimensional array. To find the largest value in the second row of array X, we would write:

```
320 LET CS = 1
330 LET XS = X(2, 1)
340 FOR C = 2 TO 4
350    IF XS <= X(2, C) THEN 380
360    LET CS = C
370    LET XS = X(2, C)
380 NEXT C
```

This is exactly the same as searching a one-dimensional array as described in Section 9-5. To search the *entire* array, we must add an outer loop to sum over the rows. This is done as follows:

```
315 LET RS = 1
320 LET CS = 1
330 LET XS = X(1, 1)
335 FOR R = 1 TO 3
340    FOR C = 1 TO 4
350       IF XS <= X(R, C) THEN 380
360       LET CS = C
365       LET RS = R
370       LET XS = X(R, C)
380    NEXT C
385 NEXT R
```

Note that we have also added a marker (RS) for the row subscript because we will need to know *both* subscripts in order to have the position of the largest value in X.

We can sum a two-dimensional array, either over the entire array or by rows or columns. The sum of the elements in the second row of X can be found by:

```
210 FOR C = 1 TO 4
220    LET S = S + X(2, C)
230 NEXT C
```

We can find the sums for all the rows by:

```
200 FOR R = 1 TO 3
210    FOR C = 1 TO 4
220       LET SR(R) = SR(R) + X(R, C)
230    NEXT C
240 NEXT R
```

This accumulates the sum of the elements in row 1 and places it in SR(1). The sum for row 2 is stored in SR(2), and that for row 3 in SR(3). The sums of the columns can be similarly found by:

```
300 FOR C = 1 TO 4
310    FOR R = 1 TO 3
320       LET SC(C) = SC(C) + X(R, C)
330    NEXT R
340 NEXT C
```

Both row and column sums can be accumulated within the *same* set of loops; we will see how this is done below.

As a final example of accumulating sums in this section, the row and column sums can be accumulated and stored within the same two-dimensional array as the data that is being summed. We did this with one-dimensional arrays and made use of that *zeroth* location. We could do it again here, but let us take a different approach. Suppose that the array X had been dimensioned as 4 by 5 to allow for an extra row and column. We would still read the data into X in the same way; however, now we have space in X to store row and column sums (or other special values) as needed. The following program reads X, accumulates row and column sums, and prints X with the sums. The output follows the listing.

	Col. 1	Col. 2	Col. 3	Col. 4	Row sums
Row 1	23	54	12	-7	82
Row 2	14	8	-11	43	54
Row 3	3	13	-27	15	4
Column sums	40	75	-26	51	140

FIGURE 12-5
Array X with row and column sums

```
10 REM  SUMMING A TWO-DIMENSIONAL ARRAY
20 REM
30 DIM X(4,5)
40 FOR R = 1 TO 3
50    FOR C = 1 TO 4
60       READ X(R, C)
70    NEXT C
80 NEXT R
90 FOR R = 1 TO 3
100    FOR C = 1 TO 4
110       LET X(R, 5) = X(R, 5) + X(R, C)
120       LET X(4, C) = X(4, C) + X(R, C)
130    NEXT C
140    LET X(4, 5) = X(4, 5) + X(R, 5)
150 NEXT R
160 FOR R = 1 TO 4
170    FOR C = 1 TO 5
180       PRINT X(R, C),
190    NEXT C
200 NEXT R
210 DATA 23,54,12,-7
220 DATA 14,8,-11,43
230 DATA 3,13,-27,15
240 END
```

```
23             54             12            -7             82
14             8             -11             43            54
3              13            -27             15            4
40             75            -26             51            140
```

Lines 40 to 80 load X but only in the first three rows and four columns. Lines 90 to 150 accumulate the totals. Row totals are summed at line 110 and placed in the extra, or fifth, column. Column totals are found at 120 and stored in the extra, or fourth, row. The sum of all the elements of the array (except the sums) is found and stored in the unused position X(4, 5) at line 140 by accumulating the sum of all the row sums. This last value could have been found by adding the column sum or *all* the elements of the array individually. The array is printed as shown by lines 160 to 200. The arrangement of the array is illustrated in Figure 12-5.

12-5 AN EXAMPLE: ABSENTEE ANALYSIS REPORT

This example illustrates the use of table searches with two-dimensional arrays and applications of the techniques for finding sums by rows and columns.

Problem: The dean of Peckham College needs a program to analyze student absentee data for any given 10-week quarter. Absentee figures are available on a daily basis as shown in Table 12-3. The program should read and print the input data along with totals for each week, each day of the week, and the entire quarter. At the end of the report, the following summary information should be printed: (1) the numbers of absentees and the weeks with the largest and smallest numbers of absentees, (2) the numbers of absentees and the

TABLE 12-3

Data for Absentee Analysis Report

Week Number	Number of Absentees for				
	Monday	Tuesday	Wednesday	Thursday	Friday
1	329	349	220	246	315
2	300	273	217	247	275
3	365	265	245	287	360
4	309	241	259	299	351
5	361	356	265	211	395
6	375	295	212	305	365
7	325	312	265	276	342
8	322	352	287	311	425
9	326	301	269	264	294
10	305	354	301	265	317

days of the week with the largest and smallest numbers of absentees, and (3) the numbers of absentees and specific days with the most and least absentees.

The solution to this problem is outlined below. Several steps that relate to previously studied procedures, such as table searches, have been summarized as a single step for simplicity.

1. Dimension the day name array and absentee data array. The latter should be dimensioned to have an extra row and column to serve as total accumulators for weekly and daily totals.
2. Set the elements of the sixth column of the absentee data array (used for weekly totals) to zero.
3. Set all but the last element of the eleventh row of the absentee data array (used for daily totals) to zero. (Why all but the *last* element?)
4. Load the day name array.
5. Print main and column headings.
6. Load the absentee data array. As the data is read into the array, perform steps 7 to 9. When all data has been read, go to step 10.
7. Update weekly (row) totals and place the sums in the respective positions in the last column.
8. Update daily (column) totals and place the sums in the respective positions in the last row.
9. Update the sum of *all* absentees (all elements of the array) and place this sum in the last element of the last row (column).
10. Print the absentee array showing the week number and all totals.
11. Search the last column of the absentee data array to find the highest and lowest weekly numbers of absentees and the weeks in which they occurred.
12. Print the highest and lowest weekly total absentees along with the weeks in which they occurred.
13. Search the last row of the absentee data array to find the highest and lowest daily numbers of absentees and the days of the week on which they occurred.
14. Print the highest and lowest daily total absentees and the days of the week on which they occurred.
15. Search absentee array (except total row and column) to find the single days of highest and lowest absentees and the number absent on these days.
16. Print days of highest and lowest absentees and number absent on each day.
17. Stop.

This procedure is pictorially illustrated in detail by the flowchart in Figure 12-6.

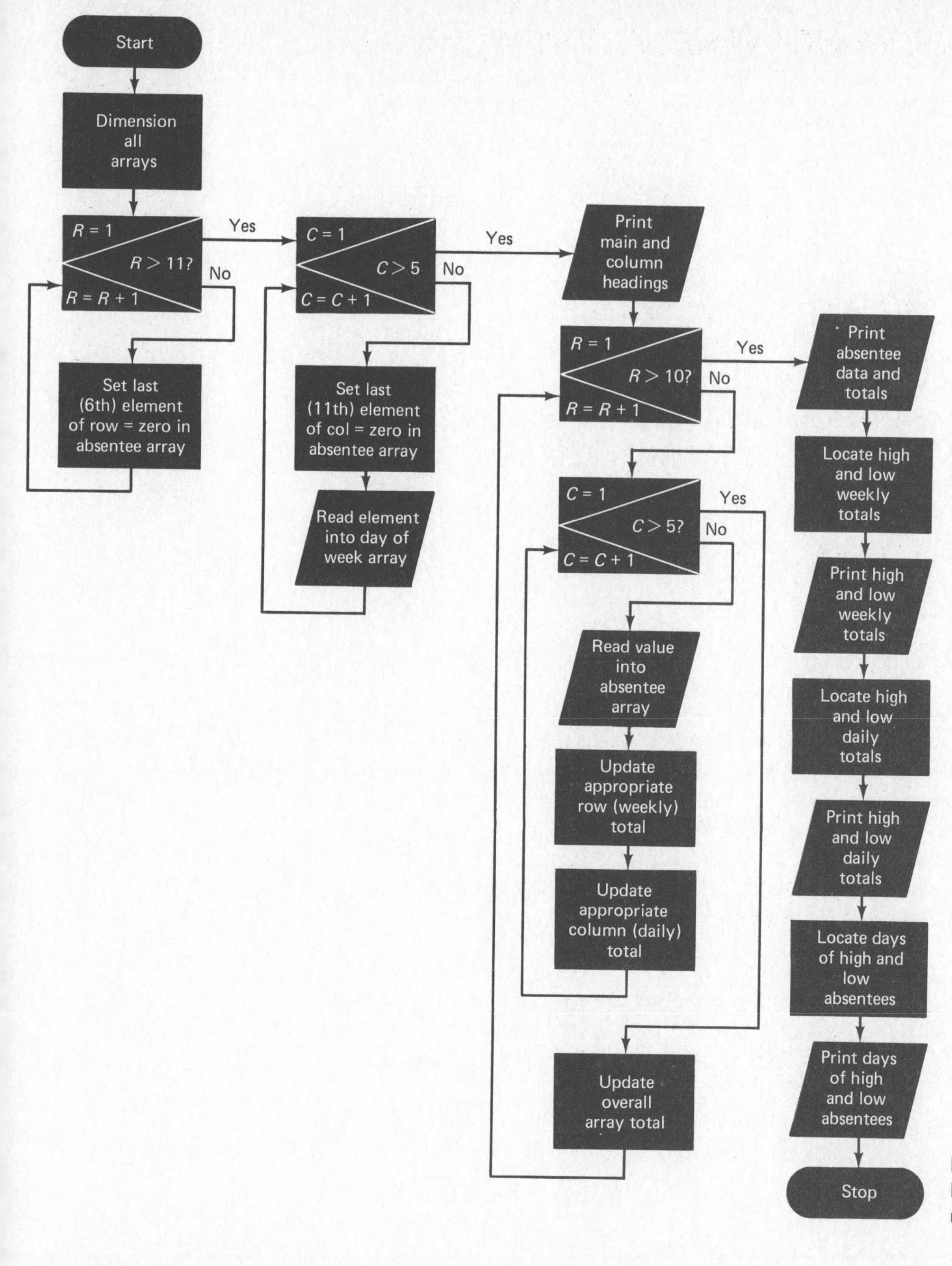

FIGURE 12-6
Flowchart for absentee analysis report example

This problem uses only two arrays as dimensioned at line 200.

```
200 DIM D$(5), A(11, 6)
```

D$ simply holds the names of the 5 days of the week. Array A will hold the absentee data which, as can be seen from Table 12-3, will require ten rows and five columns (a 10 by 5 array). We have dimensioned A as 11 by 6 to provide for an extra row and column for weekly and daily totals. Of course, this could have been done differently, with the sums being placed into one-dimensional arrays, say W and D. Then, line 200 would read:

```
200 DIM D$(5), A(10, 5), W(10), D(5)
```

with the overall total stored in a nonsubscripted variable. You may wish to use this alternative approach in other problems: however, for the present, the subject is *two-*

dimensional arrays; therefore, we will concentrate on techniques for data handling with that arrangement.

The row and column that will accumulate the totals are set to zero by lines 210 to 270.

```
210 FOR R = 1 TO 11
220    LET A(R, 6) = 0
230 NEXT R
240 FOR C = 1 TO 5
250    LET A(11, C) = 0
260    READ D$(C)
270 NEXT C
```

The first loop, lines 210 to 230, sets all elements of the *sixth* column to zero. Note that the column number is fixed at 6, and we step through the row numbers. This is done with a *single* loop as with a one-dimensional array. Lines 240 to 270 accomplish the same result for the elements of the *eleventh* row. Line 260 loads the day name array. This might have been placed in a separate loop; however, since both loops involved exactly *five* elements, one loop can do both jobs. We can do this at this point because we only have to take C up to 5. In the first loop, R went all the way to 11, so A(11, 6) was set to zero; thus we do not have to do it again in the second loop.

The next part of the program prints headings; this involves nothing new. The absentee data is loaded into the array and all totals accumulated by lines 450 to 520:

```
450 FOR R = 1 TO 10
460    FOR C = 1 TO 5
470       READ A(R, C)
480       LET A(R, 6) = A(R, 6) + A(R, C)
490       LET A(11, C) = A(11, C) + A(R, C)
500    NEXT C
510    LET A(11, 6) = A(11, 6) + A(R, 6)
520 NEXT R
```

This section is identical to lines 90 to 150 of the short program near the end of Section 12-4 *except that the* READ *statement has been incorporated into the loops with the statements that update the totals so that one set of loops performs double duty*. Note that the overall array total (line 510) is placed in the "last" array element at A(11, 6). The absentee data along with all of the totals (one array!) are printed at lines 560 to 660.

The search for the highest and lowest weekly absentee totals and the corresponding weeks is accomplished by the following set of statements:

```
700 LET HR = 1
710 LET LR = 1
720 LET H = A(1, 6)
730 LET L = A(1, 6)
740 FOR R = 2 TO 10
750    IF A(R, 6) <= H THEN 780
760    LET H = A(R, 6)
770    LET HR = R
780    IF A(R, 6) => L THEN 810
790    LET L = A(R, 6)
800    LET LR = R
810 NEXT R
```

If this looks familiar, it should. This is exactly the same procedure that we used to find the highest and lowest scores and the corresponding test subject area in the Placement Test Report example in Section 9-8. Because we are searching only the sixth column, we hold that fixed and vary only the row numbers; this is, again, like a one-dimensional process.

Note at line 740 that we search only to row 10 because there are only 10 weeks in the quarter. (If you do not remember the above procedure, stop here and review that portion of the example in Section 9-8.) The results of this search are printed at lines 850 to 900. Lines 940 to 1050 perform an identical search but for the daily totals in the last row. These results are printed by lines 1090 to 1130. Finally, lines 1170 to 1340 perform a search of the entire absentee data array (except for the total row and column) to find the time and number of the most and least absentees on a single day. The logic is the same as for the search routine previously used with the single exception that we now have to keep track of *two* subscripts. The nested FOR–NEXT loops step through the row *and* column subscripts; note that the upper limits on the loop counters do not include the last row or column. Within the inner loop, whenever a higher or lower value is found, we must keep track of both the row and column position; this is seen at lines 1270 and 1280 for higher values and at 1310 and 1320 for lower values. The results of this search are printed by lines 1380 to 1420.

Before leaving this example, a word regarding the printing of the report is in order. You have probably noted that the report was printed in pieces throughout the program. The headings were done at the beginning with each section of the report being printed as it was produced. This method was used here because it allowed certain variables, specifically those in the search routines, to be used more than once but with the same or similar meaning. This simplified matters somewhat by reducing the total number of variables of which we had to keep track. Clearly, the entire report could have been printed at one time at the end of the program. The only change that would be necessary to do this (other than moving the PRINT statements) would be to change the variables used to keep track of the high and low values and subscripts in the search routines so that there would be no duplications.

The complete program listing and a run are given below.

```
 10 REM   ABSENTEE ANALYSIS REPORT
 20 REM
 30 REM   VARIABLES ARE DEFINED AS --
 40 REM
 50 REM            D$ = DAYS OF WEEK ARRAY
 60 REM             A = NUMBER OF ABSENTEES ARRAY
 70 REM             R = ROW COUNTER
 80 REM             C = COLUMN COUNTER
 90 REM            HR = HIGH ROW MARKER
100 REM            LR = LOW ROW MARKER
110 REM            HC = HIGH COLUMN MARKER
120 REM            LC = LOW COLUMN MARKER
130 REM             H = HIGH VALUE MARKER
140 REM             L = LOW VALUE MARKER
150 REM
160 REM   DIMENSION ARRAYS.  SET LAST ROW AND COLUMN
170 REM   EQUAL TO ZERO TO SERVE AS TOTAL ACCUMULATORS.
180 REM   LOAD DAYS OF WEEK ARRAY.
190 REM
200 DIM D$(5), A(11, 6)
210 FOR R = 1 TO 11
220    LET A(R, 6) = 0
230 NEXT R
240 FOR C = 1 TO 5
250    LET A(11, C) = 0
260    READ D$(C)
270 NEXT C
280 REM
290 REM   PRINT HEADINGS
300 REM
310 PRINT TAB(28); "ABSENTEE ANALYSIS REPORT"
320 PRINT
```

```
330 PRINT
340 PRINT " WEEK"; TAB(28); "NUMBER OF ABSENTEES FOR";
350 PRINT TAB(73); "WEEKLY"
360 PRINT "NUMBER";
370 FOR C = 1 TO 5
380   PRINT TAB(12 * C); D$(C);
390 NEXT C
400 PRINT TAB(73); "TOTALS"
410 PRINT
420 REM
430 REM READ ABSENTEE DATA AND ACCUMULATE ALL TOTALS
440 REM
450 FOR R = 1 TO 10
460   FOR C = 1 TO 5
470     READ A(R, C)
480     LET A(R, 6) = A(R, 6) + A(R, C)
490     LET A(11, C) = A(11, C) + A(R, C)
500   NEXT C
510   LET A(11, 6) = A(11, 6) + A(R, 6)
520 NEXT R
530 REM
540 REM  PRINT ABSENTEE DATA AND TOTALS
550 REM
560 FOR R = 1 TO 11
570   IF R = 11 THEN 600
580   PRINT " "; R;
590   GOTO 620
600   PRINT
610   PRINT "TOTALS";
620   FOR C = 1 TO 6
630     PRINT TAB(12 * C + 1); A(R, C);
640   NEXT C
650   PRINT
660 NEXT R
670 REM
680 REM  LOCATE HIGHEST AND LOWEST WEEKLY TOTALS
690 REM
700 LET HR = 1
710 LET LR = 1
720 LET H = A(1, 6)
730 LET L = A(1, 6)
740 FOR R = 2 TO 10
750   IF A(R, 6) <= H THEN 780
760   LET H = A(R, 6)
770   LET HR = R
780   IF A(R, 6) => L THEN 810
790   LET L = A(R, 6)
800   LET LR = R
810 NEXT R
820 REM
830 REM  PRINT HIGHEST AND LOWEST WEEKLY TOTALS
840 REM
850 PRINT
860 PRINT
870 PRINT "LARGEST WEEKLY TOTAL OF ABSENTEES --"; H;
880 PRINT "-- OCCURRED ON WEEK NUMBER"; HR
890 PRINT "SMALLEST WEEKLY TOTAL OF ABSENTEES --"; L;
900 PRINT "-- OCCURRED ON WEEK NUMBER"; LR
910 REM
920 REM  LOCATE HIGHEST AND LOWEST DAILY TOTALS
930 REM
940 LET HC = 1
950 LET LC = 1
```

```
 960 LET H = A(11, 1)
 970 LET L = A(11, 1)
 980 FOR C = 2 TO 5
 990   IF A(11, C) <= H THEN 1020
1000   LET H = A(11, C)
1010   LET HC = C
1020   IF A(11, C) => L THEN 1050
1030   LET L = A(11, C)
1040   LET LC = C
1050 NEXT C
1060 REM
1070 REM  PRINT HIGHEST AND LOWEST DAILY TOTALS
1080 REM
1090 PRINT
1100 PRINT "LARGEST TOTAL BY DAY OF ABSENTEES --";
1110 PRINT H; "-- OCCURRED ON "; D$(HC)
1120 PRINT "SMALLEST TOTAL BY DAY OF ABSENTEES --";
1130 PRINT L; "-- OCCURRED ON "; D$(LC)
1140 REM
1150 REM  LOCATE DAYS OF HIGHEST AND LOWEST ABSENTEES
1160 REM
1170 LET HR = 1
1180 LET LR = 1
1190 LET HC = 1
1200 LET LC = 1
1210 LET H = A(1, 1)
1220 LET L = A(1, 1)
1230 FOR R = 1 TO 10
1240   FOR C = 1 TO 5
1250     IF A(R, C) <= H THEN 1290
1260     LET H = A(R, C)
1270     LET HR = R
1280     LET HC = C
1290     IF A(R, C) => L THEN 1330
1300     LET L = A(R, C)
1310     LET LR = R
1320     LET LC = C
1330   NEXT C
1340 NEXT R
1350 REM
1360 REM  PRINT DAYS OF HIGHEST AND LOWEST ABSENTEES
1370 REM
1380 PRINT
1390 PRINT "MOST ABSENTEES ON ONE DAY --"; H;
1400 PRINT "-- OCCURRED ON "; D$(HC); " OF WEEK NUMBER"; HR
1410 PRINT "LEAST ABSENTEES ON ONE DAY --"; L;
1420 PRINT "-- OCCURRED ON "; D$(LC); " OF WEEK NUMBER"; LR
1430 REM
1440 REM  DATA FOR DAYS OF WEEK ARRAY
1450 REM
1460 DATA "MONDAY","TUESDAY","WEDNESDAY","THURSDAY","FRIDAY"
1470 REM
1480 REM  ABSENTEE DATA LIST TO BE PROCESSED
1490 REM
1500 DATA 329,349,220,246,315,300,273,217,247,275
1510 DATA 365,265,245,287,360,309,241,259,299,351
1520 DATA 361,356,265,211,395,375,295,212,305,365
1530 DATA 325,312,265,276,342,322,352,287,311,425
1540 DATA 326,301,269,264,294,305,354,301,265,317
1550 END
```

```
                              ABSENTEE ANALYSIS REPORT

 WEEK                         NUMBER OF ABSENTEES FOR                              WEEKLY
NUMBER      MONDAY       TUESDAY      WEDNESDAY    THURSDAY      FRIDAY            TOTALS

  1          329          349           220          246           315              1459
  2          300          273           217          247           275              1312
  3          365          265           245          287           360              1522
  4          309          241           259          299           351              1459
  5          361          356           265          211           395              1588
  6          375          295           212          305           365              1552
  7          325          312           265          276           342              1520
  8          322          352           287          311           425              1697
  9          326          301           269          264           294              1454
  10         305          354           301          265           317              1542

TOTALS       3317         3098          2540         2711          3439             15105


LARGEST WEEKLY TOTAL OF ABSENTEES -- 1697 -- OCCURRED ON WEEK NUMBER 8
SMALLEST WEEKLY TOTAL OF ABSENTEES -- 1312 -- OCCURRED ON WEEK NUMBER 2

LARGEST TOTAL BY DAY OF ABSENTEES -- 3439 -- OCCURRED ON FRIDAY
SMALLEST NUMBER BY DAY OF ABSENTEES -- 2540 -- OCCURRED ON WEDNESDAY

MOST ABSENTEES ON ONE DAY -- 425 -- OCCURRED ON FRIDAY OF WEEK NUMBER 8
LEAST ABSENTEES ON ONE DAY -- 211 -- OCCURRED ON THURSDAY OF WEEK NUMBER 5
```

12-6 INPUT/OUTPUT WITH MAT STATEMENTS

Many versions of BASIC provide a special set of statements collectively referred to as **MAT** (for MATrix) statements. A **matrix** may be thought of as any two-dimensional array. For most of the special matrix operations described in the next section, the arrays *must* be numeric; however, for simple input or output of data, the matrix (array) may be string.

There are three special MAT statements for input or output of data. These are **MAT READ**, **MAT INPUT**, and **MAT PRINT** as shown in Table 12-4 along with their analo-

TABLE 12-4

MAT Input/Output Statements

MAT Form	Manual Form
120 MAT READ X	100 FOR R = 1 TO 3 110 FOR C = 1 TO 4 120 READ X(R, C) 130 NEXT C 140 NEXT R
120 MAT INPUT X	100 FOR R = 1 TO 3 110 FOR C = 1 TO 4 120 INPUT X(R, C) 130 NEXT C 140 NEXT R
220 MAT PRINT X	200 FOR R = 1 TO 3 210 FOR C = 1 TO 4 220 PRINT X(R, C) 230 NEXT C 240 NEXT R

gous "manual" statements. (Some BASICs also provide a MAT PRINT USING.) As can be seen from the table, each MAT statement performs the same function as stepping through the array, subscript by subscript, using the nested FOR–NEXT loops. Note that the MAT statements reference the entire array with no need for subscripts. However, with this convenience, we must sacrifice a little flexibility in that all three of the statements shown in Table 12-4 *always process the data in* ***row-priority*** *order*. The convenience of the statements will become more apparent as we continue through this and the next section; however, as a first look, consider the following simple program:

```
 10 REM   INPUT/OUTPUT WITHOUT MAT STATEMENTS
 30 DIM X(3, 4)
 40 FOR R = 1 TO 3
 50    FOR C = 1 TO 4
 60       READ X(R, C)
 70    NEXT C
 80 NEXT R
 90 FOR R = 1 TO 3
100    FOR C = 1 TO 4
110       PRINT X(R, C)
120    NEXT C
130 NEXT R
140 DATA 23,54,12,-7
150 DATA 14,8,-11,43
160 DATA 3,13,-27,15
170 END
```

Using the MAT statements, this can be written as:

```
 10 REM   INPUT/OUTPUT WITH MAT STATEMENTS
 20 REM
 30 DIM X(3, 4)
 60 MAT READ X
110 MAT PRINT X
140 DATA 23,54,12,-7
150 DATA 14,8,-11,43
160 DATA 3,13,-27,15
170 END
```

These two programs will give exactly the same output.

More than one array name can appear in the variable list of any one of the above three MAT statements; however, in such a case, the data is read or printed in a different way than with nested FOR–NEXT loops. Suppose that we wish to read data into three arrays, A, B, and C. To do this using the MAT READ (or MAT INPUT) statement, we simply write:

```
100 MAT READ A, B, C
```

This will read *all* of the elements of A, then all of B, and finally all of C. The data must be listed in that order with the elements of A first, B second, and C third, all in row-priority order. It is not necessary that the arrays all be of the same size for this procedure to be used. To do this with FOR–NEXT loops would be somewhat more complex (see Section 12-2).

The MAT PRINT statement at line 110 of the above program:

```
110 MAT PRINT X
```

will print X in row-priority order with one element to a print line. If the statement is terminated with a comma as:

```
110 MAT PRINT X,
```

then X will be printed with one *row* to a print line. If there are more elements in a row than print zones, then the extra items will be "reflected" back to the next print line as described in Section 3-5. Ending the MAT PRINT statement with a semicolon has a similar effect except that the elements of X are printed in a *compact* format.

More than one array can be printed by a single MAT PRINT statement. The statement:

```
MAT PRINT A, B, C
```

will print all elements of A with one element to a line, then B, then C in the same way. Ending the statement with a comma:

```
MAT PRINT A, B, C,
```

will cause the three arrays to be printed in the same order but in *rows*. Some BASICs will automatically insert a blank line between each array in the print list.

As a final note on MAT input/output, the above MAT statements can be used to read or print one-dimensional arrays, even in the same list with two-dimensional ones. However, as noted in Section 12-2, when MAT statements are used with a one-dimensional array, it is treated as a row vector; that is, as if it is a two-dimensional array with a single row.

12-7 MAT OPERATIONS AND FUNCTIONS

There are a number of special **MAT operations** and **functions** that are available for working with *numeric* arrays as matrices. This section will be devoted to a quick description of the most commonly used matrix operations and functions. For many of the operations, a manual form using FOR–NEXT loops is provided for comparison. Most of the background relating to matrix operations that you will need will be outlined in this section as we go along. However, if you are not already familiar with matrix operations or if you feel that you need some review, you may wish to consult an elementary math text for a more detailed discussion. Ask an instructor in the math department for an appropriate reference.

Two MAT functions, **ZER** and **CON**, are similar. ZER is used to set all elements of a matrix equal to zero, while CON sets all elements equal to one. Both functions are very easy to use. The matrix V is set to zero and F to one, by

```
140  MAT V = ZER
150  MAT F = CON
```

The matrices V and F will then be something like the following:

$$V = \begin{bmatrix} 0 & 0 & 0 & 0 \\ 0 & 0 & 0 & 0 \\ 0 & 0 & 0 & 0 \end{bmatrix} \quad \text{and} \quad F = \begin{bmatrix} 1 & 1 & 1 & 1 & 1 \\ 1 & 1 & 1 & 1 & 1 \end{bmatrix}$$

Of course, whatever was stored in V or F is now lost.

In Section 12-2, we saw how to form the transpose of an array. The function **TRN** generates the transpose of a matrix. The following statement gives T as the transpose of X:

```
150  MAT T = TRN(X)
```

Using the array for X given in Section 12-2, we have:

$$X = \begin{bmatrix} 23 & 54 & 12 & -7 \\ 14 & 8 & -11 & 43 \\ 3 & 13 & -27 & 15 \end{bmatrix} \quad \text{and} \quad T = \text{TRN}(X) = \begin{bmatrix} 32 & 14 & 3 \\ 54 & 8 & 13 \\ 12 & -11 & -27 \\ -7 & 43 & 15 \end{bmatrix}$$

Rows and columns are simply switched. Compare this to X and T as shown in Figures 12-2 and 12-3.

The fourth MAT function, **IDN**, creates an **identity matrix** that has ones along the **diagonal** (row number = column number) and zeros elsewhere. This function defines an identity matrix by:

```
430  MAT I = IDN
```

which generates a matrix I of the form:

$$I = \begin{bmatrix} 1 & 0 & 0 & 0 \\ 0 & 1 & 0 & 0 \\ 0 & 0 & 1 & 0 \\ 0 & 0 & 0 & 1 \end{bmatrix}$$

Obviously, an identity matrix must always be **square**; that is, it must have the same number of rows as columns. The identity matrix plays a similar role in matrix operations to that of the number 1 in regular arithmetic. Table 12-5 illustrates these four MAT functions and their equivalent FOR–NEXT loops.

TABLE 12-5

MAT Functions

MAT Form	Manual Form
120 MAT V = ZER	100 FOR R = 1 TO 3 110 FOR C = 1 TO 4 120 LET V(R, C) = 0 130 NEXT C 140 NEXT R
100 MAT F = CON	80 FOR L = 1 TO 5 90 FOR N = 1 TO 3 100 LET F(L, N) = 1 110 NEXT N 120 NEXT L
150 MAT T = TRN(X)	130 FOR R = 1 TO 3 140 FOR C = 1 TO 4 150 LET T(C, R) = X(R, C) 160 NEXT C 170 NEXT R
430 MAT I = IDN	410 FOR J = 1 TO 10 420 FOR K = 1 TO 10 430 LET I(J, K) = 0 440 IF J = K THEN LET I(J, K) = 1 450 NEXT K 460 NEXT J

One matrix can be set equal to another by the statement:

```
260 MAT R = W
```

which makes R identical to W. The statement:

```
375 MAT H = K * G
```

where H and G are matrices and K is a numeric constant causes all elements of matrix H to be multiples of those of G, with K being the multiplier. Thus, if G is given by:

$$G = \begin{bmatrix} 3 & 5 & 2 & 6 \\ 1 & 0 & 3 & -2 \\ 8 & -4 & 1 & 4 \end{bmatrix}$$

and K is 3, then H will be:

$$H = 3 \times G = \begin{bmatrix} 3 \times 3 & 3 \times 5 & 3 \times 2 & 3 \times 6 \\ 3 \times 1 & 3 \times 0 & 3 \times 3 & 3 \times (-2) \\ 3 \times 8 & 3 \times (-4) & 3 \times 1 & 3 \times 4 \end{bmatrix} = \begin{bmatrix} 9 & 15 & 6 & 18 \\ 3 & 0 & 9 & -6 \\ 24 & -12 & 3 & 12 \end{bmatrix}$$

Two matrices, A and B, can be added (**matrix addition**) or subtracted (**matrix subtraction**), forming sum and difference matrices, S and D, as follows:

```
240 MAT S = A + B
360 MAT D = A - B
```

Each element of S will be the sum of the corresponding elements of A and B, while the elements of D are the difference of those of A and B. For example, suppose that A and B are:

$$A = \begin{bmatrix} 2 & 7 \\ 4 & 3 \\ 1 & -5 \end{bmatrix} \quad \text{and} \quad B = \begin{bmatrix} 4 & 0 \\ 5 & -2 \\ 6 & 1 \end{bmatrix}$$

then S and D are found as follows:

$$S = A + B = \begin{bmatrix} 2 + 4 & 7 + 0 \\ 4 + 5 & 3 + (-2) \\ 1 + 6 & -5 + 1 \end{bmatrix} = \begin{bmatrix} 6 & 7 \\ 9 & 1 \\ 7 & -4 \end{bmatrix}$$

and

$$D = A - B = \begin{bmatrix} 2 - 4 & 7 - 0 \\ 4 - 5 & 3 - (-2) \\ 1 - 6 & -5 - 1 \end{bmatrix} = \begin{bmatrix} -2 & 7 \\ -1 & 5 \\ -5 & -6 \end{bmatrix}$$

Clearly, these last four operations require that all matrices within a given MAT statement be dimensioned exactly the same way. For example, S, A, and B must all have the same number of rows and the same number of columns. Several matrix operations are illustrated in Table 12-6 along with their manual counterparts.

TABLE 12-6

MAT Operations

MAT Form	Manual Form
220 MAT R = W	200 FOR J = 1 TO 12 210 FOR K = 1 TO 7 220 LET R(J, K) = W(J, K) 230 NEXT K 240 NEXT J
340 MAT H = K * G	320 FOR X = 1 TO 6 330 FOR Y = 1 TO 4 340 LET H(X, Y) = K * G(X, Y) 350 NEXT Y 360 NEXT X
210 MAT S = A + B	190 FOR R = 1 TO 5 200 FOR C = 1 TO 8 210 LET S(R, C) = A(R, C) + B(R, C) 220 NEXT C 230 NEXT R
210 MAT D = A - B	190 FOR R = 1 TO 9 200 FOR C = 1 TO 15 210 LET D(R, C) = A(R, C) - B(R, C) 220 NEXT C 230 NEXT R
540 MAT P = N * M	510 FOR R = 1 TO 3 520 FOR C = 1 TO 2 530 FOR E = 1 TO 4 540 LET P(R, C) = P(R, C) + N(R, E) * M(E, C) 550 NEXT E 560 NEXT C 570 NEXT R

Now we come to the product of two matrices (**matrix multiplication**). Suppose that we wish to multiply the matrices N and M to get P. The MAT statement for this is:

```
540 MAT P = N * M
```

This is *not* simply the product of the corresponding elements of the two matrices to be multiplied. Unfortunately, it is somewhat more complex. The elements of the product matrix P are found by multiplying rows from the first matrix by columns of the second, element by element, and summing the individual products. Thus, P(R, C) would be row R from N times column C from M, with each element of the row from N being multiplied by its corresponding element from the column in M. Clearly, N must have the same number of *columns* as M has *rows*. The product matrix will have the number of rows that N has and the number of columns of M. In general, we can write:

$$P(J, L) = N(J, K) \times M(K, L)$$

Let us look at an example. Consider matrices N and M given by:

$$N = \begin{bmatrix} 1 & 4 & 2 & -3 \\ 5 & 0 & 2 & 3 \\ 3 & -2 & 1 & 4 \end{bmatrix} \quad \text{and} \quad M = \begin{bmatrix} 3 & 6 \\ -4 & 2 \\ 7 & 0 \\ 5 & 3 \end{bmatrix}$$

The product P is given by:

$$P = N \times M = \begin{bmatrix} 1 \times 3 + 4 \times (-4) + 2 \times 7 + (-3) \times 5 & 1 \times 6 + 4 \times 2 + 2 \times 0 + (-3) \times 3 \\ 5 \times 3 + 0 \times (-4) + 2 \times 7 + 3 \times 5 & 5 \times 6 + 0 \times 2 + 2 \times 0 + 3 \times 3 \\ 3 \times 3 + (-2) \times (-4) + 1 \times 7 + 4 \times 5 & 3 \times 6 + (-2) \times 2 + 1 \times 0 + 4 \times 3 \end{bmatrix}$$

which, when the arithmetic is computed, gives:

$$P = \begin{bmatrix} -14 & 5 \\ 44 & 39 \\ 44 & 26 \end{bmatrix}$$

Note that while matrix addition and subtraction may be done in any order, multiplication may not. In fact, unless the matrices are square, they will multiply only in one way.

Division of two matrices cannot be done directly. We can, however, find the **inverse** of a matrix by using the **INV** function.

```
220  MAT Z = INV(L)
```

This gives a matrix Z which is the inverse of L. That is, if we multiply L times Z, we will get the identity matrix. (This is analogous to multiplying a number, such as 5, by its multiplicative inverse, 1/5, to get 1.) Therefore, if we wish to divide matrix H by matrix L, we would first find the inverse of L (call it Z) and multiply this by H. This would be done by the following two MAT statements:

```
330  MAT Z = INV(L)
340  MAT D = H * Z
```

(Remember that H and Z may multiply in only one way.)

As an example of the use of matrices in the solution of a problem, let us find the values of x, y, and z that satisfy the following system of linear equations:

$$\begin{aligned} x + 8y - 3z &= 17 \\ 4x - 2y + z &= 8 \\ 2x - 7y + 5z &= -11 \end{aligned}$$

The left sides of all three equations can be written as the product of a square (3 by 3) matrix C that contains the coefficients of the variables and a column vector V containing x, y, and z. The right sides would be a single column vector D containing 17, 8, and -11. In matrix form, the above equations would be:

$$\begin{bmatrix} X + 8Y - 3Z \\ 4X - 2Y + Z \\ 2X - 7Y + 5Z \end{bmatrix} = \begin{bmatrix} 1 & 8 & -3 \\ 4 & -2 & 1 \\ 2 & -7 & 5 \end{bmatrix} \times \begin{bmatrix} X \\ Y \\ Z \end{bmatrix} = \begin{bmatrix} 17 \\ 8 \\ -11 \end{bmatrix}$$

The values of x, y, and z can then be found from V by multiplying D by the *inverse* of C. That is $C \times V = D$ or $V = C^{-1} \times D$. (C^{-1} represents C inverse.) The following program will solve the above system of equations for x, y, and z:

```
10 REM  SOLVING A SYSTEM OF 3 LINEAR EQUATIONS
20 REM
30 DIM C(3, 3), V(3, 1), D(3, 1)
40 MAT READ C, D
50 MAT I = INV(C)
```

```
60 MAT V = I * D
70 MAT PRINT V
80 DATA 1,8,-3,4,-2,1,2,-7,5,17,8,-11
90 END
```

The output will be:

```
 3
 1
-2
```

(If you have ever solved such a system by one of the several longer algebraic methods, you will very much appreciate the power afforded by the above short program!)

Before ending our discussion of MAT operations, it should be mentioned that some MAT statements and functions permit an array to be redimensioned. For example, the following MAT READ:

```
100  DIM A(12, 15)
              :
220  MAT READ A(10, 12)
```

will cause A to be redimensioned to 10 by 12 at line 220 as it is read. If an array is redimensioned, the new dimensions apply to all following uses of that array until it is again redimensioned by another MAT operation. The MAT INPUT statement and the ZER, CON, and IDN functions can also be used to redimension arrays. When redimensioning an array with a MAT statement or function, the subscript(s) may be any numeric constant, variable, or mathematical expression. (Redimensioning is tricky, and caution is advised with regard to its use. It can lead to unexpected difficulties for the inexperienced programmer.)

TROUBLESHOOTING

Each of the following programs contains an error that prevents it from executing properly. Explain *specifically* what the problem is and what must be done to correct it. To assist you, a sample of what would happen should you attempt to run the program is provided after each listing. Refer to Appendix D for an explanation of BASIC error messages.

1.

```
 10 REM  TROUBLESHOOTING PROBLEM 12-1
 20 REM
 30 REM        A = AN ARRAY
 40 REM
 50 DIM A(4, 5)
 60 FOR R = 1 TO 5
 70   FOR C = 1 TO 4
 80     READ A(R, C)
 90   NEXT C
100 NEXT R
110 FOR R = 1 TO 5
120   FOR C = 1 TO 4
130     PRINT A(R, C)
140   NEXT C
150 NEXT R
160 DATA 2,5,4,7,3,-5,4,-2,1,5
170 DATA 1,8,6,-5,4,3,3,3,2,-7
180 END

Subscript Out of Range in Line 80
```

2.

```
 10 REM  TROUBLESHOOTING PROBLEM 12-2
 20 REM
 30 REM       S$ = STUDENT NAME ARRAY
 40 REM        G = GRADE ARRAY
 50 REM
 60 DIM S$(4), G(4, 3)
 70 FOR R = 1 TO 4
 80   READ S$(R)
 90   FOR C = 1 TO 3
100     READ G(R, C)
110   NEXT C
120 NEXT R
130 FOR R = 1 TO 4
140   PRINT S$(R),
150   FOR C = 1 TO 3
160     PRINT G(R, C),
170   NEXT C
180 NEXT R
190 DATA "T SMITH",77,85,92
200 DATA "R LEWIS",64,86,73
210 DATA "W JONES",93,89,95
220 DATA "M KELLY",78,66,83
230 END
```

```
T SMITH        77             85             92             R LEWIS
 64            86             73            W JONES          93
 89            95            M KELLY         78              66
 83
```

3.

```
 10 REM  TROUBLESHOOTING PROBLEM 12-3
 20 REM
 30 REM       S$ = STUDENT NAME ARRAY
 40 REM        G = GRADE ARRAY
 50 REM        A = AVERAGE GRADE ARRAY
 60 REM
 70 DIM S$(4), G(4, 3), A(4)
 80 FOR J = 1 TO 4
 90   READ S$(J)
100   FOR K = 1 TO 3
110     READ G(J, K)
120     LET A(K) = A(K) + G(J, K) / 3
130   NEXT K
140 NEXT J
150 FOR X = 1 TO 4
160   PRINT S$(X),
170   FOR Y = 1 TO 3
180     PRINT G(X, Y),
190   NEXT Y
200   PRINT A(X)
210 NEXT X
220 DATA "T SMITH",77,85,92
230 DATA "E LEWIS",64,86,73
240 DATA "W JONES",93,89,95
250 DATA "M KELLY",78,66,83
260 END
```

```
T SMITH        77             85             92             104
E LEWIS        64             86             73             108.667
W JONES        93             89             95             114.333
M KELLY        78             66             83             0
```

4.

```
 10 REM  TROUBLESHOOTING PROBLEM 12-4
 20 REM
 30 REM       C$ = TYPE CAR ARRAY
 40 REM        M = MILES DRIVEN ARRAY
 50 REM        T = TOTAL MILES DRIVEN ARRAY
 60 REM       HM = HIGHEST TOTAL MILES DRIVEN
 70 REM       LM = LOWEST TOTAL MILES DRIVEN
 80 REM       HA = HIGH MILES TOTAL MARKER
 90 REM       LA = LOW MILES TOTAL MARKER
100 REM
110 DIM C$(4), M(4, 4)
120 FOR J = 1 TO 4
130   READ C$(J)
140   FOR K = 1 TO 3
150     READ M(J, K)
160     LET M(J, 4) = M(J, 4) + M(J, K)
170   NEXT K
180 NEXT J
190 LET HA = 1
200 LET LA = 1
210 LET HM = M(1, 1)
220 LET LM = M(1, 1)
230 FOR A = 1 TO 4
240   FOR B = 1 TO 4
250     IF M(A, B) <= HM THEN 280
260     LET HM = M(A, B)
270     LET HA = A
280     IF M(A, B) => LM THEN 310
290     LET LM = M(A, B)
300     LET LA = A
310   NEXT B
320 NEXT A
330 PRINT "LOWEST TOTAL MILES DRIVEN IS"; LM;
340 PRINT "BY THE "; C$(LA)
350 PRINT "HIGHEST TOTAL MILES DRIVEN IS"; HM;
360 PRINT "BY THE "; C$(HA)
370 DATA "CHEVROLET",239,316,277
380 DATA "DODGE", 198,266,381
390 DATA "MERCURY",288,192,411
400 DATA "FORD",215,258,402
410 END

LOWEST TOTAL MILES DRIVEN IS 192 BY THE MERCURY
HIGHEST TOTAL MILES DRIVEN IS 891 BY THE MERCURY
```

5.

```
 10 REM  TROUBLESHOOTING PROBLEM 12-5
 20 REM
 30 REM          A = A MATRIX
 40 REM          B = ANOTHER MATRIX
 50 REM          T = TRANSPOSE OF B
 60 REM          P = PRODUCT OF A AND T
 70 REM
 80 DIM A(3, 5), B(3, 2), T(2, 3), P(2, 5)
 90 MAT READ A, B
100 MAT T = TRN(B)
110 MAT P = A * T
120 MAT PRINT P
130 DATA 3,6,5,2,-8,7,6,11,-3,4
140 DATA 1,0,3,5,0,-2,5,1,1,7,2
150 END

Illegal MAT Operation in Line 110
```

IMPORTANT TERMS

After studying this chapter, you should be familiar with the meaning and use of the following terms and BASIC statements:

Two-dimensional array
Row
Column
Row vector
Column vector
Row-priority order
Column-priority order
Transpose of array (or matrix)
Summing by rows
Summing by columns
Searching by rows
Searching by columns
Matrix
MAT statements
MAT READ
MAT INPUT
MAT PRINT
MAT operations
MAT functions
ZER function
CON function
TRN function
IDN function
Identity matrix
Diagonal of a matrix
Square matrix
Matrix addition
Matrix subtraction
Multiplying a matrix by a numeric constant
Matrix multiplication
INV function
Inverse of a matrix
Redimensioning an array with MAT operations

EXERCISES

1. Write DIM statements to dimension the following arrays:
   (a) A that is 5 by 7 and T with 15 elements.
   (b) B$ with 25 elements, Y with 9 rows and 14 columns, and JP with 30 rows and 3 columns.
   (c) F with 12 rows and 20 columns, a row vector V with 16 elements, and a square array SQ with 6 rows.
   (d) A column vector C with 12 elements, S with 8 rows and 12 columns, and the transpose of S.
   (e) A square array Q with 12 columns, X with 4 rows and 8 columns, Y with 8 rows and 6 columns, and Z that is the matrix product of X and Y.
2. Write BASIC statements to perform the following tasks:
   (a) Read an array with 5 rows and 15 columns.
   (b) Print columns 1, 3, 5, and 7 of a 4 by 7 array.
   (c) Place zeros in the first row of a 12 by 16 array.
   (d) Add the elements of the ninth row of a 15 by 12 array.
   (e) Add all *positive* elements of a 6 by 9 array.
   (f) Count the zeros in a 20 by 30 array.
   (g) Find the largest element in the third column of a 9 by 7 array.
   (h) Add the elements along the diagonal of a square array.
   (i) Find the product of any matrix and its transpose.
   (j) Print a 9 by 9 array with two digits to indicate the row and column number of each element.
3. Determine whether or not each of the following pairs of matrices can be multiplied and, if so, the dimensions of the product matrix.
   (a) V(2, 4) and R(4, 3)
   (b) A(2, 5) and B(3, 5)
   (c) F(4, 7) and H(7, 11)
   (d) K(6, 4) and P(3, 6)

For Exercises 4 to 8, give the output that will be produced by the given programs. Then, type the programs into the computer, run them, and check the actual outputs against your predictions.

4.
```
 10 DIM A(4, 5)
 20 FOR J = 1 TO 4
 30   FOR K = 1 TO 5
 40     READ A(J, K)
 50   NEXT K
 60 NEXT J
 70 FOR J = 1 TO 5
 80   FOR K = 1 TO 4
 90     PRINT A(K, J),
100   NEXT K
110   PRINT
120 NEXT J
130 DATA 2,5,4,6,3,4,-2,5,7,-5
140 DATA 1,9,-7,4,4,2,6,-1,0,3
150 END
```

5.
```
 10 DIM T(5, 4), S(5)
 20 FOR J = 1 TO 5
 30   FOR K = 1 TO 4
 40     READ T(J, K)
 50     LET S(J) = S(J) + T(J, K)
 60   NEXT K
 70 NEXT J
 80 FOR J = 1 TO 5
 90   FOR K = 1 TO 4
100     PRINT T(J, K),
110   NEXT K
120   PRINT S(J)
130 NEXT J
140 DATA 2,5,4,6,3,4,-2,5,7,-5
150 DATA 1,9,-7,4,4,2,6,-1,0,3
160 END
```

6.
```
 10 DIM T(6, 5)
 20 FOR J = 1 TO 5
 30   FOR K = 1 TO 4
 40     READ T(J, K)
 50     LET T(J, 5) = T(J, 5) + T(J, K)
 60     LET T(6, K) = T(6, K) + T(J, K)
 70   NEXT K
 80   LET T(6, 5) = T(6, 5) + T(J, 5)
 90 NEXT J
100 FOR J = 1 TO 6
110   FOR K = 1 TO 5
120     PRINT T(J, K),
130   NEXT K
140 NEXT J
150 DATA 2,5,4,6,3,4,-2,5,7,-5
160 DATA 1,9,-7,4,4,2,6,-1,0,3
170 END
```

7.
```
 10 DIM D(6, 4)
 20 FOR N = 1 TO 6
 30   FOR M = 1 TO 4
 40     READ D(N, M)
 50   NEXT M
 60 NEXT N
 70 LET HN = 1
 80 LET LN = 1
 90 LET HN = 1
100 LET LM = 1
110 LET HD = D(1, 1)
120 LET LD = D(1, 1)
130 FOR N = 1 TO 6
140   FOR M = 1 TO 4
```

```
150     IF D(N, M) <= HD THEN 190
160     LET HD = D(N, M)
170     LET HN = N
180     LET HM = M
190     IF D(N, M) => LD THEN 230
200     LET LD = D(N, M)
210     LET LN = N
220     LET LM = M
230     NEXT M
240 NEXT N
250 PRINT "LOWEST VALUE IS "; LD;
260 PRINT "AT ROW"; LN; "AND COLUMN"; LM
270 PRINT "HIGHEST VALUE IS"; HD;
280 PRINT "AT ROW"; HN; "AND COLUMN"; HM
290 DATA 4,6,3,-8,6,5,3,8,-5,3,11,4
300 DATA 6,0,3,-1,5,6,5,-9,7,1,-5,3
310 END
```

8.
```
10 DIM A(2, 3), B(2, 3)
20 DIM S(2, 3), T(3, 2), P(2, 2)
30 MAT READ A, B
40 MAT S = A + B
50 MAT T = TRN(B)
60 MAT P = A * T
70 MAT PRINT S, P
80 DATA 2,4,1,3,-2,3,5,-3,0,4,2,3
90 END
```

PROGRAMMING PROBLEMS

Write programs in BASIC to accomplish the tasks described by each of the following problems. Be sure to carefully document each program and include all appropriate report headings and other literals.

1. Write a program that will store the products of the row and column numbers in the elements of a 12 by 12 array. Print the array so that one row will fit on one print line.
2. The array that you constructed for Problem 1 can be used for constructing a multiplication table. Revise your program to include an appropriate heading for a 12 by 12 multiplication table and to show the two numbers that are being multiplied. This means printing column numbers across the top of the table and row numbers down the left side.
3. Write a program to set up a 7 by 5 array and use the random number function to place random numbers in each element of the array. Print the array with one row to a line.
4. Revise your program for Problem 3 to accumulate the sums of the rows and columns and store these in an extra column and row in the same array. Print the resulting array with one row to a line.
5. Employees at a certain factory are paid at an hourly rate according to the following table:

Shift Code	Experience Factors					
	1	2	3	4	5	6
1	5.50	6.00	6.75	7.50	8.50	9.74
2	5.75	6.50	7.50	8.50	9.75	11.00
3	6.00	7.00	8.25	9.50	10.75	12.25

Write a program to process the data below and print each employee's name, shift code, experience factor, hourly rate, hours worked, and total pay to include overtime for all hours over 40.

Employee Name	Shift Code	Experience Factor	Hours Worked
A. R. Phillips	2	3	38
T. N. Smith	1	4	44
L. A. Fuller	2	2	40
T. T. Bowen	3	5	37
P. B. Davison	1	1	40
L. C. Greene	1	4	45
H. A. Sutton	3	3	32
R. D. Carson	1	2	39
F. S. Johnson	2	6	43
T. C. Kingwood	3	1	38

6. A certain wholesale electronics company makes several special items, most of which are available with three possible voltage adapter options. The cost of each item with the various adapters is shown below. A −1 indicates that an item is not available with that particular adapter.

Item Description	12 VDC	110 VAC	220 VAC
B/W 12" TV	89.50	79.50	79.50
Color 5" TV	339.00	325.00	325.00
Emergency Light	35.00	45.00	−1
S/W Radio	219.50	235.00	235.00
12" B/W Monitor	−1	125.00	125.00
Portable Stereo	155.00	170.00	−1

The program that is needed is to process the orders for one day and produce a Daily Sales Report. Input will be the item number (as row number), voltage option (as column number), and number of items ordered. Detailed lines should be printed showing the item description, voltage, unit price, quantity ordered, and total cost. If an item is not available with the requested voltage, the message VOLTAGE NOT AVAILABLE should appear on the line following the description. If more than 10 of any one item are ordered, a 10 percent discount is given. Input data is provided below.

Item Number	Voltage Option	Quantity Ordered	Item Number	Voltage Option	Quantity Ordered
1	2	16	2	1	8
6	2	18	5	3	1
4	2	5	3	1	24
6	1	48	1	1	12
5	2	6	2	2	3
3	3	6	4	1	3

7. A Daily Sales *Summary* Report is also needed for the wholesale electronics company described in Problem 6. The report is to print for each possible combination of an item and voltage, the total number of items sold, and the total income from each item. Totals are also to be printed for the total number and income for each item for all voltage options.

8. Revise the example in Section 9-4 for the Gasoline Sales Report to process all input data and sums in one two-dimensional array. The output should remain the same as that shown in the example.

9. Revise the Grade Analysis Report for Problem 3 of Chapter 9 to process all test grades and averages in a single two-dimensional array.

10. Revise the program for the Gopher Green Golf Course (Problem 4, Chapter 9) using one two-dimensional array.
11. The manager of the Gopher Green Golf Course (Problem 4, Chapter 9) has decided that he needs more data to evaluate the course. Write a program to provide the data previously requested plus the following: the percentages of times that the pros scored over, even, or below par on all holes; the average of the course scores for all pros; and the percentage that the pros' average deviated from the course par. (The course par is the sum of the pars for the individual holes.) This should be done with one two-dimensional array.
12. Rewrite the program for Problem 14 of Chapter 9 using one two-dimensional array to process the test data.
13. Revise the program for Problem 16 of Chapter 9 to process the judges' scores in a single two-dimensional array.
14. It has been found that the analysis of the data by the Placement Test Report given in Section 9-8 is not sufficient for the needs of the university; additional information is needed. The dean has requested that a second program be written that will provide the following additional data: the names and scores of the individual students having the highest and lowest total scores, the name of the student and the score and section of the test for the student scoring highest on an *individual* section of the test, and the name of the student and the score and section of the test for the student scoring lowest on an *individual* section of the test. Revise the program in Section 9-8 using a two-dimensional array for the test data and sums to provide the additional information requested.
15. Albatross Airlines has twelve daily flights which are shown in the table below along with the type of plane used and the fares for the four classifications of seats.

Fare Schedule for Albatross Airlines

Flight Number	Type Plane	Fares for Class of			
		Special	Economy	First	Executive
122	727	$221.50	$249.00	$411.70	$444.90
218	747	478.00	509.00	845.65	886.00
283	737	365.55	401.50	648.00	702.00
309	727	202.45	248.05	462.50	511.25
411	727	312.45	348.50	500.00	539.55
454	747	488.90	524.05	850.00	920.00
510	737	328.40	360.00	577.50	603.75
521	727	241.50	278.00	498.00	555.50
639	747	401.35	451.65	768.15	810.00
701	737	331.00	353.50	506.60	550.00
732	727	189.00	212.50	330.00	365.00
769	727	279.85	304.15	515.40	545.25

The administrators of Albatross need a report to project the probable income for a day by flight and fare class, assuming full planes. The maximum number of seats available on each *type* of plane is given below.

Available Seats by Plane Type

Type Plane	Maximum Number Seats Available for	
	Economy Class	First Class
727	190	20
737	225	30
747	360	60

Special fare tickets are counted as economy; it is assumed that 40 percent of all economy seats will be sold as special fares. Likewise, executive fares are counted as first class with the assumption that 20 percent of first class will be booked as executive. The income expected for each class for each flight is calculated as the fare times the available seats. (Remember that economy will be those seats left *after* the special fares, and first class will be those seats remaining after executive tickets.) Sums are to be accumulated for the total amount to be expected from each flight, each class, and the entire day.

16. Write a program to solve the following system of four linear equations:

$$\begin{aligned} 5x - 4y + 2z - w &= 38 \\ x + 2y + 9z - 4w &= 5 \\ 2x + 3y - 7z - 2w &= -19 \\ 3x + y - 6z + 5w &= 15 \end{aligned}$$

17. For the matrix M given by:

$$M = \begin{bmatrix} 1 & 0 & -1 & 2 \\ 3 & 1 & 2 & 1 \\ 2 & 3 & 0 & -1 \\ 1 & 3 & -2 & 3 \end{bmatrix}$$

write a program to evaluate the expression:

$$M^3 + 3 \times M^2 - M$$

18. For the matrix M given in Problem 17, write a program to verify whether or not the following relationships are true (I = identity matrix, M^{-1} = the inverse of M, and M^T = the transpose of M):

(a) $M \times I = I \times M = M$ (b) $(M^{-1})^{-1} = M$

(c) $M \times M^T = M^T \times M$ (d) $(M^T)^T = M$

(e) $M \times M^{-1} = M^{-1} \times M = I$

19. Matrix multiplication can be used to find row and column sums. Multiplication of a matrix by a row vector with all elements equal to 1 will produce a row vector whose elements are *column* sums. Likewise, multiplication by a column vector of 1's will yield a column vector whose elements are *row* sums. Rewrite the Gasoline Sales Report from Section 9-4 using matrix multiplication to accumulate the row and column sums.

20. Use matrix operations as described in Problem 19 to process the data for the Grade Analysis Report from Problem 3 of Chapter 9.

CHAPTER 13

ADVANCED PROGRAMMING TECHNIQUES

This chapter is devoted to the study of several advanced programming procedures that will greatly enhance your ability to solve complex programming problems. We will first look at a faster technique for performing table searches, followed by a survey of some of the more commonly used methods for sorting data into a certain sequence. Finally, we will expand upon our previously acquired skills by examining three-dimensional arrays and multilevel control break programs.

13-1 THE BINARY SEARCH

In Section 9-5, we studied a method for searching a table to find a specific value. We did this by comparing each element in the table with the known value, beginning with the first and continuing with each in turn until a match was found. This is known as a **sequential search** in that the table is searched, element by element, in sequence. This may be desirable or even necessary in some cases; however, for many applications, there is a better and faster way. This is the **binary search**.

In a binary search, all elements of the table to be searched must be in a specific numeral order such as increasing or decreasing sequence. (If they are not in such a sequence, then they may be sorted, as we will see in Sections 13-2 and 13-4.) The middle element of the table is first found and compared to the known value. From this, assuming that the middle element did not match, we know we need to continue our search above or below the middle element. Next, the middle element of the half of the table that we decide to search is found and compared to the known value. Again, assuming that this does not provide a match, we now know in which half of *half* the table to search. This process of checking the middle element and dividing the table into halves continues until there is only one element left.

As a very simple example of how a binary search works, suppose that we have the numbers 101, 102, 103, . . . , 123 stored in the positions 1 through 23 of array A. Let us locate 115. [We know that it is at A(15), but let us find it using the binary search.] We first find the middle element; this will be A(12), or 112. Since 115 is greater than A(12), we know that it must be in the *lower* half of the table, A(13) through A(23). The middle element of this half of the table is A(18), or 118. However, 115 is *less than* A(18), hence our value must be between A(13) and A(17). The middle of this section is A(15), or 115, which is our value. If the value had not been found at this point, we would simply continue the procedure, and it would be located shortly. Note that we only had to make *three* comparisons to find a match with the binary search; *fifteen* would have been needed with a sequential search. This is illustrated in Figure 13-1.

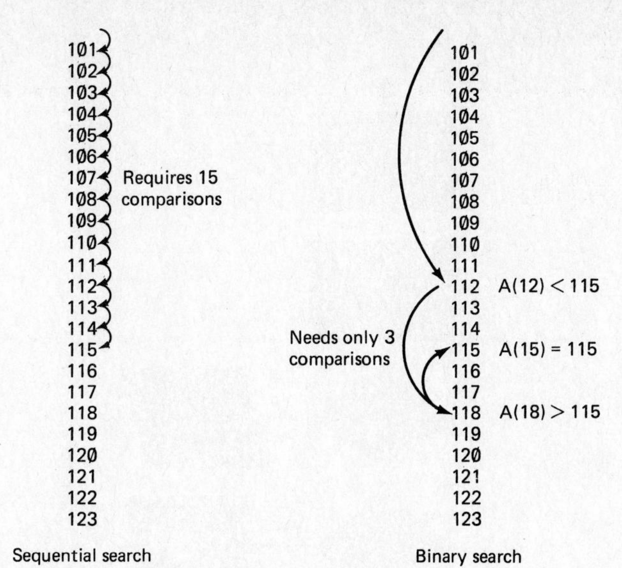

FIGURE 13-1
Comparison of sequential and binary searches

The above binary search of array A with 23 elements can be accomplished by the following sequence of statements:

```
500 LET F = 1
510 LET L = 23
520 LET M = INT((F + L) / 2)
530 IF V = A(M) THEN 600
540 IF F => L THEN 620
550 IF V < A(M) THEN 580
560 LET F = M + 1
570 GOTO 520
580 LET L = M - 1
590 GOTO 520
600 PRINT "VALUE FOUND AT ELEMENT NUMBER"; M
610 GOTO 630
620 PRINT "VALUE NOT FOUND"
630 (Next Statement)
```

The variables F and L are used to mark the first and last elements in the section of the table that is being searched. At the beginning of the search, these are set equal to 1 and 23, respectively, at lines 500 and 510. Line 520 locates the middle element, while line 530 checks to see if a match has been found. If a match is found, an appropriate message is printed at line 600 and the search is ended. If no match is found, line 550 checks to see if the desired value, V, is in the upper half of the array. If so, the last element marker, L, is reset at line 580 to one *above* the previous middle element. Otherwise, the value must be in the lower half. The first element marker, F, then is reset at line 560 to one *below* the previous middle element. A new middle element is found and checked for a match, and the process is repeated until either a match is located or the elements are exhausted with no match found. This latter condition is detected by line 540 when the first to be checked is at or beyond the last. This procedure is illustrated in Figure 13-2.

The above search is for a table whose elements are in **ascending** order—arranged from the smallest to the largest. The same procedure may be used for a **descending** sequence (largest to smallest) by simply reversing the inequality at line 550 from less than to greater than.

You may be wondering why one would want to use the binary search when it takes more program statements to execute and requires that the data be in a certain order. The answer is a simple one—speed. While the speed advantage of the binary search may not be clear for small arrays, it becomes obvious when we consider larger ones. Some data is

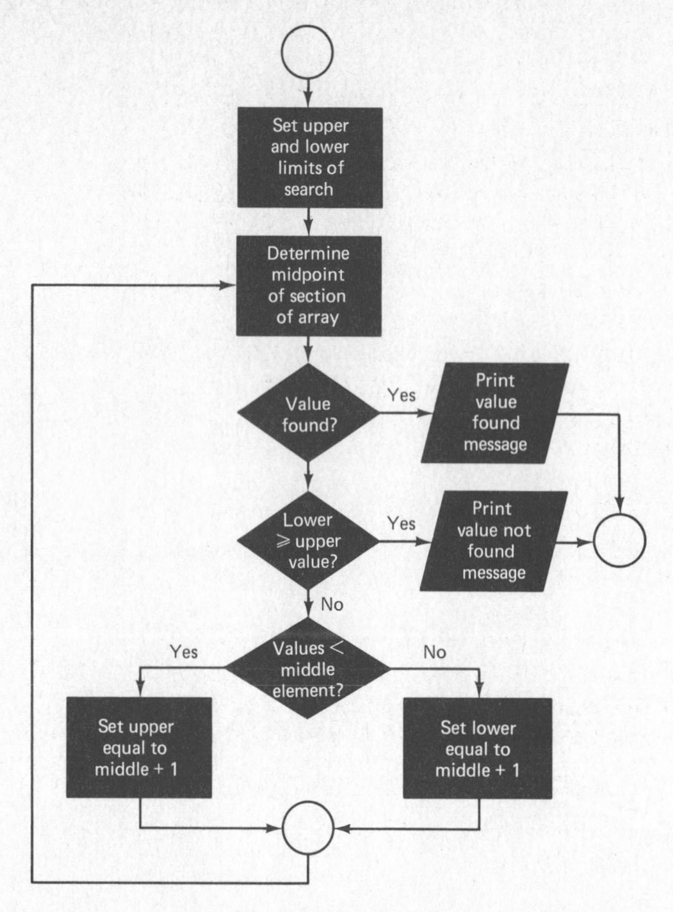

FIGURE 13-2
Flowchart for binary search

given on this in Table 13-1. The first column gives the size of the table in the number of elements to be searched. The second column gives the *average* number of comparisons that will be needed to find a match with a sequential search. Some values will be located very quickly near the top of the table, while others will be near the bottom and will take much longer to find. The numbers in the table illustrate the fact that with a sequential search the *average* position at which any element is to be found is midway through the number of elements to be searched. The last column gives the *maximum* number of comparisons needed with a binary search. These figures reflect the number of times a table with the given number of elements can be *halved*. It should be clear from Table 13-1 that the larger the table the more advantageous a binary search is.

TABLE 13-1

Speed of Sequential and Binary Searches Compared

Number of Elements Searched	Average Comparisons Necessary with a Sequential Search	Maximum Comparisons Needed with a Binary Search
10	5	4
50	25	6
100	50	7
500	250	9
1000	500	10
5000	2500	13
10000	5000	14
50000	25000	17

13-2 THE BUBBLE SORT

Of course, to use the binary search, the data in the section of the table to be searched must be in order. If it is not, then it can be **sorted** into the required sequence by one of several available methods. Probably the simplest method and the one most frequently used by most beginning programmers is the **bubble sort** (sometimes called the **exchange method** or **nested-loop interchange sort**). This procedure will be described in this section. Several other sorting techniques will be outlined in Section 13-4.

The bubble sort can be used to rearrange a series of values so that they are in an ordered sequence, such as ascending or descending with numerical data or alphabetical with string values. The basic idea is to compare one value in the sequence to the next. If they are in the proper order, do nothing; if they are not, exchange them. This procedure is repeated until all values are in the proper order. Let us look at an example for sorting the six-element array R, which contains the following values:

$$R(1) = 23 \quad R(4) = 87$$
$$R(2) = 59 \quad R(5) = 11$$
$$R(3) = 30 \quad R(6) = 45$$

into ascending sequence so that the smallest value will be first and the largest last. The first step is to construct a FOR–NEXT loop that will perform one pass through the array comparing each pair of elements and exchanging pairs that are in the wrong order. This is accomplished by the following:

```
330 FOR K = 1 TO 5
340    IF R(K) <= R(K + 1) THEN 380
350    LET E = R(K)
360    LET R(K) = R(K + 1)
370    LET R(K + 1) = E
380 NEXT K
```

Each element is compared to the next one by line 340. If the elements are in the proper order (a true condition), then the next pair is tested. If the elements are not in the proper sequence (condition is false), then lines 350 to 370 exchange the values. (Some BASICs provide a SWAP statement for this operation. See Appendix A.) Note that the FOR–NEXT loop ranges only up to 5; the subscript K + 1 takes in the last element. The arrangement of the values in the array is shown in Table 13-2 for one pass through the elements. With one pass, the largest element has been ''pushed'' to the bottom of the array. The larger elements are slowly moving downward while the smaller ones are ''bubbling'' upward.

We must now go through the array again to push the next-to-the-largest element into the next-to-last position, and then again for the next largest element, and so forth until the array is in order. This can be done with an outer loop to cause the above loop to be

TABLE 13-2

Effect of One Pass Through Array R

Element Number	Original Array	Arrangement After Comparison Number				
		1	2	3	4	5
1	23	23	23	23	23	23
2	59	59	30	30	30	30
3	30	30	59	59	59	59
4	87	87	87	87	11	11
5	11	11	11	11	87	45
6	45	45	45	45	45	87

repeated. However, note that once a ''largest'' element has been pushed to the bottom of the array, it need not be included in a subsequent comparison, so with each repetition of the above loop, the upper limit can be decreased by one. This is all put together in the following set of statements:

```
320 FOR J = 1 TO 5
330    FOR K = 1 TO 6 - J
340       IF R(K) <= R(K + 1) THEN 380
350       LET E = R(K)
360       LET R(K) = R(K + 1)
370       LET R(K + 1) = E
380    NEXT K
390 NEXT J
```

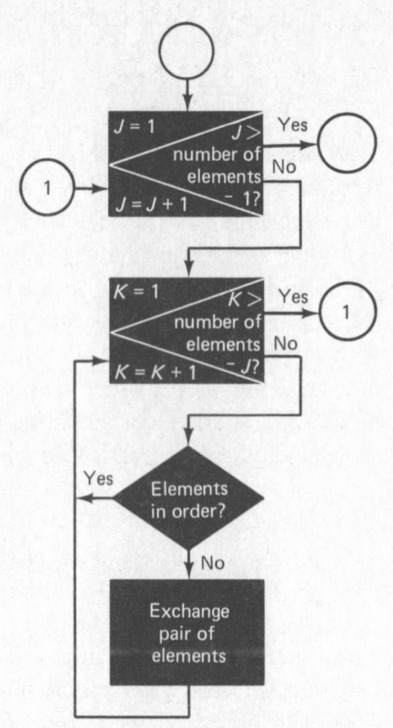

FIGURE 13-3
The bubble sort, simple form

The inner loop is the same as above except that the upper limit for K has been set to 6 − J so that it will *decrease* by one with each pass. The outer loop counts the passes. This procedure is illustrated in Figure 13-3. The effect on the elements of R is shown in Table 13-3.

The above sort was for an *ascending* sequence. To obtain a descending order, all that is required is to reverse the inequality in line 340. Of course, much larger arrays can be as easily sorted by merely changing the upper limits on the FOR–NEXT loops.

As a final point on the bubble sort, an examination of Table 13-3 will show that *no* exchanges occurred during the last pass through R. When an array is checked with no exchanges, it is in the desired order and no further checks are necessary. We can modify the above sort routine by introducing a flag (see Section 8-7) to check for any pass through the array in which no element exchanges occur. This is done as follows:

```
310 LET J = 1
320 LET F = 0
330 FOR K = 1 TO 6 - J
340    IF R(K) <= R(K + 1) THEN 390
350    LET E = R(K)
360    LET R(K) = R(K + 1)
370    LET R(K + 1) = E
380    LET F = 1
390 NEXT K
400 LET J = J + 1
410 IF F <> 0 THEN 320
```

We first set the flag to zero at line 320. The array is then checked as before to see if the elements are in the proper order. If an exchange takes place, the flag is changed at line 380. At line 410, a check is made to see if the flag has been changed; that is, if an exchange of elements has occurred. If it has, the array is checked again; if not, the sort is completed. This process is illustrated in Figure 13-4.

TABLE 13-3
Effect of Repeated Passes Through Array R

Element Number	Original Array	Arrangement After Pass Number				
		1	2	3	4	5
1	23	23	23	23	11	11
2	59	30	30	11	23	23
3	30	59	11	30	30	30
4	87	11	45	45	45	45
5	11	45	59	59	59	59
6	45	87	87	87	87	87

13-3 AN EXAMPLE: CUSTOMER ACCOUNT UPDATE

The example that follows illustrates the use of both the bubble sort and the binary search. When to use a sequential or binary search is also explored.

Problem: A certain company needs a program to process the purchases and payments made by its regular customers for a single day. All regular customers have their account ID numbers and balances stored in a customer master file. Each day's transactions are recorded with the account number and payment or purchase; payments are indicated as a negative value and purchases as positive. All transactions are to be input interactively and processed with the following actions taken:

1. The balance in the master table is to be continually updated.
2. All accounts that were updated are to be printed along with the balances at the beginning and end of the day.
3. Any transaction with an unidentified ID number should also be listed with an appropriate message.
4. Totals should be printed for the number of accounts processed, the number of transactions, and the total of the new balances of the *accounts* processed at the end of the day.

The master table should be sorted with the bubble sort and then searched with the binary method. Data for the master table is provided in Table 13-4, and transaction data to be processed is in Table 13-5.

The solution to this problem is outlined as follows:

1. Dimension arrays for account number and balance in master table and for account number and new and old balances in transaction table to 100 values.

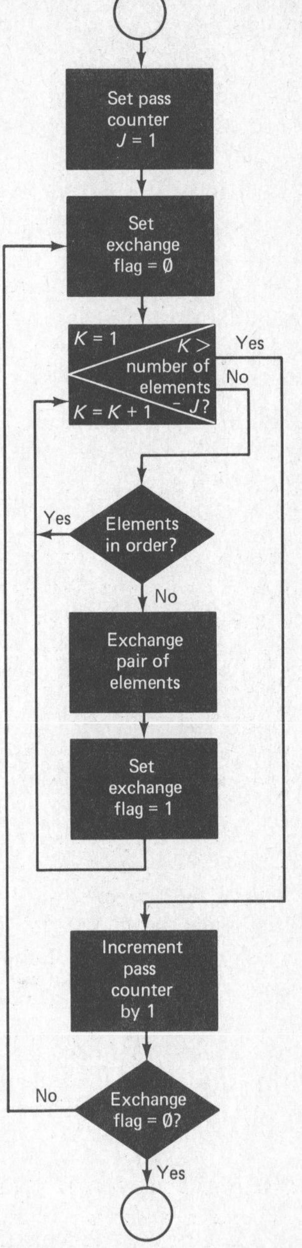

FIGURE 13-4
More efficient bubble sort

TABLE 13-4
Data for Master Table for Customer Account Update Problem

Customer Number	Previous Balance	Customer Number	Previous Balance	Customer Number	Previous Balance
10119	$235.29	16100	$ 0.00	19882	$2893.03
10213	29.22	12193	16.50	12982	129.73
21092	119.02	12165	2374.66	11488	21.57
11291	19.00	22176	297.59	22392	6.50
11829	329.75	22187	679.39	10883	34.94
14922	78.94	13273	98.35	14533	490.33
12001	119.27	12677	110.00	12884	0.00
22087	201.46	13882	10.02	18773	22.50

TABLE 13-5
Transaction Data for Customer Account Update Problem

Customer Number	Amount of Transaction	Customer Number	Amount of Transaction
11829	$ 100.00	11929	$ 115.75
12677	−25.00	14533	−200.00
11488	55.75	16100	50.00
16100	25.50	22087	−100.00
16100	−30.00	12677	45.00
19882	−500.00	12165	250.00
10119	−100.00	12165	−600.00
22392	−6.50	16100	125.00

2. Load master table. Mark the number of accounts in the table.
3. Set total accumulators for the number of accounts processed, the number of transactions, and the totals of new balances to zero.
4. Sort master table to put account numbers in ascending order.
5. Set the number of elements in the transaction table to zero.
6. Input a customer account number and transaction.
7. Check for the last record. When found, go to step 25; otherwise, go to the next step.
8. Execute a binary search of the master table to locate the customer account number.
9. If the number is found, go to step 14.
10. Add 1 to the number of elements in the transaction table.
11. Store the customer account ID number in the transaction table.
12. Set the current balance in the transaction table to −1.
13. Go to step 6.
14. If this is the first account to be processed, go to step 17.
15. Search the transaction table to determine whether the account has been previously processed.
16. If the account number is found, go to step 21.
17. Add 1 to the number of elements in the transaction table.
18. Store the customer account ID number in the transaction table.
19. Set the previous balance in the transaction table to that stored in the master table.
20. Add 1 to the number of accounts processed.
21. Add the amount of the transaction to the corresponding value in the master table.
22. Set the current balances in the transaction table equal to the updated value from the master table.
23. Add 1 to the number of transactions.
24. Go to step 6.
25. Print main and column headings.
26. Print the transaction table.
27. Find the sum of all current balances from the transaction table.
28. Print totals for the number of accounts processed, transactions, and the current balances of accounts processed.
29. Stop.

This procedure is illustrated pictorially by the flowchart shown in Figure 13-5.

The program is routine; there is nothing new through line 360. All arrays are dimensioned at line 280.

```
280  DIM  ID(100), B(100), NM(100), PB(100), CB(100)
```

ID and B will hold the account ID numbers and balances for all customers in the master table. NM, PB, and CB are for the account numbers and previous and current balances for the day's transactions for the transaction table. Since we do not know how many values will be in these two tables, we must dimension for a sufficiently large value. The number of accounts in the master table will be determined by the same method used for processing the invoices for Cindy's Cameras in Section 9-6. Another procedure will be used for the transaction table.

We will begin our analysis with the bubble sort routine at lines 400 to 530 which sorts the master table into ascending order by customer account ID number. The routine is written as:

```
400 LET J = 1
410 LET FL = 0
420 FOR K = 1 TO NX - J
430    IF ID(K) <= ID(K + 1) THEN 510
440    LET E = ID(K)
450    LET ID(K) = ID(K + 1)
```

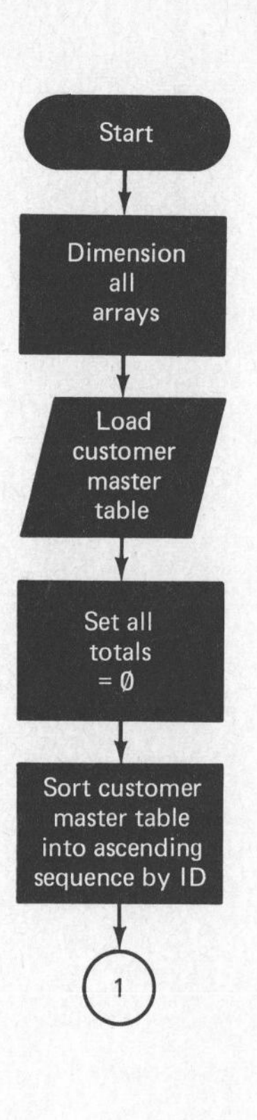

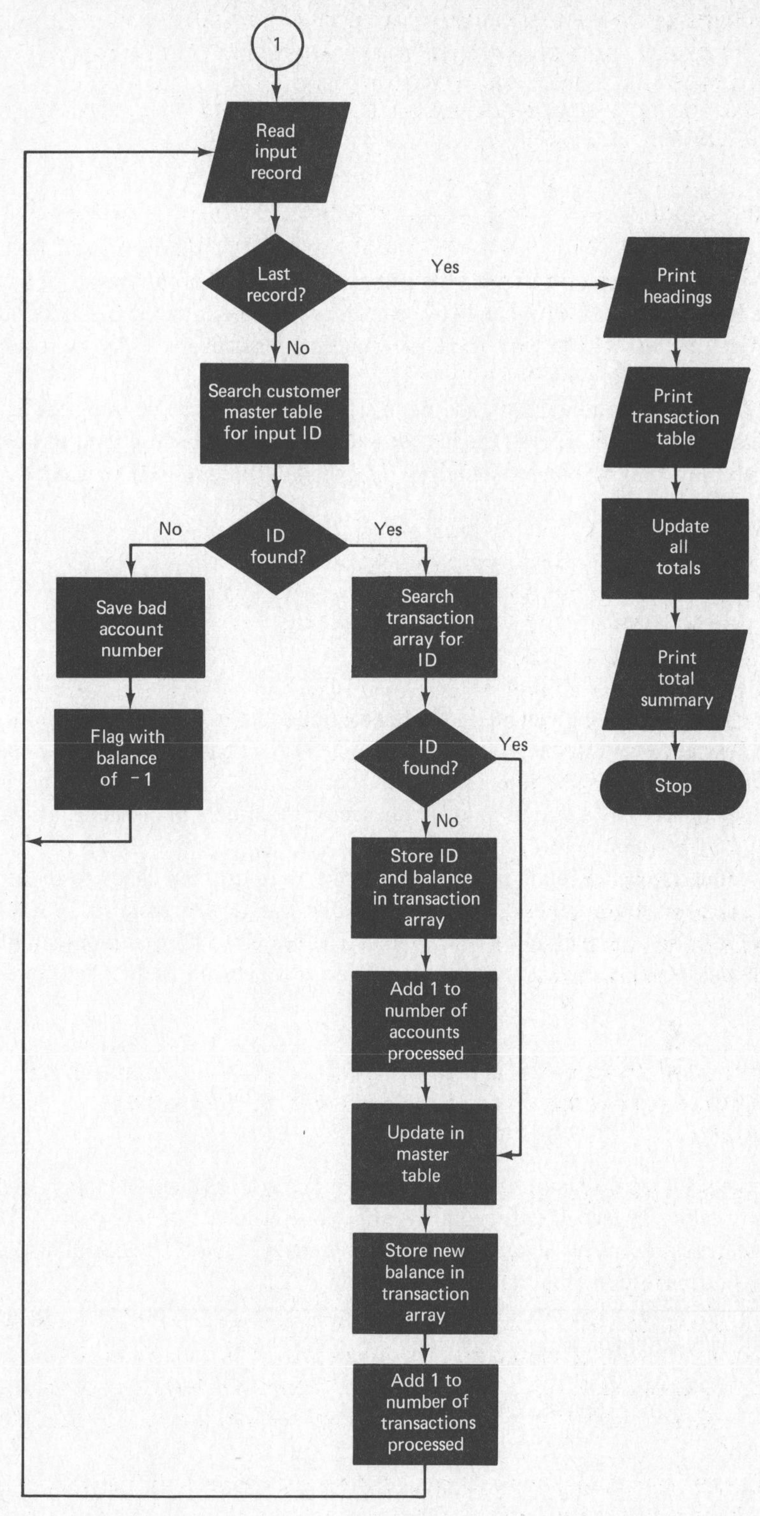

FIGURE 13-5 Flowchart for customer account update example

```
460     LET ID(K + 1) = E
470     LET E = B(K)
480     LET B(K) = B(K + 1)
490     LET B(K + 1) = E
500     LET FL = 1
510  NEXT K
520  LET J = J + 1
530  IF FL <> 0 THEN 410
```

This is exactly the same as the revised bubble sort given at the end of the last section, with the exception of lines 470 to 490. When two account numbers are found to be out of order, they are switched at lines 440 to 460. The corresponding balances must also be reversed; this is done at lines 470 to 490.

A transaction is input at line 580, and the master table is searched, using the binary method, at lines 630 to 720. This is exactly the same procedure as described in Section 13-1. If an account number is *not* found in the master table, it is processed by the following short section:

```
760  LET S = S + 1
770  LET NM(S) = IN
780  LET CB(S) = -1
790  GOTO 580
```

The subscript that counts the elements in the transaction table is first incremented by 1. (Note that it was set to zero in the beginning at line 570.) The bad account ID number is stored in the table at line 770. At line 780, the current balance is set to -1 (any negative value would do) to serve as a *flag* to indicate the account numbers in the table which are bad.

If the account number *is* found in the master table, we must then check to see if that account has already been processed and placed in the transaction table. If it has, we simply update it; if not, we will add it to the table. The search of the transaction table to see if the account has already been added to the table is processed at lines 940 to 970:

```
840  IF S = 0 THEN 910
850  FOR N = 1 TO S
860     IF NM(N) = IN THEN 990
870  NEXT N
```

This is a simple sequential search, which is sufficient because this table is much smaller than the master table. In fact, it will begin with only one account, then two, then three, etc. Binary searches are most advantageous for large arrays. (Note, line 840 skips the search when the transaction table has no accounts in it.)

If an account number has not already been placed in the transaction table, then the following sequence of statements is executed:

```
 910 LET S = S + 1
 920 LET NM(S) = IN
 930 LET PB(S) = B(M)
 940 LET TA = TA + 1
 950 LET N = S
          :
 990 LET B(M) = B(M) + P
1000 LET CB(N) = B(M)
1010 LET TT = TT + 1
1020 GOTO 580
```

Line 910 increments the subscript that locates the new account in the transaction table by 1 so it will not overwrite the last account. The next two lines place the account number and balance (before the transaction) into the proper position in the transaction table. (Remember that M locates the account in the *master* table.) Line 940 adds 1 to the total number of accounts processed. The balance in the *master* table is updated at 990 and then placed in the transaction table as the current balance at 1000. The total number of transactions is incremented at 1010. Note that at line 860, when the transaction table is searched and an account is found to already be in the table, a branch to line 990 occurs. The subscript N at 1000 indicates the location of the previous account. If it is a new account, N is set equal to S at 950.

When all of the transactions have been processed, the transaction table must be printed, and the sum of the new balances for the accounts processed must be found. The headings are first printed at lines 1090 to 1140. Then the table is printed and sums are accumulated as follows:

```
1190 FOR N = 1 TO S
1200    IF CB(N) => 0 THEN PRINT NM(N), "$"; PB(N), "$"; CB(N)
1210    IF CB(N) < 0 THEN PRINT NM(N), "*** INVALID ID NUMBER ***"
1220    IF CB(N) < 0 THEN 1240
1230    LET TP = TP + CB(N)
1240 NEXT N
```

Each account in the table is printed by line 1200 unless it has been flagged as an invalid account number by a −1 for the current balance. In this case, an error message is printed by line 1210. The same loop is used to sum the balances by line 1230. Invalid accounts are omitted from the sum by 1220. The final totals are printed by 1290 to 1310.

A complete listing and run follow:

```
 10 REM  CUSTOMER ACCOUNT UPDATE
 20 REM
 30 REM  VARIABLES ARE DEFINED AS --
 40 REM
 50 REM          ID = CUSTOMER ID IN MASTER TABLE
 60 REM           B = CUSTOMER BALANCE MASTER TABLE
 70 REM          NM = ID NUMBERS OF TRANSACTIONS ARRAY FOR PRINTING
 80 REM          PB = PREVIOUS BALANCE ARRAY FOR PRINTING
 90 REM          CB = CURRENT BALANCE ARRAY FOR PRINTING
100 REM          IN = CUSTOMER ID
110 REM           P = PAYMENT OR PURCHASE
120 REM          TA = TOTAL NUMBER OF ACCOUNTS PROCESSED
130 REM          TT = TOTAL NUMBER OF TRANSACTIONS
140 REM          TP = TOTAL AMOUNT DUE FROM ALL TRANSACTIONS
150 REM          NX = NUMBER OF ITEMS IN CUSTOMER MASTER TABLE
160 REM           S = ITEM COUNTER IN TRANSACTIONS ARRAYS
170 REM          FL = FLAG TO CONTROL BUBBLE SORT
180 REM     N AND K = LOOP COUNTERS
190 REM           J = LOOP CONTROL FOR SORT
200 REM           E = EXCHANGE VARIABLE IN SORT
210 REM           F = FIRST ELEMENT MARKER FOR BINARY SEARCH
220 REM           L = LAST ELEMENT MARKER FOR BINARY SEARCH
230 REM           M = MIDDLE ELEMENT MARKER FOR BINARY SEARCH
240 REM
250 REM  DIMENSION ARRAYS, LOAD MASTER TABLE,
260 REM  AND SET TOTAL ACCUMULATORS TO ZERO
270 REM
280 DIM ID(100), B(100), NM(100), PB(100), CB(100)
290 FOR N = 1 TO 100
300    READ ID(N), B(N)
310    IF ID(N) < 0 THEN 330
320 NEXT N
330 LET NX = N - 1
```

```
    LET TA = 0
350 LET TT = 0
360 LET TP = 0
370 REM
380 REM  SORT MASTER TABLE INTO ASCENDING ORDER BY CUSTOMER ID
390 REM
400 LET J = 1
410 LET FL = 0
420 FOR K = 1 TO NX - J
430   IF ID(K) <= ID(K + 1) THEN 510
440   LET E = ID(K)
450   LET ID(K) = ID(K + 1)
460   LET ID(K + 1) = E
470   LET E = B(K)
480   LET B(K) = B(K + 1)
490   LET B(K + 1) = E
500   LET FL = 1
510 NEXT K
520 LET J = J + 1
530 IF FL <> 0 THEN 410
540 REM
550 REM  INPUT DATA AND CHECK FOR END OF PROCESSING
560 REM
570 LET S = 0
580 INPUT "ENTER TRANSACTION"; IN, P
590 IF IN < 0 THEN 1060
600 REM
610 REM  PERFORM BINARY SEARCH TO FIND CUSTOMER ID IN MASTER TABLE
620 REM
630 LET F = 1
640 LET L = NX
650 LET M = INT((F + L) / 2)
660 IF IN = ID(M) THEN 840
670 IF F => L THEN 760
680 IF IN < ID(M) THEN 710
690 LET F = M + 1
700 GOTO 650
710 LET L = M - 1
720 GOTO 650
730 REM
740 REM  PROCESS INVALID CUSTOMER ID NUMBERS
750 REM
760 LET S = S + 1
770 LET NM(S) = IN
780 LET CB(S) = -1
790 GOTO 580
800 REM
810 REM  PLACE CUSTOMER ID, PREVIOUS BALANCE, AND
820 REM  UPDATED BALANCE INTO TRANSACTION TABLE
830 REM
840 IF S = 0 THEN 910
850 FOR N = 1 TO S
860   IF NM(N) = IN THEN 990
870 NEXT N
880 REM
890 REM  ADD ACCOUNTS TO TRANSACTIONS TABLE
900 REM
910 LET S = S + 1
920 LET NM(S) = IN
930 LET PB(S) = B(M)
940 LET TA = TA + 1
950 LET N = S
960 REM
```

```
 970 REM  BEGIN UPDATE OF PREVIOUSLY PROCESSED ACCOUNTS
 980 REM
 990 LET B(M) = B(M) + P
1000 LET CB(N) = B(M)
1010 LET TT = TT + 1
1020 GOTO 580
1030 REM
1040 REM  PRINT HEADINGS
1050 REM
1060 PRINT
1070 PRINT
1080 PRINT
1090 PRINT "       CUSTOMER ACCOUNT UPDATE"
1100 PRINT
1110 PRINT
1120 PRINT "CUSTOMER", "PREVIOUS", "CURRENT"
1130 PRINT " NUMBER", "BALANCE", "BALANCE"
1140 PRINT
1150 REM
1160 REM  PRINT TRANSACTION TABLE AND ACCUMULATE TOTAL
1170 REM  OF NEW BALANCES FOR ACCOUNTS WITH TRANSACTIONS
1180 REM
1190 FOR N = 1 TO S
1200   IF CB(N) => 0 THEN PRINT NM(N), "$"; PB(N), "$"; CB(N)
1210   IF CB(N) < 0 THEN PRINT NM(N), "*** INVALID ID NUMBER ***"
1220   IF CB(N) < 0 THEN 1240
1230   LET TP = TP + CB(N)
1240 NEXT N
1250 REM
1260 REM  PRINT SUMMARY TOTALS
1270 REM
1280 PRINT
1290 PRINT "TOTAL ACCOUNTS PROCESSED ="; TA
1300 PRINT "TOTAL TRANSACTIONS ="; TT
1310 PRINT "TOTAL AMOUNT DUE = $"; TP
1320 REM
1330 REM  DATA FOR CUSTOMER MASTER TABLE
1340 REM
1350 DATA 10119,235.29,10213,29.22,21092,119.02,11291,19.00
1360 DATA 11829,329.75,14922,78.94,12001,119.27,22087,201.46
1370 DATA 16100,0,12193,16.50,12165,2374.66,22176,297.59
1380 DATA 22187,679.39,13273,98.35,12677,110.00,13882,10.02
1390 DATA 19882,2893.03,12982,129.73,11488,21.57,22392,6.50
1400 DATA 10883,34.94,14533,490.33,12884,0,18773,22.50,-1,0
1410 END

ENTER TRANSACTION? 11829, 100
ENTER TRANSACTION? 12677, -25
ENTER TRANSACTION? 11488, 55.75
ENTER TRANSACTION? 16100, 25.50
ENTER TRANSACTION? 16100, -30
ENTER TRANSACTION? 19882, -500
ENTER TRANSACTION? 10119, -100
ENTER TRANSACTION? 22392, -6.5
ENTER TRANSACTION? 11929, 115.75
ENTER TRANSACTION? 14533, -200
ENTER TRANSACTION? 16100, 50
ENTER TRANSACTION? 22087, -100
ENTER TRANSACTION? 12677, 45
ENTER TRANSACTION? 12165, 250
ENTER TRANSACTION? 12165, -600
ENTER TRANSACTION? 16100, 125
ENTER TRANSACTION? -1, 0
```

```
   CUSTOMER ACCOUNT UPDATE


CUSTOMER       PREVIOUS       CURRENT
 NUMBER        BALANCE        BALANCE

 11829         $ 329.75       $ 429.75
 12677         $ 110          $ 130
 11488         $ 21.57        $ 77.32
 16100         $ 0            $ 170.5
 19882         $ 2893.03      $ 2393.03
 10119         $ 235.29       $ 135.29
 22392         $ 6.5          $ 0
 11929         *** INVALID ID NUMBER ***
 14533         $ 490.33       $ 290.33
 22087         $ 201.46       $ 101.46
 12165         $ 2374.66      $ 2024.66

TOTAL ACCOUNTS PROCESSED = 10
TOTAL TRANSACTIONS = 15
TOTAL AMOUNT DUE = $ 5752.34
```

13-4 OTHER SORTING TECHNIQUES

The bubble sort is popular because it is easy to learn and understand; however, it is not very fast or efficient. There are many other sorting methods available. While an entire book could easily be devoted to a discussion of sorting, space will permit us to examine only a few. In this section, we will take a quick look at several other widely used sorting techniques. We will not be able to develop these to the extent that we did the bubble sort. If you wish further information on advanced sorting methods, ask your instructor to recommend one of the references available in your library.

All sort routines that we will examine in this section will use the array R that we sorted in Section 13-2 by the bubble sort. We will also sort R into ascending order as we did before. This should help you in comparing the various techniques.

One procedure—only slightly more efficient than the bubble (about 20 to 25 percent faster), and requiring *twice* as much memory—is the **selection sort**. This can be written as follows:

```
300 FOR J = 1 TO 6
310    LET M = 100
320    FOR K = 1 TO 6
330       IF M <= R(K) THEN 360
340       LET M = R(K)
350       LET S = K
360    NEXT K
370    LET RS(J) = M
380    LET R(S) = 100
390 NEXT J
```

This procedure begins by assigning a value that is known to be larger than any value in R to the variable M. The array is then searched and the *smallest* value is found and assigned to M. This value is then assigned to the first element of the **sorter array** RS at line 370. At line 380, the smallest value is replaced by the original large value so that it will no longer be the smallest value. The process is then repeated to find the next to smallest value in the original array. This value is assigned to the second element of RS. The procedure continues until the last or largest element of R is placed in the last element of RS. This

TABLE 13-6

Effect of Selection Sort on Array R

Element Number	Original Arrays R	Original Arrays RS	Pass 1 R	Pass 1 RS	Pass 2 R	Pass 2 RS	Pass 3 R	Pass 3 RS	Pass 4 R	Pass 4 RS	Pass 5 R	Pass 5 RS	Pass 6 R	Pass 6 RS
1	23	0	23	11	100	11	100	11	100	11	100	11	100	11
2	59	0	59	0	59	23	59	23	59	23	100	23	100	23
3	30	0	30	0	30	0	100	30	100	30	100	30	100	30
4	87	0	87	0	87	0	87	0	87	45	87	45	100	45
5	11	0	100	0	100	0	100	0	100	0	100	59	100	59
6	45	0	45	0	45	0	45	0	100	0	100	0	100	87

procedure is illustrated in Figure 13-6. The contents of R and RS for each pass through R are shown in Table 13-6.

Another relatively simple procedure that is about two to three times as fast as the bubble sort is the **maximum–minimum interchange** method. This method simply searches an array to locate the largest and smallest values. The smallest value is then interchanged with the first in the array and the largest with the last. The array is then searched again, except for the first and last elements, to find the next largest and smallest values, which are then interchanged with the values next to the respective ends. This

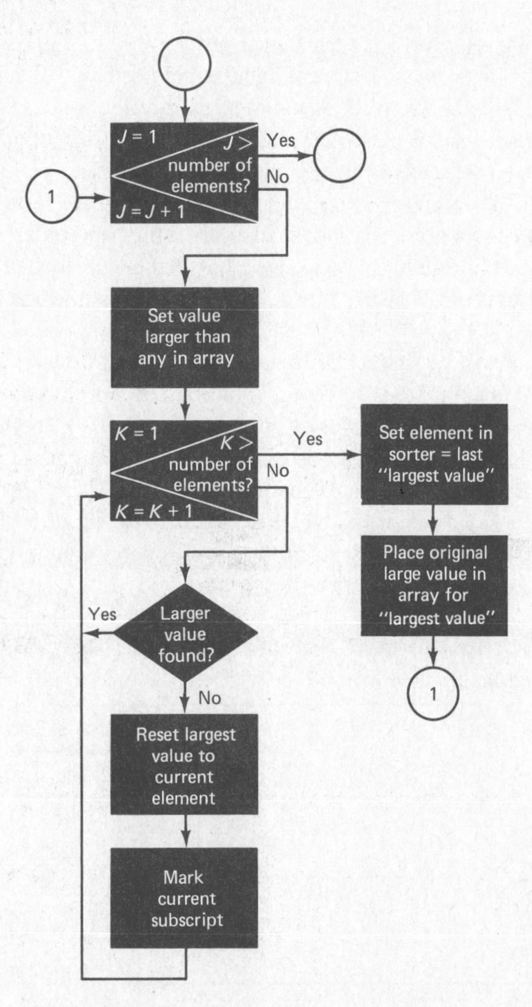

FIGURE 13-6
Flowchart for the selection sort

procedure continues until the entire array has been sorted with small values to one end and large to the other. This sort routine can be written as follows:

```
300 LET N = 6
310 FOR J = 1 TO INT(N / 2)
320    LET MN = J
330    LET MX = J
340    LET RN = R(J)
350    LET RX = R(J)
360    FOR K = J + 1 TO N - J + 1
370      IF RN <= R(K) THEN 400
380      LET RN = R(K)
390      LET MN = K
400      IF RX => R(K) THEN 430
410      LET RX = R(K)
420      LET MX = K
430    NEXT K
440    IF MX = J THEN MX = MN
450    LET E = R(MN)
460    LET R(MN) = R(J)
470    LET R(J) = E
480    LET E = R(MX)
490    LET R(MX) = R(N - J + 1)
500    LET R(N - J + 1) = E
510 NEXT J
```

This procedure is relatively routine, with a search by the loop at 360 to 430 to find the largest and smallest values in the array. These are then exchanged with the end elements at lines 440 to 500. Line 440 checks to see if the maximum value moves when the smallest one is swapped. As each pair of extreme values is found and placed at the ends of the array, the two elements at the ends need no longer be included in any future searches, and the array effectively "shrinks" by two elements with each pass. Note that the limits on the counter of the inner loop take this into account. Thus, the outer loop which controls the number of passes through the loop need only count up to half the elements in R. This is outlined in Figure 13-7. The pattern of the data in R with each pass is shown in Table 13-7.

The **insertion sort** is approximately as fast as the maximum-minimum interchange method but a little more complex in nature. It is, however, important as a preliminary to the very efficient Shell sort that will follow. The idea behind the insertion sort is that a list of values can be sorted by beginning from one end and inserting each element into the list in its proper position. In other words, the second element is compared to the first and the two switched if necessary, but these two elements will now be in the proper order. The third is then compared to the second and, if necessary, to the first to determine its posi-

TABLE 13-7

Effect of Maximum-Minimum Interchange Sort on Array R

Element Number	Original Array	Arrangement After Pass Number		
		1	2	3
1	23	11	11	11
2	59	59	23	23
3	30	30	30	30
4	87	45	45	45
5	11	23	59	59
6	45	87	87	87

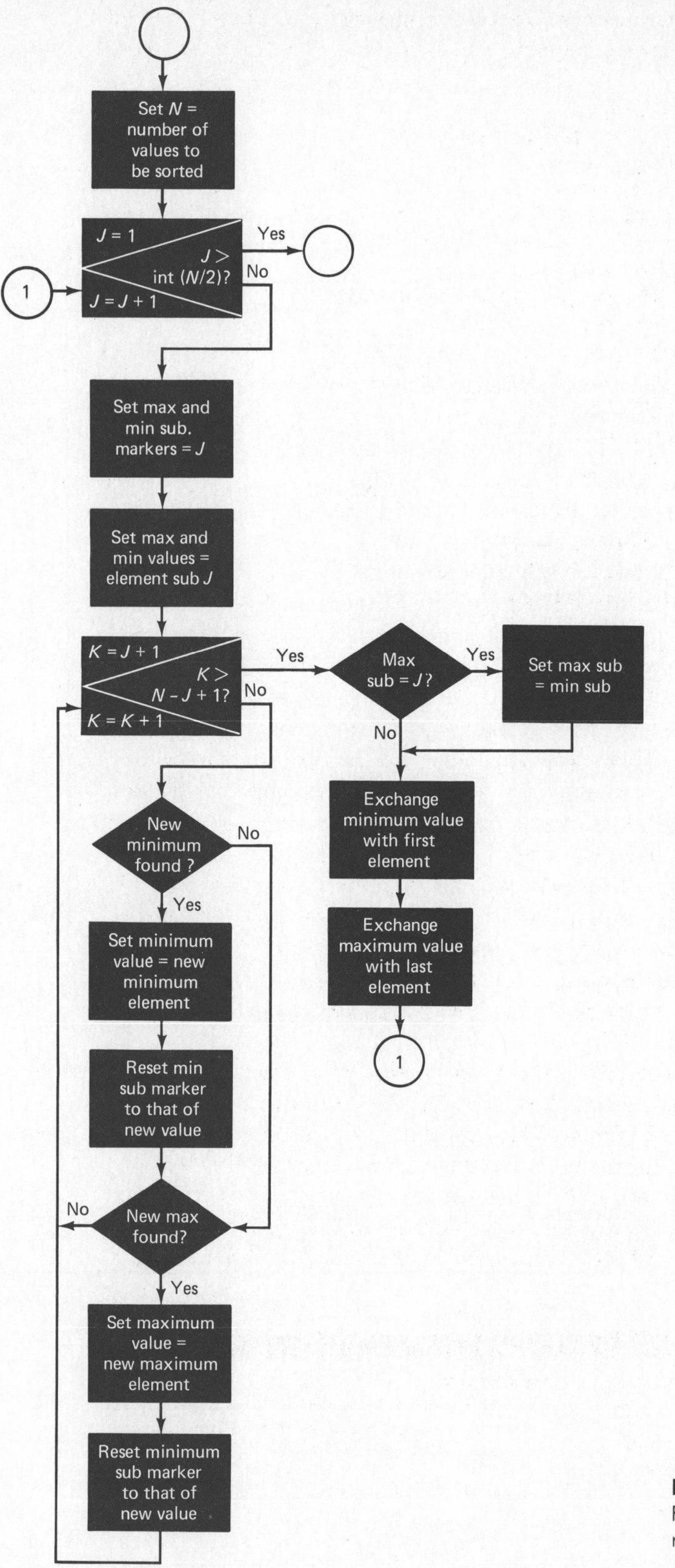

FIGURE 13-7
Flowchart for maximum-minimum interchange sort

tion. This will give three elements in order. This process continues through the entire array. It can be written as follows:

```
300 FOR J = 1 TO 5
310    LET E = R(J + 1)
320    FOR K = J TO 1 STEP -1
330       IF E => R(K) THEN 360
340       LET R(K + 1) = R(K)
350    NEXT K
360    LET R(K + 1) = E
370 NEXT J
```

When the list has J elements, the element to be inserted, E, is set equal to element J + 1 at line 310. It is then compared to all the preceding elements in the list by lines 320 to 350. Once its proper place is found, it is inserted by line 360. Until then, the other elements are moved down in the array to make a place for the new entry; this is done at line 340. The insertion sort is shown in the flowchart in Figure 13-8. The movement of the data in array R is illustrated in Table 13-8.

The bubble sort is inefficient because of the large number of comparisons and exchanges that are required to sort an array. The alternative methods discussed thus far in this section improve on this to some degree, but none approaches the relatively high efficiency of the **Shell sort** (named for its author, Donald Shell). The bubble and other sort routines lose efficiency because they only compare and exchange adjacent elements. (The maximum-minimum interchange sort begins to get away from this to some extent.) The Shell sort divides a list into large sections and compares, exchanging if necessary, respective elements. For example, our array R would first be divided into halves, R(1) through R(3) and R(4) through R(6) and compared as follows:

R(1) ⟷ R(4)
R(2) ⟷ R(5)
R(3) ⟷ R(6)

After swaps are made moving smaller values to the lower end and larger to the upper, the process is repeated with the array divided into thirds. This gives:

R(1) ⟷ R(3) ⟷ R(5)
R(2) ⟷ R(4) ⟷ R(6)

For R, the next step is an element-by-element comparison. At each step, we are using an insertion sort *within each sublist*. However, since the elements initially are moved much

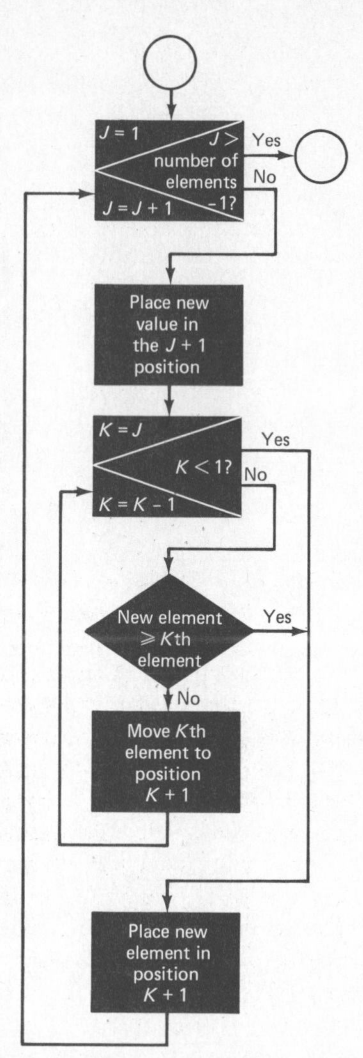

FIGURE 13-8
Flowchart for insertion sort

TABLE 13-8
Effect of Insertion Sort on Array R

Element Number	Original Array	Arrangement After Pass Number 1	2	3	4	5
1	23	23	23	23	11	11
2	59	59	30	30	23	23
3	30	30	59	59	30	30
4	87	87	87	87	59	45
5	11	11	11	11	87	59
6	45	45	45	45	45	87

further toward their proper position, the process is much faster in the end. The method can be written in BASIC as follows:

```
300 LET N = 6
310 LET I = N
320 LET I = INT(I / 2 +.5)
330 FOR J = 1 TO I
340    FOR K = J TO N - I STEP I
350       LET E = R(K + I)
360       FOR L = K TO 1 STEP -I
370          IF E => R(L) THEN 400
380          LET R(L + I) = R(L)
390       NEXT L
400       LET R(L + I) = E
410    NEXT K
420 NEXT J
430 IF I > 1 THEN 320
```

The similarity to the insertion sort is clear. The outer loop controls the division of the array list into sublists. This is outlined in the flowchart in Figure 13-9. The arrangement of the elements of R for each pass is shown in Table 13-9.

All of the techniques discussed thus far are fine for sorting a single list or a table that requires sorting in only one way. Suppose we have a table or two-dimensional array for which we wish to sort two columns (or rows) in two *different* ways. Clearly, we cannot sort the table by rearranging it in two ways at once. The way to solve this problem is to use a **pointer method** procedure. This is accomplished by setting up a separate array known as the **pointer array**, the *elements* of which give the sorted sequence of the elements of the original array. In other words, if the fifth element of the array to be sorted should be first, then the first element of the pointer array will be 5. If the third element should be next, then the second element of the pointer array will be 3, and so forth. Each column or row of a two-dimensional array can be separately sorted in any desired sequence using the pointer technique. The following assumes that our array R is the third column of a two-dimensional array. R is sorted as before and the proper sequence is indicated by the pointer array P.

```
200 FOR X = 1 TO 6
210    LET P(X) = X
220 NEXT X
                 :
300 FOR J = 1 TO 5
310    LET L = J
320    FOR K = J + 1 TO 6
330       IF R(P(L), 3) <= R(P(K), 3) THEN 350
```

TABLE 13-9

Effect of Shell Sort on Array R

Element Number	Original Array	Arrangement After Pass Number 1	2	3
1	23	23	23	11
2	59	11	11	23
3	30	30	30	30
4	87	87	45	45
5	11	59	59	59
6	45	45	87	87

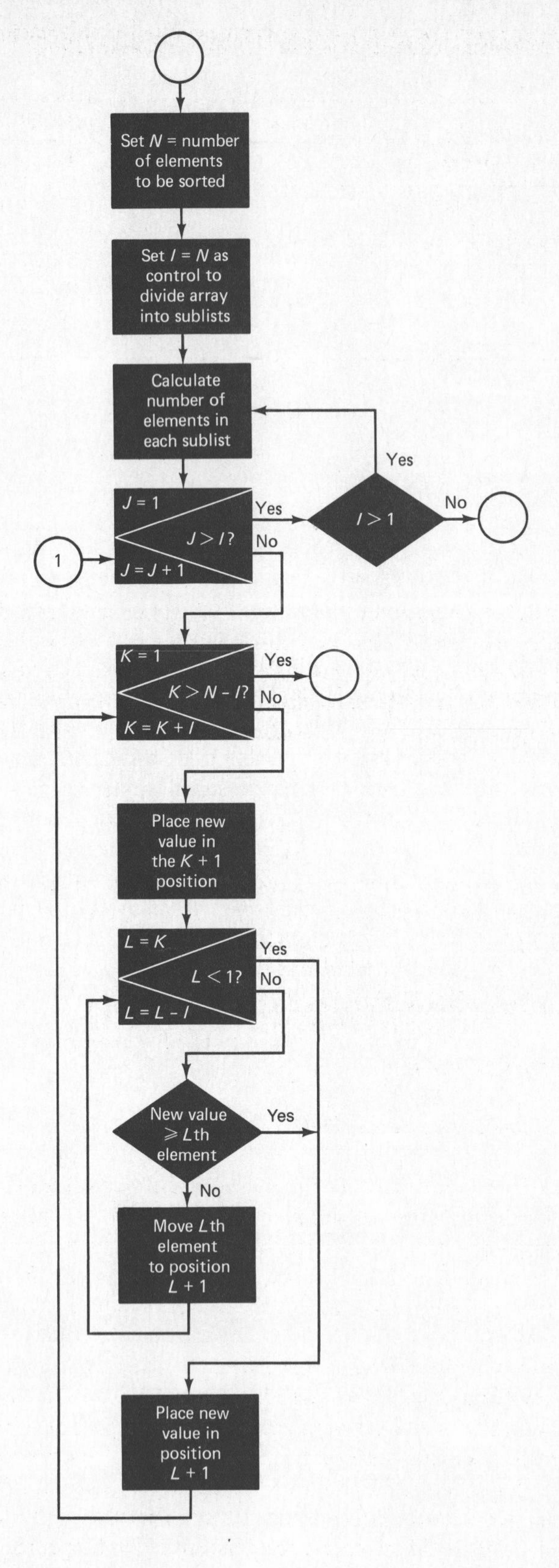

FIGURE 13-9
Flowchart for Shell sort

TABLE 13-10

Use of Pointer Array to Sort R

Element Number	Array R	Original Array P	Arrangement After Pass Number 1	2	3	4	5
1	23	1	5	5	5	5	5
2	59	2	2	1	1	1	1
3	30	3	3	3	3	3	3
4	87	4	4	4	4	6	6
5	11	5	1	2	2	2	2
6	45	6	6	6	6	4	4

```
340        LET L = K
350     NEXT K
360     LET E = P(J)
370     LET P(J) = P(L)
380     LET P(L) = E
390 NEXT J
```

This is relatively straightforward. The pointer array is first loaded with elements as if R is already in order. A search is then conducted to find the smallest element of R. Note that P is used as a subscript for R at line 330. That is its function. Following the search, the order of P is adjusted. This process is outlined in the flowchart in Figure 13-10. The sequence of the elements of the pointer array as it is constructed is shown in Table 13-10. (Remember that R does not change.)

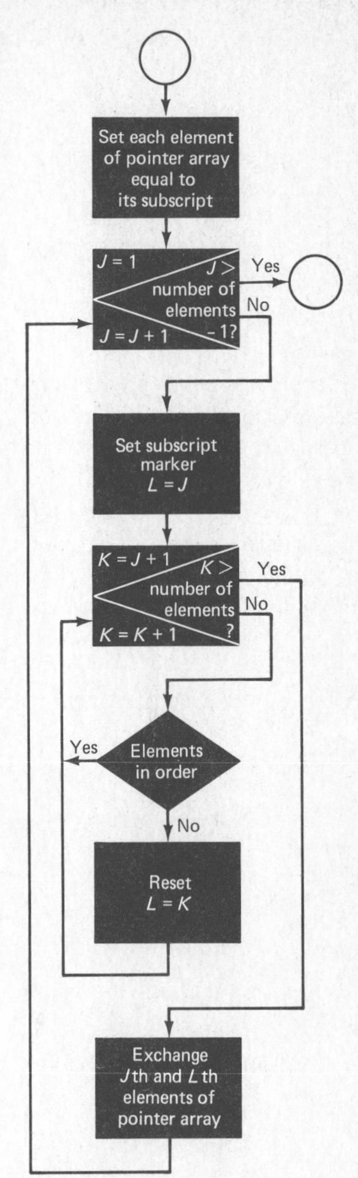

FIGURE 13-10
Flowchart for sorting by pointer method

13-5 THREE-DIMENSIONAL ARRAYS

Three-dimensional arrays are processed much the same as two-dimensional ones except that there is an additional dimension (subscript) to process, referred to as the **level**. The general form of a three-dimensional subscripted variable is:

variable(sub1, sub2, sub3)

which corresponds to the more familiar notation:

variable(row, column, level)

The level adds the third dimension to the array and is a little more difficult to envision than rows and columns alone. It can be thought of as similar two-dimensional arrays, one on top of the other. For example, suppose that we have a three-dimensional array with four rows, five columns, and three levels (a 4 by 5 by 3 array). This would be like *three* two-dimensional 4 by 5 arrays, with the first being at level 1, the second or middle at level 2, and the last at level 3.

Let us look at two possible uses of three-dimensional arrays from the last chapter. The three 3 by 4 two-dimensional arrays that were used to accumulate totals in the Telephone Usage Report in Section 12-3 might have been processed as a single 3 by 4 by 3 three-dimensional array. As another example, look once again at the Absentee Analysis Report produced in Section 12-5. Suppose that the dean of Peckham College wished to process absentee data for the last six quarters rather than just one, and to extend the analysis to include quarterly totals. This could, of course, be done with two-dimensional arrays, but the best way would be to use a single three-dimensional array with the same number of rows and columns as before but with seven levels, six for the quarterly data and one for the totals. This would be an 11 by 6 by 7 array.

All input/output and other processing with three-dimensional arrays is like that with two-dimensional ones except that there is one additional subscript to process. To load a 4 by 5 by 3 array in **level-priority order** (with row-priority within a level) would be written as:

```
200 FOR L = 1 TO 3
210    FOR R = 1 TO 4
220       FOR C = 1 TO 5
230          READ X(R, C, L)
240       NEXT C
250    NEXT R
260 NEXT L
```

Of course, you may process the array in row- or column-priority order by simply changing the order of the loops. The same precaution, however, applies as with two-dimensional arrays. *Be very sure that you know in which order you are processing the data. You may load an array in any way that you wish, but once loaded, if you try to retrieve the data in the wrong order, you will only get a mess.*

Three-dimensional arrays may be searched, summed, sorted, or otherwise processed as a whole; by *all* rows, columns, or levels; or by a *single* row, column, or level. The following finds the largest element on the seventh level of an array and its location:

```
300 LET RS = 1
310 LET CS = 1
320 LET XS = X(1, 1, 7)
330 FOR R = 1 TO 3
340    FOR C = 1 TO 4
350       IF XS <= X(R, C, 7) THEN 390
360       LET CS = C
370       LET RS = R
380       LET XS = X(R, C, 7)
390    NEXT C
400 NEXT R
```

Note the similarity of this and the routine in Section 12-4 that searched an entire two-dimensional array.

We may find the individual sums of all the columns by:

```
400 FOR C = 1 TO 5
410    FOR L = 1 TO 3
420       FOR R = 1 TO 4
430          LET SC(C, L) = SC(C, L) + X(R, C, L)
440       NEXT R
450    NEXT L
460 NEXT C
```

Remember that while there are only five columns on any one level, there are three levels, so there is a total of *fifteen* columns in all. In the above, these are placed in an appropriate 5 by 3 two-dimensional array. The sum of all elements of X can be found by replacing line 430 in the last set of statements with:

```
430 LET S = S + X(R, C, L)
```

An example should clarify the processing of three-dimensional arrays and their possible uses.

13-6 AN EXAMPLE: BASEBALL BUDGET CUTS

The example presented in this section illustrates the use of three-dimensional arrays for processing data and accumulating totals. A special use for sorting is also shown.

Problem: The Swampville Polecats, a *very* minor league baseball team has fallen on hard times. Due to decreasing attendance at the games and rising costs, the coach and general manager (who is also the water, bat, and ball boy) have decided to make some roster cuts. The team has been carrying six players who play the outfield at various times. It has been decided to reduce this number to four. In order to retain the best players, the coach needs a computer program to analyze the six players' performances over the last six seasons. Input for each player will be each season's batting average, number of home runs, number of RBIs (runs batted in), and number of fielding errors. The coach has devised a formula that he feels will help determine the four top players. His formula calculates a total performance score for each player as follows:

$$s = 1000a + 20h + 5b - 15e$$

where a = sum of all batting averages for all six seasons
h = total number of home runs hit in six seasons
b = total RBIs accumulated in six seasons
e = all errors committed in six seasons
s = total performance score

In addition, the coach feels that outstanding performances should be rewarded. An extra 1000 points is to be added to the scores of players having the highest average, number of home runs, number of RBIs, and *lowest* number of errors *in a single season*. The output should be simply the names of the two players to be cut. The input data is given in Table 13-11.

The solution to this problem is briefly outlined below.

1. Dimension arrays for the players' names, the performance data, and the calculated scores. Allow extra space in the performances array for totals.
2. Load the player name array.
3. Set the section of the performance array reserved for totals to zero.
4. Load the performance data array.
5. Accumulate totals for all data of each player for all six seasons.
6. Calculate each player's performance score.
7. Search each level of the performance array and determine which player has the highest yearly value for batting average, home runs, and RBIs, and lowest number of errors.
8. For the players found in the last step, add 1000 to their performance scores.

TABLE 13-11

Player Performance Data for Baseball Budget Cut Problem

Player's Team Nickname	Batting Average, Home Runs, RBIs, and Fielding Errors for Year Number						Player's Team Nickname	Batting Average, Home Runs, RBIs, and Fielding Errors for Year Number					
	1	2	3	4	5	6		1	2	3	4	5	6
Slidecrazy	.223	.218	.182	.209	.253	.211	Rubberbat	.201	.184	.179	.226	.198	.216
	5	4	2	0	5	3		0	2	1	3	1	1
	42	43	34	36	59	40		46	39	39	53	47	43
	6	7	2	8	3	4		4	7	5	4	3	6
Tanglefoot	.312	.294	.278	.303	.307	.300	Bullmoose	.302	.263	.298	.311	.278	.288
	22	11	19	19	15	21		23	19	17	26	20	15
	102	92	89	81	99	89		83	79	77	95	74	68
	27	41	37	31	21	33		18	23	11	31	27	17
Butterglove	.242	.216	.231	.201	.221	.229	LeJochque	.276	.248	.299	.245	.306	.266
	8	3	6	0	5	3		12	11	14	8	12	5
	52	45	50	41	47	52		59	57	71	55	79	70
	11	11	7	13	6	8		8	9	9	11	15	8

9. Find the two players with the lowest performance scores.
10. Print the names of the two players found in the last step.
11. Stop.

This procedure is illustrated in Figure 13-11.

Steps 1 through 5 above are translated into the following program statements:

```
250 DIM N$(6), P(6, 7, 4), S(6)
260 FOR R = 1 TO 6
270    READ N$(R)
280    FOR L = 1 TO 4
290       LET P(R, 7, L) = 0
300       FOR C = 1 TO 6
310          READ P(R, C, L)
320          LET P(R, 7, L) = P(R, 7, L) + P(R, C, L)
330       NEXT C
340    NEXT L
350 NEXT R
```

At line 250, we have dimensioned the performance data array with six rows for the six players, seven columns for the six seasons and one for the totals, and four levels, one for each type of data to be processed. Line 310 loads this array in row-priority with level priority within rows. The totals are accumulated into the seventh column at 320, which has just been set to zero at 290. The name array is loaded at 270. (Of course, all of this could have been done using separate loops, but the above construction is much more efficient.)

The performance score is calculated by lines 390 to 450.

```
390  FOR R = 1 TO 6
400     LET A = P(R, 7, 1)
410     LET H = P(R, 7, 2)
420     LET B = P(R, 7, 3)
430     LET E = P(R, 7, 4)
440     LET S(R) = 1000 * A + 20 * H + 5 * B - 15 * E
450  NEXT R
```

The four assignment statements at 400 to 430 are inserted to simplify the expression in 440. R identifies the row or the player. The sums for the four types of data are stored at the four levels, hence S stores the performance for each player. This is not the final result because the players with the best seasonal values for the four areas must be found. This is found by searching each level of the array separately as follows:

```
500 FOR L = 1 TO 4
510    LET RS = 1
520    LET PM = P(1, 1, L)
530    FOR R = 1 TO 6
540       FOR C = 1 TO 6
550          IF L < 4 AND PM => P(R, C, L) THEN 590
560          IF L = 4 AND PM <= P(R, C, L) THEN 590
570          LET RS = R
580          LET PM = P(R, C, L)
590       NEXT C
600    NEXT R
610    LET S(RS) = S(RS) + 1000
620 NEXT L
```

Lines 510 to 600 constitute a basic sequential search of one level of the array. The outer loop causes the search to be repeated for all four levels. Line 550 states that for the first

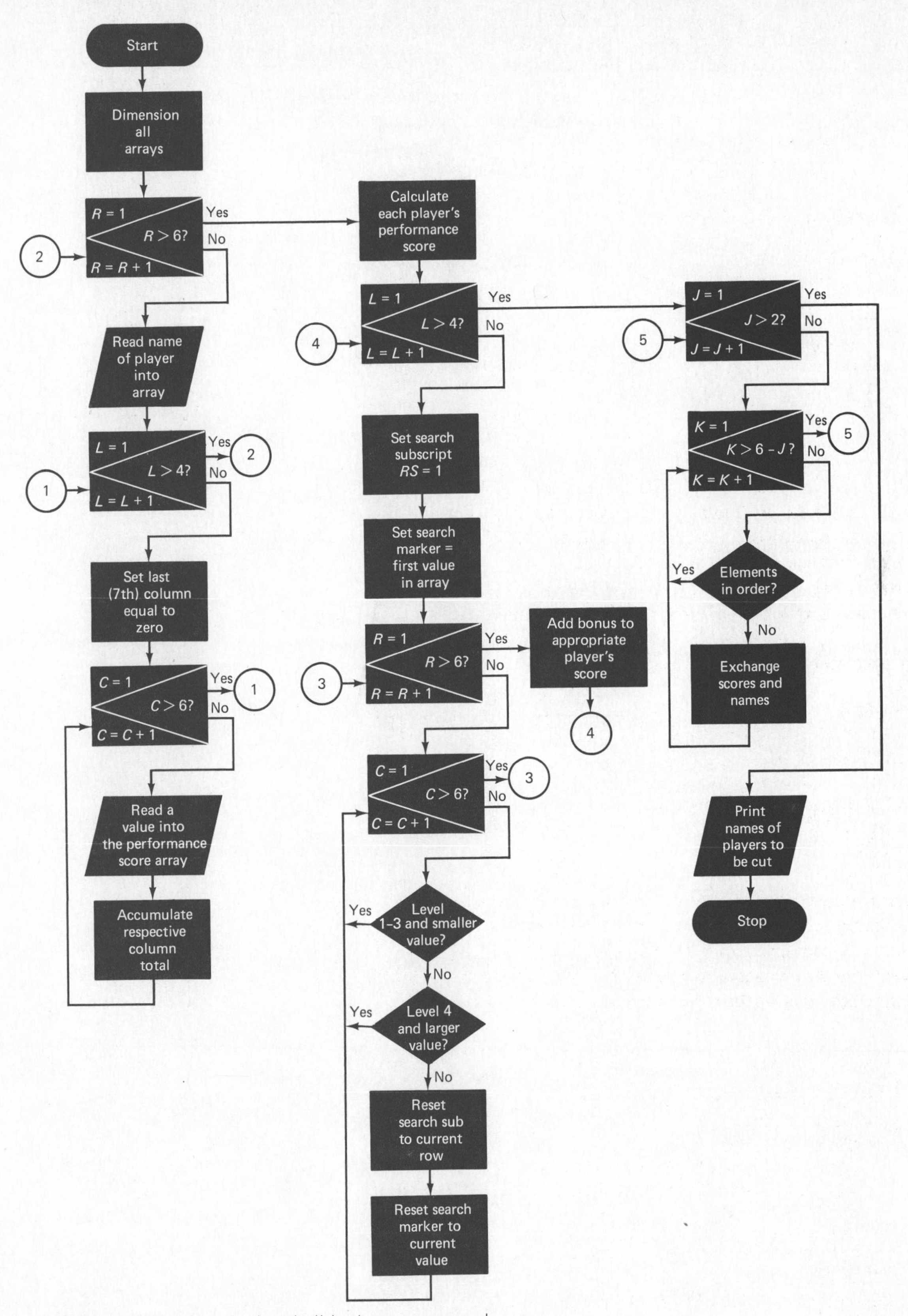

FIGURE 13-11 Flowchart for baseball budget cuts example

three levels, we are searching for the *largest* value, while 560 causes the search of the fourth level to be for the *smallest* one. After a search of each level is completed, the bonus is added to the proper player's total score at line 610.

This completes the processing of the performance data and the determination of the performance scores. All that remains is to find the two players with the lowest scores. There are many ways of doing this. The procedure used here is to sort the data to push the two lowest scores to the bottom of the array. This is done at lines 660 to 760.

```
660 FOR J = 1 TO 2
670    FOR K = 1 TO 6 - J
680       IF S(K) => S(K + 1) THEN 750
690       LET EX = S(K)
700       LET S(K) = S(K + 1)
710       LET S(K + 1) = EX
720       LET EX$ = N$(K)
730       LET N$(K) = N$(K + 1)
740       LET N$(K + 1) = EX$
750    NEXT K
760 NEXT J
```

Note that this is a straightforward bubble sort for *descending* order, except that at line 660 we pass through the array only *twice* because we need only the *two* lowest values. The unlucky players' names are printed by lines 800 to 830.

A complete listing and run follow.

```
 10 REM   BASEBALL BUDGET CUTS
 20 REM
 30 REM   VARIABLES ARE DEFINED AS --
 40 REM
 50 REM         N$ = ARRAY FOR NAMES OF PLAYERS
 60 REM          P = ARRAY FOR PERFORMANCE STATISTICS
 70 REM          S = ARRAY FOR PERFORMANCE SCORE
 80 REM          A = TOTAL BATTING AVERAGE
 90 REM          H = TOTAL NUMBER OF HOME RUNS
100 REM          B = TOTAL NUMBER OF RBI'S
110 REM          E = TOTAL NUMBER OF FIELDING ERRORS
120 REM          R = ROW COUNTER
130 REM          C = COLUMN COUNTER
140 REM          L = LEVEL COUNTER
150 REM    J AND K = LOOP COUNTERS
160 REM         EX = EXCHANGE VARIABLE FOR SCORE ARRAY
170 REM        EX$ = EXCHANGE VARIABLE FOR NAME ARRAY
180 REM         RS = SEARCH SUBSCRIPT
190 REM         PM = SEARCH MARKER
200 REM
210 REM   DIMENSION AND LOAD ALL ARRAYS.  SET THE
220 REM   SEVENTH COLUMN OF PERFORMANCE ARRAY TO
230 REM   ZERO AND ACCUMULATE THE RESPECTIVE TOTALS.
240 REM
250 DIM N$(6), P(6, 7, 4), S(6)
260 FOR R = 1 TO 6
270    READ N$(R)
280    FOR L = 1 TO 4
290       LET P(R, 7, L) = 0
300       FOR C = 1 TO 6
310          READ P(R, C, L)
320          LET P(R, 7, L) = P(R, 7, L) + P(R, C, L)
330       NEXT C
340    NEXT L
350 NEXT R
360 REM
```

```
370 REM  CALCULATE THE PLAYERS' SCORES
380 REM
390 FOR R = 1 TO 6
400   LET A = P(R, 7, 1)
410   LET H = P(R, 7, 2)
420   LET B = P(R, 7, 3)
430   LET E = P(R, 7, 4)
440   LET S(R) = 1000 * A + 20 * H + 5 * B - 15 * E
450 NEXT R
460 REM
470 REM  SEARCH FOR PLAYERS WITH HIGHEST PERFORMANCES
480 REM  IN EACH AREA AND ADD BONUSES TO TOTAL SCORES
490 REM
500 FOR L = 1 TO 4
510   LET RS = 1
520   LET PM = P(1, 1, L)
530   FOR R = 1 TO 6
540     FOR C = 1 TO 6
550       IF L < 4 AND PM => P(R, C, L) THEN 590
560       IF L = 4 AND PM <= P(R, C, L) THEN 590
570       LET RS = R
580       LET PM = P(R, C, L)
590     NEXT C
600   NEXT R
610   LET S(RS) = S(RS) + 1000
620 NEXT L
630 REM
640 REM  DETERMINE THE TWO PLAYERS WITH THE LOWEST SCORES
650 REM
660 FOR J = 1 TO 2
670   FOR K = 1 TO 6 - J
680     IF S(K) => S(K + 1) THEN 750
690     LET EX = S(K)
700     LET S(K) = S(K + 1)
710     LET S(K + 1) = EX
720     LET EX$ = N$(K)
730     LET N$(K) = N$(K + 1)
740     LET N$(K + 1) = EX$
750   NEXT K
760 NEXT J
770 REM
780 REM  PRINT THE UNLUCKY PLAYERS NAMES
790 REM
800 PRINT "THE TWO UNLUCKY PLAYERS THAT MUST BE CUT ARE --
810 PRINT
820 PRINT , N$(6)
830 PRINT , N$(5)
840 REM
850 REM  DATA TO BE PROCESSED
860 REM
870 DATA "SLIDECRAZY",.223,.218,.182,.209,.253,.211
880 DATA 5,4,2,0,5,3,42,43,34,36,59,40,6,7,2,8,3,4
890 DATA "TANGLEFOOT",.317,.294,.278,.303,.307,.300
900 DATA 23,11,19,19,15,21,102,92,89,81,99,89,27,41,37,31,21,33
910 DATA "BUTTERGLOVE",.242,.216,.231,.201,.221,.229
920 DATA 8,3,6,0,5,3,52,45,50,41,47,52,11,11,7,13,6,8
930 DATA "RUBBERBAT",.201,.184,.179,.226,.198,.216
940 DATA 0,2,1,3,1,1,46,39,39,53,47,43,4,7,5,4,3,6
950 DATA "BULLMOOSE",.302,.263,.298,.311,.278,.288
960 DATA 23,19,17,26,20,15,83,79,77,95,74,68,18,23,11,31,27,17
970 DATA "LEJOCHQUE",.276,.248,.299,.245,.306,.266
980 DATA 12,11,14,8,12,5,59,57,71,55,79,70,8,9,9,11,15,8
990 END
```

```
THE TWO UNLUCKY PLAYERS THAT MUST BE CUT ARE --

                RUBBERBAT
                BUTTERGLOVE
```

13-7 MULTILEVEL CONTROL BREAK PROCESSING

As we saw in Section 8-7, control break processing involves the temporary interruption of one process for another, usually caused by a change in some key variable. In Section 8-8, we examined an example of a **single-level** control break program, or one in which the break takes place with a change in only one variable. If more than one variable is involved, we normally have what is known as a **multilevel** control break. In Section 8-7 a single-level control break was described in which the average daily sales for the salespersons in a store were processed with control breaks being taken with a department change. Suppose that this is a large store with several branches. We might also process by branch, taking another control break with a branch change, while continuing to take control breaks for department changes within each branch. This would be an example of a problem with *two* levels. Maybe we have a *very* large store with locations in several cities. Now, along with the changes for departments and branches, we can take a control break with a change in the city. This adds a *third* level. Although there is no limit to the number of levels that such a problem can have, three to four levels is the practical limit before the processing becomes too involved to be easily handled.

Basically, the additional levels are processed in a similar manner to the first one. That is, a control break is caused to occur whenever a change in some key variable is detected. This is normally found by comparing the value just read to that saved in the compare variable. Although there are many techniques for processing multilevel control breaks, possibly the best is by the use of subroutines in which higher level breaks call successively lower ones. In the above example, if there is a city change, before we can print city summary data, we must print the results for the last branch processed, so that routine is called. However, before the branch data can be printed, we must print the information for the last department, hence we call the routine that does that. Each total line is then printed in the proper order. It is this procedure that we will use in the example in Section 13-8.

13-8 AN EXAMPLE: MOVIE ATTENDANCE SUMMARY REPORT

An example of a two-level control break is presented in this section. We will employ subroutines and the modular approach (see Chapter 10) in the solution to this problem.

Problem: A certain movie production company needs a computer program to process the weekly attendance data for its new movies as they are shown around the country. Most of the movies are shown in more than one theater in each of several cities at the same time. The attendance data for one week is given in Table 13-12. The report is to be **group printed** (see Problem 18, Chapter 8) by city for each movie, giving only one print line for each city in which a movie is shown. This line should indicate the movie, city, number of theaters showing the movie, and total attendance. After all cities in which a movie has been shown have been processed, the total number of cities, theaters, and attendance for that movie should be printed. At the end of the report, the total number of movies, cities, theaters, and attendance for all movies is to be printed. Finally, the movie name should be **group indicated** (see Problem 20, Chapter 8).

We shall take a somewhat different approach to the solution of this problem. As was stated in Section 13-7, this type of program is most easily solved by the use of subroutines. Therefore, rather than the usual solution outline and flowchart, we will divide this program into modules and construct an organizational diagram much as we did for the examples in Chapter 10.

As with all modular programs, this one will have a main program module from which

TABLE 13-12

Data for Movie Attendance Summary Report Problem

Name of Movie	City Name	Theater Number	Atten-dance	Name of Movie	City Name	Theater Number	Atten-dance
Last Days of Earth	St. Louis	01772	1882	Larry Loves Lucy	Dallas	49923	676
Last Days of Earth	St. Louis	12783	982	Larry Loves Lucy	Dallas	54432	989
Last Days of Earth	St. Louis	32576	2911	Devil's Diner	Seattle	08993	793
Last Days of Earth	Memphis	27822	3288	Devil's Diner	Seattle	28893	4893
Snakebit	Atlanta	29011	302	Devil's Diner	Seattle	49920	2883
Snakebit	Atlanta	32902	2309	Devil's Diner	New York	33288	3988
Snakebit	Atlanta	40023	1465	Devil's Diner	New York	42402	1928
Snakebit	Miami	11928	3599	Devil's Diner	New York	73888	4509
Snakebit	Miami	32255	2892	Devil's Diner	New York	74883	2872
Snakebit	Houston	30992	3902	Devil's Diner	New York	98566	1892
Snakebit	Mobile	59002	2903	Devil's Diner	Chicago	19739	2991
Snakebit	Mobile	69336	4029	Devil's Diner	Chicago	39837	5873

all processing is controlled. This module will call those that process the control break. The organization of the program modules is as follows:

```
Main program module
    Call subroutine to print headings and
        initialize values
    If movie change, call subroutine to process
        movie change
    If city change, call subroutine to process
        city change

Module to print headings and initialize values
RETURN

Module to process movie change
Call subroutine to process city change
If end of processing, call subroutine to
    process final totals and end
RETURN

Module to process city change
RETURN

Module to process final totals and end
RETURN
```

This organization is shown in the diagram in Figure 13-12.

The main processing module is written as follows:

```
260 GOSUB 340
270 READ M$, C$, T, A
280 IF M$ <> MS$ THEN GOSUB 480
290 IF C$ <> CS$ THEN GOSUB 710
300 LET CT = CT + 1
310 LET CA = CA + A
320 GOTO 270
```

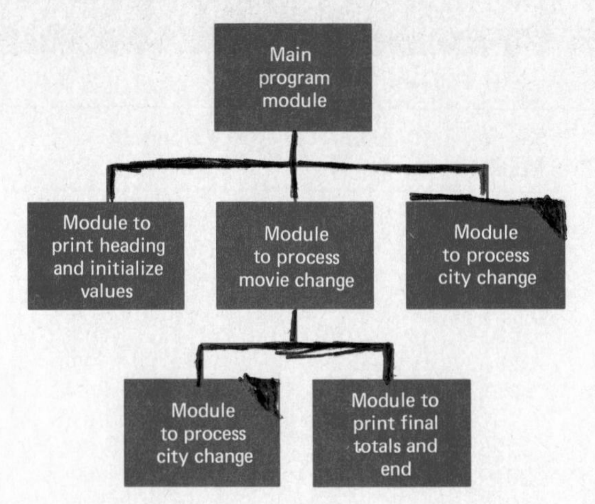

FIGURE 13-12
Organizational diagram for movie attendance summary report example

The first task is to call the subroutine that prints the headings and initializes all values. After a record is read, a check is made at line 280 for a movie change. If one has occurred, then the subroutine that processes it is called. If the movie has not changed, then a check is made at line 290 for a city change. As we will see below, if the movie changes, then so does the city; therefore, that subroutine is called from the movie change subroutine and the city name updated. This means that if the subroutine at 280 is called, the one at 290 will not be because it was in the movie change subroutine. Lines 300 and 310 update theater and attendance totals for a city. Note that there is no PRINT statement; this is because we will not print until all theaters for a city have been processed.

The module for processing a city is written as:

```
730 IF FG$ <> "YES" THEN LET P$ = " "
740 LET FG$ = "NO"
750 PRINT P$; TAB(26); CS$; TAB(44); CT; TAB(56); CA
760 LET MC = MC + 1
770 LET MT = MT + CT
780 LET MA = MA + CA
790 LET CT = 0
800 LET CA = 0
810 LET CS$ = C$
820 RETURN
```

The first three lines print the city summary line with the movie name group indicated. This means that after a control break for a movie change, the movie name is printed only on the first line and is suppressed thereafter until a new movie name is printed. This causes the output to be as follows:

```
SNAKEBIT                  ATLANTA          3          4076
                          MIAMI            2          6491
                          HOUSTON          1          3902
                          MOBILE           2          6995
```

This is opposed to having the movie name SNAKEBIT appear on every line. This is controlled by the flag FG$, which is set equal to YES whenever there is a movie change (and at the beginning of the program) and NO otherwise. Lines 760 to 780 update the totals for number of cities and theaters and attendance for a movie. The next two lines reset the total accumulators for the next city. Line 810 stores the new city name in the compare variable.

The module for processing the headings and initializing values has nothing worth special note except that *both* compare variables for the movie and city names have been initialized at lines 430 and 440. The module that processes movie changes is:

```
500 IF FL$ <> "FIRST" THEN 540
510 LET FL$ = "NOT FIRST"
520 LET CS$ = C$
530 GOTO 660
540 GOSUB 710
550 PRINT
560 PRINT TAB(12); "TOTALS"; TAB(28); MC; TAB(44); MT; TAB(56); MA
570 PRINT
580 LET TM = TM + 1
590 LET TC = TC + MC
600 LET TT = TT + MT
610 LET TA = TA + MA
620 IF M$ = "STOP" THEN GOSUB 840
630 LET MC = 0
640 LET MT = 0
650 LET MA = 0
660 LET MS$ = M$
670 LET FG$ = "YES"
680 LET P$ = M$
690 RETURN
```

The first four lines take care of processing the first record. Line 540 calls the subroutine that processes a city change. *Whenever there is a change in a movie, we must first print the totals for the last city for the previous movie*. Lines 580 to 610 update the grand totals for all movies, while the accumulators for a single movie are reset at 630 to 650. Line 620 checks for the end of processing. The new movie name is stored in the compare variable at 660, and the group indication flag is set at 670. The movie name is placed in the print variable at 680 so it will print. Note that it is cleared at line 730 when FG$ <> "YES" so it will no longer print. At the end of processing, the final totals are printed beginning at line 860. Note that M$ = "STOP", used to signal the end of the data, is at first treated as just another movie name change until line 620 detects it and directs processing to the proper place.

A complete program listing and run follow.

```
 10 REM  MOVIE ATTENDANCE SUMMARY REPORT
 20 REM
 30 REM  VARIABLES ARE DEFINED AS --
 40 REM
 50 REM         M$ = MOVIE NAME
 60 REM         C$ = CITY NAME
 70 REM          T = THEATER NUMBER
 80 REM          A = ATTENDANCE AT ONE THEATER
 90 REM        MS$ = SAVE AREA FOR MOVIE NAME
100 REM        CS$ = SAVE AREA FOR CITY NAME
110 REM        FL$ = FIRST RECORD FLAG
120 REM         P$ = PRINT VARIABLE
130 REM        FG$ = GROUP INDICATION CONTROL FLAG
140 REM         CT = TOTAL THEATERS IN ONE CITY FOR ONE MOVIE
150 REM         CA = ATTENDANCE IN ONE CITY FOR ONE MOVIE
160 REM         MC = TOTAL CITIES SHOWING ONE MOVIE
170 REM         MT = TOTAL THEATERS SHOWING ONE MOVIE
180 REM         MA = TOTAL ATTENDANCE FOR ONE MOVIE
190 REM         TM = TOTAL MOVIES
200 REM         TC = TOTAL CITIES SHOWING ALL MOVIE
210 REM         TT = TOTAL THEATERS SHOWING ALL MOVIES
220 REM         TA = TOTAL ATTENDANCE FOR ALL MOVIES
230 REM
240 REM  MAIN MODULE TO CONTROL PROCESSING
```

```
250 REM
260 GOSUB 340
270 READ M$, C$, T, A
280 IF M$ <> MS$ THEN GOSUB 480
290 IF C$ <> CS$ THEN GOSUB 710
300 LET CT = CT + 1
310 LET CA = CA + A
320 GOTO 270
330 REM
340 REM  MODULE TO PRINT HEADINGS AND INITIALIZE VALUES
350 REM
360 PRINT TAB(17); "MOVIE ATTENDANCE SUMMARY REPORT"
370 PRINT
380 PRINT
390 PRINT TAB(6); "MOVIE"; TAB(28); "CITY";
400 PRINT TAB(41); "THEATERS"; TAB(54); "ATTENDANCE"
410 PRINT
420 READ CT, CA, MC, MT, MA, TM, TC, TT, TA
430 LET MS$ = "SAVE"
440 LET CS$ = "SAVE"
450 LET FL$ = "FIRST"
460 RETURN
470 REM
480 REM  MODULE TO PROCESS MOVIE CHANGE
490 REM
500 IF FL$ <> "FIRST" THEN 540
510 LET FL$ = "NOT FIRST"
520 LET CS$ = C$
530 GOTO 660
540 GOSUB 710
550 PRINT
560 PRINT TAB(12); "TOTALS"; TAB(28); MC; TAB(44); MT; TAB(56); MA
570 PRINT
580 LET TM = TM + 1
590 LET TC = TC + MC
600 LET TT = TT + MT
610 LET TA = TA + MA
620 IF M$ = "STOP" THEN GOSUB 840
630 LET MC = 0
640 LET MT = 0
650 LET MA = 0
660 LET MS$ = M$
670 LET FG$ = "YES"
680 LET P$ = M$
690 RETURN
700 REM
710 REM  MODULE TO PROCESS CITY CHANGE
720 REM
730 IF FG$ <> "YES" THEN LET P$ = " "
740 LET FG$ = "NO"
750 PRINT P$; TAB(26); CS$; TAB(44); CT; TAB(56); CA
760 LET MC = MC + 1
770 LET MT = MT + CT
780 LET MA = MA + CA
790 LET CT = 0
800 LET CA = 0
810 LET CS$ = C$
820 RETURN
830 REM
840 REM  MODULE TO PROCESS FINAL TOTALS AND END
850 REM
860 PRINT "TOTALS FOR ALL MOVIES SHOWN --
870 PRINT
880 PRINT TAB(7); TM; TAB(28); TC; TAB(44); TT; TAB(56); TA
```

```
 890 GOTO 1200
 900 RETURN
 910 REM
 920 REM  DATA TO BE PROCESSED
 930 REM
 940 DATA 0, 0, 0, 0, 0, 0, 0, 0, 0
 950 DATA "LAST DAYS OF EARTH", "ST. LOUIS", 01772, 1882
 960 DATA "LAST DAYS OF EARTH", "ST. LOUIS", 12783, 982
 970 DATA "LAST DAYS OF EARTH", "ST. LOUIS", 32576, 2911
 980 DATA "LAST DAYS OF EARTH", "MEMPHIS", 27822, 3288
 990 DATA "SNAKEBIT", "ATLANTA", 29011, 302
1000 DATA "SNAKEBIT", "ATLANTA", 32902, 2309
1010 DATA "SNAKEBIT", "ATLANTA", 40023, 1465
1020 DATA "SNAKEBIT", "MIAMI", 11928, 3599
1030 DATA "SNAKEBIT", "MIAMI", 32255, 2892
1040 DATA "SNAKEBIT", "HOUSTON", 30992, 3902
1050 DATA "SNAKEBIT", "MOBILE", 59002, 2903
1060 DATA "SNAKEBIT", "MOBILE", 69336, 4092
1070 DATA "LARRY LOVES LUCY", "DALLAS", 49923, 676
1080 DATA "LARRY LOVES LUCY", "DALLAS", 54432, 989
1090 DATA "DEVIL'S DINER", "SEATTLE", 08993, 793
1100 DATA "DEVIL'S DINER", "SEATTLE", 28893, 4893
1110 DATA "DEVIL'S DINER", "SEATTLE", 49920, 2883
1120 DATA "DEVIL'S DINER", "NEW YORK", 33288, 3988
1130 DATA "DEVIL'S DINER", "NEW YORK", 42402, 1928
1140 DATA "DEVIL'S DINER", "NEW YORK", 73888, 4509
1150 DATA "DEVIL'S DINER", "NEW YORK", 74883, 2872
1160 DATA "DEVIL'S DINER", "NEW YORK", 98566, 1892
1170 DATA "DEVIL'S DINER", "CHICAGO", 19739, 2991
1180 DATA "DEVIL'S DINER", "CHICAGO", 39837, 5873
1190 DATA "STOP", "XXX", 0, 0
1200 END
```

```
                MOVIE ATTENDANCE SUMMARY REPORT


    MOVIE                 CITY          THEATERS     ATTENDANCE

LAST DAYS OF EARTH       ST. LOUIS          3           5775
                         MEMPHIS            1           3288

           TOTALS           2               4           9063

SNAKEBIT                 ATLANTA            3           4076
                         MIAMI              2           6491
                         HOUSTON            1           3902
                         MOBILE             2           6995

           TOTALS           4               8           21464

LARRY LOVES LUCY         DALLAS             2           1665

           TOTALS           1               2           1665

DEVIL'S DINER            SEATTLE            3           8569
                         NEW YORK           5           15189
                         CHICAGO            2           8864

           TOTALS           3               10          32622

TOTALS FOR ALL MOVIES SHOWN --

     4                      10              24          64814
```

TROUBLESHOOTING

Each of the following programs contains an error that prevents it from executing properly. Explain *specifically* what the problem is and what must be done to correct it. To assist you, a sample of what would happen should you attempt to run the program is provided after each listing. Refer to Appendix D for an explanation of BASIC error messages.

1.

```
 10 REM   TROUBLESHOOTING PROBLEM 13-1
 20 REM
 30 REM           N = ANY ARRAY OF NUMBERS
 40 REM           E = VALUE TO BE FOUND IN N
 50 REM           M = LOCATION OF E IN N
 60 REM          NX = NUMBER OF ELEMENTS IN N
 70 REM
 80 DIM N(100)
 90 FOR X = 1 TO 100
100    READ N(X)
110    IF N(X) < 0 THEN 130
120 NEXT X
130 LET NX = X - 1
140 INPUT "ENTER NUMBER TO BE FOUND"; E
150 PRINT
160 LET F = 1
170 LET L = NX
180 LET M = INT((F + L) / 2)
190 IF E = N(M) THEN 260
200 IF F => L THEN 280
210 IF E < N(M) THEN 240
220 LET F = M + 1
230 GOTO 180
240 LET L = M - 1
250 GOTO 180
260 PRINT "VALUE FOUND AT ELEMENT NUMBER"; M
270 GOTO 300
280 PRINT "VALUE NOT FOUND"
290 DATA 23,15,77,39,7,45,57,11,64,55,82,13,5,27,8,-1
300 END

ENTER VALUE TO BE FOUND? 45

VALUE NOT FOUND
```

2.

```
 10 REM   TROUBLESHOOTING PROBLEM 13-2
 20 REM
 30 REM           N = AN ARRAY OF NUMBERS
 40 REM          NX = THE NUMBER OF ELEMENTS IN N
 50 REM
 60 DIM N(100)
 70 FOR X = 1 TO 100
 80    READ N(X)
 90    IF N(X) < 0 THEN 110
100 NEXT X
110 LET NX = X - 1
120 LET J = 1
130 LET F = 0
140 FOR K = 1 TO NX
150    IF N(K) <= N(K + 1) THEN 200
160    LET E = N(K)
170    LET N(K) = N(K + 1)
180    LET N(K + 1) = E
190    LET F = 1
```

```
200 NEXT K
210 LET J = J + 1
220 IF F <> 0 THEN 130
230 PRINT "THE SORTED ARRAY IS --"
240 PRINT
250 FOR X = 1 TO NX
260   PRINT N(X);
270 NEXT X
280 DATA 23,15,77,39,7,45,57,11,64,55,82,13,5,27,8,-1
290 END

THE SORTED ARRAY IS --

-1  5  7  8  11  13  15  23  27  39  45  55  57  64  77
```

3.

```
 10 REM  TROUBLESHOOTING PROBLEM 13-3
 20 REM
 30 REM       TR = AN ARRAY
 40 REM       TS = SORTED VERSION OF TR
 50 REM        M = VALUE FOR SELECTION SORT
 60 REM
 70 DIM TR(8), TS(8)
 80 FOR Z = 1 TO 8
 90   READ TR(Z)
100 NEXT Z
110 FOR J = 1 TO 8
120   LET M = 100
130   FOR K = 1 TO 8
140     IF M <= TR(K) THEN 170
150     LET M = TR(K)
160     LET S = K
170   NEXT K
180   LET TS(J) = M
190   LET TR(S) = 100
200 NEXT J
210 FOR Z = 1 TO 8
220   PRINT TS(Z);
230 NEXT Z
240 DATA 73,8,119,47,81,-11,98,17
250 END

-11  8  17  47  73  81  98  100
```

IMPORTANT TERMS

After studying this chapter, you should be familiar with the meaning and use of the following terms:

Sequential search
Binary search
Ascending order
Descending order
Sort
Bubble sort
Exchange method
Nested-loop interchange sort
Selection sort
Sorter array
Maximum-minimum interchange sort
Insertion sort
Shell sort
Pointer method
Pointer array
Three-dimensional array
Level
Level-priority order
Single-level control break
Multilevel control break
Group printed
Group indicated

EXERCISES

1. Write DIM statements for the following arrays:
   (a) F with 6 rows, 3 columns, and 12 levels
   (b) NM with 9 rows and columns and 5 levels
   (c) SR$ with 3 rows, 7 columns, and 4 levels
2. Write BASIC statements to accomplish the following tasks:
   (a) Load a 5 by 3 by 4 array in column-priority with level-priority within columns.
   (b) Find the smallest element in the fifth row of a 6 by 7 by 6 array.
   (c) Find the column totals of a 5 by 4 by 7 array.
   (d) Count the zeros in the second and fifth levels of a 4 by 7 by 5 array.
   (e) Print a 4 by 5 by 3 array one level at a time as if it were three two-dimensional arrays.

For Exercises 3 to 5, give the output that will be produced by the given programs. Then type the program into the computer, run them, and check the actual outputs against your predictions.

3.
```
 10 DIM H(100)
 20 FOR X = 1 TO 100
 30    READ H(X)
 40    IF H(X) < 0 THEN 60
 50 NEXT X
 60 LET HX = X - 1
 70 FOR J = 1 TO HX - 1
 80    FOR K = 1 TO HX - J
 90       IF H(K) => H(K + 1) THEN 130
100       LET E = H(K)
110       LET H(K) = H(K + 1)
120       LET H(K + 1) = E
130    NEXT K
140 NEXT J
150 PRINT "THE SORTED ARRAY IS --"
160 PRINT
170 FOR X = 1 TO HX
180    PRINT H(X);
190 NEXT X
200 DATA 19,79,51,83,34,62,25,13,-1
210 END
```

4.
```
 10 DIM X(3, 4, 2)
 20 FOR A = 1 TO 3
 30    FOR B = 1 TO 4
 40       FOR C = 1 TO 2
 50          LET X(A, B, C) = A + B + C
 60       NEXT C
 70    NEXT B
 80 NEXT A
 90 FOR A = 1 TO 3
100    FOR C = 1 TO 2
110       FOR B = 1 TO 4
120          PRINT X(A, B, C);
130       NEXT B
140       PRINT
150    NEXT C
160    PRINT
170 NEXT A
180 PRINT
190 FOR C = 1 TO 2
200    FOR B = 1 TO 4
210       FOR A = 1 TO 3
```

```
220          PRINT X(A, B, C);
230        NEXT A
240        PRINT
250      NEXT B
260      PRINT
270 NEXT C
280 END
```

5.
```
 10 DIM V(8), S(8)
 20 FOR X = 1 TO 8
 30    READ V(X)
 40    LET S(X) = X
 50 NEXT X
 60 FOR J = 1 TO 5
 70    LET L = J
 80    FOR K = J + 1 TO 8
 90       IF V(S(L)) <= V(S(K)) THEN 110
100       LET L = K
110    NEXT K
120    LET E = S(J)
130    LET S(J) = S(L)
140    LET S(L) = E
150 NEXT J
160 FOR X = 1 TO 8
170    PRINT V(S(X));
180 NEXT X
190 DATA 15,63,44,79,20,11,71,58
200 END
```

PROGRAMMING PROBLEMS

Write programs in BASIC to accomplish the tasks described by each of the following problems. Be sure to carefully document each program and include all appropriate report headings and other literals.

1. Write a program that will search an array for a specific element by both the sequential and binary methods to permit you to time (as with a stopwatch) the relative speeds of the searches. Your program should first load the array, pause and allow you to input the element to be found, and then search for the element by each method. You should insert some interruption into the program so that you will know when the first method is completed and the second is to begin. Try this with an array of 1000 elements and increase the number as the speed of your system permits. (You may load the array in any way you wish, but remember that it must be sorted for the binary search. A simple method would be to load each element of the array with its subscript.)
2. Modify the program on invoice preparation for Cindy's Cameras presented in Section 9-6 to search the inventory table using a binary search.
3. Write a program to sort and print the list of seniors at Primate College (see Problem 5, Chapter 9) in descending order by GPA.
4. Write a program to read a list of students' names and test grades, calculate the average of the tests for each student, and print the students' names and averages in descending order by average. Use the data for Problem 4, Chapter 7.
5. Write a new program for the air pollution report example (see Section 6-4) to print the following two lists: (1) city names and average pollution counts for each city and (2) the days and average counts for each day, with both lists sorted in descending order by count.
6. Write a program that will load an array with a series of random integers and then sort the array by each of the following sorting techniques: bubble, selection, maximum-minimum interchange, insertion, and Shell. Run the program and sort the array by each method, timing each to obtain a relative comparison of the speeds for different

sorting procedures. Try this for an array of 100 elements and then increase the number as the speed of your system permits. (This would be an excellent chance to practice writing a menu-driven program.)

7. Write a program that will unsort or scramble a series of values. One way to do this is to read a series of random numbers into a second array of equal size so that one random number corresponds to each value of your original list. Now, sort the random numbers, exchanging both the values in the random number array and your original list. You supply a list of values to unsort.
8. Rewrite the program for the Customer Account Update example presented in Section 13-3 to read all of the day's transactions at once and presort this data into the same order as the customer master table before it is processed. The output should be the same as that shown in the example.
9. Write a grade report that will read nine weekly grades for a series of students into a two-dimensional array. The report should permit the interactive entry of a student's name and provide a list of that student's grades in descending order along with the week number in which each grade was scored. Use the data for Problem 3, Chapter 9.
10. The dean of Rockhead College (see Problem 10, Chapter 7) wishes to have another program to analyze the list of potential graduates. The dean wants to be able to list the seniors in order by GPA, total hours, or GPA in the major. Write a menu-driven program that will permit the dean to sort and print the list of seniors in ascending order by any of these three methods.
11. Modify the program for the Telephone Usage Report example in Section 12-3 as suggested in Section 13-5 to use a single three-dimensional array for all totals.
12. Thingamajigs, Ltd. makes a very exclusive line of thingamajigs that come in any combination of three sizes and four styles. The unit price and quantity in stock for each combination is given in the table below.

Size Code	Style Codes 1	2	3	4
1	14.75	15.50	17.00	19.25
	116	82	65	63
2	16.00	17.50	18.75	20.75
	82	56	71	49
3	17.25	18.75	21.50	23.25
	42	34	31	39

A Sales Summary Report is needed that presents the total sales, total number shipped, and total number back-ordered for each combination of sizes and styles. (See table below.) The total sales represents the sales from *all* orders whether the particular item is available for immediate shipment or must be back-ordered. Items ordered that are in the inventory can be shipped immediately, but if more of a certain

Size No.	Style No.	Quantity Purchased	Size No.	Style No.	Quantity Purchased	Size No.	Style No.	Quantity Purchased	Size No.	Style No.	Quantity Purchased
1	3	12	2	4	12	1	1	5	3	1	10
3	1	15	2	4	9	1	3	12	2	2	8
3	1	10	3	3	6	1	1	7	2	2	12
3	4	6	1	3	20	2	3	12	2	4	12
1	3	24	3	3	15	3	1	12	1	1	12
3	3	15	2	4	20	1	1	15	2	2	15
1	3	25	1	1	15	1	2	12	1	2	6
3	3	10	2	3	6	1	4	12	1	2	10
2	4	24	2	3	12	2	1	9	3	1	6
1	1	10	3	1	5	2	3	10	3	4	15

item is ordered than is in the stock, then the excess must be recorded separately as back-ordered. The inventory table above should be processed as a 3 by 4 by 2 array. The totals should be processed as a 3 by 4 by 3 array.

13. Modify your program for Problem 12 to include the following additional information: (1) the size and style combination that was ordered in the largest quantity, (2) the size that was ordered in the largest number for all styles, and (3) the style that was ordered in the largest number for all sizes.

14. Local scientists wish to determine the hottest time of the day during a certain time of the year. They have set up five sensors at different locations to measure the temperature at hourly intervals from noon to 5:00 p.m. for a 1-week period. The data that was gathered is given in the table below. Write a program to process this data and determine (1) the day, time, and sensor number of the highest temperature reading and (2) the time of the highest average temperature for all days and sensors. Only these two results need be printed.

Time of Day	Sensor Number	Temperature Readings for Mon.	Tue.	Wed.	Thu.	Fri.	Sat.	Sun.	Time of Day	Sensor Number	Temperature Readings for Mon.	Tue.	Wed.	Thu.	Fri.	Sat.	Sun.
Noon	1	88	83	89	93	88	84	87	3 PM	1	92	90	93	98	97	90	93
	2	87	83	87	91	88	79	85		2	91	92	94	97	95	84	95
	3	89	84	89	95	87	85	87		3	93	92	93	99	94	83	90
	4	86	81	84	89	88	85	85		4	89	92	92	96	95	82	90
	5	89	86	90	93	85	86	86		5	90	91	90	97	92	82	90
1 PM	1	90	86	92	95	93	89	91	4 PM	1	93	89	91	95	95	86	90
	2	88	87	89	93	91	90	88		2	92	90	92	96	95	82	94
	3	83	91	90	95	92	90	83		3	87	90	89	95	93	81	87
	4	81	89	89	92	92	89	90		4	90	89	89	94	93	80	88
	5	88	89	91	96	89	89	88		5	91	89	87	94	90	81	87
2 PM	1	92	89	92	97	96	92	92	5 PM	1	90	87	90	94	93	84	90
	2	89	89	91	95	93	87	93		2	92	86	90	95	92	81	91
	3	89	90	93	98	93	85	90		3	88	88	87	95	91	82	88
	4	86	92	91	94	94	88	91		4	87	88	86	95	92	78	86
	5	89	90	92	97	91	85	90		5	88	87	89	93	89	80	86

15. The table below gives enrollment data for the Division of Natural Sciences of Primate College for the current quarter. Write a program to process the data, accumulating totals for instructor, department, and the division. A detailed line for each course taught should be printed reflecting the input data. When there is an instructor change, the total number of classes and students taught should be printed for that instructor. At each department change, the total number of instructors, classes, and students

Department Name	Instructor Name	Class Number	Number in Class	Department Name	Instructor Name	Class Number	Number in Class
Biology	I Phrogge	BIO 101	37	Mathematics	A Ritmatik	MAT 101	41
Biology	I Phrogge	BIO 101	34	Mathematics	A Ritmatik	MAT 101	37
Biology	Y Jerminate	BIO 235	21	Mathematics	A Ritmatik	MAT 201	23
Biology	Y Jerminate	BIO 331	16	Mathematics	A Ritmatik	MAT 491	1
Biology	Y Jerminate	BIO 497	3	Mathematics	T Hearum	MAT 111	31
Biology	U Deena	BIO 481	6	Mathematics	T Hearum	MAT 311	13
Chemistry	E Lecktron	CHE 101	28	Mathematics	T Hearum	MAT 441	9
Chemistry	E Lecktron	CHE 101	33	Physics	Q Foton	PHY 211	21
Chemistry	E Lecktron	CHE 211	17	Physics	Q Foton	PHY 301	12
Chemistry	B Burhner	CHE 111	31	Physics	E Jewele	PHY 446	6
Chemistry	B Burhner	CHE 341	12	Physics	E Jewele	PHY 451	2

should be printed. Both the instructor and departmental names should appear in the respective minor total lines. At the end of the report, totals should be printed for the number of departments, instructors, classes, and students in all classes. The division name should appear somewhere in the report.

16. Another Sales Commission Summary Report is needed for Steve's Stereos (see Problem 13, Chapter 9) except that the new report must process sales commissions for more than one day, providing summary data for each salesperson for one day and totals for all salespersons for each day. For each salesperson, the report should print *one* line (group printed) giving the date (group indicated), the salesperson's name, total items sold, total sales, and total commission earned. At the end of each day, values for total sales and commissions paid and average sales and commission per salesperson should be printed. At the end of the report, final totals should provide the number of days processed, total sales and commissions, and average daily sales and commissions. Use the inventory table for Steve's Stereos given at the end of Chapter 9 and the commission rate table in Problem 13 of Chapter 9. The inventory table should be searched using the binary method. Sales data is given below.

Date of Sale	Salesperson Name	Item Number	Quantity Sold	Date of Sale	Salesperson Name	Item Number	Quantity Sold
6/21/84	H Truman	120002	1	6/23/84	M Kline	114299	1
6/21/84	H Truman	114299	1	6/23/84	M Kline	121178	1
6/21/84	H Truman	156643	2	6/23/84	M Kline	246689	1
6/21/84	L Perry	112892	1	6/23/84	M Kline	246690	1
6/21/84	L Perry	219928	6	6/23/84	H Truman	156877	1
6/21/84	F Wilson	110234	1	6/23/84	H Truman	135288	2
6/21/84	F Wilson	219930	2	6/23/84	H Broche	110234	1
6/21/84	F Wilson	237783	1	6/23/84	H Broche	112892	1
6/22/84	L Perry	132822	1	6/23/84	H Broche	121178	1
6/22/84	L Perry	246690	1	6/23/84	H Broche	129002	1
6/22/84	H Broche	182001	1	6/23/84	H Broche	142882	2
6/22/84	F Wilson	112892	1	6/24/84	L Perry	142882	2
6/22/84	W Dawson	135288	1	6/24/84	F Wilson	127338	1
6/22/84	W Dawson	219930	1	6/24/84	F Wilson	201190	1

17. Write a program to print a Product Sales Summary Report for the Miracle Machine Co., Inc. This will be a triple-level control break with the first level occurring whenever there is a change in the office number. This will result in a minor total line that is group printed by office number and gives the district number (group indicated), the city name (also group indicated), the office number, and the total number of salespersons and machines sold. The second control break takes place when the city changes. This will result in a total line that gives the city name and totals for the number of offices, salespersons, and machines sold in the city. The third-level break results from a change in the district number. This total line will give the district number and totals for the number of cities, offices, salespersons, and machines sold. At the end of the report, final totals should be printed to provide company totals for number of districts, cities, offices, salespersons, and machines sold. Sales data is provided in the table on page 363.

District Number	City Name	Office Number	Salesperson Number	Machines Sold	District Number	City Name	Office Number	Salesperson Number	Machines Sold
1	Albany	13	116527	12	2	Detroit	17	539267	25
1	Albany	13	134366	32	2	Detroit	17	567331	4
1	Albany	63	210708	6	2	Detroit	44	028449	31
1	Albany	63	298557	15	2	Detroit	44	328755	24
1	Albany	63	399678	27	2	St. Paul	09	298810	17
1	Hartford	22	038892	45	2	St. Paul	09	329022	34
1	Hartford	22	287745	35	2	St. Paul	09	482228	17
1	Hartford	22	428875	41	2	St. Paul	32	211190	32
1	Hartford	42	137008	28	3	Denver	75	190229	8
1	Hartford	57	112055	25	3	Denver	75	278992	27
1	Hartford	57	287745	25	3	Seattle	55	339932	17
1	Hartford	78	429075	37	4	Richmond	14	118920	12
1	Hartford	78	537788	17	4	Richmond	14	138829	21
1	Pittsburgh	11	377882	34	4	Richmond	14	432288	5
1	Pittsburgh	31	278845	23	4	Houston	33	289011	22
1	Pittsburgh	31	376408	14	4	Houston	74	298820	31
2	Cleveland	19	102993	43	4	Houston	74	428839	7
2	Cleveland	19	298225	22	4	Houston	88	218992	12
2	Cleveland	36	229066	25	4	Houston	88	378829	27
2	Cleveland	36	438292	9	4	Houston	88	379226	19
2	Cleveland	36	538823	28	4	Memphis	40	281192	17
2	Cleveland	36	598302	13	4	Tampa	53	389235	21
2	Cleveland	49	289401	24	4	Tampa	53	492109	5
2	Detroit	17	466688	16	4	Tampa	91	229810	28

CHAPTER 14

FILE PROCESSING

Up to this point, we have discussed the input of data by either incorporating it within the program or entering it interactively from the terminal. Output of results has been restricted to either the terminal or printer. This is not always the best choice, and there are other options available. In this chapter, we will describe the input, processing, and output of data using files in which the data has been stored on special storage devices, such as magnetic tapes or disks, collectively known as auxiliary storage (see Section 1-2).

All through our study of BASIC, the many variations of the language from one computer system to another have been continually emphasized. It will be no different with file processing. Unfortunately, this particular area is probably the least standard of all. While reading this chapter, it should be remembered that all concepts presented will apply to your system in general, but many may vary significantly in the syntax of the specific statements that are available for accomplishing the job.

14-1 THE CONCEPT OF A FILE

Let us begin by examining the way data is normally organized for processing. Suppose that we are processing employee payroll data in which we will input for each employee the name, social security number, hours worked, pay rate, and number of deductions. Each individual value that is to be processed for each employee is referred to as a **field**. Thus, there are five fields to be read for each employee. These five fields compose an employee's pay **record**. All of the pay records will make up the employee pay **file**. All files that are required for the processing of the employee's pay data are collectively referred to as the **data base**.

More generally, we can say that a data base is all the data required for a particular application (which may be simple or very complex). The data base is subdivided and organized into files according to the general nature and intended use of the data. Each file is composed of a set of related records, each of which is in turn broken down into individual fields that correspond to each data value to be processed. For example, at your college, all the data needed to operate the school makes up the data base. This includes information on such things as academic work, tuition and other charges, financial aid data, faculty and staff payroll, alumni records, and much more. This data is organized into files. Files relating to academic matters are kept by the dean and registrar. The business office maintains files that contain information on each student's financial and faculty payroll data. The alumni director will obviously have charge of the alumni files, and so forth. Certain files may be shared or accessed by more than one office. There may be a student master information file that contains such personal data on each student as home address, nearest relative, medical data, etc. This information, at least in part, may be needed by several different offices at the college. If a common master file is used, then the data need not be duplicated in each file where it is needed. This is part of the idea of a data base, the sharing of common information. Each file is broken into records, one or more for each student (or other person) represented. The student master information file described above would contain individual master information records for each student. Each of these records would be composed of the specific data on each student that is to be included in the file; several possible items were mentioned above.

Such files are normally stored on magnetic tape or disk. Since BASIC is designed to function in an interactive environment, disks are most frequently used and will be discussed here. You may already be asking, ''Why use files? What is wrong with the methods we have been using?'' To answer the second question first, there is nothing wrong with the methods that we have been using; however, files provide a new degree of flexibility in programming and handling data that cannot be ignored. As to why or when we would want to use files, consider the following situations. If we have a long program with many records (a large file) to be processed, it is possible that both the program and the data will not fit into the computer's main memory simultaneously. With a **data file**, we can input the program and read and process the data file from the disk one record at a time. Suppose that we wish to process the same data by more than one program. If we type the data into the programs, we must retype it into *every* program. With a file, all the programs can read the same data file. With files, the output from one program can easily serve as the input to another by simply printing the output to a data file and then reading it with the second program. To do this without files would require retyping the output into the second program as data. There are many other possible applications, but you should begin to get the idea by now.

So far, we have been talking only of *data files*. A program may be also stored on the disk as a **program file** for future use. Text files for use with a word processor are another example. (Actually text files serve as data for the word processor's program. All files may be very generally classified as either data or program.) You may have already been creating program files, especially if you are using a compiled BASIC. The procedure for creating and naming files varies with the individual computer operating system that is in use; however, most file names (technically called **file specifications**) are of a form similar to

filename.filetype

where **filename** is a user-defined (you choose it) name for the file, usually limited to six or eight characters, and **filetype** (or **file extension**)—usually up to three characters—identifies the type of file that *filename* is. For example, a BASIC program file that processes payroll data might be called:

```
PAYROLL.BAS
```

where PAYROLL is the name of the file, and BAS identifies the file to the computer as being in *BAS*IC. If PAYROLL had been written in a language other than BASIC, say COBOL, then the above might be written as:

```
PAYROLL.COB
```

The COB designates a COBOL file.

We might have several files that are to be processed by PAYROLL.BAS. The individual employee weekly payroll data might be in one file while an employee master file may have to be referenced for personal data such as address and number of deductions. Tax rate tables may be in yet another file. Finally, in addition to the printed output, a disk file of employee pay data may be needed for future reference. This means *four* data files that might be called:

```
EMPWORK.DAT
EMPMASTR.DAT
TAXRATE.DAT
EARNINGS.DAT
```

From the names of the files, can you determine which will correspond to each of the four files described above? (Two files with different filetypes may have the same filename. In other words, PAYROLL.BAS and PAYROLL.DAT are different files. However, the practice of using the same filename, even with different filetypes, can cause problems on most systems—and may not be allowed on some—and should be avoided.)

Most of our work with files in this chapter will concern data files. In Section 14-8 we will look briefly at a technique called *chaining* that permits one BASIC program to call and run another that has been stored as a file. Data in files can be organized in many ways, but such files can be generally classified as sequential, random, or indexed according to how the data is accessed in the file. Most versions of BASIC support both sequential and random file organization; these will be described in detail. Only a few BASICs offer true indexed files. Indexed file processing is, however, a very important technique that is standard with many other languages, such as COBOL. We will therefore discuss indexed file processing in general and see how to simulate indexed files with BASICs in which they are not offered.

14-2 PROCESSING SEQUENTIAL FILES

Data is organized and processed in a **sequential file** much the same way as it is in DATA statements within the BASIC program. Each record is stored and read one after the other. The first record is processed, then the second, third, etc. If you need to work with the one-hundredth record in a file, then you must first read through the preceding 99 records to get to it. This is a relatively simple way to set up a file, which is, in turn, normally fairly easy to process. The disadvantage of sequential files is the difficulty in getting to records near the middle or end of a large file when the earlier records are of no interest. The solution to this problem is the random file, which we will discuss in Section 14-5. Random files, however, are much more difficult to process than sequential ones.

Before any file can be processed, it must be **opened**. This is done with the **OPEN** statement. One common form of this statement for sequential files is:

ln **OPEN** "I/O", *#channel number, "filename"*

where "I" or "O" designates the files as *i*nput or *o*utput, **channel number** assigns a specific number to the file, and **filename** is the file's disk-file name, including the file type. The channel number can be any of the available numbers (10 to 20 channels are available on most systems) which has not been used for another file. The number, once assigned, will remain with that file until it is closed (see below). The following are typical OPEN statements:

```
110 OPEN "I", #1, "ACCOUNT.DAT"
200 OPEN "O", #3, "EMPPAY.DAT"
```

(While we will use the form of the OPEN statement given above, there are many other forms found with various BASICS. One common alternative form would express the above two OPEN statements as follows:

```
110 OPEN "ACCOUNT.DAT" FOR INPUT AS FILE 1
200 OPEN "EMPPAY.DAT" FOR OUTPUT AS FILE 3
```

The similarity should be clear. Even if the OPEN with your BASIC is different, it should be very comparable to the one above.)

Data is read or input into the computer's memory from a sequential file one record at a time by the **INPUT #** statement, which has the general form:

ln **INPUT** *#channel number, variable list*

Here, *channel number* is the number assigned in an OPEN statement to the file to be read, and *variable list* is a list of the variables in one record. To read one record from file number 4 would be:

```
240  INPUT #4, N$, H, K, Y
```

Similarly, a record is printed to a file by the **PRINT #** statement, which has the form:

ln **PRINT** *#channel number, print list*

This should be clear. We will have more to say about this statement later. (PRINT # USING is also available on many systems.)

Once a file has been processed, it must be **closed**. This is done with the **CLOSE** statement, which is:

ln **CLOSE** *channel numbers*

where *channel numbers* is a list of all of the channel numbers (with the #) of the files to be closed separated by commas. To close files that were opened with channels 1, 2, and 5, the close statement would be

```
550  CLOSE #1, #2, #5
```

A CLOSE with *no* channel numbers will close *all* open files. Once a file has been closed, it cannot be processed any further unless it is reopened.

Let us look at some simple examples of file processing. The first program creates a file, ALUMNI.DAT, from a list of data in a program. It is as follows:

```
 10 REM  CREATING A SEQUENTIAL FILE
 20 REM
 30 OPEN "O", #1, "ALUMNI.DAT"
 40 READ N$, ST$, CL$, CN
 50 PRINT #1, N$; ","; ST$; ","; CL$; ","; CN
 60 IF N$ <> "END" THEN 40
 70 DATA "R MURPHY", "CT", "1978", 100
 80 DATA "T GILBERT", "NY", "1976", 0
 90 DATA "T YOUNG", "MA", "1978", 10
100 DATA "E DANIELS", "NY", "1980", 1000
110 DATA "T REESE", "RI", "1981", 0
120 DATA "P KELLOGG", "NY", "1979", 25
130 DATA "END", "0", "0", 0
140 CLOSE #1
150 END
```

The file is opened for output using channel 1 at line 30. Line 40 reads a record from the data list and line 50 prints it to the file. Line 60 checks for the sentinel record. This is a different place for this, but we want the sentinel record to be printed to the file so we can find its end. If we do not stop trying to read data at the end of the file, we will get an **Input Past End** error, which is analogous to the now familiar Out of Data error. The PRINT statement looks a little different with the semicolons and commas in quotes. This is to print the data to the file in compact form, as close together as possible, but with separators (the commas) between each value. Other methods may be used, but the above procedure should work on most systems. The file generated will look like this:

```
R MURPHY,CT,1978, 100
T GILBERT,NY,1976, 0
T YOUNG,MA,1978, 10
E DANIELS,NY,1980, 1000
T REESE,RI,1981, 0
P KELLOGG,NY,1979, 25
END,0,0, 0
```

Compare the file to the DATA statements above. (Note that the quotes around the string values in the DATA statements are not transferred to the data file. If you create a data file with a screen editor, as you may be doing with your programs, you may use the quotes with string values in the file if you wish.)

The next program reads and prints the data from a file. It is as follows:

```
10 REM   READING FROM A SEQUENTIAL FILE
20 REM
30 OPEN "I", #1, "ALUMNI.DAT"
40 INPUT #1, N$, ST$, CL$, CN
50 IF N$ = "END" THEN 80
60 PRINT N$, ST$, CL$, CN
70 GOTO 40
80 CLOSE #1
90 END
```

Here, we are reading the file that we created above. It is opened at line 30 and a record from the file is read at line 40. The sentinel record is tested at 50 and a line printed at 60. The output is a simple printout:

```
R MURPHY       CT              1978              100
T GILBERT      NY              1976              0
T YOUNG        MA              1978              10
E DANIELS      NY              1980              1000
T REESE        RI              1981              0
P KELLOGG      NY              1979              25
```

Sequential files may be searched much as we would search an array. We could search the file ALUMNI.DAT for specific records. The following program searches the file and prints only the records of those alumni who have contributed at least $100 to the alumni fund.

```
 10 REM   SEARCHING A SEQUENTIAL FILE
 20 REM
 30 OPEN "I", #1, "ALUMNI.DAT"
 40 INPUT #1, N$, ST$, CL$, CN
 50 IF N$ = "END" THEN 90
 60 IF CN < 100 THEN 40
 70 PRINT N$, ST$, CL$, CN
 80 GOTO 40
 90 CLOSE #1
100 END
```

```
R MURPHY       CT              1978              100
E DANIELS      NY              1980              1000
```

This is very similar to the last program except that a line is printed at line 70 only when the condition at 60 is false.

As a final example in this section of processing sequential files, consider the process of updating a sequential file. To do this, we must read each record in the file, make whatever changes are necessary and then *print the new record to a second file*. Updating a sequential file always requires that a new file be used for printing the updated records. With sequential files, we cannot print to the same file from which we are reading. Consider the following example in which we enter the name of an alumnus and a contribution to be added to prior contributions.

```
 10 REM  UPDATING A SEQUENTIAL FILE
 20 REM
 30 OPEN "I", #1, "ALUMNI1.DAT"
 40 OPEN "O", #2, "ALUMNI2.DAT"
 50 PRINT "ENTER ALUMNUS NAME AND CONTRIBUTION"
 60 INPUT NA$, C
 70 INPUT #1, N$, ST$, CL$, CN
 80 IF N$ = "END" THEN 130
 90 IF N$ <> NA$ THEN 110
100 LET CN = CN + C
110 PRINT #2, N$, ST$, CL$, CN
120 GOTO 50
130 CLOSE #1, #2
140 END
```

The input file is opened as ALUMNI1.DAT—which is the same as ALUMNI.DAT—at line 30 and the output as ALUMNI2.DAT at 40. The name of the alumnus whose contribution is to be updated along with the new contribution is input at line 50. A record from ALUMNI1.DAT is read at line 60 and a check is made for a match with the input name at 80. If no match is found, the old record is simply printed to the new file, ALUMNI2.DAT, with no change. If a match is found, then the total contribution is updated at 90 before the record is printed. The output will produce a file that is identical to ALUMNI1.DAT except for the record that has been changed. If T REESE has donated $20, that record will now appear as:

```
T REESE        RI              1981              20
```

The last program assumes only *one* pass through the input file. If more than one name is to be input, then the program must be run again because we cannot "back up" in a sequential file. There are, however, some ways to avoid this problem. If a file needs to be processed more than once, it can be closed and reopened. This will start the **file pointer** (similar to the data pointer described in Section 4-1) back at the top of the file. Also, some BASICs provide a version of the **RESTORE** statement (see Section 4-1) that is of the form:

ln **RESTORE** *#channel number*

This can be used to reset the file pointer to the top of the file corresponding to the specified channel number.

14-3 ERROR TRAPPING

Many versions of BASIC provide features for detecting certain errors connected with sequential file processing, commonly referred to as **error trapping**. One such feature available on some systems is the **EOF** (for end of file) function, which is used to detect the end of a file. This function has the general form:

EOF*(channel number)*

where the channel number (no #) is that of the file, the end of which we wish to locate. This works very much like the sentinel record that we used in the last section except that (1) no actual record is required to test for the end of the file and (2) the test of the EOF function should *always* be placed *before* the INPUT # statement that reads from the file. The program in Section 14-2 that searched the file ALUMNI.DAT can be rewritten to use the EOF function as follows:

```
 10 REM  SEARCHING A SEQUENTIAL FILE
 20 REM
 30 OPEN "I", #1, "ALUMNI.DAT"
 35 IF EOF(1) THEN 90
 40 INPUT #1, N$, ST$, CL$, CN
 60 IF CN < 100 THEN 35
 70 PRINT N$, ST$, CL$, CN
 80 GOTO 35
 90 CLOSE #1
100 END
```

The sentinel record will, of course, be omitted from the data file because it is no longer required.

Another, more general, error trapping method that is available with many BASICs is the **ON ERROR GOTO** statement. This statement has the general form:

ln1 **ON ERROR GOTO** *ln2*

where *ln2* is the program line number to which a branch should occur whenever an error condition is detected. The ON ERROR GOTO statement must be placed early in a program or subroutine before all statements in which errors might arise. A special form of the statement:

ln **ON ERROR GOTO** 0

is used to terminate processing whenever an error occurs. Likewise, the **RESUME** statement can be used to resume processing at any point in the program. It has the form:

ln1 **RESUME** *ln2*

where *ln2* is the line number of the statement where processing should resume following the error condition. If no line number is specified (RESUME) or a zero is used (RESUME 0), then processing will return to the statement at which the error occurred. RESUME NEXT will return execution to the *next* statement following the one causing the error.

Two special *variables,* **ERR** and **ERL**, are frequently used in conjunction with the ON ERROR GOTO statement to process different error conditions. When an error is detected by the ON ERROR GOTO, the number of the error is assigned to ERR and the line number at which it occurred is assigned to ERL. (Error number will vary with the BASIC in use. See your instructor for a list of error codes for your system.) A test can then be made to see if a specific error, such as end-of-file, has occurred and at what point in the program.

```
                 :
100  ON ERROR GOTO 500
110  (Statements to process data)
                 :
                 :
500  IF ERR <> 62 THEN ON ERROR GOTO 0
510  PRINT "PREMATURE EOF AT LINE"; ERL
520  RESUME 600
                 :
```

Whenever an error condition is detected following line 100, a branch occurs to line 500. If the error is not code 62 (here assumed to be end-of-file), processing is immediately terminated. If the error is end-of-file or code 62, then the message at line 510 is printed with the appropriate line number indicated, and processing is resumed at line 600. Following a branch to an error handling routine as at lines 500 to 520, each branch in the routine must be appropriately terminated by an ON ERROR GOTO 0, RESUME, IF–THEN, GOTO, or other control statement. Failure to do so will result in either improper processing or an error message.

14-4 AN EXAMPLE: COMBINING INVENTORY LISTS

The example in this section illustrates many of the features of sequential file processing. Basically, two files are combined and updated at the same time with an accompanying printout that documents the various actions taken.

Problem: The Termite Furniture Company has been operating two stores; however, due to rather poor business, the owner has decided to close one store and combine the inventories of the two stores. Both stores have been carrying the same basic items but not necessarily at the same price. Also, some items that have not sold well at one or both stores have been listed as discontinued in the corresponding inventory lists. The owner has requested a program that will process the two current inventory lists and produce the following two outputs:

1. There should be a new inventory file made up from the two individual store inventories as follows:
   (a) Each item must appear in the new inventory file with the combined stock of both stores and the *lower* of the two unit costs.
   (b) If an item has been discontinued at only one store, values for the store at which it is still stocked are to be listed in the file.
   (c) Items discontinued at *both* stores should be dropped entirely from the new file.
2. The second report is a printed one that reflects the new inventory file as described above but with the following additions:
   (a) The status of each item in (b) and (c) above is to be given. A message should appear on the printout stating that the item has been DISC. AT STORE # or DISC. AT BOTH STORES.
   (b) Totals are to be printed for the numbers of items discontinued at store 1 only, at store 2 only, and at both stores and for the total of items and number of all items in the inventory.

The inventory lists for both stores are given in Table 14-1.

The solution to this problem is outlined as follows:

1. Print main and column headings.
2. Open input files for the two current inventories and one output file for the combined listing.
3. Set all total accumulators to zero.
4. Check for end of files with the EOF function. At the end, go to step 26.
5. Read a record from each inventory file.
6. If the item has been discontinued from either store, go to step 13.
7. Add the two quantities in both inventories.
8. Determine the lower unit cost.
9. Write a record to the combined inventory file.
10. Print a line of the visual report.
11. Update the totals for number of items and total stock of all items.
12. Go to step 4.

TABLE 14-1

Input Data for Combining Inventory Lists Problem

Inventory for Store Number 1				Inventory for Store Number 2			
Stock Number	**Description of Item**	**Unit Cost**	**Quantity in Stock**	**Stock Number**	**Description of Item**	**Unit Cost**	**Quantity in Stock**
111402	Twin Bed	189.50	2	111402	Twin Bed	189.50	5
113778	Telephone Table	28.75	9	113778	Telephone Table	28.75	7
114887	Bookcase	139.90	4	114887	Bookcase	129.90	3
116605	Long Sofa	319.00	3	116605	Long Sofa	329.00	5
118442	Brass Ashtray	Discontinued		118442	Brass Ashtray	Discontinued	
119882	Easy Chair	325.00	9	119882	Easy Chair	319.90	15
120019	Double Bed	229.95	6	120019	Double Bed	229.95	4
121278	Straight Chair	54.50	23	121278	Straight Chair	54.00	21
121771	China Cabinet	309.95	5	121771	China Cabinet	309.90	6
122803	Table Lamp	67.75	12	122803	Table Lamp	67.75	16
124337	Area Rug	77.50	9	124337	Area Rug	77.50	7
127633	Stereo Cabinet	99.00	6	127633	Stereo Cabinet	99.00	3
128992	Small Desk	169.90	2	128992	Small Desk	Discontinued	
128992	Wall Mirror	Discontinued		128992	Wall Mirror	Discontinued	
131101	Wood Rocker	115.50	11	131101	Wood Rocker	112.50	17
131290	Dining Set	459.00	1	131290	Dining Set	469.90	3
132788	End Table	99.00	22	132788	End Table	99.00	16
133788	Short Sofa	267.90	6	133788	Short Sofa	259.90	5
136770	King-size Bed	Discontinued		136770	King-size Bed	525.00	2
137422	Dresser	199.95	13	137422	Dresser	199.00	11
138771	Magazine Rack	37.50	5	138771	Magazine Rack	37.50	7
140255	Lamp Table	135.50	12	140255	Lamp Table	135.50	13
141622	Lawn Set	219.25	3	141622	Lawn Set	219.25	3
142105	Hat Rack	49.00	7	142105	Hat Rack	Discontinued	

13. If the item has been discontinued from stock at both stores, go to step 23.
14. If the item was discontinued only at store 2, go to step 19.
15. Write a record to the combined inventory file.
16. Print a line of the visual report with the appropriate message.
17. Update the totals for number of items and total stock of all items and the number of items discontinued from store 1.
18. Go to step 4.
19. Write a record to the combined inventory file.
20. Print a line of the visual report with the appropriate message.
21. Update the totals for number of items and total stock of all items and the number of items discontinued from store 2.
22. Go to step 4.
23. Print a line of the visual report with the appropriate message.
24. Update the total number of items discontinued from both stores.
25. Go to step 4.
26. Print all totals.
27. Close all files.
28. Stop.

This solution is illustrated by the flowchart in Figure 14-1.

We begin by printing headings at lines 270 to 340. The three files are opened for processing at lines 380 to 400.

```
380 OPEN "I", #1, "INVEN1.DAT"
390 OPEN "I", #2, "INVEN2.DAT"
400 OPEN "O", #3, "INVEN.DAT"
```

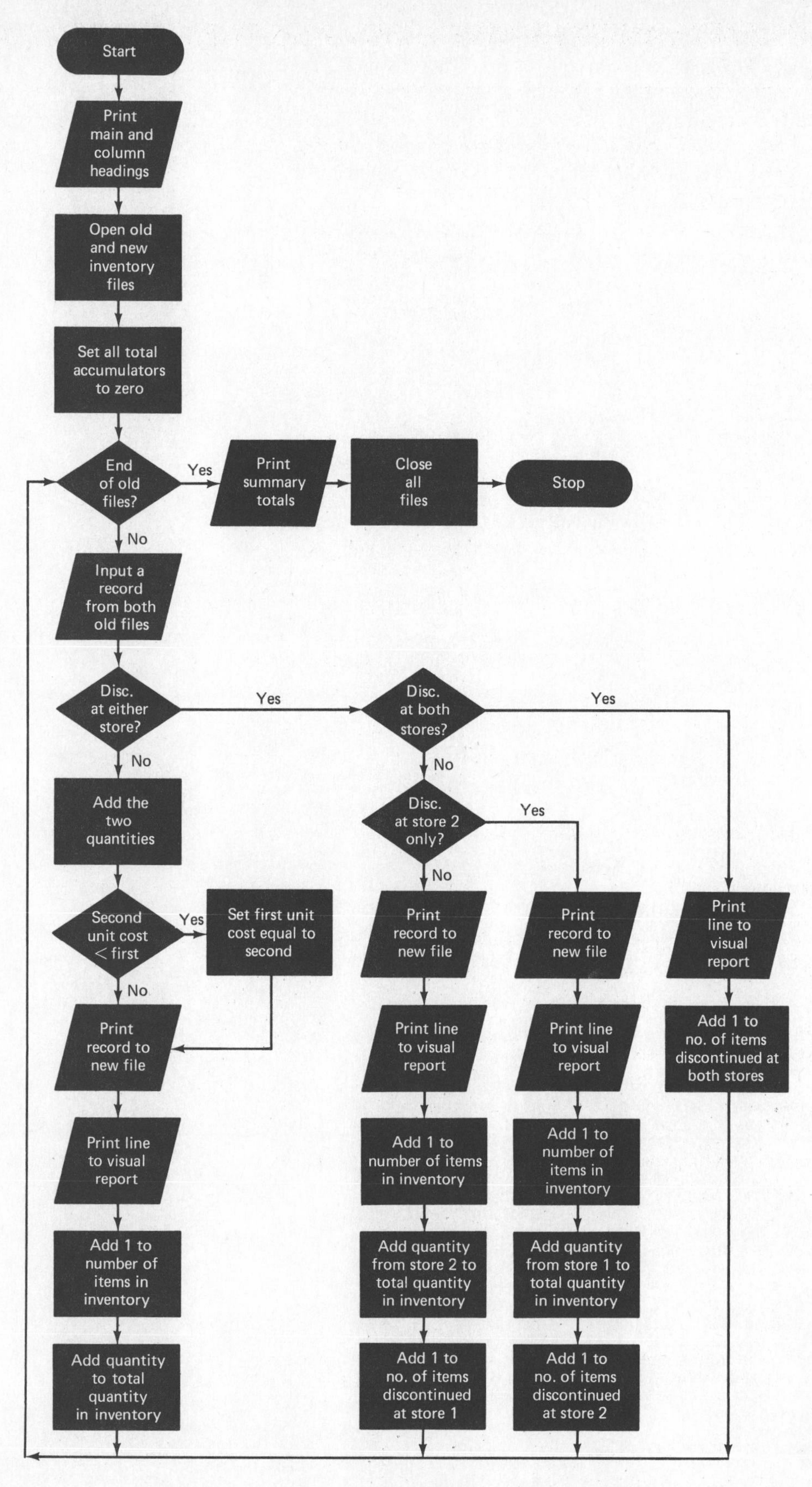

FIGURE 14-1
Flowchart for combining inventory lists example

The two files INVEN1.DAT and INVEN2.DAT are opened as input files with channel numbers 1 and 2 as shown. These will correspond to the inventory files of stores 1 and 2, respectively. The combined inventory file is opened as output file INVEN.DAT with channel number 3. All total accumulators are initialized to zero at lines 410 to 450.

Before continuing with the program analysis, let us pause for a moment to look at the actual files that are to be processed. These are shown in Figure 14-2*a* and 14-2*b*. Note that an item that has been marked as discontinued in Table 14-1 has been "flagged" as having a quantity in stock of −1. We will use this quantity of −1 to detect discontinued items. The unit cost has also been entered as 9999 so that the unit cost at the other store will be certain to be lower.

We begin processing the two inventory files at line 500. The end-of-file check is made at 500, and a record is read from each file at 510 and 520.

```
500  IF EOF(1) AND EOF(2) THEN GOTO 960
510  INPUT #1, N1, D1$, U1, Q1
520  INPUT #2, N2, D2$, U2, Q2
```

As mentioned in the last section, when using the EOF function, the end-of-file check is made *prior* to the file record being read. At line 500, we have checked to ensure that the end-of-file occurs for both files at the same time because we know that the two inventories should have the same number of entries.

Once two records have been read from the two files, they are processed beginning at line 570.

```
570 IF Q1 = -1 OR Q2 = -1 THEN 680
580 LET Q1 = Q1 + Q2
590 IF U2 < U1 THEN LET U1 = U2
600 PRINT #3, N1; ","; D1$; ","; U1; ","; Q1
610 PRINT N1; TAB(15); D1$; TAB(35); "$"; U1; TAB(50); Q1
620 LET T = T + 1
630 LET S = S + Q1
640 GOTO 500
```

First, a check is made to see if the item is out of stock at either store; if it is, then a branch to line 680 occurs to process those special cases. Otherwise, the quantities at both stores are added at 580. Line 590 determines the lower unit cost. U1 is assumed to be the lower

```
111402, TWIN BED, 189.50, 2
113778, TELEPHONE TABLE, 28.75, 9
114887, BOOKCASE, 139.90, 4
116605, LONG SOFA, 319.00, 3
118442, BRASS ASHTRAY, 9999, -1
119882, EASY CHAIR, 325.00, 9
120019, DOUBLE BED, 229.95, 6
121278, STRAIGHT CHAIR, 54.50, 23
121771, CHINA CABINET, 309.95, 5
122803, TABLE LAMP, 67.75, 12
124337, AREA RUG, 77.50, 9
127633, STEREO CABINET, 99.00, 6
128922, SMALL DESK, 169.90, 2
128992, WALL MIRROR, 9999, -1
131101, WOOD ROCKER, 115.50, 11
131290, DINING SET, 459.00, 1
132788, END TABLE, 99.00, 22
133788, SHORT SOFA, 267.90, 6
136770, KING-SIZE BED, 9999, -1
137422, DRESSER, 199.95, 13
138771, MAGAZINE RACK, 37.50, 5
140255, LAMP TABLE, 135.50, 12
141622, LAWN SET, 219.25, 3
142105, HAT RACK, 49.00, 7
```

(*a*) File for Store 1
INVEN1.DAT

```
111402, TWIN BED, 189.50, 5
113778, TELEPHONE TABLE, 28.75, 7
114887, BOOKCASE, 129.90, 3
116605, LONG SOFA, 329.00, 5
118442, BRASS ASHTRAY, 9999, -1
119882, EASY CHAIR, 319.90, 15
120019, DOUBLE BED, 229.95, 4
121278, STRAIGHT CHAIR, 54.00, 21
121771, CHINA CABINET, 309.90, 6
122803, TABLE LAMP, 62.75, 16
124337, AREA RUG, 77.50, 7
127633, STEREO CABINET, 99.00, 3
128922, SMALL DESK, 9999, -1
128992, WALL MIRROR, 9999, -1
131101, WOOD ROCKER, 112.50, 17
131290, DINING SET, 469.90, 3
132788, END TABLE, 99.00, 16
133788, SHORT SOFA, 259.90, 5
136770, KING-SIZE BED, 525.00, 2
137422, DRESSER, 199.00, 11
138771, MAGAZINE RACK, 37.50, 7
140255, LAMP TABLE, 135.50, 13
141622, LAWN SET, 219.25, 3
142105, HAT RACK, 9999, -1
```

(*b*) File for Store 2
INVEN2.DAT

```
111402 ,TWIN BED, 189.5 , 7
113778 ,TELEPHONE TABLE, 28.75 , 16
114887 ,BOOKCASE, 129.9 , 7
116605 ,LONG SOFA, 319 , 8
119882 ,EASY CHAIR, 319.9 , 24
120019 ,DOUBLE BED, 229.95 , 10
121278 ,STRAIGHT CHAIR, 54 , 44
121771 ,CHINA CABINET, 309.9 , 11
122803 ,TABLE LAMP, 62.75 , 28
124337 ,AREA RUG, 77.5 , 16
127633 ,STEREO CABINET, 99 , 9
128922 ,SMALL DESK, 169.9 , 2
131101 ,WOOD ROCKER, 112.5 , 28
131290 ,DINING SET, 459 , 4
132788 ,END TABLE, 99 , 38
133788 ,SHORT SOFA, 259.9 , 11
136770 ,KING-SIZE BED, 525 , 2
137422 ,DRESSER, 199 , 24
138771 ,MAGAZINE RACK, 37.5 , 12
140255 ,LAMP TABLE, 135.5 , 25
141622 ,LAWN SET, 219.25 , 6
142105 ,HAT RACK, 49 , 7
```

(*c*) Combined file
INVEN.DAT

FIGURE 14-2
Sequential data files for combined inventory list problem

unless U2 is found to be, in which case U1 is set equal to U2. A record is written to the combined inventory file at 600, and a line is written to the visual (printed) output at 610. Totals for number of items and total stock are updated and processing returned for a new record from each file.

Lines 500 to 640 are executed until an item is found to have been discontinued at one or both stores, at which time a branch occurs to the routine beginning at line 680.

```
680 IF Q1 = -1 AND Q2 = -1 THEN 900
690 IF Q2 = -1 THEN 800
700 PRINT #3, N1; ","; D1$; ","; U2; ","; Q2
710 PRINT N1; TAB(15); D1$; TAB(35); "$"; U2; TAB(50); Q2;
720 PRINT TAB(60); "DISC AT STORE NO. 1"
730 LET T = T + 1
740 LET S = S + Q2
750 LET T1 = T1 + 1
760 GOTO 500
```

At first, a check is made to see if the item has been discontinued from both stores; if so, processing is directed to line 900. Next, a check is made at line 690 to determine at which store the item has been discontinued. If it is store 2, then this is processed at line 800. The remainder of the above set of statements writes a line to the combined file, prints a line to the visual record (note the message), and updates the proper totals for items discontinued at store 1. Lines 800 to 860 perform the identical task for items discontinued at store 2. Finally, items discontinued at both stores are processed at lines 900 to 920.

```
900  PRINT N1; TAB(15); D1$; TAB(60); "DISC AT BOTH STORES"
910  LET TB = TB + 1
920  GOTO 500
```

Note that only a line to the visual report is printed and the total number of items discontinued from both stores updated.

The final totals are printed from 960 to 1080. Line 1090:

```
1090  CLOSE #1, #2, #3
```

closes all files. This could have been placed before the totals were printed, but there is no reason to do so here.

A complete listing and run follow. The combined inventory file, INVEN.DAT, is shown in Figure 14-2*c*.

```
 10 REM   COMBINING INVENTORY LISTS
 20 REM
 30 REM   DISK FILES ARE DEFINED AS --
 40 REM
 50 REM    INVEN1.DAT = INVENTORY LIST FROM STORE 1
 60 REM    INVEN2.DAT = INVENTORY LIST FROM STORE 2
 70 REM     INVEN.DAT = COMBINED INVENTORY LIST FOR BOTH STORES
 80 REM
 90 REM   VARIABLES ARE DEFINED AS --
100 REM
110 REM           N1 = STOCK NUMBER FROM STORE 1
120 REM           N2 = STOCK NUMBER FROM STORE 2
130 REM          D1$ = ITEM DESCRIPTION FROM STORE 1
140 REM          D2$ = ITEM DESCRIPTION FROM STORE 2
150 REM           U1 = UNIT PRICE FROM STORE 1
160 REM           U2 = UNIT PRICE FROM STORE 2
170 REM           Q1 = QUANTITY IN STOCK FROM STORE 1
180 REM           Q2 = QUANTITY IN STOCK FROM STORE 2
190 REM            T = NUMBER OF ITEMS IN COMBINED INVENTORY
```

```
200 REM          S = TOTAL STOCK OF ALL ITEMS IN INVENTORY
210 REM         S1 = NUMBER OF ITEMS DROPPED FROM STORE 1
220 REM         S2 = NUMBER OF ITEMS DROPPED FROM STORE 2
230 REM         SB = NUMBER OF ITEMS DROPPED FROM BOTH STORES
240 REM
250 REM  PRINT HEADINGS
260 REM
270 PRINT TAB(15); "COMBINED INVENTORY LISTING"
280 PRINT
290 PRINT
300 PRINT " STOCK"; TAB(16); "DESCRIPTION"; TAB(37); "UNIT";
310 PRINT TAB(47); "QUANTITY"
320 PRINT " NUMBER"; TAB(18); "OF ITEM"; TAB(37); "COST";
330 PRINT TAB(47); "IN STOCK"
340 PRINT
350 REM
360 REM  OPEN FILES AND INITIALIZE TOTALS
370 REM
380 OPEN "I", #1, "INVEN1.DAT"
390 OPEN "I", #2, "INVEN2.DAT"
400 OPEN "O", #3, "INVEN.DAT"
410 LET T = 0
420 LET S = 0
430 LET T1 = 0
440 LET T2 = 0
450 LET TB = 0
460 REM
470 REM  CHECK FOR END OF FILES AND
480 REM  READ A RECORD FROM EACH FILE
490 REM
500 IF EOF(1) AND EOF(2) THEN GOTO 960
510 INPUT #1, N1, D1$, U1, Q1
520 INPUT #2, N2, D2$, U2, Q2
530 REM
540 REM  PROCESS RECORDS WITHOUT EXCEPTIONS AND
550 REM  WRITE RECORD TO COMBINED FILE AND REPORT
560 REM
570 IF Q1 = -1 OR Q2 = -1 THEN 680
580 LET Q1 = Q1 + Q2
590 IF U2 < U1 THEN LET U1 = U2
600 PRINT #3, N1; ","; D1$; ","; U1; ","; Q1
610 PRINT N1; TAB(15); D1$; TAB(35); "$"; U1; TAB(50); Q1
620 LET T = T + 1
630 LET S = S + Q1
640 GOTO 500
650 REM
660 REM  WRITE OUTPUT FOR ITEMS DISCONTINUED AT STORE 1
670 REM
680 IF Q1 = -1 AND Q2 = -1 THEN 900
690 IF Q2 = -1 THEN 800
700 PRINT #3, N1; ","; D1$; ","; U2; ","; Q2
710 PRINT N1; TAB(15); D1$; TAB(35); "$"; U2; TAB(50); Q2;
720 PRINT TAB(60); "DISC AT STORE NO. 1"
730 LET T = T + 1
740 LET S = S + Q2
750 LET T1 = T1 + 1
760 GOTO 500
770 REM
780 REM  WRITE OUTPUT FOR ITEMS DISCONTINUED AT STORE 2
790 REM
800 PRINT #3, N1; ","; D1$; ","; U1; ","; Q1
810 PRINT N1; TAB(15); D1$; TAB(35); "$"; U1; TAB(50); Q1;
820 PRINT TAB(60); "DISC AT STORE NO. 2"
830 LET T = T + 1
```

```
 840 LET S = S + Q1
 850 LET T2 = T2 + 1
 860 GOTO 500
 870 REM
 880 REM  WRITE OUTPUT FOR ITEMS DISCONTINUED AT BOTH STORES
 890 REM
 900 PRINT N1; TAB(15); D1$; TAB(60); "DISC AT BOTH STORES"
 910 LET TB = TB + 1
 920 GOTO 500
 930 REM
 940 REM  PRINT TOTAL SUMMARY, CLOSE FILES, AND END
 950 REM
 960 PRINT
 970 PRINT
 980 PRINT "NUMBER OF ITEMS DROPPED FROM STOCK AT STORE 1 ONLY"
 990 PRINT "BUT RETAINED IN THE COMBINED INVENTORY ="; T1
1000 PRINT
1010 PRINT "NUMBER OF ITEMS DROPPED FROM STOCK AT STORE 2 ONLY"
1020 PRINT "BUT RETAINED IN THE COMBINED INVENTORY ="; T2
1030 PRINT
1040 PRINT "NUMBER OF ITEMS DROPPED FROM STOCK AT BOTH STORES"
1050 PRINT "AND FROM THE COMBINED INVENTORY ="; TB
1060 PRINT
1070 PRINT "NUMBER OF ITEMS IN THE COMBINED INVENTORY =";T
1080 PRINT "TOTAL STOCK OF ALL ITEMS IN INVENTORY ="; S
1090 CLOSE #1, #2, #3
1100 END
```

```
              COMBINED INVENTORY LISTING


 STOCK          DESCRIPTION            UNIT      QUANTITY
 NUMBER           OF ITEM              COST      IN STOCK

 111402         TWIN BED             $ 189.5        7
 113778         TELEPHONE TABLE      $ 28.75        16
 114887         BOOKCASE             $ 129.9        7
 116605         LONG SOFA            $ 319          8
 118442         BRASS ASHTRAY                                DISC AT BOTH STORES
 119882         EASY CHAIR           $ 319.9        24
 120019         DOUBLE BED           $ 229.95       10
 121278         STRAIGHT CHAIR       $ 54           44
 121771         CHINA CABINET        $ 309.9        11
 122803         TABLE LAMP           $ 62.75        28
 124337         AREA RUG             $ 77.5         16
 127633         STEREO CABINET       $ 99           9
 128922         SMALL DESK           $ 169.9        2        DISC AT STORE NO. 2
 128992         WALL MIRROR                                  DISC AT BOTH STORES
 131101         WOOD ROCKER          $ 112.5        28
 131290         DINING SET           $ 459          4
 132788         END TABLE            $ 99           38
 133788         SHORT SOFA           $ 259.9        11
 136770         KING-SIZE BED        $ 525          2        DISC AT STORE NO. 1
 137422         DRESSER              $ 199          24
 138771         MAGAZINE RACK        $ 37.5         12
 140255         LAMP TABLE           $ 135.5        25
 141622         LAWN SET             $ 219.25       6
 142105         HAT RACK             $ 49           7        DISC AT STORE NO. 2


NUMBER OF ITEMS DROPPED FROM STOCK AT STORE 1 ONLY
BUT RETAINED IN THE COMBINED INVENTORY = 1
```

```
NUMBER OF ITEMS DROPPED FROM STOCK AT STORE 2 ONLY
BUT RETAINED IN THE COMBINED INVENTORY = 2

NUMBER OF ITEMS DROPPED FROM STOCK AT BOTH STORES
AND FROM THE COMBINED INVENTORY = 2

NUMBER OF ITEMS IN THE COMBINED INVENTORY = 22
TOTAL STOCK OF ALL ITEMS IN INVENTORY = 339
```

14-5 PROCESSING RANDOM FILES

A **random file** (also referred to as a **direct access file**) is one in which any record can be accessed at any time without having to go through all the preceding ones. If you need to make a change in the 100th record of a certain random file, you can go directly to that record. This provides for much more versatile processing capabilities, but unfortunately, such files are more difficult to program. The point was made at the very beginning of this chapter that BASICs are probably *least* standard with respect to the syntax of the statements used to process files. This is especially true with regard to random files. We will generally follow the procedures used by only one form of the language. While your BASIC may vary significantly in the structure of a given statement or the specific statements required to process the files, the basic concepts should be the same.

As with sequential files, random files must first be opened with an OPEN statement. The form of this statement is somewhat different for random files; in general, it is:

ln **OPEN** *"R", #channel number, "filename", record length*

where *"R"* designates the file as *r*andom, and **record length** gives the length of a record in characters. The remainder of the statement has the same meaning as before. An example would be something like:

```
110 OPEN "R", #3, "GPALIST2.DAT", 60
```

which opens the file GPALIST2.DAT as random, with a record length of 60 characters, and using channel 3. An alternative form of this statement found on *some* other systems is

```
110 OPEN GPALIST2.DAT AS FILE 3
```

We shall continue to use the first format. Random files are closed in exactly the same way and with the same statement as sequential ones. In fact, both random and sequential files may be closed with the same CLOSE statement.

In addition to opening a random file, we must also specify each field that will make up the record and its exact length. This is done by means of the **FIELD** statement. The general form for the FIELD statement is:

ln **FIELD** *#channel number, field description list*

where each **field description** is separated from the next by a comma and has the form:

field length **AS** *field name*

All **field names** must be string; we will discuss this more below. Suppose that the file GPALIST2.DAT given above has records with six fields as described in Table 14-2. This would be translated into a FIELD statement as:

```
130 FIELD #3, 20 AS N$, 9 AS C$, 12 AS MA$, 12 AS MN$, 3 AS H$, 4 AS G$
```

TABLE 14-2

Fields for Each Record in File GPALIST2.DAT

Item Represented by Field	Variable Used	Field Length
Student's name	N$	20
Classification	C$	9
Major	MA$	12
Minor	MN$	12
Total hours earned	H$	3
Current GPA	G$	4

Note that the same channel number as was used in the OPEN statement appears at the beginning of the field description list. If you add all of the field lengths, you will get 60, the value specified at the end of the OPEN statement above.

We obtain a record for processing from a random file by means of the **GET** statement which has the form:

ln **GET** *#channel number, record number*

where the **record number** is used to specify which record in the file we wish to retrieve. The record number is more commonly known as the **key** or **pointer** and is normally linked to one of the fields in the record, known as the **key field**, from which it is calculated—often by a very complex formula. At this time, we will not be concerned with *how* the record number is obtained but will simply assume that we already know it. In the next section, we will learn a relatively simple technique for finding a record by using an index file (or array).

A record may be placed in a random file at a specified record number by the **PUT** statement, which is:

ln **PUT** *#channel number, record number*

The following skeletal program will open the file GPALIST2.DAT, described above, format the record fields, fetch record number 317 for processing, and return the result to the same record number in the file.

```
                                   :
110  OPEN "R", #3, "GPALIST2.DAT", 60
130  FIELD #3, 20 AS N$, 9 AS C$, 12 AS MA$, 12 AS MN$, 3 AS H$, 4 AS G$
                                   :
220  GET #3, 317
                                   :
430  PUT #3, 317
                                   :
```

What occurs between statements 220 and 430 is frequently the tricky part with random files.

When a record is retrieved from a random file, it is placed in a special area of memory known as a **buffer**. Before it can be written back to the file, all fields that have been removed from the buffer (processed in *any* way) must first be placed back in the buffer. This is accomplished by means of the **LSET** and **RSET** statements. Remember that we said earlier that all fields in a random file must be defined as string. These two statements assign string values to the previously defined field variables to be left-justified (LSET) or right-justified (RSET). Both statements have the general form:

ln **xSET** *field variable = string value*

where *x* is either L or R, *field variable* is any variable defined in a FIELD statement, and *string value* is any string constant or variable. Suppose that we wish to change a record in the file GPALIST2.DAT. We would first input the new data, transfer these to the buffer and the proper variable names of the record, and then write the record to the file. This is outlined by the following statements:

```
                    :
170 INPUT NI$, CI$, M1$, M2$, HI$, GI$
                    :
350 LSET N$ = NI$
360 LSET C$ = CI$
370 LSET MA$ = M1$
380 LSET MN$ = M2$
390 RSET H$ = HI$
400 RSET G$ = GI$
                    :
430 PUT #2, 295
                    :
```

The choice of whether to use LSET or RSET is arbitrary.

Each record of the file GPALIST2.DAT has two fields, H$ and G$, that would probably have to be treated as numeric. In order to handle numeric data with a random file, special conversion functions are available to convert the numeric values to and from the string values in the buffer. To convert a value in the buffer to numeric, we use either **CVI**, **CVS**, or **CVD**. To convert a numeric value to string in order to be placed in the buffer, we use either **MKI$**, **MKS$**, or **MKD$**. These six functions are summarized in Table 14-3. We will use only the single-precision functions, CVS and MKS$, which are sufficient for most work. To modify the above to input *numeric* values for total hours earned and GPA, we would write:

```
                    :
170  INPUT NI$, CI$, M1$, M2$, H, G
                    :
                    :
390  RSET H$ = MKS$(H)
400  RSET G$ = MKS$(G)
                    :
430  PUT #2, 295
                    :
```

Lines 390 and 400 place the numeric values H and G into the buffer as strings for proper storage in the file. Likewise, numeric values in the file can be retrieved from the buffer for processing by use of the CVS function. (These functions are *not* the same as VAL and STR$ and should not be confused with them.)

We will conclude this section with an example. Let us look once again at our simple file, ALUMNI.DAT, from Section 14-2. The following program permits the direct updating of records in the file without the creation of a new file.

TABLE 14-3

Numeric Buffer Data Conversion Functions

Action of Functions	Functions	Type of Numeric Data Handled	Maximum Characters
Converting from buffer to numeric value	CVI	Integer	2
	CVS	Single-precision	4
	CVD	Double-precision	8
Converting from numeric value to buffer	MKI$	Integer	2
	MKS$	Single-precision	4
	MKD$	Double-precision	8

```
 10 REM  UPDATING A RANDOM FILE
 20 REM
 30 OPEN "R", #1, "ALUMNI.DAT", 19
 40 FIELD #1, 9 AS N$, 2 AS ST$, 4 AS CL$, 4 AS CN$
 50 PRINT "ENTER RECORD NUMBER (NUMBER = -1 TO END)
 60 INPUT RN
 70 IF RN = -1 THEN 200
 80 PRINT "ENTER CONTRIBUTION"
 90 INPUT C
100 GET #1, RN
110 LET CN = CVS(CN$)
120 LET CN = CN + C
130 RSET CN$ = MKS$(CN)
140 PUT #1, RN
150 PRINT
160 PRINT "RECORD NUMBER"; RN; "UPDATED AS'
170 PRINT N$, ST$, CL$, CN
180 PRINT
190 GOTO 50
200 PRINT
210 PRINT ">>>  END OF PROCESSING  <<<"
220 CLOSE #1
210 END
```

A record number (RN) and contribution (C) are input at lines 60 and 90. The corresponding record is retrieved from the file by line 100. Line 110 converts the contribution field from its string value in the buffer to numeric form. The new contribution is added to the old at 120 and placed back into the buffer as a string field at 130. The updated record is written back to the file by 140. Since the other fields in the record were not processed or removed from the buffer, they did not have to be replaced. A typical run would be as follows:

```
ENTER RECORD NUMBER (NUMBER = -1 TO END)
?  1
ENTER CONTRIBUTION
? 25

RECORD NUMBER 1 UPDATED AS
R MURPHY     CT            1978           125

ENTER RECORD NUMBER (NUMBER = -1 TO END)
?  4
ENTER CONTRIBUTION
? 200

RECORD NUMBER 4 UPDATED AS
E DANIELS    NY            1980           1200

ENTER RECORD NUMBER (NUMBER = -1 TO END)
?  6
ENTER CONTRIBUTION
? 15

RECORD NUMBER 6 UPDATED AS
P KELLOGG    NY            1979           40

ENTER RECORD NUMBER (NUMBER = -1 TO END)
? -1

>>>  END OF PROCESSING  <<<
```

Compare the three records updated above to the originals given in Section 14-2.

Two additional functions that may be available on your system are **LOC** and **LOF**. These are both of the form:

LO*x(channel number)*

where *x* is either C or F. LOC returns the number of the record last processed, and LOF returns the total number of records in the file with the indicated channel number.

14-6 THE USE OF INDICES

Indexed files make use of a special supplementary file known as the **index file**, the individual records of which serve as pointers to specific records in the larger random file. Each **index** is linked to a record in the random file through some key field in the record. By either knowing or finding the proper index, you can go directly to the proper record in the random file. As stated in the first section of this chapter, most BASICs do not support true indexed file organizations; however, we can easily simulate these files.

Perhaps the simplest way to set up an index "file" is to create an array, the elements of which contain the key fields of the records in a random file. This means very simply that the *subscripts* of the index *array* will correspond to record numbers and point to the proper records in the random file. (Compare this technique to the pointer method for sorting arrays described at the end of Section 13-4.) We can set up and use an index array to update our file ALUMNI.DAT from the last section as follows:

```
 10 REM  UPDATING WITH AN INDEX ARRAY
 20 REM
 30 OPEN "R", #1, "ALUMNI.DAT", 19
 40 FIELD #1, 9 AS N$, 2 AS ST$, 4 AS CL$, 4 AS CN$
 50 DIM IX$(6)
 60 FOR J = 1 TO 6
 70    GET #1, J
 80    LET IX$(J) = N$
 90 NEXT J
100 PRINT "ENTER ALUMNUS NAME (NAME = 'END' TO END)
110 INPUT NA$
120 IF NA$ = "END" THEN 300
130 FOR J = 1 TO 6
140    IF NA$ = IX$(J) THEN 180
150 NEXT J
160 PRINT "    NAME NOT IN FILE -- RE-ENTER"
170 GOTO 100
180 PRINT "ENTER CONTRIBUTION"
190 INPUT C
200 GET #1, J
210 LET CN = CVS(CN$)
220 LET CN = CN + C
230 RSET CN$ = MKS$(CN)
240 PUT #1, J
250 PRINT
260 PRINT "RECORD NUMBER"; J; "UPDATED AS'
270 PRINT N$, ST$, CL$, CN
280 PRINT
290 GOTO 100
300 PRINT
310 PRINT ">>>  END OF PROCESSING  <<<"
320 CLOSE #1
330 END
```

The index array is created at lines 60 to 90 using the alumni name as the key field. Note that to do this, we have stepped through the random file as if it were sequential. This is possible, but slow and not very practical for very large files because each record in a random file requires a separate disk access. Once the index array has been created, it can be kept in memory and searched at will at the speed of the CPU, which is much faster. Next we enter the name of the alumnus instead of the record number, which is much more practical. The index array is searched to find the location (record number) of the name at 130 to 150. The remainder of the program is essentially the same as that at the end of the last section. If we enter names instead of record numbers, we will get exactly the same output as before.

Clearly, an index array can easily be set up for more than one key field for the same file to provide random access by multiple keys. Generally, if the file is not too large and the computer's memory not too restricted, all index arrays can remain resident in the main memory for immediate and fast searches. If not, one or more of the arrays can be saved to the disk as a sequential file to be retrieved or searched as needed.

14-7 AN EXAMPLE: TRAFFIC VIOLATION REPORT

The following example illustrates both random file processing and the use of indexes for locating records.

Problem: The sheriff of Tinytown has recently started issuing parking tickets to the local citizens. Not being accustomed to such things, many of the local folk have been ignoring the little slips of paper, acquiring repeated tickets, and not paying their fines. The sheriff needs a computer program that will assist him in tracking down the repeated violators. He has three files that must be processed. There is a listing of all license numbers of those to whom tickets have been issued within the last week. A second file contains a summary of all previously issued tickets and unpaid fines; each ticket is a $5.00 fine. This file lists the license number, number of tickets issued, and total of fines due. Finally, there is a master file that contains a listing of each local resident's license number, name, street address, and type of auto. (The sheriff is aware that *everyone* in Tinytown has received at least one ticket by now.) The sheriff wants a list of all persons who have either accumulated 12 or more tickets or have at least $25.00 in unpaid fines. The printout should give for each violator satisfying one or both of these conditions the full data from the master file plus the number of tickets issued and total fines due. Totals should be printed for the number of warnings issued, the total number of tickets and unpaid fines charged to those receiving warnings, and the total number of tickets and unpaid fines charged to all violators. The data for the three files is given in Tables 14-4, 14-5, and 14-6.

The solution to this problem is outlined as follows:

1. Print the main and column headings.
2. Open the master and previous violator files as random access files.
3. Format the fields for the records of the master and previous violator files.
4. Dimension the arrays to serve as the index arrays for the master and previous violator files.

TABLE 14-4

License Numbers for New Tickets Issued

License Number	License Number	License Number	License Number	License Number	License Number
KZH683	DTD778	SJJ099	BAT211	LOH446	RUS884
DTD778	ESE372	TTY684	KZH683	DTD778	YDY311
PLL388	WWH505	BTS902	RUS884	KJK382	KZH683
RUS884	PLL388	ESE372	RUS884	BAT211	KZH683
AYC332	SJJ099	PLL388	DTD778	NNK302	DOG392
KZH683	LOH446	GSN744	BAT211	RUS884	YDY311

TABLE 14-5

Listing of Previous Tickets and Unpaid Fines by Violator License Number

License Number	Previous Tickets	Unpaid Fines	License Number	Previous Tickets	Unpaid Fines
TTY684	3	15	KJK382	3	0
FIJ392	3	0	NNK302	7	0
YDY311	1	5	SJJ099	3	15
DTD778	13	65	CAT289	8	30
NNR399	1	0	ESE372	5	0
WWH505	5	0	BTS902	3	0
GSN744	1	0	LOH446	4	20
DQR328	3	15	CUC119	12	0
RUS884	8	25	RKK384	4	20
PLL388	2	0	KZH683	15	75
AGE283	5	0	AYC332	1	5
BAT211	11	55	DOG392	2	10

TABLE 14-6

Data for Master File for Traffic Violator Problem

License Number	Registered Owner	Street Address	Description of Auto
AGE283	R T Daniels	212 Tolbert St	81 Datsun
RUS884	T N Thomas	1473 S Elm St	78 Chevrolet
NNR399	W L Peterson	82 Main St	80 Cadillac
BTS902	A N Lewis	Little Creek Rd	72 Ford Trk
YDY311	R C Fieldman	311 Apple Dr	84 T-bird
DTD778	E S Cousins	512 Brown St	65 Dodge
ESE372	S L Andrews	76 N Broad	79 Dodge
SJJ099	A H Broderick	221 Teake Dr	82 Porsche
LOH446	T B Greene	399 Rice St	77 Toyota
BAT211	W L Jacobs	1117 Oakleaf Lane	81 Buick
TTY684	E T Upton	712 Apple Dr	81 Continental
DQR328	S F Freeman	1016 S Elm St	74 Mustang
WWH505	W T Wiley	619 Ropper Dr	80 Plymouth
CAT289	N N Dickson	Millcreek Rd	78 Mercury
KZH683	T K Boyd	288 N Elm St	80 Oldsmobile
AYC332	R O Willis	Millcreek Rd	70 GMC Trk
PLL388	E D Benhamin	Hwy 90 N	69 Chevrolet
KJK382	T W Silvers	754 Brown St	82 Datsun
FIJ392	G N Dodd	Little Creek Rd	81 Ford
RKK384	N A Franklin	131 N Broad	79 Cadillac
CUC119	P A Edwards	701 Pine Lane	73 VW Beetle
NNK302	R A Innis	619 Teake Dr	84 Mercedes
DOG392	L C Black	1192 Oakleaf Lane	80 Ford
GSN744	B M Edge	Millcreek Rd	80 Dodge Trk

5. Build index arrays for master and previous violator files.
6. Open new ticket file as an input, sequential file.
7. If end-of-file, go to step 15.
8. Read a record from the new ticket file.
9. Search the index array for the previous violator file for the corresponding license number. When a match is found, fetch the corresponding record from the previous violator file.
10. Convert the number of tickets and amount of unpaid fines to numeric values.
11. Add 1 to the number of tickets issued and 5 to the total unpaid fines.

12. Replace updated values for number of tickets and unpaid fines to the buffer as string values.
13. Write the updated record back to the previous violator file.
14. Go to step 7.
15. Close ticket file.
16. For each record in the previous violator file, perform steps 17 to 25.
17. Fetch a record from the previous violator file.
18. Convert the number of tickets and amount of unpaid fines to numeric values.
19. Add the number of tickets and amount of unpaid fines to the totals for all violators.
20. If number of tickets is less than 12 and amount of unpaid fines is less than 25, go to step 25.
21. Add 1 to number of violators to receive a warning.
22. Add number of tickets and amount of unpaid fines to totals for violators receiving a warning.
23. Search the index array for the master file for the corresponding license number. When a match is found, fetch the corresponding record from the master file.
24. Print a line listing information on a violator to receive a warning.
25. If more records remain in previous violator file, go to step 17.
26. Print total summary.
27. Close master and previous violator files.
28. Stop.

This is illustrated in the flowchart in Figure 14-3.

We begin our analysis of this problem at steps 2 and 3, which are programmed as:

```
460  OPEN "R", #1, "VIOLATOR.DAT", 14
470  OPEN "R", #2, "MASTER.DAT", 50
480  FIELD #1, 6 AS L$, 4 AS TT$, 4 AS TF$
490  FIELD #2, 6 AS LN$, 13 AS N$, 17 AS AD$, 14 AS A$
```

The file VIOLATOR.DAT is opened at line 460 as a random file using channel number 1 and with a record length of 14 characters as described at line 480. Similarly, the file MASTER.DAT is opened at 470 using channel 2 and having a 50 character record length described at line 490. The third file will be sequential and will be opened later when needed.

The two index arrays are created by the following loop:

```
530 DIM V$(24), M$(24)
540 LET JX = 24
550 FOR J = 1 TO JX
560   GET #1, J
570   LET V$(J) = L$
580   GET #2, J
590   LET M$(J) = LN$
600 NEXT J
```

Line 540 set the number of elements in the two files. (Remember, everybody in town has received at least one ticket, so the two files have the same number of records.) The loop at lines 550 to 600 counts through the records of the files *sequentially*. A record from the previous violator file, VIOLATOR.DAT, is read at line 560 and the license number assigned to the corresponding index array element at 570. Lines 580 and 590 do the same job for the master file, MASTER.DAT.

Now that we have the index arrays set up, we are ready to begin to process the actual

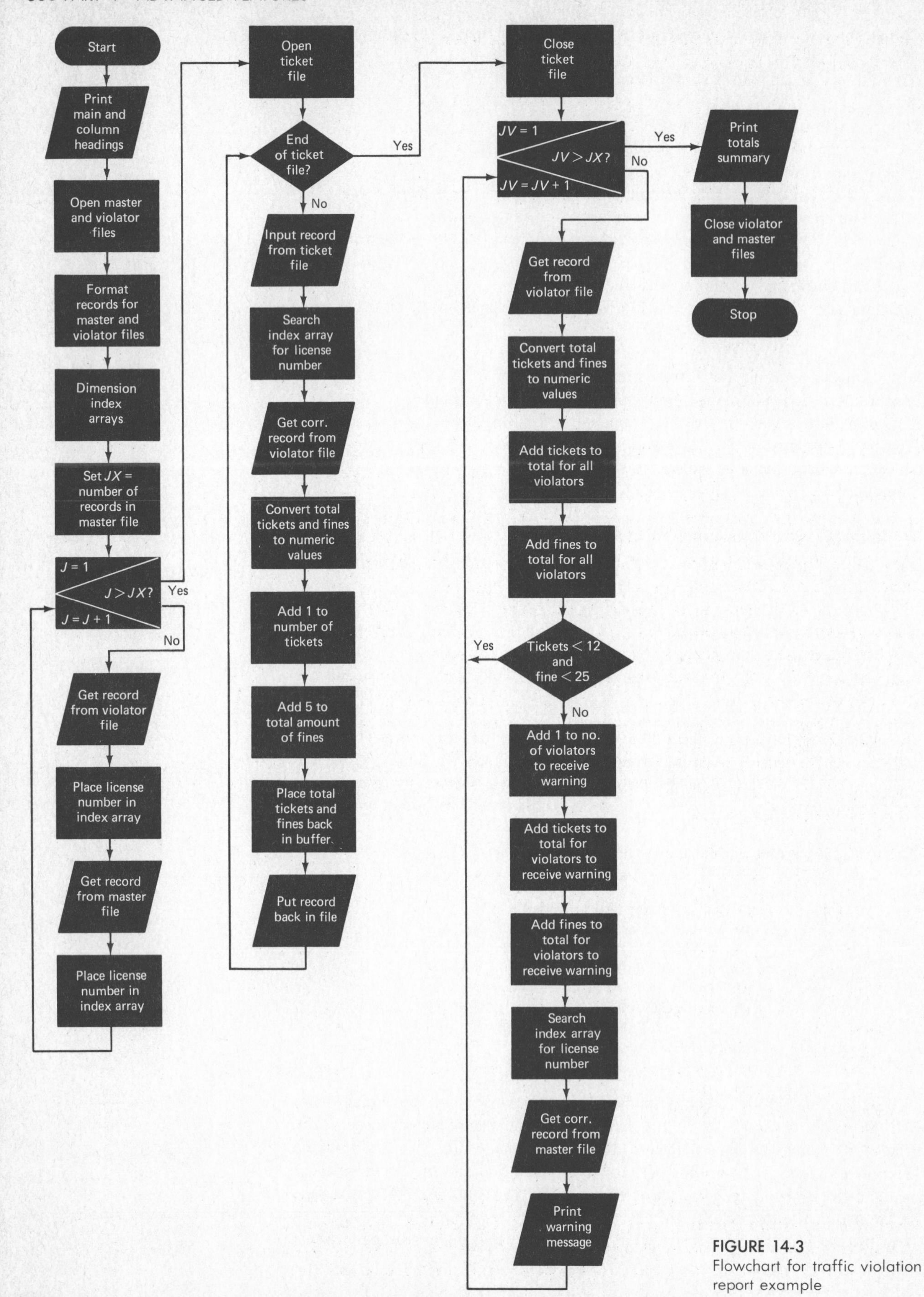

FIGURE 14-3
Flowchart for traffic violation report example

program data. First, we must update the previous violator file using the new ticket data from the ticket file. This is done at lines 640 to 790.

```
640 OPEN "I", #3, "TICKET.DAT"
650 IF EOF(3) THEN 810
660 INPUT #3, NL$
670 FOR JV = 1 TO JX
680    IF NL$ = V$(JV) THEN 700
690 NEXT JV
700 GET #1, JV
710 LET TT = CVS(TT$)
720 LET TF = CVS(TF$)
730 LET TT = TT + 1
740 LET TF = TF + 5
750 RSET TT$ = MKS$(TT)
760 RSET TF$ = MKS$(TF)
770 PUT #1, JV
780 GOTO 650
790 CLOSE #3
```

The new ticket file is opened as an input, sequential file, TICKET.DAT, at line 640. Basically, the above is a loop in which we read records from the ticket file and update the corresponding record in the previous violator file. A record from TICKET.DAT is read at 660 and the record with the same license number in VIOLATOR.DAT is found and read at lines 670 to 700. Lines 710 and 720 convert the string values for the total number of tickets and amount of unpaid fines from the buffer to numeric values. The numeric values are updated at 730 and 740 by adding 1 to the number of tickets and 5 (dollars) to the fines. The updated values are then placed back into the buffer as strings by lines 750 and 760 and the record written back to VIOLATOR.DAT by 770. When the end-of-file occurs, TICKET.DAT is closed at line 790 because we no longer need it.

Now that the violator file has been brought up to date, we can check to see who has enough tickets or fines to receive a warning. We do this by reading and checking each record of VIOLATOR.DAT one at a time as if it were a sequential file. The loop for this is at lines 860 to 1040.

```
 860 FOR JV = 1 TO JX
 870    GET #1, JV
 880    LET TT = CVS(TT$)
 890    LET TF = CVS(TF$)
 900    LET TA = TA + TT
 910    LET FA = FA + TF
 920    IF TT < 12 AND TF < 25 THEN 1040
 930    LET W = W + 1
 940    LET TW = TW + TT
 950    LET FW = FW + TF
 960    FOR JM = 1 TO JX
 970       IF L$ = M$(JM) THEN 990
 980    NEXT JM
 990    GET #2, JM
1000    PRINT LN$; TAB(15); A$; TAB(38); TT; TAB(52); "$"; TF
1010    PRINT TAB(15); N$
1020    PRINT TAB(15); AD$
1030    PRINT
1040 NEXT JV
```

A record of VIOLATOR.DAT is fetched at line 870 and the total number of tickets and amounts of fines converted to numeric values at 880 and 890. The next two lines, 900 and 910, update the total number of tickets and unpaid fines for all violators. Line 920 checks to see if a warning should be printed. If not, then the next record is read and processed. If so, then lines 930 to 950 update the totals for the number of warnings printed and the total tickets and unpaid fines by those violators receiving warnings. Lines 960 to 990 find and fetch the corresponding record from the master file. The remaining lines above print the warning message. This loop is repeated until the entire violator file has been processed. At the end, the final totals are printed at lines 1080 to 1140, and the two open files are closed at 1150.

A complete listing and run follow:

```
 10 REM   TRAFFIC VIOLATION REPORT
 20 REM
 30 REM   DISK FILES ARE DEFINED AS --
 40 REM
 50 REM    VIOLATOR.DAT = PREVIOUS TRAFFIC VIOLATORS
 60 REM      MASTER.DAT = MASTER LIST OF LOCAL RESIDENTS
 70 REM      TICKET.DAT = LATEST TICKETS ISSUED
 80 REM
 90 REM   VARIABLES ARE DEFINED AS --
100 REM
110 REM          JX = NUMBER OF ENTRIES IN MASTER & VIOLATOR FILES
120 REM          V$ = INDEX ARRAY FOR VIOLATOR FILE
130 REM          M$ = INDEX ARRAY FOR MASTER FILE
140 REM          L$ = LICENSE NUMBER IN VIOLATOR FILE
150 REM         LN$ = LICENSE NUMBER IN MASTER FILE
160 REM         NL$ = LICENSE NUMBER IN TICKET FILE
170 REM          TT = TOTAL NUMBER OF TICKETS ISSUED TO VIOLATOR
180 REM         TT$ = TT AS STORED IN VIOLATOR FILE
190 REM          TF = TOTAL AMOUNT OF UNPAID FINES BY VIOLATOR
200 REM         TF$ = TF AS STORED IN VIOLATOR FILE
210 REM           W = TOTAL NUMBER OF WARNINGS ISSUED
220 REM          TW = TOTAL NUMBER OF TICKETS ISSUED TO WARNEES
230 REM          FW = TOTAL OF UNPAID FINES BY WARNEES
240 REM          TA = TOTAL TICKETS BY ALL VIOLATORS
250 REM          FA = TOTAL UNPAID FINES BY ALL VIOLATORS
260 REM          N$ = NAME FROM MASTER FILE
270 REM         AD$ = ADDRESS FROM MASTER FILE
280 REM          A$ = TYPE OF AUTO FROM MASTER FILE
290 REM          JV = LOCATION OF RECORD IN VIOLATOR FILE
300 REM          JM = LOCATION OF RECORD IN MASTER FILE
310 REM           J = LOOP COUNTER
320 REM
330 REM   PRINT HEADINGS
340 REM
350 PRINT TAB(17); "TRAFFIC VIOLATION REPORT"
360 PRINT
370 PRINT
380 PRINT "LICENSE"; TAB(19); "VIOLATOR"; TAB(37); "TICKETS";
390 PRINT TAB(51); "UNPAID"
400 PRINT "NUMBER"; TAB(16); "IDENTIFICATION"; TAB(37); "ISSUED";
410 PRINT TAB(51); "FINES"
420 PRINT
430 REM
440 REM   OPEN AND FORMAT RANDOM FILES
450 REM
460 OPEN "R", #1, "VIOLATOR.DAT", 14
470 OPEN "R", #2, "MASTER.DAT", 50
480 FIELD #1, 6 AS L$, 4 AS TT$, 4 AS TF$
490 FIELD #2, 6 AS LN$, 13 AS N$, 17 AS AD$, 14 AS A$
500 REM
510 REM   DIMENSION AND SET UP INDEX ARRAYS
520 REM
530 DIM V$(24), M$(24)
```

```
540 LET JX = 24
550 FOR J = 1 TO JX
560   GET #1, J
570   LET V$(J) = L$
580   GET #2, J
590   LET M$(J) = LN$
600 NEXT J
610 REM
620 REM  UPDATE VIOLATOR FILE WITH NEW TICKET DATA
630 REM
640 OPEN "I", #3, "TICKET.DAT"
650 IF EOF(3) THEN 790
660 INPUT #3, NL$
670 FOR JV = 1 TO JX
680   IF NL$ = V$(JV) THEN 700
690 NEXT JV
700 GET #1, JV
710 LET TT = CVS(TT$)
720 LET TF = CVS(TF$)
730 LET TT = TT + 1
740 LET TF = TF + 5
750 RSET TT$ = MKS$(TT)
760 RSET TF$ = MKS$(TF)
770 PUT #1, JV
780 GOTO 650
790 CLOSE #3
800 REM
810 REM  FOR EACH RECORD IN VIOLATOR FILE WITH EXCESSIVE
820 REM  TICKETS AND/OR UNPAID FINES, PRINT PERSONAL DATA
830 REM  FROM MASTER FILE ALONG WITH APPROPRIATE VIOLATION
840 REM  SUMMARY INFORMATION.
850 REM
860 FOR JV = 1 TO JX
870   GET #1, JV
880   LET TT = CVS(TT$)
890   LET TF = CVS(TF$)
900   LET TA = TA + TT
910   LET FA = FA + TF
920   IF TT < 12 AND TF < 25 THEN 1040
930   LET W = W + 1
940   LET TW = TW + TT
950   LET FW = FW + TF
960   FOR JM = 1 TO JX
970     IF L$ = M$(JM) THEN 990
980   NEXT JM
990   GET #2, JM
1000  PRINT LN$; TAB(15); A$; TAB(38); TT; TAB(52); "$"; TF
1010  PRINT TAB(15); N$
1020  PRINT TAB(15); AD$
1030  PRINT
1040 NEXT JV
1050 REM
1060 REM  PRINT TOTAL SUMMARY, CLOSE FILES, AND END
1070 REM
1080 PRINT
1090 PRINT "TOTAL NUMBER OF PERSONS RECEIVING WARNING ="; W
1100 PRINT "     TOTAL TICKETS ISSUED TO WARNEES ="; TW
1110 PRINT "     TOTAL UNPAID FINES BY WARNEES = $"; FW
1120 PRINT
1130 PRINT "TOTAL TICKETS ISSUED TO ALL VIOLATORS ="; TA
1140 PRINT "TOTAL UNPAID FINES DUE FROM ALL VIOLATORS = $"; FA
1150 CLOSE #1, #2
1160 END
```

```
                    TRAFFIC VIOLATION REPORT

LICENSE               VIOLATOR             TICKETS        UNPAID
NUMBER             IDENTIFICATION          ISSUED         FINES

DTD778          65 DODGE                     17           $ 85
                E S COUSINS
                512 BROWN ST

RUS884          78 CHEVROLET                 13           $ 50
                T N THOMAS
                1473 S ELM ST

BAT211          81 BUICK                     14           $ 70
                W L JACOBS
                1117 OAKLEAF LANE

SJJ099          82 PORSCHE                   5            $ 25
                A H BRODERICK
                221 TEAKE DR

CAT289          78 MERCURY                   8            $ 30
                N N DICKSON
                MILLCREEK RD

LOH446          77 TOYOTA                    6            $ 30
                T B GREENE
                399 RICE ST

CUC119          73 VW BEETLE                 12           $ 0
                P A EDWARDS
                701 PINE LANE

KZH683          80 OLDSMOBILE                20           $ 100
                T K BOYD
                288 N ELM ST


TOTAL NUMBER OF PERSONS RECEIVING WARNING = 8
    TOTAL TICKETS ISSUED TO WARNEES = 95
    TOTAL UNPAID FINES BY WARNEES = $ 390

TOTAL TICKETS ISSUED TO ALL VIOLATORS = 159
TOTAL UNPAID FINES DUE FROM ALL VIOLATORS = $ 535
```

14-8 CHAINING

In Section 14-1, we said that *programs* can also be treated as files. Frequently, it is convenient (or necessary) to run one program from another, a process defined as **chaining**. This may be because processing the data in a program may lead to several alternatives which will require that other programs be processed. It may be that to process the data all in one program would require a program that would be too large to fit into the computer's memory.

One method that is available with many versions of BASIC by which one program can cause another to be executed is by means of the **CHAIN** statement. The basic form of this statement is:

ln1 **CHAIN** *"program name", ln2*

where *program name* is the name of the new program to be executed, and *ln2* is the line number of the new program at which execution should begin if other than at the beginning. If the optional line number is omitted, then the new program will begin to run from the first executable statement. The following set of statements will run the program, PROG2.BAS, from the first program (PROG1.BAS) and then return to PROG1.BAS to line 350, the line following that from which it "chained in" the second program.

```
 10  REM   THIS IS PROGRAM 1
            :
            :
340  CHAIN "PROG2.BAS"
350  (Next statement)
            :
            :
600  END
```

```
 10  REM   THIS IS PROGRAM 2
            :
            :
220  CHAIN "PROG1.BAS", 350
            :
300  END
```

In order to call a program with the CHAIN statement, it must have been saved to the disk as a program file.

One problem with most CHAIN statements is that as one program replaces another in memory, so do the values for all variables. This means that the values assigned to the variables in one program are not automatically transferred to the other program. There are several possible solutions for this. One is a very simple option for the CHAIN statement that is available with a few versions of the statement. This is the **ALL** option that is simply added to the end of the statement. That is, typing line 340 in program 1 above as:

```
340  CHAIN "PROG2.BAS", ALL
```

will cause all values of the variables to be transferred to program 2. Similarly, line 220 in program 2 should be:

```
220  CHAIN "PROG1.BAS", 350, ALL
```

to return the values to program 1. If this option is not provided, it is possible that your BASIC makes use of the **COMMON** statement (borrowed from FORTRAN), which permits selected variables to be passed between programs.

One method that can be used regardless of whether the ALL option or COMMON statement is available is to simply write a file to the disk that will contain all values needed by the second program just before chaining in a program. The second program need only read this file. Files need only be repeated, written to, and read from as each successive program is chained.

TROUBLESHOOTING

Each of the following programs contains an error that prevents it from executing properly. Explain *specifically* what the problem is and what must be done to correct it. To assist you, a sample of what would happen should you attempt to run the program is provided after each listing. Refer to Appendix D for an explanation of BASIC error messages.

1.

```
10 REM   TROUBLESHOOTING PROBLEM 14-1
20 REM
30 REM          N$ = NAME
40 REM         SS$ = SOCIAL SECURITY NUMBER
50 REM           A = AGE
```

```
 60 REM
 70 OPEN "I", #1, "FILE1.DAT"
 80 IF EOF THEN 120
 90 INPUT #1, N$, A, SS$
100 PRINT SS$, N$, A
110 GOTO 80
120 CLOSE #1
130 END
```

```
Syntax Error in Line 80
```

2.

```
 10 REM  TROUBLESHOOTING PROBLEM 14-2
 20 REM
 30 REM         N$ = NAME
 40 REM        SS$ = SOCIAL SECURITY NUMBER
 50 REM          A = AGE
 60 REM
 70 OPEN "I", #1, "FILE1.DAT"
 80 OPEN "O", #2, "FILE2.DAT"
 90 IF EOF(1) THEN 140
100 INPUT #1, N$, A, SS$
110 IF A => 65 THEN PRINT #1, N$, A, SS$
120 PRINT SS$, N$, A
130 GOTO 90
140 CLOSE #1
150 END
```

```
Bad File Mode in Line 110
```

3.

```
 10 REM  TROUBLESHOOTING PROBLEM 14-3
 20 REM
 30 REM         N$ = DONOR NAME
 40 REM     PC/PC$ = PREVIOUS CONTRIBUTIONS
 50 REM     LC/LC$ = LAST CONTRIBUTION
 60 REM
 70 OPEN "R", #1, "DONOR.DAT", 28
 80 FIELD #1, 20 AS N$, 4 AS PC, 4 AS LC
 90 PRINT "ENTER RECORD NUMBER AND CONTRIBUTION"
100 PRINT "  RECORD NUMBER = -1 TO END)
110 INPUT R, LC
120 IF R = -1 THEN 200
130 GET #1, R
140 LET PC = CVS(PC$)
150 LET PC = PC + LC
160 RSET PC$ = MKS$(PC)
170 RSET LC$ = MKS$(LC)
180 PUT #1, R
190 GOTO 90
200 CLOSE #1
210 END
```

```
Type Mismatch in Line 80
```

IMPORTANT TERMS

After studying this chapter, you should be familiar with the meaning and use of the following terms and BASIC statements:

Field
Record
File
Data base
Data file
Program file
File specification
Filename
Filetype
File extension

Sequential file
Opening a file
OPEN statement
Channel number
INPUT # statement
PRINT # statement
Closing a file
CLOSE statement
Input Past End error
File pointer
RESTORE # statement
Error trapping
EOF function
ON ERROR GOTO statement
RESUME statement
ERR and ERL variables
Random files
Direct access files
Record length
FIELD statement
Field description
Field length
Field name
GET statement
Record number
Key
Pointer
Key field
PUT statement
Buffer
LSET and RSET statements
CVI, CVS, CVD functions
MKI$, MKS$, MKD$ functions
LOC and LOF functions
Indexed files
Index file
Index
CHAIN statement
ALL option
COMMON statement

EXERCISES

1. Write OPEN statements for each of the following files. In the case of a random file, also write the accompanying FIELD statement.
   (a) FILE.TXT as a sequential file for input
   (b) CHAP14.DOC as a sequential file for output
   (c) PAYDED.DAT as a random file with a record with field of 25, 15, 9, 13, and 4 characters
   (d) EMPMSTR.DAT as a random file with a record with fields of 20, 20, 15, 2, 4, 11, 10, and 2 characters
2. Explain the action of each of the following statements:
   (a) `210 PRINT #3, B$, F, J5, V$`
   (b) `175 GET #6, 211`
   (c) `1120 CLOSE`
   (d) `450 LET D = CVS(F$)`
   (e) `190 ON ERROR GOTO 780`
   (f) `575 RESUME 230`
   (g) `450 PUT #3, FA`
   (h) `290 LSET V$ = K$`
   (i) `600 IF ERR = 39 AND ERL = 370 THEN RESUME`
   (j) `410 LSET A3$ = MKS$(TR)`
   (k) `520 ON ERROR GOTO 0`
   (l) `375 CHAIN "ACCRCV.BAS", ALL`

PROGRAMMING PROBLEMS

Write programs in BASIC to accomplish the tasks described by each of the following problems. Be sure to carefully document each program and include all appropriate report headings and other literals.

1. Write a program that reads names from one sequential file—in first name, middle initial, last name order—and writes the names to a second file with last name first, then first name and middle initial.

2. Write a program to create a sequential mailing label file that can be used to print mailing labels. Each record should contain a name, street address, city, state, and zip code. Once the file has been created, labels should be printed according to one of the following options, which should be menu-selected: (1) print all labels, (2) print only those labels with a specified zip code, (3) print only those labels within a given state, or (4) print an individual label selected by name. Labels should be printed with the name on the first line, street address on the second, and city, state, and zip code on the third. At least one blank line should appear between addresses. Use 15 to 20 names and addresses of your friends and classmates as data.
3. Redo Problem 5 at the end of Chapter 9 using a single sequential file to store the data to be processed.
4. Write a program to convert the combined inventory file in the example in Section 14-4 from a sequential file to a random file. Your program should input records from the sequential file and then write them to a random file.
5. Using the random file that you created in Problem 4, write a program that updates the quantity in stock for an item by either adding or subtracting items from the inventory for that item. As each item is processed, the proper record in the file should be updated. When processing is completed, the updated file should be printed for verification. Data is provided below.

Items Sold from Inventory		Items Added to Inventory	
Stock Number	Total Quantity	Stock Number	Total Quantity
111402	2	111402	5
113778	3	119882	12
116605	1	120019	12
119882	5	121278	24
120019	2	127633	3
121278	14	128922	2
121771	1	131101	12
122803	4	131290	2
124337	2	132788	12
131101	6	133788	1
132788	12	136770	2
137422	2	141622	6
140255	3	142105	5

6. Repeat Problem 5 but process all data, including the inventory file, using *sequential* files.

Problems 7 to 9 make use of the inventory table for Steve's Stereos given at the end of Chapter 9. For these problems, this table should be treated as a random file.

7. Revise Problem 11 at the end of Chapter 9 by processing the inventory table as a random file and the daily sales data as a sequential file. The output should produce both the printed report as described in the previous problem as well as updating the inventory file.
8. Redo Problem 12 from Chapter 9 using a sequential file for the sales data as presented in the table.
9. Rewrite Problem 13 from Chapter 9 using disk files rather than arrays. You will need three files for this one: the random file for the inventory table, the sequential file for the sales data, and a random file for the commission data.
10. Redo problem 7 from Chapter 9 using files for the data. Use whatever types of files for the data you feel are best.

11. Rewrite Problem 8 from Chapter 9 using files. Use whatever file organizations you think best.
12. Revise Problem 2 to provide the additional options of adding or deleting names from the file.
13. The City College Library is having a hard time keeping track of its books which have been checked out or returned. Write a program to create and maintain a library circulation report file that will assist the library with this task. The file should have records that contain the following fields: book title, author, catalog number, person checking book out, date to be returned. The program should be menu-driven and provide the following options: (1) add a book (record) to the file, (2) delete a book (record) from the file, (3) determine if a book is in the file (you determine how this search should be made), (4) determine if a specific person has any books on loan, (5) list all books on loan, and (6) list all overdue books. To gather data for this one, go to your library, copy data for 15 to 20 books from the card catalog, and add appropriate names and dates.

CHAPTER 15

CASE STUDIES

Textbook problems are fine for practice, but real-life situations rarely resemble the idealistic situations that are normally encountered in such problems. While most of the problems that you have solved up to this point have been based on practical situations, it was not feasible to present large problems in the individual chapters. That would have obscured the specific concepts that were being emphasized in that particular chapter and made it more difficult to master them. However, now that you have mastered much of BASIC, you are ready to tackle larger, more complex programs. Such programs, presented as a learning tool, are loosely called *case studies*. These are normally oriented toward practical situations and require the combination of several programming techniques to achieve a successful solution. This chapter presents six such case studies.

15-1 SAVING AT THE LAST NATIONAL BANK

In order to attract more large depositors, the Last National Bank is offering, for a limited time only, a series of special certificates as described in Table 15-1. In addition, for each type of certificate shown in the table, any investment will earn an extra 0.5 percent for every *multiple* of the minimum that it is *over* the minimum, up to a maximum of an extra 3 percent. In other words, an investment of $100,000 in a type 3 certificate exceeds the minimum by $75,000 which is three times the minimum of $25,000. This means an extra $3 \times 0.5\% = 1.5\%$ or a total of $13.0\% + 1.5\% = 14.5\%$ paid on that investment. No extra interest is paid for fractions of the minimum investment.

The president of the bank has requested a program be written that will assist the bank employees in providing customers with information on the new certificates. The program should permit interactive input of certificate type and amount of intended investment. The program should then calculate and print the following information: minimum investment required, amount to be invested, basic interest, interest to be paid, maturity period, method of compounding, and maturity value. Editing checks should be made on both

TABLE 15-1

Descriptions of Available Certificates

Certificate Type Number	Minimum Deposit	Annual Rate	Time to Maturity	Compounding Period
1	$10,000	12.0%	18 months	Monthly
2	$10,000	12.5%	30 months	Daily
3	$25,000	13.0%	24 months	Monthly
4	$25,000	14.0%	48 months	Daily
5	$50,000	15.5%	60 months	Daily

TABLE 15-2

Certificate Inquiry Data to Be Processed

Certificate Type Number	Intended Investment	Certificate Type Number	Intended Investment
3	$ 25,000	2	$ 50,000
2	$ 20,000	4	$ 85,000
3	$ 15,000	1	$ 15,000
4	$ 40,000	6	$250,000
2	$ 10,000	3	$ 45,000
4	$130,000	1	$ 5,000
5	$ 50,000	2	$100,000
1	$ 30,000	5	$120,000

input fields. If the certificate number is invalid, the message INVALID CERTIFICATE NUMBER—PLEASE REENTER should be printed. If the amount to be invested is below the minimum required investment, then only the minimum investment and amount to be invested are to be printed along with the message BELOW REQUIRED MINIMUM INVESTMENT for that entry.

After all inquiries have been made, a summary is to be printed that gives the total number of inquiries of each certificate type and the projected investment amount as well as totals for the number of inquiries and projected investments for all certificates. Inquiries that involved an invalid certificate number or an amount below the minimum investment are not to be included in any totals. Data to be processed is provided in Table 15-2.

15-2 SELLING DIRT-A-WAY VACUUM CLEANERS

The Dirt-a-way Vacuum Cleaner Company still sells its line of machines door to door. The company offers five different models of cleaners as described in Table 15-3.

All salespersons are assigned a specific territory located in one of six national regions as given in Table 15-4. To simplify recordkeeping, each salesperson also has an identification number, as listed in Table 15-5.

Each salesperson is to be paid a weekly commission, based on the total sales from all vacuums sold, at the rate of 7 percent for the first $2500 sold and 9 percent for all sales over $2500. Any salesperson selling $5000 or more in one week will earn a $100 bonus.

Up until now, all sales data has been compiled by hand on a monthly basis; however, due to declining sales, the president of the company has asked that a computer program be prepared that will give him a weekly sales report. Input data, given in Table 15-6, will be the region number, salesperson's number, and the total number of machines sold for each model in order from model 1 through model 5. The total sales and commission earned for each salesperson is to be calculated. A detailed line giving the region name (group indi-

TABLE 15-3

Names and Unit Prices for Vacuum Cleaners

Model Number	Model Name	Unit Price
1	Port-a-Vac	$ 39.90
2	Super-broom	$ 59.90
3	Standard	$ 99.90
4	Heavy-duty	$139.90
5	Super-deluxe	$189.90

TABLE 15-4

Sales Regions

Region Number	Designation
1	New England
2	Atlantic
3	Southern
4	Mid-Western
5	Mountain
6	Pacific

TABLE 15-5

Salespersons' Numbers and Names

Number	Name	Number	Name	Number	Name
1145	L. R. Irvin	2282	S. B. Watson	4162	R. D. Spencer
1278	P. N. Baldwin	2322	F. K. Kramer	4287	K. K. Tyler
1453	J. Q. Smith	2350	R. R. Jones	4478	B. C. Woodward
1556	C. C. Wilkenson	2377	L. L. Drapper	4671	W. N. Johnson
1677	E. R. Tower	3472	W. A. Sykes	4782	T. T. Ishimoto
1819	Y. S. Harris	3491	E. B. Harris	4790	F. D. Scott
2001	A. C. Clarke	3592	R. T. Rodriguez	5173	H. B. Franklyn
2011	R. E. Price	3813	E. S. Milkes	5278	A. N. Lee
2199	A. M. Cummings	3900	W. A. Smith	5317	E. E. Freeman
2203	J. N. Lopez	4110	T. C. Craddock	5478	H. C. Ackerman

cated), salesperson's name, total sales, and commission earned is to be printed for each salesperson. Whenever there is a change in region, a control break is to be taken giving both the total sales and average sales per salesperson for the region being printed. When all regions have been processed, the following information should be printed: (1) the total numbers sold and models for which the greatest and least number of vacuums were sold, (2) the total sales for all regions and models, (3) the name of the salesperson with the highest weekly sales total along with the total sales and region in which the sales were made, (4) the name of the region with the largest weekly *total* sales and the total, and (5) the region with the highest *average* weekly sales and the average.

15-3 VOTING IN PIGWALLOW COUNTY

The county clerk of Pigwallow County has finally given up trying to maintain the voter registration records by hand and has requested that the data processing department prepare a program that will assist him with that task. You have been assigned the job of preparing this program.

The records for each voter in the master voter table contain the following values: name with last name first, street address, telephone number, party affiliation, and year

TABLE 15-6

Regional Sales Data for One Week

Region Number	Salesperson Number	Total Sold for Model Number					Region Number	Salesperson Number	Total Sold for Model Number				
		1	2	3	4	5			1	2	3	4	5
1	2011	8	4	8	1	5	4	2282	11	9	8	5	7
1	3900	1	2	9	4	7	4	4110	7	2	9	9	1
1	1145	7	7	7	5	8	4	1556	3	4	9	7	8
1	4162	2	9	7	1	5	4	1677	8	4	7	6	2
1	2199	5	1	6	2	4	4	5278	4	3	5	9	5
1	1278	14	6	5	3	11	5	3472	7	7	0	1	4
2	2203	3	8	9	0	3	5	5317	2	8	5	6	4
2	3813	3	7	11	5	0	5	1819	4	2	0	4	7
2	4287	8	1	4	8	1	5	2001	9	3	6	6	8
2	4478	5	6	7	9	3	6	3592	5	11	6	7	14
2	5173	9	8	0	2	1	6	4790	7	9	0	7	2
3	2350	9	4	10	9	2	6	1453	6	3	0	3	0
3	5478	11	12	4	11	17	6	2322	1	6	2	11	7
3	4671	12	8	6	5	7	6	2377	8	2	11	8	3
3	4782	8	6	4	11	6	6	3491	3	8	2	7	1

when last voted. The party affiliation is expressed as one of the following:

"R" for Republican

"D" for Democrat

"O" for party other than Republican or Democrat

"I" for independent

The data for the master voter table is given in Table 15-7.

The requirements of the program are that it be menu-driven and provide the following options:

1. List a particular voter's current status.
2. Permit a change in an individual voter's record.
3. Delete an individual voter from the list.
4. Add a new voter to the master list.
5. Purge the list of all voters who have not voted since a specified year.

TABLE 15-7

Data for Master Voter Table

Name of Voter	Street Address	Telephone Number	Party Affil.	Last Voted
Burke, Gayle	556 Airey Dr	526-9444	O	1982
Burke, Larry N.	556 Airey Dr	526-9444	I	1977
Carroll, Ed R.	772 5th Av	388-0029	R	1985
Cohn, R. T.	112 Nancy Lane	388-2992	R	1984
Cohn, R. T.	231 Nancy Lane	388-9291	R	1985
Cohn, Ruth	231 Nancy Lane	388-9291	R	1985
Hanson, Lisa	290 8th Av	526-0117	I	1982
Hanson, Lisa	N Pine Ridge	272-8821	D	1984
Hanson, Paul H.	N Pine Ridge	272-8821	D	1984
Jones, T. L.	411 8th Av	526-5574	R	1977
Jones, Tom	516 Houser St	526-0702	R	1982
Jones, Tom	767 Battle Lane	446-2955	I	1984
Jones, Sara J.	767 Battle Lane	446-2955	I	1984
King, Lloyd S.	82 Nancy Lane	446-9228	R	1984
Lindsey, L. A.	51 Front St	526-0221	D	1981
Murphy, Allan D.	45 Front St	526-8990	R	1984
Murphy, Linda K.	45 Front St	526-8990	D	1982
Owens, Janice	414 Gill St	446-7222	D	1984
Owens, R. Harry	414 Gill St	446-7222	D	1980
Peters, Ellen	Lakeview Hwy	272-6606	D	1982
Reed, W. Neil	217 Perry Av	446-7336	D	1977
Rivers, R. R.	929 17th St	446-0339	R	1980
Rivers, Terisa	1127 Yancy St	388-1992	R	1976
Rivers, T. Y.	1127 Yancy St	388-1992	D	1981
Smith, Ellen	627 Moffet Dr	526-9337	I	1984
Smith, John R.	421 Lowery Dr	388-3544	D	1984
Smith, John W.	828 Battle Lane	446-2232	R	1982
Smith, John W.	617 Lowery Dr	388-1922	R	1980
Smith, John W.	672 Moffet Dr	526-9337	I	1984
Smith, W. H.	461 Alto Way	388-4923	O	1978
Thomas, John T.	212 King St	526-2883	D	1984
Tyler, Mary C.	771 Airey Dr	526-0021	D	1984
Wade, Wendy K.	416 Perry Ave	446-5502	I	1976
Wise, P. T.	411 Eagle Dr	446-4439	O	1984
Wise, Peter D.	411 Eagle Dr	446-7882	D	1977
Zachry, Gwen M.	Lakeview Hwy	272-3374	R	1984

6. List all voters with a given party affiliation.
7. Select *at random* and print a specified number of records from the master voter list for possible jury duty.
8. List all voters in the table.
9. Terminate the program.

Let us look at each of these options separately.

Option 1. This provides the ability to list a particular voter's current record for review. Care must be taken, however, to list the *correct* voter's record. There may be more than one person with the same name. There are several possible approaches to this. All records with the indicated name might be listed. Another and better method (see below) would be to request a second value (such as street address) against which to check the records whenever more than one is found. You decide the best way to handle this problem.

Option 2. It is likely that a voter will have a new name, street address, telephone number, or party affiliation. This option should allow for a change in any (or all) of these values. Once again, you must be certain that you have the correct record before any changes are made. (A submenu might be a good approach to this section.)

Option 3. This option will permit a single name to be removed from the voter list. Again, be sure that you are removing the correct name from the list. This can be done in a number of ways. If you leave an unused record (a ''hole'') in the middle of the list, be sure to mark it in some way. It can be used for option 4.

Option 4. Whenever new people register to vote, they must be added to the list. This option provides for this. Such records can be added to the end of the list or placed in unused spaces vacated by options 3 or 5. Of course, a check should be made to ensure that the new voter is not already on the list.

Option 5. In most areas, a person's name is removed from the list of eligible voters if a vote has not been cast within a certain period of time. This selection will permit the master voter table to be purged of all inactive voters.

Option 6. It might be necessary, such as for primaries, to have a list of voters who belong to a certain party. This option will allow such a list to be generated.

Option 7. Most counties select potential jurors from the list of registered voters. This option will provide for a *random* selection of a specified number of persons from the master voter list. The records selected will be printed.

Option 8. This will print the *entire* master voter table.

Option 9. This is self-explanatory.

The program should obviously permit interactive input of the required options and the data to be processed. A suggested list of options and accompanying data (as required) are given in Table 15-8. (Note: This problem can be accomplished using arrays; however, if you have studied Chapter 14, you may wish to use a random file.)

15-4 SOMETHINGORTHEOTHER, INC.

The production manager of Somethingortheother, Inc., has requested a program to produce an analysis of the production of somethingortheothers over a 1-week period. The company works on a three-shift, 24-hour production schedule with three assembly lines

TABLE 15-8

Jobs to Be Processed

Option Number	Data Required for Processing (if any)		
1	Reed, W. Neil	217 Perry Av	
4	Miller, Karen A.	212 Ellis Av	446-9277 R
2	Jones, Tom	516 Houser St	Change R to I
1	Jones, Tom	516 Houser St	
3	Smith, John W.	617 Lowery Dr	
5	All who did not vote in 1980 or since.		
4	Thomas, Betsy K.	45 Corbot Dr	388-2667 I
2	Smith, John W.	828 Battle Lane	
	New values:	N Pine Ridge	272-2256
2	Hanson, Lisa	290 8th Av	
	New values:	Carroll, Lisa	
		772 5th Av	388-0029
1	Hanson, Lisa	772 5th Av	
3	Rivers, Terisa	1127 Yancy St	
6	Independents		
7	6 names, addresses, and telephone numbers.		
8			
9			

running for the first two shifts but only two are in operation during the third shift, the third line being closed for routine maintenance. The first shift operates from 7:00 a.m. to 3:00 p.m., the second from 3:00 p.m. to 11:00 p.m., and the third from 11:00 p.m. to 7:00 a.m. Production data as total somethingortheothers produced by all lines in operation is available for 2-hour intervals. Data for one 1-week period is given in Table 15-9.

The report must provide the following information regarding the production of somethingortheothers:

1. The production per line for each period and day
2. The total production per line for the full week for each time period
3. The total production for each day
4. The time periods in which the highest and lowest total weekly productions per line occurred and the total productions per line during these periods
5. The days of the week on which the highest and lowest total productions occurred and the production values

TABLE 15-9

Somethingortheother Production Data

Time Period	Number Produced on				
	Monday	Tuesday	Wednesday	Thursday	Friday
7– 9 a.m.	45	49	52	51	48
9–11 a.m.	47	49	51	52	50
11– 1 p.m.	45	51	53	51	52
1– 3 p.m.	42	48	52	50	49
3– 5 p.m.	46	52	51	49	46
5– 7 p.m.	48	53	52	47	44
7– 9 p.m.	49	54	51	50	45
9–11 p.m.	45	52	48	46	43
11– 1 a.m.	29	33	34	32	29
1– 3 a.m.	30	35	33	32	27
3– 5 a.m.	31	34	35	31	28
5– 7 a.m.	30	34	32	32	28

6. The time periods and days at which the highest and lowest productions per line occurred and the productions per line
7. For each individual shift, the days of the week on which the highest and lowest total productions per line occurred and the total productions per line on these days

15-5 WHATCHAMACALLITS, INC.

Whatchamacallits, Inc., carries a very exclusive line of whatchamacallits that come in four styles, five colors, and three sizes. The unit prices and quantities in stock for each whatchamacallit are given in Tables 15-10 and 15-11, respectively.

Whatchamacallits, Inc., needs a program that will process its orders at the end of each day providing both a detailed report of the daily sales by customer and a daily sales summary. Input consists of order records that contain the customer's account number; code numbers for style, color, and size; and the quantity ordered. Sales data for one day's sales is given in Table 15-12. It is not in any specific sequence and must be sorted to be in order by the customer's account number.

Each *detailed* line of the detailed report should give the customer's account number

TABLE 15-10

Unit Price Table for Whatchamacallits

Style Number	Size Number	Color Number 1	2	3	4	5
1	1	23.56	24.67	25.78	31.67	32.87
	2	37.65	38.06	39.28	50.33	55.43
	3	43.24	45.64	48.66	70.76	80.43
2	1	33.58	36.05	39.00	46.49	54.76
	2	48.65	51.46	52.99	63.79	71.46
	3	61.88	64.91	69.16	78.05	84.40
3	1	41.61	42.45	44.12	53.46	58.44
	2	49.34	51.68	55.01	70.55	85.10
	3	64.33	71.62	75.12	86.21	95.07
4	1	49.61	53.80	60.83	76.88	83.94
	2	67.73	70.56	76.80	85.94	94.66
	3	86.12	94.38	106.54	112.56	125.81

TABLE 15-11

Quantity Price Table for Whatchamacallits

Style Number	Size Number	Color Number 1	2	3	4	5
1	1	122	116	95	56	115
	2	46	81	110	31	40
	3	31	12	73	102	69
2	1	130	109	81	46	68
	2	38	46	81	75	47
	3	99	73	61	84	61
3	1	41	126	84	67	115
	2	94	56	110	49	63
	3	91	19	35	42	26
4	1	38	105	84	61	35
	2	84	23	76	38	95
	3	24	61	50	73	27

TABLE 15-12

Purchase Data by Individual Whatchamacallits Ordered

Account Number	Style	Color	Size	Unit Cost	Account Number	Style	Color	Size	Unit Cost
112738	3	2	2	20	190105	3	2	3	14
329882	1	5	3	15	112738	3	2	3	10
367448	1	5	3	5	137782	3	5	2	9
112738	1	3	2	12	190105	4	1	3	25
190105	4	2	3	5	228394	3	5	2	8
177781	3	5	2	6	190105	2	1	3	28
112738	4	3	3	13	137782	4	4	3	22
137782	2	4	1	24	190105	4	2	2	12
329882	4	2	3	3	228394	5	3	2	20
137782	1	1	3	5	329882	3	2	1	14
137782	1	2	3	15	137782	3	1	3	12
228394	3	4	3	16	228394	1	1	1	25
137782	3	2	1	10	278296	2	1	3	15
112738	2	5	2	15	329882	2	4	2	7
137782	1	5	2	6	112738	4	5	2	12
190105	1	4	2	7	137782	1	4	2	2
137782	1	1	1	10	112738	2	1	2	5
177781	2	3	2	15	329882	3	4	3	22
367448	1	3	4	20	137782	1	2	1	10
177781	4	4	3	10	137782	3	3	3	10
190105	2	5	3	12	329882	2	3	3	5
190105	1	1	3	17	367448	2	2	1	8
329882	4	1	3	20	367448	3	2	2	11
190105	1	5	1	30	177781	4	2	2	16
137782	2	3	4	18	367448	4	4	1	15

and name (both group indicated), quantity ordered, unit cost, and total cost. The data should be properly edited for the three codes. In the event of an improper style, color, or size code, a message indicating which code was invalid should be printed following the customer's name. To prepare the detailed sales report, each order must be processed against the inventory as follows:

1. The quantity ordered of a given whatchamacallit must be checked against the quantity in stock to see that a sufficient supply of the specific whatchamacallit is in stock to make shipment.
2. The quantity in stock must be updated as each order is processed.
3. If a specific whatchamacallit is out of stock (quantity = 0), then the message OUT OF STOCK should appear at the end of the line.
4. If there is an insufficient number of a particular whatchamacallit in stock to fill an order, the number in stock is to be shipped with the message INCOMPLETE at the end of the line.
5. The total cost for each whatchamacallit ordered is to be calculated as the unit cost times the number *actually shipped*. This means that if an item is out of stock, there is no charge to the account at this time. For incomplete shipments, charges are made only for those items that are in stock for immediate shipment.
6. Whenever there is a change in customer account number, the total cost of each order is to be calculated as the sum of the total costs for all whatchamacallits charged to that account number. The total charges should be checked against the account credit status given in Table 15-13. The credit status codes have the meanings given in Table 15-14. Depending on the code, the appropriate message should be printed on the minor total line except that for a code of R, a message will be printed only when the credit line of $1000 is exceeded.

TABLE 15-13

Customer Name and Credit Status Listed by Account Number

Account Number	Customer Name	Credit Status	Account Number	Customer Name	Credit Status
112738	Gibson's 5/10	U	254883	Elson's	U
137782	ShopMart #1	U	278296	Gina's Gifts	N
145883	E-Z Buy #3	U	287902	ShopMart #5	U
177781	Ellerbee's	R	301111	Larry's Lot	N
182992	Eastside Hdwr	N	308992	Lewis & Sons	U
190105	E-Z Buy #6	U	312788	T. C. Minns	U
209110	Telman's	W	329882	E-Z Buy #2	U
216744	Smith Gen St	R	347882	Hamm's Hdwr	R
228394	Yancy's Toys	R	367448	Teri's Things	W
237992	Coleman 5/10	R	375933	Farkhar's	U

TABLE 15-14

Meaning of Credit Status Codes

Code	Meaning	Action	Message
U	Unlimited	No action needed	None needed
R	Restricted	No credit over $1000	OVER CREDIT LINE
W	Withdrawn	Credit unavailable	PREPAYMENT ONLY
N	Not rated	Request references	REQUEST REFERENCES

The daily total report is to be processed as follows. Totals for the number *ordered* for each style, color, and size combination are to be printed as well as the totals for the number of each style in all colors and sizes, each color in all sizes and styles, and each size in all colors and styles. The total income from *all* whatchamacallits *shipped* in any style, color, and size should also be printed.

15-6 FACULTY RATINGS AT PROXIMA COLLEGE

The students at Proxima College are required to evaluate their instructors at the end of each quarter. The evaluation forms ask the students to rate the instructors from 1 to 5, where 1 is poor and 5 is outstanding, in each of the following four categories:

A. Faculty accessibility
B. Quality of instruction
C. Fairness of exams
D. Overall challenge

The dean of the college has requested a program that will produce a summary of the quarterly ratings. Two reports are required: a detailed report that provides a summary of ratings by category and score by class, and a general overall summary by instructor.

All evaluation forms contain an instructor number, class number, and four numbers corresponding to the four rating categories described above. The forms are turned in at random so the data is not in any specific order and must be sorted by instructor number and by class number for each instructor. For each class, the total number of each rating should be accumulated as well as an average rating for each category. The average is calculated as the sum of the number of each rating times the rating divided by the total number of ratings for that category. Suppose that 20 students are in one class, and, for faculty accessibility, the ratings total zero 1's, three 2's, nine 3's, six 4's, and two 5's.

The average rating would be calculated as:

$$\frac{0 \times 1 + 3 \times 2 + 9 \times 3 + 6 \times 4 + 2 \times 5}{20} = 3.35$$

This should be repeated for each of the four categories for that class. Finally, a total rating score for a class is found as the sum of the average scores for the four categories.

The detailed report should print the above summary of the rating data by instructor and class with the instructor name group indicated. For each class, a set of detailed lines with a format something like the following should be printed:

Inst. Name (group ind.)	Class Listing	List Category of Rating	List Total Number of Ratings in Category	Give All Average Scores

List Total Rating Score Last

Here is a sample of how a typical set of lines might appear.

```
R E LANGLEY    HIS 102    FAC ACCESS      0  3  9  6  2     3.35
                          QUAL OF INSTR   1  4  7  5  3     3.25
                          FAIR OF EXAMS   0  4  7  6  3     3.4
                          OVRLL CHALL     2  4  6  4  4     3.2
                          TOTAL RATING                     13.2
```

Note that R E LANGLEY will be printed only if this is the first class listed for that instructor. Instructor names and class listings are given in Tables 15-15 and 15-16.

All input data (see Table 15-17) should be carefully edited for invalid ratings. Any record that contains a rating other than 1, 2, 3, 4, or 5 in *any* of the four categories should be discarded entirely from the survey, with none of the other ratings on that record processed, even if correct.

TABLE 15-15

Instructor Numbers and Names

Number	Name
116	K. A. Peoples
303	Y. L. Utley
319	W. W. Nash
471	H. A. Williams
588	R. E. Ashford
615	F. C. Luckus
737	D. S. Craine

TABLE 15-16

Class Numbers and Listings

Number	Listing	Number	Listing	Number	Listing
1230	Mat 101	4154	His 251	8655	Edu 451
1817	Eng 212	4411	Bio 221	8866	Eng 491
2002	Bio 101	4882	Psy 201	8933	Bio 451
2265	His 101	6476	Edu 345	9125	Che 497
3257	Eng 101	7115	Che 301	9611	Soc 201
3888	Che 101	7647	His 201	9947	Edu 491

TABLE 15-17

Instructor Rating Survey Data

Inst. Num.	Class Num.	Rat. For Cat. A	B	C	D	Inst. Num.	Class Num.	Rat. For Cat. A	B	C	D	Inst. Num.	Class Num.	Rat. For Cat. A	B	C	D
471	3257	4	4	3	2	615	2002	1	1	2	3	615	2002	4	3	4	5
116	1230	1	2	2	1	737	8655	3	3	2	2	737	6476	4	4	3	4
303	3888	2	1	1	2	615	8933	5	4	4	5	588	7647	3	2	4	3
471	3257	2	1	3	2	588	2265	4	4	3	4	588	2265	2	3	2	4
615	2002	2	1	1	2	471	3257	3	1	2	3	615	4411	4	4	3	3
615	2002	2	2	1	2	471	3257	3	2	1	4	588	7647	1	2	1	1
303	3888	3	2	2	1	303	3888	3	4	4	3	615	2002	1	1	2	3
588	4154	2	1	1	2	303	3888	1	1	2	0	471	3257	1	1	2	3
319	4882	5	5	5	4	737	6476	4	4	4	3	588	4154	5	4	4	3
319	9611	4	4	5	4	471	3257	2	4	3	2	116	1230	4	3	2	1
303	7115	5	5	4	5	319	9611	4	4	4	5	615	2002	4	5	5	3
116	1230	4	5	4	4	615	4411	4	5	5	4	615	2002	1	2	1	1
471	3257	3	2	1	3	116	1230	4	3	3	4	116	1230	4	4	3	4
588	7647	3	3	3	4	116	1230	5	4	3	4	116	1230	3	4	3	3
116	1230	1	3	2	2	588	4154	4	5	4	5	588	2265	4	3	3	4
303	3888	4	3	3	5	615	2002	3	3	4	3	615	2002	3	4	4	2
615	2002	2	3	2	3	615	4411	4	3	3	3	588	2265	1	2	3	2
615	2002	1	2	1	1	615	4411	3	2	1	4	319	4882	5	4	3	4
471	3257	1	1	2	1	588	2265	3	4	4	2	319	4882	5	4	4	4
737	9947	3	2	2	3	303	7115	4	5	4	4	471	3257	2	1	3	1
588	2265	2	1	1	2	471	1817	3	4	5	4	588	2265	2	1	1	2
737	6476	4	5	4	5	116	1230	4	4	4	5	303	9125	5	5	5	5
615	2002	2	2	3	2	615	8933	5	4	4	4	588	2265	3	2	2	3
588	2265	4	3	2	2	588	2265	3	4	3	3	471	1817	4	4	2	3
615	8933	4	4	4	3	303	3888	4	5	3	4	615	2002	4	3	4	4
588	2265	4	3	4	4	116	1230	5	4	4	4	319	9611	4	5	5	4
588	4154	3	3	4	5	471	3257	1	2	2	1	471	1817	4	2	4	4
588	7647	3	4	4	5	471	1817	3	4	4	4	588	2265	5	4	5	5
588	2265	4	3	3	4	615	2002	2	1	1	2	471	1817	4	3	4	5
319	4882	5	5	5	5	471	3257	2	1	3	4	471	1817	3	2	1	2
615	2002	3	4	4	3	303	3888	2	4	4	3	319	9611	3	4	4	4
303	7115	5	5	4	5	588	2265	3	2	3	2	116	1230	2	3	4	2
116	1230	5	4	4	5	471	8866	3	2	2	3	588	4154	4	3	3	4
588	4154	2	3	3	1	319	9611	5	4	4	4	116	1230	5	5	3	4
319	9611	4	3	3	4	737	8655	5	4	4	5	588	7647	2	3	3	2
615	2002	2	3	2	4	588	7647	4	4	3	4	471	3257	3	2	3	3
303	3888	2	1	3	1	471	1817	3	3	4	3	471	3257	2	3	1	3
116	1230	1	2	1	1	303	3888	3	4	4	3	471	1817	4	2	3	4
319	4882	5	4	4	5	319	4882	5	5	3	4	615	4411	3	2	3	1
588	7647	2	4	4	3	116	1230	4	4	3	4	116	1230	4	2	8	4
471	3257	1	1	2	1	737	6476	5	4	4	5	303	3888	3	3	3	4
116	1230	4	3	4	5	303	7115	4	4	5	5	471	3257	1	2	1	1
737	6476	4	4	3	4	615	2002	3	2	3	3	471	3257	2	1	1	3
116	1230	1	1	1	1	615	2002	1	3	2	2	588	2265	4	5	4	5
319	4882	5	4	5	4	303	3888	4	3	3	1	471	2357	3	3	2	1
303	3888	5	4	4	5	471	8866	1	2	3	3	588	2265	4	3	3	4
588	2265	4	5	5	4	615	4411	4	4	4	2	303	7115	5	4	4	5

After all classes have been processed, a second report is required. This one is to list each instructor by name along with a final rating score, which is calculated as the average of the total rating scores for all classes taught. The instructors should be listed *in order* from the one with the highest score to the one with the lowest.

APPENDIX A
SUMMARY OF BASIC STATEMENTS

The following is a list of the most frequently encountered BASIC statements. These are given in the form that is common to the widest variety of BASICs. Whenever applicable, alternative forms of a statement have been provided. The following general terms are used:

var = any variable

num = a numeric variable

mat = a matrix variable

str = indicates a string value

exp = any mathematical expression

lit = any literal of the appropriate type

val = any data value

ln = any BASIC statement line number

sub = a subscript

ch = a file channel number

filespec = a file specification

Only a brief description of each statement is given here. Refer to the appropriate section of the text for a detailed description of the function and uses of each.

CHAIN

ln1 CHAIN "filespec", *ln2*, ALL

Enables a second program to be executed from the first. The two options following the file specification permit execution to begin at any line number, *ln2*, in the second program and allow *all* variables to be passed from one program to the other.

CHANGE

ln CHANGE *str* TO *num array*

Stores the ASCII codes for each character of *str* in the corresponding elements of a numeric array.

ln CHANGE *num array* TO *str*
Builds *str* from the ASCII codes stored in a numeric array.

CLOSE

ln CLOSE *ch1, ch2, ch3, . . .*
Closes the files with the specified channel numbers, *ch1, ch2, ch3,* etc. If no channel numbers are listed, then *all* open files are closed.

DATA

ln DATA *val1, val2, val3, . . .*
Lists the input data values to be read by variables in READ statements.

DEF FN

ln DEF FN*x(var1, var2, var3, . . .) = exp*
Used to define special, user-defined function FN*x*.

DIM

ln DIM *var1(sub1), var2(sub2), var3(sub3), . . .*
Specifies dimensions of *sub1, sub2, sub3,* . . . for arrays *var1, var2, var3,* . . . .

END

ln END
Provides a logical end to the program.

FIELD

ln FIELD *#ch, num1* AS *str1, num2* AS *str2, . . .*
This statement is required on many systems to describe the format of the fields in the records of random files. For a record in a file with the indicated channel number, each field is assigned a string variable, *str,* which will require *num* characters.

FOR/NEXT

ln1 FOR *num = exp1* TO *exp2* STEP *exp3*
:
ln2 NEXT *num*
Creates a loop in which the numeric variable, *num,* goes from the initial value of *exp1* to the final value, *exp2,* in increments of *exp3*. The STEP is optional and, if omitted, is assumed to be 1.

GET

ln GET *#ch, exp*
Fetches record number *exp* from a random file with channel number *ch*.

GOSUB

ln1 GOSUB *ln2*
Directs the program to a subroutine at *ln2*. *See* RETURN.

GOTO

ln1 GOTO *ln2*
Causes an unconditional branch to *ln2*.

IF–GOTO

ln1 IF *condition* GOTO *ln2*
Causes a conditional branch to *ln2* when the *condition* has a truth value of true.

IF–THEN

ln1 IF *condition* THEN *ln2*
Same as IF–GOTO

ln IF *condition* THEN *statement*
The *statement* is executed when the *condition* has a truth value of true.

INPUT

ln INPUT *var1, var2, var3, . . .*
Used for the interactive input of values for *var1, var2, var3,* etc., directly from the screen.

ln INPUT *"str lit"; var1, var2, var3, . . .*
Same as above INPUT except that the *str lit* provides a message prompt.

INPUT #

ln INPUT *#ch, var1, var2, var3, . . .*
Used to read one record of a sequential file with the specified channel number. (Although it is called *INPUT,* the action of this statement is more nearly like that of the READ statement than the INPUT.)

LINE INPUT

ln LINE INPUT *str var*
Used for the interactive input of a single string *str var* directly from the screen. No automatic prompt is supplied, but the string may contain any characters, including commas, quotation marks, and colons. Also found as LINPUT and INPUT LINE.

ln LINE INPUT *''str lit''; str var*
Same as above LINE INPUT except that the *str lit* provides a screen prompt.

LINE INPUT #

ln LINE INPUT *#ch, str var*
Similar to the first form of the above LINE INPUT statement except that the string is read from one record of the designated disk file.

LET

ln LET *var = lit*
Assigns a literal to a variable.

ln LET *var1 = var2*
Assigns the value of *var2* to *var1*.

ln LET *var = exp*
Evaluates a mathematical expression and assigns the result to the variable *var*.

LSET/RSET

ln L/RSET *str1 = str2*
Used to place string values into the record buffer for random files. LSET causes values to be *left*-justified, and RSET *right*-justifies them.

MAT

ln MAT *mat1 = mat2*
Assigns the value of *mat2* to *mat1*.

ln MAT *mat = mat exp*
Evaluates a matrix expression and assigns the result to the variable, *mat*.

MAT INPUT

ln MAT INPUT *mat1, mat2, mat3, . . .*
Used for the interactive input of matrix variables, *mat1, mat2, mat3,* etc., directly from the screen.

MAT PRINT

ln MAT PRINT *mat1, mat2, mat3, . . .*
Prints matrices *mat1, mat2, mat3,* etc.

MAT PRINT USING

ln1 MAT PRINT USING *format/ln2, mat1, mat2, mat3, . . .*
Prints the matrices, *mat1, mat2, mat3,* etc., using the specified format. (*See* PRINT USING)

MAT READ

ln MAT READ *mat1, mat2, mat3, . . .*
Used to assign values from those listed in DATA statements to matrix variables, *mat1, mat2, mat3,* etc., for processing.

ON ERROR GOTO

ln1 ON ERROR GOTO *ln2*
Used to direct the program to an error trapping routine at *ln2* whenever any error condition is detected. If ln2 = 0, then processing is terminated.

ON–GOTO

ln ON *exp* GOTO *ln1, ln2, ln3, . . .*

Causes a branch to *ln1, ln2, ln3,* etc., for truncated values of *exp* equal to 1, 2, 3, etc. Also found as ON–THEN and GOTO–ON.

ON–GOSUB

ln ON *exp* GOSUB *ln1, ln2, ln3, . . .*

Same as ON–GOTO except the branch is to a subroutine at the respective line numbers. Also found as GOSUB–ON.

OPEN

ln OPEN ''I/O'', *#ch,* ''filespec''

This form of the OPEN statement is for sequential files. It specifies whether the file is for input (''I'') or output (''O''), the channel number, and the file specification.

ln OPEN ''R'', *#ch,* ''filespec'', *record length*

This form for random files is similar to the above except that it is denoted as random (''R'') and a record length is specified.

OPTION BASE

ln OPTION BASE *0/1*

Used to set the lower bound of the subscript of an array at either 0 or 1.

POKE

ln POKE *(exp1, exp2)*

Places the character with the ASCII code specified by *exp2* into memory address given by *exp1*. Most frequently found on microcomputer BASICs.

PRINT

ln PRINT *var1/lit1, var2/lit2, var3/lit3, . . .*

Prints a list of values assigned to variables and/or literals to the screen.

PRINT #

ln PRINT *#ch, var1/lit1, var2/lit2, var3/lit3, . . .*

Same as PRINT except that the output is directed to the file opened with the indicated channel number.

PRINT USING

ln PRINT USING *format, var1, var2, var3, . . .*

Prints the values of *var1, var2, var3,* etc., using the format description at the beginning of the variable list.

ln1 PRINT USING *ln2, var1, var2, var3, . . .*

:

ln2: format description

Same as the above PRINT USING except that the format description is given at line number *ln2*.

PRINT # USING

ln1 PRINT *#ch* USING *format/ln2, var1, var2, var3, . .*

Same as PRINT USING except that the output is directed to the file opened with the indicated channel number.

PUT

ln PUT *#ch, exp*

Stores record number *exp* to a random file with channel number *ch*.

RANDOMIZE

ln RANDOMIZE

Used on some systems in conjunction with the RND function to ensure a different random sequence.

READ

ln READ *var1, var2, var3, . . .*

Used to assign values from those listed in DATA statements to variables *var1, var2, var3,* etc., for processing.

REM

ln REM *comment*

Used to insert *comments* into the program listing. Some systems permit the use of special symbols such as the exclamation point (!) or apostrophe (') in place of REM.

RESET

ln RESET

Causes values read from the READ statements to be read from the beginning of the data list.

RESTORE

ln RESTORE

Same as RESET.

RESTORE #

ln RESTORE *#ch*

Resets pointer for the file with the indicated channel number to the beginning of the file.

RESUME

ln RESUME

Causes processing to resume at the line at which it was interrupted following an error trapping procedure.

ln1 RESUME *ln2*

Same as the above form except that processing is directed to the line number *ln2*. If ln2 = 0, then the effect is the same as the first form.

ln RESUME NEXT

Resumes processing at the next line following that at which the interruption occurred.

RETURN

ln RETURN

Signals the end of a subroutine and returns processing to the line following the GOSUB that called the subroutine. *See* GOSUB.

STOP

ln STOP

Causes a break in processing.

SWAP

ln SWAP *var1, var2*

Exchanges the values of *var1* and *var2*.

APPENDIX **B**

BASIC LIBRARY FUNCTIONS

Below is a list of the most frequently encountered BASIC library functions. For the functions listed, the following general terms are used:

num = any numeric variable or constant

exp = any mathematical expression

str = any string expression.

mat = any matrix expression

While the form of the functions may vary with the version of BASIC that is in use, the general meaning should not. In many cases, alternative forms of the same (or similar) functions are provided for reference with different systems. Not all of the functions listed below have been discussed in this text, and your BASIC will not include all of them either. You may, on the other hand, have additional ones not given. Consult your instructor for a list of the specific functions available on your system.

MATHEMATICAL FUNCTIONS

ABS(exp)	Takes the absolute value of *exp*.
ACOS(exp)	Returns in radians the arccosine for $-1 \leq exp \leq 1$.
ASIN(exp)	Returns in radians the arcsine for $-1 \leq exp \leq 1$.
ATN(exp)	Returns in radians the arctangent of *exp*.
COS(exp)	Returns the cosine for *exp* in radians.
COSH(exp)	Returns the hyperbolic cosine of *exp*.
DEG(num)	Converts *num* from radians to degrees.
EXP(exp)	Raises the natural base *e* to the *exp* power.
FIX(exp)	Same as INT for $exp \geq 0$. For $exp < 0$, INT returns the next lower integer, while FIX returns the next larger integer.
FP(exp)	Returns the *fractional* part of *exp*. Gives the same result as exp − INT(exp) for $exp \geq 0$.

INT(exp)	Returns the truncated value of *exp*.
LGT(exp)	Returns the logarithm base *10* for $exp > 0$.
LOG(exp)	Gives the natural (base *e*) logarithm for $exp > 0$.
LOG2(exp)	Returns the logarithm base *2* for $exp > 0$.
LOG10(exp)	Same as LGT.
MAX(exp1, exp2)	Returns the maximum of the two values *exp1* and *exp2*.
MIN(exp1, exp2)	Returns the minimum of the two values *exp1* and *exp2*.
MOD(num1, num2)	Returns the integer remainder of the division of *num1* by *num2*. (MOD is implemented with some BASICs as an arithmetic operator.)
PI	Gives the value of $\pi = 3.141592654 \ldots$. The number of digits returned will depend on the system.
RAD(num)	Converts *num* from degrees to radians.
RND/RND(exp)	Generates a random number between 0 and 1. The exact response of RND to the values of *exp* will depend on the version of BASIC that is in use. Many versions do not require an argument for RND.
SGN(exp)	Returns the sign of *exp* according to the following: Returns 1 when $exp > 0$ Returns 0 when $exp = 0$ Returns −1 when $exp < 0$
SIN(exp)	Returns the sine for *exp* in radians.
SINH(exp)	Returns the hyperbolic sine of *exp*.
SQR(exp)	Returns the square root for $exp \geq 0$.
TAN(exp)	Returns the tangent for *exp* in radians.
TANH(exp)	Returns the hyperbolic tangent of *exp*.

MATRIX FUNCTIONS

CON	Stores the constant one (1) in each element of a matrix.
DET	Returns the determinant of the matrix last operated on by INV.
IDN	Sets a matrix equal to the identity matrix in which the elements along the diagonal are all equal to one, while all other elements are zero.
INV(mat)	Returns the inverse of *mat*.
NUM	Used to record the number of elements input into a matrix. (A few systems use NUM in place of the VAL function.)
TRN(mat)	Returns the transpose of *mat* in which the rows and columns have been reversed.
ZER	Causes all elements of a matrix to be set equal to zero.

STRING FUNCTIONS

ASC(str)	Gives the ASCII code for the first character in *str*.
CHR$(exp)	Returns a single ASCII character corresponding to the value of *exp*.
CPY$(str, exp1, exp2)	Returns *exp2* characters beginning at the *exp1* position from the left of *str*.
INDEX(str1, str2)	Determines whether or not *str1* contains *str2* and, if so, at what position in *str1*. Sometimes written in the shorter form IDX.
INSTR(exp, str1, str2)	Similar to INDEX except the search of *str1* begins at the position specified by *exp*.
LCASE(str)	Converts all upper case characters in *str* to lower case. Also found as LCS.
LEFT$(str, exp)	Returns the first *exp* characters of *str* beginning from the left. Also found as LEFT.
LEN(str)	Returns the length (in characters) of *str*.
MID$(str, exp1, exp2)	Same as CPY$. Also found as MID.
ORD(str)	Same as ASC.
POS(str1, str2, exp)	Same as INSTR.
RIGHT$(str, exp)	Returns the first *exp* characters of *str* beginning from the right. Also found as RIGHT.
SEG$(exp1, exp2)	Similar to MID$ except that *exp2* gives the *end* of the string that is returned rather than its length.
SER(str1, str2)	Same as INDEX.
STR$(exp)	Converts a numeric expression to a string expression.
SPACE$(exp)	Causes the insertion of *exp* spaces.
STRING$(exp, "str")	PRINTS the single character, *str*, *exp* times. The string character can be represented by its ASCII code *not in quotes*.
UCASE(str)	Converts all lower case characters in *str* to upper case. Also found as UCS.
VAL(str)	Converts a string expression to a numeric one provided *str* contains only numeric characters.

FILE-HANDLING FUNCTIONS

CVI/S/D(str)	Converts a string value from the record buffer to numeric. The three forms, CVI, CVS, and CVD return integer, single-precision, and double-precision values, respectively.
EOF(num)	Detects the end of file with channel number *num*.
ERR/ERL	Two special *variables* which, when used in conjunction with an error-trapping procedure, are automatically assigned the values of the error code (ERR) and the line number (ERL) at which the error occurred.

LOC(num) Returns the current record number of file number *num*.

LOF(num) Returns the number of records in file number *num*.

MKI/S/D$(num) Converts a numeric value to string for placement in the record buffer. The three forms, MKI$, MKS$, and MKD$ convert integer, single-precision, and double-precision values, respectively.

INPUT/OUTPUT FUNCTIONS

INKEY$ Permits the entry of a character from the terminal *during program execution* without having to press the RETURN key.

INPUT$(num) Permits the entry of *num* characters from the terminal without having to press the RETURN key.

PEEK(exp) Gives the ASCII code for the character located at the memory address given by *exp*. Most frequently found on microcomputer BASICs.

SPC(exp) Similar to SPACE$ except this function may only be used in a PRINT statement.

TAB(exp) Positions a variable or literal at the column in a print line given by *exp*. May only be used in a PRINT statement.

CLOCK FUNCTIONS

CLK Gives the current time of day as a string value in hours, minutes, and seconds in a 24-hour format something like hh:mm:ss.

DATE$ Gives the current date as a string value as month, day, and year in a format something like mm-dd-yyyy. Some systems use DATE.

TIME Similar to CLK except that the current (or elapsed) time is given in seconds as a real number. Also found as TIM.

TIME$ Same as CLK.

APPENDIX C

COMMON INTERACTIVE SYSTEM COMMANDS

When you sit down before a terminal to write a BASIC program, you must first log-on to the system. This procedure is different for all computers, but it is usually fairly simple. On a small microcomputer, you may have to do no more than turn the computer on and BASIC will be brought up automatically. On larger multiuser systems, it may be necessary to enter a user name and/or password and then call up BASIC. It is not possible to give any types of details of what you will have to do for this procedure because they vary so widely with computer systems.

Once you have logged onto the system and have BASIC, there are a number of system commands used for working with your BASIC program that are fairly uniform among the various versions of BASIC. The most common of these are listed in this appendix along with a brief explanation of each. However, you should remember that these commands *will* vary with the version of BASIC that is in use. You may not have some of those given below, and you may have others that are not listed. Also, the various options listed for some of the commands will vary with the version of BASIC.

AUTO Used to obtain automatic line numbering.

Options:

- AUTO — Begins numbering at the next or a preset beginning line with a default increment, usually 10.
- AUTO *ln1, ln2* — Begins numbering at *ln1* with increment *ln2*.

BYE Used to leave BASIC.

CLEAR Used to clear the current program workspace and allow another program to be entered.

CONT Used to continue a BASIC program at the point of interruption following a STOP statement or other nonterminal break in processing.

DELETE Used to delete part or all of a program from memory. (Sometimes used to delete programs from the disk.)

Options:

- DELETE — Deletes the entire program.

DELETE *ln*	Deletes only the statement at line number *ln*.
DELETE *ln1–ln2*	Deletes all statements with line numbers from *ln1* through *ln2*. Some systems will use DELETE *ln1, ln2* for this operation.
DELETE *–ln*	Deletes all statements from the beginning of the program through that with line number *ln*.
DELETE *ln–*	Deletes all statements from that with line number *ln* to the end of the program.

ERASE Used to delete a file from the disk.

FILES Used to obtain a listing of disk files available to the user.

KILL Same as ERASE.

LIST Used to list part or all of a program to the screen.

Options:

LIST	Lists the entire program.
LIST *ln*	Lists only the statement at line number *ln*.
LIST *ln1–ln2*	Lists all statements with line numbers from *ln1* through *ln2*. Some systems will use LIST *ln1, ln2* for this operation.
LIST *–1n*	Lists all statements from the beginning of the program through that with line number *ln*.
LIST *ln–*	Lists all statements from that with line number *ln* to the end of the program.

LOAD Used to load a program from a disk file into memory. It will normally be followed by a file reference and possible options that depend on the system that is in use.

NEW Same as CLEAR.

RENAME Used to change the name of a program.

RENUMBER Used to renumber the lines of a program.

Options:

RENUMBER	Renumbers all lines and line references beginning with a certain default line, such as 10 or 100, and using a set increment, usually 10.
RENUMBER *ln1, ln2, ln3*	Renumbers all lines beginning with the old number *ln2* with the new number *ln1* using the increment *ln3*.

RESEQUENCE Same as RENUMBER.

RUN Causes the program to be executed.

SAVE Used to save a program from memory to a disk file. It will normally be followed by a file reference and possible options that depend on the system that is in use.

SCRATCH Same as ERASE.

SYSTEM Same as BYE.

UNSAVE Same as ERASE.

APPENDIX **D**

SUMMARY OF BASIC ERROR MESSAGES

A list of the most commonly encountered BASIC error messages is given below along with a brief explanation of each. The exact wording of the message or how specific it is will vary with the version of BASIC that is in use. Some BASICs will even give error message codes or numbers which have to be referenced in the language manual. In any case, the *general meaning* of the error messages which you encounter should be the same as (or very close to) the ones listed below. The messages have not been separated into categories, such as syntax, runtime, and system, because some error messages may appear as different types depending on the particular version of BASIC or whether an interpreter or compiler is in use.

Dimension too Large — Indicates that an array has been defined for too many elements or for too many dimensions.

Division by Zero — Occurs whenever the denominator in a calculation involving division has a value of zero.

END Not Last — Signals that the END statement is not the last statement in the program on those systems that require it to be.

Field Overflow — Indicates that more characters were allocated in a FIELD statement than were specified as the record length in the corresponding OPEN statement.

File Not Found — Refers to an attempt to load a file that does not exist into the BASIC workspace.

File Not Opened — Signals an attempt to process a file that has not been opened.

FOR without NEXT — Signals an attempt to execute a FOR–NEXT loop without a NEXT statement.

Illegal Constant — Indicates a number that is either out of the allowed bounds or of illegal format.

Illegal Function Call — Occurs whenever the argument of certain functions assumes an invalid value, such as a negative value, in the TAB, SQR, or LOG functions. May appear as Value out of Range error.

Illegal Instruction — Indicates that a statement is not a legal BASIC instruction. Check for typing errors.

Illegal MAT Operation — Refers to any of the many things that can go wrong when executing MAT statements. Most frequently, it will result from a dimension problem where matrices have dimensions that are incompatible with certain arithmetic operations.

Illegal Relation — Indicates an illegal use of one of the relational operators in the condition of an IF–THEN statement.

Illegal Variable — Indicates the use of an illegal variable name.

Input Past End — Signals an attempt to read a sequential file past the end of file. Similar to Out of Data for READ/DATA statements.

Invalid Command — Refers to an attempt to use an invalid system command or an invalid format of a system command.

Invalid File Mode — Signals an attempt to process a file that has been opened as sequential using random file procedures or vice versa. May also refer to syntax errors in file processing statements, especially the OPEN.

Invalid File Number — Refers to an attempt to process a file with a channel number that is unavailable. May also occur if the file has not been opened.

Invalid Line Number — Signals an attempt to use an invalid line number, either of incorrect format or out of range.

Invalid Subscript — In some cases, the same as Subscript out of Range. In others, refers to invalid subscript expressions or numbers of subscripts.

Invalid Input — Signals an attempt to enter invalid data with the interactive INPUT statement.

Missing Argument — Occurs when an expression contains a function with no argument when one or more is required.

Missing Operand — Indicates the presence of an operator without an operand as with two adjacent arithmetic operators.

NEXT without FOR — Signals an attempt to execute a FOR–NEXT loop without a FOR statement. Can also occur with an illegal branch *into* a FOR–NEXT loop.

Out of Data — Refers to an attempt, using a READ statement, to read values that are beyond those present in the data list of the DATA statements.

Out of Memory — Signals that the available program memory has been used. May also result from too many variables, excessively large arrays, or too many nested loops.

Overflow	Signals that a numerical value has exceeded the maximum allowed value, the size of which will depend on the BASIC that is in use.
Redimensioned Array	Two different DIM statements list the same array. May also occur when a DIM statement is used to dimension an array after it is used with the default dimension.
RESUME without Error	A RESUME statement is encountered without having been preceded by an error trapping procedure.
RETURN without GOSUB	Occurs when a RETURN statement is encountered without a corresponding GOSUB statement.
String too Long	Indicates that a string value is longer than the version of BASIC allows.
Subscript out of Range	Indicates that the value for the subscript for a subscripted variable is beyond the maximum range allowed in the DIM statement.
Syntax	Usually refers to a structural mistake such as a misspelled command, missing parentheses or punctuation, or an improperly constructed statement. Some systems use this error message as a catch all category for problems that are not covered by other messages.
Type Mismatch	Refers to an attempt to mismatch a variable type; for example, trying to assign string data to a numeric variable or vice versa.
Undefined Function	Signals an attempt to use a user-defined function before the function has been defined with the DEF statement.
Undefined Image	The image line for a PRINT USING statement has been omitted, the incorrect reference line number given, or the colon (:) that signals the image line omitted.
Undefined Line	Refers to an attempt to branch to or otherwise reference a nonexistent line number.
Underflow	Signals that a numeric value is less than the minimum allowed value, the size of which will depend on the BASIC that is in use. On some systems, this will result in a value of 0 being assigned to the offending variable.
Value out of Range	Signals an attempt to use a value beyond that allowed by certain statements or functions, such as the ON–GOTO statement or TAB function. May appear as Illegal Function Call error.
What? Huh?	Signals an error condition for which BASIC has no preprogrammed error code or message.

APPENDIX E

ASCII CHARACTER CODES

The most frequently used ASCII characters and the corresponding codes in decimal form are given in Table E-1.

TABLE E-1

Most Frequently Used ASCII Characters and Corresponding Codes

<table>
<tr><th>Decimal Code</th><th>ASCII Character</th><th>Decimal Code</th><th>ASCII Character</th><th>Decimal Code</th><th>ASCII Character</th></tr>
<tr><td>0</td><td>Null</td><td>58</td><td>:</td><td>93</td><td>]</td></tr>
<tr><td>7</td><td>Bell</td><td>59</td><td>;</td><td>94</td><td>^</td></tr>
<tr><td>8</td><td>Backspace</td><td>60</td><td>⟨</td><td>95</td><td>_</td></tr>
<tr><td>9</td><td>Horiz. Tab</td><td>61</td><td>=</td><td>96</td><td>`</td></tr>
<tr><td>10</td><td>Line Feed</td><td>62</td><td>⟩</td><td>97</td><td>a</td></tr>
<tr><td>11</td><td>Vert. Tab</td><td>63</td><td>?</td><td>98</td><td>b</td></tr>
<tr><td>12</td><td>Form Feed</td><td>64</td><td>@</td><td>99</td><td>c</td></tr>
<tr><td>13</td><td>Carr. Rtn.</td><td>65</td><td>A</td><td>100</td><td>d</td></tr>
<tr><td>27</td><td>Escape</td><td>66</td><td>B</td><td>101</td><td>e</td></tr>
<tr><td>32</td><td>Blank</td><td>67</td><td>C</td><td>102</td><td>f</td></tr>
<tr><td>33</td><td>!</td><td>68</td><td>D</td><td>103</td><td>g</td></tr>
<tr><td>34</td><td>"</td><td>69</td><td>E</td><td>104</td><td>h</td></tr>
<tr><td>35</td><td>#</td><td>70</td><td>F</td><td>105</td><td>i</td></tr>
<tr><td>36</td><td>$</td><td>71</td><td>G</td><td>106</td><td>j</td></tr>
<tr><td>37</td><td>%</td><td>72</td><td>H</td><td>107</td><td>k</td></tr>
<tr><td>38</td><td>&</td><td>73</td><td>I</td><td>108</td><td>l</td></tr>
<tr><td>39</td><td>'</td><td>74</td><td>J</td><td>109</td><td>m</td></tr>
<tr><td>40</td><td>(</td><td>75</td><td>K</td><td>110</td><td>n</td></tr>
<tr><td>41</td><td>)</td><td>76</td><td>L</td><td>111</td><td>o</td></tr>
<tr><td>42</td><td>*</td><td>77</td><td>M</td><td>112</td><td>p</td></tr>
<tr><td>43</td><td>+</td><td>78</td><td>N</td><td>113</td><td>q</td></tr>
<tr><td>44</td><td>,</td><td>79</td><td>O</td><td>114</td><td>r</td></tr>
<tr><td>45</td><td>-</td><td>80</td><td>p</td><td>115</td><td>s</td></tr>
<tr><td>46</td><td>.</td><td>81</td><td>Q</td><td>116</td><td>t</td></tr>
<tr><td>47</td><td>/</td><td>82</td><td>R</td><td>117</td><td>u</td></tr>
<tr><td>48</td><td>0</td><td>83</td><td>S</td><td>118</td><td>v</td></tr>
<tr><td>49</td><td>1</td><td>84</td><td>T</td><td>119</td><td>w</td></tr>
<tr><td>50</td><td>2</td><td>85</td><td>U</td><td>120</td><td>x</td></tr>
<tr><td>51</td><td>3</td><td>86</td><td>V</td><td>121</td><td>y</td></tr>
<tr><td>52</td><td>4</td><td>87</td><td>W</td><td>122</td><td>z</td></tr>
<tr><td>53</td><td>5</td><td>88</td><td>X</td><td>123</td><td>{</td></tr>
<tr><td>54</td><td>6</td><td>89</td><td>Y</td><td>124</td><td>|</td></tr>
<tr><td>55</td><td>7</td><td>90</td><td>Z</td><td>125</td><td>}</td></tr>
<tr><td>56</td><td>8</td><td>91</td><td>[</td><td>126</td><td>~</td></tr>
<tr><td>57</td><td>9</td><td>92</td><td>\</td><td>127</td><td>Delete</td></tr>
</table>

GLOSSARY

Absolute value The magnitude of a number without sign.
Accumulator A variable used for keeping track of a continuing total.
Ada A recently developed programming language that is well suited for structured program development. Ada is named for Ada Lovelace, a nineteenth-century pioneer in programming theory.
Address The number associated with each location in main memory.
ALGOL ALGOrithmic Language; one of the earliest high-level languages, it was designed primarily for mathematical applications.
Algorithm A procedure for accomplishing a task.
Alphanumeric value *See* String value.
ALU *See* Arithmetic/logic unit.
ANSI The American National Standards Institute, which works to establish basic standards for many programming languages and for other areas.
Argument A value on which a function operates.
Arithmetic operations Any operation involving one or more of the five fundamental arithmetic operators. This is one of the three fundamental types of operations.
Arithmetic operators The operators used in arithmetic operations and in constructing mathematical expressions. These are given in Table 5-1.
Arithmetic/logic unit (ALU) The section of the CPU that performs all arithmetic and logic operations.
Array An orderly list of values that may be individually referenced and used.
Array element A member of an array.
Ascending order Increasing from smallest to largest.
ASCII American Standard Code for Information Interchange, one of the 8-bit systems for coding data currently in common use, especially with I/O devices and small computers. *See* Appendix E for a list of ASCII codes.
Assembler A program that translates a source program written in assembly language to a machine language object program.
Assembly language An intermediate-level but machine-dependent language that employs mnemonics and operational codes in place of the binary codes used by machine languages.
Auxiliary storage A method of storing data outside of the CPU for later retrieval and processing. The most common examples are magnetic tape and disk.
BASIC Beginner's All-purpose Symbolic Instruction Code, the first language developed for interactive processing and instruction in programming, it has now become the most widely used language on microcomputers.
Batch system A method of processing data in which a number of jobs are submitted at one time and then processed in sequence.
Binary code A code written in the binary or base 2 number system.
Binary search A table search that is performed by repeatedly dividing the table into smaller and smaller halves.
Bit A binary digit, either 0 or 1.
Boolean expression *See* Compound condition.
Bubble sort One of the simplest but slowest sorting techniques. It works by repeatedly exchanging adjacent elements in an array to ''push'' the smallest or largest to one end, one element at a time.
Buffer A special area of memory set aside for a particular purpose, such as providing an intermediate area for records from random files.
Bug An error in a program.
Byte A group of bits (usually 8) that make up one character.
Case study A problem, usually based on a realistic situation, normally requiring the combination of several programming (or other) techniques to achieve a solution.
Central processor unit (CPU) The heart of the computer in which all data processing takes place.
Channel number A number used to designate and reference a disk file.
Classifying A method of processing in which data is placed into certain categories according to specific conditions.
COBOL COmmon Business Oriented Language, a language designed specifically for processing business-related problems.
Column A vertical arrangement of data. In two-dimen-

sional arrays, columns are designated by the second subscript.

Column-priority order Processing a two-dimensional array by columns.

Column vector A two-dimensional array with only one column.

Compiler A program that translates the source program written in a high-level language to an object program in machine code.

Compound condition Two or more conditions connected by logical operators.

Computer program A program written to be executed on a computer.

Computerphobia The fear of computers.

Concatenation The combination of two or more strings to build a larger string.

Concatenation operator A special operator that permits concatenation.

Condition *See* Logical expression.

Conditional branch A change in the flow of program execution depending on the results of the test of the truth value of a logical expression.

Constant A value that does not change.

Control break A type of processing in which one procedure is temporarily interrupted for another whenever there is a change in some control field.

Control field A key field used to signal that a control break should be taken.

Control unit A section of the CPU that directs and coordinates all computer operations and components.

Controlling module The section of a modular program that serves to coordinate all other modules.

Counter A type of accumulator that ''counts'' or keeps track of the number of something, such as the number of records processed.

CPU *See* Central processor unit.

Data Values to be processed.

Data base All the data necessary for a particular application.

Data editing Checking to catch potential errors in data values.

Data name A name to which data values are assigned.

Data value A value to be processed or produced as the result of processing.

Debug Find errors (bugs) in computer programs.

Decision table A table of the various decisions or program branches that will be required, often used as a basis for program design.

Default A special value or condition automatically assumed unless another is specifically assigned.

Descending order Decreasing from largest to smallest.

Destructive read A method of data input in which the new values assigned to one or more variables replace the previous ones in memory.

Detailed line A print line that prints information about one input record.

Dimension Indicates the maximum number of elements in an array.

Direct access files Any type of file organization in which a record may be accessed directly, without passing through all preceding ones. Often used interchangeably with random file.

Double-precision A format in which numeric data is expressed with an extended number of significant digits—up to 16 on some systems.

Dummy argument An argument of a user-defined function that assumes the value of the corresponding variable whenever the function is called.

Error trapping A procedure that incorporates a special routine into a program that permits errors to be analyzed, such as for type and location, and appropriate action taken rather than simply aborting processing whenever an error is detected.

Exception report A report in which only results that satisfy certain conditions are printed.

Executable statements BASIC statements, such as READ, PRINT, and GOTO, which cause an action to occur.

Exponential notation A format for expressing numeric values in which a number is expressed as the product of a number greater than or equal to 1 but less than 10 and ten to a power.

Fatal error An error that causes program termination.

Field One data value

File A collection of related records

File specification Includes both the filename and filetype, usually in the form *filename.filetype,* sometimes preceded by a device code.

Filename The user-designated name for a disk file, usually 1 to 8 characters.

Filetype Identifies the file as to its intended use or function.

Flag A special variable the value of which is used to direct processing.

Flowchart A pictorial representation of an algorithm.

FORTRAN FORmula TRANslation; the first high-level programming language to be developed, it was designed primarily for mathematical, scientific, and engineering applications.

GIGO Garbage-in-garbage-out.

Global variable A variable that remains the same in meaning throughout the program.

Group indicated Printing a value only on the first of several consecutive print lines on which it is to appear. Most frequently used with control break programs.

Group printed Printing a line only after a series of records for a certain key field have been processed. Similar to a summary report but normally used for control break programs.

Hard copy A printed copy of output from a computer.

Hardware The physical components of a computer system, such as CPU, printer, VDT, auxiliary storage devices, etc.

High-level language A programming language, such as BASIC, COBOL, or FORTRAN, that permits computer instructions to be written in a form that humans can easily understand.

I/O device Any device used for input (I) of data to a computer system or output (O) of information from the system.

I/O operations Any operation that involves input and/or output of data. This is one of the three fundamental types of operations.

Increment A set value by which an accumulator is changed. *See* Step.

Index A variable used to indicate a specific position within an array or file. Index also refers to a loop counter. *See* Pointer.

Indexed files A file organization in which records are located through an index which is linked to a key filed in each record.

Infinite loop A loop that is repeated without end.

Information The results of successfully processing data.

Initialize To set an initial condition, such as setting a total accumulator to zero.

Instruction Directions to perform a specific operation.

Interactive system A system that provides (almost) immediate responses to inquiries to the data base.

Interpreter A program that translates and executes a program written in a high-level language line by line with no object program being created. Many BASICs are run with interpreters.

K An abbreviation for 2^{10} or 1024 storage locations.

Key field Any field that is used as a control for processing.

Left-justified Positioned as far to the left as possible.

Level Refers to the third dimension in three-dimensional arrays, indicated by the third subscript.

Level-priority order Processing a three-dimensional array by levels.

Library function *See* Special function.

Limit check An edit check to determine if a certain value falls within reasonable limits.

Literal A constant used in a program.

Local variable A variable that is restricted to a certain line or section of a program and cannot be referenced throughout the remainder of the program. In BASIC, such variables are normally restricted to dummy arguments of user-defined functions.

Logic error An error that results from an incorrect flow of data through the program. Such errors are not detected by the compiler or interpreter.

Logic operations An operation that involves the test of the truth value of a logical expression. This is one of the three fundamental types of operations.

Logical expression An expression that is either true or false.

Logical negation Reversing the truth value of a logical expression.

Logical operator An operator, such as NOT, AND, or OR, which combines logical expressions to form other logical expressions, usually giving compound conditions.

Loop A series of instructions that are repeated.

Loop counter A counter used to control and/or exit from a loop.

Machine language The lowest level of programming language in which instructions are written in binary code that is directly interpreted by the computer.

Machine-independent Easily transported from one machine to another.

Machine-specific Locked to one machine or one type of machine.

Macro A single instruction that performs several operations.

Main memory The section of the CPU in which data and programs are stored for processing.

Mathematical expression Any grouping of numeric constants, variables, or functions connected with arithmetic operators.

Matrix A two-dimensional array.

Menu A list of available program options.

Menu-driven A program that is run from a menu.

Merging Combining two or more lists of data to form a single list.

Message prompt A screen prompt that supplies a specific message.

Microprocessor A small, but frequently very powerful, processor unit found in microcomputers and small electronic devices.

Minor totals Totals that are printed when a control break is taken.

Mnemonic A memory aid.

Modular program A program that is structured entirely in modules.

Module A set of statements that performs one or more basic tasks.

Nesting Placing one group of statements within another, such as one FOR–NEXT loop within another or one subroutine within another.

Nonexecutable statements Statements, such as REM and DATA, that do not cause action to occur and therefore do not affect the flow of a program. Such statements can, with a few restrictions, be placed anywhere in a program.

Numeric value A value that is to be treated as a number. Only numeric values may be used in arithmetic operations.

Object program The machine language image that is produced whenever a program is successfully compiled or assembled.

Parameter One of a special set of variables that control the solution to a problem.

Pascal The first high-level programming language developed specifically for structured programming.

Pointer A variable that indicates the position or location of a certain value, as in a data list, array, or file. *See* Index.
Print zones The five sections of the screen (or printer page), usually 13 to 16 columns wide, that are automatically provided by the PRINT statement.
Program A set of instructions for accomplishing a specific task.
Pseudocode The statement of an algorithm in English-like sentences.
Radian A method of angular measure. 2π rad = 360°, or 1 rad = 57.29577951°.
Random files A file organization in which any record can be retrieved without having to process all of the preceding ones.
Range check An edit check to verify that a certain value falls within a known range of values.
Record A set of related fields.
Relational operator An operator used to construct a logical expression. In BASIC, there are six such operators as given in Table 4-2.
Reserved word A series of characters that have a special meaning in BASIC and therefore cannot be used for a variable or anything else other than the intended use.
Right-justified Positioned as far to the right as possible.
Rounding The process of adding 0 to the last significant digit to be retained if the next digit (the one to be dropped) is in the range 0 to 4, and adding 1 to the last significant if the next one is in the range 5 to 9.
Row A horizontal arrangement of data. In two-dimensional arrays, rows are designated by the first subscript.
Row-priority order Processing a two-dimensional array by rows.
Row vector A two-dimensional array with only one row.
Runtime error A physical error in the program that is not detected until the program is actually run.
Scientific notation *See* Exponential notation.
Screen prompt A symbol sent to the screen to signal the user to enter data or take other action.
Secondary storage *See* Auxiliary storage.
Seed An initial value required by some random number functions.
Sentinel record A special record at the end of a data list or file that is used to detect the end of the list.
Sequential file A file organization in which records are stored and must be processed in a specific order.
Sequential search A table search in which the known value is compared to each element in the table, one by one, until a match is found.
Shell sort One of the fastest, most efficient sorting procedures. It achieves its speed by comparing and exchanging widely spaced values as compared to most sorting methods which only work with adjacent values.
Significant digit A digit that may be considered to be accurate.
Single-precision The normal format used by most BASICs for displaying numeric data. It will provide from 6 to 9 significant digits.
Software A general term used to refer to computer programs.
Sorting The process of arranging a list of values into a specific sequence.
Source program The program entered directly into the computer in an assembly or high-level language.
Special function A function built into BASIC for special processing of data.
Step The value by which the loop index or counter is changed. *See* Increment.
Stored program concept The idea that programs can be stored in main memory along with the data.
String value A data value that may contain any printable character and that cannot be treated as numeric.
Subroutine A set of statements within a program that performs a single task. Normally a subroutine is called from elsewhere in the program, with control returning to the line following that from which it was called after the subroutine is completed.
Subscript A value that indicates a specific location in an array.
Subscripted variable A variable used to define an array, any one value of which designates one element of the array.
Substring A section of a string.
Summary report A report that prints totals or other summary data.
Switch *See* Flag.
Syntax error An error in a program that results from a misspelling or other grammatical error.
System command An instruction directly to the computer's operating system.
Table One or more related arrays, usually processed as a unit.
Test value A value used to test for an upper limit, as in the FOR–NEXT loop.
Three-dimensional array An array defined with three subscripts designating rows, columns, and levels.
Time-sharing system A system in which several users interact simultaneously with the CPU by sharing its resources, speed, and other capabilities.
Trailer record *See* Sentinel record.
Transpose Interchanging rows and columns of an array.
Troubleshoot *See* Debug.
Truncation The act of dropping digits from a number, leaving the last remaining significant digit unchanged (not rounded off).
Truth value The value of a logical expression. Must be either true or false.
Two-dimensional array An array defined with two subscripts designating rows and columns.

Unconditional branch An interrupt in and redirection of the program that takes place under any condition.
Updating The process of using new data to bring old values up to date.
User-defined function A function defined by the programmer for a special use.
Value check An edit check that ensures that a value is one of a known set of allowed values.
Variable A data name the value of which may change during processing.
VDT Visual Display Terminal, sometimes referred to as a CRT.

INDEX